THE COUNTRY HOUSES OF JOHN F. STAUB

NUMBER ELEVEN

SARA AND JOHN LINDSEY SERIES

IN THE ARTS AND HUMANITIES

THE COUNTRY HOUSES OF

John F. Staub

STEPHEN FOX

Color Photography by RICHARD CHEEK

Texas A&M University Press College Station

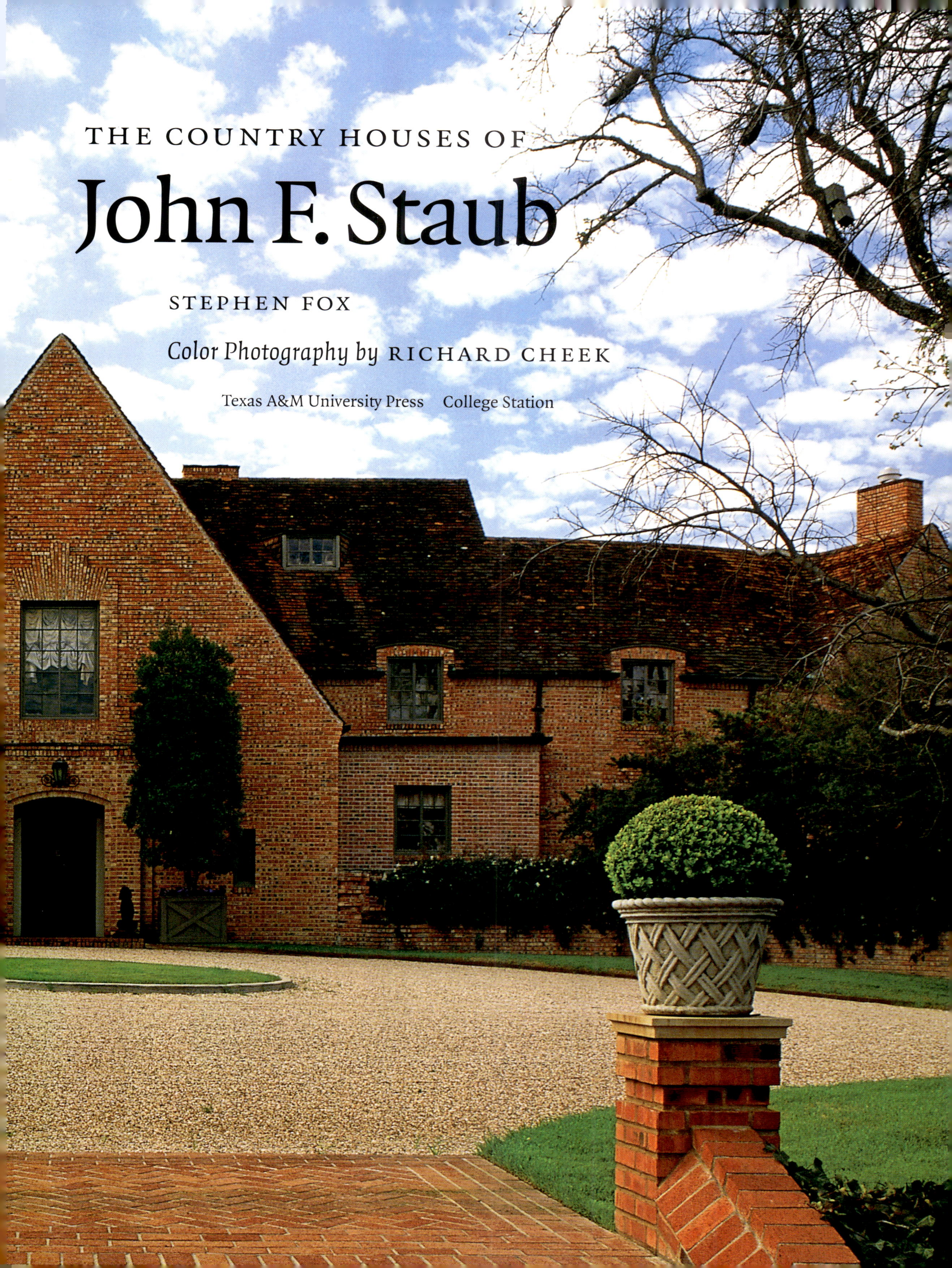

Manufactured in China by Everbest Printing Co. through Four Colour Imports

First edition

The paper used in this book meets the minimum requirements of the American National Standard for Permanence of Paper for Printed Library Materials, z39.48-1984. Binding materials have been chosen for durability.

∞

LIBRARY OF CONGRESS CATALOGING-IN-PUBLICATION DATA

Fox, Stephen, 1950-

The country houses of John F. Staub / Stephen Fox ; principal photography by Richard Cheek. — 1st ed.

p. cm. — (Sara and John Lindsey series in the arts and humanities ; no. 11)

Includes bibliographical references and index.

ISBN-13: 978-1-58544-595-0 (cloth : alk. paper)

ISBN-10: 1-58544-595-9 (cloth : alk. paper)

1. Staub, John F., 1892-1981—Criticism and interpretation. 2. Architecture, Domestic—Texas—Houston. 3. Architecture—Texas—Houston—20th century. 4. Eclecticism in architecture—Texas—Houston. 5. Houston (Tex.)—Buildings, structures, etc. I. Cheek, Richard. II. Title.

NA737.S635F69 2007

728′.09764411—dc22 2007003217

CONTENTS

List of Illustrations vii

Preface xiii

Chapter 1. John F. Staub, Houston, and the Social Construction of Upper-Class Identity 1

Chapter 2. Broadacres 17

Chapter 3. River Oaks 67

Chapter 4. Small Houses 113

Chapter 5. Grand Houses 135

Chapter 6. Country Retreats 211

Chapter 7. Typification, Consensus, and the River Oaks House 245

Chapter 8. Regionalism 261

Chapter 9. The Contemporary and the Palladian 289

Chapter 10. Architecture, Social Construction, and the Country Houses of John F. Staub 335

Notes 345

Bibliography 371

Index 381

LIST OF ILLUSTRATIONS

CHAPTER 1
John F. Staub 1
Courtlandt Place, Houston. Entry piers, 1910, demolished 3
"River Oaks: Live Where You Play." River Oaks Corporation advertisement 4
Howard Barnstone, John F. Staub, and David Courtwright in the garden at Bayou Bend, 1976 5
"The Little New York of the South" advertisement for the Second National Bank 6
Aerial view of the Rice Institute campus, Houston, 1920 8
Aerial perspective of Main Boulevard, Hermann Park civic arena, Houston 8
Hugo V. Neuhaus House, Shadyside, Houston, 1919–23, Harrie T. Lindeberg, architect 9
Kenneth E. Womack House, Shadyside, Houston, 1921–23, Harrie T. Lindeberg, architect 9
William S. Farish House, Shadyside, Houston, 1921–25, Harrie T. Lindeberg, architect 10
D. D. Peden House, Shadyside, Houston, 1921–24, Harrie T. Lindeberg, architect 10
"Houston's Cradle of Culture and Environs." 11
Modern Houston. Gulf Building, Houston. Vincent Maragliotti, painter, 1929 12
"Combining Beauty with Utility," E. M. Schiwetz, *Houston Gargoyle* 4 13
"Harmony without Monotony," E. M. Schiwetz, *Houston Gargoyle* 4 14

CHAPTER 2
Broadacres, view looking west on North Boulevard 16–17
Plat map of Broadacres, 1923 18
Aerial view of Hermann Park, 1925 19
Palmer Hutcheson House, Broadacres, 1924–25, John F. Staub, architect. Detail of north-facing street elevation 22
Hutcheson House, detail of chimney 23
Hutcheson House, south-facing garden elevation 24
Hutcheson House, detail of dormer window 24
Hutcheson House, first- and second-floor plans 25
Hutcheson House, detail of arched window 27
William S. Cochran House, Broadacres, 1925–26, John F. Staub, architect. First- and second-floor plans 28
Cochran House, south-facing street elevation 29
Cochran House, detail of entrance alcove 29
Cochran House, detail of chimney 30
C. Milby Dow House, Broadacres, 1926–27, John F. Staub, architect. Vista of the house from Parkway 32–33
Dow House, north-facing front elevation 34
Dow House, side entrance to kitchen wing with garage beyond 34
Joseph A. Tennant House, Broadacres, 1926–27, John F. Staub, architect. Detail of south-facing garden elevation with arches of fig ivy by J. Allen Myers Jr., landscape architect 36–37
Tennant House, first- and second-floor plans 37
Tennant House, north-facing street front 38
Tennant House, east side elevation 38–39
Tennant House, entrance hall 40–41
Tennant House, detail of antique mantle installed in living room 42
Tennant House, detail of garden loggia 43
Tennant House, dining room 44
Tennant House, view from dining room to garden 45
Kemp S. Dargan House, Broadacres, 1929–30, John F. Staub, architect. North-facing street elevation 46–47
Dargan House, detail of backlit ceiling light above stair 47
Dargan House, view from living room window to south-facing rear lawn 48
Dargan House, detail of transom above entrance door 49
Dargan House, detail of circular window in entrance hall 49
Dargan House, detail of stair newel post 50
Dargan House, detail of master bathroom 51
Dargan House, detail of wood mantle in master bedroom 52
Col. Rudolph C. Kuldell House, Broadacres, 1928–29, John F. Staub, architect. South-facing street elevation 53
Kuldell House, first- and second-floor plans 53
Kuldell House, detail of brick bonding patterns at dining room window bay 54
Kuldell House, detail of gable and chimney stack above dining room 54
Kuldell House, detail of timbered bay above entrance 55
Kuldell House, detail of brick bonding patterns above living room window 55
Kuldell House, looking from rear garage toward north-facing rear elevation 56
Kuldell House, detail of brick-framed dining room window bay 57
Kuldell House, detail of terra-cotta shingle tile roof 58
Kuldell House, detail of side-gabled roof above entrance porch showing lapping of roof tiles 58

Kuldell House, detail of east side gables showing brick (foreground) and tile (background) facing 58
Kuldell House, view from attic window toward west side of Cochran House 59
Kuldell House, entrance hall 60
Kuldell House, detail of casement windows in living room 60
Kuldell House, detail of carved wood bracket in living room 61
Kuldell House, oak overmantle in living room. Peter Mansbendel, carver 62
Kuldell House, detail of living room mantle and fireplace surround 62
Kuldell House, detail of breakfast room windows 63
Kuldell House, pantry 64
Kuldell House, detail of front door pull and lock plate 65
Kuldell House, detail of daughters' bathroom 66

CHAPTER 3

River Oaks Gate Pier, River Oaks Boulevard near Locke Lane, 1925, John F. Staub, architect 67
Will C. Hogg 69
Ima Hogg in the living room at Bayou Bend, 1952 69
Plat map of Country Club Estates, 1924 71
Aerial view looking north down River Oaks Boulevard toward River Oaks Country Club, 1926 72
Aerial view of River Oaks, Buffalo Bayou Park–Allen Parkway, and Downtown Houston 74
River Oaks Country Club, Houston, 1923–24, John F. Staub, architect. Demolished 74
Country Club Estates House (Redbird House), River Oaks, 1925, Briscoe and Dixon, architects 75
Country Club Estates House (River Oaks Latin Colonial House), River Oaks, 1925, John F. Staub, architect 75
Cleveland Sewall House, River Oaks, 1923–26, Cram and Ferguson, architects 76
William L. Clayton Summer House, River Oaks, 1924, Briscoe and Dixon, architects 77
"Latin Colonial Architecture in the Southwest," *Civics for Houston* 1 (Feb. 1928): 6 79
A meeting of the Houston Symphony Society at Bayou Bend, c. 1935. 80
Ima Hogg House, Bayou Bend, Homewoods, River Oaks, 1926–28, John F. Staub and Birdsall P. Briscoe, architects 81
Bayou Bend, entrance front. 82–83
Bayou Bend, garden front 84
Bayou Bend, garden portico and terrace 85
Bayou Bend, view from hall toward Diana Garden 86
Bayou Bend, view from bachelors' porch toward East Garden 87
Bayou Bend, view from living room toward dining room 88
Bayou Bend, view from bachelors' living room through the library toward the living room 89
Bayou Bend, first- and second-floor plans 89
Bayou Bend, detail of dining room mantle and painted wallpaper by William Mackay 90
Bayou Bend, view from Miss Hogg's sitting room toward passage that leads down to bachelors' wing 91
Bayou Bend, servants' bathroom in basement 92
Bayou Bend, view through breakfast room bay window toward Diana Garden 92–93
Bayou Bend, detail of fanlight above entrance front door 95
Bayou Bend, detail of acroterion above garden portico 96
Bayou Bend, detail of garden portico door 97
Bayou Bend, detail of garden terrace bay window 98
Bayou Bend, detail of living room doorway 100
River Oaks gate piers, 1925, framing view of River Oaks Community Center, Houston, 1927, John F. Staub and Charles W. Oliver, architects 101
Junior League Building, Houston, 1929, John F. Staub, architect. Altered. Sketch of Stuart Avenue elevation 101
Joseph H. Chew House, River Oaks, 1925, John F. Staub, architect. Street front 102–103
Hubert B. Finch House, River Oaks, 1926–27, John F. Staub, architect. Street front 105
John S. Mellinger House, River Oaks, 1930, John F. Staub, architect. Street front 106–107
Mellinger House, detail of front door 108
Mellinger House, detail of back door 109
Mellinger House, view from dining room into living room 110
Mellinger House, first- and second-floor plans 110

CHAPTER 4

"Playtime in River Oaks," E. M. Schiwetz. *Houston Gargoyle* 4 112
Bungalow house, Houston, 1920, Thomas and Van Santen, architect-builders 113
River Oaks Latin Colonial House (David M. Picton Jr. House), River Oaks, 1925, John F. Staub, architect 115
Latin Colonial House, first- and second-floor plans 115
Latin Colonial House, hall and stair 116
River Oaks Early Republic House (Hugh Potter House), River Oaks, 1925–26, John F. Staub, architect 118
Latin Colonial House, living room 119
Mrs. John F. Staub House, River Oaks, 1925–26 120–121
Staub House, first- and second-floor plans 122
Staub House, living room 123
Dr. C. M. Griswold House, River Oaks, 1933, Stayton Nunn, architect 125
George R. Brown House, River Oaks, 1932–33, J. T. Rather Jr., architect 125

Clark Hardison House, Braeswood, 1929, Carl Mulvey, architect 126
Ballinger Mills Jr. House, Galveston, 1939, Cameron Fairchild, architect 126
H. Q. Hickman House, River Oaks, 1927, Hiram A. Salisbury, architect. Demolished 127
First-prize design: Honeymoon Cottage, 1928, Vance D. Phenix and E. M. Schiwetz, architects 128
William C. Helmbrecht House, Galveston, 1928, John F. Staub, architect 130–131
Helmbrecht House, detail of shutters 132
Helmbrecht House, detail of oval window 133
Dr. Edward Randall Jr. House, Galveston, 1928, John F. Staub, architect 134
Helmbrecht House, first- and second-floor plans 134

CHAPTER 5
J. Robert Neal House, River Oaks, 1931–33, John F. Staub, architect. Detail of pediment-capped window above entrance portal 135
E. E. Bewley House, River Crest, Fort Worth, 1926–28, John F. Staub, architect. Entrance elevation 137
Morris E. Berney House, River Crest, Fort Worth, 1915–16, Adler and Dangler, architects 138
Mrs. Neil Anderson House, River Crest, Fort Worth, 1916–17, Adler and Dangler, architects 138
Bewley House, vista from entrance front looking toward Trinity River 139
Bewley House, detail of basement-level garage and rubble-stone foundations 140
Bewley House, south lawn elevation 140–141
Bewley House, detail of south gable 142
Bewley House, detail of loggia 143
Bewley House, first- and second-floor plans 143
Bewley House, detail of stair rail 144
John King House, River Crest, Fort Worth, 1928, John F. Staub, architect 146–147
Herman Gartner House, River Crest, Fort Worth, 1929–30, John F. Staub, architect 148
Gartner House, first- and second-floor plans 148
Gartner House, detail of gable 149
Gartner House, detail of entrance portal 150
Gartner House., detail of door plate and handle 151
Gartner House, detail of oval window and wrought-iron grille 152
J. Robert Neal House, River Oaks, Houston, 1931–33, John F. Staub, architect. Entrance forecourt 154–155
Perspective drawing of the street front of the Neal House, entrance driveway and forecourt, and great lawn, 1932, Olmsted Brothers, landscape architects 156
Neal House, east elevation looking toward great lawn 157
Neal House, west lawn elevation viewed from the Venetian temple installed by Olmsted Brothers 158
Neal House, first- and second-floor plans 159
Neal House, axis of view from the garden room through the living room toward the front doors. The front doors replaced Staub's originals 160
Neal House, antique mantle installed in living room 161
Neal House, antique mantle installed in garden room 161
Neal House, staircase with eighteenth-century French wrought-iron rail 162
Neal House, dining room 163
Neal House, detail of carved stone pediment on garden elevation 164
Hugh Roy Cullen House, River Oaks, Houston, 1933–35, John F. Staub, architect. East elevation 166–167
Cullen House, first- and second-floor plans 168
Cullen House, north elevation facing motor court 170–171
Cullen House, south elevation facing garden 171
Cullen House, living room 172–173
Cullen House, entrance hall and stair 174
Cullen House, library 175
Cullen House, view through aligned doorways 175
Cullen House, gallery 175
Cullen House, view from music alcove in living room to garden allée 176
Cullen House, dining room 176
Cullen House, detail of stair rail 177
Cullen House, detail of front door 178
Cullen House, detail showing vaulted ceiling above stair 179
Stephen P. Farish House, Homewoods, River Oaks, Houston, 1934–36, John F. Staub, architect. Entrance (west) elevation 180–181
Farish House, detail of black-painted shutters 182
Farish House, detail of cast- and wrought-iron stanchion silhouetted against white-painted brick background 183
Farish House, living room 184
Farish House, detail of antique mantle installed in living room 184
Farish House, stair with view into library 185
Farish House, vista from living room through dining room to breakfast room 186
Farish House. Garden (east) elevation 187
Farish House, detail of china cabinet inset in dining room window aperture 187
J. Cooke Wilson House, Beaumont, 1935–37, John F. Staub, architect. Garden (south) elevation 188–189
Wilson House, entrance (north) elevation 190
Wilson House, detail of stair rail 191
Wilson House, detail of marble- and glass-framed fireplace opening in garden room 191

Alex Camp House, Dallas, 1936–38, John F. Staub, architect. Entrance (south) elevation 193
Camp House, north elevation overlooking White Rock Lake 193
Camp House, first- and second-floor plans 194
Camp House, view through dining room toward White Rock Lake with steel-framed windows slid into side pockets 195
Camp House, entrance alcove 196
Camp House, living room looking toward entrance hall 196
Camp House, detail of marble- and bamboo-framed fireplace in morning room 197
Camp House, morning room looking toward rear terrace and guest room 197
James O. Winston Jr. House, Houston, 1938–39, John F. Staub, architect. Entrance (north) elevation and forecourt 198–199
Winston House, entrance foyer looking toward staircase 200
Winston House, detail of stair rail and riser returns 201
Winston House, detail of library mantle 202
Winston House, vista through cross hall and foyer toward staircase 203
Winston House, first- and second-floor plans 203
Winston House, detail of antique mantle installed in living room 204
Winston House, living room 204–205
Winston House, dining room 206
Winston House, detail of front elevation showing marble belt course and brick relieving arch 207
Winston House, detail of front elevation showing carved marble panel beneath first-floor windows and iron handrail 207
Winston House, garden (south) elevation 208–209

CHAPTER 6
Wiess Stables, Houston, 1930, John F. Staub, architect. Cupola and weathervane 211
Bay Ridge shoreline and cottages seen from Galveston Bay, Morgan's Point, Texas 212
Frank N. Bullock Bay Cottage, Bay Ridge, 1928, John F. Staub, architect. Detail of entrance (northwest) elevation 213
Bullock Bay Cottage, detail of elliptical pediment showing lone stars 214
Bullock Bay Cottage, shore (southeast) elevation 215
Bullock Bay Cottage, view from rear loggia toward Galveston Bay and the Houston Ship Channel 216
W. T. Carter Jr. Lodge, Houston, 1929–30, John F. Staub, architect 218
Carter Lodge, views of living room 219
Wiess Stables, Houston, 1930, John F. Staub, architect. First-floor plan 221
Wiess Stables, entrance (southeast) front with swimming pool and bath house to the left 222–223
Wiess Stables, view from living room to swimming pool and bath house 224
Wiess Stables, detail of sallyport portal 225
Wiess Stables, view from living room toward tack room 226
Wiess Stables, detail of split brick fireplace surround in living room 227
Wiess Stables, view of southwest flank showing rear stable wing 228–229
Olga Wiess (right) and friends at the Stables, 1931 229
Raymond H. Goodrich House, Houston, 1932, John F. Staub, architect. Entrance (north) elevation 230–231
Goodrich House, view of living room looking toward entry 232
Goodrich House, detail of living room fireplace 233
Aerial view of Ernest Bel Fay House, Houston, 1937–38; John F. Staub (center) and Albert Bel Fay House (upper right corner), 1939, John F. Staub, architect. Demolished, c. 1940 234
Fay House, first- and second-floor plans 235
Ernest Bel Fay House, garden (south) front looking toward Buffalo Bayou 236–237
Fay House, second-floor living room 238
Fay House, detail of molded fascia in living room 239
Bayou Club, first- and second-floor plans 240
Bayou Club, Houston, 1938–40, John F. Staub, architect. Entrance (north) elevation 240
Bayou Club, south elevation and swimming pool 241
Bayou Club, second-floor Lounge 242–243
Bayou Club, first-floor Grill Room 243
Bayou Club, detail of fireplace surround in Grill Room 244

CHAPTER 7
George S. Heyer House, River Oaks, Houston, 1935–37, John F. Staub, architect. Detail of iron-framed light fixture above front door 245
David D. Bruton House, River Oaks, Houston, 1933–34, John F. Staub, architect. Entrance (north) elevation 248–249
Bruton House, first- and second-floor plans 250
Robert H. Bowles House, River Oaks, Houston, 1935–36, John F. Staub, architect. Entrance (north) elevation 251
Bowles House, end elevation of east wing, added to the house by Staub for its second owner, Patrick R. Rutherford 251
George S. Heyer House, River Oaks, Houston, 1935–37, John F. Staub, architect. Entrance (north) elevation 252–253
Heyer House, detail of cast aluminum stair rail 254

Heyer House, first- and second-floor plans 255
Heyer House, garden (south) elevation 256-257
Heyer House, view from garden terrace toward avenue of live oak trees planted by Fleming and Sheppard, landscape architects 257
Harry C. Hanszen House, Homewoods, River Oaks, 1930–31, John F. Staub, architect. Extensively altered 258
Wallace E. Pratt House, Homewoods, River Oaks, Houston, 1931–33, John F. Staub, architect. Demolished 259
Dolores Welder House, River Oaks, Houston, 1935–36, John F. Staub, architect. Demolished 260

CHAPTER 8
Dan J. Harrison House, Homewoods, River Oaks, Houston, 1938–39, John F. Staub, architect 261
Tom Scurry House, River Oaks, Houston, 1936–37, John F. Staub, architect 264
Kellum-Noble House, Sam Houston Park, Houston, 1847. Francis Mc Hugh, builder. Exterior elevations 265
Scurry House, view of south elevation from side garden 266
Scurry House, first- and second-floor plans 267
John M. Jennings House, River Oaks, Houston, 1937–38, John F. Staub, architect. Street elevation 268
Fleming Summer House, river front 268–269
Lamar Fleming Jr. Summer House, Hunt, Texas, 1937–38, John F. Staub, architect. View of terrace facing river 270- 271
South fork of the Guadalupe River 271
Fleming Summer House, entrance front 272–273
Fleming Summer House, dog trot entrance passage 274
Fleming Summer House, detail of limestone corbels at eaves line 275
Fleming Summer House, second-floor sleeping loft 275
Fleming Summer House, first-floor plan 276
Fleming Summer House, living room 276
Fleming Summer House, bedroom 277
Fleming Summer House, detail of fossilized limestone fireplace surround in bedroom 277
Dan J. Harrison House, Homewoods, River Oaks, Houston, 1938–39, John F. Staub, architect. Entrance (west) elevation 278–279
Harrison House, garden (east) elevation with reflecting pool and azalea parterres by Fleming and Sheppard, landscape architects 280
Harrison House, first- and second-floor plans 280
Harrison House, detail of service-wing entrance 281
Andrew Jackson Wray House, Shadyside, Houston, 1938–39, John F. Staub, architect. Street front 282–283
Wray House, first- and second-floor plans 284
Wray House, garden elevation 285
Wray House, view from dining room into rear garden 286

CHAPTER 9
James A. Elkins Jr. House, Houston, 1958–61, Staub, Rather and Howze, architects. Detail of stair rail 289
Robert D. Straus House, River Oaks, Houston, 1937, John F. Staub, architect. Street front 291
Straus House, first- and second-floor plans 292
Straus House, detail of front door 293
Straus House, living room as furnished by T. H. Robsjohn-Gibbings 294
Straus House, library as furnished by T. H. Robsjohn-Gibbings 295
Straus Recreation House, 1939, John F. Staub, architect. East elevation 296
Straus Recreation House, interior 296
W. L. Moody III House, Galveston, 1937–38, John F. Staub, architect. Detail of entrance portal 298
Anne Burnett Windfohr House, Westover Hills, Texas, 1938–39, John F. Staub, architect. Entrance front 298–299
Windfohr House, detail of stair rail 300
James A. Elkins Jr. House, River Oaks, Houston, 1947–48, Staub and Rather, architects. Street elevation 303
Elkins House, detail of entrance bay 304
Elkins House, detail of living room fireplace surround 305
Elkins House, detail of stair rail 306
Robert Gregory House, Pinewood Estates, Houston, 1952–53. Staub, Rather and Howze, architects. Demolished 307
Rienzi, Homewoods, River Oaks, Houston, 1952–54, Staub, Rather and Howze, architects. Entrance (south) elevation 308–309
Three sketches by Harris Masterson describing his conception of his house, undated, c. March 1952 310
Rienzi, preliminary site plan 311
Rienzi, floor plan 312
Rienzi, entrance hall 313
Rienzi, looking from bar across living room to north-facing terrace 314–315
Rienzi, bathroom 316
Rienzi, garden (north) elevation and terraces seen from bayou glade 318
Ben M. Anderson House, Tall Timbers, River Oaks, Houston, 1956–58, Staub, Rather and Howze, architects. Entrance (south) elevation 320–321
Anderson House, detail of entrance portal 321
Anderson House, detail of grill 322
Anderson House, floor plan 322
Anderson House, living room 323
Anderson House, rear (north) 324
James A. Elkins Jr. House, Houston, 1958–61, Staub, Rather and Howze, architects. Detail of entrance elevation 326–327

Elkins House, vista from entrance cross hall toward living room 328–329
Elkins House, staircase 329
Elkins House, terrace beneath cantilevered bedroom wing 330
Albert Bel Fay Bay House, Kemah, Texas, 1960–61, Staub, Rather and Howze, architects. Floor plan 332
Fay Bay House, detail of outdoor chimney 333

CHAPTER 10

Bayou Bend, detail of stair 335
C. Milby Dow House, detail of stair 337
Rudolph C. Kuldell House, detail of stair 339
J. Robert Neal House, detail of stair 341
Alex Camp House, detail of stair 342

PREFACE

This book began in 2001 in response to the unavailability of Howard Barnstone's book *The Architecture of John F. Staub: Houston and the South*, published in 1979. Barnstone's book was a classic. It was one of the works that in the 1970s led to a revision in the critical standing of architects of Staub's generation, and it was the first book to be published on the work of a Houston architect. *The Architecture of John F. Staub* went through two printings. After Howard Barnstone's death in 1987, however, no effort was made to reprint the book once it was sold out. By the 1990s available copies were being sold for escalating sums. The Houston architect H. Davis Mayfield III proposed to John H. Lindsey, who had been instrumental in securing support for the publication of Barnstone's book, that it be republished by Texas A&M University Press, which John Lindsey was instrumental in founding. Charles Backus, director of Texas A&M University Press, secured publication rights to *The Architecture of John F. Staub* from the original copublishers, the University of Texas Press and the Museum of Fine Arts, Houston. John Lindsey, Dave Mayfield, and Charles Backus felt that an addendum to Barnstone's book might be useful and that new photographs were warranted. This led to my involvement in the project as well as that of the distinguished photographer Richard Cheek. Richard Cheek has established his authority as the foremost photographic interpreter of the American country house. His work with Mark Alan Hewitt, who wrote most of the manuscript for *The Architect and the American Country House, 1890–1940* while an assistant professor of architecture at Rice University, as well as his contributions to William B. O'Neal and Christopher Weeks's *The Work of William Lawrence Bottomley in Richmond*, Roger G. Reed's *A Delight to All Who Know It: The Maine Summer Architecture of William R. Emerson*, and John M. Bryan's *Maine Cottages: Fred L. Savage and the Architecture of Mount Desert* made Richard Cheek an obvious choice. His exploratory visit to Houston on a rainy December weekend in 2001 proved fortuitous in two respects. It led to the decision to produce a new book, which would be illustrated with all new color photography by Richard Cheek, rather than attempt to add to or revise Barnstone's work. It also led to the involvement of the Houston landscape historian Susan Keeton as project coordinator.

In order to distinguish this book from Barnstone's book, we decided that a smaller selection of houses would be included. This meant that difficult choices had to be made in determining which houses to focus on. Consequently there are many significant Staub houses in Houston that are not represented in this book. It also meant that only a handful of Staub's houses outside Houston have been included.

Another pressing decision involved content: how was this book to be different from Barnstone's? Because I had worked for Howard Barnstone during part of the time he was preparing his book and assisted him in that process, it would have been difficult for me to challenge his findings or interpretations even had I wanted to. What precisely was there to say about the country houses of John F. Staub that Barnstone had not said already? My response to this question has been to explore a line of inquiry that fascinated Howard Barnstone: the social dimension of Staub's architectural practice. John Staub was a "society architect." His clients were the social elite of Houston, and Staub bore special responsibility for the ways in which his clients were represented to the nation at large as national news media began to take notice of Houston in the 1930s and 1940s. I proposed to Texas A&M University Press that this book examine the ways in which Staub's country houses constructed a collective identity for Houston's social elite that represented them as an upper class and that it examine how his houses sought to mold their occupants into patrician "subjects"—ideal personifications of an American upper class—through spatial organization, architectural composition, proportion, and decoration. A rich array of interdisciplinary literature combining architectural history, anthropology, and sociology, which was just beginning to take shape in the 1970s, has enabled me to expand upon Barnstone's insights and look critically at Staub's houses to understand how they socially constructed upper-class space in Houston. This book is not a biography of John Staub. It is a book about his buildings and how these buildings functioned as outward and visible signs of what George E. Marcus calls the intangible "social architecture" that gave them meaning.

All books are collaborations and this work is no exception. Many people have contributed to making this book a reality, some knowingly, others indirectly.

Thanks are due to Sara Houstoun and John H. Lindsey, who grew up as close friends of the Staubs and their children, for their generous, patient, and unfailingly encouraging support of this project. Mr. and Mrs. Lindsey quietly but substantially continue the implicit civic project materialized in John Staub's houses: making Houston a more humane and more beautiful city in which to live by their consistent and magnanimous support of good causes.

H. Davis Mayfield III was a moving force not only in bringing this project into being but also in ensuring that it was undertaken with the seriousness that John Staub's architecture merits.

Richard Cheek's amazing photographs reveal new insights into what makes Staub's work exceptional. His commitment to this project and his eagerness and enthusiasm for thinking over the social ramifications of the American country house, especially in its Texan incarnations, made our collaboration lively and stimulating.

Susan Keeton made everything important and necessary happen. Her knowledge and love of Houston and of its landscape heritage meant that she was always ready to ruminate on and debate questions of the "social architecture" embedded in John Staub's domestic architecture.

The Anchorage Foundation of Texas made it possible for me to participate in this project, for which I am deeply grateful. Thanks to Anne S. Brown, founder and president, the foundation's directors Le Roy Melcher III, Pierre S. Melcher, Marc Melcher, Pierre M. Schlumberger, and Jody Blazek, staff member Patsy Guerrero, and friend Peter Hoyt Brown.

Madeleine Callery Hussey and Nancy Staub Callery generously and enthusiastically shared recollections of their grandparents Madeleine Delabarre and John F. Staub.

Kate Sayen Kirkland undertook the difficult job of recommending how the manuscript could be cut after I wrote too much. Many thanks for her judiciousness, patience, and tact. Thanks also to Karl Laurence Kilian for reading the manuscript.

I am fundamentally indebted to a broad range of scholars. Although footnotes cite specific sources, I want to acknowledge especially those who have had a formative influence on this book. The Austin architect and architectural historian James Robert Coote gave a lecture on Staub's work for the Harris County Heritage Society in March 1982 in which he talked about the material components of Staub's houses—floorboards, hardware, light fixtures, plumbing fixtures—in ways that forcibly made me aware that Staub's mastery of style and planning were underpinned by the material attributes of his houses and that these had to be taken into account. Conversations with Mark Hewitt during the preparation of his book on the American country house first brought the concept of identity as a social construct to my attention and gave me insight into how the discourse of social Darwinism provided an epistemological basis for American architectural criticism during the country house era. Joel Warren Barna's book *The See-Through Years: Creation and Destruction in Texas Architecture and Real Estate, 1981–1991* impelled me to ask what the mythic dimension of Staub's houses might be. Steven A. Moore's book *Technology and Place: Sustainable Architecture and the Blueprint Farm* is a compelling demonstration of how a thesis can be methodically developed and critically explored to examine the social, political, and economic dimensions of an architectural site. As is evident from the frequency with which it is cited, the dissertation "Sacred Modern: An Ethnography of an Art Museum" by Pamela G. Smart has been enormously important in stimulating my awareness of key concepts in contemporary anthropology and how these can be applied to an analysis of Houston's history and culture. The business-professional-political histories that Joseph Pratt, professor of history at the University of Houston, and Harold A. Hyman, William P. Hobby professor emeritus of history at Rice University, have published since the 1980s broadened and deepened my comprehension of how Staub's houses fit into the bigger economic and political picture that his Houston clients were instrumental in constructing, as have those of Don E. Carleton, director of the Center for American History at the University of Texas at Austin, and James A. Tinsley, professor emeritus of history at the University of Houston. David G. McComb's histories of Houston and Galveston remain indispensable. Harold L. Platt's political history of Houston during the New South era has yet to be surpassed.

Trying to write thoughtfully about "society" and social class has been made much easier thanks to the exceptional work of four authors: Nelson W. Aldrich Jr. and his *Old Money: The Mythology of America's Upper Class*, Richard L. Bushman and his *The Refinement of America: Persons, Houses, Cities*, George E. Marcus and his *Lives in Trust: The Fortunes of Dynastic Families in Late Twentieth-Century America*, and Suzannah Lessard and her *The Architect of Desire: Beauty and Danger in the Stanford White Family*. In addition, *Harvard Design Magazine*, edited by William S. Saunders and Nancy Levinson, devoted its summer 2000 issue to the topic "Design and Class." The contributions of Michael Benedikt, Suzannah Lessard, Penny Sparke, and Margaret Crawford proved especially rewarding in thinking about Staub and his houses.

K. Michael Hays's book *Modernism and the Posthumanist Subject: The Architecture of Hannes Meyer and Ludwig Hilberseimer* represents an enormous contribution to contemporary architectural historiography in its rigorous and innovative examination of how architecture interacts with the social imagination. Alexander Tzonis and Liane Lefaivre explicate architecture with clarity, profundity, and precision in their book *Classical Architecture: The Poetics of Order*. Ptolemy Dean's keen attentiveness to the spatial structuring and material articulation of buildings makes his *Sir John Soane and the Country Estate* a case study in how works of architecture can be examined and interpreted to understand what makes them singular and extraordinary.

Other scholars and architects to whom I am indebted are Rolf Achilles for an introduction to Lake Forest, Illinois, and its architecture; Anthony Alofsin for his epic work on Frank Lloyd Wright; Juan Ignacio Barragán Villarreal for many thought-provoking exchanges about architectural practice in Monterrey, Nuevo León, and Texas; Ellen Beasley for her pioneering work on architecture and social history in Galveston; Wayne Bell and Frances Chamberlain for introducing me to the country houses of Austin; Sadie Gwin Blackburn for making me aware of the critical importance of landscape in architecture and community development; Bradley Brooks for his work on the Beaumont country houses of Owen J. Southwell; Vincent B. Canizaro for giving me the opportunity to think critically about regionalism in architecture; Chris Carson for the opportunity to learn about San Antonio architecture first-hand; Stephanie Hetos Cocke for sharing with me her research and writing on the architecture and social history of San Antonio; Margaret Culbertson for her work on early-twentieth-century housing in Texas; Jane Anderson Curtis for her work on the gardens of Bayou Bend and for making a copy of Jon Emerson and Suzanne Turner's historic landscape report available to me; Cheryl Caldwell Ferguson for her important work on Texas suburban communities and the history of River Oaks; John C. Ferguson for his work on Atlee B. and Robert M. Ayres; Mary Carolyn Hollers George and W. Eugene George for their work on O'Neil Ford and the architectural culture of twentieth-century Texas; Lisa Germany for her work on Harwell Hamilton Harris; Christopher Gray for his work on elite residential development in the United States; W. Mark Gunderson for giving me a greater appreciation of the architecture of Fort Worth; Kenneth Hafertepe for his work on place, mythology, and politics in the architecture of Texas; Jay C. Henry for his work on twentieth-century architecture in Texas; Lynn M. Herbert for her work on modernist culture in Houston; Dorothy Knox Howe Houghton for her work on the social history of Houston; Marguerite Johnston for her work on the social history of Houston; Barry J. Kaplan and Orson Cook for their work on Houston neighborhood history; Kate Sayen Kirkland for her meticulous work on the Hogg family as Progressive-era philanthropists; Lila Knight for facilitating my access to the Alexander Architectural Archive at the University of Texas at Austin; Ben Koush for his work on modern architecture in Houston; Scott Reagan Miller for his work on the architecture of MacKie and Kamrath; Jeffrey Karl Ochsner for his work on twentieth-century American architecture; Howard Perkins for introducing me to the architecture and social history of Beaumont; Camille Wells for her insights into the social history of eighteenth-century Virginia architecture; Frank D. Welch for his work on Philip Johnson and the architectural culture of Texas in the second half of the twentieth century; Dan Wigodsky for his readiness to drop everything to architecturally tour San Antonio; and Ann Quin Wilson for her work on the Hogg Building, its architect, and architecture.

I am very fortunate to have colleagues and collaborators whose knowledge, insights, and ideas have enriched my thinking, especially Cameron Armstrong, Ellen Beasley, Dana Cuff, William Curtis, Anthony E. Frederick, Marta McBride Galicki, Diane Yvonne Ghirardo, Richard Holley, Richard Ingersoll, Carlos Jiménez, Peter Flagg Maxson, Gerald Moorhead, John Kaliski, Lars Lerup, Rafael Longoria, William O. Neuhaus III, Peter C. Papademetriou, Charles A. Perlitz III, Barrie Scardino, Anderson Todd, Emily Todd, Drexel Turner, William F. Stern, Frank D. Welch, Celeste Williams, and Russell Windham.

Many friends and colleagues have contributed ideas that, in one form or another, found their ways into this work. For the stimulus of their observations and thoughts I thank Martha and James Alexander, George Barnstone, Gertrude Barnstone, Willis Barnstone, Minnette B. Boesel, Frank Briscoe Jr., Roxanne Casscells, Barry Caver, Patsy Cravens, Leslie Barry Davidson, Emilie Farenthold, Frances Tarlton Farenthold, Laura Furman, Lee Govatos, Theodore B. Gupton, Olive S. Hershey, Terrell James, Richard P. Keeton, Inez Rather Lasell, Lynn D. Lasher, Richard Longstreth, Marley Lott, Virginia McAlester, Selden Wallace Morales, Robert C. Richter Jr., Ann Swain, Phoebe Tudor, Lucie Wray Todd, Martha Claire Tompkins, Bettie Ward, Linda Gale and Mark W. White, Evangeline Loessin Whorton, Marion M. Wilcox, Joanne Seale Wilson, and David G. Woodcock.

I especially want to acknowledge Howard Barnstone, who gave me the opportunity to work on his book, and John F. Staub, who was as exceptional a gentleman as he was an architect. Nina J. Cullinan and Hugo V. Neuhaus Jr. kindly shared their personal memories of Shadyside and its early architecture. Lucile Mellinger Harris, Caroline Wiess Law, and Carol Austin Straus talked about their architectural experiences with John Staub. The pioneering work of William H. Jordy and David Gebhard in the 1960s greatly expanded the ways architectural historians were willing to think about twentieth-century American architecture. The *samizdat* essays that Colin Rowe wrote for fun when he lived in Texas in the 1950s are amazing for their prescience in anticipating critical interpretative methodologies that took form in the 1970s.

A number of institutions and organizations have been exceptionally supportive of my efforts to learn more about John Staub and the historical contexts affecting his career.

I am grateful to the School of Architecture at Rice University, its dean, Lars Lerup, associate dean, John J. Casbarian, and Doris Anderson, administrator, its faculty, staff, and students; the Fondren Library at Rice University, especially the Brown Art and Architecture Library, Jet Prendeville, art librarian; the Woodson Research Center, Lee Pecht, head of special collections, Amanda Focke, Philip Montgomery, and Lisa Moellering; and the library's Government Publications and Microforms collection; as well as the Rice Historical Society and its board of directors, especially Karen Hess Rogers, John B. Boles, Ray Watkin Strange, Joyce Winning Nagle, Lee Chatham Seureau, Nancy Boothe, Neal Heaps, and Helen Lawrence-Toombs.

I am grateful to the Gerald D. Hines College of Architecture at the University of Houston and its dean, Joe Mashburn, associate deans, Lannis Kirkland and Trang Phan, faculty, staff, students, and especially its visual resources curator, Jean Krchnak, Catherine Essinger, architecture and art library coordinator, and Tee Thach, librarian; as well as the university's M. D. Anderson Library and the Houston Teachers Institute of the university's Honors College.

The Museum of Fine Arts, Houston, has made possible opportunities to think and write about the architectural histories of Bayou Bend and Rienzi, for which I thank Peter C. Marzio, director of the museum, Katherine S. Howe, director of Rienzi, Bonnie Campbell, director of the Bayou Bend Collection and Gardens, Kathleen B. O'Connor, former education director of Bayou Bend and her predecessor Nancy E. Packer as well as Michael K. Brown, curator of the Bayou Bend Collection and Garden. The research and writings of David B. Warren, the first curator, then the first director, and now director emeritus of Bayou Bend, on the collection, the house, the gardens, and Ima Hogg are invaluable, as are the work of Emily Ballew Neff, curator of American painting and sculpture, on Will C. Hogg, and of Katherine S. Howe on Harris Masterson and his collection, house, and gardens. Elizabeth Bellows made it possible for me to explore Bayou Bend with Jim See of Bellows, Inc., while it was under restoration.

The Houston Metropolitan Research Center of the Houston Public Library is the fundamental source of research material on the history of Houston. I am grateful to Ron Drees, architectural archivist, and his predecessors Steven Strom and Michael E. Wilson. I am deeply indebted to the Texas and Local History Component of the research center, its manager, Steven Hill, and staff, Jennifer Sheehan, Fred Mondrit, and Fred Parris, and former staff members Ellen Hanlon, Will Howard, Douglas Weiskopf, and Doris Glasser.

The Rice Design Alliance has facilitated my traveling to Boston, Charleston, Chicago, Los Angeles, Mexico City, Miami, Phoenix, Savannah, and Seattle to experience their country place communities and country houses. I am grateful to Linda Sylvan, executive director, Kathryn Fosdick and Carrie R. Carpenter, program administrators, Mary Swift, membership coordinator, and Lynn Kelly, tour coordinator.

The Houston Seminar has facilitated my traveling to Des Moines and northeast Iowa, Fort Worth, Galveston, Los Angeles, the Northern Neck of Virginia, San Antonio, and Santa Fe to visit works of architecture. I especially thank Jacqueline André Schmeal, Nona Carmichael, Nancy Philen Thompson, Beverly Ramírez, Josephine Powell Smith, and Barbara S. Sklar. Marion Knox Barthelme, Anne S. Brown, Elizabeth H. Carrell, Bettie Cartwright, Emilie S. Kilgore, Gaye V. McCullough, Evelyn Thomas Nolen, Jane H. Gregory, Mary Lynch Kurtz, and other directors of the Houston Seminar have been unstinting in their generous support of my research as has Stuart Hudson, executive director.

Preservation Dallas, its director, W. Dwayne Jones, and survey manager, Katherine Dyll Seale, enabled me to become much better acquainted with Dallas and its remarkable architecture through their tours both formal and spontaneous. Thanks also to Ann Abernathy, David Griffin, Robert L. Meckfessel, Douglas Newby, and Ralph Randall.

Historic Fort Worth, its director, Jerre Tracy, staff historian Susan Allen Kline, former president Malinda Crumley, and directors Judith Singer Cohen and Gail Landreth not only invited me to lecture, along with Peter Maxson, on the country houses of John Staub but very generously supported this project by providing accommodations for Richard Cheek and Susan Keeton in June 2002. Thanks also to Joseph Minton.

The Dixon Gallery and Gardens in Memphis and the McFaddin-Ward House Historical Museum in Beaumont enabled me to learn more about those cities and their country houses.

In choosing to make Staub's country houses the focus of its first Texas study tour in March 2006, the Institute of Classical Architecture–Classical America facilitated access to ten Staub houses and three institutional buildings in three intensive days, revealing the depth and variety of Staub's architecture. Special thanks to William Curtis and Russell Windham, Houston hosts for the visit, Gilbert P. Schafer III, chairman of the institute's board of directors, fellows and public program committee co-chairs William Brockschmidt and Courtney Coleman, and fellow John Woodrow Kelley, as well as Thomas Hayes of Classical Excursions, and participants Rhett Butler, Jeffrey Davis, Richard Dragisic, Virgil McDowell, Helen and Sandy McNabb, Steven M. Salny, Bailey Sharp, and Lloyd Zuckerberg.

The Cultural Landscape Foundation held its fall 2005 directors' meeting in Houston, setting the stage for interpretive tours that put Staub's buildings into the broader context of Houston's city, community, and landscape planning history. Special thanks to Charles A. Birnbaum, founder, and directors Mac Keith Griswold, Susan Keeton, Douglas Reed, and Suzanne L. Turner.

Essential in bringing this book to fruition was the generosity of owners of John Staub's houses who welcomed exploratory visits and Richard Cheek's photography. Without their kind indulgence, this project would not have been possible. Profound thanks to Mr. and Mrs. Ben M. Anderson, the president, director, and manager of the Bayou Club, Mr. and Mrs. Frank W. Bellows, Mr. and Mrs. Alfredo Brener, Ms. Bonnie Campbell and Mr. Michael K. Brown of the Bayou Bend Collection and Gardens of the Museum of Fine Arts, Houston, Mr. and Mrs. George S. Craft, Mr. James A. Elkins Jr., Mr. and Mrs. James A. Elkins III, Ms. Carolyn Farb, Mrs. Ernest B. Fay, Ms. Marie Fay Evnochides of the Fay School, Mr. and Mrs. James C. Flores, Ms. Burdine Anderson Giese, Mr. and Mrs. Ben Guill, Mr. and Mrs. P. J. Murphey Harmon, Mr. and Mrs. Brantly Harris Jr., Mr. and Mrs. Dan J. Harrison III, Mr. and Mrs. John Havens, Henry C. Hirtz, Ms. Katherine S. Howe of Rienzi, the Museum of Fine Arts, Houston, Mr. and Mrs. Peter Jameson, Mr. and Mrs. George Jewell, Mr. and Mrs. Rob L. Jones, Mrs. Theodore N. Law, Mr. and Mrs. Kenneth A. Moffet, Ms. Marian Fay Momsen, Mr. and Mrs. Edward C. Norwood, Mrs. Kenneth Dale Owen, Mr. and Mrs. Jeffrey R. Parsons, Mr. and Mrs. Matthew Prucka, Mr. and Mrs. Harry M. Reasoner, Ms. Gay Roane, Ms. Susan Kister and Mr. George J. Ruel, Mr. and Mrs. Christopher Sarofim, Mr. and Mrs. Don W. Short, Mr. and Mrs. Matthew R. Simmons, and Mr. and Mrs. Peter S. Wareing.

In Beaumont, thanks are due to Mary Olson, M.D., and Mr. Jeffrey L. Fritz. Special thanks to Laura Lee and William J. Graber III, M.D., who opened many doors in Beaumont. In Dallas, the Dallas Arboretum and its president, Mary Brinegar. In Fort Worth thanks to Mr. and Mrs. John Oudt, Mrs. Alfred McKnight, Ms. Gail Landreth, Mr. and Mrs. Richard W. Moncrief, and Mrs. Richard Hunter Barrett; special thanks to Louise Kuehn and Gordon Appelman. In Galveston thanks to Mr. Risher Randall, Mrs. Martin L. Towler, and Mary Walker-Chyle, M.D. In Hunt, Texas, thanks to Mrs. Samuel N. Sprunt. In Kemah, Texas, thanks to the Hon. and Mrs. Bill King and Mr. and Mrs. Stephen Evnochides. In Morgan's Point, Texas, thanks to Ms. Lillian H. Bean. In Victoria, Texas, thanks to Mrs. Patrick H. Welder Jr. and Mr. and Mrs. Thomas C. Tyng. Special thanks to Ann Alcorn. In Knoxville, Tennessee, thanks to Mr. and Mrs. William Ross McNabb.

Susan Bielstein of the University of Chicago Press, Holly Carver of the University of Iowa Press, and Jan Cigliano of the Princeton Architectural Press provided valuable guidance in the publication process.

Finally, thanks are due to Charles Backus of the Texas A&M University Press and his very professional staff of editors, designers, and marketers. Thanks especially to the anonymous readers for their perceptive criticisms and generous endorsements.

CHAPTER 1 : JOHN F. STAUB, HOUSTON, AND THE SOCIAL CONSTRUCTION OF UPPER-CLASS IDENTITY

John F. Staub

This book about the country houses of Houston architect John F. Staub seeks to go beyond the discourse of style as a way to understand and evaluate architecture. Le Corbusier's assertion in 1923 that "the 'styles' are a lie" bespoke the frustration of several generations of nineteenth- and twentieth-century architectural reformers with a system of knowledge that privileged what, in practice, seemed most superficial and interchangeable about modern buildings: the historical sources on which their compositional and decorative attributes were modeled.[1] John F. Staub, a twentieth-century American eclectic architect, had a long and distinguished career designing modern houses based on historical models, precisely the sort of buildings that his near contemporary Le Corbusier sought to dismiss. The guiding thesis of this book is not that the styles are a lie but that they were only part of the crucial architectural task in which John Staub, his eclectic peers, and their predecessors were involved: the social construction through architecture of upper-class-ness. This book analyzes the ways Staub's country houses socially constructed upper-class "identity" (identity involves the formation of community around shared beliefs and claims to belonging) and sought to sustain upper-class "subjects" (subjects are idealized personifications of identity positions) from the 1920s through the 1950s.[2] This interpretation seeks to demonstrate that the practices associated with architectural design—site planning and spatial organization, massing and composition, building finishes and details, as well as the application of style—were the material media through which Staub advanced the social construction of upper-class identity and subjectivity. The perceptible beauty of Staub's country houses was meant to sustain mythic identities that legitimized his clients' social standing, linked them to other elites in a process of mutual reinforcement, and edified and inspired them to become upper-class subjects by internalizing the mythical virtues and manners imputed to the highest order of social classification: integrity, courage, wisdom, generosity, grace, and charm.[3] This book examines the social construction through architecture of the upper-class representational style that the social historian Nelson W. Aldrich Jr. categorizes as "patrician."[4] Analysis will demonstrate how the sense of style these houses, as objects, "materialized" (that is, made materially tangible), constructed an identity for, and lent cohesion to Houston's entrepreneurial elite in the second quarter of the twentieth century.

John Fanz Staub was born on September 12, 1892. He was the third generation of his family to live in the east Tennessee railroad city of Knoxville.[5] His family's wealth, modest by comparison to that of some of his future clients, was formed by his paternal grandfather, Peter Staub, a Swiss-German immigrant tailor who came to Knoxville in 1856. During the period of the New South following the Civil War, Peter Staub's business and real estate investments carried him to good fortune and respectability (he was twice elected mayor of Knoxville). John Staub's father, Fritz, operated Peter Staub's best-known business, Staub's Opera House. John Staub's mother, Anna Cornelia Fanz, was also from a Knoxville Swiss-German family.[6] By the time of John Staub's childhood, his family had crossed the threshold of ethnic insularity and had been absorbed into Knoxville's small-town Southern elite, as indicated by Anglicizing the pronunciation of Staub ("stawb"); the marriage of his mother's younger sister, Emma Fanz, to Albert G. Hope, a Knoxville jeweler and a great-great-grandson of Thomas Hope, an English-born carpenter and joiner who had been Knoxville's first architect at the turn of the nineteenth century; and their membership in St. John's Episcopal Church.[7] Staub graduated from the University of Tennessee in Knoxville, where he studied mathematics, in 1913. Staub told his biographer, the Houston architect Howard Barnstone, that a house his parents built near the university campus in the 1900s and sketching trips with a college drawing class to old towns in east Tennessee stimulated his interest in architecture. Staub spent the summer of 1913, following his graduation, giving dancing lessons to sons and daughters of his parents' friends at the Knoxville Country Club. Staub's grace as a dancing partner would stand him in good stead throughout his life.[8]

From 1913 to 1916, Staub studied architecture at the Massachusetts Institute of Technology, a favorite destination of aspiring Southern architects. He earned a bachelor's of science degree in architecture in 1915 and a master's degree in 1916. Through a sequence of fortuitous connections Staub was able to obtain an interview with, and be hired by, the New York country house architect Harrie T. Lindeberg, for whom he worked from 1916 to 1917 and again from 1919 to 1923 after two years of service as a U.S. Navy combat aviator during World War I.[9] Lindeberg, an alumnus of McKim, Mead and White's office, began his practice in 1906. By 1916, he was one of the most influential country house architects in the United States.[10]

The memoir that Alexandra Fatio compiled about her father, the architect Maurice Fatio, a Swiss immigrant who worked in Lindeberg's office in 1920–21, corroborates what Staub told Howard Barnstone about Lindeberg's practice. In letters written to his parents in Switzerland, Fatio complained that Lindeberg paid his draftsmen miserably but also reported that he was alert to their talents, entrusted them with design responsibility, and encouraged and supported them when they were ready to begin their own practices.[11] Lindeberg's origins were obscure (Staub recalled that Lindeberg's draftsmen joked among themselves that his father, a Swedish immigrant, was a masseur in Bergen Point, New Jersey, where Lindeberg was born).[12] Yet beginning with the Stillman House in Pocantico, New York, a job that he seems to have taken from McKim, Mead and White's office, Lindeberg reinvented himself not just as a gentleman but also as an arbiter of style to his upper-class clientele.[13] In Lindeberg's office, Staub worked on Wyldwood, the country place of Clyde M. Carr in Lake Forest, Illinois, of 1916, the Lisbeth Ledyard House in Stockbridge, Massachusetts, of 1917, the Frederic G. Achelis House in Greenwich, Connecticut, of 1919, Tangley Oaks, the Philip D. Armour III country place in Lake Bluff, Illinois, of 1922, and the Seth E. Thomas Jr. country place in Morristown, New Jersey, of 1925.[14]

The years Staub spent in Harrie T. Lindeberg's office in New York seem to have crystallized his abilities as an architect and his sensitivity to the nuances of country house practice. In 1921, Lindeberg asked Staub to go to Houston with his young bride, Madeleine Louise Delabarre of Conway, Massachusetts, a graduate of what is now the Parsons School of Design in New York, to whom Staub had been introduced in 1916 and whom he married in 1919. A commission Lindeberg received for a house in Houston had led to two additional commissions because of the enthusiasm of Lindeberg's initial client. Staub told Barnstone he had been on the verge of leaving Lindeberg's office to return to Knoxville, where he had been offered a position in the firm of Barber and McMurry, Knoxville's leading architects.[15] Deferring this prospect, Staub moved to Houston, expecting to stay two years at the most.

What Staub encountered in Houston, and what caused him to remain there, was not simply professional opportunity but also the possibility of functioning, like Lindeberg, as an arbiter of taste, style, and form. As a country house architect in the 1920s and 1930s, Staub was responsible for formulating a representational style that enabled Houston's elite to affiliate with an American patrician class. An analysis of Staub's career demonstrates that this upper class was, especially in its representational aspect, a mythical

Courtlandt Place, Houston. Entry piers, 1910, demolished.
Illustrated City Book of Houston, 170.

construct, what the cultural historian Richard L. Bushman describes as a "convenient identity and definition of position in the confusing fluidity of a democratic society," the latter phrase an apt description of the entrepreneurial city of Houston during most episodes of its history.[16]

Staub liked to remember that his wife Madeleine so charmed Lindeberg's Houston clients and their wives that as the three (eventually four) Lindeberg-designed houses in Houston were nearing completion in 1923, two of these clients got Staub the commission to design a clubhouse for the River Oaks Country Club, a new golf club being organized west of Houston.[17] The clubhouse commission enabled Staub to open his own office in the Union National Bank Building, where one of Lindeberg's Houston clients had provided him with office space. Staub's first employee was his eventual partner, John Thomas Rather Jr. Among his employees in the 1920s, 1930s, and 1940s were the Houston architects Charles H. Kiefner, Vance D. Phenix, Milton B. McGinty, Albert Howze, Donald Barthelme, and William C. Caldwell.[18]

During the 1920s, Staub's houses in Houston were concentrated in the city's new elite neighborhoods. He designed one house in the earliest of these neighborhoods, Courtlandt Place, a St. Louis–like private street developed in 1907, as well as six houses in the private place subdivision of Broadacres, developed in 1923.

The neighborhood with which he became especially identified was River Oaks, where the country clubhouse was built. Development of its first section, Country Club Estates, began in 1924 under the direction of Will, Mike, and Ima Hogg, and their associate Hugh Potter. It was for Miss Hogg and her brothers that Staub designed his first major country house, Bayou Bend, between 1926 and 1928.

Although Staub's office occasionally produced institutional buildings and small commercial buildings, it was with the country house that he made his reputation. By the end of the 1920s, Staub was being commissioned to design country houses in Galveston and Fort Worth, Texas. His work was published in the regional architectural press, especially the Atlanta-based *Southern Architect and Building News*, and in such nationally circulated magazines as *House Beautiful* and *House and Garden*. The Houston Metropolitan Research Center, the archival collection of the Houston Public Library, contains the largest collection of Staub's architectural drawings.[19] By reviewing sets of construction documents for Staub's houses in the collection, it is possible to understand why Staub told Howard Barnstone that as an architect he worked "awfully hard." It is not simply the number of drawings generated for a single house but also the intensity with which window sections, for instance, were detailed that make one aware that the material presence of Staub's houses, although not emphasized perceptually, depended on the rigor, thoroughness, and deliberation with which the parts of each house were designed and constructed.

The Great Depression crippled the practices of architects in Houston as in other parts of the United States. Although Staub remembered the early 1930s as a time of professional anxiety, he received his most exceptional commissions between 1930 and 1935. After 1935, as Houston's economy began to recover, Staub reached his peak as an architect and as an arbiter of style for Houston's elite. River Oaks was where Staub made his mark on Houston, designing twenty-one houses there between 1930 and 1941. At the same time, Staub began to design country retreats in the pine forest along Buffalo Bayou west of Houston as well as substantial country houses in Dallas, San Antonio, Fort Worth, Beaumont, Galveston, and Victoria, Texas; Shreveport, Louisiana; and Knoxville and Memphis, Tennessee. The most signifi-

"River Oaks: Live Where You Play." River Oaks Corporation advertisement. The Campanile, 1928. Fondren Library, Rice University.

cant instance of national recognition for Staub came in the form of a profile of his work published in January 1942 in the architectural magazine *Pencil Points.*

Staub spent most of the years of World War II on active duty in the U.S. Naval Reserves.[20] Resuming practice with his partner J. T. Rather Jr. in 1944, Staub continued to concentrate on the design of houses as Rather expanded the firm's production to include buildings at Rice University, the University of Texas at Austin, the University of Houston, and the Texas Medical Center in Houston. In the postwar period, Staub, although only in his fifties, began to exhibit a loss of direction as he struggled to come to terms with the "contemporary" trend in postwar domestic architecture. The collapse of the consensus on the legitimacy of the country house after World War II was mirrored in Staub's architectural uncertainty as he explored such new house typologies as the ranch house in the late 1940s and early 1950s. In the mid-1950s he formulated a one-story suburban house type that merged the ranch house and the classical pavilion. The "Palladian" ranch house made it possible for Staub to return to the design of houses based on historical models with a measure of conviction that had waned in the late 1940s.

Staub designed his last house in 1961. He retired from practice in 1963 and used his free time to travel with his wife. John Staub was gregarious. He and Madeleine Staub were members of the Bayou Club and the Paul Jones Dance Club.[21] Tom Rather's declining health in the late 1960s forced Staub to resume greater involvement in the management of the firm. Following Rather's death in 1968, Staub and his surviving partner, Albert Howze, dissolved the firm of Staub, Rather and Howze and closed its office.

In the early 1970s, William A. Wareing III, the son of Staub's elder daughter, Nancy, and her husband, William Wareing Jr., and a student of architecture at the University of Texas, proposed that a book about his grandfather's work be published. One enthusiastic supporter was the Houston insurance executive John H. Lindsey, a contemporary and friend of Staub's children. Billy Wareing had had polio as a child, and his health was precarious. While staying with his grandparents in Houston in 1973 so he could look for an architectural job, Billy Wareing died. His death galvanized the effort to compile a book on John Staub's work. John Lindsey and Caroline Wiess Law were instrumental in involving the Museum of Fine Arts, Houston, as sponsor, raising the funds, and securing the participation of Howard Barnstone, one of Houston's best-known modern architects, as author. Barnstone worked avidly for five years with the photographers Rob Muir and Rick Gardner and research associates David T. Courtwright, a historian, and Jerome Iowa, an architect and architectural historian, on *The Architecture of*

From right to left: Howard Barnstone, John F. Staub, and David Courtwright in the garden at Bayou Bend, 1976, Courtesy Houston Chronicle

John F. Staub, which was published by the University of Texas Press and the Museum of Fine Arts in 1979.[22]

John Staub participated in the preparation of the book and took great pride in the result. It was the first book to be published on the career of a Houston architect, and it marked the beginning of serious scholarship on the architectural history of Houston.

John Staub died on April 13, 1981, after a short illness; Madeleine Staub died five months later.[23] Their house was acquired by their grandson Peter Staub Wareing and his wife, Elizabeth Blanton. Peter Wareing is the brother of William Wareing III and one of the four children of Nancy Staub and William Wareing. Another Staub grandchild, Nancy Staub Callery, one of the three daughters of Madeleine and John Staub's younger daughter, Caroline, and her husband, Charles Callery, became an architect and practices in Seattle, Washington, with Bassetti Architects. The three children of Madeleine and John Staub's son, Dr. John Delabarre Staub, and his wife, Alice York, are, like their father, involved in health care professions.

Since John Staub's death, five of his Houston houses have been demolished, and at least seven have suffered alterations extensive enough to call their integrity into question. Because Houston has an ineffective historic preservation ordinance, the fate of other houses will continue to hang in the balance. At the same time, four of Staub's houses (Bayou Bend, Rienzi, the Camp House in Dallas, and the Dixon House in Memphis) have become house museums.

Houston, the largest city in Texas and by 1990 the fourth largest city in the United States, seems like an unlikely place for John Staub to have had a flourishing career. Houston is notorious as the only major city in the U.S. never to have adopted a zoning code. It is flat, hot, humid, and sprawling. The civility, composure, and proportioned assurance of Staub's country houses bespeak another Houston, one not immediately apparent to first-time visitors or even to Houstonians who live on the city's boundless periphery. Staub's country houses implicitly propose a utopia: the American garden-suburban idyll of the late nineteenth and early twentieth centuries.[24] That the civic landscape of Houston was being reorganized in the 1910s and 1920s to support such a construct becomes evident when Staub's houses are experienced in their spatial contexts.

When Madeleine and John Staub arrived in Houston in November 1921, it was the third largest city in Texas, with a population of 138,276. By 1930, a decade of sustained economic and population growth had enabled Houston, with a population of 292,352, to surpass Dallas and San Antonio to become the largest city in Texas and, after New Orleans, the second largest city in the South.[25]

THE LITTLE NEW YORK OF THE SOUTH

"The Little New York of the South" advertisement for Second National Bank. *Houston* 1 (June 1930): 41.

Founded in August 1836, Houston was named for Sam Houston, the flamboyant military and political leader who commanded the Texan army at the Battle of San Jacinto in April 1836, when Anglo-Texan rebels surprised and captured the Mexican general Antonio López de Santa Anna, forcing him to concede the independence of Texas from Mexico. The founders of Houston, two brothers from New York, A. C. Allen and J. K. Allen, named their new town on Buffalo Bayou (a small river that empties into Galveston Bay) for Sam Houston, who had become the first president of the Republic of Texas. Sam Houston returned the favor by supporting the town's designation, from 1837 to 1839, as provisional capital of the Republic of Texas.[26] During the nineteenth century, Houston was economically subordinate to the Gulf coast port city of Galveston, fifty miles to the southeast. Beginning in the 1850s Houston's business elite laid the foundation for their city's economic ascent by promoting, investing in, and building railroads, which facilitated the transportation of cotton, Texas' most important cash crop, from the fields to Houston for processing and transshipment to buyers in the northeastern United States and Europe. By the time of the Civil War, a nascent system of railroads emanated from Houston.[27] Spurred by competition with Galveston, Houston entrepreneurs constructed consensus around projects of economic expansion and diversification during the New South period, encouraging emergent entrepreneurs to headquarter their businesses in Houston. By welcoming and absorbing emergent elites in the 1880s and 1890s, especially entrepreneurs in the East Texas timber industry, Houston's business leaders made their city seem more appealing than Galveston (which Houstonians stigmatized as rigid, stratified, and hostile to newcomers).[28] By 1900 Houston had surpassed Galveston in population.

Three critical events at the beginning of the twentieth century set the economic stage for Staub's career in Houston. In September 1900, Galveston, which occupies a barrier island in the Gulf of Mexico, was devastated by a hurricane that killed fifteen percent of the city's population.[29] In January 1901, an enormous reservoir of oil was discovered at Spindletop near Beaumont, eighty miles east of Houston, precipitating an outburst of oil exploration and production along the Texas Gulf coast and other promising sites in Louisiana and Oklahoma.[30] Houston's business leaders acted decisively to persuade oilmen to locate their businesses in Houston. Three of the newly organized "majors"—the vertically integrated oil companies—established regional headquarters in Houston: the Texas Company (Texaco) in 1908, the Gulf Oil Companies (now Chevron-Texaco) in 1916, and the Humble Oil and Refining Company (now ExxonMobil) in 1917.[31] The devastation of Galveston worked to Houston's advantage by strengthening the argument of Houston businessmen for a deep-draught ship channel through Galveston Bay and up Buffalo Bayou that would permit maritime traffic to bypass the port of Galveston and transform Houston into an inland seaport. Between 1902 and 1914 the U. S. Army Corps of Engineers constructed the fifty-mile-long Houston Ship Channel. Its completion coincided with the outbreak of World War I in Europe.[32] Houston's railroad connections, shipping facilities, oil refineries, and cotton warehouses meant that the city and its economy were positioned to profit from wartime demand. During the 1920s, these economic activities cohered to accelerate Houston's expansion. The economic historian Joseph Pratt called the 1920s the "golden age" of the cotton exporting business in Texas.[33] Oil exploration, processing, and marketing surged during the 1920s, as did Houston's real estate and construction markets. John Staub's Houston clients during the 1920s tended to come from established local families or, if newcomers, were affiliated with established businesses. Their sources of wealth were the cotton trade, banking, law, real estate, insurance, and retail trade. Not until the 1930s, when oil, replacing cotton, became dominant in the Texas economy, did oil outrank all other sources of wealth among Staub's clients.[34]

Staub's client base shifted in the 1930s in response to the emergence of a new oil elite. Houston was so fluid socially that by the 1930s emergent elites from the first two decades of the century—such as the real estate developer, banker, and eventual cabinet secretary Jesse H. Jones, the international cotton merchant William L. Clayton, and the oilmen J. S. Cullinan (founder of the Texas Company) and William S. Farish, R. Lee Blaffer, and Harry C. Wiess (three of the nine cofounders of the Humble Oil and Refining Company)—had metamorphosed into established elites. Harrie T. Lindeberg's initial client in Houston, the stock and bond broker Hugo V. Neuhaus, and Staub's clients, Will C. Hogg and his sister Ima Hogg, demonstrated that architectural patronage could function as what the anthropologist Pamela G. Smart calls an "instrument in the formation of a public" and as a "technology of self-fashioning" in order, as the cultural historian Penny Sparke discerned, "to underscore and to disguise a social transition marked by the acquisition of 'taste.'"[35] From the 1900s through the 1930s the formation of such new collectives as the River Oaks Country Club contributed to the social construction of an upper class in Houston. Cultural institutions (the Museum of Fine Arts, the Houston Symphony Orchestra, the Little Theater), schools (Kinkaid School), neighborhoods, even religious bodies (especially Christ Church, Houston's oldest Episcopal parish, and Palmer Memorial Church, an Episcopal parish organized in 1929), functioned as sites capable of framing those affiliated with them as a Houston upper class. Staub's architectural association with the River Oaks Country Club, the Houston Riding and Polo Club, the Tejas Club, the Bayou Club, the Junior League of Houston, Palmer Memorial Church, Christ Church, and the Museum of Fine Arts contributed to the construction of class solidarity through buildings and spaces that identified their members and supporters as superior and refined.[36]

Houston architecture during the early twentieth century kept pace with the city's emergence from provincial status. During the nineteenth century, it had been unusual for out-of-state architects to design buildings in Texas. A rare exception was McKim, Mead and White's house for the banker George Sealy in Galveston of 1891.[37] By 1910, the practice of hiring metropolitan architects was becoming increasingly common in Houston. D. H. Burnham and Company of Chicago designed the eleven-story Scanlan Building of 1909, briefly the tallest in Houston. Jarvis Hunt of Chicago designed the nine-story Southern Pacific Building of 1911. Warren and Wetmore of New York were responsible for Union Station of 1911, the thirteen-story Texas Company Building of 1915, and a small (by their standards) but locally influential country house for T. J. Donoghue, executive vice president of Texaco of 1916 in Courtlandt Place. The St. Louis architects Mauran, Russell and Crowell designed the twelve-story Union National Bank Building of 1912 and the seventeen-story Rice Hotel of 1913 for Jesse H. Jones.[38] At the south end of Main Street, Edgar Odell Lovett, who in 1908 resigned his professorship of mathematics at Princeton University to become president of what is now Rice University, retained the Boston architects Cram, Goodhue and Ferguson to plan Rice's 288-acre campus and design its initial buildings, which were completed when the university opened in 1912.[39]

The Rice Institute (as it was originally called) had an extraordinary impact on the imagination of Houston's Progressive era elite that extended beyond Cram's bold, exotic, neo-Byzantine architecture. Rice caused Houston's business leaders to realize what could be achieved by systematically integrating architectural design, landscape planting, and city planning. In 1915, the St. Louis landscape architect George E. Kessler was retained by the City of Houston to prepare a master plan for the newly acquired Hermann Park, adjacent to the Rice Institute campus, and to transform the two-lane, unpaved extension of Houston's Main Street, which ran between the park and campus, into the tree-lined Main Boulevard.

Kessler used Cram's planning model of axial avenues of live oak trees (the totemic Southern tree) to impose a new sense of rhythm, measure, and proportion in what was still largely open countryside. So compelling was Kessler's planning regimen that J. S. Cullinan hired Kessler in 1916 to lay out the private place neighborhood of Shadyside, with frontage on the parkway section of the new Main Boulevard.[40] Cullinan treated Shadyside as a proprietary venture rather than a speculative real estate deal. He sold building sites only to "congenial parties."[41] At Kessler's recommendation, Cullinan hired the St. Louis architect James P. Jamieson to design his house. The Houston architects Birdsall P. Briscoe, Alfred C. Finn, and William Ward Watkin (whom Cram had sent to Houston to oversee construction of Rice's buildings and who remained at Rice to become the first professor of architecture) designed country houses for other Shadyside families. The stockbroker Hugo V. Neuhaus outflanked these residents by commissioning Harrie T. Lindeberg to design his house. Neuhaus then secured additional commissions for Lindeberg in Shadyside from the cotton exporter Kenneth E. Womack and the oilman William S. Farish. Another house commission, from the wholesale merchant D. D. Peden, and extensive alterations and additions to the five-year-old house of Farish's partner, Harry C. Wiess, brought the number of Lindeberg's Shadyside commissions to five.[42]

Aerial view of the Rice Institute campus, Houston, 1920. Woodson Research Center, Fondren Library, Rice University.

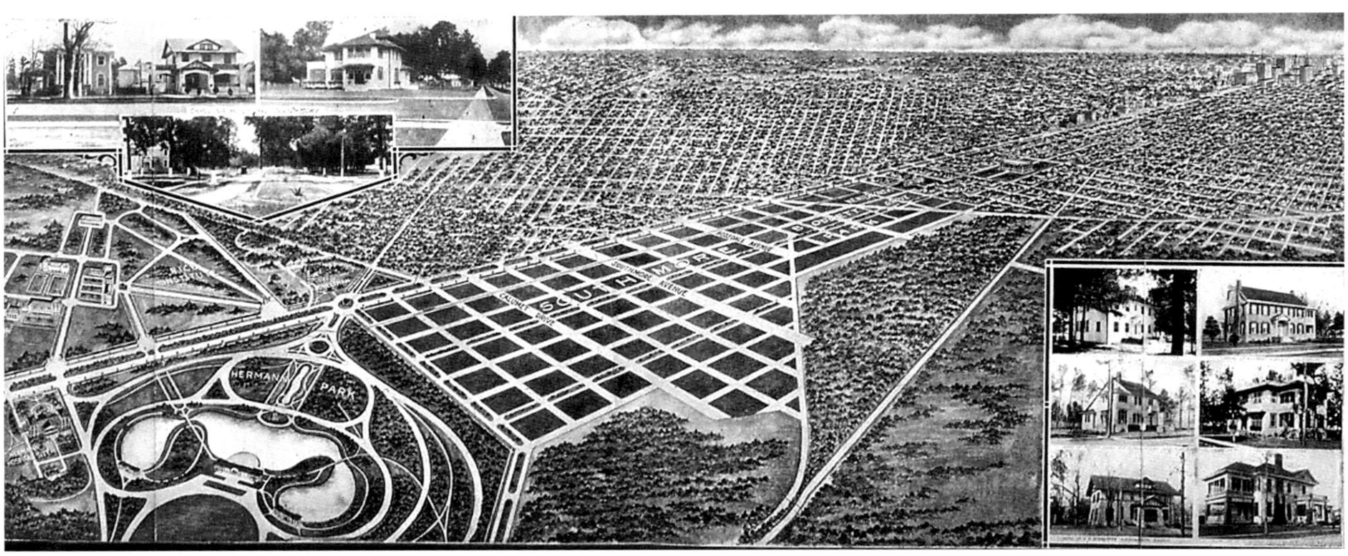

Aerial perspective of Main Boulevard, Hermann Park civic arena, Houston. Houston City Directory, 1915. *Advertisement for H. F. MacGregor real estate interests.*

The installation of avenues of live oaks to construct axes of directed movement and vision and to shape volumes of shaded space to compensate for the flatness of the terrain was repeated in new subdivision development in the early 1920s in what *The Houston Gargoyle* (Houston's short-lived version of the *New Yorker*) humorously called "Houston's Cradle of Culture" near Rice, Hermann Park, and Shadyside.[43] This was where the spatial matrix for Staub's Houston, a modern garden city, took shape.

The historical context for evaluating the houses Staub designed in the Cradle of Culture and other Houston neighborhoods involves the "country house," an elite house type of the late nineteenth and early twentieth centuries, and historical eclecticism, the practice of adapting historical models to modern architectural programs.[44] A more elusive context involves the ways that the country house and historical eclecticism supported the social construction of upper-class identity and subject positions. An analysis of Staub's country houses demonstrates how he "spatialized" (to spatialize is to make something perceptible in space through the organization of spaces) upper-class identity and subjectivity in his houses through practices derived from the discipline of classical architecture. American country houses, which the architectural historian Mark Alan Hewitt divides into three historical phases—the stately home of the 1890s to 1900s; the country manor of the 1900s to 1920s; and the suburban country house of the 1920s to 1940s—differed architecturally in their degrees of ostentation and in their architects' attitudes toward the appropriation of historical models.[45] What these country houses shared was a tacit commitment to the social construction of spatial settings capable of identifying and sustaining an upper class in a democratic republic. This commitment constituted the implicit social program of the American country house. One factor that makes Staub's houses so remarkable is the facility and ingenuity he displayed in "naturalizing" this social program, so that it never seems to stand out as an objective. It is through beauty, generosity, propriety, and precision that Staub's domestic architecture makes a case for the relevance and legitimacy of the subject positions identifying an American patrician class, the lady and gentleman.[46] As Hewitt also discerned, an evolutionary consciousness underpinned the construction of "tradition" in the architecture of the country house, evident in the recurring use of Darwinian terminology—"stage," "development," "adaptation"—in American architectural criticism of the period.[47] Evolutionary rhetoric indicates the extent to which retrospective architectural imagery masked the modernity of the country house, an apparent "critique of modernity" shaped by "the modern imperative of rationalization," as Pamela Smart has observed.[48] The dualities

Hugo V. Neuhaus House, Shadyside, Houston, 1919–23, Harrie T. Lindeberg, architect. Photograph by Calvin Wheat, Civics for Houston, 1928.

Kenneth E. Womack House, Shadyside, Houston, 1921–23, Harrie T. Lindeberg, architect. Photograph by Paul Hester, Houston Architectural Survey, *vol. 5, 1228.*

William S. Farish House, Shadyside, Houston, 1921–25, Harrie T. Lindeberg, architect. Photograph by Paul Hester, Houston Architectural Survey, *vol. 5, 1169.*

D. D. Peden House, Shadyside, Houston, 1921–24, Harrie T. Lindeberg, architect. Photograph by Calvin Wheat, Civics for Houston *1 (May 1928): 11.*

"Houston's *Cradle of Culture and Environs*." Houston Gargoyle 5 [May 1, 1932]: 11.

Modern Houston. *Gulf Building, Houston. Vincent Maragliotti, painter, 1929.*
Alfred C. Finn Collection, Mss 19–333, Houston Metropolitan Research Center, Houston Public Library.

modernity-tradition, present-past, and patrician-democratic were to be negotiated through the construction of continuity.

The construction of spatial continuity, so critical to urban reform programs during the Progressive era of the early twentieth century, is a recurring phenomenon in Staub's houses.[49] Continuity between a house and its landscape setting and between houses and their neighborhood overcame the pervasive feeling of spatial monotony due to the lack of topographic variation and of trees characteristic of the Gulf coastal plain. The systematic way that Staub used axes of movement and view to frame subjective perceptions of scale, proportion, and rhythmic measure outside and inside his houses constructs sensations of continuity. He naturalized houses by opening their reception rooms to light, view, and (of overriding importance in Houston before air-conditioning) the prevailing southeast Gulf breeze. On many of Staub's house sites, landscape architects reinforced the construction of continuity by designing gardens based on the projection of axes of movement and view from inside his houses. The systematic application of techniques for constructing continuity was explicit, and the result was to transform barren, spatially monotonous subdivision lots into verdant, spatially buoyant landscape settings. The systematic construction of spatial continuity produced subjective emotional experiences of wholeness, completeness, and belonging.[50] Spatial continuity identified the houses, the neighborhoods, and the people associated with them as superior in their capacity to transform the landscape with hierarchically consistent gradations of scale, proportion, and rhythmic measure. Inside houses, Staub constructed continuity with the same means as outside. Axes of movement and view through houses produce perceptions of deep interior space that are emotionally affecting. These perceptions transform movement through houses into procession, ritualizing the experience of occupying Staub's houses and reinforcing the implicit construction of patrician subjectivity.[51]

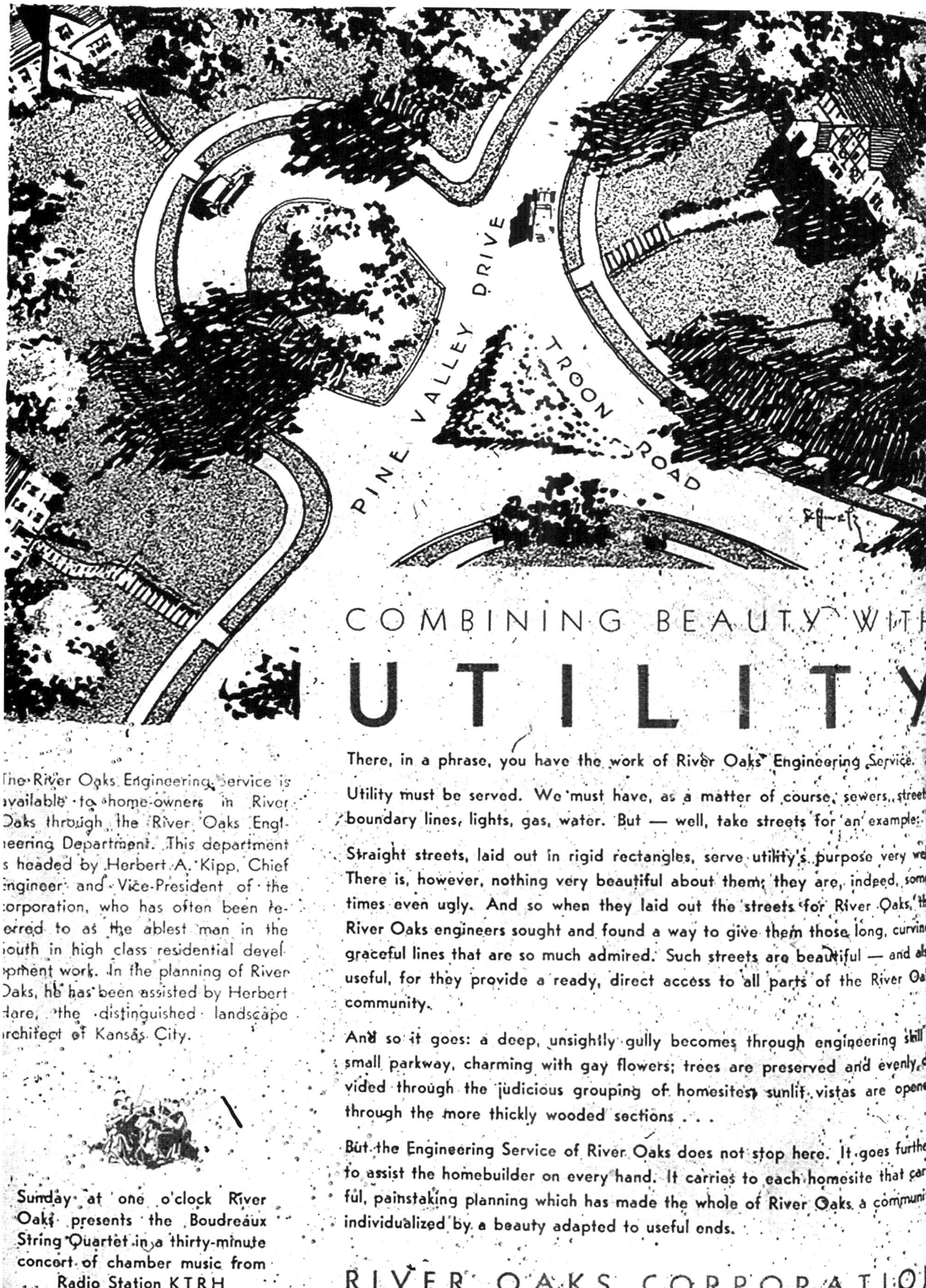

"Combining Beauty with Utility," E. M. Schiwetz, Houston Gargoyle 4 (Nov. 29, 1931): back cover.

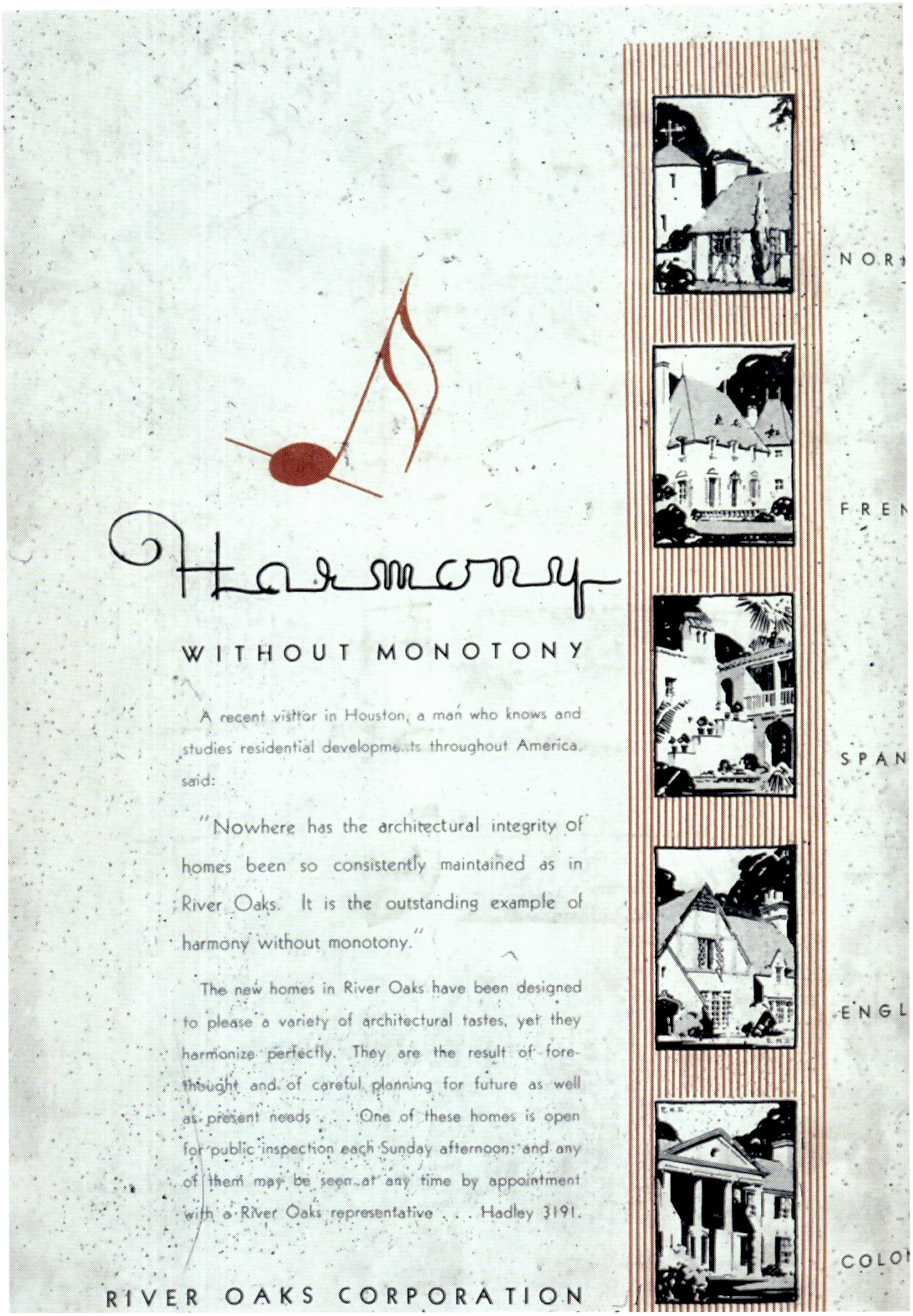

"*Harmony without Monotony,*" E. M. Schiwetz, Houston Gargoyle 4 *(June 14, 1931): back cover.*

The construction of spatial sensations of generosity is another feature of Staub's houses. Generosity (as well as discretion, composure, and liveliness) is a spatially felt intimation of the virtues—the good form—of the people who inhabit such settings. Barnstone described the bodily experience of moving through a Staub interior as the "divine float."[52] This description evokes the visceral sensation of weightlessness and levitation one can feel in Staub's houses. Lightening one's experience of space and stimulating sensations of liberation and delight through proportion were ways that Staub rendered houses as simultaneously authoritative and joyful.[53] He complemented visual perceptions of beauty with bodily sensations of delight. The capacity that architecture has to make its inhabitants feel good and enhance their senses and imagination reinforced the social construction of upper-class-ness in American country houses. Upper-class domestic architecture was identified with restraint and dignity.[54] It was emotionally exhilarating but in ways that feel decorous and measured. Another sensation that one becomes aware of in Staub's houses is his propensity for coupling feelings of monumentality and intimacy. His ability to fuse these seemingly opposed sensations reinforces the upper-class identity and subject positions under construction in Staub's houses. This fusion of opposites bespeaks the authenticity of the subject positions that the houses materialize as they perform these identifying virtues (personal nobility and genuineness) spatially.[55] It is through such spatial sensations that the fictional subjects of these houses, the lady and gentleman, can seem to be embedded in the architecture, making implicit claims about the authenticity of both the architecture and its subjects.

Staub constructed identity and subject positions that materialized his clients' individual ways of life with subtlety and imagination. He did this by regulating degrees of individuality and typification in his designs.[56] Typical forms (such as the ways certain rooms are related to each other in the plans of his houses and the material finishes associated with libraries, living rooms, and entrance halls for example) come to connote class identity through repetition.[57] Staub repeatedly put history to work to imagine, and image, the kind of city Houston might be if imbued with well-defined spatial hierarchies that systematically constructed continuity. His houses performed the identifying patrician themes of legitimacy, propriety, and decorum. They spatially played out claims to belonging.[58] They composed difference to represent class distinction within houses, neighborhoods, and the city.[59] With respect to the historical models on which their designs were based, they fluently translated images of patriarchal authority into modern usage.

There was much that Staub's houses ignored. Their perspective was elitist and premised on hierarchical social gradation based on economic disparity. Racial segregation was accepted as normative and unproblematic. Yet because their beauty is profound and spatially palpable, Staub's houses compel admiration and respect. They conserve a mythical aura of decorum, propriety, and grace that promises to confer legitimacy upon their occupants as deserving subjects of American upper-class identity. They teach their occupants how upper-class-ness is to be lived, and lived in proximity to.[60] Examining these houses in their neighborhood settings and in the context of their clients' aspirations demonstrates how Staub repeatedly sought to resolve the contradictions of country house planning—adapting historical models to contemporary uses and alien sites so seamlessly that the mechanics of this operation remain imperceptible—so that they implicitly justify constructing upper-class-ness in a democratic republic constituted on the proposition that all citizens are equal. In this context, style stands out as the medium through which the resolution of contradictions was to be performed. Style was not a lie so much as it was, in the psychological sense, a fetish, useful for diverting criticism away from the social operation the country house carried out: legitimizing class privilege and prerogative. Constructing upper-class identity with beauty and instilling upper-class subjectivity with composure called for spatial invention and material resourcefulness.[61] These are the qualities that stand out in Staub's architecture and enabled him to frame, magnify, and identify a patrician class in Houston from the 1920s through the 1950s.

Broadacres, view looking west on North Boulevard.

CHAPTER 2 : BROADACRES

Broadacres is a thirty-four-acre, single-family residential neighborhood three miles southwest of downtown Houston and five blocks west of Main Boulevard and the Museum of Fine Arts. It was cooperatively developed in 1922–23 by seventeen property owners led by James A. Baker Jr., a partner in the law firm of Baker, Botts, Parker and Garwood.[1] The subdivision's flat, treeless site was improved with a street and lot plan designed by the architect William Ward Watkin.[2] As a diagram, Watkin's plan was almost mechanical in its straightforwardness: two parallel divided boulevards, North and South, joined on the east by a cross street bounding a small neighborhood park containing a tennis court and on the west by a cross boulevard, West. The subdivision plat contained twenty-five house sites, most of them slightly less than an acre in size.

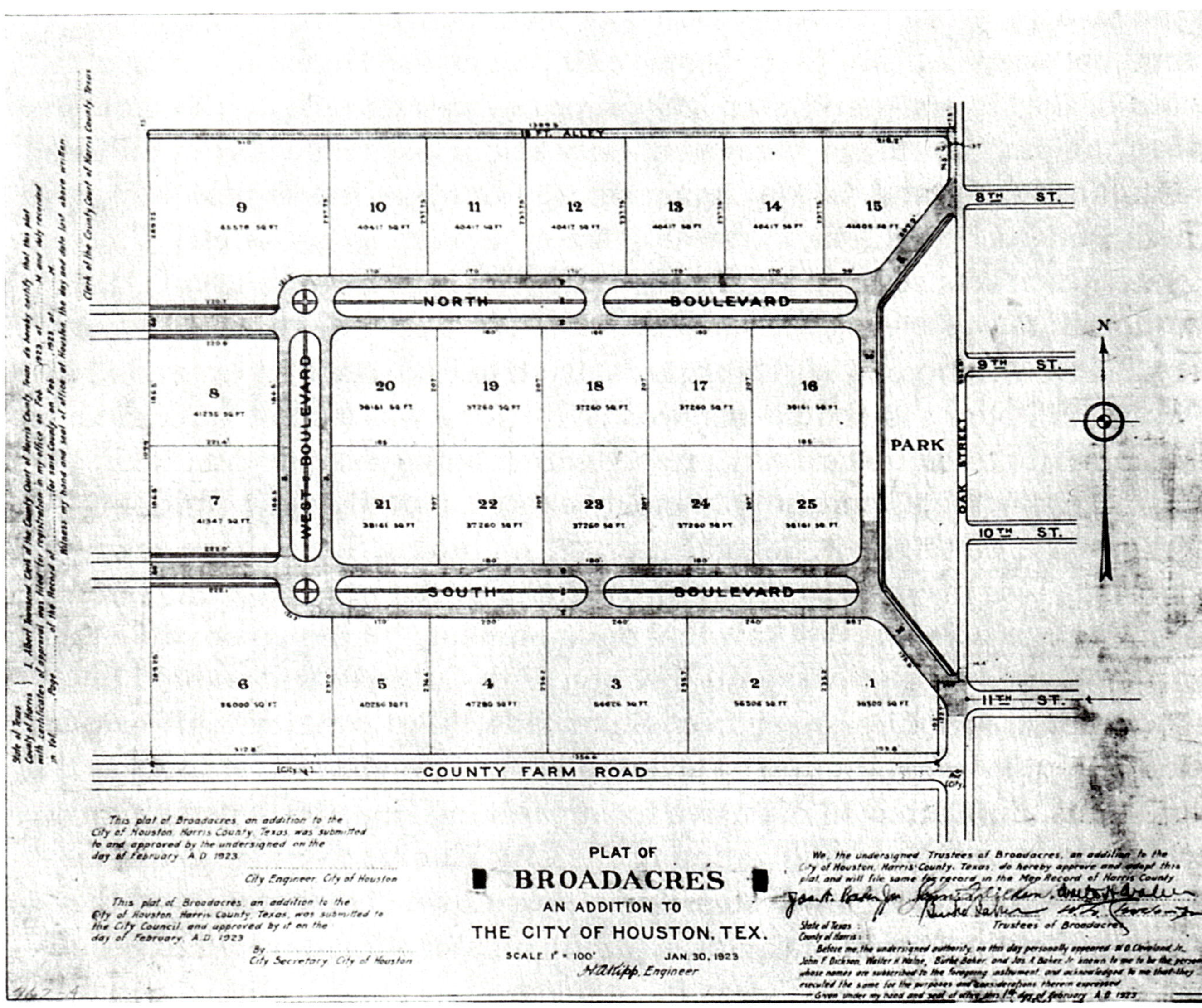

Plat map of Broadacres, 1923.

Aerial view of Hermann Park, 1925. Broadacres is in the upper left corner. Quarterly Municipal Review of Houston 1 *(April–May–June 1925).*

As aerial photographs from the late 1920s and early 1930s show, Broadacres and the territory surrounding it were painfully bare of vegetation. The substantial brick and stucco-faced houses built there during the 1920s loomed improbably over the coastal plain. What is not visible in these archival images, because they were so small, are the live oak trees installed as part of Watkin's design. Staggered rows of live oaks, six across, were planted in the wide median esplanades and along the outer curb lines of the boulevards. As these trees matured and their canopies took shape, they radically transformed perceptions of space in Broadacres.

Today, the neighborhood is an extraordinary park. Six of the eighteen houses built in Broadacres before 1930 were designed by Staub. Broadacres demonstrates how, from the beginning of his career, Staub used the country house as an instrument to construct a myth of patrician superiority that bestowed upper-class identity on his Houston clients and instilled in them the subjective discipline, attitudes, and expectations needed to sustain this construction. Broadacres also demonstrates how Staub's country houses operated as part of a broader consensus, evident in the work of other architects and in the spatial structure of the neighborhood, that conferred legitimacy on Houston's elite as civic leaders by framing them in settings of exceptional beauty and spatial coherence.

Watkin symbolized his clients' aspirations for Broadacres by systematically coding its space as high status, a challenge given the monotonous conditions prevailing when improvements began. Watkin had the streets graded low, so that, from the boulevards, house sites appear to occupy raised terraces. All sidewalks in the neighborhood were paved with red brick laid in a herringbone pattern. Pairs of brick piers at the four points of entry identified Broadacres as a private place. Broadacres's tennis court and park, occupying the equivalent of two house sites, spatially registered elite recreational pastimes and leisure. The live oak avenues of Broadacres are a triumph of naturalization. They construct long passages of spatial continuity, a volumetric correlate of community identity, and rhythmically instill spatial measure and proportion.[3] In Broadacres, house fronts are aligned in rows. Yet the live oaks of North and South Boulevards layer the monotonous space of the coastal plain and frame individual house fronts, breaking down the perception of serial repetition. Watkin fluently translated the space-shaping and whole-making practices his mentor Ralph Adams Cram introduced to Houston at the Rice Institute to construct a spatial matrix that, as the trees matured, framed, magnified, and identified the residents of Broadacres as a Houston upper class.

Broadacres was a proprietary undertaking rather than a speculative venture. Like its Houston antecedents, Courtlandt Place and Shadyside, it was never advertised and the codevelopers controlled first-time lot sales. Broadacres was quite consistent socially. It had no Jewish residents and only one Catholic household. House builders during the 1920s were more likely to be from established elite families than emergent elites. By 1930, only one oilman—Frank Prior Sterling, a cofounder, director, and vice president of the Humble Oil and Refining Company—had built a house in Broadacres.[4] The neighborhood's economic base represented Houston's economy of the 1920s: varied but ultimately tied to the commodities trade (cotton, lumber), transportation, manufacturing, banking, insurance, and the professions. The last category was especially pertinent because three partners in the Baker and Botts law firm were among the eighteen families who built houses in Broadacres in the 1920s.

Kenneth Lipartito and Joseph Pratt's history of Baker and Botts makes it possible to examine Broadacres in the broader context of Houston's (and Texas') political economy in the 1920s. Baker and Botts was Houston's first corporate law firm. It traced its origin to a law practice organized in Houston in 1865.[5] In 1872, Judge James A. Baker, a lawyer from Alabama then practicing in Huntsville, Texas, seventy miles north of Houston, joined the firm, which in 1875 was reorganized as Baker and Botts.[6] Baker's son, also called James A. Baker (but more commonly identified as Capt. James Baker to distinguish him from both his father and his eldest son, James A. Baker Jr.), joined the firm in 1887. During Captain Baker's tenure—he remained active until his death in 1941—what became Baker, Botts, Baker and Lovett (from 1893 to 1904), then Baker, Botts, Parker and Garwood (from 1904 to 1931), then Baker, Botts, Andrews and Wharton (from 1931 to 1946) was structured as the professional equivalent of a vertically integrated corporation to enable partners to offer clients an array of specialized legal services.[7]

Palmer Hutcheson, a partner in Baker, Botts, Parker and Garwood, and his wife, Eleanor Thomson, were Staub's first clients for a house in Houston. Staub told Howard Barnstone that Eleanor Hutcheson and Madeleine Staub became good friends when both lived in the South End in the early 1920s, the Hutchesons at Main Street and Eagle Avenue, the Staubs in an apartment on Elgin Avenue between Main and Fannin Streets.[8] Eleanor and Palmer Hutcheson were from established families. Hutcheson—named for his mother's brother, William H. Palmer, a son-in-law of the nineteenth-century Houston banker B. A. Shepherd—was descended from Virginian immigrants to Houston in all lines. His father, Joseph C. Hutcheson, a graduate of the University of Virginia's law school, had represented Houston in the Texas legislature and the U.S. Congress. Palmer Hutcheson's elder half-brother, Joseph C. Hutcheson Jr., had been appointed U.S. District Court judge for the Southern District of Texas by Pres. Woodrow Wilson in 1918. Although born in Houston, Hutcheson was educated at the Hill School, Princeton University, and the University of Texas law school. He was a parishioner of Christ Church, Houston's oldest Episcopal parish. At the time he built his house in Broadacres, Hutcheson won election to the board of trustees of the Houston Independent School District as an opponent of the Ku Klux Klan.[9] Eleanor Thomson Hutcheson was the great-granddaughter of a Tennessean who came to Mexican Texas in the 1830s. Her father, an Austin lawyer, had been appointed by Woodrow Wilson as U.S. minister to Colombia. Mrs. Hutcheson's cousin was H. B. Thomson, Dallas' foremost country house architect, and, like Staub, a graduate of the Massachusetts Institute of Technology.[10]

Palmer Hutcheson's professional and personal background indicates a family tradition of dedication to the law combined with a history of public service and leadership also reflected in his wife's family. Hutcheson was "old" Houston. His descent was Southern and of the most venerable sort, Virginian. His religion and educational formation affiliated him with institutions that conserved and disseminated patrician identity in a national context. His role as a lawyer was to serve Baker and Botts's corporate clients by ensuring that their businesses operated within the framework of Texas law and counseling either adjustments in business practices, or adjustments to state law, to maintain compliance. In this context, the house Staub designed for Eleanor and Palmer Hutcheson functioned ideologically to reinforce and represent Hutcheson's patrician virtues—trustworthiness, honesty, integrity, wisdom—coded in the recognizable forms of colonial sobriety (shingled colonial house type) and Georgian honor (the scrolled pedimented entrance portal). As the Hutcheson House was joined by other country houses in the 1920s, the entire neighborhood of Broadacres attained a collective identity that emphasized—through the beauty and decorum of individual houses and their systematic integration into a hierarchical landscape order that moved in rhythmically measured sequences from the space of each country house, to its garden, to the space of the community, to the space of the planned garden city—the discernment, authority, and what Bushman called "radiance" of its residents.[11] By 1930, Broadacres collectively displayed its residents as a Houston upper class. None of the families who built houses there figured as singular architectural patrons. It is the extraordinary collective impact that Broadacres's landscape still exerts that makes it such an instructive example of how elite community was socially constructed in Houston through architecture and landscape architecture during the 1920s.

Staub, like Watkin, dealt resourcefully with the spatial contradictions involved in transforming a blank rectangular tract on the coastal plain into an arboreally lush, upper-income residential enclave. The Hutcheson House and the other houses Staub designed in Broadacres reveal, on examination, how he systematically developed the class implications of Watkin's subdivision and planting plan to advance the program of socially constructing upper-class identity by working imaginatively with limiting conditions. The Hutcheson House was planned and built in 1924–25 for $32,600 according to figures that Staub compiled for most of his houses built before 1940. At a time when a two-story, brick-veneered wood-frame house for a middle-income Houston family could cost less than $10,000, the Hutcheson House was not cheap. However, it was the only one of the eighteen houses built in Broadacres before 1930 with wood facing and seems to have been the least expensive. The house was constructed by Christian J. Miller, a Danish immigrant and a Houston builder Staub came to value highly.[12]

The Hutcheson lot lay on the south side of North Boulevard. This gave it the most desirable orientation for an in-town country house in Houston, since the rear of the house faced south into the prevailing southeast breeze. By 1930, all the south-side lots in Broadacres had been improved with houses (some of the north-side lots would not be built on until the 1950s). Its location gave Staub the opportunity to endow the house with one of the identifying features of the country house: double fronts. Staub extended the Hutcheson House along its east-west axis, parallel to the street, while limiting it to a depth of one- to one-and-a-half rooms on its north-south axis, a pattern that would prevail in elite domestic architecture in Houston during the interwar period. Standing in front of the house, one can literally look through it. This organization not only worked to stimulate ventilation, it treated the house as a screen that shielded the backyard from the street, and it employed what the architectural historian and critic Colin Rowe described as the technique of "authenticating" to adapt the Connecticut colonial historical model to the flat landscape and hot, humid climate of Houston.[13] In addition to the house, Staub designed a two-story, two-car garage with a servants' apartment above and to one side a stall for the Hutcheson children's horse, the only stable in Broadacres and another element authenticating its identity as a country house. The garage was located in the southwest corner of the lot, aligned with the house's west-side service wing. Staub composed the street front of the Hutcheson House in a pattern repeated in all his symmetrically organized Broadacres houses: a five-bay central block offset with advancing (or in some cases receding) wings, a pattern rescued from monotony by advancing or recessing the flanking wings to animate the planar house front spatially.

The symmetrical, horizontally extended street front of the Hutcheson House performed themes of stability, permanence (immeasurably assisted by the maturing of the live oak matrix), authority (Staub's chastened version of an eighteenth-century colonial scrolled pediment frames the front door; a pair of tall, slender, slab-like chimneys of textured orange-red clinker brick frames the central block), and belonging (adaptation to site and climate). Surfacing the house with wood shakes imbued it with individuality, as did the row of five shuttered, high-set, horizontally elongated second-story windows set in a lateral band in the central block. These windows are very important. Because they produce a broader band of wall between first- and second-floor openings than would more conventional six-over-six-pane sash windows, they reinforce the compositional theme of lateral extension and code the front of the Hutcheson House as "humble." Humility performed understatement and restraint, key attributes of patrician identity.[14] In the design of the Hutcheson House, Staub's capacity for systematic integration enabled him to make architecture out of the resolution of issues of site planning and climatic responsiveness that cohered to identify the patrician themes of propriety, proprietary belonging, and legitimacy accruing from generational continuity.

The garden "front" of the Hutcheson House is more conventional in appearance than the street elevation: a two-story, five-bay, symmetrical Georgian house front with six-over-six-pane sash windows on the second floor mirroring those on the first floor and attic-level dormer windows, with the central block outflanked by one-story wings (one originally an open

Palmer Hutcheson House, Broadacres, 1924–25, John F. Staub, architect. Detail of north-facing street elevation.

Hutcheson House, detail of chimney.

loggia) capped by Chinese Chippendale railings. The formality of this side of the house stresses the consistency of its owners' patrician identity by being no less, and perhaps even slightly more, ceremonious than the street front, although to avoid pretension the central door is a pair of French doors framed by a flat architrave. The assertion of consistent character performed by the architecture advances arguments about the propriety, decorum, and authenticity of its occupants.

Staub spatially embedded the myth of harmonious hierarchical community within his houses by qualifying their primary formal order with secondary "interruptions," intricately interlocking reception, family, and serving spaces in plan, section, and elevation so that something made of parts is experienced as whole and complete.[15] Interruptions offset formality with spontaneity by juxtaposing service-related uses and reception spaces. At the Hutcheson House, Staub used symmetry on the street front to mask the fact that, for climatic reasons, the ground-floor serving spaces were grouped on the west side of the house (to the right of the front door), so that it is the kitchen in its outflanking wing on the west that balances the library in its outflanking wing on the east. On the side elevation of the offset west wing, Staub revealed interior complexities by positioning a pair of slender casement windows, not visible if the house is viewed head-on, whose head and sill heights differ from adjacent, larger, street-facing windows to articulate the presence of first- and second-floor bathrooms inside. These windows come as a surprise to a visitor approaching the front door. They rescue the ceremonial aspects of the design from monotony and affirm the necessity of making practical adjustments to sustain patrician identity.

The reception spaces (entrance hall, living room, dining room) perform themes of hospitality and composure, beginning with the three-and-a-half-foot-wide paneled front door, which materializes security and generosity. The hall is twelve-and-a-quarter feet wide and fourteen-and-a-quarter feet long. It establishes a sense of spatial generosity and ease that permeates the reception rooms of the Hutcheson House. The upward spiral of the circular stair introduces a dynamic counterpoint in the space. It rises next to a street-facing window and leads to an upper hall lit by the horizontal second-floor windows, so that the entrance hall is amply illuminated with reflected north light. Staub aligned the front door, double doors from the hall to the dining room, and the pair of French doors opening from the dining room to the garden to construct a long visual passage that traverses the house, channeling perception and movement much as Watkin's live oak trees do outside.

In the living room symmetry constructs a sensation of composure. The fireplace wall—the architectural focus of the living room—is a thick, brick-cored wall. Doorways to the library and loggia are recessed in alcoves within the thick-

Hutcheson House, south-facing garden elevation.

Hutcheson House, detail of dormer window.

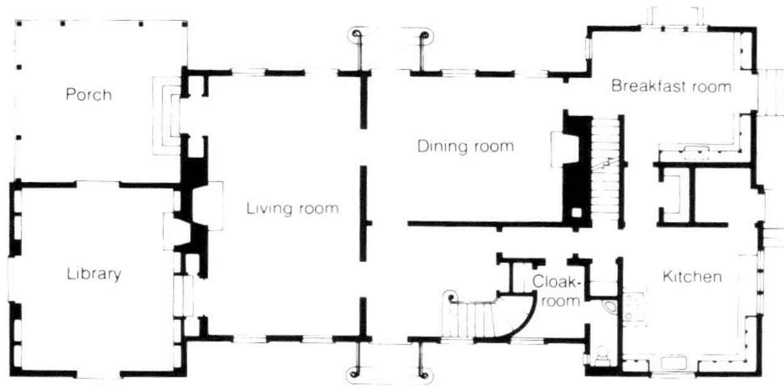

First-floor plan

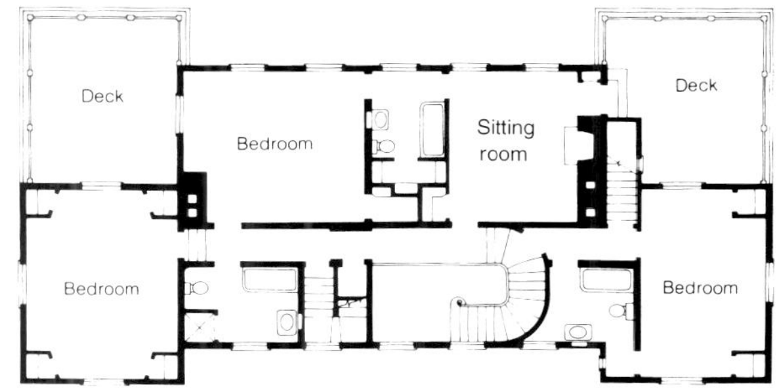

Second-floor plan

Hutcheson House.

ness of the wall, with cabinets faced with louvered doors inserted in the reveals of the alcoves. The depth of the fireplace wall spatially embodies the strength and security of the house. Oak strip floors outlined with perimeter borders run the long dimension of each room, as Lindeberg advised was good form.[16] Staub composed the west end wall of the dining room (which is fifteen feet, nine inches wide, with the room's long dimension measuring twenty feet, nine inches) with a fireplace stationed between a pair of shallow recessed arches incised into another thick, brick-cored wall plane. One of the arches is discretely fitted with a door to the breakfast room and pantry. The shallowness of the recesses and the verticality of the arches subtly convey a quality of intimate monumentality, a paradoxical association of two sensations that Staub managed to sustain proportionally. Staub reinforced this perception by lowering horizon lines in the dining room, depressing window sills, chair rails, and the glass panes in the French doors to increase the sense of height in the room, which like the living room and hall is nine feet high. Because the French doors and the two windows overlook the south-facing garden, the dining room is brightly lit during the day. Shallowly incised panels are set beneath the window sills in the living and dining rooms. These delicately but crisply articulate a sense of planar stationing, composing window openings to enhance decorum within the rooms. The perceptual qualities of lightness, grace, ceremoniousness, composure, and spatial exhilaration with which Staub imbued the reception rooms of the Hutcheson House inform and sustain patrician subjectivity. The use of such framing devices as double doors, aligned openings, and symmetrical interior elevations suggest a "ritualization" of the activities of daily family life.[17] Staub's manipulation of proportions to construct a sensation of loftiness in rooms with ceilings that are only minimally high is subliminally experienced as elevating. Such minor details as panels beneath windows and delicately profiled doorknobs, precisely because they materialize refinement without attracting attention, sustain intimations of patrician subjectivity.

Even for an elite family such as the Hutchesons (who had three young sons when they moved into the house), there were limits on the ceremoniousness with which daily life was lived. Staub's treatment of the library established its identity as overlapping the reception and family spheres of the house. The location and detailing of libraries was one of the most variable elements in Staub's houses, a clue to how different clients chose to use this particular space: as a family sitting room, a private sanctum, or overflow space from the living room when entertaining. The Hutcheson library is two steps down from the living room, set at grade and on level with the loggia, with which it is paired in plan. It is directly accessible from the living room but has a contrasting spatial character. The library is paneled in red gum with a dark polished finish rather than the light-reflecting finishes of the reception rooms. The fireplace is not centered. Staub customarily paired fireplaces in reciprocal back-to-back arrangements in his houses. Sometimes those in libraries adjoining living rooms were centered on the library wall, at other times they were off center. Here, the off-center location intimates the less formal, family-oriented use of the room in contrast to the formality of the adjoining reception rooms. The loggia is paved with black slate, grounding this roofed, open air space and materially suggesting its transition between interior and garden.

In the service sector of the Hutcheson House, Staub's use of spatial dialectics as a way to distinguish between the character of different parts of the house is accentuated. The cloak room and toilet behind the main stair exemplify Staub's skill in investing serving spaces with eccentricities that contrast with the serene regularity of reception spaces. In the cloak room, the backside of the wall that follows the curve of the stair scoops out a negative space so that in plan the room expands outward from its entrance door. This maneuver permitted Staub to encompass one of the street-facing first-floor windows and maintain external symmetry. The toilet compartment, lit by the side-facing casement, is slotted into a corner of the west kitchen wing. In plan, this compartment aligns with the stacked basement stair/back stairway behind the west fireplace wall. The combination of geometric play and geometric rigor that the negative curve of the cloakroom and the alignment of stairs and toilet compartment displays represents Staub's versatility as a dancer and mathematician. By constructing a spatial poetics of surprise and discovery, Staub imbued his houses with sensations of spontaneity. By resolving the disposition of nonhonorific uses with geometric clarity, he registered depth of character, consistency, and discipline as additional subjective attributes. Staub almost always prefaced the guest toilet compartment with a larger cloakroom, a layering of space that Barnstone identified as essential to instilling upper-class subjectivity.

The kitchen is located in the northwest corner of the Hutcheson House. To ensure the best ventilation and exposure to the reception rooms, the kitchen was relegated to the least desirable corner of the house, with exposure to the west sun and no direct access to the prevailing southeast breeze. The ceiling height above the west-side downstairs spaces stepped down to eight feet, spatially coding this portion of the house as subservient. Separate exterior entrances were provided for the breakfast room (the most family-oriented of the west-side rooms and the only one with southern exposure and a view of the garden) and the kitchen porch, explicitly distinguishing between the family and their servants and tradespeople. Because it is likely that domestic servants and many of the tradespeople who would use the kitchen porch entrance were African American, spaces in Staub's houses were additionally coded as white and black.

The second floor of the Hutcheson House mirrors the logic of first-floor spaces. Staub positioned three bedrooms and a sitting room (as labeled in his floor plans) for access to the prevailing breeze. A cross-hall, the main stair, and bathrooms serving the outer-wing bedrooms were slotted into a lateral band behind the street front of the house. The cross-hall was subdivided by doorways that permitted spaces to be used in combination or separately. Staub would frequently subdivide corridors with portals and arches to frame passage and impose rhythm and measure that, implicitly, informed occupants' sense of subjectivity. The main stair also breaks at an upper landing, reflecting the sectional step from a nine-foot ceiling height down to an eight-foot ceiling height on the floor below. As a result of this stepped section, the west-wing bedroom and its adjoining bathroom gained an extra foot of head height. Staub intensified this volumetric experience by carrying the ceilings of both east and west-wing bedrooms up under the gabled roofs in tray profiles that spring from shallow, symmetrically stationed closets framing alcoves within each bedroom. Constructing more activated sections than in the reception rooms below and layering space in second-floor bedrooms were techniques Staub used to endow his houses with spatial variety, surprise, and individuality. Arched windows, centered beneath the gable ends of these wings, externalize this internal spatial composition.

Michael Benedikt observed that when works of architecture are praised or criticized, the terminology used in articulating judgments often seems more relevant to characterizations of people than buildings.[18] The words that emerge in describing the Hutcheson House externally and internally evoke the subject and identity positions embedded in its architectural design. Staub demonstrated with the Hutcheson House his capacity to integrate reception, family, and service spaces in a unified work and to naturalize historical models by rationally and rigorously adapting them to limiting conditions. Hierarchical layering and dialectical contrasts provided a methodical basis for spatially organizing the house. Staub addressed and resolved the practical contradictions inherent in applying an eighteenth-century Connecticut colonial model to twentieth-century Houston and building a country house in the city. In doing so he implicitly offered the house as a model for transposing stylish metropolitan architectural practices to the Texas Gulf coast and naturalizing—Houstonizing—them so that they became part of the social fabric of Houston.

Staub's next Broadacres house was quite different from the Hutcheson House. It was designed for Annie Martin and William S. Cochran. Cochran was a vice president and director of the First National Bank as well as president of the Republic Box Company of Texas. He was also a director of the Houston Land and Trust Company, the Peden Iron and Steel Company, the Houston Drug Company, and the Southern Brass and Manufacturing Company. His father, O. L. Cochran, a native of Tennessee, had operated an insurance agency and a cotton factorage business in Houston before becoming president of Houston's oldest chartered bank, the First National Bank, which William Cochran's maternal grandfather, B. A. Shepherd, founded. William Cochran's aunt, Manilla Shepherd, had married Palmer Hutcheson's uncle, William H. Palmer. Cochran was a member of the Houston Country Club, the Houston Yacht Club, and the newly organized Houston Riding and Polo Club; Annie Cochran, who like her husband had grown up in Houston, would become a member of the Garden Club of Houston. Mr. and Mrs. Cochran and their two children, William Jr. and Jane, were parishioners of Christ Church. The Cochran House was designed and built in 1925–26 on South Boulevard at a cost of $51,000. Chris J. Miller was the builder.[19] The Cochran House demonstrates Staub's virtuosity in constructing picturesqueness as an apparently natural, and therefore authentic, response to limiting circumstances.

The Cochran lot is on the north side of South Boulevard. This meant that its reception rooms and bedrooms had to

Hutcheson House, detail of arched window.

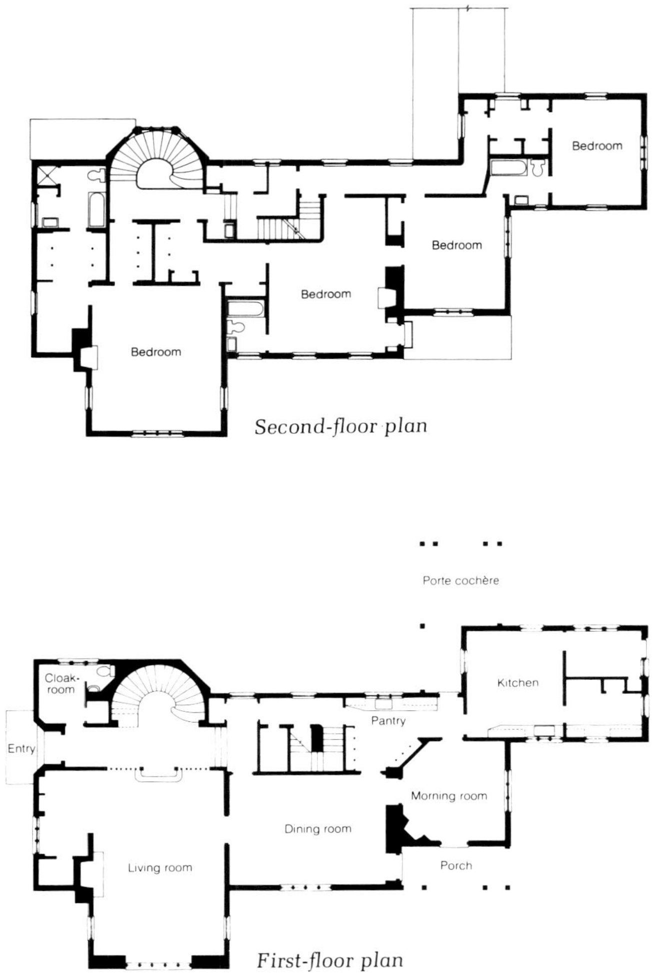

William S. Cochran House, Broadacres, 1925–26, John F. Staub, architect.

face the street to have access to the prevailing breeze. Staub generated picturesqueness by responding spatially to climatic conditions and hierarchical distinctions involving the reception, family, and serving spaces of the house. Staub sited the one- to one-and-a-half-room-deep house in the middle of its broad, flat lot, extending the plan along an east-west axis. He offset the plan in stepped formation to give the large living room on the west, an intermediate dining room, a morning room on the east, and the kitchen wing on the northeast multiple exposures to the prevailing southeast breeze. Upstairs bedrooms located above these first-floor spaces likewise have two, and in some cases, three exterior exposures. Along the north (rear) side of the house, backing up to the reception rooms, a lateral band of circulation begins with the front door (located on the west side of the house) and concludes in the kitchen wing on the east. Staub keyed the sectional organization of the house to its offset plan. The gabled wall of the projecting wing containing the living room, with master bedroom above, rises highest. As the house begins to step back in plan on the east, the roofline steps down in section. The two-story, three-car garage-apartment building near the rear, northeast corner of the lot concluded this rhythmic sequence of offset wings and descending ridge heights.

Staub treated the street front of the Cochran House as its garden front. Annie Cochran reinforced this fiction by planting a ligustrum hedge along the street line, just behind the live oak trees, to screen the front yard from the street. Staub placed the front door on the west side elevation of the Cochran House. Visitors arrive at the door by car rather than walking up a sidewalk from the front curb as in a city house. There is a graveled motor court with a turnaround, which Mrs. Cochran planted with hedge rows in a circular pattern, in the rear, northwest corner of the property. A brick wall and porte cochère screen the motor court from the garage-apartment building and its service court, although the motor court borrows the end elevation of the garage as an architectural backdrop. Dedicating the backyard to the circulation of cars and interposing screen walls, roofed passages, and hedge rows filled up and layered the empty space of the flat lot to reinforce the country house fiction. Staub detailed the side-facing entrance alcove with an arch constructed of receding brick voussoirs, its spring line and cap keyed with thin slices of slate. Staub quoted the English country house architect Edwin L. Lutyens with this detail, confirming the Cochran House's identity as a country house by affiliating it with the work of the architect considered to be the greatest contemporary exponent of the Anglo-American country house.

Staub constructed belonging at the Cochran House by naturalizing a medieval European historical model that might otherwise have seemed especially inappropriate for reproduction on the Gulf coastal plain through rigorous and

Cochran House, south-facing street elevation.

Cochran House, detail of entrance alcove.

Cochran House, detail of chimney.

imaginative adjustment to climate, site, and a spatial dialectic of honor and service. He spatially structured the design in response to the same conditions that affected the design of the symmetrical, colonial-type Hutcheson House. The typological, formal, and spatial reversals evident in comparing the two houses could be construed as logical, objective responses to differences in site and orientation. The Cochran House is notable for its austerity, achieved by Staub's use of thin steel casement windows and his avoidance (with judicious exceptions) of architectural decoration. Themes of planarity and plainness advance implicit arguments for the characters of the people who live there. The preference for plain statement and the rejection of ostentation and pretension bespeak honesty, sobriety, and rectitude, all desirable characteristics in a banker. The Cochran House performed the same identifying patrician virtues as the Hutcheson House; that the two houses are totally different architecturally could be construed as an expression of their owners' individuality. The Cochran House is capable of dramatic moments. When Staub designed the Kuldell House on the lot west of the Cochran House in 1928, he offset it in plan to preserve the view of the west side of the Cochran House from South Boulevard. When the setting sun strikes the mixed blend of textured orange-red brick on this side of the house, it dramatically highlights the arched entrance alcove to one side of the gabled bay and the slender, tapered chimney stack that frames it, an oblique view of the side of a house not repeated elsewhere in Broadacres.

Staub's capacity to regulate typification and individuality was evident in the next two houses he designed in Broadacres, a house on the south side of North Boulevard, designed and built in 1926 for Lucile Borden and Joseph A. Tennant and their daughter and three sons, and a house on the south side of South Boulevard designed and built in 1926–27 for C. Milby Dow, a widower, and his daughter Dagmar. Both houses were constructed by the builder Thomas M. Murray, the Tennant House for $39,640 and the Dow House for $47,046.[20] Both corresponded to the five-bay symmetrical model flanked by an offset wing (only one wing in each case, rather than a pair of wings) introduced in the Hutcheson House. Both were based on eighteenth-century English Georgian models. They contributed to the construction of upper-class identity in Broadacres by repeating the type Staub formulated for houses located on the south sides of Broadacres' two boulevards. Yet each was quite different and demonstrated the flexibility of the type as it was individualized in response to site conditions and client requirements.

The Dow House performs "belonging" through systematic integration with its neighborhood setting. Staub aligned the symmetrical front of the Dow House with the centerline of Parkway, the neighborhood cross street bounding the Broadacres tennis court park at the east end of the subdivision, so that the house front terminates the vista of those traveling south on Parkway. As the avenue of live oaks planted along Parkway matured, the tree canopy volumetrically framed this vista. Tall brick piers capped by cast stone pineapples flank the brick sidewalk leading from the curb line on South Boulevard to the front door of the Dow House to reinforce this frame. Staub treated the lines of sight and movement in Watkin's street plan as an implicit spatial armature to construct continuity between the subdivision plan and the house. He enabled the Dow House to perform belonging and permanence by locking it into place at the terminus of Parkway's oak alley. In designing the Dow House so that it complemented the spatial program of Watkin's street and planting plan, Staub contributed to the social construction of Broadacres as power space by subliminally asserting the capacity of its residents' unified (elite) consciousness to envision and produce such beauty.

Staub used austerity to reinforce assertions of understatement and reserve. The street front of the Dow House is an exercise in shallow planar relief and discrete modulation. The three-bay central register is advanced forward of flanking wings. Horizontal unity is underscored by continuous, cast stone coping along a high parapet that masks the eaves of the shallowly pitched hipped roof. A pair of slender chimneystacks frames the roof. Cast stone finials at the points of planar offset between the central register and the recessed wings and a modillioned cast stone cornice that spans only the central register underscore the lack of ornamentation on the rest of the façade. Staub deftly pulled flanking window and door openings, both in the central register and in the wings, toward the center to mobilize the façade with a hint of tension. The composition of openings surrounding the front entrance portal is balanced by the composition of openings in the wings: a pair of paneled French doors, framed within a relieving arch, centered beneath eight-over-eight-pane sash windows that are slightly wider than the six-over-six-pane windows in the central bay. The entrance steps and platform reiterate the theme of center-and-wings by opening to each side rather than on center. The entrance platform, like the flanking French doors, is rimmed with a low, delicately detailed wrought iron rail. The house is surfaced with a mixed blend of sandstruck brick, varying in tone from dark red to rose to an earthy green, that is extremely subtle. Rooted on its site and framed by the force of nature embodied in the avenue of live oak trees, the Dow House represents its occupants, and by extension the inhabitants of Broadacres, as a patrician elite in whom the nuances encoded in the composition of the house inhere.

The Dow House displays Staub's practice of spatially leavening solemnity with wit by juxtaposing reception and serving spaces. The main block is joined on its west side to a rear service wing that gave the house an L-plan configuration. Staub lowered first-floor ceiling heights in the service wing, which occasioned a two-foot step-down at the second-floor level. Staub also faceted the wall connecting the low-profiled rear service wing and the taller main block. From the street, the service wing appears to fan out from the house, breaking free of its formality and the inhibitions formal rectitude implies. Staub continued this narrative in his design of the two-story, two-car garage-apartment building at the southwest rear corner of the property. It is a neoclassical folly in which tricks of scale, embedded in the detailing of arched wood panels containing the garage doors and a pair of bull's eye windows, identify it as both the service wing's jolly companion and a retainer to the main block. Staub's ability to work out schemes of spatial organization dialectically, to stage compositional themes as narrative sequences, and to represent class difference *within* the country house intensified the capacity of his houses to project identity and sustain the construction of subjectivity. These architectural characteristics imbued Staub's houses with a sense of complexity and depth that sustained the operations of social construction they performed.

Charles Milby Dow was a contemporary of Staub's and a native of Houston.[21] His father had been a partner of Charles H. Milby (for whom Dow was named) in the firm of Milby and Dow, dealers in coal. By 1914 Dow operated a car dealership.

C. Milby Dow House, Broadacres, 1926–27, John F. Staub, architect.
Vista of the house from Parkway.

Dow House, north-facing front elevation.

Dow House, side entrance to kitchen wing with garage beyond.

What became the Dow Motor Company sold Ford and Lincoln automobiles and Fordson trucks from its showroom on the southwest edge of downtown Houston (although in 1928 the firm switched to Chevrolets). Dow was a parishioner of Christ Church. Joseph A. Tennant belonged to Houston's emergent elite rather than to its established elite. He began practice in Houston as a consulting and construction engineer in 1916.[22] Tennant's wife, Lucile Borden, was not a Houstonian, but she was from an established Texan family. Her paternal grandfather, John P. Borden, was the youngest brother of Gail Borden and Thomas H. Borden, U.S. immigrants to Mexican Texas in the 1820s, inventors, newspaper publishers, and the surveyors who laid out the Houston townsite for the Allen brothers in 1836. The Bordens were Baptists until Mrs. Tennant's father, Sidney Gail Borden, married Mary Sullivan, whose Irish immigrant family had come from New Jersey to the Irish colony of San Patricio de Hibernia on the lower Nueces River in South Texas in 1853.[23] Mary Borden was Catholic. Thereafter the branch of the family perpetuating the Borden name in Texas became Catholic.

The house Staub designed for Lucile and Joseph Tennant figures in a systematically integrated spatial hierarchy that includes its designed garden, the Broadacres neighborhood, and the more extensive complex of tree-lined thoroughfares and institutional precincts that made up Houston's notional garden city landscape of the 1920s. The Tennant garden was designed by the Bryan, Texas, landscape architect J. Allen Myers Jr. in the 1930s.[24] It was developed by projecting the axes of movement and view within Staub's house and inscribing them spatially in the landscape. This was made possible because Staub oriented the house's reception rooms—a library on the east and a dining room on the west symmetrically flanking the central living room, its long dimension parallel to the garden front of the house and inset behind a double height loggia—toward the south-facing rear of the property. Myers aligned brick-paved walks on axis with the library and dining room windows to frame a central grass panel that is continuous with the terrace of the loggia. Behind this grass terrace, tall, columnar Southern magnolia trees screen a stand of limbed-up live oaks. The massed trees form a volume of dense green shade, a vertical layer of dark space that, when seen from the loggia, works reciprocally with the volume of bright open space encompassing the flat grass panel. Myers added an additional layer to this composition by spanning the parallel brick walks with arches of fig ivy, which form virtual tunnels of directed space that can be walked through. These buoyant spatial layers modulate the flat space of the coastal plain at scales of hierarchical gradation midway between the architectural scale of the house and the community scale of Watkin's live oak avenues, which bound the east side of the house's corner lot. Myers constructed other garden rooms that expand outward from the Tennant House. But it is the south garden terrace that most inventively extends the space-shaping themes of Staub's house by layering the landscape. The impact upon the perceptions of occupants and their guests of proceeding from the tree-lined street into the graveled motor court and up to the house front, then through a pedimented front door into a proportionally orchestrated sequence of reception spaces that culminates in the rear loggia, with its vista of the garden, and then along one of the paths bounding the central grass panel is to impress a sense of privilege (on visitors) and entitlement (on residents) that derives from the rhythmic measure of these spaces and their systematic integration.[25]

The Tennant House constructs individuality in the context of patrician reserve because Staub was so inventive in his treatment of the double-fronted country house. Staub maintained neighborhood decorum on the street front of the house by composing it in the image of an early-eighteenth-century English house (the type is one repeated over and again in mid-eighteenth-century Anglo-American houses as well): a pedimented central register symmetrically flanked by hipped-roofed wings and framed by tall chimneys.[26] Staub externalized the interior organization of space on the street front with an arched window in the east wing that rises from the level of the stair landing. The street front of the house is a dialectical triumph. It maintains good form while inverting conventional room arrangements to facilitate ventilation, reformulating compositional codes with such gracefulness that a new form of practice is authorized.[27] The Tennant House constructs patrician identity by resolving formal conflict ingeniously without undermining the authority of convention. The arched window asymmetrically inserted in the symmetrically composed façade represents the tendency of Staub and his eclectic peers to treat style as the medium through which the resolution of contradiction was performed.

The Tennant House stands out among Staub's Broadacres houses because it is such a rigorous example of his design practices. The east elevation of the Tennant House is visible from West Boulevard. The view of this side elevation is not emphasized, as at the Cochran House. But it reveals the shallow, one-and-a-half-room-deep, north-south axis of the house and, in its symmetrical disposition of windows that does not privilege the center, the secondary status of the elevation when compared to the honorific street and garden fronts.

The interior organization of the house is as rigorous as its exterior composition, with circulation and services layered behind the north (street) front, and reception and domestic spaces symmetrically facing the south (rear) garden. Interior spaces in the Tennant House are slightly smaller than in Staub's other Broadacres houses. The entrance hall is eight-and-a-half-feet wide, but the presence of a pair of windows

Joseph A. Tennant House, Broadacres, 1926–27, John F. Staub, architect. Detail of south-facing garden elevation with arches of fig ivy by J. Allen Myers Jr., landscape architect.

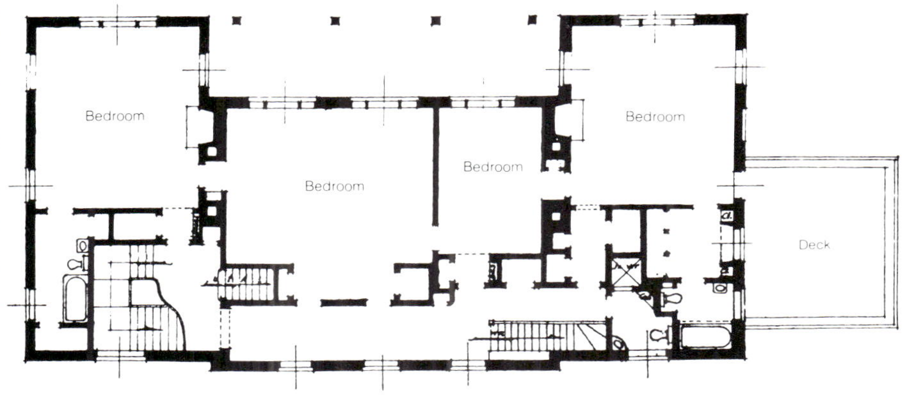

Second-floor plan

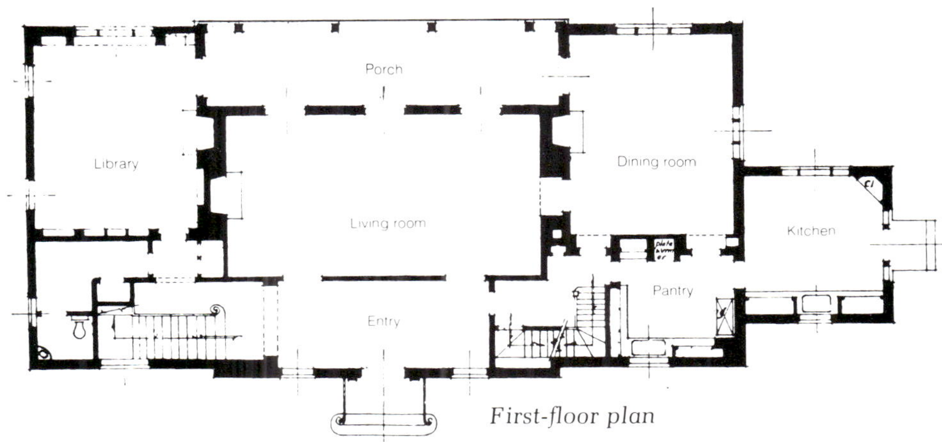

First-floor plan

Tennant House.

Tennant House, north-facing street front.

Tennant House, east side elevation.

(overleaf) Tennant House, entrance hall.

Tennant House, detail of antique mantle installed in living room.

flanking the front door, a pair of doorways fitted with double doors opening into the light-filled living room, and the stair, set at the east end of the passage with north light filtering down from the arched landing window, prevents it from feeling narrow. At the west end of the entrance hall, painted wood panels are grouped beneath a segmental arch set into the wall. Careful inspection reveals the presence of a "secret" door within the panels, which opens into the back hall, back stair, pantry, and kitchen. A segmental arch in the entrance hall symmetrically repeats the profile of the wall panel, discreetly staging movement in rhythmic intervals from the front door toward the stair and, behind it, the cloakroom and guest toilet, and the library (a polished wood-paneled room that does not open into the living room). The secret door "subjectifies" discretion in the service of necessity. Rhythmically layering space in the hall transforms passage into procession, subtly ritualizing elite experiences of daily life.

The living room of the Tennant House is symmetrical and formal. Beneath the cornice a band of fretwork subliminally charges the space with crispness. French doors open onto the loggia, its two-story height a proportional transition from the space of the living room to that of the garden terrace. Because one passes on axis from the living room to one end of the dining room through a fireplace wall (the dining room is shifted in plan: its long wall is centered on the fireplace rather than the door from the living room), the dining room possesses the sensation of being a thickly encased hollow volume. In combination with recessed openings, slender rounded and reeded jambs modulated with corner blocks, which frame door and window openings, and low-set window sills, the dining room feels both expansive and delicate, achieving the proportional sensation of monumentality suffused with intimacy palpable in the Hutcheson dining room. The three-part south-facing garden window frames the axis of fig ivy arches, integrating the space of the dining room with the receding space of the garden. In this graceful house, the dancer and the mathematician seem to complement each other's instincts. Even the pantry and kitchen are inscribed in square plans.

Also located on a south-side lot on North Boulevard was the last house Staub designed in Broadacres, for Estelle W. and Kemp S. Dargan and their daughter, Margaret, built in 1929–30 for $43,660.[28] Dargan was from Paris, Texas, in the northeast corner of the state, and a vice president of the Houston insurance company of Cravens, Dargan and Company, which his partner James R. Cravens organized in 1903. By the time they completed the house, Mr. and Mrs. Dargan were parishioners of Palmer Memorial Church; they had formerly been parishioners of Christ Church.[29]

Staub repeated his use of the five-bay symmetrical house type flanked by slender chimneystacks and offset wings at the Dargan House. Through repetition, this type can be seen as encoding an economy of meaning to "bound and conventionalize" upper-class identity in Broadacres.[30] It embodies the consensus on what a Houston upper-class house looked like. The type was individualized as an abstraction of a classical French manorial model, distinguished by Staub's use of a mixed blend of mottled orange-red brick, molded brick decorative detail, especially in the projecting polygonal entrance bay, blocky corbels, and in courses that project at intervals in vertical stacks to suggest quoins. The Dargan House possesses a more imposing scale than Staub's other Broadacres houses. The plan of the Dargan House pivots around the polygonal entrance hall, which contains a spiral stair on axis with the front door. The stair is set in an elliptical well that rises beneath a backlit ceiling light.

Tennant House, detail of garden loggia.

Projecting off the back of the stairwell is the dining room, which looks out to the south garden through a semicircular bay window. Triple-hung windows in all apertures give the room, which has three exposures, a very open feeling. The same is true of the living room, which spans between the street and garden elevations to the left of the entrance bay. Staub constructed grandeur in the Dargan House with interior symmetry, spaciousness, and ceiling heights of twelve and a half feet. Paneled double doors ceremonialize passage between rooms and thick interior walls construct sensations of solidity. Yet views through the house to the south terrace and garden prevent the interiors from feeling oppressive. Since the triple-hung windows open from floor-level sills, the polished hardwood strip floors seem to extend outward to the grass plane of the garden lawn, making the interior feel very connected with the out-of-doors despite its formality.

Staub kept details in the Dargan House simple to contrast with its expansive proportions. The three-and-a-half-foot-wide paneled front door, recessed in a pedimented, cast-stone alcove, is capped with a glass transom articulated with thin wrought iron scrolls and flanked by deeply embrasured circular windows set in the angled planes of the entrance bay. Door and window openings in the reception rooms are framed with reeded jambs and lintels. Slender cylindrical balusters supporting the delicately profiled handrail of the stair emphasize its spiral curve. Staub played the axial composure and scale of the reception rooms against the more intricate organization of serving spaces. Yet lofty ceiling heights and triple-hung windows imbue these secondary spaces with a degree of grandeur also.

Upstairs, Staub followed his customary practice of hierarchically reducing scale (ceiling heights step down to nine-and-a-half feet) and decorative detail. The master bathroom retains its original white tile dado with black border, its durable, generously proportioned plumbing fixtures, and such characteristic Staub details as the segmentally curved mirror mounted above the pedestal sink and framed between

Tennant House, dining room.

Tennant House, view from dining room to garden.

sconces. The painted wood mantle in the master bedroom pays homage to the early-nineteenth-century English neoclassical architect John Soane. Its inverted fluting, simple corner blocks, and exquisitely curved fascia, flaring out to support the thin, shallowly curved mantle shelf, intimate restraint as compellingly as other attributes of the Dargan House declaim grandeur. Subtlety and modulation were affects Staub used to imbue his houses with the subjective qualities of character, depth, and measure, qualities that could be ascribed as well to the people who lived in these houses.

Staub's penultimate house in Broadacres explored subtlety and modulation in the service of an expressive decorative program. The house for Ethelyn Cramer and Rudolph C. Kuldell, built in 1928–29 by Thomas M. Murray for $75,708, displays Staub's response to the challenge posed by clients who wanted a house that was much more luxuriantly detailed than his other Broadacres houses and had the resources to pay for it.[31]

Col. Rudolph Kuldell was vice president of the Hughes Tool Company when he built this house. A native of Pittsburgh and the son of a Methodist minister, Kuldell was a graduate of the U.S. Military Academy's Army Engineering School. He married Ethelyn Cramer, a Barnard College alumna from Portland, Connecticut, in 1912. After serving as department engi-

Kemp S. Dargan House, Broadacres, 1929–30, John F. Staub, architect. North-facing street elevation.

Dargan House, detail of backlit ceiling light above stair.

Dargan House, detail of transom above entrance door.

Dargan House, detail of circular window in entrance hall.

(opposite) Dargan House, view from living room window to south-facing rear lawn.

Dargan House, detail of stair newel post.

(opposite)
Dargan House, detail of master bathroom.

neer for the Southern District of the U.S. Army Corps of Engineers at Fort Sam Houston in San Antonio and assistant to the chief of engineers during World War I, Kuldell resigned his commission and was recruited by Howard R. Hughes in 1920 to move to Houston and become Hughes's executive assistant at the Hughes Tool Company. When Hughes died suddenly in 1924, Kuldell became general manager, then vice president, then in 1931 president of the Hughes Tool Company. Kuldell was a rigorous, disciplined, and resourceful corporate administrator. He was rapidly absorbed into both Houston's business elite (he served several terms as president of the board of directors of the Houston Chamber of Commerce) and social elite (he was a member of the Houston Country Club, the Houston Yacht Club, and the Houston Riding and Polo Club). Kuldell was also a member of the First Methodist Church, where he taught Bible classes.[32] Ethelyn Kuldell was a collector of English furniture. Staub told Howard Barnstone that Mrs. Kuldell had seen an elaborately detailed manorial style house in Los Angeles, where the Hughes Tool Company had a branch office (and where the younger Howard Hughes, the company's sole owner, lived after 1925), and had asked Staub to design one like it. Staub confided his misgivings about designing a house that might look inappropriate in Houston to Annie Cochran. He remembered Mrs. Cochran's unequivocal response: "Give those people what they want."[33] The Kuldell House demonstrates Staub's capacity to regulate decorative display by structuring it as narrative, a technique that enabled him to materialize claims to continuity and belonging.

The Kuldell property was on the north side of South Boulevard next door to the Cochran House. As at the Cochran House, Staub oriented the house's reception and family rooms to face the south front lawn, which was rimmed with a yaupon hedge along the street line to screen the front yard. The kitchen and other serving spaces were attached to the west end of the house, and a two-story, three-car garage with servants' rooms above was located in the northwest corner of the lot backing up to the Hutcheson garage. The Kuldell House is offset in plan, but this configuration was not architecturally emphasized as it was in the Cochran House.

Staub used narrative to regulate the picturesque exterior organization and opulent decorative program of the Kuldell House. He achieved narrative economy with so little display of laboriousness that one must examine the roof, with its complicated junctures, to appreciate the complex orchestration of shapes and volumes the design entailed. The production of this narrative is evident in the horizontal band that encompasses second-floor windows on all sides of the house. Staub varied decorative brick bonding patterns every time there is an offset in wall plane. The exterior of the house (like its plans) becomes more circumstantial, and picturesque, as it moves

Dargan House, detail of wood mantle in master bedroom.

from reception to service zones, with decorative detailing concentrated most intensely in the family (bedroom and bathroom) and serving sectors. The attachment of the shed-roofed back porch to the garage-apartment building, with its roofed pass-through, invokes narrative literally (and literarily) by evoking the court of a medieval English inn or manor to integrate the serving spaces of the house into a compositional whole. Narrative was a technique for picturesquely and systematically integrating cars, laundry, storage, servants, and tradespeople and the activities associated with them into elite households. The fiction was made more credible by incorporating supporting characters and their actions into the story rather than excluding or ignoring them.

It is fascinating to observe Staub's use of narrative in responding to limitations. The living room and dining room of the Kuldell House each contain a single south-facing window opening (in addition to openings on other walls). Staub made wide openings for the windows (ten feet wide in the dining room, twelve feet wide in the living room) and set their sills at the level of the baseboards. To integrate such big openings into his manorial architectural narrative, Staub carried the wall across these voids in screens of specially molded brick whose tapered profile reflects daylight back into the rooms. Steel casement windows were inserted into the compartments of the brick screens frame. The windows are fitted with retractable, roll-down insect screens, which were essential in Houston. Staub maintained the planar continuity of the Kuldell House's brick walls, and consistency with its picturesque manorial genre, without compromising the desire for abundant light and air or settling for unsatisfactory solid-to-void proportions. Staub accommodated climatic concerns without violating the premises of the stylistic model. Narrative continuity was maintained by resolving practical problems while remaining in character, as the disappearing insect screens disclose.

The Kuldell House's terra-cotta shingle tile roof was another field for materially inscribing myths of continuity and belonging.[34] Staub treated the tiles as a continuous plastic surface, visible in the valleys of intersecting roof planes; as thin slivers, visible where the lapping of tiles is exposed above the side gable over the entrance porch; even as a substitute for brick in the tile-hung wall plane of the east-facing side gable.

From inside the house, Staub used the roof to construct episodes sustaining the manorial narrative, such as a "secret" vista of the west side of the Cochran House framed between rising roof planes from a diamond-paned attic window. Staub had the terra-cotta tile installed so that at the ridge level it was fairly consistent in color. But by the time it reached eaves level its color was variegated. This technique implied that the roof had experienced differential weathering as the result of extended climatic exposure. Through evidence of the effects

Col. Rudolph C. Kuldell House, Broadacres, 1928–29, John F. Staub, architect. South-facing street elevation.

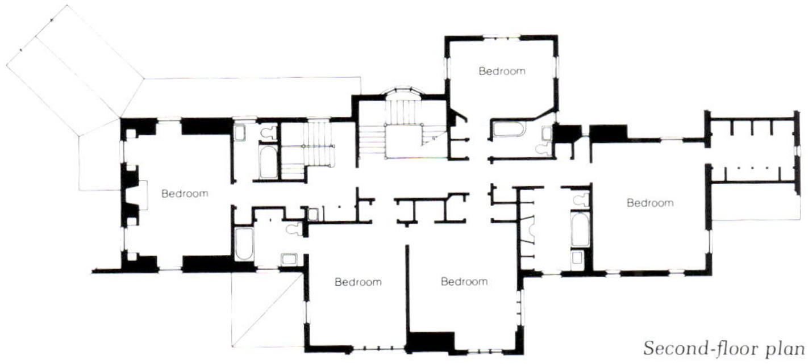

Second-floor plan

First-floor plan Kuldell House.

Kuldell House, detail of brick bonding patterns at dining room window bay.

Kuldell House, detail of gable and chimney stack above dining room.

Kuldell House, detail of timbered bay above entrance.

Kuldell House, detail of brick bonding patterns above living room window.

Kuldell House, looking from rear garage toward north-facing rear elevation.

Kuldell House, detail of brick-framed dining room window bay.

Kuldell House, detail of terra-cotta shingle tile roof.

Kuldell House, detail of side-gabled roof above entrance porch showing lapping of roof tiles.

Kuldell House, detail of east side gables showing brick (foreground) and tile (background) facing.

of nature, concession to climate (the big, south-facing windows), absorption of domestic services and technology, and decorative variation, Staub constructed a multilayered architectural narrative suggesting that this picturesque manorial style house not only belonged on the Texas Gulf coast but had long existed there. Contemporary critics of American architecture, especially of domestic architecture, recognized that the peril inherent in such blatant fictionalization was that the narratives being constructed could not be sustained. The material consistency, spatial rigor, and ingenuity required to invent period analogues of modern requirements called the economy of thematic narration into question.[35] It is a measure of Staub's skill that he could perform at this level. It is indicative of his misgivings about the social utility of such performances that it required Mrs. Cochran's admonition for him to carry out this project. Staub's virtuosity was most evident not in the profuseness of his imagination but in his sublimation of the results. The exterior surfaces of the Kuldell House impress with their richness. They cohere to compose a whole.

The interiors of the Kuldell House are more characteristic of Staub in their restraint. Twelve-and-a-half-foot-high ceilings throughout the first floor of the house ensure a sense of loftiness. Yet the house does not feel as imposing as the Dargan House. The entrance hall, which is paneled in polished oak and receives only north light, is the spatial point of confluence of the other reception rooms, which, in contrast to it, feel light and open. In the Kuldell House, one seems to move along axes of light. The big casement windows in the living room and dining room make it seem as though space in both rooms flows continuously across floor planes of wide, pegged planks to the lawn outside.

Staub modulated the white plaster wall and ceiling planes of the living room with oak piers, brackets, and beams that articulate surfaces but do not subdivide the space. The dining room was originally the most opulently finished reception room. Gilt plaster frames, wreathing openings and wall panels, and mirrors inset in paneled doors are no longer in place. Today, it is the deeply embrasured and compartmented south window and the wide floorboards that materially underpin the room's strongly felt spatial ambiance.

Secondary spaces are less solemn. The breakfast room opening off the dining room is glazed with diamond-paned windows. The use of opalescent glass especially animates the west-facing room when the sun casts shadows across the floor plane of Zenitherm, a resilient, industrially produced composition flooring material. The pantry and kitchen have been substantially preserved. They are unusually spacious because they share the same ceiling height as the first-floor reception rooms. Befitting the Kuldells' generous budget, four bathrooms serve the five second-floor bedrooms. Staub varied

Kuldell House, view from attic window toward west side of Cochran House.

Kuldell House, entrance hall.

Kuldell House, detail of casement windows in living room.

Kuldell House, detail of carved wood bracket in living room.

Kuldell House, oak overmantle in living room. Peter Mansbendel, carver.

Kuldell House, detail of living room mantle and fireplace surround.

(opposite)
Kuldell House, detail of breakfast room windows.

Kuldell House, pantry.

decorative detail, especially tile colors and patterns, to give each bathroom individuality. The house contains instances of minor thematic detailing, such as the door pull and lock plate on the inside of the thick, paneled, four-foot-wide front door, which take the form of a medieval heraldic dragon.

The Kuldell daughters' bathroom demonstrates how Staub's designs consistently instilled upper-class subjectivity in the spaces (and occupants) of his houses. Symmetry, centrality, and figuration are reiterated to underscore the privileged status of the patrician subject. The bathtub is set in a symmetrically composed alcove that projects axial composure into the room, which is not symmetrically organized. The segmentally curved mirror above the sink and the sconces flanking it frame and center. The concave profile of the dressing table and its three-part mirror enfold and reflect. Coordinating the color of the tiles with the color of the plumbing fixtures, when white was the standard color for bathrooms and their equipment, reinforced the exceptional status of the subject position being constructed here. Not only in rooms where guests were received but also in the most intimate domestic spaces of Staub's houses, the unified consciousness of the patrician subject was instilled architecturally in order to frame, magnify, and identify family members to themselves as those subjects.

At the Kuldell House, narrative functions to order and compose. Staub resolved the contradictions implicit in adapting the picturesque English manorial model to Houston and in generating a decorative program to substantiate this stylistic fiction. It was the Kuldell House's social program, however, that gave the architectural narrative its themes. The spatial components of the manorial genre, the architectural conventions for combining these components, and the varieties of material finish signifying the genre cohered to tell a story about the propriety and refinement of Colonel Kuldell and his family and to demonstrate that they belonged where they were. The house materialized the myth of the unified consciousness of the upper-class subject. By resolving contradictions through the medium of architecture, Staub allowed the issue of social class—and the legitimacy of an upper class—to remain invisibly embedded in the house rather than externalized as problematic and contentious. Style, not class, would function as the fetish to absorb criticism and deflect debate.

Kuldell House, detail of front door pull and lock plate.

Staub's six country houses in Broadacres contributed to the spatial construction of an upper-class identity for Houston's elite in the 1920s through their systematic integration of architecture with community planning and landscape architecture. Socially, they facilitated the integration of emergent elites and established elites. Ideologically, they advanced practices and models identified with the architectural culture

Kuldell House, detail of daughters' bathroom.

of metropolitan centers, especially New York. Staub's houses collectively construct a consensus in which the beauty, order, and sophistication embodied in these houses performed assertions of their owners' virtue, worthiness, and legitimacy and identified them as belonging to a superior class of people entrusted with ensuring the prosperity and well-being of the community.

Staub's country houses in Broadacres contribute to the exceptional architectural consistency of the small neighborhood and the construction of upper-class identity it advances. The beauty, groundedness, and permanence of the houses of Broadacres, and their systematic integration into a spatial matrix that, in theory, ensured continuity and coherence from the scale of the house to that of the city, enabled established elite families to assert their continued relevance and authority as civic leaders while emergent elites asserted their determination to ascend to local leadership rank.[36] As a collective response to the uncertainty that modernization provoked, the neighborhood and its houses represented elite commitment to maintaining authority by constructing a consensus on their virtues as leaders, as those who set standards for the community by building wisely, durably, and beautifully and by offering their domestic settings as models for how Houston could become more civilized as it became bigger, richer, and more modern. Staub advanced this consensus with his country houses in Broadacres, which spatially framed Houston's elite as a patrician gentry and sought to sustain this construction by instilling upper-class subjectivity in their occupants.

CHAPTER 3 : RIVER OAKS

River Oaks Gate Pier, River Oaks Boulevard near Locke Lane, 1925, John F. Staub, architect. Howard Barnstone called Staub's gate piers the "gates of paradise."

River Oaks Country Club Estates began as a 180-acre, single-family residential subdivision adjoining the 200-acre grounds of the newly organized River Oaks Country Club.[1] Planned in 1923, it lay south of Buffalo Bayou, three-and-a-half miles west of downtown Houston. Shortly after the initial developer, the Country Club Estates Company, filed the subdivision plat in May 1924, the entire subdivision was bought out by Hogg Brothers, which organized Country Club Estates, Inc. (the River Oaks Corporation after 1927), headed by the lawyer Hugh Potter, to manage development of the community. From this second beginning, River Oaks was primed to become *the* elite neighborhood of Houston. Will Hogg and his associate Hugh Potter compensated for River Oaks's problematic location west of downtown Houston (rather than south of downtown, where Broadacres, Shadyside, and Courtlandt Place lay) by projecting a vision of community intended to set it apart from these small elite neighborhoods. Through community planning, landscape design, architecture, and—most unusually in the context of earlier elite neighborhoods—advertising imagery, the River Oaks Corporation represented River Oaks not simply as a neighborhood but as a way of life. Mythic imagery was consciously and repeatedly used to construct community identity that emphasized civic idealism, elite status, and suburban exclusivity. Architecture as a representation of community identity was especially important to Will Hogg and his sister Ima Hogg. The developers of River Oaks retained Staub, Birdsall Briscoe, and Joseph W. Northrop Jr. to design a series of speculative houses in 1925 based on historic American prototypes. Ima Hogg worked with Staub on the second house to be built, which was patterned on the Spanish Creole architecture of the French Quarter of New Orleans. According to Staub, Miss Hogg coined the term "Latin Colonial" to describe this architecture, which was represented as a historic tradition especially applicable to Houston.[2] Staub subsequently designed a set of gate piers at the south entrance to River Oaks, a shopping and office center for the River Oaks Corporation, and the Hoggs' house, Bayou Bend, in the Latin Colonial style.

The Hogg siblings were emergent elites absorbed into Houston's social elite within a few years of their moving to Houston in 1906. They were originally from Quitman in East Texas, seventy-five miles east of Dallas, but had grown up in Austin after their father, James S. Hogg, a newspaper publisher and lawyer, was elected attorney general of Texas in 1886.[3] Four years later, Hogg was elected governor and served two terms from 1891 to 1895. The first Texas governor to be born in Texas, Jim Hogg embraced reform, establishing the Texas Railroad Commission to regulate railroad corporations in Texas. Hogg's wife, Sallie Stinson Hogg, died in 1895, shortly after the end of his gubernatorial career. Jim Hogg practiced law in Austin and sought investment opportunities to provide for his four children, which led him to form the Hogg-Swayne syndicate with the Fort Worth lawyer and politician James W. Swayne, the Lampasas, Texas, newspaper publisher William T. Campbell, and the Georgetown, Texas, lawyer and district judge R. E. Brooks in early 1901. Daniel Yergin, the historian of oil, remarked that J. M. Guffey (who started what became the Gulf Oil Corporation) purposefully sold the Hogg-Swayne syndicate an extremely valuable piece of production at Spindletop to ensure that Texas politicians would have an incentive not to attack out-of-state oil operators.[4] It was the Hogg-Swayne syndicate that afforded J. S. Cullinan an entry to Spindletop, leading to his formation of the Texas Company.[5] In 1901 Hogg also bought the 4,100-acre Patton plantation near West Columbia, Texas, sixty miles south of Houston.[6] An ex-sugar plantation that was never profitable after the abolition of slavery, Varner, as Hogg renamed the property after its first Anglo-American owner, was the site of unsuccessful farming and stock raising efforts before and after Jim Hogg's death in 1906.[7] Following Jim Hogg's death, Ima and Will Hogg settled in Houston. A third brother, Mike Hogg, completed his studies in Austin and the youngest, Tom, lived at Varner. Will Hogg, a lawyer, worked as a special assistant to J. S. Cullinan. Hogg was elected to the board of directors of the Texas Company shortly before Cullinan resigned in 1913, and he followed Cullinan out of the company.[8]

Ima Hogg, after her father's death, studied piano for two years in Berlin. Returning to Houston in 1909, she was one of the women who formed the Houston Symphony Orchestra Association in 1913, and she served as the association's second president.[9] In January 1918, the Tyndall-Wyoming Oil Company brought in the Tyndall-Hogg Number 2 well at Varner, vindicating Jim Hogg's conviction that the plantation lay atop a reservoir of oil. Production royalties from the resulting West Columbia oilfield were the basis of the Hogg family's fortune.[10]

Ima Hogg experienced a serious episode of depression in 1918 that compelled her to seek medical treatment in Philadelphia in 1919, where she remained under a doctor's care until 1923.[11] It was during this interval that she and Will embarked on parallel careers as collectors: Miss Hogg of seventeenth-, eighteenth-, and early-nineteenth-century American furniture and decorative art and her elder brother of American antiques and the first important collection of the art of Frederic Remington.[12] In 1918 Will Hogg considered buying the lot in Shadyside where William S. Farish would build his Lindeberg-designed house but lost the opportunity to do so because of a misunderstanding with J. S. Cullinan, who sold the lot to Farish instead.[13] Hogg undertook a radical transformation of the eighty-five-year-

Will C. Hogg. Courtesy The Museum of Fine Arts, Houston.

Ima Hogg in the living room at Bayou Bend, 1952. Photograph by Joffé. Courtesy Condé Nast.

old Patton House at Varner Plantation in 1919 and the same year tried to interest several family friends in cooperatively developing a private place neighborhood, Community Place, abutting Main Boulevard near the Museum of Fine Arts site.[14] Will and Mike Hogg built a seven-story office building in downtown Houston in 1920–21, and Hogg Brothers and the baking company executive Henry W. Stude entered the field of suburban real estate development in Houston. Their first undertaking was Norhill of 1921–22, a lower-middle-income subdivision developed in several phases, followed by Colby Court of 1923 on what was to have been the Community Place tract.[15] Between November 1923 and April 1924 the Varner Realty Company, the Hogg-Stude real estate operation, bought several tracts of land aggregating one thousand five hundred three acres on the north side of Buffalo Bayou four miles west of Main Street. These purchases comprised the easternmost extension of a dense pine forest that ran for several miles along Buffalo Bayou west of Houston, an outlier of the East Texas piney woods. In May 1924, Hogg Brothers sold this land at cost to the City of Houston and additionally donated nearly ten percent of the purchase price to the city so that it could make the first payment on the tract, which was to be dedicated as a park, Memorial Park, in memory of Houstonians killed in World War I.[16] These activities reflect Will Hogg's personal expansiveness. Like his father, Hogg was a charismatic personality: impulsive, ebullient, temperamental, and domineering. Wealth gave him the leisure and resources to pursue his interests on what must have seemed like a limitless scale.

Will Hogg's activities between 1918 and 1924—art collecting, urban real estate development, suburban community development, public space acquisition, nature conservation, and cultural philanthropy—represented his effort to construct alternatives to the course of civic development in Houston in both the public and private domains as well as to construct for himself a social role as civic visionary, using the authority that wealth and access to institutions of influence conferred for what he understood to be the public good. River Oaks and Bayou Bend, the house Staub designed for Ima, Will, and Mike Hogg, were the projects where Will Hogg's disparate activities came into focus as an integrated spatial whole. In River Oaks and at Bayou Bend one could experience the construction of new models for life in Houston based on historical myths and images that stressed themes of cultural continuity with recovered regional and national traditions spatially represented in architecture, urban design, landscape architecture, and interior design. Hogg and his allies carried out this cultural project with an unusual degree of consistency and comprehensiveness, the better to suggest that River Oaks was not simply another elite residential neighborhood but rather a model for how Houston could be modernized intelligently and responsibly.

In this respect, River Oaks can be understood as what the anthropologist Pamela G. Smart calls "an instrument in the formation of a public," material evidence of the superiority of practices Hogg and his allies advocated, meant to ensure public approbation and construct consensus on the value and effectiveness of such practices.[17] The contradictions this consensus entailed involved advancing the cause of comprehensive planning in the sociopolitical and economic context of entrepreneurial capitalism and sustaining elite prerogative without appearing to propose a hierarchical system of social classes.[18] The planning and architecture of River Oaks sought to negotiate these contradictions through objective spatial demonstrations of superiority and subjective narratives of seduction, in effect selling patrician identity and subjectivity in conformance with what had become the state of the art of American commercial advertising in the 1920s. River Oaks spatially aspired to the patrician affect of perfect integration.

According to Hugh Potter, it was he and Mike Hogg who came up with the idea of buying out the Country Club Estates Company while riding on the south bank of Buffalo Bayou, across from the Memorial Park site, on a 118-acre tract that Mike Hogg bought in March 1923 as a weekend country retreat, which he called Tall Timbers.[19] Tall Timbers lay just west of Country Club Estates and the River Oaks Country Club golf course. Will Hogg consented to their proposition on the conditions that Hogg Brothers acquire not only Country Club Estates but enough contiguous real estate to develop a comprehensively planned residential community and that Potter resign his partnership in Gill, Jones, Tyler and Potter, the law firm that had once been Hogg, Watkins and Jones, Jim Hogg's short-lived Houston law practice, and become the development company's chief executive officer.[20] Hogg Brothers bought seven hundred twenty additional acres stretching from Shepherd's Dam Road on the east to the Southern Pacific railroad tracks on the west, and from Buffalo Bayou on the north to Westheimer Road on the south. By August 1924, Hare and Hare, landscape architects and city planning consultants to Houston's Board of Park Commissioners and the City Planning Commission, were retained to prepare a master plan for the entire tract. Drawings in the Hare and Hare Collection of the Houston Metropolitan Research Center indicate that the Hare firm produced subdivision plan proposals for the River Oaks Corporation as late as April 1925.[21] But in August 1925, the Houston engineer Herbert A. Kipp, who laid out Country Club Estates and was retained by the Hoggs and Potter as consulting engineer, was made first vice president of the development company, a post he would hold until the company's dissolution in 1954.[22] Some of the major street alignments visible in Hare and Hare's studies appear in the street plan of River Oaks, but Kipp was responsible for planning the twenty subdivisions that comprise River Oaks, the last of which was platted in 1947.[23]

The site plan of Country Club Estates and the subsequent phases of River Oaks contributed to its aura of distinction. Kipp's plans spatially distinguished River Oaks from Broadacres, Shadyside, and Courtlandt Place by representing it as the country place alternative to what were antithetically construed as city neighborhoods. Kipp's plan for Country Club Estates, designed to be free-standing, was based on a curving grid of east-west streets (which he named for famous golf clubs), which gave almost all the house sites a north-south orientation and thwarted the endless vista effect that straight, urban streets produced in the coastal flatlands.[24]

Country Club Estates incorporated one urban episode, a divided boulevard (initially called Ball Boulevard after one of the investors but renamed River Oaks Boulevard by Hogg Brothers) running north-south through the center of the tract and terminated on the north by the country clubhouse site. Kipp's subdivision plat incorporated a wide variety of lot sizes, from a quarter acre along the east and west edges of the subdivision and the blocks farthest south of the country club to four acres (the two lots on either side of the boulevard bordering the country clubhouse site).

Due to Will Hogg's insistence that River Oaks not be limited to Country Club Estates, the community possessed an enormous advantage that the proprietary neighborhoods near the Museum of Fine Arts and their ancillaries lacked. It was capable of being expanded to absorb the wealth Houston continued to produce, even during the Great Depression. As an elite community that was not exclusively upper income, River Oaks proved to be more modern, dynamic, and flexible than Courtlandt Place, Shadyside, and Broadacres. Inclusiveness helped extend the demographic base and stabilize spatial representation of the myth of harmonious community. Through its identifying institutions (such as the country club), its architecture, and its advertising, River Oaks served as a template to regulate patrician formation because it offered emergent elites access to a system of representation that framed them as an upper class in Houston.

River Oaks was systematically integrated into the two-and-a-half-mile linear park and parkway drive along Buffalo Bayou that Hare and Hare designed to link the downtown civic center to Memorial Park. Upon crossing South Shepherd, the parkway drive, now called Allen Parkway, became Kirby Drive, which arced through the eastern sector of River Oaks, turning south to link the Buffalo Bayou linear park to a proposed Brays Bayou linear park and parkway four-and-a-quarter miles to the south. (South of River Oaks, Kirby Drive would be developed in the 1940s and 1950s as a commercial strip instead of a parkway boulevard.) By linking the civic

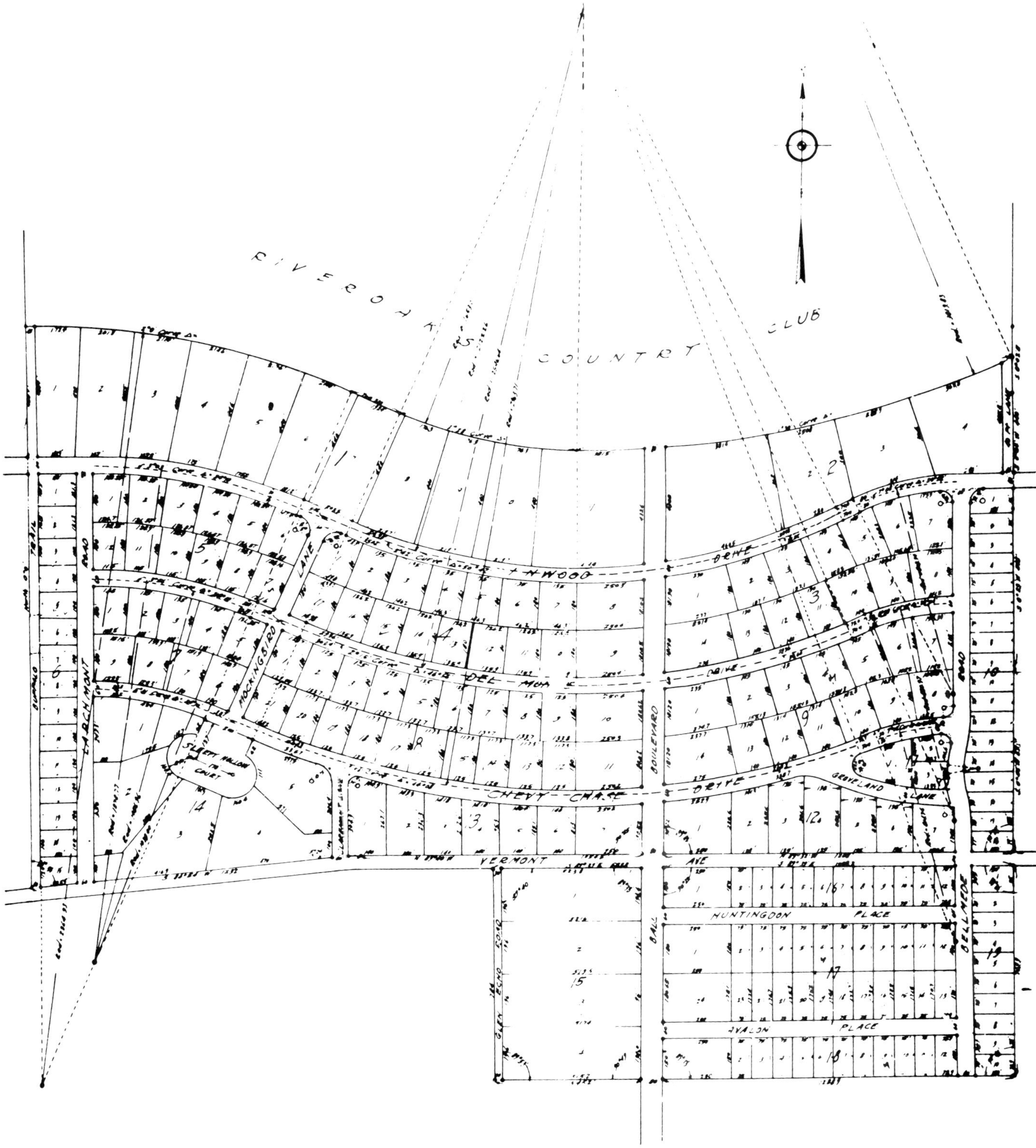

Plat map of Country Club Estates, 1924, H. A. Kipp, consulting engineer.

Aerial view looking north down River Oaks Boulevard toward River Oaks Country Club, 1926. The light-colored house facing camera in upper right was Staub's River Oaks Early Republic House, which Hugh Potter bought. The two houses near the right center were two of Joseph W. Northrup's houses for Country Club Estates. *River Oaks Magazine* 5 (May 1941).

center downtown to River Oaks and Memorial Park, Will Hogg and his cohorts systematically integrated a natural waterway prone to flooding with landscaping, public park space, and high-speed automobile circulation in an urban space design that made its appeal not only in terms of economy and efficiency but also of scenic beauty.[25] Constructing urban space as suburban scenery, indeed overlaying a new dynamic on the city—a continuous drive that minimally intersected with the existing street network to facilitate rapid mobility through a landscaped setting not previously urbanized because it had been treated as a problematic edge—differed from the more measured rhythms and proportions of the tree-lined Main Boulevard and its ancillaries. Allen Parkway introduced to Houston the modern experience of moving freely through the city at the speed of machines rather than constraining machines to operate at the tempo of the nineteenth-century city. The River Oaks Corporation's advertising brochure announcing completion of the Allen Parkway–Kirby Drive thoroughfare was illustrated with an aerial perspective by Wilfred H. Stedman that adroitly positioned River Oaks within the context of Progressive modernization.[26] Stedman's bird's-eye view underscored themes of continuity, connection, and the superior "big picture" perspective that, as Emily Neff observed, was a defining characteristic of Will Hogg's civic vision. The construction of spatial continuity that River Oaks's systematic integration into Hare and Hare's city plan portended attested to the community's superiority. River Oaks belonged to Houston of the future rather than Houston of the past. Systematically integrated into the new Houston, River Oaks comprised a "utopian fragment" constructing enlightened suburban modernity in the chaotically mixed field of the early-twentieth-century American city.[27]

Kenneth Womack seems to have been the link between Staub and the Hoggs. Staub told Barnstone that it was Womack, one of Lindeberg's Shadyside clients, an investor in the Country Club Estates Company, and founding president of the River Oaks Country Club, who got him the commission for the clubhouse as an inducement to remain in Houston rather than return to Knoxville.[28] After Hogg Brothers bought out his fellow investors in the Country Club Estates Company, Womack retained an affiliation with the River Oaks Corporation as a member of its board of directors, along with Will Clayton, who built the first house in River Oaks, and the Houston lawyer (and future mayor) Walter E. Monteith, vice president of the country club.[29]

Staub's design for the River Oaks Country Clubhouse, begun in the summer of 1923, was a stucco-walled, tile-roofed, one- and two-story building faced with a triple-arched entrance loggia. The clubhouse was domestic rather than institutional in scale. Externally, it displayed little decorative ornament.[30] Staub spatially portrayed the clubhouse's social role as a collective embodiment of elite community by designing it on an X-shaped plan, so that the entrance loggia was flanked by splayed wings that, at the terminus of River Oaks Boulevard, seemed to reach out and embrace the wide, esplanade-centered street. In its symmetry, centrality, and figuration, the country clubhouse reciprocated the symmetry and breadth of the boulevard. The clubhouse was completed in June 1924 just after Hogg Brothers bought out the Country Club Estates Company. One of the benefits of the purchase was that the club (which had signed up only three hundred members of the five hundred authorized in its charter) could immediately carry out a second phase—a ballroom—by Staub, costing $32,000, equipping it to better serve as a social and recreational center for the expanded country club community that would take shape around it.[31] Whether Staub's use of the Spanish Mediterranean genre for the country clubhouse can be attributed to Womack's influence is uncertain (Lindeberg's house for Womack was designed in the Spanish style). After the Hoggs took over River Oaks, Staub was enlisted in a new stylistic venture, the Latin Colonial, that set out to supersede the Spanish Mediterranean.

This stylistic shift suggests the Hoggs' yearning to redefine Houston culturally in ways that demonstrated their superiority as arbiters of style. Staub's facility in synthesizing a "new" eclectic alternative to the Spanish Mediterranean genre illuminates his usefulness to the Hoggs as "leading by serving" in the words of the anthropologist George E. Marcus, in order to elevate his clients' class standing.[32] Newspaper advertising for the River Oaks Corporation during the second half of 1924 listed Staub as the corporation's consulting architect.[33] Although his name ceased to appear in this capacity by January 1925, Staub, Birdsall Briscoe and his partner Sam H. Dixon Jr. and Joseph W. Northrop Jr. were recruited to design a set of speculative houses for the River Oaks Corporation in the spring of 1925. Ima Hogg worked with the architects on these houses, each of which was designed in an historic American architectural genre. Northrop's four houses were based on American Colonial and Georgian precedent.[34] Staub's biggest house of 1925–26 was designed in the neoclassical "early Republic" genre. The two most distinctive houses, Briscoe and Dixon's "Redbird House" (bought while under construction in the fall of 1925 by the oil tool equipment manufacturer William T. Campbell Jr.) and Staub's first house of 1925, were designed in the Latin Colonial style, the term Staub credited Ima Hogg with inventing.[35]

Two other Houston women built ambitious houses in River Oaks in its initial phase of development that attempted to define place culturally with architecture. Ralph Adams Cram was commissioned by the artist and patron Blanche

Aerial view of River Oaks, Buffalo Bayou Park–Allen Parkway, and Downtown Houston. Wilfred H. Stedman, April 1927, "Low Price Pre-Development Sale in River Oaks," River Oaks Scrapbooks, Houston Metropolitan Research Center, Houston Public Library, vol. 5A.

River Oaks Country Club, Houston, 1923–24, John F. Staub, architect. Demolished. Photograph by R. M. Luster in Don Riddle, River Oaks.

Country Club Estates House (Redbird House), River Oaks, 1925, Briscoe and Dixon, architects. Photograph by Paul Hester, Houston Architectural Survey.

Country Club Estates House (River Oaks Latin Colonial House), River Oaks, 1925, John F. Staub, architect. Photograph by R. M. Luster, in Don Riddle, River Oaks.

Cleveland Sewall House, River Oaks, 1923–26, Cram and Ferguson, architects. Photograph by Calvin Wheat, Civics for Houston *1 (May 1928): 4.*

Harding Sewall and her husband, the wholesale grocer and cotton factor Cleveland Sewall, to design an extraordinary Spanish style country house built in 1924–26 on a six-acre site on Inwood Drive abutting the country club.[36] The Sewall House incorporated antique furniture and decorative artifacts that Mrs. Sewall acquired in Spain and Italy with the aid of Mildred Stapley and Arthur Byne, the two leading American experts on Spanish architecture and decorative art.[37]

Will Clayton's wife, Sue Vaughan Clayton, selected a specific Southern architectural image for the country house she and her husband commissioned Briscoe and Dixon to design on another golf course lot on Inwood, completed in late 1924.[38] Built as a summer cottage, the Clayton House was modeled on Mount Vernon but adapted to the spatial requirements of a seasonal resort cottage. Mrs. Sewall and Mrs. Clayton were involved in the overlapping circles of art, architecture, collecting, and patronage with which Ima and Will Hogg were identified. Their houses demonstrate that the Hoggs operated in a climate of cultural exploration that engaged other members of Houston's elite. Although the images of tradition embodied in these houses were conservative, the independence with which they were formulated and the confidence with which they were asserted attest to a contradiction underlying eclectic traditionalism in the 1920s: it was the product of a modern imagination liberated from conformity to tradition, free to choose and invent. The Sewall House and the Clayton Summer House further put into perspective the imaginative fusion that the Latin Colonial represented in its architectural reconciliation of the building cultures of the Anglo-American South and Latin America.

The Latin Colonial fused the artistic and the patrician. It also emphasized, as Mark Alan Hewitt observed, the urbanity of its New Orleans Creole models to ground the architecture of suburbanization.[39] Staub cited the Old Absinthe House in the French Quarter of New Orleans as the model for the River Oaks Latin Colonial House (as it was called by the River Oaks Corporation), a linkage materialized in the cast-iron balcony affixed to the street front of the house.[40] Staub told Barnstone that he, Ima Hogg, and Birdsall Briscoe traveled to New Orleans by car in 1925 (an adventure before the construction of paved intercity highways; Staub especially remembered the farmer who emerged suddenly with his team from behind a screen of vegetation next to a mud hole in which their touring car was stuck and, for a fee, pulled them out).[41] In New Orleans, Staub was able to buy nineteenth-century cast-iron railings and arabesque panels salvaged by the Feitel Wrecking Company, which he incorporated in the houses and gate piers he designed for the River Oaks Corporation. The River Oaks publicity apparatus seized on this acquisition ("Antique Iron Rescued for River Oaks,"

"New Orleans Gates Are Reclaimed for Homes in Houston") to mythologize the fragments as talismans facilitating the evolutionary transmission to Houston of New Orleans's reputation for grace, style, and flair.[42] The Latin Colonial House was a material token of the River Oaks Corporation's apparent ability to fuse the bohemian and the patrician, the urban and the suburban, to achieve a synthesis between dialectical opposites and frame a community identity that appropriated the venerability, charm, and historical depth of the French Quarter, resolving stylistically the contradictions between conflicting desires for historical continuity and modernity. It demonstrated the ability of the River Oaks Corporation to "invent" a neo-traditional style that spoke architecturally to the ill-defined historical identity of Houston with more restraint than Spanish Mediterranean and more resonance than Georgian architecture.

In 1928, *Civics for Houston*, the monthly magazine published by Will Hogg's Forum of Civics, printed an essay by Staub on Latin Colonial architecture, reprinted in the *Southern Architect and Building News* in 1930. An excerpt summarizes the essay's essential points:

> One phase of the early development of the Louisiana architecture holds particular interest: that work which is Georgian in form and Latin in flavor. Most of the Latin characteristics come from the French, but the Spanish influence is seen in the use of the arch, particularly the elliptical, with and without fan-like transoms, as well as in tile roofs.
>
> This work has a very perceptible sense of order and dignified restraint, but at the same time a tropical quality of warmth and friendliness. The dignity of simplicity is mellowed by distinct elements of pictorial appeal such as the use of decorative iron in the balconies and railings, arched windows under galleries, arched gateways leading to inner courtyards. Stucco walls are pierced by balanced openings with plainly molded stucco and brick cornices. . . .
>
> The interiors are simply composed, stately in effect, high ceilinged, with prominent staircases, often gracefully curved. The openings generally extend from the floor almost to the ceiling, with windows treated like doors in the French manner. The tall openings giving abundant ventilation assist in making these houses very pleasant places in which to live.[43]

This passage reflects the fundamentally Darwinian point of view of American architectural discourse in the 1910s and 1920s. Its Darwinian premise is that "tradition" represents the evolutionary continuum of architectural expression, which is rooted in the culture of a place. This understanding of tradition as a phenomenon that could be modified to

William L. Clayton Summer House, River Oaks, 1924, Briscoe and Dixon, architects. Photography by Paul Hester, Houston Architectural Survey.

circumstances of location, environment, social customs, and human use (all categories of experience recognized in Darwinian discourse as effecting human culture) meant that tradition was understood as malleable and transmissible rather than rigid and fixed.

The building in which Staub most consistently materialized the Latin Colonial discourse was Bayou Bend, the house that Ima, Will, and Mike Hogg built between 1926 and 1928 on a fourteen-and-a-half-acre estate on Lazy Lane, the broad curving street that bisects the Homewoods section of River Oaks. Bayou Bend cost $217,164 to build, making it one of the most expensive houses constructed in Houston during the 1920s. Chris J. Miller was the general contractor and Birdsall P. Briscoe was Staub's associated architect.[44] Bayou Bend would become Ima Hogg's house. In 1927, while the house was under construction, Mike Hogg won election to a seat in the Texas Legislature and served two terms, until 1930. In July 1929, while Will Hogg was in California and Ima Hogg was traveling in the Nordic countries, Mike Hogg, then forty-four, married Alice Nicholson Frazer, a Dallas divorcée, in Galveston.[45] When Alice and Mike Hogg returned from their wedding trip, they bought a house built by the River Oaks Corporation at 2007 River Oaks Boulevard. In November 1929 Will Hogg embarked on an extended trip to Europe, where he was joined by his sister in the summer of 1930. In Baden-Baden in September 1930, Hogg suffered an attack of gallstones and, after emergency surgery, died of pneumonia at the age of fifty-five.[46]

Bayou Bend (a magic name, like River Oaks, meant to invest the landscape with poetic resonance) functioned as a technology of self fashioning because it spatially framed Will and Ima Hogg as arbiters of style, taste, and form.[47] Its beauty, spatial presence, and proportioned composure materialized authority, constructed continuity, and exuded benevolence to lend substance and legitimacy to Will Hogg's program for modernizing Houston intelligently and responsibly and Ima Hogg's for deepening and intensifying engagement with cultural practices intended to make Houston a more civilized, refined, and urbane city. Staub made real the Hoggs' fascination with historical myths and images to assert continuity between modern Houston and an imagined South, mediated through representations of "tradition" fused at Bayou Bend into an architectural whole. The unity of consciousness embedded in Bayou Bend reflected Ima and Will Hogg's virtues: altruism, liberality, magnanimity, civic idealism, and a profound awareness of the power of culture. Unlike his younger brothers, who attended Lawrenceville School, Will Hogg never attended any mid-Atlantic or New England boarding school. His formation as a patrician subject was shaped less by experience than by imagination. He was not restrained, like Mike Hogg, nor was he focused on personal preoccupations to the exclusion of public issues like the youngest Hogg brother, Tom, who lived in San Antonio rather than Houston in the 1920s.[48] It is tempting to understand Ima Hogg's involvement in the formulation of the Latin Colonial style, the planning of Bayou Bend and other houses in River Oaks, her collection of American furniture, and her developing interest in European modern art in the late 1920s as technologies of self fashioning focused on personal recovery and reconstruction.[49] Bayou Bend, through its internal coherence, consistency, and grace, enhanced the personal radiance and charisma of Will and Ima Hogg, magnifying their generosity and talents, implying a heritage of taste, culture, and refinement that belied the newness of the family's wealth.

At Bayou Bend, Will Hogg and Ima Hogg performed patrician subjectivity to enlist support in their campaigns to gentrify Houston's elite, educating them by example in superior forms of ethical responsibility and aesthetic grace that would equip them to become civic leaders. Bayou Bend served especially as a school for refining domestic style in Houston, a function fully acknowledged when Miss Hogg gave the house, its grounds, and her collection to the Museum of Fine Arts in 1957.[50] In earlier stages, this process of institutionalizing identity and subjectivity was based on the social construction of rituals that would expose not just Miss Hogg's friends but a broader public to the lessons materialized in the house, its collection, and gardens. Beginning in the early 1930s, local newspaper and magazine photographs indicate that Miss Hogg used Bayou Bend as a staging ground for organizations with which she was connected, especially the Houston Symphony Orchestra.[51] Membership and board meetings brought people (and news photographers) to Bayou Bend.

Even more important in efficiently regulating public exposure to Bayou Bend were invented rituals that sought to construct consensus around the educational mission it implicitly represented, which could function as instruments in the formation of a public willing to internalize the subject positions Bayou Bend objectified. The clearest example of such an invented ritual was the Azalea Trail, an annual "pilgrimage" to River Oaks gardens and houses first organized by the River Oaks Garden Club in 1936 that, each year, included Bayou Bend.[52] In 1939 the Garden Club of America held its annual meeting in Houston at Azalea Trail time, occasioning publication of an illustrated directory of Houston's foremost domestic gardens and a feature article in *Landscape Architecture* magazine.[53] Although such national recognition may have enhanced Miss Hogg's local role as cultural arbiter, it was the annual experience of the Azalea Trail and exposure to the magic world of Bayou Bend it afforded a middle-income Houston public that ritualized this experience and expanded

Latin Colonial Architecture in the Southwest

Exotic in Design and Color Blends With Colonial Type

JOHN F. STAUB

> *"The pursuit of fashions in style and the imitation of strange foreign things, in a cheap and hasty way, have filled the land with curious sights."*

A CONSIDERATION of the domestic work of the architects in this country during the past decade reflects the impress from recurring importations of styles developed in the past centuries in foreign lands and diverse climates, Waves of English manor houses, Spanish haciendas, Italian villas and French farmhouses have swept all sections of the United States.

It is not proposed to minimize the benefit from foreign study but rather to ask for a consideration of the architectural traditions of our own country in search for new points of view, and to urge the development of our local heritage.

The American architectural traditions most familiar to the public are those of Charleston, South Carolina. Many of us, however, err in not fully availing ourselves of a more genuine source of inspiration by overlooking the heritage of our own environment.

Shadows, cast through a wrought iron balcony, fanlights over shuttered doorways, add to the charm of the home of Mr. and Mrs. David M. Picton, Jr., of Houston.

The agencies producing architecture at any time or place are climate, available materials, methods of construction, taste of the day and the amenities of social life. Is it not wiser for us to seek inspiration in the architecture developed in our own climate with the materials at hand and adjust it to the tastes and requirements of our day, rather than to force the adaptation of types derived in foreign environments under different climatic conditions?

Architects generally agree that the most satisfactory work in domestic architecture in the United States within the past decade has developed in the environs of Philadelphia. Here has been produced a really significant architecture, because the Pennsylvanians have studied their local traditions and adapted them, in a free spirit to the changed conditions of this era.

Our Gulf Coast country possesses a rare heritage in the rich deposit of French and Spanish work and the later development of the Greek Revival. Southeast Texas is climatically associated with Louisiana rather than with Southwest Texas and New Mexico. The beautiful San Antonio Missions are evolved for an arid country. While there is some justification in a further development of this type on our sparse prairies, it is not so logical for this very humid section as is the Louisiana tradition.

One might wander far and see nothing so interesting architecturally as the Old Absinthe House of New Orleans

One of the greatest contributing factors to the romantic charm of these old houses is their color. A softness has naturally come with age, but even in their original state the same harmony with variety must have existed. Sunlit stucco walls of pale apricot pink are relieved by black lace iron work and blue-green blinds. In New Orleans a unique shade of orange was sometimes used for the trim around the openings and in small quantities, pleasingly contrasts with the blue-green blinds. On some of the plantation houses, dusty yellow stucco is combined with red brick.

The interiors are simply composed, stately in effect, high ceilinged, with prominent staircases, often gracefully curved. The openings generally extend from the floor almost to ceiling, with windows treated like doors in the French manner. The tall openings, giving abundant ventilation, assist in making these houses very pleasant places in which to live.

Here then, almost at our door, is a domestic architecture, having beauty and comfortable living as component parts, which time has proved. Surely, study of this architecture shall bring rich reward.

* * *

To those interested in study of this tradition the following are recommended:

"Architectural charm of Old New Orleans," Allison Owen, *A. I. A. the Journal of the American Institute of Architects*, October, 1913.

"Old Plantation houses in Louisiana," by Wm. P. Spratling and Natalie Scott.

"Architectural tradition in New Orleans," by N. C. Curtis, *Journal of the American Institute of Architects.* August 1925.

"The Domestic Architecture of the early American Republic," Howard Major.

"Latin Colonial Architecture in the Southwest," Civics for Houston 1 (Feb. 1928): 6.

A meeting of the Houston Symphony Society on the garden terrace at Bayou Bend, c. 1935, Houston 16 (July 1944): 8.

the public Staub's house could captivate, instruct, and persuasively subjectify. Staub's spatial approach to planning grounded and naturalized the "magical" sensations visitors were apt to experience at Bayou Bend.

The house is built on a shelf-like terrace that interrupts the downward slope of the terrain toward Buffalo Bayou. Staub employed axiality, centrality, and symmetry to order the house internally and integrate it with its site. By treating axes, centers, and symmetry as spatial conditions, Staub prevented their application from seeming diagrammatic or mechanical. Bayou Bend is double fronted. The south front functions as a full spatial stop in an entry sequence that begins at Lazy Lane. Bayou Bend is not visible from the street. The entrance drive curves around the rim of a ravine profusely planted with evergreen woodland vegetation, then divides. The lower drive approaches the house on axis, sloping down through a tunnel of trees that tightly frames a distant view of the house. The drive emerges from this tunnel into a clearing and turns, revealing the entire south front of the house, which spreads out to fill the carefully framed horizon.

Tall, limbed-up loblolly pine trees at the edge of the woods give this entry space a vertical, high-ceilinged sensation, which the house counters with its lateral spread. The symmetrical division of the house into a central block framed by tall chimney stacks, low-roofed, recessed hyphens, and narrow flanking end wings with centered frontal chimney stacks implies a volumetric reciprocity between the tall perimeter trees, the flat clearing, and the horizontal expanse of the house front. Loggias opening off the dining room and living room contained volumes of shade that accentuated the division of the house into symmetrically balanced components. Centrality is used to focus rather than insist. Axiality and symmetry regulate this sequence. Staging movement and perception endowed Bayou Bend with a layered identity that is developed at even finer scales of difference inside. Staub modulated his use of axiality and symmetry on the south front of Bayou Bend with spatial recession and projection, so that the house seems to embrace arriving visitors and the landscape as his River Oaks Country Clubhouse once did.

The north (garden) face of Bayou Bend also spreads out laterally to fill the horizon. On this elevation, which is in shadow most of the day and is customarily viewed from below, there is less volumetric recession and projection than on the south elevation so that, from a distance, the house front appears planar, a serenely dominant presence at the crest of the shelf on which it was built. The three-bay portico and the bow-fronted entrance bay inside it emphasize verticality to a greater degree than occurs on the south front of the house. The portico and bow focus the long view from the

Ima Hogg House, Bayou Bend, Homewoods, River Oaks, 1926–28, John F. Staub and Birdsall P. Briscoe, architects. Site plan. Courtesy The Museum of Fine Arts, Houston; MFAA Archives.

Bayou Bend, garden front.

(previous page) Bayou Bend, entrance front.

lower garden, the Diana Garden. Indeed, the bow front spatializes the presence of the regulating axis. The terraced garden, designed in 1937 by the Houston landscape architects Fleming and Sheppard, expands laterally as it moves axially downhill away from the house front.[54]

The east elevation of Bayou Bend (the east wing originally contained the Hogg brothers' rooms) is symmetrical, but centrality is not emphasized. Consequently, it is the landscape of the East Garden, an axial parterre designed in 1934 by the Houston landscape architect Ruth London, that asserts primacy, rather than the architecture, which functions as a planar backdrop.[55] The west elevation (the west wing contained the kitchen and housekeeper's rooms on the first floor and guest bedrooms on the second floor) is also symmetrical, but because its symmetry is not projected spatially into the landscape, it is insignificant. Movement was designed to pass laterally alongside the west wing on the downhill slope toward the garage rather than on axis with it. The spatial neutrality of the west side of Bayou Bend, where efficient servicing was the dominant concern, demonstrates by contrast how the honorific portions of Bayou Bend's landscape were powerfully spatialized by the axes, centrality, and symmetry embedded in the design of the house. Centrality, symmetry, and axiality were the optical means used to integrate architecture and landscape architecture systematically so that building and nature spatially reinforce each other. They are activated in an implicit hierarchy that privileges the north and south fronts, treats the east front as secondary, and suppresses awareness of the west front as unimportant.

Staub employed centrality, symmetry, and axiality to organize the interiors of Bayou Bend. Axes were used in plan to spatially interlock sequences of rooms. The broad entrance hall is aligned on the central axis. Doors from the entrance hall into the dining room and living room are aligned on a cross axis centered on the dining room fireplace. Consequently, visitors do not enter the living room on axis with its centrally positioned fireplace. In rooms as long as the living room (twenty feet by forty feet), Staub often deflected entry off the centerline of the room. Entering on the diagonal spatially energized one's initial experience of the room, whereas entering on the centerline tended to emphasize the planarity of the fireplace wall opposite, dividing the space into static halves.[56] From the living room, Staub organized movement in a spiraling motion through the adjacent library, the bachelors' living room with its extraordinarily intense blue-painted paneling, and the no-longer-extant bachelors' tap room in the east wing.[57] The major reception rooms, family rooms, and bedrooms were symmetrically composed in elevation along their fireplace walls, and in some instances on all four walls.

Bayou Bend, garden portico and terrace.

Bayou Bend, view from hall toward Diana Garden.

As in Staub's other houses, symmetry imparts a sense of composure and formal order to the principal rooms of the house, which Staub animated with minor deviations, as in the dining room, where the niche cupboard is balanced with the recessed French doors to the loggia. Hierarchy—gradation based on the binary opposition of high and low, better and worse, superior and inferior—was the means through which different components and spaces were coherently joined. Conjunction discloses the extent to which perceptions of continuity made it possible to understand these assemblies as wholes rather than pieces.

Staub coordinated the sequence of interiors at Bayou Bend with architectural detail to shape a spatial narrative that corresponded to Miss Hogg's interest in American furniture and artifacts. With its neoclassical decor, which Miss Hogg likened to Charleston, South Carolina, and the virtuoso coloration supplied by the artist William Mackay's painted decoration, the dining room represented one pole in an evolutionary narrative of connoisseurship and refinement.[58] From the lofty dining room, one moved on axis across the entrance hall, the most forceful space in the house, into the brightly illuminated living room, representing James River classicism of the 1760s. From the living room, movement adhered to a spiraling trajectory into the lower-ceilinged, more light absorbing, and increasingly more intimate family rooms, based on early-eighteenth-century Massachusetts precedent, to the conclusion of this evolutionary narrative, the vernacular-style tap room. As on the exterior, Staub adroitly regulated this spatial narrative by absorbing each episode into a compositional continuum based on symmetrical organization about central, figural elements while streamlining and academically "correcting" the variations in classical detailing that the original models exhibited. One result is that at Bayou Bend the reception rooms possess individual character; Staub never seems to be generating rooms merely to fill up a big house. The rhythmic techniques Staub employed, the articulate composition of shapes and subdivision of surfaces in accordance with the conventions of classical architecture, accompanied the choreography of movement in an architectural continuum through the house's reception and family rooms. Bayou Bend was imbued with narrative coherence and rhythmic continuity. Staub's application of classical practices imparted meaning and consistency to subjective experiences of the architecture. The sequence of interiors he designed constructed narratives of connectedness that not only linked the historical episodes represented by each room to one another but also to the house as a whole and to its site.

By contrasting a circumstantial treatment of the service areas of the house with the calm, limpid spaces of the reception rooms, Staub constructed an internal dialectic that is

Bayou Bend, view from bachelors' porch toward East Garden.

Bayou Bend, view from living room toward dining room.

Bayou Bend, view from bachelors' iving room through the library toward the living room.

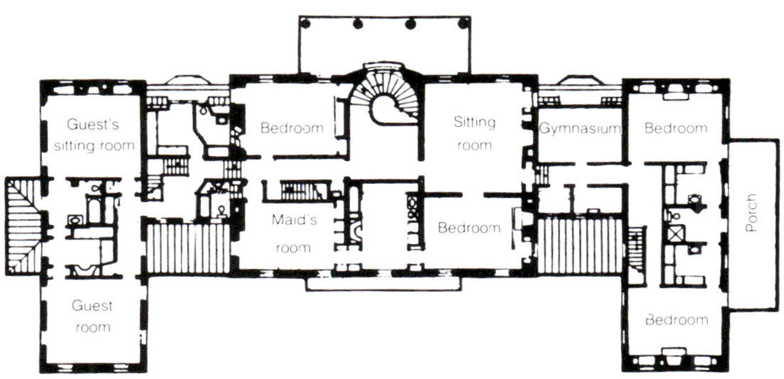

Second-floor plan

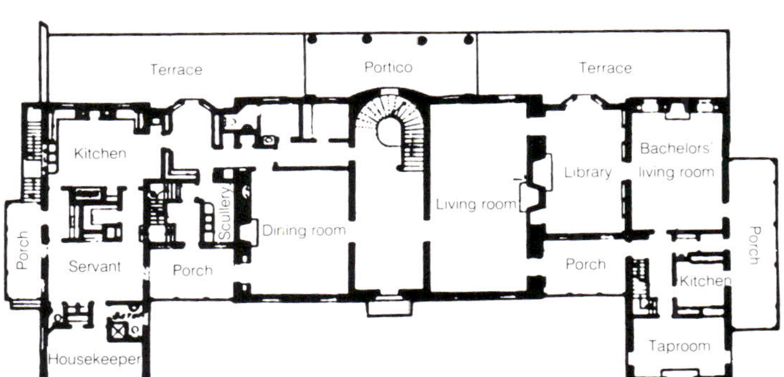

First-floor plan

Bayou Bend.

Bayou Bend, detail of dining room mantle and painted wallpaper by William Mackay.

Bayou Bend, view from Miss Hogg's sitting room toward passage that leads down to bachelors' wing.

perceptible. This technique cleverly composed and naturalized difference. Service areas tended to be intricately configured and were where Staub introduced changes in floor and ceiling levels to create spatial variety. First-floor ceiling levels of eight-and-a-half feet in the east and west wings and hyphens entailed lower second-floor levels above, necessitating interior steps.

In both plan and section Staub accentuated spatial contrasts to distinguish between reception, family, and service spaces inside Bayou Bend, contrasts coordinated with the distribution of functions and the external composition of the house. Staub carried this dialectical approach to articulating distinctions to the free-standing one- and two-story garage and servants' apartment building. The building is symmetrically organized. One-story wings outflank a central two-story block, reiterating the composition of the main house. Architectural detail, although sparing, reprises that of the main house. When the Clio Garden was redesigned by

Bayou Bend, servants' bathroom in basement.

Bayou Bend, view through breakfast room bay window toward Diana Garden.

Fleming and Sheppard in 1939, they incorporated the north wing of the garage in its upper terrace. A bounding wall with an arched gateway separating the terrace from the driveway belongs on one side to the formal world of the Clio Garden and on the other to the mundane world of the driveway.

As he customarily did, Staub aligned living rooms and bedrooms at Bayou Bend for access to the prevailing south-east breeze. Therefore, all reception rooms and all but two guest bedrooms were lined up behind the south and east fronts of the house. The kitchen, bathrooms, and corridors were lined up on the north and west sides of the house. The complicating circumstance at Bayou Bend is that the prime view is to the north toward the Diana Garden. The dining room does not have access to this view, and half the ground floor windows on the north terrace front originally opened into family or service rooms rather than into reception rooms. On the north front of Bayou Bend, Staub privileged the façade, suppressing recognition of the character of the spaces behind it. Bayou Bend exhibits the myriad ways in which Staub negotiated the ideological, stylistic, and practical issues of country house planning to shape a complexly integrated architectural design.

Essential to the aura of authority that Bayou Bend radiates was Staub's handling of scale and proportion. Barnstone noted that Staub's houses often appear diminutive in scale.[59] Bayou Bend shares this characteristic, which is true of the work of other eclectic architects of the 1920s. Only when standing next to one of the ground-floor windows in the central block is one aware of Bayou Bend's actual scale. Staub made his houses seem smaller than they were to ensure that they felt domestic rather than institutional. Scale at Bayou Bend contributes to the feeling that the house is generous and welcoming rather than pompous and pretentious. Outside and inside, the house possesses the paradoxical combination of monumentality and intimacy that is such a striking characteristic of Staub's country houses. This combination masterfully constructs subtlety. The understatement and assurance with which it expresses power connote legitimacy.

Staub's ability to move people emotionally with proportion is best experienced in the entrance hall at Bayou Bend. The entrance hall is fifteen feet wide and twelve-and-a-half feet high. Its width, its height, and its extension through the house charge the space it contains with an exhilarating ambiance, to which the ascending curve of the four-foot wide stair contributes. Staub composed and proportioned interior space to lighten and animate one's experience of the interior, producing the sensation Barnstone called "the divine float."[60] Proportion at Bayou Bend stimulates subjective feelings of buoyancy and corporeal enhancement. Staub infused space with proportion to affect bodily awareness and perform myths of security, composure, assurance, and superiority.

Staub reinforced the architectural authority of Bayou Bend through his detailing of materials and his use of color. The house's stucco surfaces respond to the movement of the sun with subtlety rather than high drama, emphasizing the material presence of the walls without making one consciously aware of them. Staub's detailing of the low, splayed base course and water table at the foot of the walls is undemonstrative yet rigorous. From the south the base course elevates the house just enough above the ground plane to prevent it from appearing to sink visually. On the north terrace front, it functions as a base mold, domesticating exterior space. Staub carefully resolved conditions where the base course intersects other protrusions, as at the front door, where it is integrated with the front step, the door sill, and the raised molded band that frames the opening. The pink-tinged, pale peach stucco (now painted pink so that it no longer possesses the iridescence of the integrally colored stucco), the window sash originally painted brown then glazed with green, the green painted louvered blinds, dark ironwork, and weathered copper roofs give Bayou Bend the "tropical quality of warmth and friendliness" that Staub admired in the Creole architecture of the French Quarter.[61] The rich rose color of the Colorado sandstone with which the north terrace is paved harmonizes with the exterior walls to reinforce a feeling of warmth.[62]

Staub told Howard Barnstone that Homewood, a neoclassical country house in Baltimore of 1803, was the model for Bayou Bend in plan: a central block flanked by narrow wings joined to the main block by low-roofed hyphens, with the disposition of openings on the principal elevations governed by centrality and symmetry.[63] However, the exterior of Bayou Bend was derived from the Spanish Creole architecture of the French Quarter, an urban vernacular of stucco-surfaced brick walls modulated by raised molded bands.[64] The exterior walls of Bayou Bend are simply detailed as flat planes of stucco-surfaced structural tile block, the material with which the walls were built. Even the columns of the north portico are detailed to suggest vernacular building rather than academic classical architecture.

Staub's affinity for vernacular building bespeaks the reverence that American eclectic architects of the 1920s had for low-style building traditions, valued for their craftsmanship, durable construction, and, as eclectic architects saw it, artless beauty.[65] However, as an academically trained architect, Staub punctuated his neo-vernacular composition with details from high-style models: the recessed, fanlit entrance portal (based on the entrance portal of the early-nineteenth-century Nathaniel Russell House in Charleston, according to Staub) and the cast stone acroteria crowning the south-facing raked parapet and the north portico, which suggest Belle Meade in Nashville, Tennessee (1853; especially the portico),

Bayou Bend, detail of fanlight above entrance front door.

and are derived from the Grecian decoration popularized by Minard Lafever in the 1830s and 1840s, as is the acroterion above the portico door.[66]

Staub adroitly dropped high style quotations into his neo-vernacular narrative to enliven the architectural fiction Miss Hogg called Latin Colonial. The cast-iron arabesques springing from lyres incorporated in the balcony, loggia, and window guardrails were, like the ironwork on the Latin Colonial House, acquired as salvage in New Orleans. The lyres intimated Miss Hogg's love of music just as the Grecian reflection of Nashville evoked association with Sam Houston, who had lived in Nashville as governor of Tennessee, and in whose bed in the Texas Governor's Mansion in Austin Miss Hogg had slept as a child. The affiliation with Sam Houston was enhanced by the extent to which the entrance hall and spiral stair echoed not only those of the Hermitage of 1821, the Nashville country house of Houston's mentor, Andrew Jackson, but also, as David Warren has observed, the Governor's Mansion in Austin of 1856.[67]

Bayou Bend, detail of acroterion above garden portico.

Staub's detailing of the projecting window bays, set into the hyphens on the north terrace front of the house, represents his use of urban spatial elements to give character to suburban architecture. The bay windows replicate the kind of shop fronts, punctuated with Lafever-inspired Grecian ornament, that might have been added to older houses in the French Quarter as they were transformed into shops. The window bays animate the terrace—where people stand, sit, and walk in close proximity to the house—in an urbane way, much as projecting shop windows might have animated a narrow sidewalk in the Vieux Carré.[68] Staub used picturesque incidents to energize the exteriors of Bayou Bend. Above the bay windows are dormer windows half hidden by parapets. Corresponding to these dormers on the south front of Bayou Bend are picturesque octagonal windows, which Staub absorbed into the compositional continuum of the house. The house appears composed from a distance yet at close hand does not seem static. The architectural fictions Staub composed were credible and compelling.

The architecture of Bayou Bend condensed southernness. Externally it combined images of Baltimore, New Orleans, and Charleston with the Greek Revival of Nashville. Spatially, it evoked nineteenth-century planters' houses with its central hall, curving stair, and columned north portico. Through architectural decoration, materials, and proportions, major rooms recalled certain places and times in eighteenth-century America. The cast iron in the balcony rail above the front entrance was from New Orleans.[69] The architectural detail of the living room, with its modillion cornice, paneled walls, and scrolled pediments framing deep-set double doors, replicated the saloon at Shirley in Charles City County, Virginia (1769). The low ceiling and pine-paneled walls of the library were based on the early-eighteenth-century Metcalf Bowler House in Portsmouth, Rhode Island, while the Hogg brothers' tap room was accorded what American antiquaries of the 1920s would have described as a "primitive" treatment. Miss Hogg's bedroom contained paneling salvaged from a house in Ipswich, Massachusetts (1740), and her adjoining sitting room contained floorboards and paneling from a late-eighteenth-century house in Salem, Massachusetts.[70] In composing an architectural summation of American style and grace, Staub "led by serving" to advance the Hoggs' agenda for constructing new models of life in Houston based on historical myths and images.[71] Bayou Bend constitutes a mythic whole.[72] Not only does it materialize a unified consciousness, it was intended to instruct and persuade and to function as an educational institution for conforming patrician subjectivity by beautifully embodying the "myth of permanence," an assertion of "order and stability in the face of cultural commodification and rapid demographic

Bayou Bend, detail of garden portico door.

Bayou Bend, detail of garden terrace bay window.

change," as the architectural historian Mitchell Schwartzer has observed.[73]

Bayou Bend tangibly represents the ideology of 1920s American eclecticism.[74] Eclecticism was motivated by the desire to fix a sense of place, to define place spatially in culturally, historically specific ways. Bayou Bend coherently represents the master myth of American eclectic architecture of the 1920s: evolution through historic continuity connected present to past rather than severing the two. There was no contradiction between modernity and tradition. Bayou Bend represents this myth in the context of twentieth-century Houston—an aggressively expanding industrial city with an underdeveloped sense of cultural identity—and of River Oaks, an elite residential community in which master planning, historically evocative domestic architecture, and social control were to guarantee the stability and peace of mind typically associated with the idea of tradition.

Architectural analysis demonstrates the underlying themes embedded in Bayou Bend. The idea of continuity is central. It figures ideologically in the stylistic narratives embodied in the exterior and interiors of Bayou Bend. It figures phenomenally in the spatial organization of the house and grounds and in the visual organization of architectural surfaces. As idea and technique, continuity stressed the importance of connecting. Making place ideologically and shaping space phenomenally were means for connecting that Will Hogg pursued systematically as a city planning advocate and enlightened developer, Miss Hogg as a collector, patron, and cultural advocate, and John Staub as an architect. The Hoggs and their architect promoted awareness and appreciation of models for modern civic and domestic life that would make Houstonians more concerned and responsible for their city and give them a more profound sense of their historical and cultural patrimony. Architectural analysis also clarifies critical issues that Bayou Bend, as a cultural model, failed to address. It represented absorption with private, domestic space. It ignored local history and local cultural inheritance. In minimizing architectural recognition of the working spaces of the house, in segregating these spaces in the most poorly ventilated portions of the house (occupied principally by African American domestic servants), and in emphasizing a genteel interpretation of vernacular architectural images, it avoided having to recognize and deal with issues of class and racial difference that, especially in a Southern city, were embedded not only in history but also in contemporary life.[75]

Authenticity was the ideological value with which Miss Hogg and Staub sought to sustain the Latin Colonial discourse at Bayou Bend. Staub's essay on the Latin Colonial style minimized the appropriateness of the Spanish Mediterranean style in order to supplant it with the Spanish Creole architecture of New Orleans, which he presented as having a more authentic connection to the Texas Gulf coast (although, historically, Houston had never been affected by it). Miss Hogg and Staub sought to buttress this discourse at Bayou Bend by building in authenticity with the cast iron and the architectural fragments from Massachusetts houses. Bayou Bend materializes the ways in which culturally ambitious Americans in the 1920s constructed meaning by their eclectic interpretations of tradition. Bayou Bend reveals the nature of this tradition to be mythical projections of selected historical episodes, which served the purpose of highlighting the taste and discernment of the patrons—Ima and Will Hogg—and the virtuosity of the architect—Staub, legitimizing them as cultural arbiters and underpinning the Hoggs' efforts to construct new models for life in Houston.

Bayou Bend is the most tangible and concentrated expression of the Hoggs' quest to reinvent Houston ideologically, to fix it with a profound, stable, historically, and ethically rooted identity that would impel Houstonians to treat their city as a forum for common action and purpose, not merely as a field for self-interested pursuit. Bayou Bend architecturally expresses the ideals and techniques of the Hoggs and Staub, as well as the anxieties and prejudices they shared with American elites of the 1920s. It materialized patriarchal authority, cultural continuity, and maternal benevolence to present itself and the world constructed around it as a counterbalance to the insecurities and instabilities of the market economy fueling Houston's expansion.[76] Bayou Bend was positioned to function as a material token symbolizing a unified consciousness. The exceptional consistency of the spatial practices that systematically integrated the house with its landscape setting and with the collection of artifacts it was designed to contain framed it as an icon of the River Oaks way of life by underpinning the myths of harmonious hierarchical community and of rituals of domesticity rooted in tradition and untainted by class hostility and invidious striving. Bayou Bend framed and magnified its occupants as patrician subjects but, in doing so, both underscored and disguised their transition in social standing from emergent elites to leaders who set the standard.[77] It empowered a new economy of cultural power to legitimize Will Hogg and Ima Hogg as arbiters of cultural authority in Houston.[78]

The paradox of Bayou Bend is that, for all its impact on local imaginations, it did not spark a Latin Colonial movement in Houston. Staub (and other Houston architects, especially in the 1930s) produced additional Latin Colonial designs, but the genre was never received in Houston as disclosing some essential but previously undiscerned identity. Staub briefly advanced the Latin Colonial as the identifying style of River Oaks with the River Oaks gate piers of 1926 and the no-longer-extant River Oaks Community Center of 1927 at River Oaks Boulevard and Westheimer Road, a shopping

Bayou Bend, detail of living room doorway.

and office complex on which he collaborated with Charles W. Oliver, the River Oaks Corporation's staff architect. The automobile-oriented community center seems to have been based on Benjamin H. Latrobe's State Bank of Louisiana Building of 1820 in the French Quarter of New Orleans. It asserted mastery of the tradition-modernity antithesis and the capacity of planning and design to "harmonize" all apparent contradictions by rigorously resolving programmatic conflict through architecture.[79]

One year after the completion of Bayou Bend, Staub designed the clubhouse of the Junior League of Houston of 1929 in the Latin Colonial style, adapting another French Quarter model, the Spanish Creole Rillieux House of 1795.

Built by the contractor Don Hall for $48,000, the Junior League Building was a rigorous adaptation of a Spanish Creole urban courtyard house to a site in the South End of Houston just outside the gates of Courtlandt Place.[80] Ruth West described the building in the *Houston Gargoyle* as "a home of friendly charm, a place of Southern hospitality, a thought of old New Orleans in this bustling city of sudden, hazardous growth."[81] The "bustling city of sudden, hazardous growth" tended to be the way Houstonians chose to mythify themselves rather than by adopting architectural codes connoting cultural conformity and stability. The houses Staub designed in River Oaks for individual clients between 1925 and 1930 more accurately represented collective attitudes about stylistic representation in Houston in the 1920s and early 1930s because they expressed individuality in the context of affirming identity. These houses negotiated difference to represent patrician identity.

The first house Staub designed in River Oaks for a private client was the picturesque manorial-type house for Rebecca Donelson and Joseph H. Chew, built in 1925 for $52,525. Thomas M. Murray was the builder.[82] The Chew House was built astride a double lot on the south side of Inwood Drive. Set amid tall pine trees, the house, which is faced with a mixed blend of orange clinker brick, a blend popular in Houston in the 1920s that Staub used often, spatially compensated for its flat site with a variety of techniques. Staub reversed planning conventions by attaching the three-car garage and servants' apartment building to the street front of the house, rotating it in plan to skew it out of alignment with the house. The point of attachment is an auto drive-through that enables cars to pass through the house and turn in a rear motor court into rear-facing garage stalls. A covered ground-floor service porch contributes an additional spatial layer to the street front of the house as it connects the kitchen wing to the pass-through and garage. Staub orchestrated roof shapes so that they rise, subside, and stretch laterally, imbuing the house with an artificial topography as if to compensate for the flat site. Staub used spatial dialectics to construct

River Oaks gate piers, 1925, framing view of River Oaks Community Center, Houston, 1927, John F. Staub and Charles W. Oliver, architects. Photograph by R. M. Luster, in Don Riddle, River Oaks.

Junior League Building, Houston, 1929, John F. Staub, architect. Altered. Sketch of Stuart Avenue elevation. Houston Gargoyle *2 (June 2, 1929): 13.*

Joseph H. Chew House, River Oaks, 1925, John F. Staub, architect. Street front.

picturesqueness. He contrasted the part of the house containing the reception rooms with the lower, spatially layered service wing, then reiterated this operation to produce additional stages of spatial subordination, so that the west end of the garage building slopes down in profile as though it were about to merge with the ground plane. Rhythmic movement, embodied in the space-embracing skew plan and the flows of the wood shingled roofs, created reciprocity between the attenuated house and its flat site.

Two houses Staub designed adhered to the Colonial genre. The house for William S. Cochran's sister and brother-in-law, Mary Alice Cochran and Hubert B. Finch, was faced with a white-painted Tuscan portico figuring against a wall plane of rose colored brick that Houston newspaper reports described as coming from Holland. Designed and built in 1926–27, the Finch House cost $60,750; Thomas T. Hopper was the builder.[83] A long, seven-bay elevation capped by a side-gabled roof causes the house front to function as a planar backdrop to the portico and the heroically scaled architrave encasing the fanlit front door. Because the site, on the south side of Inwood a half-block west of the Chew House, is a corner lot, the Finch House is seen in a three-quarter profile, with the Mockingbird Lane side elevation given focus by a second-story Anglo-Palladian window. Yet photographs from the 1920s show that the wide, green, front lawn that frames the house so persuasively as an icon of River Oaks identity today was originally heavily wooded, and the attenuated house front was glimpsed through a screen of tree trunks. The south-facing rear elevation of the L-plan house is not symmetrical. Oriented toward a garden installed in 1937 by the Lambert Landscape Company of Dallas for the second owners of the house, Madeline Welder and William A. Smith, it expresses individuality rather than typicality.[84] The interior of the house surprises because it does not correspond to the symmetrical plan implied by the front elevation. Staub constructed spatial flow by aligning double doors, opening from the entrance hall into the living room and dining room, with windows on the east and west sides of the house. The resulting cross axis of directed movement and vision animates the spacious, street-facing reception rooms. Interior fanlights above these double doors ceremonialize this spatial sequence and lighten it by emphasizing transparency and implied movement.

Staub's New England Georgian Colonial house for Marguerite Meachum and John S. Mellinger was built on a double lot at the corner of Del Monte Drive and Larchmont Road in 1930 by A. A. Bertelsen for $24,825.[85] The Mellinger House has a picture-perfect look that makes it an icon of River Oaks identity. Because the house lies on the north side of the street, Staub set it far back on the lot, framing the pristine, symmetrical, south-facing house front with an open lawn that is both deep and broad. The white-painted brick walls, white-painted pedimented doorway, and black-painted shutters with their Lindeberg-like, big-scaled louvers stand out against the green plane of the lawn and mature, free-standing shade trees that punctuate the site.

Staub used reversal as a technique at the Mellinger House to counter the serenity of the main block and prevent it from seeming too complacent. He treated the kitchen and garage wing as a dependency of the main block, attenuated in plan and stepped back behind an arched wood loggia to emphasize the lowering profile of a double-pitched roof, a single protruding dormer, and the gable of the attached, rear-facing garage, turned to confront the street. This sector of the house was expanded in the 1980s by the Houston architect Anthony E. Frederick following a schematic plan of addition Staub designed but never carried out.[86] Staub continued this approach to composing difference on the north-facing rear elevation of the Mellinger House, where a shingle-faced gabled bay containing the back "front" door, framed by an architrave less elaborate than that of the street-facing front door, overlaps the brick block.

The driveway, brought in from the side street past this door, curves to form a motor court, then continues into a walled service court accessible from the kitchen porch, terminating at the garage. This layering of space and movement plays out the fiction that the Mellinger House is a country house. On the Finch and Mellinger Houses, Staub coded symmetry, centrality, and axiality as constituents of community identity while the more relaxed organization of the side and rear faces of the houses represented individuality. Implied narratives of circumstantial development spatially underpinned and energized the "timeless" composure of façades. Ruth London's landscape design at the Mellinger House subtly emphasized spatial hierarchies. Her one formal space, a central grass panel framed by a brick walk and a low hedge of azaleas alongside the west side of the house, reproduces with planting and proportions the sensation of calmness and composure that the house emits.[87] Internally, a twelve-and-a-half-foot-wide central hall and aligned doorways that open from it into the paneled living room and the dining room construct an axis and cross axis of movement and vision to make a house that is quite compact feel spacious.

Repetition of plan types and proportions in the Mellinger and Finch Houses "effectively bounds and conventionalizes" subjective experience and socially constructed a shared identity that could be coded as patrician not only through personal association with elite owners but also, subliminally, through subjective sensations of bodily pleasure, magnification, and empowerment.[88] This coding was transmissible. It functioned as efficiently in a compact house, such as the

Hubert B. Finch House, River Oaks, 1926–27, John F. Staub, architect. Street front.

(overleaf) John S. Mellinger House, River Oaks, 1930, John F. Staub, architect. Street front.

Mellinger House, detail of front door.

Mellinger House, detail of back door.

Mellinger House, view from dining room into living room.

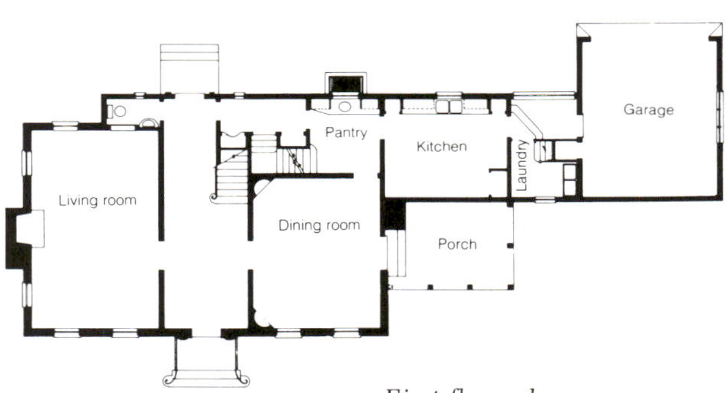

First-floor plan

Second-floor plan

Mellinger House.

Mellinger House (where, for instance, there was no library), as it did in a grand house such as Bayou Bend because of Staub's rhythmic fluency in naturalizing perceptual sensations and diagrams of order so that they never seem mechanical, repetitive, or deterministic.

Staub's River Oaks clients of the 1920s were, like his Broadacres clients, members of established Houston families. Joseph H. Chew was Kenneth Womack's partner in Sanders and Company. His father, William B. Chew, a Kentuckian who came to Houston in 1881, the year of Joseph Chew's birth, had been associated with the Sewall cotton factorage and wholesale grocery firm and had then served as president of the Commercial National Bank of Houston. Joseph H. Chew was a graduate of the Hill School. He and his wife, who was from Birmingham, Alabama, were parishioners of Christ Church and subsequently of Palmer Memorial Church, members of the Houston Country Club and of the River Oaks Country Club.[89] Hubert Finch was a vice president and director of the Union National Bank, a parishioner of Christ Church who then became a parishioner of Palmer Memorial Church, and a member of the Houston and River Oaks Country Clubs; his wife Mary Alice Cochran Finch was a granddaughter of the banker Benjamin A. Shepherd.[90] John Sweeney Mellinger was the son of the Houston jewelry store executive George J. Mellinger and grandson of the company's founder, John J. Sweeney. John S. Mellinger was secretary of the J. J. Sweeney Jewelry Company when he and his wife built their house on Del Monte Drive, the manager of his grandfather Sweeney's estate, a member of both the Houston and River Oaks Country Clubs, and a parishioner of Christ Church who did not transfer to Palmer Church.[91] Staub's River Oaks houses confirmed his clients' standings in the business and social circles of Houston in the 1920s, enabling them to advertise their patrician identity. What these houses imply is that to the extent that Staub's houses constructed a distinct identity for River Oaks, they did so in the context of affirming the patrician status of Houston's established elite.

The houses Staub designed in River Oaks in the 1920s advanced the efforts of Will Hogg, Ima Hogg, and Hugh Potter to frame the community as a charmed way of life. The River Oaks Corporation's advertising, real estate improvements, and building program demonstrate how profoundly this community undertaking was affected by a broader cultural dynamic current in the U.S. in the 1920s involving the social construction of patrician identity. The elitism of this project would seem to contradict the Hoggs' personal dedication to championing the interests and welfare of ordinary people and the dispossessed. Yet the patrician discourse on elite leadership framed privilege and exception as "gifts" that obligated their recipients to become advocates for causes that were in the public interest, even if unpopular or insufficiently appreciated.[92] For Will Hogg and Ima Hogg, privilege could be legitimized if exercised for the public good. River Oaks, Bayou Bend, Hogg's city planning and nature conservation projects, and Miss Hogg's support of music, education, art, and the formation of her collection functioned as technologies of self fashioning that identified the Hoggs, especially to themselves, as members of a conscientious and cultivated Southern elite rather than Texan new rich. What Staub offered them was the capacity to make this project visible and real in ways that were rational, rigorous, beautiful, and believable. Staub produced country houses that framed their occupants as ladies and gentlemen. When confronted with clients of exceptional ambition and imagination, he responded with buildings that condensed their aspirations in spatial settings that were compelling and persuasive. In Staub's hands, the country house was capable—given the right clients—of framing its occupants as Bayou Bend framed Will and Ima Hogg: dispensers of hospitality, connoisseurs of beauty, conservators of tradition, defenders of liberality, and guardians of the public conscience.[93]

PLAYTIME IN RIVER OAKS

The first of a series of six advertisements.

1. *Playtime in River Oaks.*
2. A Matron's Morning in River Oaks.
3. Tea-Time in River Oaks.
4. A River Oaks Evening.
5. The Day of Rest in River Oaks.
6. A Home for All Time.

River Oaks Corporation
HUGH POTTER, President

HOME and playtime! The final bell has rung at school and a crowd of ruddy cheeked youngsters pile pell mell from the door, their thoughts intent on games of prisoners' base, on tea-parties under the trees, on those mysterious, romantic adventures in which small boys delight. In merry groups of twos and threes and fours they make their way through River Oaks' wide thoroughfares. No danger here from congested traffic—River Oaks children are carefully safeguarded during every step of their homeward passage . . .

Has anyone yet been able to find anything comparable to the sheer joy of a child at play? Under the trees of River Oaks children find their perfect playground—wide spaces in which to run and romp, fresh air free from the taints of the thick life close in town, elbow room, room for a fellow to have a dog, too, for the matter of that . . .

The year 'round it's playtime in River Oaks!

"Playtime in River Oaks," E. M. Schiwetz. Houston Gargoyle 4 (Jan. 11, 1931): back cover.

CHAPTER 4 : SMALL HOUSES

Inez Rather Lasell, who lived in two houses that Staub worked on in Galveston, Texas—a house on Avenue O built in 1915, which Staub remodeled in 1933 for the cotton exporter Heinrich Renfert, and a house eight blocks away on Avenue P that he designed for Renfert's partner, William C. Helmbrecht, built in 1928—observed the difference between the two that defines the Helmbrecht House as a small house: it has no back stair.[1] Although lack of a rear service stair is only one characteristic of Staub's smaller houses, it indicates the dilemma Staub and other country house architects confronted as they sought to extend the domain of the country house to encompass middle-income suburban housing. They had to sacrifice spaces and services that socially constructed difference with the reception spaces of the house, limiting—ideologically as well as functionally—the spatial dialectics of high and low, light and dark, big and little, open and closed, regular and circumstantial that sustained the country house discourse and its classes of subjects: the lady and gentleman, the honored guest, the retainer, the servant. The incentive for reducing the country house in scale was the opportunity it offered to expand the consensus on the legitimacy of the country house discourse, using the country house as an instrument in the formation of a public that, in seeking to identify with gentility's "beautification campaign," would adopt its subject positions and reinforce its worldview.[2]

Bungalow house, Houston, 1920, Thomas and Van Santen, architect-builders. House and Garden 42 (*Aug. 1922*): 1.

The house type against which the reduced-scale country house was dialectically positioned—its "other"—was the bungalow. The bungalow was a house type formulated in the first decade of the twentieth century and promoted as a middle-income suburban house with anti-elitist associations. The identifying features of the bungalow—a one-story layout, an expansive front porch, minimization of interior hallways to maximize living space in a compact house, and indifference to historical models with invidious overtones—signaled the anti-elitism of the bungalow discourse.[3] Initially associated with the Craftsman movement and other programs of domestic reform in the United States during the Progressive era, the bungalow had been absorbed into the popular house-building culture of much of the United States, and certainly Houston, by the beginning of the 1920s. The bungalow discourse appealed to nature rather than to historical precedent. But the extent to which it succeeded in becoming a popular middle-income house type by the early 1920s compromised the terms of its appeal, as bungalows came to be affiliated with new subdivisions developed by speculative builders for the middle- and lower-middle-income residential real estate market rather than with free-spirited, artistic nonconformists. Staub's small houses of the 1920s can be analyzed to discern his spatial strategy for countering the bungalow discourse with the country house discourse, seeking to construct a new consensus on the superiority of the elite (and elitist) alternative.

In middle-income neighborhoods developed in Houston in the first half of the 1920s there were two dominant house types: the one-story bungalow and the two-story house type that Alan Gowans called the "foursquare" because of its blocky proportions.[4] Both were apt to be of wood frame construction, sheathed externally with brick. Both tended to have front porches raised several feet above the grade level of the site. Both tended to be rectangular in plan, with the long dimension of the house parallel to the side lot lines and with rooms organized in two parallel bands. In a one-story bungalow in Houston this interior arrangement tended to afford one file of rooms better access to the prevailing southeast breeze than the other file. Typically, the bedrooms (aligned front to back with a bathroom inserted in between and a short corridor, probably the only corridor in the house, paired with the bathroom to separate the private side of the house from living rooms) were placed on the side with exposure to the breeze. Living room, dining room, possibly a small pantry-breakfast nook, the kitchen, and a rear service porch were organized front-to-back parallel to the file of bedrooms. The living room was entered directly from the front porch through the front door; there was no entrance vestibule. By the mid-1920s, a free-standing, two-story, two-car garage with a two-room apartment above, located behind the back corner bedroom (the driveway provided the open space along the side lot line facilitating exposure to the prevailing breeze) was a standard feature of new speculative housing for middle-income Houstonians. Single-pane, sliding sash windows, especially those facing the street, might be ganged in pairs. The rectangular living room might contain a fireplace centered on the short end wall, flanked by built-in bookshelves with small, high-set windows above the shelves. The fireplace was ceremonial rather than functional, as the house was likely to be centrally heated with steam radiators. A wide opening, possibly not fitted with doors, connected living room and dining room. A door opened from the living room into the front bedroom; another door opened from the dining room into the short cross-hall, often opposite the bathroom door.[5]

The architects William Ward Watkin and Joseph W. Northrop Jr. designed moderately sized houses in the early 1920s that began the process of reducing the country house in scale to accommodate a middle-income constituency in Houston. Staub's small houses of the 1920s participated in this competition for formal hegemony by persuasively translating the identifying characteristics of the country house to the moderately sized, middle-income suburban house and, in the process, stigmatizing the bungalow as unfashionable, that is to say as lower middle class.

The River Oaks Latin Colonial House stands out because of the consistency with which it constructed patrician identity as a "small house," the category to which it was assigned when published in *House Beautiful* in 1927.[6] The Latin Colonial House was two stories high rather than one story high. This permitted complete separation of reception rooms and bedrooms, allowed rooms to be organized for advantageous access to the prevailing southeast breeze, and gave the compact house a greater spatial presence than a one-story house would have exerted. These attributes were facilitated by aligning the long dimension of the house with the street front rather than with the side lot lines. In place of a front porch, the Latin Colonial House had a side loggia projecting off a back corner and accessible from the living room. A second-story sleeping porch above the loggia was accessible from the master bedroom. These volumes economically expanded the size of the house while addressing the practical issue of providing open-air sitting space with three exposures. The house was set low to the ground; no entrance steps were required. The symmetrical organization of the street front and Staub's uniform treatment of openings (three fanlit first-floor openings—the center one a door, the flanking openings French doors) imbued the house with composure and a sense of scale grander than its actual size. Use of divided-light window sash rather than single-pane window sash contributed to this perception since it gave Staub more flexibility in making proportional adjustments. Ganged sash windows were rigorously avoided. The low-pitched hipped roof, the subordinate ridge heights of the offset rear loggia and kitchen wings, the slender chimney stack serving working fireplaces in the living room and the master bedroom above, even the segmental arch spanning the first-floor loggia opening subtly framed the planar front elevation. The big-scaled louvered shutters that Staub copied from Harrie T. Lindeberg and the use of the New Orleans balcony rail to cast intricate shadow patterns on the front elevation animated the façade. The pale pink integrally colored stucco wall surfaces of the house and the layered painting and glazing of wood and metal elements suffused exte-

River Oaks Latin Colonial House (David M. Picton Jr. House), River Oaks, 1925, John F. Staub, architect. Photograph by Paul Hester, Houston Architectural Survey.

rior finishes with a perceptible sense of depth.[7] In contrast to the one-story height, red wire-cut brick veneer facing, tailed rafters beneath roof eaves, front porch, and single-pane, one-over-one sash windows of the typical Houston bungalow of the early 1920s, the Latin Colonial House persuasively constructed patrician identity through its symmetry, scale gradation, and its materialization of expansiveness and understatement.

It was in the interior planning and design of the house that Staub most forcefully challenged the bungalow. The living room and dining room were each fourteen feet wide, a standard dimension in middle-income Houston houses of the 1920s. But between these rooms Staub inserted an entrance and stair hall that was ten-and-a-half-feet wide.

In terms of the bungalow, this expansive center hall represented an extravagant waste of space. Yet what it accomplished, in conjunction with a first-floor ceiling height of nine-and-a-half feet, was to endow the Latin Colonial House with a sensation of grandeur by spatially performing generosity, ceremoniousness, and the ritualized differentiation of domestic space associated with the country house. Staub

Second-floor plan

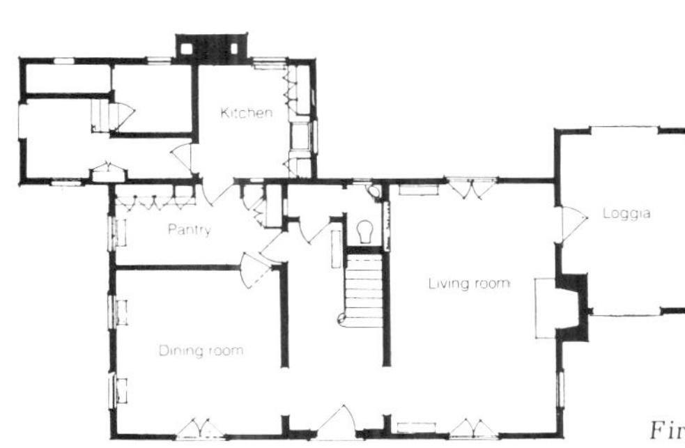

First-floor plan

Latin Colonial House, first- and second-floor plans.

Latin Colonial House, hall and stair. Photograph by Calvin Wheat, Civics for Houston *1 (Feb. 1928): 9.*

maintained this sense of spatial expansiveness in the living room and dining room through such devices as the continuity between the interior floor plane and the exterior ground plane, perceptible through the French doors, and the sense of proportioned loftiness to which the fanlights above the French doors contributed. Because the living room spanned the depth of the house, it had three exposures, which further magnified its apparent size as well as its country house–like continuity with the out-of-doors. The fireplace was centered on one of the long walls of the room, which was twenty-two-feet long. Bookshelves were recessed in the opposite long wall; the semicircular head of the recess mirrored the height and profile of the fanlights above the French doors and the opening from the entrance hall to the living room, which it balanced symmetrically, to reinforce the room's generous proportions with composure. The reeded fascias of interior window and door frames, neoclassical corner blocks where the jambs and heads framing doors intersected, the lithe cylindrical balusters supporting the stair rail, and Staub's distinctive small, globular door knobs materialized refinement at ever-finer degrees of hierarchical gradation to underpin the discourse on the superiority of the country house.

Staub designed the Latin Colonial House with amenities that comparably sized Houston houses were not as likely to contain: a downstairs lavatory and toilet beneath the stair and two bathrooms upstairs, one allocated to the master bedroom, the other shared by the two remaining bedrooms and directly accessible from each rather than from a corridor. The plans disclose the techniques Staub used to layer space in bedrooms by framing windows with pairs of shallow closets to impart a sense of depth and to frame symmetrically composed views within rooms. A comparison of the kitchen of the Latin Colonial House with that of other small Staub houses of the 1920s suggests that Staub rationalized the kitchen down to a spatial minimum (approximately nine feet by ten feet) in conjunction with the layering of service spaces (a breakfast room–pantry between the kitchen and the dining room, and a service porch with space for the boiler, recessed four steps below the first-floor level, that fired the steam central-heating system). Flues serving the boiler and the kitchen stove were consolidated in a rear chimney stack, maximized in size for architectural effect rather than minimized for economy.

Architectural gentrification came at a price. The Latin Colonial House was more expensive than a comparably sized two-story house in such 1920s neighborhoods as the Turner addition or Southampton.[8] Neither the Latin Colonial House nor Staub's other, somewhat larger Early Republic House on Chevy Chase Drive (it had a half-back stair: a back stair that ran from the first floor to the landing of the main stair, where those using the back stair transferred to the upper run of the main stair) sold immediately. The three small houses that Joseph Northrop designed for the River Oaks Corporation did sell, but his larger house was bought by its contractor, Charles J. Gerner.[9] Eight months after its completion in February 1926, Staub's Early Republic House was bought by Hugh Potter.[10] The Latin Colonial House, completed in August 1925, was bought in February 1927 by the lawyer and real estate investor David M. Picton Jr. and his wife, Martha Nance. Picton, like Potter, had studied at the University of Texas law school at the same time as Mike Hogg, then did graduate work at the Harvard Law School before returning to Texas in 1913. Since 1919, Picton had been affiliated with the Hogg family's business operations: he was president of the Varner Company, vice president of the Varner Trust Company, and legal counsel to the Varner Realty Company.[11] Before moving to River Oaks, Picton and his family lived in a bungalow on Mount Vernon Street in Rossmoyne backing up to the house on Rossmoyne Boulevard that Will, Mike, and Ima Hogg occupied from 1918 until the completion of Bayou Bend in 1928.[12] In the calculus of location, cost, and style, Staub's construction of elite identity in a small house was not sufficient to compel potential buyers in Houston's mid-range real estate market to pay extra for imaginatively elevating their social status. It initially fell to the Hoggs' network of friends and retainers to people these houses, which did facilitate the continued use of the houses as instruments in the formation of a public through publication in local and national media.[13]

The second issue of Will Hogg's short-lived magazine, *Civics for Houston*, in February 1928, featured the Latin Colonial House in a pair of articles: Staub's essay "Latin Colonial Architecture in the Southwest" and "A Blending of Periods in Harmonious Design" by Dorothy Dawes Chillman, wife of James Chillman Jr., director of the Museum of Fine Arts and, like Madeleine Staub, a graduate of the Parsons School of Design.[14] Dorothy Chillman's article was illustrated with photographs of the interiors of the Picton House. These displayed an assured, unpretentious assembly of eighteenth-century (or perhaps eighteenth-century-style) American, English, and French furniture and decorative artifacts arranged in the spare, calm style that began to be visible in illustrations in *House and Garden* in the mid-1910s, which "naturalized models of subjectivity" by performing intimations of grace, propriety, and comfort.[15]

The arrangement of furniture in the Picton living room clarifies the class challenge that the reduced-scale country house mounted against the bungalow. Staub explained to Barnstone that he tried to avoid centering the fireplace opening on the short end of a rectangular living room because it led to furniture being packed into one end of the room, congesting circulation while abandoning the other end to isolation. This practical consideration served to reinforce the spatial distinction between the country house and the bungalow, identifying the fireplace opening centered on the long wall and set flush with the wall plane as the more patrician arrangement. In the Picton living room, Staub incorporated the bookshelves (which, in a Houston bungalow, would have flanked the projecting, brick faced mantle) in a recessed niche that contributed to the spatial composure of the room, heightening its affiliation with the country house. The social practices that transpired in the living room of a bungalow and of a reduced-scale country house were probably not that different.[16] It was the spatial setting that distinguished between the elitist and anti-elitist alternatives. Staub's design of domestic space, reinforced by the choice of furniture and its arrangement in the Picton House, advanced the elitist alternative.

The house Staub designed for his family—his wife, Madeleine, and their two children, John Delabarre and Nancy—in 1925 also imaginatively condensed the country house to fit the limits of a middle-income family house. Staub told Barnstone that after he received the commission for the River Oaks Country Clubhouse he felt compelled to join the country club and buy a lot in the initial offering of house sites in Country Club Estates, although he and his wife had already acquired a lot in the Southmore addition, just north of Hermann Park, where the architects William Ward Watkin, Alfred C. Finn, and Maurice J. Sullivan built houses for their families between the mid-1910s and early 1920s.[17] Staub's River Oaks lot was on Larchmont Road, the westernmost street in Country Club Estates. After the Hoggs bought the Country Club Estates Company, then additional tracts flanking the subdivision, they had Kipp alter the Country Club Estates street plan so that Del Monte Drive, rather than dead-ending into Larchmont on the west, could continue westward. As a result, Staub gained frontage on Del Monte, enabling him to expand his lot with a sliver left over from the adjoining lot taken for the street extension and design the house so that it faced north toward Del Monte (with the rear facing south) rather than east toward Larchmont, with the rear facing west, the least desirable orientation in Houston. When the Staub House was completed in 1926, its side lot line was the west city limit line of Houston.[18]

Staub told Barnstone that he designed the house in a picturesque New England colonial style to honor Mrs. Staub's Massachusetts heritage, although the interlocked gables that face Del Monte were more akin to Lutyens than colonial Massachusetts.[19] Staub collected the service and circulation spaces of the house on its north-facing street front and compacted them into tight clusters beneath these peaks, differentiating between the band of street-facing circulation and service spaces (the entry and stairs, a paired guest toilet and

River Oaks Early Republic House (Hugh Potter House), River Oaks, 1925–26, John F. Staub, architect. Photograph by R. M. Luster, in Don Riddle, River Oaks.

Latin Colonial House, living room. Photograph by Calvin Wheat, Civics for Houston *1 (Feb. 1928): 9.*

telephone alcove, the kitchen, a miniscule pantry, and a service porch and boiler room) and the larger volumes that project from the rear of the house. Staub expanded the house's presence on Del Monte by incorporating wing walls and a freestanding two-car garage with apartment above into the street-front composition.[20] As at the Chew House, the garage was brought forward from the rear corner of the site, where it might otherwise have been built, to perform narratives of service and circumstance, expanding the degrees of hierarchical gradation built into the façade and rhythmically framing the entire street front with a low-slung, shed-roof profile on the west that mirrors the pitch of the gabled entrance bay on the east. Staub gave this small house big presence by manipulating perceptions of scale with the imposing classical entrance pediment and the high-silled shuttered windows lighting the toilet and kitchen, as well as the material contrast between the white-stained gray cypress shingles (cladding the kitchen bay, the wing walls, the garage, and the second floor) and the pink common brick facing of the entrance bay, the living room, and the tall frontal chimney stack.

As in the Latin Colonial House, the interiors of the Staub House reinforced the country house discourse on the small house. The entrance and stair vestibule is faced with dark-stained, vertical pine planking. The ceiling is low, the floor is paved with dark flagstones, and the stair, which turns at a landing to ascend beneath the inclined roof plane of the gabled entrance bay, has a steep rise. The vestibule, although lit by a window at the stair landing, is dim and enclosed, imaginatively performing "Massachusetts" and "colonial." Staub constructed the two reception rooms—the living room and dining room (there was no library or back stair)—as generously proportioned and lofty in comparison, with ceiling heights of nine feet, seven inches. Both rooms had three exposures, giving each access to the prevailing breeze. Both opened to a ten-foot-deep, south-facing, roofed porch overlooking the rear garden. The living room (which is fifteen feet by twenty-four-and-a-half feet) and dining room (which is fifteen feet by eighteen feet) are interlocked axially to sustain the perception of consistent symmetrical composure. Staub maintained this perception by symmetrically composing all four elevations of the living room (the fireplace wall, the long wall of the room, is paneled and painted a green color glazed with turquoise; the fireplace opening is flush with the wall) and three of the four walls of the dining room, which is papered above a paneled dado. Panels beneath living room and dining room windows reinforce the sense of ceremoniousness that these rooms materialize.

Mrs. John F. Staub House, River Oaks, 1925–26.

First-floor plan

Second-floor plan

Staub House.

The spatial organization of the second floor displayed Staub's ability to construct volumetric layers that implied hierarchical gradation even in tight circumstances. Staub incorporated tray ceilings in the master bedroom above the living room and his daughter's bedroom above the dining room, bringing the exterior roof planes down to low clipped eaves above interior trays, spatially intimating shelter in both rooms. (When Staub expanded the kitchen and service porch wing in 1931, after the birth of his youngest child, Caroline, he fashioned a new second-floor bedroom for his son that stepped down above the kitchen while its ceiling opened up beneath the sloping planes of the gabled roof, constructing an unanticipated episode of spatial drama.[21]) The intricacy with which he staged access to the master bedroom and girls' bedroom, so that passage moved in two stages around what the floor plan reveals was the bathtub niche in the master bathroom, demonstrated his capacity to work with space reciprocally, to resolve practical planning issues in order to shape circumstantial spaces that dialectically framed the rooms to which they gave access as ceremonial. Staub even managed to relegate closets to these "anterooms," so that interior elevations in the master and girls' bedrooms could be gracefully composed, highlighting their superiority within this micro-spatial dialectic of serving and served.

When the Staub House was published in the March 1928 issue of the *Southern Architect and Building News*, it was editorially framed as an example of the small house.[22] When it was published in the January 1928 issue of *House Beautiful*, much more emphasis was placed on its furniture and decoration.[23] The author of the *House Beautiful* article was Staub's former architecture classmate at MIT, Charles O. Cornelius, who in 1917 began the American decorative arts collection at the Metropolitan Museum of Art in New York and by 1928 was the museum's associate curator of American art.[24] Cornelius's focus on Staub's furniture bespoke Madeleine and John Staub's interest in collecting eighteenth- and early-nineteenth-century American antiques, a passion they shared

Staub House, living room.

(if on a smaller scale) with Ima and Will Hogg and in which they had been encouraged by Staub's aunt, Emma Fanz Hope of Knoxville, for whom he designed his first house, built in 1921 while he was still an employee of Lindeberg's.[25] The Staubs' collection of high style and vernacular American pieces materialized patrician identity in the 1920s. It affiliated them with the cutting edge of "traditional" taste in the United States and, like the mantle-less fireplace, declared their patrician virtues: subtlety, refinement, discretion, authenticity. By the end of the 1920s, living with American antique furniture in Houston operated as a technology of self fashioning, testifying to the cultural authority wielded by the Hoggs in defining a domestic style that might identify the superior segment of Houston's elite as an upper class.

Staub's house proved to be a more compelling model for the design of other houses than did the Latin Colonial House. The architect Hiram A. Salisbury, a graduate of Columbia University's architecture school who came to Houston in 1926 from his hometown, Omaha, Nebraska, designed at least three versions of the Staub House in River Oaks between 1930 and 1936.[26] Stayton Nunn, a graduate of Rice and a former employee of William Ward Watkin's who began his practice in 1930, designed his interpretation of Staub's house, the Dr. C. M. Griswold House of 1933, on Brentwood Drive in River Oaks.[27]

And John Thomas Rather Jr., a Rice graduate whom Staub hired in 1923 on the recommendation of James Chillman to help in producing the drawings for the River Oaks Country Clubhouse, adapted the Staub House as his model for a house on Inwood Drive next door to the Chew House. Rather designed this house for his former Rice classmate, the engineer and contractor George R. Brown, and his wife Alice Pratt in 1932–33.[28]

What these River Oaks homages to the Staub House suggest is that it operated as a persuasive model of gentility compressed into the limits of a middle-income house. The Latin Colonial House also appealed as an image of patrician propriety and composure, perhaps more so than as a symbol of local identity. One of the first houses that the Houston architect Carl Mulvey designed when he began independent practice, the Clark Hardison House of 1929 in the subdivision of Braeswood, was not only compositionally and proportionally similar to the Latin Colonial House, it was described in advertising for Braeswood as being in the "French Colonial" style.

Harvin Moore and Hermon Lloyd, two young Houston architects in partnership from 1934 to 1941, based their design of the Gillette Hill House on Looscan Lane in River Oaks of 1935–36 and of the Louis F. Fox Jr. House on Avenue O in Galveston of 1935–36 on the Latin Colonial House.[29] The architect Cameron Fairchild, who began his practice in Houston in 1925, designed the Margaret Leonard and Ballinger Mills Jr. House on Avenue O in Galveston of 1939 as his homage to the Latin Colonial House.[30]

In none of these cases was the newer house a copy of Staub so much as an adaptation of the façade composition and proportions of the original (although the cast-iron balcony was a recurring feature). Staub's houses performed myths of elite identity with such persuasiveness and charm that they recommended themselves to other Houston architects as models. Staub seems to have been the first Houston architect to whom other Houston architects deferred with such regard.

Tom Rather, who designed houses under his own name while an employee of Staub's and continued to produce his own design work under the firm name after he became Staub's partner in 1936, was responsible for more small houses than Staub, some of them smaller in size than even Staub's smallest houses (that is to say: no downstairs guest toilet and lavatory and only one upstairs bathroom). From his earliest known independent design, a two-story English Regency house for Estelle Streetman and Marion L. Lindsey on Milford Street in the Turner addition of 1926–27, Rather adhered to the spatial patterns established in Staub's houses.[31] One of Hiram Salisbury's earliest houses, the H. Q. Hickman House on Stanmore Drive in River Oaks of 1927, published in the *American Architect* in January 1928, applied the composition of interlocked gables of Staub's house to a one-story house organized on a bungalow plan: parallel back-to-front ranges with two bedrooms bracketing a bathroom on one side, and a living room–dining room–breakfast-pantry-kitchen line-up on the other.[32]

Salisbury brought the house down to grade level, substituted a side loggia for the front porch, indented the bathroom to give the bedrooms three exposures, and had the brick painted white to externally mask any trace of the bungalow. In 1928 the River Oaks Corporation and the *Houston Post-Dispatch* co-sponsored an architectural competition for an ideal small house, the Honeymoon Cottage, that could be sold for between $10,000 and $12,000 including the cost of the lot.[33] Eighty entries were received. Both the first prize and the third prize were won by Staub's draftsman Vance D. Phenix in collaboration with the artist-architect E. M. Schiwetz. Neither design was as deft in its planning as Staub typically was, but both balanced circumstantial circulation and service spaces with composed primary spaces. Phenix and Schiwetz's first-prize design even managed to insert a separate entrance vestibule, give one of the two bedrooms three exposures, and compose the living room with a paneled fireplace wall, the fireplace opening set flush with the wall and flanked by a recessed bookshelf balancing a set of double doors leading into the dining room. Staub did not

Dr. C. M. Griswold House, River Oaks, 1933, Stayton Nunn, architect. Houston 4 (*Mar. 1933*): 9.

George R. Brown House, River Oaks, 1932–33, J. T. Rather Jr., architect. Photograph by Paul Hester, Houston Architectural Survey.

Clark Hardison House, Braeswood, 1929, Carl Mulvey, architect. Houston Metropolitan Research Center, Houston Public Library.

Ballinger Mills Jr. House, Galveston, 1939, Cameron Fairchild, architect.

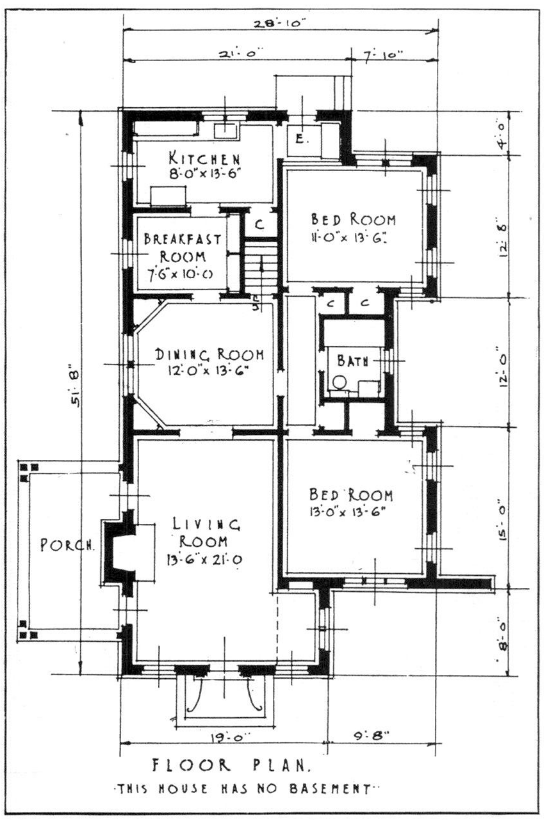

HOUSE OF H. Q. HICKMAN, HOUSTON, TEXAS

HIRAM A. SALISBURY, ARCHITECT

COMPUTATION OF CUBAGE

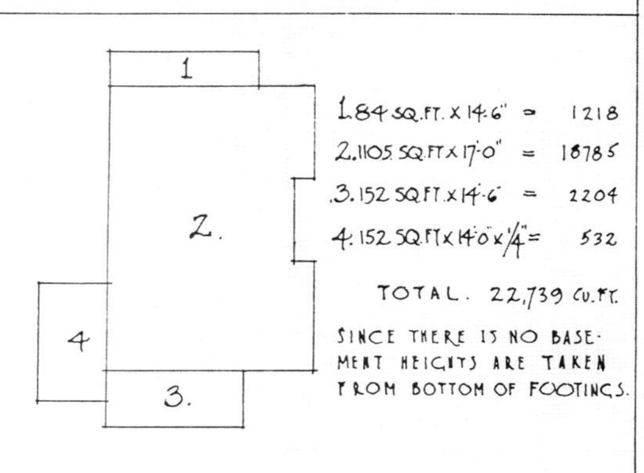

H. Q. Hickman House, River Oaks, 1927, Hiram A. Salisbury, architect. Demolished. American Architect 133 (Jan. 5, 1928): 62.

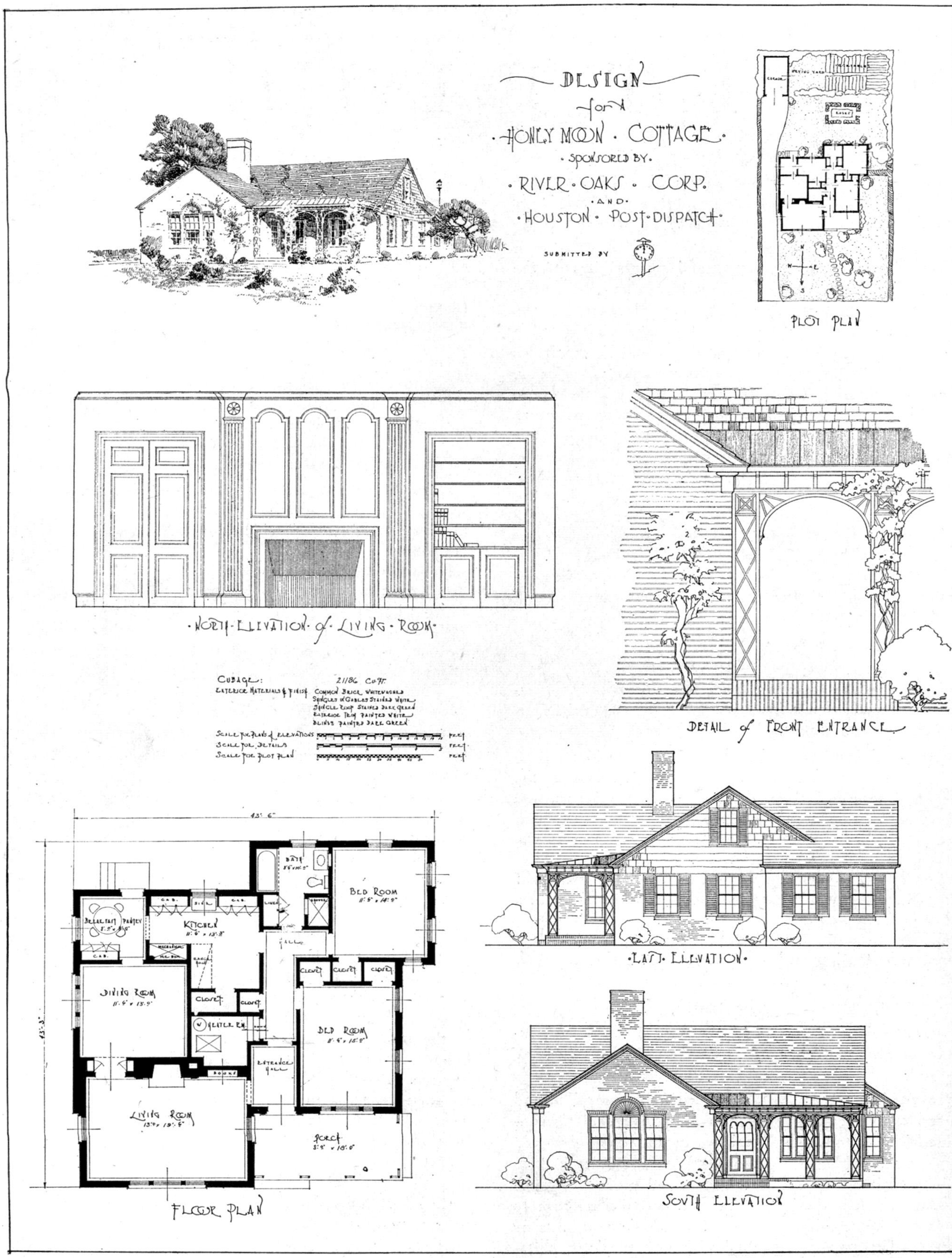

FIRST PRIZE DESIGN, BY VANCE D. PHENIX AND E. M. SCHIWETZ

HONEYMOON COTTAGE COMPETITION

First-prize design: Honeymoon Cottage, 1928, Vance D. Phenix and E. M. Schiwetz, architects. Demolished. Pencil Points 9 (July 1928): 444.

need to produce models at ever-smaller scales to influence the design of small houses that extended the country house discourse. His small houses (and Briscoe and Dixon's Redbird House, another important Houston model) demonstrated how economies of planning and scale could be achieved while sustaining the sense of composure and ceremonious distinction propagated by the country house discourse. Salisbury's gentrification of the bungalow in the Hickman House and the effort that published entries to the River Oaks Corporation's Honeymoon Cottage competition expended on avoiding the bungalow plan diagram (a spatial diagram that made sense in Houston) display the ideological shift that transpired between the second and third stages of the American country house as it moved from what Kevin Phillips described as an "architecture of polarization" (maximizing the distinctions between the country house and other house types) in its lord-of-the-manner phase to an architecture of consensus in its suburban country gentleman phase, in which the reduced-scale country house was deployed as an instrument in the formation of a public to support the legitimacy of the country house's implicit social vision of class distinction in a classless society.[34]

John Staub told Howard Barnstone that his favorite small house was one of the houses in which Inez Lasell lived, the two-story brick house he designed for Marie and William C. Helmbrecht on Avenue P in Galveston, built in 1928 for $21,547.[35] The Helmbrecht House is a condensed version of the plan type represented by the Hutcheson House, with the entrance and stair hall and the dining room parallel to each other and with both perpendicular to the long dimension of the living room, contained within a symmetrically composed exterior envelope. In part because the Helmbrecht House does not have a back stair, the dimensions of its ground floor reception rooms are larger than those of the River Oaks Early Republic House, giving the house a sense of spaciousness that makes it feel expansive and generous. Staub opened the living room and the rear-facing dining room to the backyard with shuttered French doors. Paneled interior double doors with paneled overdoors between the three reception rooms, small door knobs or levers, and a parquet floor in the living room were other material elements that subtly ceremonialized occupation of these rooms. Staub lifted the head heights of the French doors almost to the ceiling to construct a sense of scale gradation and raise the apparent height of the nine-and-a-half-foot ceilings. In place of a cornice at the top of the dining room wall, he substituted a cornice detail that seems to be derived from John Soane: a fascia band framed by molding applied to the ceiling.[36] Staub Galvestonized the Helmbrecht House by paving the entrance hall, the telephone alcove, and the dining room with white tiles keyed with smaller, diagonally rotated black tiles that Mrs. Helmbrecht salvaged from a nineteenth-century Galveston building.

Barnstone remarked on the use of shallow planar relief to frame the shuttered French doors on the Avenue P front of the Helmbrecht House and energize what otherwise would have been a flat, planar elevation.[37] The subtlety with which the big-scaled louvered shutters are texturally contrasted with walls of orange clinker brick and with which the slate-surfaced hipped roof is framed by slender chimney stacks naturalizes the architectural construction of upper-class composure.

Staub registered discretion as an upper-class virtue in the Helmbrecht House by juxtaposing symmetrical window arrangements with the distribution of interior spaces. The oval window to the right of the entrance illuminates the reception hall, its counterpart to the left the telephone alcove. The downstairs lavatory and toilet room is placed behind the French door that symmetrically balances the living room window; the glazed portion of the lavatory French door incorporates a "secret" sliding sash window. Staub even composed the driveway entrance to the kitchen with a Palladian figure, a central door with an arched transom flanked by high-set, flat-headed windows, to bestow the grace of propriety, order, and hierarchical gradation on the service sector of the house, securely integrating it into the country house discourse on the good community.

Taking advantage of the amount of space required for the boiler room downstairs, Staub organized the second floor with a spacious master bedroom and bathroom above the living room (the bedroom is approached from the upstairs stair hall through an anteroom of closets), a pair of secondary bedrooms above the dining room and pantry that share a second bathroom, and, above the kitchen and a corner of the boiler room, a small servant's bedroom (or sleeping porch) with its own compact bathroom isolated from the rest of the floor. Staub provided doors between the three family bedrooms and the shared bathroom to make it possible to pass from room to room without going out to the hall, a recurring spatial practice he described to Barnstone as occasioned by concerns for security should an intruder get into the house. Staub's skill at spatially instantiating class identity and subjectivity was inseparable from his planning rigor. His mastery at resolving practical issues of adjacency, access, storage, ventilation, and plumbing with rhythmic geometry and proportions underpinned the broader program of social construction since inadequate or defective planning would have called the social construction into question, exposing it and undermining its plausibility.

Galveston differed from Houston in that its economy in the 1920s was contracting rather than accelerating.[38] This could be inferred from the site of the Helmbrecht House, three lots in a block of the city's nineteenth-century town plan. The Helmbrecht House is surrounded by older,

(overleaf) William C. Helmbrecht House, Galveston, 1928, John F. Staub, architect.

Helmbrecht House, detail of shutters.

wood-clapboard-faced cottages and bungalows. A cast-iron fence outlining the sidewalk front of the property is an indication that the house was built in a city neighborhood rather than a country-place subdivision. In this context, the Helmbrecht House does not look as small as it might have had it been built in Houston. It also looks resolutely modern and stylish rather than homey, familiar, or old fashioned. A similar dialectical contrast adheres to the two-story brick house Staub designed three blocks away at 35th Street and Avenue P for Dr. and Mrs. Edward Randall Jr., also built in 1928 and costing $26,808.[39]

Based on the River Oaks Early Republic house type, the Randall House, by virtue of its location in a Galveston neighborhood in which Dr. Randall's forebears had lived since the 1850s, constructed family identity and spatial continuity of a kind that the urban redevelopment of Houston's elite nineteenth-century neighborhoods no longer supported. The chains of signification in which Staub's architecture was implicated could affect the meanings to be construed from his houses depending on their locales, even when, architecturally, they conformed to identical typological and stylistic models. What constituted a small house in Houston was not necessarily a small house in other Texas towns. Yet an ideological constant uniting these Galveston houses and their Houston counterparts was their discrete assertion of superiority. Staub's "architecturalization" of elite status identified the occupants of his houses as legitimate claimants to leadership, as reflected in Dr. Randall's educational and professional career.[40] A third-generation Galvestonian, he was a graduate of the Hill School and Yale University and obtained his medical education at the University of Pennsylvania, where his father had also been trained. When, the year his new house was built, Dr. Randall's father retired as professor of materia medica, therapeutics, and diagnostics at the University of Texas Medical Branch, which is located in Galveston (and of which the senior Dr. Randall had been a founding faculty member in 1891), Edward Randall Jr. succeeded to the professorship of therapeutics. Like his father, Dr. Randall served on the boards of the Sealy and Smith Foundation, the city's major medical philanthropy, the Rosenberg Library, its major cultural institution, and the vestry of Trinity Church, its oldest Episcopal parish.[41]

The Randall and Helmbrecht Houses, like Staub's own house and the Latin Colonial House, were significant because of their relatively small size and affordability when compared to the grand houses for which Staub was better known. They were Staub's contribution to the process of gentrifying the middle class.[42] Rather than simply a by-product of the trickle down from top to middle, as middle-income families sought to imitate the fashions of the rich, the "small" country house of the 1920s can be understood as

Helmbrecht House, detail of oval window.

Dr. Edward Randall Jr. House, Galveston, 1928, John F. Staub, architect.

an instrument for expanding and legitimizing elite cultural authority by recruiting a broadened constituency that would identify with this authority and absorb, naturalize, and legitimize the subject positions affiliated with it.

In Houston, River Oaks became the landscape where this process of spatial affiliation was realized in the 1930s. Although a few four-square houses were constructed in River Oaks in the 1920s, no bungalows were built there. The streets of River Oaks's affordable sections, as imaged in Buck Schiwetz's advertising illustrations for the River Oaks Corporation, were built out in the latter half of the 1930s with two-story country houses that collectively identified the families who dwelled in them as "nice" (the Houston euphemism for Anglo-Americans who were socially respectable but not rich).[43] Their children studied in the same schools (especially elementary schools) as the children of the rich, with whom they established long-term acquaintances and a sense of familiarity. They worshipped at the same churches and shared in such pastimes as hunting, golf, tennis, horseback riding, and the cultivation of flowering shrubs. Thanks to Ima and Will Hogg, nice Houston families were likely to exhibit a penchant for eighteenth- and early-nineteenth-century American antiques and were apt to grow azaleas in profusion. Staub's small country houses were important models for other Houston architects, enabling them to provide appropriate domestic accommodations that sustained their owners' social aspirations. In such smaller cities as Galveston, Staub's small country houses performed the social function his larger houses did in Houston by identifying and reinforcing the status of local elites.[44] During the 1920s the small country house was recognized in the national architectural press as a potentially problematic category that merited special attention. By addressing issues of spatial condensation and constructional economy with the imagination and rigor, Staub performed meritorious social service by demonstrating how the country house discourse and its subject positions could spatially inform the domestic life of nice families like his own and seem to democratically expand the realm of elite privilege. He demonstrated that it was possible for ladies and gentlemen to live gracefully without a back stair.

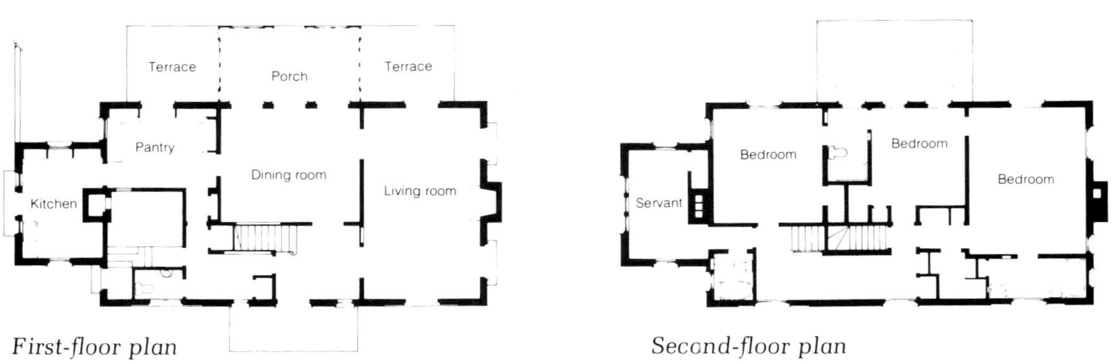

Helmbrecht House.

CHAPTER 5 : GRAND HOUSES

J. Robert Neal House, Homewoods, River Oaks, 1931–33, John F. Staub, architect. Detail of pediment-capped window above entrance portal.

If a small Staub house is one without a back stair, a grand Staub house, as the Houston architect Russell Windham observed, is one in which not only the reception rooms but bedrooms and other spaces not used for entertaining are accorded architectural decoration. Grand houses were exceptional rather than normative in Staub's practice. Yet starting with Bayou Bend in 1926 and proceeding into the 1950s Staub produced country houses that were, by Texas standards, built on a grand scale. What this qualification indicates is the exceptional status of the grand country house in Texas, the production of new wealth there notwithstanding. Staub was unusual among Texas architects in practice in the 1920s and 1930s for the number of grand houses he carried out. The few Texans prepared to build on such a scale were as likely to hire architects from New York, Boston, Chicago, or California to design their country houses as they were to hire local architects.[1] Staub's success in this small but highly visible field stemmed from his responsiveness to his clients' aspirations. His grand houses demonstrate his mastery—and discretion—at architecturally registering ambition. They consistently interpret and translate his clients' most expansive visions into houses that expressed grandeur while remaining manageable as family dwellings. This point touches on what was most problematic about these houses from a patrician perspective: their theatricality.

Staub had to negotiate between his clients' desire to be seen as grand and the risk that a house might project an identity that could not be sustained by the subjects who occupied it, alienating them within their own habitat and exposing them to ridicule.[2] By repeatedly grounding the design of his grandest houses in the disciplines that characterized his architecture—geometric rigor, rhythmic proportions, spatial clarity, openness, and generosity—Staub led by serving. He used his customary spatial practices to construct continuity between the small house and the grand house, ensuring the reality of the latter and reinforcing the country house consensus on the good community by implying that the same subject positions pertained on both ends of the axis: that there was no conflict between great wealth and "niceness." Staub's grand houses insistently construct upper-class identity as open, connected, reflective, rigorous, balanced, buoyant, and magnanimous. Despite their aristocratic theatricality, these houses also perform patrician restraint with conviction and persuasiveness. A survey of Staub's largest houses of the 1920s and 1930s indicates his versatility in accommodating his clients' programs, as well as less tangible expectations, to the production of upper-class identity. This survey also shows how Staub's conception of that identity began to change in the 1930s.

The country house Staub designed in 1926 for Martha Jennings and Edwin E. Bewley in Fort Worth, Texas, two hundred sixty miles northwest of Houston, was built between 1927 and 1928 in tandem with Bayou Bend. The Bewley House was constructed by the Fort Worth contractor Thomas S. Byrne for $83,020, making its cost slightly less than forty percent that of Bayou Bend.[3] In comparison to Staub's Houston houses of the 1920s, the Bewley House stands out because of its scale and site, a twenty-acre tract that straddles a ridge above the bank of the West Fork of the Trinity River in Fort Worth's River Crest addition. The house faces the low, extremely broad flood plain of the Trinity. Staub took advantage of these topographic conditions to construct an identity for the Bewley House as an Anglo-Texan country house that engages in a dialectical exchange with other houses in the neighborhood to enhance its grand identity.

E. E. Bewley was president of Bewley Mills, producers of flour and cornmeal, which his father, a native of Kentucky who came to Fort Worth in 1876, founded.[4] Bewley was a graduate of the University of Texas. Martha Bewley was the granddaughter of Khleber M. Van Zandt, a native of Tennessee raised in East Texas who came to Fort Worth in 1866 and in 1874 became a partner in a private bank that, in 1884, merged with the Fort Worth National Bank, of which Van Zandt served as president until his death in 1930 at the age of ninety-four. Bewley would eventually become chairman of the bank's board of directors after its merger with the Farmers and Mechanics National Bank, of which he had been an officer and director. Additionally, Bewley was an officer of several Fort Worth–based insurance companies. In 1920 Mr. and Mrs. Bewley had commissioned the Chicago architect David Adler to produce designs for them that were not built.[5] Five years earlier, Adler designed a pair of houses built next door to each other in River Crest that had the same impact on Fort Worth as Lindeberg's Shadyside houses had in Houston. These houses, for Flora Anderson and Morris E. Berney and for Mrs. Berney's mother, Mrs. Neil P. Anderson, were breathtaking demonstrations of Adler's subtlety and flair.[6] Both houses are very grand, and they enhance this aura by performing grandness with exceptional understatement and restraint. Fort Worth architects in the 1920s sought to repeat Adler's achievement in the design of other large houses in River Crest but consistently fell short. Staub took on Adler with a house that was less expensive than Adler's but that dialectically identified their one shortcoming.

River Crest is a country place subdivision planned in 1911 in conjunction with development of the River Crest Country Club.[7] It consisted of large lots, many of them sited along the bluff of the West Fork of the Trinity River. The breadth of the Trinity's flood plain and the height and relatively steep slope of the bluff gave River Crest a topographic advantage unavailable in the flat Gulf coastal plain. However, since River Crest house sites lie on the southeast bank of the river,

E. E. Bewley House, River Crest, Fort Worth, 1926–28, John F. Staub, architect. Entrance elevation.

Morris E. Berney House, River Crest, Fort Worth, 1915–16, Adler and Dangler, architects. Courtesy Doco Foto Services.

Mrs. Neil Anderson House, River Crest, Fort Worth, 1916–17, Adler and Dangler, architects. Courtesy Doco Foto Services.

houses needed to face away from the river for access to the prevailing southeast breeze. Adler located the Berney and Anderson Houses at the crest of their sites. Yet he turned the backs of both houses on the river and, in the reception rooms of the Berney House, suppressed awareness of the prospect available from the backyard. Staub rectified this circumstance at the Bewley House. He tailored the house to its site, extending its linear plan along the contour lines of the property and performing the sort of dialogue between interior and exterior rehearsed at the Cochran House in Broadacres.

Staub's choreography of movement begins at the entrance to the Bewley property on Alta Avenue, adjoining the River Crest Country Club golf course. Thick, low, tapered gate piers capped by gableted weathering of shingle tiles, with thin wedges of vertically layered tiles exposed in the plaster-filled triangle beneath the peaks of the weathering, announce a Lutyens-like invented vernacular. The piers are constructed of limestone rubble.[8] Streets in River Crest bounding the golf course are outlined with low parapet walls made of this limestone rubble. Staub appropriated an ordinary element of the local landscape that is pervasive but not architecturally emphasized to construct continuity by proposing a River Crest vernacular. The graveled entrance drive curves along the rim of the ridgeline beyond which descent toward the river plain begins, impressing the site's topography on visitors. The house, oriented north-south so that its narrow east end lies closest to the street, is set on a flat shelf. The drive curves in a gentle arc in front of the north face of the house, turning in a circular motor court centered on the Bewley House's immense, steeply raked gabled entrance bay of orange, red, and black clinker brick. The gabled bay contains a big-scaled casement window lighting the main stair, which is framed by a keystone-centered brick jack arch. Aligned beneath it is the deeply inset, segmentally arched, architrave-framed front door. The monumental scale of the gabled frontispiece serves as a backdrop to the view. The front door and stair window frame prospects across a descending sequence of natural terraces (the one closest to the driveway now containing a swimming pool) that dramatize the sweep of the landscape as it expands north toward the Trinity River flood plain.

The driveway continues beyond the circular forecourt, descending nearly ten feet below the ridgeline to the house's basement level, where Staub inserted a three-car garage. The service wing of the house curves to follow the ruling contour line before terminating above the garage. To enhance the fiction that the Bewley House grows out of its site, Staub faced the exposed basement level with River Crest limestone rubble. Staub also framed a vista of the more tranquil south side of the property, a meadow that slopes gently up and

Bewley House, vista from entrance front looking toward Trinity River.

away from the house, through the one-story loggia closest to the street.

Consistent with the scale of the house, the loggia is big. The front of the Bewley House lacks Staub's characteristic coupling of monumentality and intimacy; monumentality is stressed. Yet because the scale of the house is related to the scale of the landscape with proportional assurance, the house does not feel overblown or institutional.

Staub responded to the topographic conditions of the Bewley site by scaling the house to the landscape and using it to frame perceptions that make the setting appear dramatic, eventful, and grand from the perspective of the privileged subject. He identified the Bewley House with the country houses of Edwin Lutyens through such devices as the dominating presence of the entrance gable, the cascade of the house's shingle tile roofs, the contour of its plan, even the detailing of the terrace balustrade, affiliating it with the Anglo-American country house discourse and naturalizing this discourse by basing it on limestone rubble foundations.[9] Staub slyly challenged the neighborhood's reigning arbiters of style, the Berney and Anderson Houses, by designing the Bewley House to take advantage of site conditions and views rather than responding only to the requirements of orientation as the Adler and Dangler houses do. Staub framed openings with constructive detail that, in a Lutyens-like way, subliminally merged classical decoration with the picturesque manorial historical models on which the design of the house was based. He spatially evoked repose in the gabled east loggia, which seems to await its subjects and the social rituals enacting upper-class leisure they will perform. Staub not only internalized the dialectic between service and ceremony in the downstairs-upstairs stratification of rubble stone and brick but also in the spatial distinction between the orthogonal geometry of the parts of the house containing

Bewley House, detail of basement-level garage and rubble-stone foundations.

Bewley House, south lawn elevation.

Bewley House, detail of south gable.

Bewley House, detail of loggia.

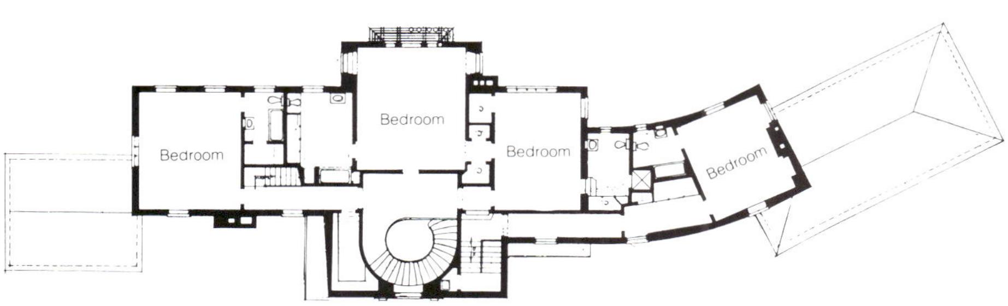

Second-floor plan

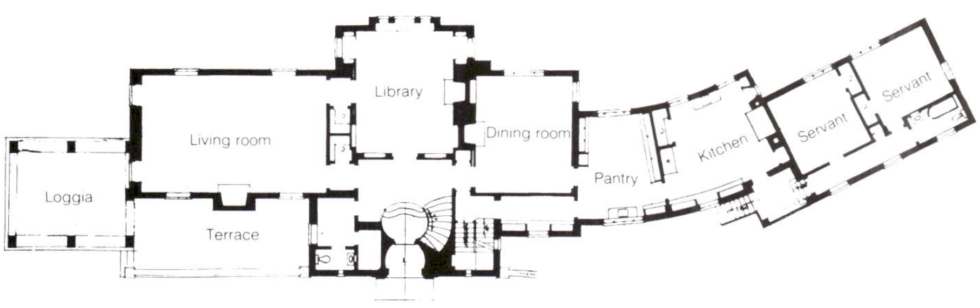

First-floor plan

Bewley House.

Bewley House, detail of stair rail.

reception rooms and family bedrooms and the radial geometry, stepped section, and myriad adjustments, offsets, and overlaps of the west service wing, coding it as subordinate but no less interesting.

Internally, the Bewley House is very subdued. Because the house is one-room deep, the living room and library have three exposures, the dining room two, and the pantry and kitchen run the shallow depth of the house. The view through the front door is a prospect of the south lawn, framed by French doors in the projecting library bay. Internally, the reception rooms are visually connected to the out-of-doors. Staub incorporated spatial practices in the Bewley House he would repeat in subsequent grand houses. Two cross axes of movement and view are opened up through the house by aligning doorways from the entrance and stair hall to the living room and dining room, and between the library and living room, in each instance projecting the cross axis outward through French doors in the east end of the living room. These cross axes construct a sense of deep interior space that is powerfully affecting. Openings between reception rooms are recessed in alcoves to stage, slow, and ritualize the movement of subjects, imbuing circulation with an intimation of procession and arresting the impulse to relentless movement. This internal dialectic between continuity and pause generates a subtle tension that energizes the composed reception rooms of the Bewley House. Wide wood plank floors emphasize breadth and generosity. The grace of simplicity is conveyed by the detailing of fireplace openings—molded marble bands framing a flush-set opening in the living room and a black marble mantle in the dining room—and of the slender wrought iron handrail and balusters outlining the Lindeberg-like stair, which ascends in a sinuous curve above the front door.

Staub carried spatial inventiveness to the second floor. Edwin Bewley Jr.'s bedroom, in the east end of the house above the living room, and a guest room at the end of the west wing have vaulted ceilings that give each a distinct volumetric identity, Edwin Jr.'s room has a low tunnel vault and the guest room a groin vault. Staub's finely tuned sense of propriety is evident in the way the guest room is both connected to, yet separable from, the family's bedrooms via the back stair and a long corridor whose length is spatially mitigated by its picturesque curvature.

Staub expanded upon, without repeating, the lessons in elite domestic style David Adler had introduced to Fort Worth in the 1910s. The extent to which the Bewley House proved to be "an educational institution" was made clear from the number of commissions Staub subsequently received from Fort Worth clients.[10] For Lorena Bain and John P. King, Staub designed a two-story-high, five-bay-wide American neoclassical house built in 1928 by the Fort Worth contractor

B. B. Adams for $52,279.[11] The symmetrically composed, brick-faced front elevation of the King House is capped by a taut, low-pitched hipped roof and articulated with slender Ionic pilasters. Shuttered twelve-pane-over-twelve-pane ground-floor windows are framed with tall architraves incorporating fluted fanlight header panels. The King House has a mannered quality, unusual for Staub, that is enhanced by a two-story-tall porte cochère that projects off the west end of the house. The vertical attenuation produced by the pilasters, the architraves, and the double-height porte cochère was Staub's response to the house's site on Crestline Road. The street, as its name implies, runs along the ridge atop the Trinity River bluff. House sites on the riverside of Crestline, such as the King property, slope down from the street to a broad shelf before descending at a steeper incline toward the river valley. Staub visually compensated for the down slope from the street, which puts the eaves line of the King House at approximately the curb level on Crestline, by accentuating the vertical, not just in the plane of the house's front elevation but volumetrically in the double-height porte cochère, so that from the street the house appears to rise rather than sink.

Staub addressed practical problems of orientation and siting in an even more extraordinary display of architectural exuberance at the Fort Worth house he designed for Elizabeth Reynolds and Herman Gartner. The Gartner House was built by B. B. Adams in 1929–30 facing the east edge of the River Crest Country Club golf course at the corner of Hillcrest Drive and Clarke Street. The site is more conventional than the estate lots on the west side of the golf course: two deep lots that back up to the middle-income McCarts addition. Like the King House, the Gartner House was not, by Staub standards, a grand house; the construction contract was for $60,000.[12] It demonstrates, though, how the grand country houses of Fort Worth "educated" elite clients, recommending spatial arrangements that framed desirable subject positions. The Gartner House also displays Staub's sensitivity to his clients in its departures from spatial practices characteristic of his houses.

As Barnstone noted, the problem affecting the Gartner property is that the street front faces west into the most intense sunlight and heat conditions.[13] Staub responded with one of his most idiosyncratic plans. The reception rooms of the Gartner House—the living room, an intermediate morning room, and the dining room—were aligned front-to-back to face the south side of the site, a broad side yard. Staub offset the layout of these rooms so that each had exposure to the east as well. Taking advantage of the shallow slope of the property from west to east, there is an interior sectional shift, a one-foot step-down from the living room to the morning room. An interior passage, accessible from the entrance and stair hall, bypasses the morning room to connect to the dining room. The ground-floor service spaces—a low-ceilinged, driveway-side entrance and guest toilet, the back stair, a pantry, and the kitchen—were aligned front-to-back along the north side of the house. On the second floor, three bedrooms—for Mr. and Mrs. Gartner, their daughter Suzanne, and a guest—were located above the reception rooms, so that each also has south and east exposure. Another sectional shift occurs with the library, one of Staub's most beguiling rooms. It is located neither on the first nor the second floors but at an intermediate level between them, accessible from a landing two-thirds of the way up the main stair, which itself is quite curious: a spiral stair that angles upward in an orthogonally planned stairwell. Staub spatialized intimacy in the library, which is an elongated octagon in plan with paneled walls and a vaulted ceiling.

The Gartner House's most extravagant feature, a cascading gabled frontispiece facing Hillcrest Drive and the golf course, exemplifies Staub's engagement with contradiction. He externalized the programmatic, planning, and sectional dissidence that results from turning the "front" of the house away from the street and toward the side yard. The bravura profile and bold scale of the gable distract attention from the collision of spaces behind it but do not conceal this collision.

The two-story stairwell to the left of the entrance (blind on the street front of the house but lit from the side by a north-facing oriel window), the mid-level library bay projecting off the north side of the house, and the two-story wing containing the living room with master bedroom above to the right of the entrance, centered on a tall, vigorously broken-out chimney stack, each receives its due. The folded plane of the side-gabled, shingle tile roof constructs the volumetric continuity that permits these conditions to be acknowledged yet contained. The commanding scale of the frontispiece, mirrored in the scale of the segmentally arched, molded sandstone entrance portal, announces the attitude of the house's reception rooms, which are imposing in their architectural decoration but not their size.

The sixteenth-century knight-in-armor front doorplate (the knight's shield flips up to reveal the keyhole) materializes a playfulness more evident in the Gartner House than in most of Staub's houses. The decorative mesh of tightly coiled wrought iron in the oval window above the entrance portal lights, yet screens, the master bathroom, reinforcing the sense that masking—disclosure through screening rather than concealment and denial—was the architectural theme of the Gartner House.

What makes the Gartner House fascinating in the context of Staub's grand houses is that it aspires to grand status through every medium but size. From the Bewley House, Staub borrowed the use of a gabled frontispiece to give the house front monumental scale and presence. The shaped,

(overleaf) John P. King House, River Crest, Fort Worth, 1928, John F. Staub, architect.

Herman Gartner House, Rivercrest, Fort Worth, 1929–30, John F. Staub, architect.

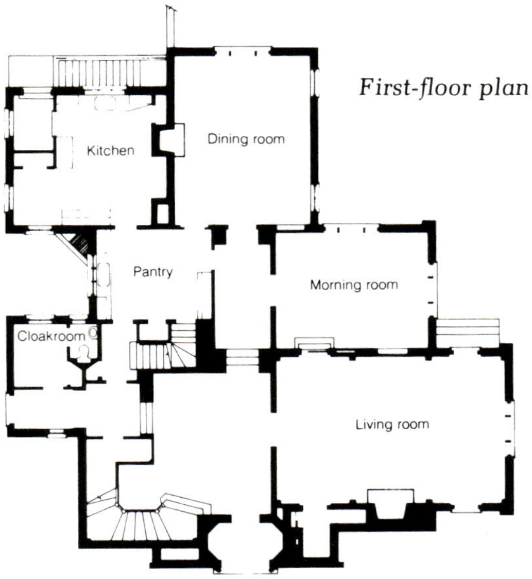

Gartner House.

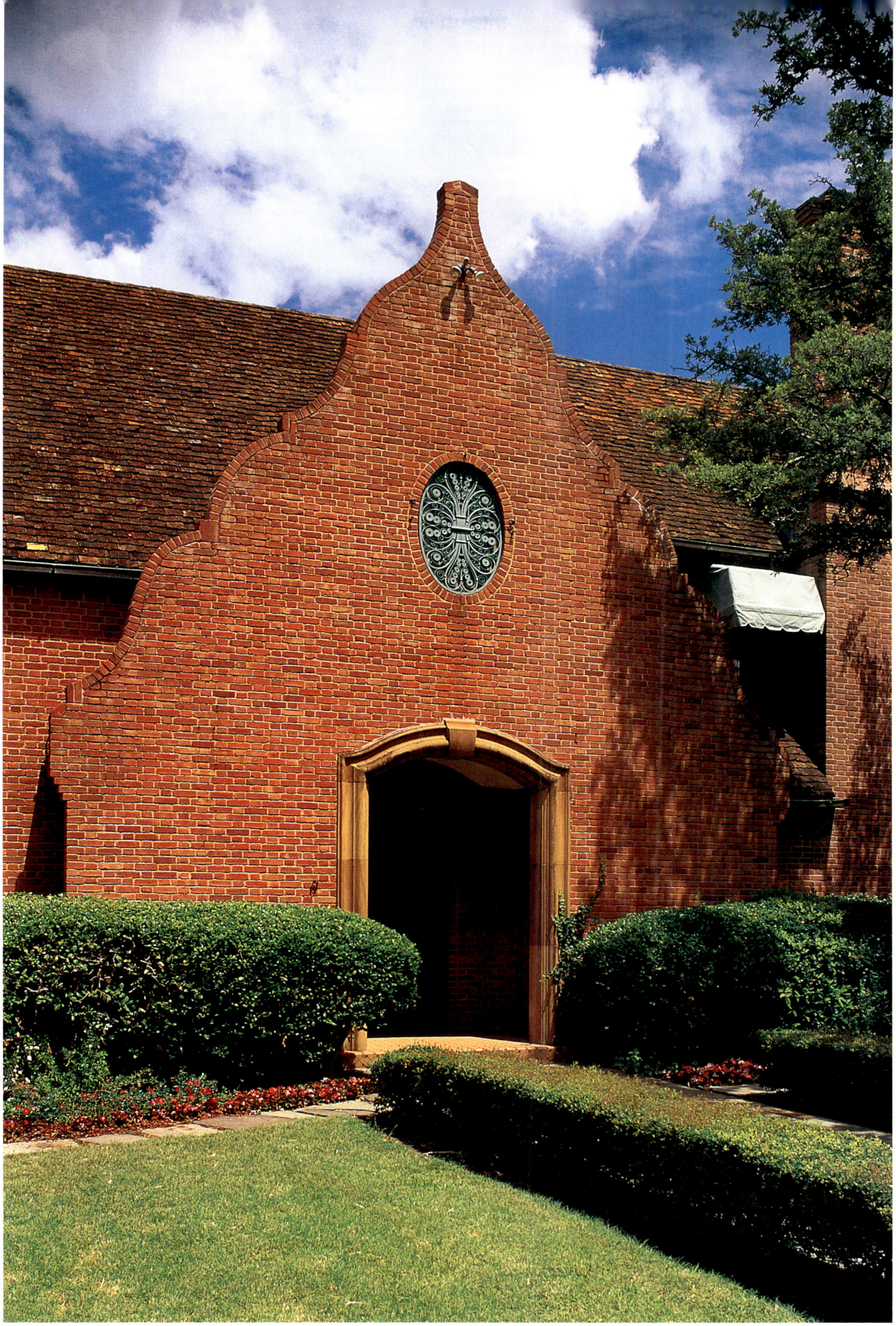

Gartner House, detail of gable.

mid-level library echoes an elliptically planned library entered from the landing level of the main stair in David Adler's Berney House. The two libraries (and the two houses) are not alike. It is rather the subject positions implicit in the intimately scaled "secret" library, suspended above grander reception rooms, that seem to have intrigued Staub's clients. The idiosyncrasies of the Gartner House suggest that Staub was responding to his clients' desire for a grandly appointed house. Even the lack of spatial continuity between its reception rooms perhaps stems from his interpretation of spatial arrangements appropriate to the way his clients lived. The Gartner House represents one of the most deliberate instances in which Staub sought to perform the resolution of contradictions through formal virtuosity. Here, architectural style figured as a kind of code both concealing and revealing the spatial operations involved in the social construction of upper-class identity and in framing subject positions to sustain assertions of superiority. Staub's unusual resort to Baroque flamboyance in designing the scalloped gable implies the scale of contradictions that confronted him in the Gartner commission and his inspired decision to tap the energies of these contradictions rather than ignore or suppress them.[14]

Staub's three Fort Worth houses of the 1920s seem keyed at a higher pitch than his contemporary Houston or Galveston houses, perhaps because of Staub's sensitivity to Fort Worth, where the elite social style is more exuberant than in Houston. During the early 1930s Staub designed additions to a house in River Crest for the lawyer George Thompson Jr., a nephew of Capt. James A. Baker of Houston. He also designed a house (that was not built) for the independent oilman Charles F. Roeser. Staub's Fort Worth clients, like most of his Houston clients of the 1920s, were identified with, if not always from, established families. All were members of the Fort Worth Club, the downtown businessmen's club, and the River Crest Country Club. Most shared a business connection with K. M. Van Zandt's Fort Worth National Bank. King, an entrepreneur from Brenham, Texas, near Houston, was founder of the King Ice Company and the King Candy Company.[15] He was a director of the Fort Worth National Bank. Herman Gartner, from Cibolo, Texas, near San Antonio, had worked as a young man for the Houston insurance firm that became Cravens, Dargan and Company.[16] He moved to Fort Worth in 1909. In 1914, the year after the organization of Mitchell, Gartner and Walton, a general insurance agency, Gartner married Elizabeth Reynolds, the daughter of Elizabeth L. Matthews and George T. Reynolds. Mrs. Gartner's father was a partner with his brother in the Reynolds Land and Cattle Company of Albany, Texas. Both brothers and their families retired to Fort Worth from their enormous cattle ranches in Shackelford and Throckmorton Counties

Gartner House, detail of door plate and handle.

(opposite)
Gartner House, detail of entrance portal.

in the early twentieth century, and Mrs. Gartner's uncle, William D. Reynolds, became a director of the Fort Worth National Bank.[17] W. D. Reynolds's daughter, Annie Merle, married Robert Ellison Harding, an officer of the bank and the brother of Blanche Harding Sewall, Ralph Adams Cram's Fort Worth–born Houston client.[18] The web of connections binding Staub's Fort Worth clients and his Houston clients and acquaintances exemplify the overlapping economic and social ties that reinforced elite standing and identity in both communities, which Staub's houses amplified and beautified.

John Staub told Howard Barnstone that the scalloped gable of the Gartner House was inspired by a seventeenth-century English house he saw during the summer of 1929 when he took a trip through Europe to examine the historic sources of the architecture he and other American country house architects had been so industriously producing during the 1920s.[19] Military service in England in World War I had given Staub little opportunity to study architectural sites and the years spent establishing his practice meant that not until 1929 did he make an effort to return to Europe for a more focused investigation. The impetus for this trip was a commission he received from the entrepreneur who was the Fort Worth counterpart of Jesse Jones, Amon G. Carter. Like Jones, Carter was a self-made man whose natural abilities as a salesman led him first into advertising, then newspaper publishing. A resident of Fort Worth since 1906, Carter worked his way up through the ranks of the advertising department of the *Fort Worth Star-Telegram* to become its president and publisher by 1923, the year after he expanded the paper into the realm of broadcasting by starting Radio WBAP.[20] In addition to his personal business activities, Carter promoted the founding and served as first chairman of the board of trustees of what is now Texas Tech University in Lubbock, Texas, its campus designed by William Ward Watkin and Sanguinet, Staats and Hedrick in 1924–25.[21] Carter also masterminded construction of the twelve-story Fort Worth Club Building in downtown Fort Worth in 1924–25 by Sanguinet, Staats and Hedrick, the most imposing urban clubhouse in Texas. Staub told Barnstone that Carter's commission had an unusual twist. Carter told Staub he was to work with his second wife, Nenetta Burton Carter, on the design of the house and give her whatever she asked for. However, Carter made clear from the outset that the house would never be built, and it was not.[22]

Staub's excursion through England, Scotland, Belgium, northern Germany, Italy, and destinations in Spain and France were reflected not only in the Tuscan villa he designed for Nenetta Carter (a reflection of the continuing appeal of Adler's Tuscan villa–style houses to Fort Worth's elite) but also in many of the grand houses he produced between late 1929 and 1935 during what turned out to be the bleakest years of the Great Depression. Staub, reflecting on his reaction to the buildings he visited and photographed in Europe, explained to Barnstone that he was seeking to avoid duplicating designs he had already produced.[23] The paradoxical opportunities with which he was presented to design especially opulent houses in the depths of the Depression enabled him to exorcise this fear. The grand houses Staub designed in River Oaks for J. Robert Neal and Hugh Roy Cullen were the most theatrical and "aristocratic" productions of his career. Both reflect the personal ambitions of the clients and the restraint Staub exercised in integrating subject positions into these very grand expressions of a desired identity.

In 1931, Marian Holt Seward and J. Robert Neal commissioned Staub to design a house on a three-and-three-quarters-acre site on Lazy Lane in the Homewoods section of River Oaks abutting the River Oaks Country Club golf course. James Robert Neal was the only surviving child of Elizabeth Mitchell and John W. Neal, who had moved to Houston in 1904 when their son was ten years old.[24] In 1886, J. W. Neal and Joel O. Cheek cofounded a wholesale grocery business in Nashville, Tennessee, that came to specialize in coffee roasting and sales as the Cheek-Neal Coffee Company, manufacturers of Maxwell House coffee.[25] After J. Robert Neal's graduation from Washington and Lee University and the Wharton School of Finance at the University of Pennsylvania, he married Marian Holt Seward, a parishioner of Christ Church, and became a vice president of Cheek-Neal, which was a family-run enterprise. By the mid 1920s, the Houston branch of the Cheek-Neal Coffee Company advertised itself as the largest coffee roasting operation in the United States west of the Mississippi River.[26] The magnitude of its operations became fully apparent in 1928 when the Postum Company (subsequently General Foods) bought the Cheek-Neal Coffee Company for $42 million, which was divided among the company's eight owners.[27] With his share of the proceeds, J. W. Neal bought controlling interest in Houston's Second National Bank. He became chairman of its board of directors and made his son a vice president. Mr. and Mrs. J. W. Neal were earnest and industrious. They were stalwart members of the Second Baptist Church and after 1928 became the primary benefactors of Memorial Hospital, Houston's Baptist hospital.[28] J. Robert Neal's very different personality and ambitions were evident in the instruction he gave Staub, in Staub's recollection, to design a "pure Louis Quinze" style house.[29] The Neal House, which was built between 1931 and 1933 by the Houston contractors West and Jensen for $169,659, would seem to have represented an unconscionable extravagance by the standards of the elder Neals.[30] The house is of reinforced concrete frame construc-

(opposite) Gartner House, detail of oval window and wrought-iron grille.

Perspective drawing of the street front of the Neal House, entrance driveway and forecourt, and great lawn, 1932, Olmsted Brothers, landscape architects. National Park Service, Frederick Law Olmsted National Historic Site.

(previous page)
J. Robert Neal House, Homewoods, River Oaks, Houston, 1931–33, John F. Staub, architect. Entrance forecourt.

tion, surfaced with Texas cream limestone and a slate roof. For Robert Neal, the house, its furnishings, and its landscape allowed him to distinguish himself from his parents and establish an aristocratic standard of domestic style in River Oaks. Unlike Bayou Bend, two house sites away, the Neal House is visible from Lazy Lane. Neal's explicit image of what he wanted in a house challenged Staub to satisfy his clients while maintaining the Houston consensus on what constituted appropriate expressions of upper-class identity.

Neal retained Olmsted Brothers of Brookline, Massachusetts, in late 1931 to plan his garden.[31] The Neal garden was the first ambitious garden to be carried out in River Oaks. When brand new, it was recognized in *Fortune* magazine as one of fourteen outstanding new country house gardens in the United States, substantiating Robert Neal's sense of stylistic leadership and stimulating Ima Hogg to begin work with the Houston landscape architect Ruth London to complete Bayou Bend's first designed garden, the East Garden, between 1932 and 1934.[32] On Staub's recommendation, Mr. and Mrs. Neal hired Jane Christian, a New York interior designer who had been a classmate of Madeleine Staub at Parsons, to design the interiors of the ground floor of the house. Miss Christian shared with Staub an economy of expression that allowed her to frame potentially troublesome, historically referential subjectivities with grace and flair.[33]

Contingency, eccentricity, and display were the bases of Staub's design of the Neal House. The splayed entry pavilion framed by the displayed wings of the dining room and library exemplify the application of these techniques. Symmetry is constructed eccentrically: it is contingent on viewers' visual adjustment and correction to make what is partial and dissimilar appear balanced and whole. The pedimented east elevation facing out to Lazy Lane, and the house's complex rear garden elevations, where the main stair bay bites into the splayed garden entrance pavilion, compel viewers not to notice the conflicts and asymmetries that abound but to edit, reframe, and perfect.[34] Staub treated composition as contingent on partial perception to spatialize the ambiguous circumstances under which a princely identity was displayed here. Rather than conceal the contradictions evident in these aspirations, Staub externalized them and, using the pretext of climatic responsiveness inherent in the house's one-room-deep, Z-plan formation, made architecture out of them.

Staub worked with his draftsmen, Milton McGinty (who had made his own European architecture tour as winner of the Rice Institute architecture department's first traveling scholarship in 1928) and Vance Phenix, to spatialize the house's eccentric, displayed plans.[35] The short main axis from the front entrance leads through the vaulted, lime-

Neal House, east elevation looking toward great lawn.

stone-paved and -cased reception hall out to the rear garden terrace, bypassing the rest of the house. An offset pair of splayed cross axes, the longer running past the staircase and library through the living room, garden room, and north terrace, and the shorter terminating in a column-framed dais above the sunken marble dining room, convey visitors to the reception rooms.

The French pavilion-and-wings organization of the Neal House gives the grandly scaled reception rooms (most with ceiling heights of thirteen feet, although the dining room is fifteen feet high) three, and in some cases four, exposures, with the major orientation being east-southeast toward Lazy Lane.

The major cross axis deflects visitors' awareness to the splayed jambs in which double doors to the library are set. This eccentric focus on the door jambs subliminally underscores the thickness and depth of the walls of the Neal House, spatializing the experience of passing from room to room and making the volumes of individual rooms seem whole, complete, and, paradoxically, simple. Parquet floors establish a continuous plane in the library, salon, and garden room. Coved ceilings subtly center and compose the large reception rooms. French doors, which slide into side pockets in the exterior walls, open these rooms to the limestone-paved and balustraded terraces with which Olmsted Brothers' designer, James F. Dawson, surrounded all of the reception rooms except the dining room.[36] On sunny days, these rooms are radiant with natural light. They feel transparent and open, a sensation enhanced by the French-style use of mirrors as architectural fixtures in most of the reception rooms, especially the long, salon-like living room. As at Bayou Bend, Staub incorporated antique artifacts in reception rooms to authenticate their Frenchness: a pair of curvilinear Numidian marble mantles in the salon, a neoclassical Numidian and white marble mantle in the garden room, and the extraordinary, flowing wrought iron rail that the limestone main stair was designed to accommodate.

The Empire-style dining room, with its Frasnes Rose marble dado and terrazzo floor and Loredo Chiaro marble columns and pilasters, is the most pretentious of the Neal House's reception rooms. It feels cold. In comparison, the garden room, where classical decor is collaged onto walls of dark blue polished plaster accented with a faceted plate glass mirror above the fireplace, feels "cool" in its sleek streamlining of historical precedent.

To compensate for the flatness of the lightly wooded site, James Dawson layered two levels of terraces along the back face of the living room wing—the upper terrace paved, the lower one planted—with the lower terrace stretching out alongside the kitchen wing and terminating in a rose garden (later replaced by a swimming pool) that stepped down

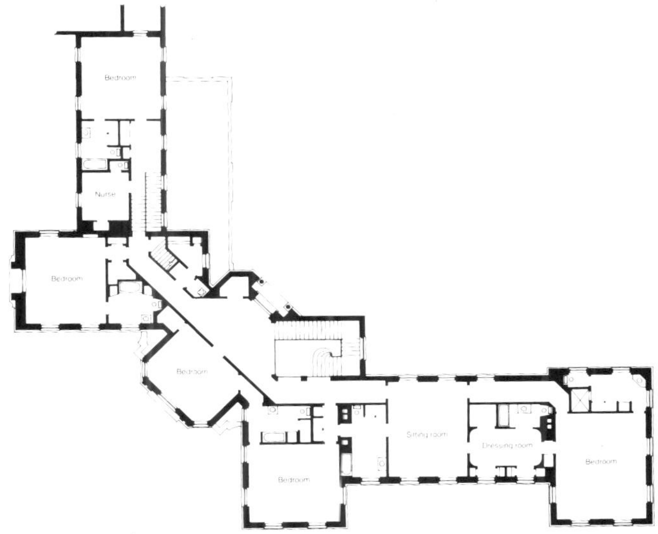

Second-floor plan

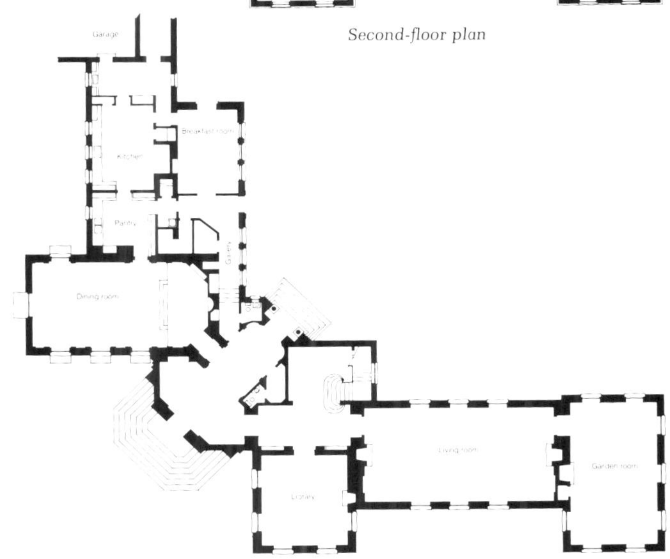

First-floor plan

Neal House.

(opposite)

Neal House, west lawn elevation viewed from the Venetian temple installed by Olmsted Brothers.

Neal House, antique mantle installed in living room.

Neal House, antique mantle installed in garden room.

(opposite) Neal House, axis of view from the garden room through the living room toward the front doors. The front doors replaced Staub's originals.

Neal House, staircase with eighteenth-century French wrought-iron rail.

to grade level. Along the north side property line a linear, hedge-enclosed flower garden rims one edge of the west lawn, which the displayed rear wings of the house frame. Olmsted Brothers marked the intersection of the two walks outlining the open edges of the lawn with a circular, domed garden temple. The walled garden court is centered on a fountain outside the garden room terrace. As inside the house, axes of movement and view imposed a coherent volumetric structure on the garden, materialized with massed evergreen plantings, terraces, balustrades, piers, walls, and walks. These framed such architectural episodes as the panels of decorative relief sculpture in the pediments above the entrance and over the living room wing, detailed by another recent Rice architecture graduate, Edward B. Arrants.[37]

The Neal House exhibited its owner's aristocratic ambitions by mobilizing eccentricity and display in an effort to naturalize the problematic building of "pure Louis Quinze" style architecture in 1933 in Houston. Staub sought to ground the evocations of a grand manner of domestic life in planimetric ingenuity, climatic responsiveness, country house openness to the out-of-doors, and a frank acknowledgement of the project's unconventionality. It was more difficult to sustain the plausibility of the identity position the historical models for the Neal House represented. What were the modern analogues of the Louis XV style? The problem such a question posed for the defense of an upper class in a democratic republic (especially in a time of severe economic contraction) was that these aristocratic identity and subject positions were so fictitious. Ima Hogg and Will Hogg used domestic architecture to materialize arguments for a civic identity for Houston and, more indirectly, advance their cultural and civic causes. Because Robert Neal did not figure as a civic leader or cultural arbiter in Houston, the social significance of his splendid house is ambiguous. The Neal House and gardens were Neal's greatest achievement. Unlike his father, he never attained standing in Houston's business community. During the one-term administration of Mayor R. H. Fonville (1937–39), Neal was appointed chairman of the city's Board of Park Commissioners. But in 1939 he was diagnosed with a brain tumor and died at the end of the year at age forty-five.[38] Neal was outlived by both his parents. It was his mother, Elizabeth Mitchell Neal (who lived until 1970), who would figure as the family philanthropist.[39] Neal's funeral was held at Second Baptist Church, suggesting the split in his allegiances between the practices of his parents' world and his seeming desire to transcend that world for an imagined realm of historical resonance, stateliness, and beauty. Marion Seward Neal owned the house until 1954, when she sold it to the independent oil producer John W. Mecom and his wife, Mary Elizabeth Withers.[40]

Neal House, dining room.

Neal House, detail of carved stone pediment on garden elevation.

The year the Neal House was completed, Staub was commissioned by Lillie Cranz and Hugh Roy Cullen to design a country house for their family that was as splendid as the Neal House. Constructed in 1934–35, also by West and Jensen, the Cullen House cost $289,852 according to Staub's office records.[41] This sum probably included the cost of furniture, other interior artifacts, and landscape improvements, which Staub's cost figure for the Neal House did not, since Hugh Roy Cullen made Staub responsible for these portions of the design. The site was the largest lot in Country Club Estates, a four-acre lot at River Oaks Boulevard and Inwood Drive flanking the River Oaks Country Clubhouse, a lot that Cullen expanded by buying the two-acre lot to the west. Although larger than the Neal property in Homewoods, the Cullen House site was more exposed to public view, which seems to have accorded with Cullen's desire to be identified as a leader and adhere to subject positions that would sustain this identity.

Cullen was an independent oil operator.[42] Born in San Antonio, he left school to go to work at age twelve. According to his biographers, Ed Wright and Theon Kilman, Cullen's brother-in-law got him a job as a cotton classer in Schulenberg, halfway between San Antonio and Houston, when he was nineteen. There he met Lillie Cranz, the daughter of a local businessman, Gustav Cranz, and the niece of

Hattie Kessler Neuhaus, the wife of W. O. Neuhaus. W. O. Neuhaus was the uncle of Lindeberg's original Houston client, Hugo Neuhaus.[43] As seems to have been the case in Schulenberg, prosperity led the Cranzes and other German-Texan families to assimilate to Anglo-American social identities. Lillie Cranz was sent to boarding school at St. Mary's Hall, the Episcopal girls' school in San Antonio.[44] In 1903 she married Roy Cullen, by then a cotton buyer in the Oklahoma Territory. The Panic of 1907 so adversely affected Cullen's cotton-buying business that he turned briefly to farming in Oklahoma before deciding in 1911 to return to Texas and enter the real estate business in Houston, where his father-in-law managed property. As Wright and Kilman wrote, Cullen's move coincided with the end of an expansionary cycle in Houston real estate.[45] Cullen then entered the oil business in 1918 as a wildcatter, using his persuasive ability to negotiate oil leases and, through observation and study, familiarize himself with topographical and geological conditions likely to indicate the presence of subsurface oil deposits. Not until 1921 did Cullen make his first successful strike, at Pierce Junction on the southern outskirts of Houston, through deep drilling in an oilfield presumed to have been exhausted.[46]

Wright and Kilman observe that deep drilling in abandoned fields became Cullen's specialty. The Houston lumberman and investor James M. West formed a partnership with Cullen to finance oil exploration in 1927.[47] In 1931, Cullen brought in his first big field at Thompsons in Fort Bend County, twenty-five miles south of Houston, which Wright and Kilman described as a $100 million field. Cullen and West sold their interest in the tract to the Humble Oil and Refining Company for $20 million in 1932. Cullen then terminated his partnership with West and organized the Quintana Petroleum Company with his son Roy G. Cullen, who had attended Rensselaer Polytechnic Institute and Rice; Isaac Arnold, an engineer and his son's Rensselaer roommate, who married Cullen's daughter Agnes; and the lawyer Harry Holmes.[48] In 1933, Quintana brought in the Tom O'Connor Field on the Tom O'Connor Ranch in Refugio County, one hundred forty miles down the coast from Houston, the largest oil discovery in southwest Texas in the first half of the twentieth century.[49] It was the sale of the Thompsons tract that prompted Cullen to buy the property in River Oaks (the family had lived since 1921 in a respectable foursquare house on Alabama Avenue in the South End) and commission a new house from Staub. The Tom O'Connor Field brought Cullen such extraordinary wealth that he came to conceive of the construction of his house "as a civic enterprise to help people who were out of work in the dark days of the depression."[50]

Staub told Barnstone that it was Lillie Neuhaus Carter, the wife of W. T. Carter Jr., who recommended Staub to Mr. and Mrs. Cullen.[51] Lil Carter's mother, Laura Boettcher Neuhaus, was the sister-in-law of two siblings of Lillie Cullen's mother in the interconnected world of Schulenberg's elite. Roy Cullen's newfound wealth notwithstanding, Mrs. Cullen's Schulenberg connections seem to have been indispensable to the family's assimilation by Houston's social elite. Roy Cullen was tough, decisive, independent, and assured. Staub's recollections to Barnstone confirm other attributes Cullen's biographers ascribed to him: honesty, fairness, confidence in the judgment of people whom he respected, and instinctive generosity.[52] Kilman and Wright emphasized the point that Cullen did not direct operations from his office in the Sterling Building in downtown Houston but participated personally in the frequently rough conditions that prevailed on his drilling sites. His biographers give the impression that Cullen would have had little time or patience for activities that didn't contribute directly to his work, not only cultural pursuits but leisure sports. The personal transformation that Staub's house and garden portended was Cullen's identification with subjective models of upper-class-ness with a conviction and purposefulness that mirrored his work ethic.

Cullen used his house and garden to frame himself as a civic leader, not just of local standing but, he seems to have hoped, of national consequence. The intimations of power that the Cullen House conveys were amplified through the Cullen's entertainments, the annual ritual of the Azalea Trail (Bayou Bend, the Neal garden, and the Cullen garden were the spectacular mainstays of the Azalea Trail into the 1950s), occasional publication, cultural patronage (Cullen was elected to the board of trustees of the Museum of Fine Arts, he was the first chairman of the board of regents of the University of Houston, and he was prevailed upon to serve as president of the Houston Symphony Society during the years of World War II), and philanthropy.[53] The year after Lillie and Roy Cullen and their two youngest daughters, Margaret and Wilhelmina, moved into the River Oaks house (their three elder children, Roy Gustav, Lillie, and Agnes, had married by 1935), Roy Gustav Cullen, then thirty-two years old, was killed in an oilfield accident.[54] Beginning with a gift to the University of Houston in 1936 to construct its first permanent building as a memorial to Roy Gustav Cullen, Mr. and Mrs. Cullen embraced philanthropy on a scale unmatched in Houston since William M. Rice had endowed the Rice Institute in 1891 and George Hermann had endowed Hermann Hospital and donated the property for Hermann Park in 1914. Although the Cullen Foundation, established in 1947 with assets then estimated to be worth $160 million, was not the first philanthropic foundation in Houston, it was the first to which the donors committed significant assets and made significant grants during their lifetimes.[55] Lillie and Roy Cullen set a standard of philanthropic beneficence

(overleaf) Hugh Roy Cullen House, River Oaks, Houston, 1933–35, John F. Staub, architect. East elevation.

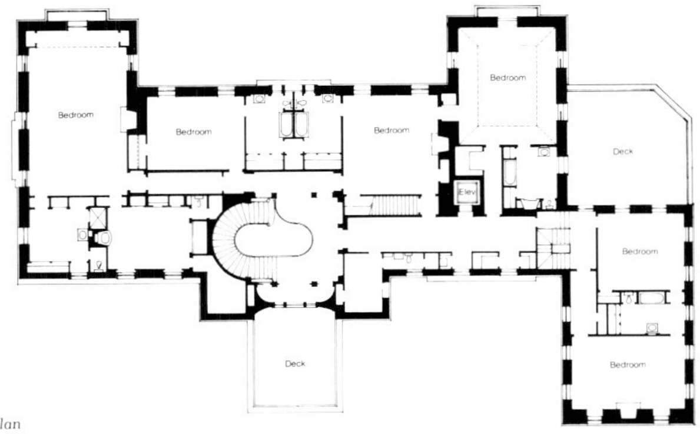

Second-floor plan

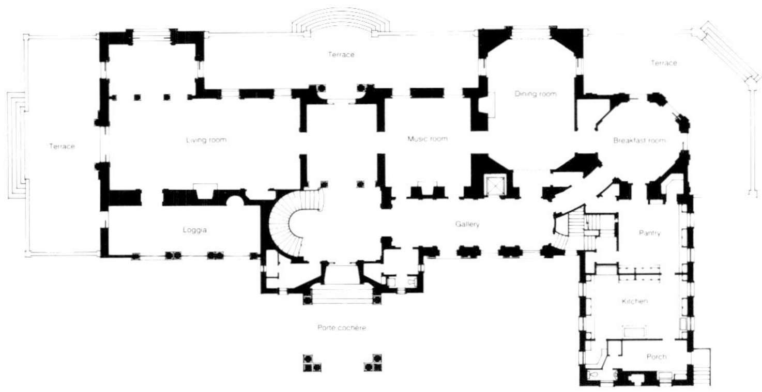

First-floor plan

Cullen House.

that did not begin to be matched in a systematic way by other Houston donors and foundations until the 1950s. Yet Staub's house and gardens did not underpin Cullen's emergence as a political leader. Jesse Jones and Will Clayton were the Houston business leaders who would ascend to national and international recognition during the Roosevelt and Truman administrations. Cullen's social vision lacked the liberality of his personal generosity. His strident opposition to the New Deal (shared by most Texas economic and political elites, including some who figured prominently in the New Deal) meant that he remained on the margins politically.[56] He used his wealth to lobby politicians and public opinion on the threats that government regulation, free trade, and socialism posed to individualism, states rights, and economic liberalism. In the early 1950s he briefly championed the activities of the U.S. senator from Wisconsin, Joseph McCarthy.[57] Staub's house spatialized the patrician virtues represented by Cullen's philanthropy and support of Houston cultural institutions, but the house's grandeur externalized the contradictions involved in seeking to legitimize aristocratic leadership in a democratic republic. The Cullen House too successfully elevated and isolated Roy Cullen to legitimize the political discourse on conservative populism he promoted.[58]

Staub's design of the Cullen House was not as complex as that of the Neal House, in part because of differences in their sites. The Cullen House had the desired north-south orientation. Staub followed the practice, established by earlier houses with corner sites on River Oaks Boulevard, of facing the house toward the east-west cross street rather than the boulevard. Automobile access to the house is from a gateway facing River Oaks Boulevard, which leads visitors into a paved motor court in what would otherwise be the backyard. The garden front of the house faces south toward Inwood. To ensure privacy, the house was set well back on its two-hundred-foot-deep site, with axially aligned gardens extending forward from the south front. Staub aligned the reception rooms in a row behind the symmetrical garden elevation. At the east end is a living room, forty-three feet, five inches by twenty-one feet, ten inches in area, with a columned music alcove projecting off the southeast end of the room. As in other ground-floor reception rooms, the ceiling is thirteen feet high. A limestone-paved and -cased loggia parallels the living room on the north overlooking the motor court. The central hall, sixteen feet wide, is subdivided by a screen of polished marble columns with Ionic capitals into an apsidal entry foyer, containing the cantilevered spiral stair, and a reception hall that opens onto the garden terrace. A whitewood-paneled library, nearly square in plan at nineteen-and-a-half feet by twenty-one feet, two inches, and the dining room, a rectangle in plan, nineteen feet, ten inches by thirty-one feet, two inches in size with chamfered corners, fill out the west end of the house. Projecting from the far west end was an octagonal breakfast room. Deeply cased doorways are aligned to form a cross axis of movement and view through the house from the breakfast room to the living room. A vaulted, cross-axial gallery with access to the library and dining room connects the entry hall to a service wing that projects off the northwest corner of the house. The living room and dining room have three exposures. Slender steel-sash windows with floor-level sills slide into side pockets, opening reception rooms to terraces on the east, south, and southwest fronts of the house. Because the north galleries are also glazed, the interiors are suffused with light. The reception rooms are exhilarating because of daylight reflecting off parquet floors in the sitting and dining rooms and the gray-and-white polished marble floors in the hall and cross-gallery.

The treatment of spaces on the first floor of the Cullen House reflects Roy Cullen's personal attributes in the straightforwardness and clarity of the plan and in the generous dimensions and expansive proportions of the reception rooms. As in the Neal House, views to the garden connect reception rooms to nature, lightening and simplifying the perceptual impact of the classical architectural decoration. In the living room, the long north wall is centered on a grandly scaled neoclassical marble mantle, flanked by pilaster-framed, solidly paneled double doors beneath arched panels. A crisp but unemphatic dado belts the lower quarter of the elevation while a neoclassical entablature, half as high as the dado, rings the top of the elevation. This frame modulates the wall plane, articulating its proportional composure. It establishes the social role of architectural decoration as the construction of a matrix that rhythmically frames and heroically elevates its subjects. Staub individualized rooms with the design of decorations. The dentils that run above the fascia band in the living room entablature are shaped like tassels. Pilasters in the dining room and second-floor stair hall have a quarter-circle plan profile and are fluted. They terminate not in outward flaring capitals (the conventional vertical terminus) but in tapered anthemia. Staub inserted air-conditioning registers in the living room entablature (the Cullen House was built with a central air-conditioning system) by reiterating the vertical fluting of the fascia band in the detailing of vertical louvers, as if to suggest the evolutionary absorption of advanced technology by "tradition." Staub streamlined tradition with his design of the sparkling crystal anthemia, mounted like jewels in lightweight, cast aluminum lyres and framed by the slender crystal balusters supporting the stair rail. The themes of sleekness and transparency that the decorative use of aluminum and crystal materialize are reiterated in the cast aluminum screen of the front door, its flanking sidelights, and segmentally arched transom, all backed with plate glass and, during the day, backlit by sunlight streaming into the entrance hall from the garden front of the house. The sidelights and transom are hinged so they can be opened to facilitate ventilation. Practical usefulness and the streamlining of decoration advance implicit arguments about the contemporary relevance of classical design practices and the capacity of their subjects to integrate modern and traditional identities. Staub's quotations of John Soane in the Cullen House, most evident in the cast plaster Greek keys encircling the shallow handkerchief vault that ceils the double-height stairwell, affiliated him with the nineteenth-century English architect who was of particular interest to eclectic architects in the early 1930s because Soane seemed to be searching for ways to reinvigorate the language of classical architecture through linear abstraction and volumetric expansion.[59]

The scale of the Cullen House and especially the cross-axial *enfilade* of aligned doorways construct monumentality, as if to magnify Roy Cullen and his guests with spatially induced sensations of empowerment. As in Staub's other grand houses, the effect is to transform movement into procession. The exteriors of the house exert the same sensation, especially the short east elevation facing River Oaks Boulevard and the long south elevation facing Inwood. The detailing of wall surfaces is simple and straightforward: a modillioned cornice supporting the eaves of the low-pitched hipped roof, a pair of belt courses—one above, the other below, the shuttered, second-floor windows—and ceremonial portals supported by single or paired Ionic columns framing ground-floor openings at center and end points. Other ground-floor windows are framed by architraves consisting of a narrow molded band capped with an anthemion in low relief, an echo of the garden door at Bayou Bend. Centrality, symmetry, and figuration, allied with the horizontality of the garden front of the Cullen House, endow it with a spatial authority Staub reciprocated in his planning of the landscape. Camellia allées were projected forward of the two wings framing the south elevation, outlining a broad central grass terrace on axis with the recessed body of the house. Another grass terrace containing an axial reflecting basin was projected forward of the east elevation of the house. The simplicity and consistency of the composition, detailing, and landscape of the Cullen House supported its assertion of formal authority, advancing a coherent identity position.

The Neal and Cullen Houses are grand. As works of architecture they continue to impress. As works of social construction they were problematic, in part because they are such accomplished works of architecture. Staub's houses were so rigorous and consistent formally that they leave no room for unintended departures from their cogently framed identity positions. The Neal House is the embodiment of a

Cullen House, north elevation facing motor court.

Cullen House, south elevation facing garden. The swimming pool terrace is an early twenty-first-century addition by the Houston landscape architects McDugald-Steele.

Cullen House, living room.

Cullen House, entrance hall and stair.

Cullen House, gallery.

(above)
Cullen House, library.
(below)
Cullen House, view through aligned doorways.

Cullen House, view from music alcove in living room to garden allée.

Cullen House, dining room.

personal vision that seems disconnected from its time and place, for all of Staub's and James Dawson's ingenuity in linking it to its site and constructing coherence through design. The Cullen House lacks the element of fantasy that is both the charm and unacknowledged contradiction of the Neal House. The identity and subject positions it advances are comprehensible and grounded. The contradictions it failed to address were to reconcile Roy Cullen's desire to be seen as grand with his concern for the welfare of ordinary people and his ambition to affect public policy. The country house was in part about disciplining and beautifying power. Cullen's house framed him as powerful. But because it did so, it framed his politics as reactionary (certainly not the interpretation he would have chosen): a bastion of privilege from which he opposed public social policies that, as a philanthropist, he funded with magnanimity. As an instrument of upper-class identity, the country house could frame the liberality of its subjects (as Bayou Bend did for Ima Hogg). It could also frame them as patrician rather than aristocratic (as Birdsall Briscoe's houses for Will Clayton did; Clayton's summer house is just two doors down from the much more imposing Cullen House). The absence of a country house could shift architectural frames of reference to other building types, for instance the skyscraper office buildings and hotels that identified Jesse Jones as a builder of cities (even though Mary Gibbs and Jesse Jones lived in a very grand penthouse apartment Staub designed for them in 1927–28 on top of the Lamar Hotel in downtown Houston). The Cullen House exposed Cullen's political pronouncements to charges of elitism. The theatrical exposition of superiority on which the grand house was premised, and its vulnerability to invidious criticism, account for the suspicion with which grandeur was regarded by American country house architects after the eclipse of the stately home era of the 1890s and early 1900s.

What distinguishes the Neal and Cullen Houses is the rigor and delight with which Staub sought, through composition, proportion, ingenious planning, and inventive detailing, to ensure the reality of each house for its occupants. Other grand country houses built in or near Houston in the late 1920s—James Ruskin's Bailey's design of the manorial-style house for John H. Kirby of 1926, Alfred C. Finn's Newport-like classical "cottage" at Bay Ridge for Ross S. Sterling of 1928, and Joseph Finger's Mediterranean villa–type ranch house for James M. West at Clear Lake of 1929—were impressive externally but developed internally with copied historical detailing and perfunctory spaces.[60] Staub's houses are neither lugubrious nor vacant. They induce sensations of excitement and enjoyment in their subjects; they make people happy to be in them. They challenge their owners, though, to be just as rigorous, enlightened, and unsentimental in their ambitions.

Cullen House, detail of stair rail.

Staub's grandest houses from the mid-1930s to the early 1940s retreated from the stylistic effusion of the Great Depression years, reflecting their clients' expectations as well as marking a simplifying trend in Staub's work after 1935. The house he designed for Lottie Rice and Stephen P. Farish on Lazy Lane in 1934, built between 1934 and 1936 by A. A. Bertelsen for $89,460, exemplified this trend.[61] Stephen Power Farish was the younger brother of William S. Farish; Lottie Rice Farish was the younger sister of Mrs. Hugo Neuhaus and the cousin of Mrs. William S. Farish. Steve Farish and another brother, Robert, came to the oilfields of Electra in northwest Texas in 1913 from the University of the South, where Steve Farish had studied engineering.[62] Both worked their way up in the oil field hierarchy. Steve Farish became a driller and Bob Farish a scouting and leasing specialist. Both brothers were affiliated with the Humble Oil and Refining Company from the time of its formation until the early 1920s, with Steve Farish departing in 1922 to organize his own drilling contracting company, FWC, with two veteran drillers, E. E. Watts and J. A. Collins; the affiliated F-W-C Royalty Company; and in 1925 the Navarro Oil Company. In 1925 Farish bought controlling interest in the Reed Roller Bit Company, which manufactured the cross-roller drilling bit used in rotary drilling equipment for oil wells. Under Farish's direction, Reed Roller Bit grew to be second in size to the Hughes Tool Company as a producer of oil field tools and technology. Farish was a sportsman and a polo player, one of the original members of the Houston Riding and Polo Club. Lottie Farish was an amateur actress. During the late 1920s and 1930s she frequently performed, sometimes in starring roles, with Frederick Leon Webster's Little Theater.[63] As might be expected given their family backgrounds, Mr. and Mrs. Farish belonged to the Houston Country Club and the River Oaks Country Club. They and their children, Stephen Jr. and Joan, were parishioners of Palmer Memorial Church.[64]

The scale of the house, which Mr. and Mrs. Farish called Ravenna, is deceptive. Staub repeated the practice he began at the Neal House of installing second-floor windows that open from floor-level sills, like those on the first floor. These visually reduce the apparent scale of the exterior elevations, which, despite the pedimented Tuscan portico on the northwest street front of the house and the even grander full-width, double-height Tuscan portico on the southeast garden elevation, does not become fully apparent until visitors approach the house and apprehend its true size. Black-painted Lindeberg shutters reinforce this perception because their big scale is consistent with the size of all other openings.

Walls of white-painted brick and roofs surfaced with cypress shingles give the Farish House an appearance of

Cullen House, stair hall with vaulted ceiling.

(opposite)
Cullen House, detail of front door.
(overleaf)
Stephen P. Farish House, Homewoods, River Oaks, Houston, 1934–36, John F. Staub, architect. Entrance (west) elevation.

Farish House, detail of black-painted shutters, concealing the window that is now a china cabinet.

self-effacing simplicity. The arabesques of anthemia in the black-painted iron stanchions are virtually the only architectural decoration except for the curved pediment framing the central door on the garden elevation.

Therefore, the spatial impact on entering the house is completely unexpected. The axial central hall, nineteen feet wide and terminating in a spiral stair, is monumental and dramatic. Arched over-doors in the hall, double-framed and inset, reproduce a design from the early-nineteenth-century Virginia house Oatlands.

The rectangular living room is isolated in a wing that outflanks the body of the house. It is approached from the entrance hall on a cross axis tunneled between the library and the cloakroom through a series of arched portals. Looking back from the living room, these portals frame a vista that penetrates the sweeping dining room and concludes in the breakfast room beyond, which is surfaced with scenic wallpaper.

The understatement with which Staub spatially embodied sensations of grandeur in the Farish House is impressive. Unlike the Neal and Cullen Houses, the exterior does little to prepare visitors for the scale of the interior, intensifying the sense of excitement and surprise that the interiors disclose. Staub built in additional surprises. A bookshelf in the paneled library and a pediment-crowned china closet in the dining room are set into window openings and hinged, so that the entire compartment—fully loaded—can be swung outward to reveal the window behind.

The entrance portico is Anglo-Palladian, complementing the symmetrical block, wing, and pavilion organization of the house. The garden portico, with its Deep South overtones (evoking the Farish family's connection to Jefferson Davis; he was the brothers' great-uncle), imbues the simple house with monumental scale and gives proportion and measure to the broad, flat backyard.

In the Farish House, as in Staub's other country houses after the mid-1930s, simplicity masked, and grandeur elevated, the occupants of these houses. Grand houses could be construed as just slightly larger versions of neighboring suburban houses rather than as radically different from them in size, expense, and pretension, architecturally implying the existence of a community that was not polarized by disparities of wealth and power. Externally, the patrician consensus on proper form was reinforced and with it the appearance of upper-class solidarity. Yet inside and behind, these houses rewarded their occupants by delivering exhilarating sensations of expansiveness, empowerment, and their logical corollary, entitlement. Staub's grand houses also demonstrate Staub's attentiveness to the nuances of his clients' personalities. The drama and surprise of the Farish House are particular to it and seem to represent Staub's interpretation of the subjective characteristics of its owners.

In the same way, the country house Staub designed in Beaumont for Mary Randolph and J. Cooke Wilson exhibits a certain idiosyncrasy within the context of the grand house that individualized the owners without overtly calling attention to them. The Wilson House was built between 1935 and 1937 for $84,750.[65] It is set in the center of a flat, rectangular city block in the Averill addition, an extension of the city's orthogonal, nineteenth-century street-and-block grid, one and three-quarters miles west of downtown Beaumont. During the consolidation that the oil industry underwent in Texas in the second decade of the twentieth century, Beaumont forfeited to Houston the opportunity it might have had to become a regional headquarters for oil businesses. Beaumont was the site of the Magnolia Petroleum Company's major refinery, served by pipeline connections to the Oklahoma oil fields, which kept the refinery operating (as it did the Texas Company's major refinery in nearby Port Arthur) after the exhaustion of Spindletop and other early oilfields along the upper Texas Gulf coast in the 1900 decade.[66] But in 1925 the city's fortunes rebounded when the Beaumont-based oil operator Marrs McLean and the driller M. Frank Yount reopened the Spindletop field with deep flank drilling.[67] Although not as momentous as the first Spindletop discovery, the reopening of the Spindletop field had a more substantive impact on the economy of Beaumont, which sprouted a skyline of downtown office and hotel buildings twelve to nineteen stories tall in the late 1920s and filled out the neighborhood where the Wilson House was built with suburban country houses for elite Beaumont families.[68] Frank Yount's two Beaumont partners built what remain the largest dwellings in the city. Mabel Lee and Talbott F. Rothwell had the Russell Brown Company of Houston design and build a ponderous three-story house in Beaumont's garden subdivision, Caldwood, in 1929.[69] The wholesale grocer John Henry Phelan, secretary-treasurer of Yount's company, and his wife, Johanna Cunningham, hired the Atlanta architect Owen J. Southwell to design their neo-Georgian country house on a flat thirty-acre tract west of the Averill addition in 1927. Completed in 1930, the Phelan House was one of if not the most expensive house built in Texas in the 1920s.[70] In comparison to the Rothwell and Phelan Houses, the Wilson House was an object lesson in architectural refinement and patrician restraint.

To avoid calling attention to the perceptual problem that extensive flatness causes, Staub sited the Wilson House in the middle of the block, giving it emphatic relationships to the parallel east-west streets, Evalon and Ashley, that its long north and south elevations face. The Houston landscape architect C. C. Pat Fleming installed allées of massed aza-

Farish House, detail of cast- and wrought-iron stanchion silhouetted against white-painted brick background.

Farish House, living room.

Farish House, detail of antique mantle installed in living room.

leas, backed by sweet gum trees, to frame the projecting end bays of the symmetrical south elevation facing Ashley Avenue and reciprocate Staub's composition of the house.

The north elevation, facing Evalon Avenue, was more complex and idiosyncratic as Staub qualified its symmetry to incorporate a shed-roofed extension of the service wing at the west end of the house, attached to a screen wall separating the motor court in front of the house from a walled west-side service court. Staub also incorporated the one- and two-story, three-car garage in this complex. Instead of setting the garage back from the street, he put it on the front property line along Evalon. Staub composed difference on the north face of the Wilson House by constructing a hierarchy of spaces that highlights the ceremonial portion of the Wilson House's north elevation, then efficiently fills up what would otherwise be a flat, vacuous plane. The Wilson House uses what Hewitt discerned as a trace of New Orleanian urbanity to construct a narrative of belonging. Staub's liberal use of wrought and cast iron reinforced the New Orleanian theme and affiliated the Wilson House with the Latin Colonial discourse on what Beaumont's historic architectural identity ought to have been. Discreetly, the Wilson House was advanced as more securely and poetically connected to the place where it was built than the larger, more opulent Phelan and Rothwell Houses.

The reception rooms of the Wilson House, like those in Staub's other grand houses, were designed for hospitality. The living room (thirty-one feet, ten inches long by sixteen feet wide) is framed by the dining room on the west and a library on the east (both eighteen feet wide and twenty-one feet long). French doors and twelve-over-twelve-pane windows opening from floor-level sills connect the house and its grounds. Cross-axes of movement and view link the dining and living rooms as well as the entry hall and an additional reception room, the garden room (which is twenty-eight feet long and seventeen feet, nine inches wide). The garden room floor is paved with polished terrazzo. Its fireplace opening is outlined with molded Stueben glass and vert antique marble.

Staub incorporated a decorative motif in the detailing of reception rooms, an unusual practice for him. This was an elongated hexagon, which appears as a border around the perimeter of the terrazzo floor, in the panels of the dining room doors, and, in a curvilinear variation, the cast-iron stair rail.

The Wilson House contains additional examples of streamlined decor: the triglyph-like returns on the edges of the stair risers and the subtly stepped profiling where walls and ceilings intersect. The latter detail is pervasive but so understated as to hardly call attention to itself. It looks modernistic but, when compared to Staub's more conventional classical decor, reads as a reduced and abstracted classicism:

Farish House, stair with view into library.

Farish House. Garden (east) elevation.

Farish House, detail of china cabinet inset in dining room window aperture.

(opposite)
Farish House, vista from living room through dining room to breakfast room.

(overleaf)
J. Cooke Wilson House, Beaumont, 1935–37, John F. Staub, architect. Garden (south) elevation.

2550

Wilson House, entrance (north) elevation.

Wilson House, detail of stair rail.

Wilson House, detail of marble- and glass-framed fireplace opening in garden room.

stacked, oversailing bands minus the decoration. This asperity did not prevent Staub from applying Ionic pilasters and an entablature to the dining room. With nonchalance, the Wilson House constructs subjects that are sophisticated, stylish, up-to-date, and liberated from the social newcomer's temptation to dress up in clichés of class identity. Spatial generosity, formal assurance, and a graceful accommodation to one's place are implicitly identified as the patrician virtues the Wilson House (and its subjects) embody.

Neither Mary nor Cooke Wilson was from Beaumont. Wilson began his working life in banking in his hometown, Meridian, Mississippi (where his father was a manufacturer of brick and tile products), before coming to Beaumont in 1902 at the age of twenty-three to represent a group of Meridian oil investors. The next year Wilson entered the oil business as an independent producer. He was involved in oil production in the Texas coastal fields and in Kansas, Oklahoma, and Louisiana. Wilson was one of the independents who pooled their interests to start the Humble Oil and Refining Company in 1917, although he withdrew, remaining in Beaumont and continuing to function as an independent. He married Mary Randolph of Sherman, Texas, in 1908, and they were the parents of four children. In addition to his oil interests, Wilson invested in other Beaumont businesses and real estate. He was a member of the Beaumont Club and the Beaumont Country Club. He and his family were parishioners of St. Mark's Episcopal Church, of which he was a vestryman.[71] Both Mary and Cooke Wilson were gardeners. The siting of the Wilson House on its block suggests that Mr. and Mrs. Wilson may have anticipated the block's future subdivision, perhaps as building sites for their children. However, during their lifetimes the block was not subdivided, functioning, at least visually, as a landscaped park in the Averill addition neighborhood.

Like Mr. and Mrs. Wilson when they built their house, Staub's clients for the grandest house he designed in Dallas, the lawyer Alex S. Camp and his wife, Roberta Coke, were middle-aged (they had no children) and required a house for entertaining. Staub told Barnstone that he took the job with some trepidation as Roberta Camp had worked with a succession of architects—H. B. Thomson of Dallas, Joseph Urban of New York, and Addison Mizner of Palm Beach—without satisfaction.[72] Staub recalled that, at a dinner party given by Mr. and Mrs. Camp, he introduced himself to another guest as Mrs. Camp's "latest" architect. Word got back to his hostess, and Staub liked to believe she went through with the house just to demonstrate she was not indecisive and capricious. The Camps' other architects had in common a reputation for designing picturesque Mediterranean-style houses. Given this commonality, what is so striking about the Camp House was Staub's construction of grandeur through austerity.

Staub extended the Camp House in a one-room-deep linear plan on a flat shelf at the crest of a long slope down to White Rock Lake, a city reservoir at the time of construction.[73] The Camps' twenty-three-acre property was on the south shore of the lake, so the house required exposures to both the south (for ventilation, although it was designed with a central air-conditioning system) and north (for the view of the lake).

The house was built on Garland Road east of downtown Dallas. In the 1920s, the garden suburb of Highland Park, north of downtown, surpassed older east-side neighborhoods, notably Munger Place, as the preferred elite neighborhood in Dallas. Mr. and Mrs. Camp demonstrated their "old Dallas" affiliation by building on the east side. As at the Farish House, the walls of the Camp House are white-painted brick. The house is lit by thin, steel-framed, floor-level windows that slide into side pockets in the walls. The windows are big in scale, as are the Lindeberg shutters with which many of the openings are outfitted. The one- and two-story house is capped with low-pitched, standing-seam copper roofs. The Camp House was designed and built between 1936 and 1938 for $80,978. D. F. Steele of Dallas was the builder.[74]

With the Camp House, Staub moved beyond the use of historical models to attempt an unmediated exposition on "good form" by spatially portraying a patrician conception of grandeur. The house's clarity, frankness, and generosity identify the "innate" virtues of the essential patrician subject, which can make such forms of social composure as symmetry seem superfluous, even affected. The reception rooms of the Camp House are not as austere as the planes and slopes of the exterior. Yet they further the social construction of elite identity by reasserting the innate stylishness of the patrician subject, constructing a subjective interiority that is complementary to the house's external aspect yet more complex in its tendency toward expansiveness, warmth, and surprise. Because of the linear plan of the Camp House, the entrance and stair hall has exposure to the north toward White Rock Lake. The vista through the front door frames the façade of the Mount Vernon–like Thomas Pickett House of 1929 on the east shore of the lake (which, by the time the Camp House was completed, had become home to Dallas's richest, most flamboyant independent oilman, H. L. Hunt).

This vista fixes the Camp House to its site by constructing visual continuity with a house whose historic model made it a Dallas landmark.[75] One way Staub imparted complex interiority to the Camp House was to subdivide the expansive interior volumes with paneled alcoves. The entrance doors are set in one such alcove. All the panels in this enclosure contain doors that conceal the compressed, but composed, spatial complexity layered behind the serene surface of the

Alex Camp House, Dallas, 1936–38, John F. Staub, architect. Entrance (south) elevation.

Camp House, north elevation overlooking White Rock Lake.

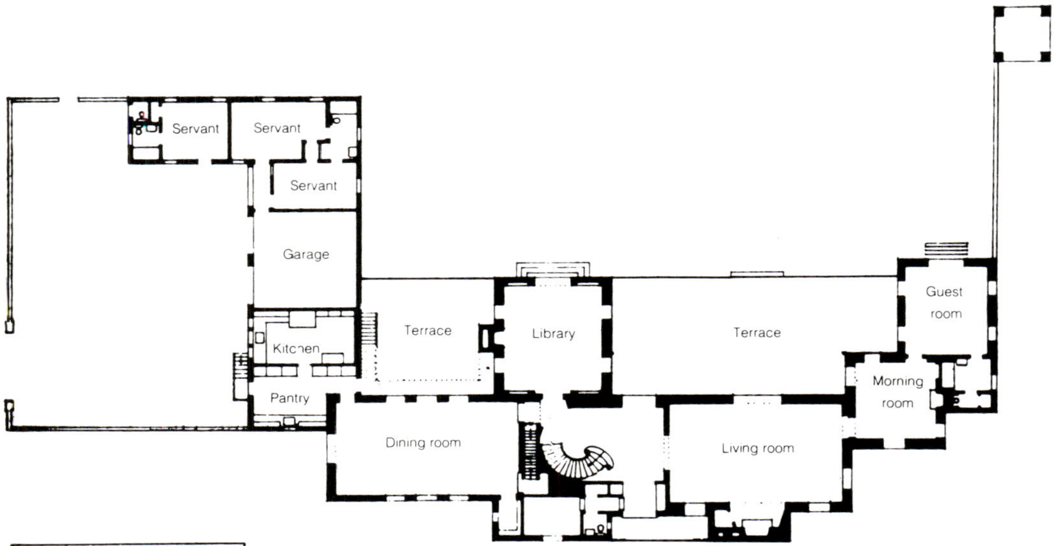

First-floor plan

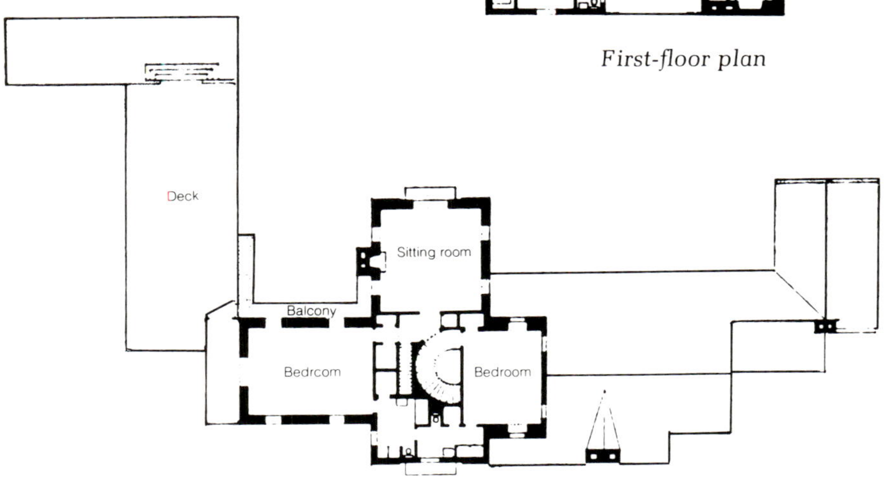

Second-floor plan

Camp House.

house, affording access not only to closets but a "secret" cloakroom and guest toilet.

The broad living room, lit from windows on three sides, contains a paneled alcove housing the mantle-less fireplace. The alcove paneling, the double doors opening into the living room, and the sheltering tray ceiling are finished with redwood, dulled with a semi-opaque finish so that its warmth is distilled and does not compete tonally with the polished wide plank floors running the long dimension of the room and continuing the axis of movement and view from the entry hall with its spiral stair.

The sliding steel and glass windows ensure that views of the landscape initially dominate visitors' impression of the living room. The scale and placement of the windows at centers and corners bring the large room into contact with daylight and the ground plane on three sides. Symmetry opens, enlightens, and discloses in the Camp living room. It fixes, centers, and composes, too, but these attributes are

Camp House, view through dining room toward White Rock Lake with steel-framed windows slid into side pockets.

Camp House, entrance alcove.

sublimated in the more obvious connections to the out-of-doors. The offset plan of the house enables subjects to move between rooms on implied diagonal paths, enhancing their awareness of the volumetric qualities of rooms. The morning room, offset between the living room and the guest bedroom at the east end of the house, has four exposures as a result.

Its exotic identity is encoded in its reflective silver-leaf ceiling, hand-blocked wallpaper, and bamboo moldings. Polished parquet floors and the monumental scale of the windows contribute to the complex experience of this space, which is simultaneously intimate and exposed, accessible yet precious. Because the morning room connects the living room to the guest room, the complex feelings engendered by this simple, square-planned room are enhanced by the projection of interior vistas through adjacent rooms as well as to the out-of-doors. The library, with its walls of flush-set, polished harewood, and the dining room, which at thirty-five feet in length is one foot longer than the living room, feel very open to the landscape. The spatial fluidity of the interiors and the consistency and continuity of proportions and finishes enable this long house to be experienced as a whole rather than a sequence of parts.

Yet, as Staub's set of architectural drawings of the Camp House disclose, the design took shape in a discontinuous process of revision, expansion, and simplification. After the construction contract was awarded in February 1937, spaces were reshuffled, with the kitchen and pantry being relegated to the garage wing so that the dining room could

Camp House, living room looking toward entrance hall.

occupy what was to have been the service wing. What was originally to have been the dining room became the library, and what was to have been the library became the morning room. Alternative study sketches document the process by which the front entrance portal migrated from a conventional, historically modeled design to a much simpler and more rigorous design during July and August 1937. Notations on these sketches indicate that Roberta Camp was very involved in this process. Alternative sketch perspectives and elevations by Staub's associate, Donald Barthelme, from August through October 1937 for the new dining room and library display the process of simplifying what, initially, were exuberant modernistic decorative themes. Most dramatic was the redesign of the main stair in November 1937. After the house was completed, chromium-plated brass stair rails were replaced with the present redwood rails following numerous alternative studies by Barthelme between October 1938 and January 1939. Rather than confusing and compromising Staub's design, these alterations consistently clarified and refined it. The spatial construction of an essential patrician subjectivity at the Camp House emerged from a process of negotiation between client and architect.[76]

Camp House, detail of marble- and bamboo-framed fireplace in morning room.

The Camp House is episodic but not picturesque. It persuasively presents itself as noble and rigorous, not through decoration but through the spatial construction of implied subjects whose personal qualities could not be otherwise if they were to do justice to this house. The house spatially encourages and rewards its inhabitants for internalizing and

Camp House, morning room looking toward rear terrace and guest room.

enacting patrician subject roles so that they too, as Aldrich might observe, can be blessed by the grace of upper-class magnanimity, composure, and beauty that the country house was designed to bestow.

When completed in 1939, Staub's grand country house for Ella Rice and James O. Winston Jr. lay in the country west of Houston. The house, which cost $95,340, was built by Pete Miller on a small estate bordering Buffalo Bayou.[77] The Winston property had been part of the weekend place owned by Will and Steve Farish, where they stabled horses. It bordered the weekend place of Lil Neuhaus and W. T. Carter Jr. and was adjacent to Olga and Harry Wiess's weekend place. Ella Winston was the younger sister of Libbie Farish. Before her marriage to James Winston in 1933, she had been married to Howard Hughes. Although Winston was born in Massachusetts, his parents were from Virginia. He was a graduate of the University of Virginia and the Harvard Business School. Winston worked for the Irving Trust Company in New York until he married Ella Rice. During the 1930s and early 1940s he was vice president and treasurer of the Navarro Oil Company and treasurer of the F-W-C Royalty Corporation. After Steve Farish sold these companies to the Continental Oil Company during World War II, Winston joined Russell R. Rowles in founding the investment banking firm of Rowles, Winston and Company. Mr. and Mrs. Winston had two young sons at the time they moved into the house; their daughter was born several years later.[78]

James O. Winston Jr. House, Houston, 1938–39, John F. Staub, architect. Entrance (north) elevation and forecourt.

The Winston House is grand: it signifies patrician standing with formal restraint. Staub told Barnstone that its formality and reserve reflected his assessment of his clients' personalities. As was typical of Staub, the Winston House constructs grandness dialectically by elaborating circumstance and leavening formality with spatial surprise. The layering of spaces at the north-facing main entrance exemplifies these practices. Paneled double doors are set in a cast stone alcove. This sequence of shallow layers made it possible for Staub to insert windows lighting the women's and men's guest toilets in the recesses of the alcove. Inside the front doors, a cylindrical entrance foyer is articulated with Ionic pilasters and ceiled with a shallow domical vault.

The foyer receives daylight from interior spaces to either side: the staircase, which is a separate room, and a cross-hall leading to the living room on the east side of the house. The staircase is extraordinary. Within what appears from outside to be two stories, Staub eliminated the second floor to make a very tall double-height space.

The stair advances a few steps up to a landing platform (from which the men's toilet is entered), then turns for a long run up to the second floor, displaying the ascending, diagonally inclined, interlocking frets of the dark-blue-painted Chinese Chippendale stair rail that dominates the

Winston House, entrance foyer looking toward staircase.

high, north-lit room. The cross-hall leads past a secluded, mahogany-paneled library overlooking the south rear lawn; this was James Winston's preserve.

Outside the cross-hall door to the library, Staub inserted closets to either side of one of the windows on the north elevation of the house, framing an alcove that brings daylight into the cross-hall. The closets were equipped to contain Winston's hunting guns and his whiskey. At the terminus of the cross-hall, the living room occupies a high-ceilinged, one-story wing with four exposures. The architectural set piece of the room is a grandly scaled, eighteenth-century English white marble mantle piece with relief sculpture in the frieze and fluted black marble columns.

However, it is the shallow-coved ceiling, which ascends to a rectangular central panel, that spatially embodies the room's sense of centeredness and belonging. Nine-over-nine-pane wood windows, which open from floor-level sills, complement this spatial operation by imbuing the room (which is twenty feet, seven inches wide and thirty-seven feet long) with a scale that feels generous rather than simply big. It is the connection of the Winston House to its site, not the opulence of its interior architecture, that registers in the living room.

The dining room is hidden at the center of the house. It lies behind the circular entrance foyer and is accessible only from the staircase and the cross-hall. To compensate for having only one exposure (although it is southern exposure), the south wall of the dining room expands outward in a bow front. Nine-over-nine-pane windows in the bow slide up into jib-head pockets above the headers to open the room to the garden terrace. Staub decorated the dining room with a dentiled cornice, a chair rail, architraves framing interior doors, and fluted quarter-circle pilasters flanking the windows that frame into architraves. Here again, it is the space of the room, and its country house connection to the out-of-doors, that animate it.

Staub treated the north and south elevations of the Winston House differently in response to site conditions. Until the Winston property was subdivided in 1997 (the price paid for preserving and rehabilitating Staub's house), a circuitous drive took arriving motorists somewhat out of their way in order to turn them around in a hairpin curve and bring them up to the north front on axis with a low-walled motor court framed by the out-flanking one-story wings. The right-hand wing, which mirrors the living room wing on the left, contains a special one-car garage behind the noble three-part window and a second floor, housing a servant's room, concealed behind the tall parapet (second-story windows appear on the return face of this wing, looking toward the front door, just to indicate the sleight of hand being played). Staub superimposed horizontal belt courses of white marble, decorated with fluted panels framed by carved rosettes underneath the sills of second-floor windows and blocky modillions in the entablature above, on the brick walls of the north elevation.

The marble bands step back off the advanced center bay of the house front, then belt the one-story wings to ensure horizontal continuity. Marble panels carved with swags in high relief and a centered medallion are set in shallow recesses beneath the sills of first-floor windows framing the columned and pedimented entrance portal and putting architectural emphasis at the point where visitors approach the front wall. There, the mixed blend of sandstruck pale orange and purple brick with "grapevine" mortar joints comes into focus. The rough texture of the brick, its color variations, the subliminal horizontal emphasis achieved by interposing header courses at every seventh brick course, and shallow planar relief animate the material background of the wall, subtly energizing the field that the white marble grid of honor frames and articulates.

The garden elevation of the Winston House looks out across a lawn that slopes gradually down to Buffalo Bayou. From the house and lawn, the bayou channel is concealed by dense, riparian woodland vegetation. The lawn is bracketed by a mixture of deciduous shade trees and tall, slender loblolly pine trees. The garden elevation retains traces of honorific architecture, notably the pair of one-story, cast-stone loggias framing the central block. It is the elemental geometry of the central block, its recessed wings and rounded central bay secured by tall, bounding chimney stacks, that compose the house and establish its authority when seen from the down slope of the lawn. Everything is held in equilibrium. The parts add up to a whole. Pursuing this straightforward approach, Staub composed a myth of stability, nobility, and belonging in his design of the Winston House. The house's construction of upper-class identity is grounded in emphasis on the typical rather than expressions of singularity. As he so often balanced perceptual sensations of monumentality and intimacy, here Staub balanced sensations of grandeur and everydayness to portray spatially the authenticity, connectedness, naturalness, even simplicity, of grandeur. The interior is the zone of individuality and adjustment to circumstance. The exterior of the Winston House instructs upper-class subjects (as well as the subjects of other social classes) in the mythic virtues identifying a Houston upper class. Its sobriety, propriety, expansiveness, assurance (and inner richness) say: this is what we look like; this is who we are.

The Winston House, no less than the Camp, Wilson, and Farish Houses, asserts the value of a patrician consensus on limits that countered aristocratic assertions of mastery. Staub's grand houses of the 1920s and 1930s can be seen, in historical perspective, as enacting a sequence of

Winston House, detail of stair rail and riser returns.

Winston House, vista through cross hall and foyer toward staircase.

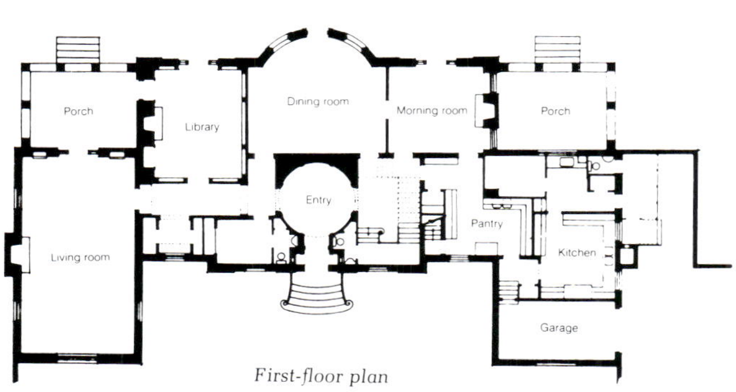

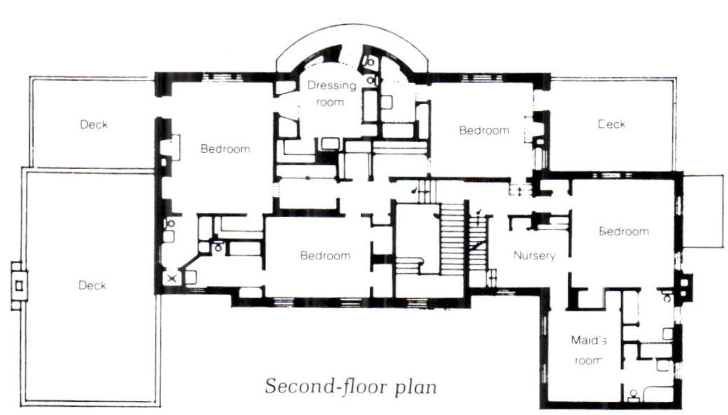

Winston House.

(opposite) Winston House, detail of library mantle.

Winston House, detail of antique mantle installed in living room.

Winston House, living room.

Winston House, dining room.

Winston House, detail of front elevation showing marble belt course and brick relieving arch.

Winston House, detail of front elevation showing carved marble panel beneath first-floor windows and iron handrail.

Winston House, garden (south) elevation.

propositions on hypothetical upper-class identity positions. The most unabashedly aristocratic—the Neal and Cullen Houses—grew out of the stylistic eclecticism of the 1920s. They represented positions that could not be sustained socially because their credibility depended on maximizing class distinction, on emphasizing what separated the upper class from other social classes and aggrandizing the differences. The Farish, Wilson, Camp, and Winston Houses countered with a reinforcement of the consensus on limits by disciplining extravagance, emphasizing austerity as an identifying upper-class virtue, and modeling a representational style that valued the typical more than the singular. This position situated upper-class identity in relation to a hierarchy of social classes, emphasizing continuity, belonging, and propriety to stress interclass connections, minimize conflict, and sustain social cohesiveness (and the prerogatives of the upper class within this construct) to preserve a social role for the grand country house.

The Bewley House constructed upper-class identity through architectural affiliation with the English country houses of Lutyens and their U.S. counterparts by Lindeberg and Adler. Staub demonstrated his facility at naturalizing the Anglo-American country house in a Texan context at the Bewley House in his invention of a River Crest vernacular, highlighting style as the arena in which the resolution of contradictions could be performed. The Neal and Cullen Houses tested Staub's ability to manage contradiction through a regime of formal rigor. As he did at the Gartner House, Staub used contradictions pertaining to the commission as a source of formal energy in the Neal House. It was the contradictions involving subjectivity that resisted architectural sublimation: the uncertainty of how courtly splendor or exquisite domestic intimacy translated to the circumstances affecting American elites in the early 1930s. The Cullen House framed Roy Cullen as grand but for that reason could not also credibly frame him as a populist. Staub's subsequent grand houses of the 1930s reflect a reappraisal of upper-class identity. Identity positions shift from subjects based on personality to subjects based on character and, consequently, from eclectic exuberance to formal sobriety.[79] Subtlety, refinement, and restraint had to be internalized as virtues rather than sported as stylistic flourishes. Staub's versatility, his concern for avoiding repetition, and the responsibility he felt for producing houses that were specific to their owners enabled him to continue to lead by serving, reinterpreting the country house in a lower key so that it might continue to perform efficiently as an instrument of upper-class taste and power.

CHAPTER 6 : COUNTRY RETREATS

Wiess Stables, Houston, 1930, John F. Staub, architect. Cupola and weathervane.

Bay Ridge shoreline and cottages seen from Galveston Bay, Morgan's Point, Texas. The Ross S. Sterling Cottage of 1928 by Alfred C. Finn is on the right. Photo courtesy Doco Foto Services.

As the Winston House demonstrates, Staub did design houses that qualified as country houses in the literal sense: houses built outside the limits of cities and their garden suburbs. These houses and other domestically scaled buildings not intended primarily for residential use also construct class identity in their exurban or resort settings. These retreats display Staub's inventiveness in distinguishing exurban houses from suburban houses. They reflect his attentiveness to the special qualities of the places where they were built in his effort to naturalize their designs. And they exhibit the seeming ease with which he produced houses responsive to client and programmatic requirements that consistently reinforced upper-class identity.

In the 1890s, as the construction of new short-haul railroad lines systematically connected cities and towns in the coastal plain of Texas, resort communities began to be developed on coastal bays along the Gulf of Mexico. This process was set back by the Panic of 1893 but rebounded in the first decade of the twentieth century.[1] One such community was the Bay Ridge Park Association, located twenty-four miles east of Houston on a ridge, twenty to twenty-five feet high, on the west shore of Galveston Bay just below Morgan's Point, where Buffalo Bayou and the San Jacinto River empty into the bay.[2] The association was organized in 1890 by twelve Houston families who subdivided a forty-acre tract on which they built cabin-like cottages intended for summer occupancy, with a centrally located pavilion for communal meals. By the late 1890s, less rustic cottages were being constructed in the subdivision of Bay Ridge Park, which association members platted in 1893, and the adjoining Woodbridge and Grandview additions of 1896. Peter Flagg Maxson, in a historical account of the community's development, noted that Woodbridge, Grandview, and later subdivisions followed the pattern established at Bay Ridge Park: long lots fronting on the bay, with outbuildings for servants and livestock on the landward side of Bay Ridge Road, which ran parallel to the shore and bisected the lots. By 1910 owners were building substantial Craftsman cottages at Bay Ridge. These cottages conformed to prevailing locational patterns—houses faced the water and the Gulf breeze and turned their backs on the road—but their occupants did not imitate the communal practices of the Bay Ridge Park Association. Amid the cottages were boarding houses, such as Mrs. Vinson's, and even corporate camps. The Peden Iron and Steel Company maintained a "club" for its employees on a wooded tract in the Grandview addition that possessed a long, gradual incline down to the Bay Ridge beach. At the end of 1927 the company sold the property to Frank N. Bullock of Houston, president of the Park Realty and Investment Company and vice president of the Eagle Petroleum Company.[3]

Frank N. Bullock Bay Cottage, Bay Ridge, 1928, John F. Staub, architect. *Detail of entrance (northwest) elevation.*

Bullock Bay Cottage, detail of elliptical pediment showing lone stars.

Bullock commissioned Staub to design a bay cottage for himself, his wife Laura, and their three children, Dorothy, Herman, and Ray.

Ross Sterling owned two hundred acres at Bay Ridge with six acres of frontage on the bay, the largest tract along Bay Ridge Road. In 1925 Sterling and his wife began to plan construction of a cottage next to one of the raised, Craftsman-type cottages where they had summered.[4] Working with Alfred C. Finn, Finn's residential designer Robert Smallwood, and the landscape architects Hare and Hare, Mr. and Mrs. Sterling built an enormous, two-and-a-half-story, limestone-faced classical house, completed in 1928, that was said to be modeled on the White House (its monumental bay-front portico replicates the lake front of Charles A. Platt's country house, Gwinn, outside Cleveland, Ohio, of 1908).[5] Because the broad site has few trees, the Sterling Bay Cottage is starkly silhouetted against the horizon.

The Houston banker and confectioner W. H. Irwin built a stucco-faced tile-roofed Spanish-Mediterranean cottage two lots away from the Sterling Cottage in 1927–28.[6] Designed by Joseph Finger, the Irwin Bay Cottage was not grandiose, but it did portend the suburbanization of domestic architecture in Bay Ridge, although true to bay-front practices Finger opened the water-front of the house with a second-story veranda over an open ground-floor arcade.

Staub negotiated identity in the design of the Bullock Bay Cottage, which was built in 1928. He differentiated the Bullock cottage from other new cottages by constructing continuity and belonging with Bay Ridge. The hipped-roof house is faced with cypress shingles. The front door, facing Bay Ridge Road, is capped by inset arched panels, the outer panel decorated with alternating triglyphs and stars (the Lone Star had been a popular icon on late-nineteenth-century Texan buildings). Pilaster strips with block capitals frame the front door and the windows to either side on the symmetrically composed street elevation. The windows are peculiar. They are two-pane-over-two-pane sash windows, uncharacteristically narrow for Staub and vertically attenuated. The Bullock Cottage contributed to the architectural suburbanization of Bay Ridge (its street front, for instance, is the front elevation). But it pretends otherwise. The shingles affiliated the house with the tradition of elite but unpretentious shingle-sided summer cottages associated with the New England shore, emphasizing the house's identity as a resort cottage rather than a suburban country house. The stars signified Texas identity.[7]

The odd two-over-two windows were appropriated from the Victorian builders' vernacular visible in the oldest cottages at Bay Ridge.[8] Given the disdain with which Victorian architecture was treated in the 1920s, it is remarkable that

Bullock Bay Cottage, shore (southeast) elevation.

Staub sought to claim a Bay Ridge heritage for the Bullock Cottage by including this quirky detail, which is incorporated without fanfare, as though the house had been built by one of the La Porte, Texas, contractors who constructed other Bay Ridge cottages around 1900. While the Sterling Cottage ostentatiously flaunts its dependence on Charles Platt, and Finger's Irwin House sought affiliation with the Mediterranean resort architecture of Palm Beach and Santa Barbara, Staub naturalized the Bullock Cottage in its Bay Ridge setting by pursuing a strategy of authentication. Implicitly, a class identity position was being advanced. The Bullock Bay Cottage was patrician in its subordination of style to the characterful imperative of community solidarity and its claim of belonging. The house seeks to fit in rather than stand out. The design demonstrates Staub's capacity for making homeliness stylish.

The Bullock Cottage is unusual in the context of Staub's houses because it does not have an entrance hall; the front door opens directly into the living room. The ground-floor plan is based on the Hutcheson-Helmbrecht model but reversed. In the bay house, a screened loggia facing the sloping rear lawn and the water occupies the place of the entrance and stair hall in the Hutcheson-Helmbrecht model. Staub detailed the living room of the Bullock Cottage with more flair than the exterior might suggest. Paneled wood walls are modulated with pilasters framing window and door openings. Peter Maxson observed that because the humidity level on the bay is consistently higher than in the city, older Bay Ridge houses often had dark-stained wood interiors to prevent the damp and mildew problems to which wallpaper was liable and to shade interiors against the intense summer sunlight reflecting off the bay.[9] Here too Staub appeared to accede to "traditional" Bay Ridge practices. The rear loggia of the Bullock Bay Cottage is screened with ornamental woodwork in a Chinese Chippendale pattern of intersecting diagonals, elongated octagons, and elongated diamonds. This matrix uses architecture to compose and proportion views of the lawn, the beach, and the bay in order to frame perception, experience, identity, and subjectivity. Photographs of Houstonians at the bay published in summer numbers of the *Houston Gargoyle* might show children barefooted and dressed for play.[10] Adults, however, tended to be photographed in light-toned attire, with women wearing high-heeled shoes, to signify summer leisure but also the aura of composure that identified them as patrician subjects belonging to the class of people who, even in the season of relaxation, were decorous and refined.

In 1926 Staub designed a stable for Frankie Carter and Robert D. Randolph to house Deke Randolph's polo ponies on a wooded site along Buffalo Bayou and what is now South Post Oak Lane. The Randolph Stable, like Susan and William L. Clayton's summer house in River Oaks, was an early example of a tendency among Houston's elite to invest in the construction of building types for recreational and leisure pursuits that reinforced claims to upper-class status. In the late 1920s, the pine forest along Buffalo Bayou upstream from Memorial Park became the favored place for elite Houston families to buy multi-acre tracts and develop weekend places for horseback riding.[11] Staub was at first called on to provide retreats for country entertaining (the area is about four-and-a-half miles northwest of Broadacres and only one-and-a-half miles northwest of River Oaks). Increasingly, though, in the 1930s he had clients like Mr. and Mrs. Winston who wanted year-round houses in the country. As at the bay, Staub displayed his inventiveness by designing country retreats that satisfied his clients' practical requirements while also legitimizing them as an upper class, not only because they had the resources to sustain such activities as horseback riding but also because they internalized subject positions involving equestrian activities that identified them as stylish, sophisticated, and refined. Several of Staub's clients, by using their retreats to extend hospitality to their friends, formulated a consensus on social style with which Staub's buildings became identified. The spatial generosity, material resourcefulness, and assured ambiance characteristic of Staub's architecture supported and sustained this consensus. Staub's country retreats materialized a seemingly charmed way of life that flourished in the interwar period yet proved quite fragile as Houston's postwar expansion resulted in the intensive suburbanization of its former countryside.

Staub's first architecturally significant commission for a country retreat came from Frankie Carter Randolph's sister-in-law and brother, Lillie Neuhaus and William T. Carter Jr. Built in 1929 by the contractor Pete L. Nelson for $42,000, the Carter Lodge (as the Carters called it) was described in the real estate section of the *Houston Post-Dispatch* as a "club house," the first phase of a one-hundred-acre tract being planned by Hare and Hare on which, it was reported, Mr. and Mrs. Carter would eventually build a country house and a private airport.[12] Carter, the eldest son of the lumberman and banker W. T. Carter, was then president of the W. T. Carter Lumber and Building Company, which he ran with his brother Aubrey L. Carter and his brothers-in-law Haywood Nelms and R. D. Randolph. He was chairman of the board of directors of the Federal Trust Company and the Carter Investment Company and a commissioner of the Houston Harris County Ship Channel Navigation District.[13] As president of the Houston Airport Corporation, Carter built the first modern airport in Houston on Telephone Road in 1927; ten years later he sold it to the City of Houston to form the nucleus of what became William P. Hobby Airport.[14] Adjacent

(opposite) Bullock Bay Cottage, view from rear loggia toward Galveston Bay and the Houston Ship Channel.

House Beautifu
June, 193

Photographs by Edison Studio

THE HOUSE OF W. T. CARTER, JR., IN HOUSTON

JOHN F. STAUB, ARCHITECT

Walls of native stone and brick whitewashed, roof of split-wood shingles weathered, shutters and door of moss green glazed with natural wood color, characterize this house. The living-room has two French doors opening on to a terrace on the south side, making a cross draft in this room and also in the master's bedroom. Awarded Honorable Mention in our 1931 Competition

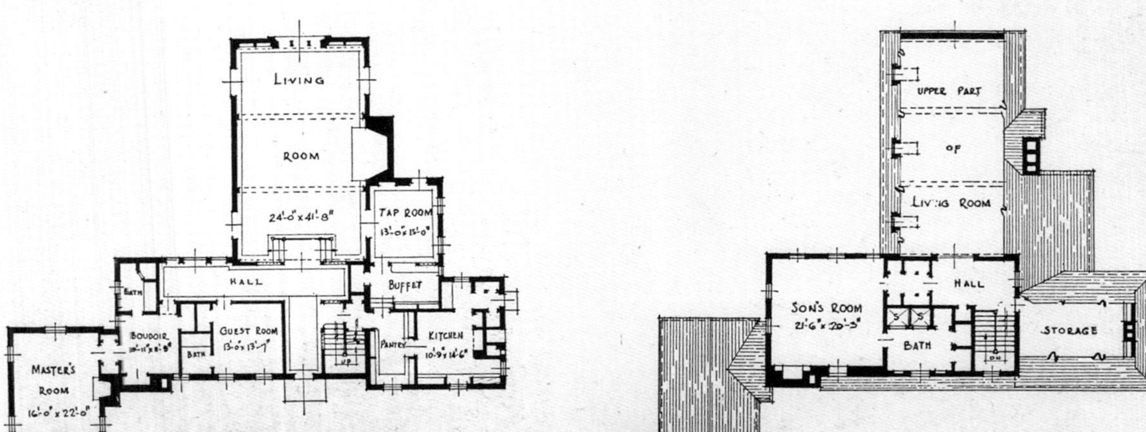

W. T. Carter Jr. Lodge, Houston, 1929–30, John F. Staub, architect. House Beautiful 71 (June 1932): 439.

USE BEAUTIFUL
, 1932

The living-room is entered by a double stairway from the hall. It has exposed framing timbers of hewn oak weathered and waxed, and the attractive fireplace pictured above. The timbered opening in the gable on the second floor makes a musician's balcony of the second floor hall

Carter Lodge, views of living room. House Beautiful 71 (June 1932): 440.

to the airport, Carter developed the residential subdivision of Garden Villas in 1925. Described in a sales brochure as a "model planned community," Garden Villas featured curving streets, large lots, and frontage on Sims Bayou.[15] Reflecting its location in southeast Houston, Garden Villas was marketed to lower-middle-income families. Deed restrictions on its house sites permitted fruit, vegetable, and poultry production to supplement household income. Garden Villas advertised itself as based on English garden city models.[16] This suggests the extent to which the garden city planning ethos permeated American residential real estate practices in the 1920s and attests to Carter's astuteness in adopting such practices to competitively advance Garden Villas' prospects, especially since it was not an elite community.

Carter was born in Polk County in East Texas, eighty-five miles northeast of Houston, where his father's lumber milling operations were centered, and lived there until the family moved to Houston in 1903. He was a graduate of the University of Chicago.[17] Lillie Carter was the daughter of Laura Boettcher and J. Victor Neuhaus. Born in Hackberry, Texas, one hundred miles west of Houston, she grew up in Houston.[18] Lillie and W. T. Carter and their two sons, William T. III and Victor, lived in Courtlandt Place alongside Carter's sisters, Mrs. Randolph, Mrs. Judson Taylor, and Mrs. J. J. Carroll; his mother, Maude Holley Carter; and Lil Carter's uncle Charles L. Neuhaus, the father of Harrie Lindeberg's client, Hugo Neuhaus. Mr. and Mrs. Carter were members of the Houston Country Club and parishioners of Palmer Memorial Church. Lil Carter and her sister-in-law Agnese Carter Nelms followed the examples of Ima and Will Hogg by becoming collectors of eighteenth-century American furniture. Mr. and Mrs. Carter outfitted the lodge with rustic American pieces combined with overstuffed upholstered furniture.

Staub made rustic conviviality the theme of the Carter Lodge. The lodge was organized around a two-story living room, twenty-four feet wide and forty-one feet, eight inches long, with exposed oak structural timbers framing the walls and roof. Queen trusses span the width of the room to support the open roof structure and timber plank ceiling. Since the living room projects off the back of the lodge, it has three exposures. French doors on the long walls and a central, arched window on the end wall containing casements in wood-framed compartments open onto terraces. These look down on Newman Branch, which flows into Buffalo Bayou, and Lake Carter, an artificial lake Hare and Hare formed by damming the branch. Wide plank floors; wide, bevel-edged shiplap siding; and the immense scale of the exposed brick fireplace, which is centered on the long north wall of the room, construct proportionally integrated fields that materialize breadth and generosity in the lodge living room. Visitors entering through the front door walk down a short hall to a balustraded landing centered on one end of the living room.

From the landing they perceptually experience the volume, scale, and dim, lustrous tones of the living room before turning to the left or right to descend into the room. A "taproom" (as it was labeled) to one side of the hearth, served by a bar framed with structural timbers and in-filled with balustraded screens, functioned as a space for dispensing food and drinks. It felt quite different from the dining room of a suburban house. The lodge had a master bedroom suite and a guest room on the ground floor and a sleeping loft on the second floor. But spatially it was organized to distinguish it from Staub's houses. The exterior of the east-facing front of the lodge, with its layered and stepped roof planes, advancing and receding wall planes, and a complexly profiled corner chimney stack spatially suggested improvisation rather than composure. The west-facing rear of the lodge implied through its massing that the gable-ended living room was the regular core to which irregular, shed-roofed wings were subsequently attached. The living room, furnished with big case pieces, ladder-back chairs, a dining table seating twelve, and a huge sofa covered in flame-stitched upholstery, was a very consoling space. It registered familiarity, comfort, and hospitality on an expansive scale. The Carter Lodge asserted (even more charmingly inside than outside) that this is what a Houston upper class in the country looks like.

Staub's skill in composing social settings through architecture is especially evident in the stable he designed for Olga and Harry Wiess on their country retreat in Memorial. Designed and built in 1930–31 for $29,055, the brick building consisted of a stable with twelve stalls, a tack room and adjoining bedroom in a wing to one side of a central access way, and a living room and small kitchen in a wing to the other side, arranged in a T plan.[19] There were a pair of dressing rooms and toilets for guests, and a groom's apartment on the second floor above the central access way. To one side of the building, on axis with the short end of the living room wing, are a swimming pool and a free-standing bath house.

The Stables, as Mr. and Mrs. Wiess called the building, became a de facto clubhouse for their friends, whom they invited to Sunday open houses to ride, play tennis or cards, swim, and socialize. "It's where all the fun in Houston happened," John Staub told Howard Barnstone.[20] The Stables framed Olga and Harry Wiess as radiant hosts who dispensed hospitality with style. It is intriguing to examine the Stables in relation to Mr. and Mrs. Wiess's personal progress as architectural clients. In 1911, two years after their marriage, they built a two-story, flat-roofed, foursquare-type house in the McFaddin addition in Beaumont.[21] When they moved to Houston in 1920, they built a much larger and more expensive Italian villa–type house in Shadyside

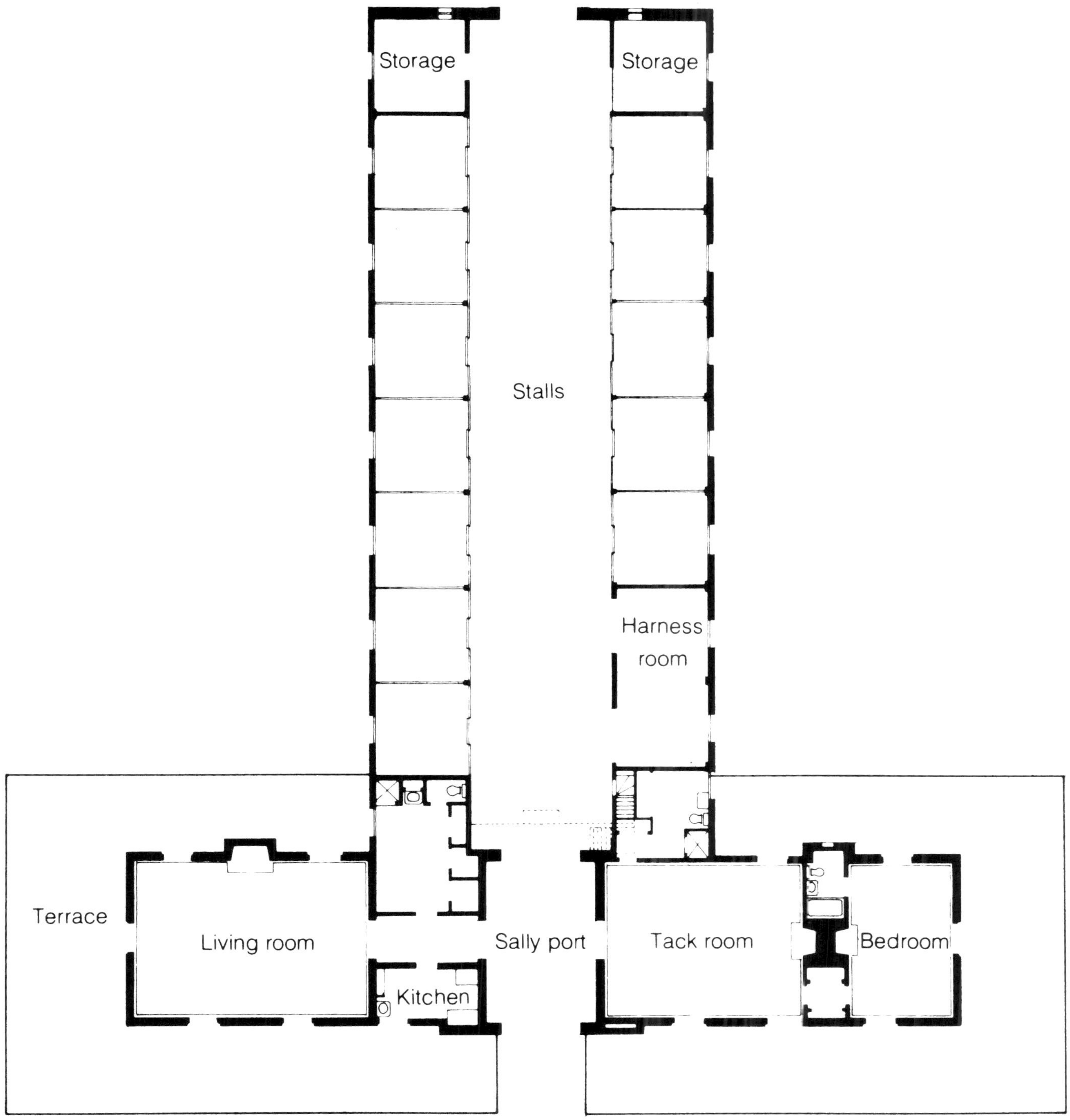

First-floor plan. Wiess Stables, Houston, 1930, John F. Staub, architect.

designed by William Ward Watkin.[22] But just as their Beaumont house must have seemed less than stylish by the time they moved to Houston, so the sophistication of their Shadyside house waned in comparison to Lindeberg's houses in Shadyside. Lindeberg altered and added to the Wiess House in 1925 to construct grandly scaled, proportioned, and decorated spaces through which they and their dinner guests did indeed process as they moved from Lindeberg's spacious new living room to their amplified and redecorated dining room.[23] At the Stables, Staub planned for entertaining that was to be more casual, relaxed, and outdoor-oriented than in Shadyside. Yet he impressed the building with a sense of style that reflected the social style of Olga and Harry Wiess, just as the Carter Lodge reflected the personalities of Lil and W. T. Carter.

The Stables possesses the curious and affecting attribute Staub so often built into his domestic architecture. It is monumental and intimate simultaneously. Although the building is spacious in size, it feels diminutive in scale. Experiencing this paradoxical sensation was essential if visitors were to surrender to the magic spell of the architecture and become its willing subjects. The fun with which John Staub associated the Stables was experienced by its beneficiaries as a kind of social grace, made possible by the resources and liberality Olga and Harry Wiess possessed, which they shared with their friends. Through this social process, the building was invested with expectations on the part of the people who were most often recipients of the Wiess family's hospitality as well as those who might have experienced such entertainments infrequently or only knew of them by hearsay: a consensus on what constituted stylish recreation in Houston and where it was to be enjoyed. Over time, the Stables acquired a mythic aura. Invocation of its name could summon images of stylish country camaraderie, where the elite of Houston (or at least some of them) enjoyed life as well as the pursuit of riches.[24]

How Staub fashioned the Stables as an instrument of mythic resonance that supported and legitimized an upper class in Houston can be demonstrated by analysis. Symmetry was the technique with which Staub grounded the perception of order that underpins the building's sense of authority and composure. On the flat site, symmetry in elevation distinguished and clarified the Stables in its woodland surroundings, especially the gabled frontispiece framed by thick chimney stacks and the hipped-roof wings. Symmetry in plan was reiterated in the organization of major interior spaces, reproducing Staub's mechanism of order with a consistency that simplified perception and subliminally but unambiguously distinguished what was worth seeing and knowing from what was accounted secondary. The main axis, which led from the front entrance (the sallyport) into

Wiess Stables, entrance (southeast) front with swimming pool and bath house to the left.

Wiess Stables, view from living room to swimming pool and bath house.

Wiess Stables, view from living room to swimming pool and bath house.

the stable, aggrandized the building's identification with horses and riding. The cross axis of movement and view running from the tack room through the living room then outdoors across the swimming pool to the symmetrical bath house experientially unified the social spaces of the Stables.

The process of framing that the two axes achieved spatially emphasized the key spaces and associated recreational experiences (and personalities) that the Stables housed while editing out the services and subjects (the grooms and other attendants) who sustained the Stables' operations. The fusion of monumentality and intimacy makes the symmetry of the Stables seem playful rather than pompous. It is authoritative in a stylishly low-key, uninsistent way.

Staub's choice and detailing of building materials supported these themes. The building is faced with brick laid in running bond, with header courses at every seventh course underscoring horizontal continuity. White painted brick materializes simplicity and reinforces the distinctive presence and defined profile of the Stables in its green setting. The sallyport door, the segmentally arched French doors in the wings of the building, the parapet of the central gable, and the upper shafts of the chimney stacks are framed with thin Roman brick in a mixed blend emphasizing dark red.

The Roman brick stands out vividly against the white-painted walls. Its thinness and elongation embody exquisiteness and refinement. The use of Roman brick for the segmental arches and the channeled frame surrounding the sallyport door rhythmically articulates and proportions the white wall planes. Advancing the frontispiece forward of the flanking wings, steeply raking the inclination of its gable, and slightly flaring the clipped eaves of the roofs of the wings spatially portray symmetry, centrality, and figuration, producing sensations of clarity, subtlety, and the intimation of delight. Equilibrium is sustained. The Stables are neither too formal nor too winsome. They radiate charm, modeling one of the most admired attributes of the ideal patrician subject. These qualities pertain in the living room and former tack room. Exterior finish materials are used in the Stables' interiors to identify the non-domestic nature of the building (the tack room even has brick-paved floors).

The use of Roman brick to construct mantles in the living room and tack room is an inspired example of materializing the Stables' identity as an alternative to suburban domesticity. Whereas a more finely differentiated hierarchy of materials might distinguish dualities in a suburban house (inside versus outside, brick exterior walls versus marble or wood mantles, marble mantle in downstairs reception room versus wood mantle in upstairs bedrooms), the use of "outdoor" materials in the interiors of the Stables underlines its difference from a suburban house in precisely those instances where it is most house-like. The one-room depth

Wiess Stables, detail of sallyport portal.

of the wings, especially as seen from the swimming pool and bath house, was a subliminal marker of the less complex (and therefore freer, more spontaneous) program of this non-house. The unarticulated elevations of the stall wing and Staub's straightforward design of the timber post structural system that carries its wider roof span materially code the stall portion of the building as "background" meant to recede behind the foreground of the façade and the wings.[25]

The subliminal urbanity of the Stables stood for the urbane, stylish, and refined social practices that transpired there and, by extension, the patrician subjects enacting them, subjects just as assuredly at home in the country as in the city. The clock face in the gabled frontispiece represents a paradoxical intrusion of time and its commensurate values into the realm of the timeless, complementing the gilded weathervane atop the octagonal cupola. These symbols of limits grounded the mythical world of the Stables and reminded Harry Wiess and his business peers that a return to the real world of capitalist production awaited. They represented Staub's practice of countering flights of fantasy in his buildings with phenomenal experience, proportioning and rationing fantasy so that it enlivened without undermining and destabilizing patrician authority.

The Stables spatially registered Olga Wiess's fondness for riding. It spatially registered Harry Wiess's social identity in a more complex way. Under Wiess's auspices as vice president of the Humble Oil and Refining Company until 1937, then as president from 1938 to 1948, Staub produced two prototype designs for service stations for the Humble Oil and Refining Company, one in 1929 and a second in 1938, and he collaborated with Kenneth Franzheim on the design of the first corporate office building constructed in Houston after the onset of the Great Depression, the seventeen-story Humble Tower of 1933–35.[26] Staub designed the parish house of Palmer Memorial Church of 1929–30, for which Wiess chaired the parish building committee, and the Fondren Library at Rice University of 1945–49 while Wiess served as trustee in charge of the university's committee on buildings and grounds.[27] Staub would design a pair of houses for Wiess's youngest daughter Margaret and her husband, James A. Elkins Jr., and alter Lindeberg's Peden House for his eldest daughter, Elizabeth, and her husband, Lloyd H. Smith. Among these architectural commissions, the Stables stood out as the one with which Harry Wiess had the closest personal identification and which represented him as friend and host rather than as corporate executive or institutional trustee. The number and variety of building projects on which Wiess and Staub were associated was unusual in Staub's career. They represent Staub's versatility as an architect and the bonds of respect, trust, and admiration that linked him to his client; they also indicate how buildings

Wiess Stables, detail of split brick fireplace surround in living room.

(opposite)

Wiess Stables, view from living room toward tack room.

Wiess Stables, view of southwest flank showing rear stable wing.

Olga Wiess (right) and friends at the Stables, 1931.
Photograph by R. M. Luster, Houston Gargoyle *4 (Mar. 22, 1931): 17.*

could reflect different aspects of a client's social identity and sustain multiple subjectivities related to domestic life, social life, business and professional careers, and institutional affiliations.

The Stables displayed Staub's capacity for projecting personal identity that served his clients' agendas, whether these involved a family dwelling or more complex aspirations to civic and social leadership. It demonstrated Staub's skill and insight at negotiating social identity not only through the media of brick and wood but through such intangible phenomena as composition, proportion, and affect. It disclosed his ability to encode buildings with spatial and material nuances that imbued them with differentiated character. The Stables and the Carter Lodge projected a social vision of upper-class country life on the edge of Houston that affiliated Houston's elite with those of the country place suburbs of Boston, New York, Philadelphia, Chicago, and San Francisco and suggested an amplification of the country house way of life beyond the spatial context of Houston's garden-suburban neighborhoods. Two houses Staub designed along Buffalo Bayou in the 1930s for Mr. and Mrs. Raymond H. Goodrich and Mr. and Mrs. Ernest Bel Fay qualified as country-houses-in-the-country when they were built. Each performed its country identity in distinctive ways to suggest that the range of identity positions available in the country were as varied and diverse as those associated with Houston's suburban neighborhoods.

Esther Whinery and Raymond Goodrich built their Staub-designed house on the south side of Buffalo Bayou near the north end of what is now South Post Oak Lane, across the bayou from the Wiess Stables property. A ravine, thirty feet deep in places and requiring a bridge so the driveway can span it, meanders through the east half of the long site. Staub set the Goodrich House on the back, western, half of the property so that it seems isolated in the woods. Encircled by subdivisions and apartments in the 1950s and overshadowed by high-rise office and apartment towers in the 1970s, the Goodrich House still feels very remote from its immediate surroundings, buried in a Connecticut country glade as imagined on the semitropical Gulf coast. Staub constructed the Goodrich House as country colonial with such spatial sensitivity that it is the house's present setting, not the house, that seems anomalous. Raymond Goodrich was the son of a dentist from Norman, Oklahoma, and a graduate of the University of Oklahoma and Harvard University. Goodrich and his brother Robert were petroleum geologists, as was the husband of his elder sister Nell, Everette Lee De Golyer. Goodrich worked for the Humble Oil and Refining Company as division geologist for the Gulf coast region until the late 1920s when he negotiated what turned out to be a productive lease for himself.[28] By the time Goodrich

Raymond H. Goodrich House, Houston, 1932, John F. Staub, architect. Entrance (north) elevation.

Goodrich House, view of living room looking toward entry.

built his country house, he was an independent oil operator. Constructed in 1932, the Goodrich House was the first house Staub designed for year-round occupancy in the Post Oak Road area. The rigor, imagination, and tact with which Staub adapted the Connecticut colonial model to a Southern bayou woodland setting bespoke his effort to construct patrician identity through strategies of naturalization and authentication that call almost no attention to themselves.

The house is two stories high and of wood frame construction. The entrance elevation, which faces north, consists of a pair of gabled wings of different heights framing a recessed, one-and-a-half-story central range. The central range contains the front door and three three-over-six-paned sash windows set below an upper row of shuttered three-over-three sash windows. The low roofline of the central range and the low-set second-floor windows construct humility, as in the Hutcheson House. The wall plane of the second floor projects out almost imperceptibly above the first-floor wall plane. The first-floor wall surface of the central range, the first-floor level of the gabled east wing, and the entire elevation of the slightly lower gabled west wing are faced with bevel-edged vertical siding. The second level of the central range is finished with flush boarding. And the second story of the east wing is faced with horizontal clapboards. These variations in the size of windows, in roof height, roof pitch, and type of wood siding construct a narrative of episodic construction. The mid-eighteenth-century-style paneled front door, framed with a flat transom and bracketed by fluted pilasters with medallion caps, is the sole instance of decoration. The interior continues this theme.

The entrance hall is paved with flagstone like the exterior doorstep, complementing the hall's dark, polished plank walls and the tight dimension of the stair, which rises immediately inside the front door alongside the back of an exposed brick chimney stack. The sensation is quite similar to Staub's own house, even though the Goodrich House is larger. The living room is the space in which Staub carried his country colonial fiction to summation. The room feels almost square in plan since it is much broader in relation to its length than was customary in Staub's living rooms. It is also unusually low ceilinged. The windows in the room (five openings across the east-facing garden elevation) rise almost to the ceiling. But their sills are elevated well above the wide plank floor to construct a uniform interior horizon line and a sense of spatial containment. The fireplace and mantle, centered on the long west wall of the room, proportionally comply with these high-set arrangements. The fireplace opening is positioned off center in an exposed brick chimney below the centered mantle shelf. The mantle shelf projects directly from the wall. There is actually no mantle; the brick chimney is framed instead by a molded band. A smooth fascia between the molding and the mantle shelf merely implies the existence of a mantle. The walls are surfaced with light-stained, wax-coated, vertical pine planking, the beveled edges of the planking rhythmically proportioning the space with visually unobtrusive but precisely articulated moldings.

The material attributes of the exterior and interior of the Goodrich House cohere to construct a myth of country life in Houston that is all the more seductive because it ran counter to Staub's expected practices. The house lacks the composed façades with which Staub's Broadacres and River Oaks houses maintained civic decorum, even when based on picturesque models. This lack of composure identifies it as a "country" country house. Its episodic character, registered in the varieties of its wood siding, and its humility, achieved through the dimensioning and arrangement of windows, reinforces the house's rustic identity. It is the living room, though, that consummates this pastoral myth. Its breadth, its spatial containment, its wood plank finish, and bookshelves recessed in the shorter north and south end walls imply that this is a multipurpose room where a range of family activities can occur, not a specialized drawing room to be used only for formal entertaining. It emits strong sensations of country unpretentiousness through its elevated interior horizon line and low-seeming ceiling. The room is symmetrically composed, but the effect is one of subliminal order rather than of ceremonial formality. The low-style character of the living room is consistent with the perceptions the outside of the house instills in subjects, imbuing the "story" the architecture tells with spatial plausibility and charm. The rigor and consistency with which unpretentiousness, stability, and belonging are constructed in the Goodrich House make it extraordinarily impressive as a model that finely differentiates between a country house in a garden suburb and a country house in a rural exurb. The Carter Lodge, the Wiess Stables, and the Goodrich House are arcadian pastorales. They spatially embody the myth of a refined, civilized, and cultivated manner of life lived in nature, a stylish rustication of the country house practices with which Houston's social elite identified in the 1920s.

Goodrich House, detail of living room fireplace.

By the later 1930s, Staub's exurban country houses participated in the process of simplification also visible in his grand houses. These houses explore an identity position that emphasizes typicality and internalizes nuances keyed to family and individual identity but subordinates them to a consensus on what constitutes appropriate expressions of propriety and belonging. Staub's two-story country house for Carolyn Grant and Ernest Bel Fay exemplified this trend. Like the Goodrich House, the Fay House constructed an image of country life along Buffalo Bayou, Houston-style. Staub based its design on a historical model but manipulated the model to naturalize its transformation into a twentieth-century

Aerial view of Ernest Bel Fay House, Houston, 1937–38; John F. Staub (center) and Albert Bel Fay House (upper right corner), 1939, John F. Staub, architect. Demolished, c. 1940. Photograph courtesy of Marie Fay Evnochides.

suburban house. Carolyn Grant was the daughter of Homoiselle Randall and John F. Grant. Her father owned a chain of retail lumberyards that stretched across Texas.[29] Born in Galveston, she grew up at Grantlands, a country house Birdsall Briscoe designed for her parents in 1925 on what was then the southern edge of Houston.[30] Ernest Bel Fay managed the John F. Grant Lumber Company. His parents, Marie Bel and Charles S. Fay, were from Louisiana. Ernest Fay grew up in New Orleans but moved with his family to Houston when his father was made vice president and traffic manager of the Southern Pacific Lines' Texas and Louisiana subsidiaries.[31] In 1930–31, Fay's aunt, Katherine Bel, and her husband, Harry C. Hanszen, built a grand house by Staub on Lazy Lane in the Homewoods section of River Oaks. Fay was a graduate of Harvard University; Carolyn Fay was a graduate of Vassar College. The year of their marriage, 1937, they commissioned Staub to design their house on the west side of a fifteen-acre tract that Fay and his brother, Albert Bel Fay, bought from their friends, Tina Cleveland and Dudley Sharp, near the Wiess Stables.[32] The Fay property slopes down to the north edge of Buffalo Bayou. It was bounded on the east by what is now North Post Oak Lane. The house was built in 1937–38 for $33,627.[33] Staub sited it just beyond the crest of the property as it begins to descend to the wooded bayou channel. The north portion of the Fay tract was a flat, treeless pasture.

The Fay House embodies the type of the Buffalo Bayou country house. It is extended in plan along its east-west cross axis but is shallow on its north-south axis. Entrance is from the north. The reception rooms and bedrooms face south toward the bayou and into the prevailing southeast breeze. A two-story veranda, accessible from reception rooms through twelve-over-twelve-pane windows that slide up into pockets above the window opening, spans the rear garden elevation of the main block.

In a memoir prepared in 1987, Mrs. Fay wrote that Staub modeled the design on low-style, Louisiana Creole planters' houses to acknowledge Ernest Fay's Louisiana background.[34] From the entrance side, the house is horizontal and low set; it appears to subside into the site. From the bayou side on the downhill slope, square brick piers supporting the wood-decked veranda and wood colonnettes carrying the veranda's shed roof appear to lift the house. The long, low-pitched gabled roof of the house is framed by brick end chimneys. With the exception of the projecting angled bay centered inside the veranda and big-scaled Lindeberg shutters fram-

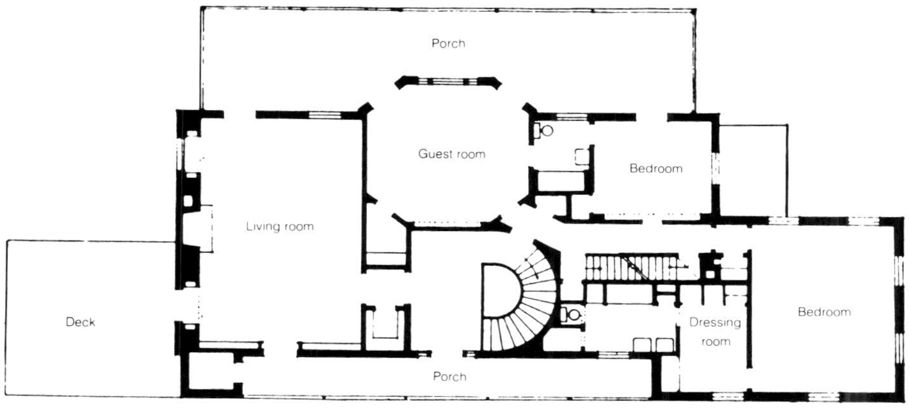

Second-floor plan

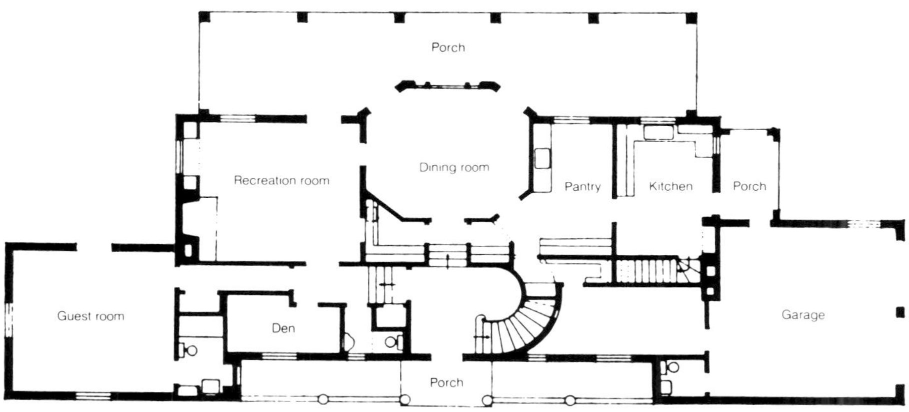

First-floor plan

Fay House.

ing windows not protected by the veranda, the Fay House is unassuming. In making use of a regionally resonant historical model—a rural rather than urban version of the Latin Colonial—Staub emphasized typicality and suppressed architectural incident.

The interior organization of the Fay House is more complex than the exterior suggests, especially because the living room is on the second floor. Other reception rooms—Ernest Fay's game room, where he displayed his collection of model sailing yachts (Ernest and Albert Fay sailed competitively), and an octagonal dining room behind the projecting central bay—are downstairs, as are the kitchen, pantry, and a two-car garage in the west wing. Staub incorporated level changes on the ground floor so that the house steps down with the slope of the land, affording higher ceilings in the game room, dining room, and a guest bedroom in the east wing. He deftly organized circulation to separate reception spaces on the second floor from the family's three bedrooms. The living room is a generous, high-ceilinged space nineteen feet wide and twenty-seven feet, eight inches long.

Staub inserted bookshelves into the reveals of window and door openings in the living room's long fireplace wall to induce a sense of spatial layering in the simply composed room. Architectural decoration was consistent with the straightforwardness of the exterior: Staub framed openings with reeded jambs and headers joined by corner blocks, as one might find in a nineteenth-century Louisiana house, combined with a Soane-like reeded fascia banding the edges of the ceiling. Carolyn Fay wrote that the living room was the space to which she and her husband most often gravitated. But she indicated that during their nearly forty-nine-year tenure in the house, they shifted room uses as their family expanded to three children with a live-in nurse and then contracted once the children grew so that, as she put it, ". . . we have lived all over the house—and loved it."[35]

The Fay House was carefully tailored to fit the circumstances of Carolyn and Ernie Fay's life. Yet Staub submerged expressions of singularity in the plan to emphasize a spatial theme of timeless simplicity that evokes nostalgia but not sentimentality. The historically resonant identity the house projects differs from that of the more idiosyncratic Goodrich House and Carter Lodge. The Fay House performs patrician superiority through self-effacement because it appears to be unconcerned with competitively asserting its owners' wealth, status, or political and social prerogatives. Yet its inner layering sustained Carolyn Fay's interest in and involvement with

Ernest Bel Fay House, garden (south) front looking toward Buffalo Bayou.

the insights of the Swiss psychologist Carl G. Jung, which led her to organize the Jung Educational Center of Houston in 1958.[36]

Staub's design of the Bayou Club framed his clients as a collective, not to the city at large (like most of these retreats, the clubhouse is not visible from a public thoroughfare) but to the members themselves. The Bayou Club's social role was to edify and inspire its members, their families, and guests. Staub's building was an instrument for elevating the collective consciousness of its members. Of the club's seventy-nine charter members, twenty-one were Staub's clients; his own membership raised the number to twenty-two.[37] The Bayou Club was formed in part to supplement the Houston Country Club, to which most of its members belonged. It economized by not having a golf course. It was identified instead with polo and functioned as a successor to the Houston Riding and Polo Club, which had disbanded. The club's organizers bought a sixty-one-acre tract filling out the northwest corner of Memorial Park.[38] The club's allusive name notwithstanding, the property has no frontage on Buffalo Bayou. The clubhouse was built in the wooded western sector of the tract while the more open eastern sector was developed with tennis courts, a polo field, stables for members' horses, and a blacksmith shop. Fleming and Sheppard were the landscape architects. The clubhouse was designed and built between 1938 and 1940 for a cost of $84,320.[39]

Staub based the design of the clubhouse on the model of the Louisiana Creole planter's house. It conformed to the type of the Buffalo Bayou country house in its double-fronted organization, its elongated east-west cross axis and compressed north-south axis, and its double-level, south-facing veranda (supplemented with a pedimented, north-facing portico incorporating a porte cochère and a second-story deck).

The main block is symmetrical on its long north and south elevations. A hipped roof flares out just above the eaves lines to enhance the building's horizontal elongation. Chimneys at the peaks of the roof ridge reinforce centrality. Twelve-over-twelve-pane windows framed by white-painted Lindeberg shutters predominate on the exterior of the main block, proportionally diminishing the apparent scale of the building so that it appears house-like. A slightly narrower two-story west wing with a lower ridgeline contains the men's locker room on the ground floor and the kitchen and serving areas on the second floor (and originally an apartment for the manager). The white entrance portico on the north (backed up with white-painted brick in the entrance bay) and the long veranda on the south (also highlighted by white-painted brick inside the veranda) stand out against a mixed blend of rose, lavender, and orange colored brick and the intense green of the loblolly pine trees that tower above

Fay House, second-floor living room. Photograph courtesy of Marie Fay Evnochides.

the clubhouse. Symmetry is projected from the building into the landscape to mark an axial path from the north for arriving motorists. On the south, symmetry is spatially enhanced by a clearing in the forest that contains a rectangular swimming pool bordered by a broad, brick-paved terrace outfitted for dining, framed in turn by an open lawn in which limbed-up trees were discreetly planted in sequence and where a low bounding wall separates the pastoral landscape of the enclosure from the natural landscape of the forest.

The interior of the building is organized on two floors. A stair at one end of the lateral entrance hall leads to a second-floor card room in the southeast corner of the building and the lounge, a generously proportioned but simply detailed room for receptions, large parties, and other special events. At forty-nine feet, two inches in length and twenty-six feet, eight inches in width, it has the feel of an enlarged living room from one of Staub's houses. The lounge spans the width of the club building so it receives south and north light and has access to the front portico and rear veranda.

Discreetly monumental fireplaces centered on the short ends of the room provide a focus for seating arrangements. A tray ceiling underneath the slope of the roof contributes to the lounge's sense of ceremoniousness and centeredness. Polished oak strip floors materially connote sturdiness. The heart of the club is its downstairs common rooms, the grill room and the veranda.

These ground-floor spaces as well as the entry corridor are paved with dark polished brick. Structural bearing walls are of white-painted brick. Interior partitions are finished with vertical pine planks, lightly stained and wax-coated. Openings are shuttered with solid plank pine shutters, and the ceiling is the exposed underside of the dark-stained, pine, second-floor structure. At one end of the grill room is an open cocktail bar incorporating a streamlined clock face; at the other end of the room (which is as long as the lounge above) is a large fireplace let directly into the brick wall. The fireplace opening is framed with stretcher and header courses of unpainted brick interlined with thin courses of slate. The veranda contains a pair of cast-in-place concrete stairs, stained the same color as the floor, that rise symmetrically from either end of the veranda to the second floor.

As a description of its interiors makes clear, the Bayou Club signifies its country retreat status by incorporating the palette of durable, precisely detailed, slightly rustic materials Staub had used to construct patrician identity along Buffalo Bayou since the late 1920s. The building is not plain, but decoration is kept to a minimum. It is the expansive proportions of its ceremonial spaces, the familiarity of its casual social spaces, the assurance with which it claims a place in its landscape setting, and its aura of composure that enable the club house to be categorized as "typical" of the class

Fay House, detail of molded fascia in living room.

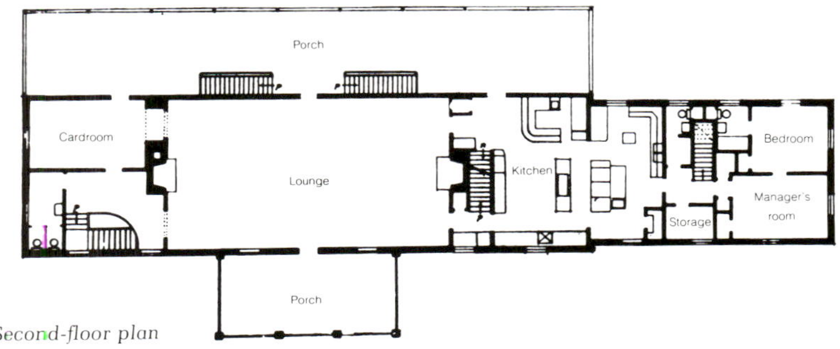

Second-floor plan

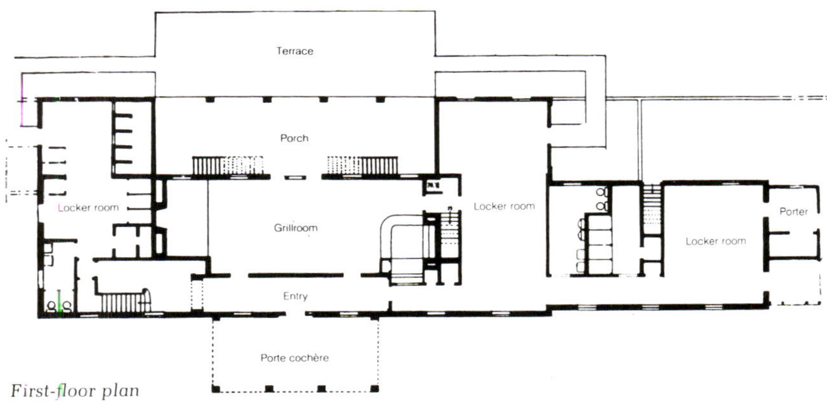

First-floor plan

Bayou Club.

Bayou Club, Houston, 1938–40, John F. Staub, architect. Entrance (north) elevation.

Bayou Club, south elevation and swimming pool.

Bayou Club, second-floor Lounge.

Bayou Club, first-floor Grill Room.

of dwellings and allied domestic buildings that, thanks to Staub, spatially identified a Houston upper-class presence in the countryside west of Memorial Park in the 1930s and 1940s. As a work of architecture, it encourages, inspires, and consoles. Architecturally the Bayou Club functions along the lines of George Marcus's description of a trust: it works to maintain continuity, sustain belonging, and preserve identity by ensuring that succeeding generations will embrace what it offers.[40]

Staub's involvement with the social construction of a new architectural category of upper-class exurban dwelling in Houston—the country retreat—took form on what were the outskirts of Houston in 1930. Yet residential subdivisions began to be platted in tandem with the country retreats, the earliest being the banker J. M. Jackson's Memorial Park Estates, announced at the end of 1935 and wedged in between the Stables, the Dudley Sharp place, and the Fay brothers' site.[41] Briar Hollow, north of San Felipe Road and just across the Southern Pacific tracks from River Oaks, began to be developed as a country place neighborhood in 1936, although it was never platted as a subdivision and never had deed restrictions.[42] West Oaks, which straddles South Post Oak Lane near the Randolph Stables, was put on the market in 1938.[43] The allure of country living (and the competition it was beginning to represent) led Hugh Potter to develop Mike Hogg's Tall Timbers retreat as the Tall Timbers sections of River Oaks in 1939 and 1941. Asphalt-topped roads, open drainage ditches, and the lack of sidewalks and curbs identified Tall Timbers as the country

Bayou Club, detail of fireplace surround in Grill Room.

place section within River Oaks. Yet by 1940 first Steve Farish, then in 1941 Will Farish, subdivided their country place into the subdivision of Bayou Woods, and in 1945 W. T. Carter Jr. began redevelopment of the Carter Lodge tract as the subdivision of Sherwood Forest. Urban expansion and the profits it afforded meant that what a report in the *Houston Post-Dispatch* in 1928 called the "millionaire country estate section" along Buffalo Bayou west of Memorial Park had a very short life span.[44] The rapid absorption of these country retreats and the elite pastimes with which they were associated by Houston's suburban real estate market demonstrated that the "other" that menaced the social construction of patrician identity and subjectivity in Houston came not from outside the elite but from within. Upper middle-income postwar suburbanization isolated most of Staub's country retreats on greatly reduced pieces of property. While most of Staub's buildings have survived, they failed to accomplish the critical social task of instilling the sort of "disinterested" values with which the country life movement was identified during the Progressive era and by which it sought legitimation.

CHAPTER 7 : TYPIFICATION, CONSENSUS, AND THE RIVER OAKS HOUSE

George S. Heyer House, River Oaks, Houston, 1935–37, John F. Staub, architect. Detail of iron-framed light fixture above front door.

During the 1930s, River Oaks realized Hugh Potter's ambitions. It eclipsed rival neighborhoods to become Houston's foremost elite neighborhood, although it never achieved Will Hogg's ambition of becoming the model of good community planning that the rest of Houston might follow. Between 1930 and 1941, twenty-two houses designed by Staub were built in River Oaks.[1] In this time period, nine of his firm's houses as well as the Stables and the Bayou Club were constructed in the Post Oak Road, Memorial Drive, and Briar Hollow areas west of River Oaks. Only one Staub house was built in the South End neighborhoods, in Shadyside, even though residential construction, which ebbed throughout Houston in the first half of the decade, rebounded in 1935. What stands out about Staub's River Oaks houses is how some among them began to be affected by the phenomenon of typification. As with other buildings by Staub where emphasis was placed on the typical rather than the singular, this practice suggests the extent to which he demonstrated his virtuosity by emphasizing type over individuality. Each house is different. But difference is formally subordinated to the repetition of a type. Staub's use of repetition to imply the formation of upper-class identity is at its most assured in these houses. The self-effacement characteristic of Staub's houses in the 1930s was especially evident in these River Oaks houses, which tended to resolve planning issues in similar ways based on site orientation. Barnstone noted a sense of relaxation in Staub's design work after the sequence of opulent houses designed and built between 1930 and 1935. This relaxation reflected a general trend toward simplification in American eclectic architecture of the 1930s and early 1940s. Yet because of Staub's clientele, this trend also warrants examination in extra-architectural terms to observe how it corresponded to adjustments in the economy of Houston and Texas that occurred in the 1930s. In this respect, Staub's fascination with an architecture of typological repetition mirrors the emergence of a new consensus among Houston's economic elite in the wake of the Great Depression.

In 1939, an article on Texas in *Fortune* magazine reported: "they tell you in Houston 'this is the city that never knew the depression.'"[2] As the unnamed author observed, this phrase underestimated the impact of the Great Depression on Houston's economy, especially after the expansionary cycle of the 1920s. McComb, in his history of Houston, noted that during the 1920s the value of new building permits rose from $10,398,000 in 1921 to $35 million in 1925 and peaked in 1929 at $35,320,000. In contrast, the value of new building permits issued in Houston in 1932 was $2.9 million. McComb charted the recovery of Houston's economy through a rise in building permits to $18.5 million for 1936 and $25 million for 1938, a figure that would not be surpassed until after World War II.[3] Yet Buenger and Pratt observe that some sectors of Houston's economy, notably the cotton-buying business, were hit hard.[4] How Houston's entrepreneurial elite dealt with the crisis that the collapse of the stock market portended illustrates the critical role of consensus formation in making a local recovery possible. Two episodes exemplify the construction of consensus under conflicted circumstances.

Between October 25 and October 27, 1931, Jesse H. Jones convened a marathon conference of Houston business leaders in his office to work out a plan of economic restructuring among Houston banks and corporations to assume the liabilities of two banks that were insolvent, one of them being the Houston National Bank, the second-oldest chartered bank in Houston. Intense ideological and personal conflicts existed among these leaders. Some believed that a bank failure was the most efficient way to address irresponsible management practices and investment policies. Jones, who was deeply mistrusted by some participants because of his past business practices, argued that the failure of two banks could cause a run on all Houston banks and destabilize small-town Texas banks that had correspondent relationships with Houston banks. Bank failures would injure Houston's reputation among national financial institutions and prospects for regional economic recovery. Jones persuaded the consenting business leaders to pressure the dissenters into adding liabilities to those they were already struggling with, finding new owners to recapitalize the Houston National Bank, and agreeing to allow Jones's National Bank of Commerce to absorb the other bank. Jones's efforts to reassure major New York, Chicago, and Pittsburgh bankers as well as corporations with substantial investments along the Texas Gulf coast of the success of this operation sustained confidence in Houston's banking and corporate community. It also gave Jones such stature that the next year Pres. Herbert Hoover appointed him to the Reconstruction Finance Corporation, despite Jones's prominence as a Democrat, and Franklin D. Roosevelt, after his inauguration in March 1933, named Jones chairman of the Reconstruction Finance Corporation, a position he retained until 1945, even while serving the Roosevelt administration concurrently as federal loan administrator and eventually as secretary of the Department of Commerce.[5]

A number of Staub's most prominent clients were involved in a protracted economic, political, and ideological conflict over oil and natural gas prorationing by the states and the U.S. Department of the Interior. Between 1931 and 1934, as the Depression precipitated a crisis in the U.S. oil industry because of mounting production and diminishing markets, the Texas legislature tried to regulate oil production by limiting the amount of oil and natural gas that could be extracted within certain time intervals. Independent oil operators defied the Texas Railroad Commission, the state regulatory agency to which the Texas Legislature assigned authority for regulating various phases of the oil and natural gas industry, by producing oil so far in excess of market demand that the price of oil fell from just under one dollar per barrel to ten cents, and for "hot" oil—illegally produced or stolen oil—four cents per barrel.[6]

Ross Sterling, who served one term as governor in 1931 and 1932, twice called the Texas Legislature into special session to pass legislation authorizing the Railroad Commission to set proration limits, only to have these measures overruled in court challenges brought by oilmen opposed to production controls. After Franklin Roosevelt took office in 1933, representatives of the major oil corporations sought federal intervention. Continued readjustments on the part of the Texas Legislature and the U.S. Congress led to the crafting of laws that withstood court challenges in 1934 and 1935, leaving oilfield regulation in the hands of state commissions but reinforced by the federal government's authority to regulate interstate commerce and ensure consistent enforcement policies and practices. Proration tied to market demand was successfully implemented by the end of 1934 in Texas, with the result that the price of oil returned to the one dollar per barrel level. The period from 1935 to 1945 was the golden age of the Texas oil industry.[7]

The demonstrated ability of prorationing to rapidly stabilize oil prices, the Railroad Commission's success in authorizing production practices that conserved oil and natural gas reserves instead of wastefully depleting them, and the increasing sophistication of the scientific practices and technology used in oil exploration seemed to confirm the pro-regulationist position, the stance associated with the major vertically integrated oil companies and especially with William S. Farish.[8] The leading independent oilman to figure as a proponent of regulation was Charles F. Roeser of Fort Worth, for whom Staub designed a house that was not built.[9]

Don E. Carleton in his biography of the independent oilman Jubal R. Parten, one of the leaders of the anti-regulatory movement, repeatedly cites Staub's clients Hugh Roy Cullen, Mike Hogg, and Dan J. Harrison as foremost among the Houston oilmen opposed to government regulation.[10] The extent to which these opponents eventually conceded the economic usefulness of conservation practices can be inferred from the fact that the authors of Cullen's authorized biography, published in 1954, never mention the prorationing controversy.[11] In the Houston banking crisis and the Texas proration controversy, consensus was not achieved between like-minded parties but by conflicting interests. The practice of constructing economic and political consensus was the technique that an emerging segment of Houston's entrepreneurial elite identified with in the 1930s.

In his history of the Houston law firm of Vinson and Elkins, Harold M. Hyman tied the rise to influence and power of an emerging generation of entrepreneurs in the 1930s to wealth-producing activities they pursued aggressively but that also reflected a measure of collective deliberation. Hyman focuses on Judge James A. Elkins, co-founder of the Vinson and Elkins law firm and of what in 1934 became the City National Bank. What set Judge Elkins apart from the business and professional leaders who were Staub's clients in the 1920s were his aggressive business style and his disinterest in conforming to the subject position of the gentleman. In place of patrician Southern courtliness, Elkins substituted an ethic of personal honesty, reliability, and trust; a commitment to serving the clients of Vinson and Elkins and the City National Bank unfailingly; and a small-town subject position that Hyman characterized as the "sly hick."[12] Elkins defined an intensely personal business and professional style that challenged the Progressive ethos of hierarchy, systematization, objectivity, and rational planning.

In this context, Staub's fascination with typification can be interpreted as a spatial reflection of the process of consensus formation that marked Houston's business style in the 1930s. Of the twenty-two houses Staub designed in River Oaks in the 1930s, fourteen were for clients whose wealth derived directly or indirectly from oil. This economic pattern, which was very different from that of the 1920s, also held true for his houses in other Houston neighborhoods and outside Houston. Repetition, rationalization, and restraint produced a semblance of formal order signifying upper-class consensus on the virtues and practices from which Staub's clients benefited economically during the Great Depression, masking the extent to which this consensus was centered on financial self-interest and involved unresolved intra-elite ideological conflicts. Although the nature of their stylistic expression changed after the exuberant houses of the early 1930s, Staub continued to design houses that performed the resolution of contradictions symbolically by naturalizing style in the site-specific circumstances in which the houses were given form. In this way his houses of the 1930s—most visibly so in River Oaks—served his clients by constructing class identity and the appearance of class solidarity through their formal beauty and coherence as well as edifying and, through their spatial organization and proportional composition, inspiring owners to internalize upper-class subject positions.

Between 1933 and 1935 Staub designed three houses along Inwood Drive in River Oaks that are variations on a typological theme. They are based on the Hutcheson House type: a symmetrically composed rectangular block with offset wings in which a living room running front-to-back is perpendicularly paired with a dining room spanning the length of the central block. Each house lies on the south side of the street, so that reception rooms and bedrooms can open toward the rear garden. What is fascinating is how Staub chose to articulate individual differences reflecting client requirements and budgets in the context of a strongly defined type. The emphasis on typicality in these houses suggests an optimal architectural resolution of issues of planning and spatial organization. It suggests as well an optimal architectural resolution of the spatial representation of patrician identity and subjectivity, as though a measure of individual anonymity affirmed the class status of these houses even more effectively.

The two-story, four-bedroom house for Harriet M. and David D. Bruton was designed and built in 1933–34 for $32,930. Pete Miller was the general contractor.[13] David Bruton was an independent oil operator who had formerly worked as a lease man for the oil operators Erwin Smith and C. E. Gates.[14] The Bruton House appears to be quite straightforward: a simplified, more austere brick version of the Hutcheson House.

The house's compositional subtleties emerge on analysis. Staub's use of raised horizontal brick bands staged differences in sill levels between the five shuttered second-floor windows in the recessed central block and larger, lower-set windows in the outflanking wings. Staub constructed rhythmic variations by juxtaposing the trio of large, three-part openings on the ground floor of the central block with the band of proportionally related windows above, reiterated in the relationship between the hipped-roofed central block and the subordinate peaks of the hipped-roofed wings. He countered the dominant horizontality of the house front with the pair of vertical chimney stacks projecting forward from the re-entrant angles where the wings connect to the central block. Vertical slot windows inset in the chimney stack to the right of the front door suggest interior spatial surprises. The presence of two pairs of brick gate piers on the front sidewalk line of the property, detailed to match the house, and of a third pair aligned with terraced, brick-edged planting beds in front of the house, gives the Bruton House the intimation of urbanity with which Staub instilled a strong sense of spatial layering in suburban houses. The house's second owners, Olga and Harry Wiess's daughter Caroline and her husband, the lawyer William H. Francis Jr., had the landscape architect C. C. Pat Fleming install a brick-paved motor court in place of the original circular drive and tree-studded lawn.[15] Fleming's intervention enhanced the sense of subtly staged spatial layers that frame perceptions of what initially seems to be an uncomplicated symmetrical house

David D. Bruton House, River Oaks, Houston, 1933–34, John F. Staub, architect. Entrance (north) elevation.

Bruton House.

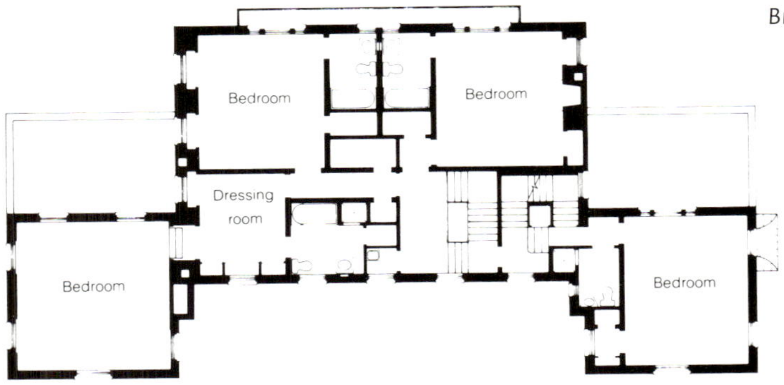

Second-floor plan

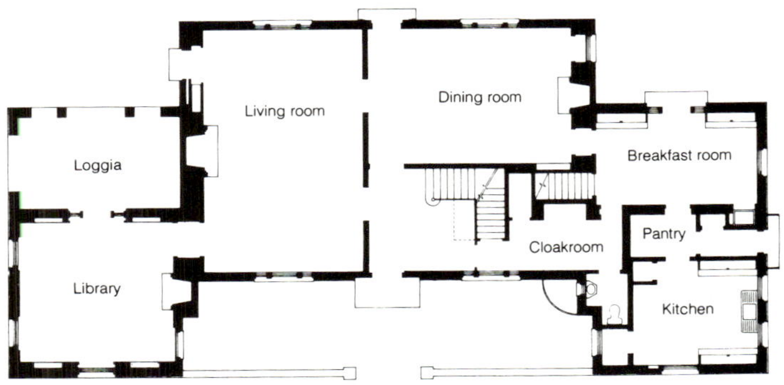

First-floor plan

front. Staging underpins the Bruton House's performance of composure with means that are so minimal they seem to disappear. Staub spatialized symmetry at the Bruton House with these techniques to materialize understatement, economy, and restraint as identifying patrician virtues.

On the same block of Inwood several lots to the west, Staub designed a slightly larger house for Ethel and Robert H. Bowles in 1935, completed in 1936 for $33,533. It was also built by Pete Miller. Robert Bowles was a geologist for the Standard Oil Company of Kansas.[16] Of the three Inwood Drive houses, the Bowles House is the only one that deviated from the Hutcheson House plan. The front door of the Bowles House is not centered on the symmetrically massed front elevation. From its off-center location, it opens into a wide hall that runs front to back, parallel to the living room in the advancing wing to the left of the front door. The stair parallels the front-to-back alignment of the entrance hall, rising to return in a landing above the front door. The dining room fills out the balance of the recessed central block. It is an elongated octagon in plan. For the house's second owners, Elizabeth Traylor and Patrick R. Rutherford (Rutherford was an independent oilman, president of the Rutherford Drilling Company and the San Patricio Drilling Company when he bought the house in 1941), Staub added a square-planned, two-story wing to the east end of the house, containing a paneled library on the ground floor.[17]

Staub used shallowly relieved brick banding to articulate the wall planes of the Bowles House. A low-key contrapuntal rhythm is established between segmentally arched second-floor windows on the outflanking wings, square-headed windows in all other openings, and the front door, framed by a classically detailed architrave with scrolled volutes and capped by a semicircular fanlight articulated with wrought iron. The progression from flat to segmental to semicircular profiles is effective because it is subtle and unstressed. The architrave framing the door is the only bit of "architecture" on the front of the Bowles House. Its scale is monumental, giving it a surprising degree of spatial presence and authority at close hand. Staub emphasized symmetry on the front of the Bowles House by asserting it volumetrically, then displacing it with the asymmetrical front door. Roofing over the recessed central range to insert a second-story iron balcony railed with black-painted cast iron, used also in second-floor balconies projecting from the wings, furthered this process of constructing individuality in the context of typological repetition. The design of the landscape was Pat Fleming's first job in Houston.[18] He reiterated the simplicity of the house's design by outlining the east side and rear lawn with broad brick walks. The walks border wide peripheral planting beds, where massed plantings spatially frame the back lawn as a plane of grass punctuated with free-standing oak and magnolia trees.

Robert H. Bowles House, River Oaks, Houston, 1935–36, John F. Staub, architect. Entrance (north) elevation.

Bowles House, end elevation of east wing, added to the house by Staub for its second owner, Patrick R. Rutherford.

In using cast and wrought iron to code the Bowles House as Latin Colonial, Staub gave it a more precise stylistic identity than the Bruton House. The appeal the Bowles House exerted was evident in the extent to which its design was replicated, and not only in River Oaks. Mr. and Mrs. Jacob L. Eisen built a slightly reduced version of the Bowles House in 1937 in the Beaumont neighborhood where the Cooke Wilson House was constructed. Twenty-five years later at the southern end of the Texas Gulf coast, Mary Altman and Frank D. Yturria built their house in the Brownsville neighborhood of Río Viejo in homage to the Bowles House.[19] Staub's ability to condense sensations of propriety, proprietary belonging, grace, and beauty in his country houses was so compelling that it inspired others to reproduce this design in order to possess its charisma. Typification aided the transmission process. The design of the Bowles House was specific but not idiosyncratic. The conciseness and coherence with which it spatially portrayed consensus on what constituted an architecture of patrician identity in Texas gave the house architectural authority.

The third house in this series was built next door to the Bruton House. It was designed and constructed between 1935 and 1937 for Jane Gregory and George S. Heyer. George Heyer was a Houstonian whose father, a New Orleans–born druggist and patent medicine formulator, opened a drug store in Houston in the mid-1880s, which George Heyer's mother operated after her husband's death in 1900. Heyer was a graduate of the University of Texas.[20] Jane Gregory Heyer was from Austin, the daughter of Julia Nalle and Thomas Watt Gregory. Mrs. Heyer's father, an Austin lawyer, was attorney general of the United States during the two terms of Woodrow Wilson's presidency.[21] George Heyer had been in the cotton business. During the 1920s he and his family lived in Liverpool, where he was associated with a Liverpool-based cotton merchant and exporting firm with offices in Memphis and Houston. Following his mother's death in 1926, Heyer returned to Houston. After one year in the cotton business, he entered the oil business as manager of the Cranfill-Reynolds Company, an oil production and marketing company that became the General Crude Oil Company, with George Heyer as its president, in 1934.[22]

Although there is not much difference in the size of the reception rooms of the Heyer, Bruton, and Bowles Houses, the Heyer House, which cost $92,656, was more expensive to build than the other two because of George Heyer's insistence on noncombustible construction. The house was equipped with a duct system for central air-conditioning although, initially, not with the necessary equipment.[23] Such interior finishes as marble paving in the entrance hall and parquet floors in other reception rooms gave the Heyer House a material likeness to Staub's grand houses. Mr. and

George S. Heyer House, River Oaks, Houston, 1935–37, John F. Staub, architect. Entrance (north) elevation.

Heyer House, detail of cast aluminum stair rail.

Mrs. Heyer had Staub incorporate eighteenth-century marble mantles they acquired in England in the living room and dining room. The slender stiles of the stair rail are cast aluminum as is the delicate English Regency period detail with which the rail is decorated.[24]

Staub told Barnstone that during construction Mrs. Bruton showed up on the job site one day to remonstrate with him for reproducing the design of her house for the Heyers.[25] Mrs. Bruton's sense that typification infringed on her prerogatives as a client indicates the extent to which Staub's project was apt to contradict the expectations of owners intent on singular rather than collective representation. The adjoining houses explore typification and the social construction of patrician identity with subtlety. Repetition involves rhythm, measure, and proportion as means to assert a unifying suburban architectural order.

The houses also differ from each other. The flanking wings of the Heyer House are recessed slightly behind the central block rather than advanced forward of it. The classical frame of pilasters and entablature articulating the central range gives the street front of the Heyer House a more focused composition and more monumental scale than the horizontally aligned Bruton House. Where the repetition is most direct—as in the three-part windows framed by segmentally arched panels and the solidly paneled front door with rectangular transom and overhead iron lantern in the central block—the variations between the two houses are most obvious. The jambs and headers of the Heyer windows are more articulated than those of the Bruton House. The front door is framed by a classically detailed architrave rather than paneled insets. And the overdoor lantern is detailed with crisply streamlined Greek keys that step out to spatially reciprocate the curve of the pediment. The houses exhibit variety of personality. Each reassures, though, with a representation of character that identifies each with patrician virtue.[26]

The landscape architects C. C. Fleming and Albert E. Sheppard designed the south-facing rear garden of the Heyer property, which comprises a pair of lots, one behind the other.[27] The resulting depth gave Fleming and Sheppard the opportunity to install an allée of live oak trees in the backyard to frame the symmetrically composed garden elevation of the house and, from its cast-iron loggias and flagstone terraces, construct a volume of shade and directed vision that makes the Heyer House feel grand. Bounding the flat ground plane with broad flagstone paths and massed evergreen plantings systematically integrates the composed exterior spaces of the Heyer House with its composed elevations and composed interior spaces. The subtle projection of power radiating from axes of order that construct and control perceptible volumes of space animates these River Oaks houses,

Heyer House.

Second-floor plan

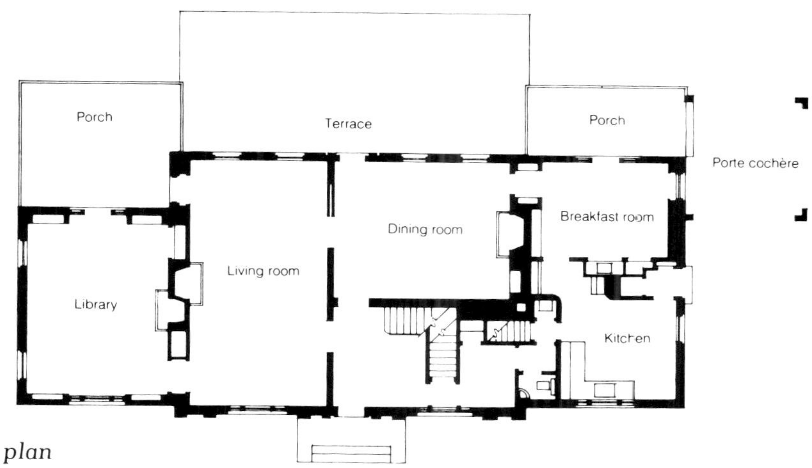

First-floor plan

most forcefully at the Heyer House. Staub relied on typification to shape an architectural consensus on elite identity in River Oaks in the 1930s that only indirectly acknowledged wealth and power. Wealth and power were much more likely to be embedded in his houses—in the authority with which they occupied their sites and interacted with their landscape settings; their solid construction, thick walls, and wide front doors; their proportioned beauty; their internal coherence and ceremoniousness; the precision with which decorative detail was designed and executed—than displayed ostentatiously.

The Bruton House and a slightly earlier River Oaks house, designed for Mary Vandenberge and George A. Hill Jr. in 1931 and completed in 1932 by the builder E. B. Crawford for $33,000, paralleled the design and construction of such grand River Oaks houses as the Katherine Bel and Harry C. Hanszen House of 1930–31 on Lazy Lane in Homewoods (which cost $107,977) and the Neal, Cullen, and Farish Houses.[28] Together with two of the most distinctive houses Staub produced—a Regency pavilion for Pearl Stuckey and Wallace E. Pratt at the corner of Lazy Lane and Inwood Drive in Homewoods, designed and built in 1931–33 for $42,495, and a Spanish-style patio-centered house on one of the most

Heyer House, garden (south) elevation.

Heyer House, view from garden terrace toward avenue of live oak trees planted by Fleming and Sheppard, landscape architects.

Harry C. Hanszen House, Homewoods, River Oaks, 1930–31, John F. Staub, architect. Extensively altered. Photograph by Sylvia Saunders.

Wallace E. Pratt House, Homewoods, River Oaks, Houston, 1931–33, John F. Staub, architect. Demolished. River Oaks Magazine 5 (May 1941).

arresting sites in River Oaks at Pine Valley Drive and Troon Road for Dolores Welder and William J. Crabb, designed and built in 1935–36 for $50,911—these houses represent Staub's simultaneous exploration of designs based on typification and individual exception.[29]

The two streams visible in Staub's River Oaks houses of the first half of the 1930s—the exceptional houses (Hanszen, Pratt, Neal, Cullen, Crabb) and those that engaged typification (Hill, Bruton, Bowles, Heyer)—converged in the Farish House, a grand house that Staub identified as "typical" with white-painted brick walls, black-painted ironwork, and second-story windows opening from the floor and framed by Lindeberg shutters. The Farish House demonstrated that grandness was compatible with typification, a proposition on

Dolores Welder House, River Oaks, Houston, 1935–36, John F. Staub, architect. Demolished. River Oaks 3 *(May 1939)*: 11.

which Staub expanded in the design of the Wilson House in Beaumont and the Camp House in Dallas. Staub's River Oaks clients in the 1930s were not as homogeneous as his Houston clients of the 1920s had been. They were far less likely to be from established Houston families and indeed might even be newcomers to the city. Some were from elite backgrounds, others were not. In this context, typification served Staub and his clients by constructing an upper-class identity position that was flexible, unpretentious, and—in the midst of the Great Depression—could be sustained socially. Through an aesthetic of self-effacement, Staub led by serving to construct an architectural consensus around images of dignity, propriety, and responsibility that, through the process of typification, stressed reasonableness rather than extravagance and commonality rather than polarization.

CHAPTER 8 : REGIONALISM

Dan J. Harrison House, Homewoods, River Oaks, Houston, 1938–39, John F. Staub, architect.

In January 1942 Staub's work received the only extended critical assessment published during his working career. James Chillman Jr., director of the Museum of Fine Arts and associate professor of architecture at the Rice Institute, wrote about Staub's houses for an occasional series called "The Architect and House" in *Pencil Points*, a nationally circulated architectural journal that in 1945 changed its name to *Progressive Architecture*. Chillman's essay was insightful and deliberately constructed. Like Staub's houses, its straightforward prose style masked a more complex argument. Chillman sought, implicitly rather than explicitly, to defend Staub against charges that his houses were stylistically dependent on historical models, built for rich people only, and out of touch with contemporary realities. To align Staub's houses with a consensus ideologically acceptable to a sufficient percentage of Chillman's presumed readers to make the argument persuasive, he framed Staub's architecture with the term "regionalism." Chillman then spent much of the rest of the essay qualifying his interpretation of regionalism to justify this categorization.[1]

During the 1930s, the consensus that sustained the eclectic adaptation of historical models for new building design in American architecture during the 1920s was challenged. Rationalist architectural criticism of the eclectic country house in the late 1920s and early 1930s focused on the practice of adapting historical models. But the ideal subjects of the country house, the lady and gentleman, and the hierarchical class structure with which they were identified were also being challenged. American architects sensitive to charges of antiquarianism but not prepared to accept the alternative of European rationalism and its democratic-socialist subjects tried to secure an ethically defensible position by readjusting familiar architectural practices rather than rejecting them. They constructed apologies for elite identity positions cloaked in their critics' rhetoric. In this context, regionalism can be understood as a defense against the formulation of new subject and identity positions through architecture, especially through domestic architecture.

Regionalism in architecture involved the observation that forms of cultural production—such as buildings—exhibited material consistencies based on construction, typology, and spatial organization that pertained over contiguous geographical areas.[2] Staub and Ima Hogg's invention of a Latin Colonial discourse in the mid-1920s qualified as a proto-regionalist project. It was Staub's contemporary, the Dallas architect David R. Williams, who became the principal exponent of regionalism in Texas architecture between 1928 and 1933.[3] Staub was one of the architects to whom Williams gave collections of snapshots of houses in Fredericksburg, Castroville, San Antonio, San Augustine, and other locales in an effort to promote wider knowledge of these buildings.[4]

Staub's affiliation with regionalism differed from that of David Williams and his protégé O'Neil Ford. In considering this episode in the history of Texas architecture, Peter C. Papademetriou distinguished between a "formal regionalism," which Williams propagated and to which he remained loyal, and a "regionalist functionalism," the position toward which Ford and Arch B. Swank, his partner from 1937 to 1941, moved in their buildings.[5] It is tempting to describe Staub's practice as formal regionalism grounded in the discipline of regionalist functionalism. But in reviewing the houses and other buildings Staub designed in the 1930s and early 1940s that displayed regionalist inclinations, his underlying concern appeared to be the maintenance of elite identity positions. This was the program that sustained Staub's regional eclecticism.

In 1936, Texans observed the one-hundredth anniversary of Texas' independence from Mexico, and Houston celebrated the centenary of its founding. Preparations had been underway for the Texas Centennial since the early 1930s, reinforcing the regionalist impulse in Texas architecture. The Historic American Buildings Survey, the New Deal program begun in 1934 and administered by the National Park Service that hired unemployed architectural draftsmen to document the historic architecture of the United States, also contributed to an awareness of regional historical architecture.[6] In 1936 Staub designed four houses in the regionalist genre that the real estate section of the *Houston Post* described as the "Texas Farm House." Of these, the house for Sarah Chambers and Tom Scurry, built by the Morgan-Bouiffle Company in 1936–37 for $20,085, adhered to formal regionalist practice by being based on a specific historical model.[7] It also adhered to regional functionalist practice because Staub reinterpreted the historical model in response to a rational analysis of conditions of siting and climatic orientation. Staub's client, Tom Scurry, was a partner in the law firm of Baker, Botts, Andrews and Wharton, which he joined in 1929 on moving to Houston from Dallas. Scurry specialized in work for Baker and Botts's oil and gas clients.[8] By 1937 he had been elected to the board of directors of one of Baker and Botts's most important corporate clients, the Houston Lighting and Power Company. Scurry's paternal grandfather and great-uncle, who came to Texas in the 1830s from Tennessee, were active in public affairs in the 1840s and 1850s and died during the Civil War while serving as Confederate officers. Scurry County in North Texas was named for his great-uncle.[9] Staub used a Texas regional model in designing the Scurry House to code his client's illustrious Texas connections and "naturalize" Mr. and Mrs. Scurry as Houstonians.

Staub told Barnstone that his model for the Scurry House was the oldest building in Houston, the Kellum-Noble House of 1847, located in Sam Houston Park.[10] The Kellum-Noble House was atypical of mid-nineteenth-century Houston houses. It was built of brick rather than wood. It is a five-bay-wide, symmetrical, two-story house based on a center passage plan rather than a three-bay-wide town house based on a side passage plan. Like rural planters' houses, but unlike town houses, it was encircled by two-story galleries supported on brick piers. The Kellum-Noble House is not a grand house. In 1936, the year that Woodlief F. Brown documented it for the Historic American Buildings Survey, the Kellum-Noble House was used as a park service building, not the historic house museum it became after 1958 when it was restored for the Harris County Heritage Society by Harvin C. Moore.[11]

Staub saw in the Kellum-Noble House a model for a historically resonant regional house despite the fact that it was plain rather than picturesque. Staub authenticated his appropriation of this model by spatially reinterpreting the Kellum-Noble House in the process of transposing it to River Oaks.

The Scurry House was built on Larchmont Road, a block south of Staub's house. The lot has an east-west orientation rather than the north-south orientation standard for most lots in River Oaks. As Barnstone observed, Staub, rather than reproducing the symmetrical front elevation of the Kellum-Noble House, rotated the historical model so that its L-plan rear elevation became the street front of the Scurry House.[12] This placement enabled Staub to give the living room and dining room three exposures each and to use the L-plan, inset, two-story gallery to shade the south and east faces of the house. Views from the living room and dining room are directed toward the south-facing side garden.

These reception rooms and the three bedrooms on the floor above were oriented for access to the prevailing southeast breeze. Visitors enter the house by walking the length of the nine-and-a-half-foot-wide, brick-paved gallery to the front door, which is located at the juncture of the wings, where the back door of the Kellum-Noble House is located. By taking the historic model through a sequence of reversals based on a functional response to climate, view, and plan, Staub constructed a regional identity authentically. What was also notable about the house, its compact size notwithstanding, is that the reception rooms were generous in size (the living room is seventeen feet, four inches by twenty-seven feet in dimension, the dining room fifteen feet, four inches by nineteen feet, and the entrance and stair hall nine feet, four inches wide). There is a rear entry from the driveway, a visitor's toilet beneath the stair, and even an offset alcove passage between the center hall and the dining room, providing the ceremonious spatial layers of a larger country house. Although the Scurry House had neither a library nor a back stair, Staub preserved the spatial amenities that authenticated its identity as a gentleman's house as well as a Houston house.

The Scurry House was the least expensive house Staub designed in River Oaks in the 1930s. It was the prototype for another compact house he designed for Ann G. and John M. Jennings on Troon Road in the eastern sector of River Oaks, built in 1937–38 for $21,745 (the Jennings House was the third least expensive Staub house built in River Oaks in the 1930s).[13]

Staub told Barnstone that the historical model for the Jennings House was the Larkin House in Monterey, California, of 1834.[14] In the late 1920s the Larkin House became the progenitor of the Monterey style, which was promoted as the regional vernacular of California in opposition to the Spanish Mediterranean genre, which had been especially identified with California architecture in the 1920s.[15] The Jennings House incorporates an inset gallery abutting an asymmetrical, street-facing end bay, the identifying feature of the Monterey style (although it is not a feature of the Larkin House). In other respects—white-painted brick walls, the detailing of ground-floor brick piers supporting the gallery, exposing the underside of the timber-framed gallery deck, and the profile of the low-pitched, wood-shingled hipped roof—the Jennings House represented a closer study of the back of the Kellum-Noble House than did the Scurry House. The appeal of the historic models for these houses was that in their simplicity (in comparison to the period style houses of the 1920s) they represented patrician identity by implying continuity with rediscovered American regional traditions. Adapting the historic model in response to site-specific local conditions guaranteed their authenticity architecturally and, through the logical deduction inherent in Chillman's argument, the authenticity of the class identity embedded in them.

One of Staub's most compelling regionalist works was a summer house he designed in 1937 for Clare Knowles and Lamar Fleming Jr., on a 240-acre tract on the south fork of the Guadalupe River outside Hunt, Texas, 275 miles northwest of Houston.

Fleming was vice president of Anderson, Clayton and Company at the time the house was built; he became president of the corporation when Will Clayton retired in 1940 and then chairman of its board of directors from 1953 to 1960.[16] Clare Fleming was English, from Hoylake in Cheshire. She met Lamar Fleming in Italy just after World War I, where he represented Anderson, Clayton. The son of a cotton merchant, Fleming had been born in Augusta, Georgia. He spent his childhood in New York City, then at Middlesex School in Concord, Massachusetts. Fleming attended

19

Kellum-Noble House, Sam Houston Park, Houston, 1847. Francis Mc Hugh, builder. Exterior elevations. Photo courtesy Doco Foto Services.

Harvard for two years before striking out on his own to join Anderson, Clayton in Oklahoma City in 1911. Will Clayton sent the twenty-two-year-old Fleming to Milan in 1914. After their marriage in 1920, Mr. and Mrs. Fleming lived in Milan, then in Liverpool from 1922 to 1924. They came to Houston in 1924 with two young sons; their two daughters were born in Houston.[17] The Flemings' house was built in 1937–38 for $35,600. Thomas Jensen, formerly of West and Jensen of Houston, was the builder.[18] Like the Bullock Cottage at Bay Ridge, the Fleming Summer House demonstrates Staub's sensitivity to the cultural as well as natural landscape in which the house is set.

Hunt lies in the Texas Hill Country thirty miles southwest of Fredericksburg. The stream-like channels of the Guadalupe River (which, upriver from Hunt, is divided into north and south forks) course through terrain that, near the river channels, is wooded with scrubby vegetation indicative of a climate that is much drier than that of Houston and the humid coastal plain. While summer temperatures in the Hill Country are as hot as those in Houston during the day, the region's lower humidity and cooler temperatures at night made it seem very appealing as a resort, as does its hilly topography, where shelf-like limestone outcroppings are especially visible along the river.[19] A twentieth-century

(opposite) Tom Scurry House, River Oaks, Houston, 1936–37, John F. Staub, architect.

Scurry House, view of south elevation from side garden.

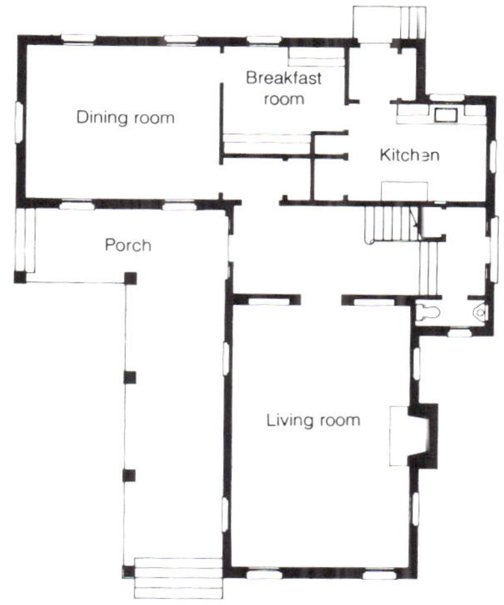

First-floor plan

Second-floor plan

Scurry House.

John M. Jennings House, River Oaks, Houston, 1937–38, John F. Staub, architect. Street elevation. Courtesy Doco Foto Services.

feature of the landscape is the low-water crossing, a concrete platform bridge without railings engineered to allow water to course continuously over the roadway, so that cars seem to drive through the river rather than over it. Together with highways slotted into the river valleys, low-water crossings give the landscape around Hunt, even when experienced from a car, a sense of intimacy not typical of most of the rest of Texas. Staub's siting and design of the Fleming House made visitors especially aware of these characteristics.

The house was built on a bluff above the river channel, high enough to remain above the normally placid Guadalupe when it floods yet without losing the sensation of being intimately connected to it. The bluff is on the east bank of the Guadalupe, but the road to Hunt lies on the west bank. The two are connected by an unpaved drive that runs across a flat meadow in the river bottom to a low-water crossing fording the stream, then, with a ninety-degree turn, up a steep incline between the river channel and the face of a limestone outcropping. At the crest of the slope, the drive enters the woodland and circles in front of the house. The offset wings of the one- and one-and-a-half-story, gable-roofed house rise in section and expand outward in plan in a telescoping formation as the terrain slopes down from the approach drive. Repetition of shingled roof planes and thick chimney stacks rhythmically constructs this formation. Entrance is not through a front door but an open-air "dogtrot" passage that penetrates the house where the middle one-story wing adjoins the one-and-a-half-story wing (in Staub's plans this passage is labeled a "trot"). The passage opens onto a

Fleming Summer House, river front.

Lamar Fleming Jr. Summer House, Hunt, Texas, 1937–38, John F. Staub, architect. View of terrace facing river.

South fork of the Guadalupe River.

Fleming Summer House, entrance front.

Fleming Summer House, dog trot entrance passage.

west-facing terrace overlooking the wooded riverbank; doors to the living and breakfast rooms in the one-and-a-half-story wing are inside the passage, as are those to the bedrooms in the one-story wings. The walls of the house are built of long, thin slabs of limestone laid in running bond. In color, texture, and formation, they resemble the outcropping that frames the approach drive. The one-and-a-half-story wing contains three square-proportioned second-level windows on its east elevation like those on the Hutcheson House and the Carter Lodge. In conjunction with the house's limestone walls and gabled roof profiles, the windows evoke the Sunday Houses of Fredericksburg, a distinctive, local, late nineteenth-century cottage type built by German-Texan farm families, who occupied them when they came to town for Saturday market days and Sunday worship.[20]

At the Fleming House, Staub, in the Darwinian sense, "developed" the Sunday House model. He naturalized the Fleming House by detailing the limestone walls to look like the landscape and fitting its spatial organization to the lay of the land. The two-room-deep floor plan of the one-and-a-half-story wing, with its long, west-facing living room paired with a kitchen and breakfast room; the exposed stair that climbs up one wall of the breakfast room; the sleeping loft above the living room, lit by dormer windows; and the profile of the shed-roofed veranda of the living room terrace can all be likened to Fredericksburg models.[21]

These operations underpinned Staub's reversal of the Fredericksburg Sunday House theme to materialize the Fleming House's identity as a Hill Country retreat for a modern city family seeking the isolation and peace of the country in summer. By resorting to such authenticating practices, Staub achieved the rational translation of a historically resonant, materially radiant building type to modern use, fulfilling the regionalist myth of an approach to cultural continuity that dialectically acknowledges difference in order to construct a modern synthesis.

The interiors of the Fleming Summer House are consistent with the exterior. All perimeter walls are load-bearing, eighteen-inch-thick, limestone cavity walls exposed inside as well as outside. They radiate the heat of the day at night but retard interior heat gain during the daytime. Non-masonry partitions and ceilings are of pine siding. In the living room, which is nineteen feet, four inches wide by thirty-six feet long and has an eleven-foot-high ceiling, the partitions are of molded and tongued vertical boards of clear white pine, finished with a thin coat of shellac, a coat of stain, and a coat of wax. The ceiling is of V-joint, tongue-and-groove white pine boards, similarly finished. Random-width plank doors with forged hardware sustain the rustic theme without veering into the theatrical. French doors or twelve-over-twelve-pane windows rising from floor-level sills enable the house

Fleming Summer House, detail of limestone corbels at eaves line.

Fleming Summer House, second-floor sleeping loft.

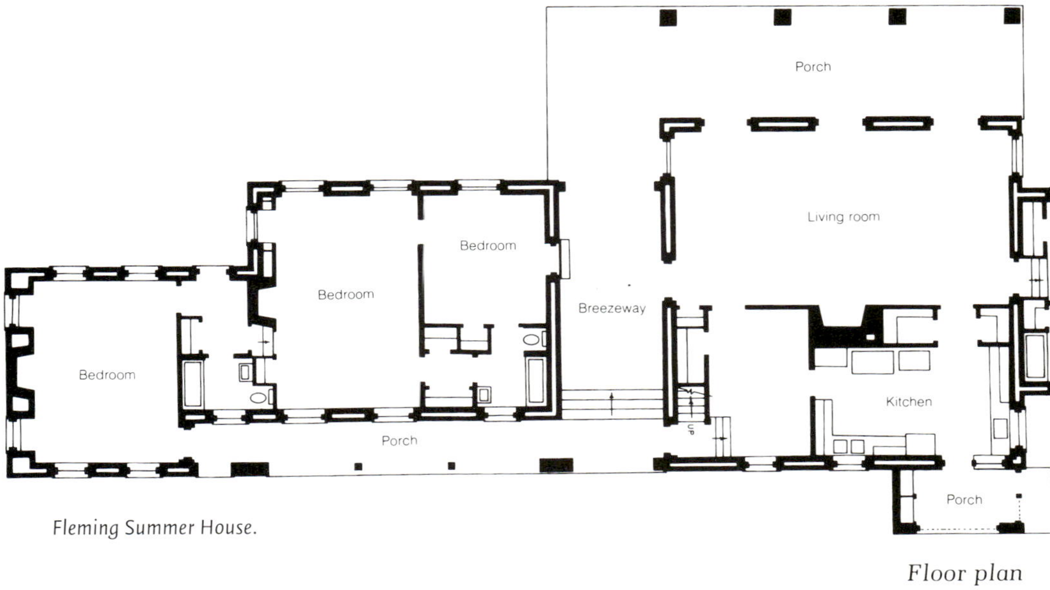

Fleming Summer House.

Fleming Summer House, living room.

Fleming Summer House, bedroom.

Fleming Summer House, detail of fossilized limestone fireplace surround in bedroom.

to be completely opened to the outdoors; cordovan-colored cement tile floors contribute to the muted ambience of the living and breakfast rooms and experientially unify the four-level ground floor of the house. The offset plan not only facilitated ventilation and adjustment to the sloping site, it enabled flexible use of the Fleming House, whether crowded with children's friends who might arrive unannounced or accommodating only Mr. and Mrs. Fleming. The Fleming House seems smaller on the outside than it does inside. The south bedroom wing is banked into the ground, and the eaves of the low-pitched roof seem to rest on the heads of the windows and doors, intimating a more diminutive scale than actually exists. The house possesses a rigor-to-charm ratio that dialectically grounds delight in the ingenuity with which the site-specific conditions of firmness and commodity are addressed architecturally.

The Fleming Summer House is materially real (Staub told Barnstone with satisfaction that the Fleming House was designed with the limestone, which had been quarried near Del Río, Texas, on the Río Grande one hundred miles west of Hunt, laid on the bed to emphasize its load-bearing function).[22] It applies historical models functionally (such as the dogtrot entrance passage) rather than as formal images. It is a seasonal retreat rather than a suburban house, and it frames its subjects accordingly: no façade, no front door, no ceremonial entrance hall, no intervening pantry, the stair is in the breakfast room, the back terrace is the outdoor living room, the bedrooms are not sequestered, interior finishes underpin its lodge-like identity and its code of relaxed formality. It integrates these formal, spatial, and material elements into a house that performs continuity, belonging, authenticity, and superior entitlement with understatement, restraint, and hospitable grace. Yet in the spatial layers that insulate bedrooms, the generous dimensions of the house's living room and terraces, the forged metal hardware, and even the discreet difference in scale and joining between the pine siding in the expansive living room and in the breakfast room, Staub built in nuances that materially code patrician identity in the Fleming House.

Staub's adherence to a regionalist discourse seems to have been linked to his interpretation of his clients' inclinations rather than to doctrines of cultural propriety and restrictions on the application of historical models. His fondness for Texan historical models coincided with the trend toward typological repetition in his houses, visible in his use of white-painted brick and black-painted ironwork. Yet as such Latin Colonial designs as the Wilson House and the Bowles House demonstrate, he did not exclude a wider range of models that could be coded as Southern if not specifically Texan. The house Staub designed for Ethel Hedeman and Dan J. Harrison on Lazy Lane, built in 1938–39

Dan J. Harrison House, Homewoods, River Oaks, Houston, 1938–39, John F. Staub, architect. Entrance (west) elevation.

Harrison House, garden (east) elevation with reflecting pool and azalea parterres by Fleming and Sheppard, landscape architects.

Second-floor plan

Harrison House. First-floor plan

Harrison House, garden (east) elevation with reflecting pool and azalea parterres by Fleming and Sheppard, landscape architects.

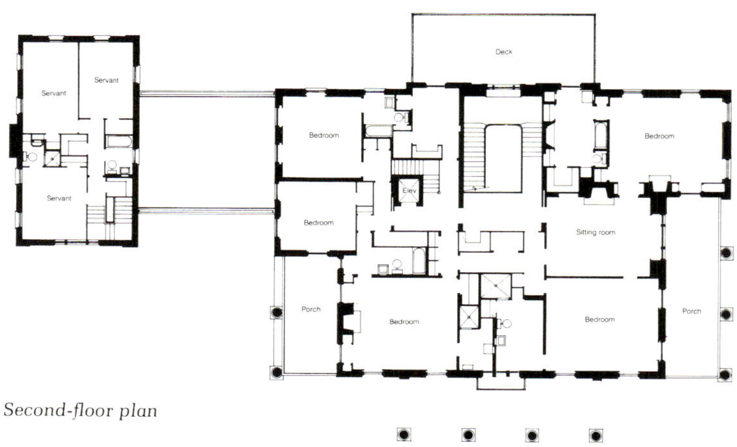

Second-floor plan

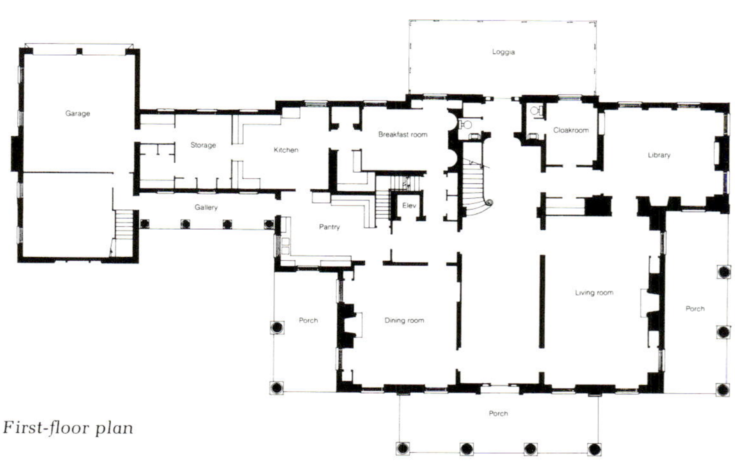

Harrison House.

First-floor plan

Harrison House, detail of service-wing entrance.

by A. A. Bertelsen for $126,918, was an example of what Houston newspaper real estate reports of the 1930s routinely described as the "Southern Colonial" style.[23]

Staub told Barnstone his model for the Harrison House was Concord in Natchez, Mississippi, a late-eighteenth-century raised Creole planter's house with perimeter galleries that had been amplified in the early nineteenth century with a low-pitched pedimented portico attached to the front of the house.[24] It was the profiles of the portico of Concord, its side-gabled roof framed by chimney stacks, and its shed-roofed galleries, that Staub adapted for the Harrison House. In place of full galleries, the Harrison House possesses two-story porches on the south and north sides of the house. A one-story, black, cast-iron loggia was appended to the rear garden elevation. The Harrison House is of steel-framed construction with reinforced concrete floor and roof slabs. It was equipped with a central air-conditioning system and a passenger elevator.

Staub's application of a Southern regional model seems to have been keyed to Mrs. Harrison's family connection to Mississippi. Her parents were from Yazoo City, although she had grown up in Beaumont. Dan Harrison was a lawyer who had been born near Georgetown, Texas, north of Austin, and grew up in Lampasas, Texas, northwest of Austin and Georgetown, as Patrick J. Nicholson wrote in his biography of James S. Abercrombie, Harrison's partner during the 1930s and early 1940s.[25] Completing law school at the University of Texas in 1904, Harrison moved to Liberty, Texas, between Houston and Beaumont, where he practiced law, held public office, and entered the oil exploration business. Harrison formed the Harrison Oil Company, of which Mrs. Harrison was an officer. In 1926 the Harrisons moved to Houston, and in 1929 Harrison and J. S. Abercrombie began their association in an oil exploration business. Harrison and Abercrombie brought in, with E. L. De Golyer's Atlatl Royalty Company, the Old Ocean oil and gas field in Brazoria County sixty miles south of Houston in 1934.[26] J. S. Abercrombie and his associates, including Joseph A. Tennant, designed a model pumping system at Old Ocean, completed in 1938, to conserve and maximize the field's producing potential.[27] In 1942 Harrison sold his interest in Old Ocean to the Magnolia Petroleum Company, since 1925 the Texas subsidiary of the Standard Oil Company of New York (subsequently Mobil), for $27 million.[28] Dan Harrison served as a regent of the University of Texas from 1941 to 1944. He and Mrs. Harrison were members of the Houston Country Club and the River Oaks Country Club, and Mrs. Harrison belonged to the River Oaks Garden Club.[29]

Andrew Jackson Wray House, Shadyside, Houston, 1938–39, John F. Staub, architect. Street front.

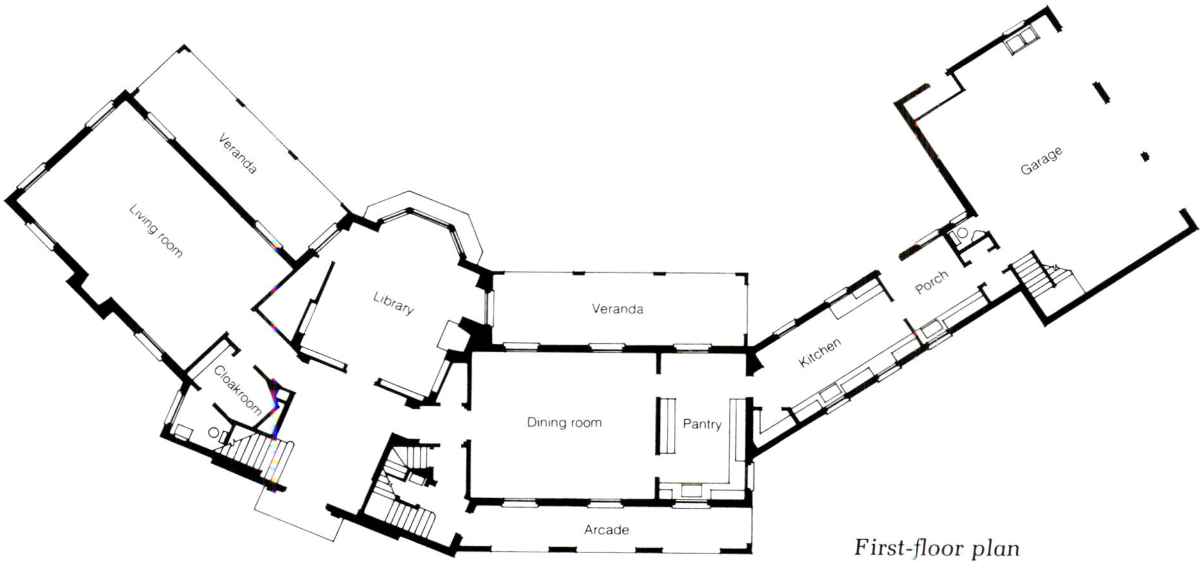

First-floor plan

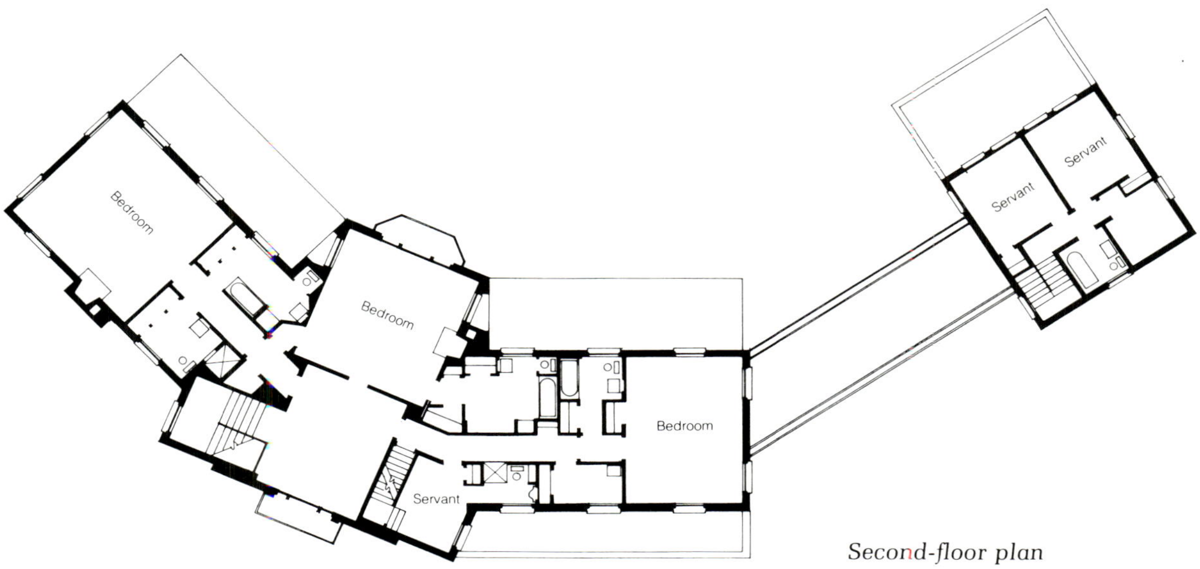

Second-floor plan

Wray House.

Wray House, garden elevation.

Wray House, view from dining room into rear garden.

The Harrison House is firmly planted on its flat, lightly wooded, four-acre site. The Ionic columns supporting the portico and the side porches give the west-facing street front monumental presence, although in closer proximity to the house the columns perform a reversal in perception, diminishing the apparent scale of the house front. As on the Farish House next door, white-painted brick, black-painted Lindeberg shutters, and twelve-over-twelve-pane windows that open from floor-level sills on both floors imbue the front elevation with a very even scale. The house is solid and relatively plain. The east-facing garden elevation is less reserved. The fanlight of the central stair window, which protrudes into the zone of the central pediment and is framed by a relieving arch, activates the garden elevation. Proportionally, the rear of the house feels like a weightier version of the garden elevation of the Bayou Club. The symmetry of the garden elevation is enhanced spatially by a rectangular, forty-two-foot-long, brick-lined reflecting pool terminating in a stepped brick fountain. The pool is flanked by parallel rows of low azalea and taller ligustrum hedges, all part of Fleming and Sheppard's landscape design. This ensemble compensates for the flatness of the site by integrating the Harrison House and its landscape.[30] Internally, the organization of house was quite simple, with a fifteen-and-a-half-foot-wide hall running on axis through the center, a living room and a mahogany-paneled library fitted into externally expressed volumes on the south side of the hall, and a dining room and pantry-kitchen-back stair (and elevator) spatial complex fitted on the north side, with service spaces spilling into a one-story hyphen linking the house to a two-story pavilion to the north containing two garage stalls and servants' bedrooms. A freestanding, three-car garage building occupied the northeast corner of the property.

Because of the proximity of the Harrison and Farish Houses and their typological and material similarity, what is striking is how different they are. The Harrison House possesses none of the effervescence and flair of the Farish House. It is grand but in a subdued, even predictable way. By 1941 Mr. and Mrs. Harrison's garden had joined those of their neighbors Miss Hogg, Mrs. Neal, Mr. and Mrs. Hanszen, and Mr. and Mrs. Farish as a regular stop on the annual Azalea Trail.[31] After World War II, their son Dan Harrison Jr. married Mary Alice Finch, the daughter of Staub's early River Oaks clients Mary Alice Cochran and Hubert B. Finch, thereby absorbing the family into "old" Houston.[32] However, neither Dan Harrison nor his family called any attention to themselves. The solemnity and uncomplicated certainty of their house seem to have reflected their personal attributes.

Staub's resort to Latin Colonial regionalism in the house he designed for Margaret Cullinan and Andrew Jackson Wray in Shadyside related more to a problematic site condition than an assessment of his clients. The lot is pie-shaped: two interior lot lines meet at a right angle and are joined by a north-facing arc, which outlines the street front of the flat lot. Staub folded the house into a series of one-room-deep facets that fan out to follow the curve of Remington Lane. This angular configuration spatially complements the curvature of the street in an urbane way, giving the two-dimensional diagram of Kessler's subdivision plan a volumetric dimension. The house screens the south-facing rear garden from the street and facilitates through ventilation. Reflecting the rigor characteristic of Staub's practice, formal regionalism and regionalist functionalism are fused in the Wray House.

The plan of the house is a blunt cruciform. The living room, the dining room, and the library open onto rear, brick-paved verandas through twelve-over-twelve-pane windows that slide up into jib-head pockets. The Wray House spatially conveys a sense of generous ease and welcome that begins with Fleming and Sheppard's wide brick sidewalk. The entrance bay is the pivot point about which Remington Lane seems to turn.

Staub underscored the bay's centrality with double doors set beneath a transom and a tripart second-story window in a segmentally arched panel. Delicate cast ironwork in the balcony rail, the transom, and the lanterns flanking the front doors accentuates the planar solidity of the façade. An arcade screening the dining room from the west afternoon sun adds a shallow layer of space not repeated on the street front of the north-facing living room wing, giving the Wray House an episodic spatial quality, to which the kitchen wing and garage contribute. The facility with which the reception rooms can be opened to the rear lawn makes the house feel spontaneous, despite the formality of the decor. In contrast to the rustic Creole models on which the Ernest B. Fay House and the Bayou Club were based, the Wray House seems urbane (if not strictly urban) in its Latin Colonial guise.

Staub's uses of regionalism varied from house to house, just as his choice of regionalist models varied. In the Harrison House, a Southern Colonial regional model constructed an identity tied to its owners' family history and, indirectly, more personal attributes. At the Wray House, Staub used the urbane regionalism of the Latin Colonial to enable the house to spatially negotiate the curve of Remington Lane and perform community continuity. The two houses frame upper-class subject positions that are similar, yet emphasis and nuance vary from house to house, indicating the precision with which Staub spatialized subjectivity for his clients. The Harrison House is conventional in its formality: fixed, determined, and established. The Wray House surprises: it is long on the outside, transparent inside, with unexpected angled passages connecting the reception rooms to the entrance hall and with the primary family room, the library, located at the center of the house, where it is immediately accessible to arriving visitors. Jack Wray's gregariousness seems implicit in the library's centrality. Wray worked for Kemp Dargan's insurance company, Cravens, Dargan and Company, when the house was built in 1938–39 by the general contractor P. H. Fredricks for $51,992.[33] After returning to Houston from military service during World War II, Wray started his own general insurance agency, which became Wray, Couch and Elder. In 1930 Wray, who was from Waco, Texas, and had spent much of the 1920s working in oil fields in Texas, Louisiana, and New Mexico, married Margaret Cullinan, one of Lucie Halm and J. S. Cullinan's three daughters. Margaret Wray was a graduate of Smith College. She, her elder sister Nina, and her younger sister Mary were founding members of the Junior League of Houston. Mr. and Mrs. Wray acquired the lot in Shadyside on which they built their house after J. S. Cullinan's death in 1937.[34]

The choices that Staub's regionalist practices entailed contradicted a fundamental tenet of the regionalist discourse. As framed by David Williams and O'Neil Ford around 1930, Texas Regionalism countered the eclecticism of 1920s American domestic architecture.[35] For Staub, eclecticism—the practice of selecting among styles—was implicit in the variety of historical models he adapted for his clients in the 1930s and early 1940s. The claim of ethical certainty inherent in architectural consistency, as advocated by Williams and Ford, did not resonate with Staub. Despite his investment in regionalist practices, Staub subordinated the construction of narratives of place-based identity through architecture to the construction of identity positions that enhanced and stabilized his clients' class affiliation. To this end, the regional styles in which Staub designed in the 1930s and early 1940s never represented exclusionary claims. They were means to an end rather than ends in themselves. The forms Staub's regionalist houses were committed to conserving and sustaining were social forms, not architectural forms.

For a time in the 1930s the discourse of regionalism seemed to strike a progressive balance in American architecture between the eclectic practices of the 1920s and European rationalism and other modernist tendencies. It preserved in modified form the adaptation of historical models to contemporary uses that appeared to spatially perform place-based narratives of cultural belonging and cultural continuity. As Staub's houses demonstrate, the discourse of regionalism was sufficiently flexible to accommodate a limited eclecticism. Staub's houses also demonstrate that in the hands of an ingenious architect regionalism could be inflected to emphasize different themes. It was especially useful for naturalizing newcomers and symbolically transforming them into old-timers. It could spatially portray the cultural identity of its owner, assertions of superior cultural discernment and integrity, and the construction of place. These variations demonstrate how Staub adapted regionalist models to specific circumstances rather than taking regionalism as a basic architectural premise. Staub's selective use of regionalism can be interpreted as an indication of his primary commitment to shaping an architecture of upper-class identity. He explored the application of regionalist models when they supported his primary goal, but, as with his use of other stylistic genres, regionalist genres were subordinated to the representation of social forms.

CHAPTER 9 : THE CONTEMPORARY AND THE PALLADIAN

James A. Elkins Jr. House, Houston, 1958–61, Staub, Rather and Howze, architects. Detai of stair rail.

In the final two decades of Staub's practice, changing architectural and social paradigms portended a crisis for him and other country house architects. At the midpoint of the twentieth century, the country house became unsustainable as an architectural paradigm. It was succeeded not by a new and reformed generation of country houses but by the modern movement in architecture, which ideologically rejected the elitist premises on which the country house was based. Staub's houses of the late 1940s and early 1950s suggest that he keenly experienced this crisis as he explored various suburban house types in an effort to come to terms with changed circumstances. What Staub's explorations also reveal are the dialectical cultural politics involving modernism, tradition, and the range of alternatives categorized at the time as "contemporary," which occupied an ambivalent terrain between the more clearly defined poles of this debate. As a survey of Houston architecture at the middle of the twentieth century makes clear, the debates, even though articulated in terms of style, were as much about social identity and subject positions as about architecture. These arguments assumed special urgency because of the social-democratic, antihierarchical bias of interwar European rationalism and the egalitarian modernism that Frank Lloyd Wright called "Usonian."

The cultural politics of mid-century Houston underscore what must have been disorienting to Staub and his country house contemporaries. By 1945, the cultural tide had turned. Eclectic architects were no longer part of the mainstream. Staub remained in practice until 1963, and his firm continued to produce buildings until 1968. Yet James Chillman's tribute to Staub in *Pencil Points* in 1942 marked what, in retrospect, was the end of the country house era. Staub and his partners never lacked for work in the postwar period. But, as Barnstone observed, they were professionally marginalized because their dependence on historical models meant that they did not conform to the modernist consensus on the ethical unacceptability of such practices.[1] In the late 1940s and early 1950s, Staub sought to resist marginalization and re-situate his practice in this new mainstream. He did this by exploring the contemporary genre in domestic architecture in an effort to accommodate his work to the changed paradigms of American architecture.[2] His exploration of the contemporary ranch house type stands out in this respect. It was to be through a merger of the traditional and the contemporary in the design of the house for Carroll Sterling and Harris Masterson III—Rienzi of 1952–54 in River Oaks—that Staub achieved the accommodation that seemed to suit him and his clients. A late, provocative design for a large modern house for Margaret Wiess and James A. Elkins Jr. of 1958–61 reengaged the debate on upper-class social identity and subject positions in mid-century modern Houston architecture.

Staub's first modern house was his most frequently published house of the 1930s. When Staub designed the one- and two-story house for Carol Austin and Robert D. Straus on a lot on Larchmont Road bordering his backyard in early 1937, it followed Harvin Moore and Hermon Lloyd's one- and two-story modernistic house for Doris and Virgil Childress on Locke Lane of 1936 as one of the earliest modern houses in River Oaks.[3] The Straus House, which was built by Pete Miller for $20,690, making it the second-least-expensive house Staub designed in River Oaks in the 1930s, was equipped with a central air-conditioning system and had a backyard swimming pool.[4] In the 1940s Carol and Robert Straus retained the New York interior designer T. H. Robsjohn-Gibbings to design interiors in the compact house. In 1939, they had Staub design a freestanding, one-room, flat-roofed recreation house adjoining the swimming pool. The Straus Recreation House was one of the finest modern buildings produced in Houston in the interwar period.[5] In 1941, Staub added a two-story wing to the back of the house to provide a pair of children's bedrooms. Fleming and Sheppard designed gardens for the small site. By the time André Kertész photographed the Straus House for publication in the March 1950 issue of *House and Garden*, Mr. and Mrs. Straus had complemented their modern architecture and furniture with a significant collection of modern paintings and sculpture by Milton Avery, Max Beckmann, Yasuo Kuniyoshi, Loren MacIver, Henry Moore, Robert Motherwell, Umberto Romano, Frederic Taubes, and Karl Zerbe.[6] Yet in 1950 when Mr. and Mrs. Straus decided to build a larger house in Briar Hollow, they retained Hermon Lloyd and his partner W. B. Morgan as their architects, because, as Mrs. Straus remembers, her husband did not think John Staub could design a modern house.[7]

Among Staub's River Oaks clients of the 1930s, Mr. and Mrs. Straus stood out. They were young (Robert Straus was thirty when he moved into his house). A graduate of the University of Pennsylvania, Straus came to Houston in 1929 to head the Houston branch of his family-owned business, the Straus-Frank Company. Founded in 1870, the Straus-Frank Company had been a manufacturer of harnesses and leather products until the 1910s when it was reorganized to become a distribution company. Its most advertised products by 1930 were radios. Since the 1910s, it had distributed automotive parts, which eventually became the focus of the company's business. Under Straus's direction, the Straus-Frank Company in 1933 became the distributor for Carrier Corporation heating and air-conditioning equipment in Houston, just as air-conditioning, incorporating humidity control, became commercially available. Straus was one of the air-conditioning pioneers of Houston.[8] If the technology with which he was identified could not claim to affect the economy of

Robert D. Straus House, River Oaks, Houston, 1937, John F. Staub, architect. Street front. Photograph by Elwood M. Payne, River Oaks Magazine *4 (Mar. 1940): 14.*

Houston to the same extent as cotton, timber, oil, natural gas, railroads, and shipping, it did radically alter the conditions under which people lived and worked in Houston. Air-conditioning allowed Houstonians to escape the oppressive humidity that made Houston's hot summers and summer-like autumns so insufferable and produced such demoralizing conditions as mildew. The extent to which air-conditioning was regarded as a technology of deliverance in Houston is attested by the Chamber of Commerce's monthly magazine, *Houston*, which from 1933 to the mid-1950s published an annual air-conditioning theme issue.[9]

Robert Straus was both a technological modernizer and an exponent of modernism in art and design. He was one of the incorporators of Houston's Contemporary Arts Association in 1948.[10] Staub's house accommodated his clients' penchant for modernity in a dialectic of tradition and modernity, suggesting that modernity developed out of and was continuous with tradition. The house front was an abstracted, pedimented two-story bay, framed by advancing, flat-roofed, one-story wings.[11] The white-painted brick of the Straus House affiliated the house with the process of typification associated with Staub's other River Oaks houses of the 1930s. Yet within this framework of continuity, the Straus House stood out. The square panel of glass block above the wide front door, the grid of translucent cast-glass panels set in the door, and the running band of Greek key molding that framed the door gave the house a hermetic appearance, underscoring its most radical departure from convention: the absence of windows.

The Straus lot had the same problem as the Scurry lot a block away: it had an east-west orientation rather than a north-south orientation. Central air-conditioning eliminated this problem. Staub used symmetry and the lack of transparency to construct a modern identity for the Straus House. He incorporated a two-car garage in the body of the house and faced the garage stalls toward Larchmont in order to

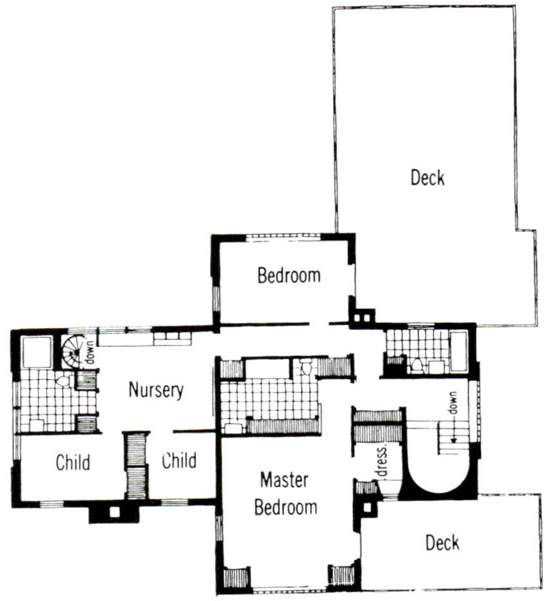

Second-floor plan

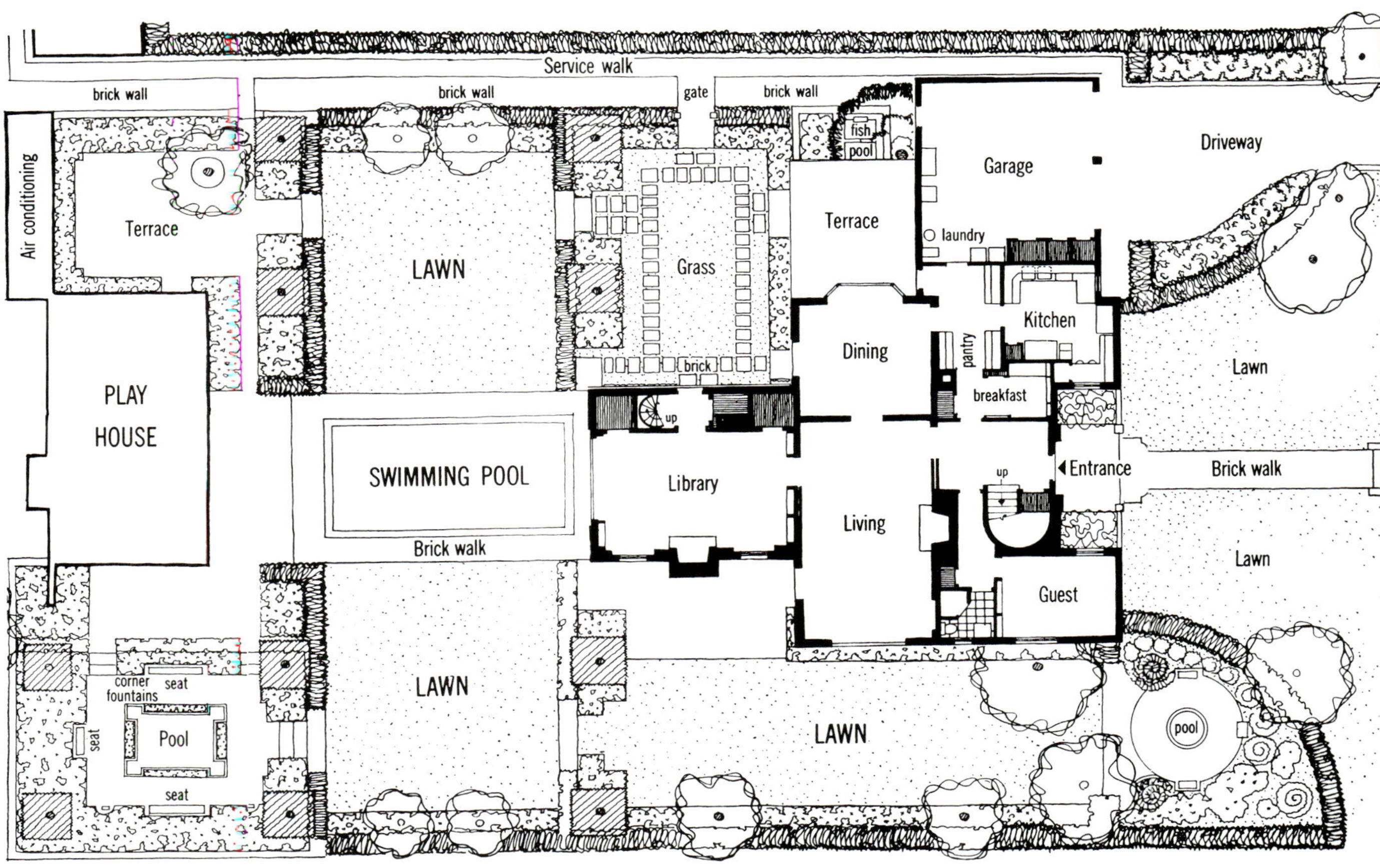

Landscape and first-floor plan

Straus House..

conserve backyard space. The garage wing, to the north, is considerably longer than the south wing that frames the pedimented entrance bay. Pat Fleming screened the garage with a tall hedge, restoring the illusion of symmetry to the street front of the house.[12] Staub's negotiation of symmetry and non-symmetry in the Straus House suggests his initial approach to modernism. Elimination of referential details and an even more extreme reduction to material essentials than marked other Staub houses of the 1930s emerge as his instruments for constructing a modern identity for the Straus House in the context of historical continuity. The Straus House's visual solidity and opacity (rather than its penetrability and transparency) were additional dualities that Staub negotiated to construct the Straus House as modern.

This process was apparent inside. The living room and dining room were detailed with cornices that, as Barnstone observed, were like classical guttæ subtracted from a Doric entablature.[13] The fireplace opening in the living room was rimmed with glass and stainless steel moldings. The dining room walls were finished with reflective silver Chinese tea-chest paper. The ground-floor library, part of the 1941 rear wing addition, had a floor and ceiling of cork that complemented the flush redwood plywood siding and backlit, octagonally framed shadow boxes in which Mr. and Mrs. Straus displayed Chinese statuary and books.[14] The symmetrical composition of the reception rooms, their sense of spatial amplitude (notable especially because the rooms were relatively small by Staub standards), and an ingenious north-south cross axis of light and view that opens the paired living and dining rooms to the outdoors demonstrated the assurance with which Staub constructed patrician domestic space within limits. The interior architecture of the house was consistent with the sensibility of Robsjohn-Gibbings, whose lithe, elongated walnut-framed chairs, sofas, ottomans, and tables, including a surreal, glass-topped table, "harmonized" with the Straus's eighteenth-century English dining room furniture.[15] The Straus House and its contents constructed modernism as an evolutionary extension of tradition. Classically derived practices ensured that all parts cohered to shape a whole. Staub's architecture framed his clients as exceptional, yet within an economy of meaning that materially asserted their claims to belonging. The negotiation of difference seemed to make it possible for the house to stand out and fit in simultaneously.

The recreation house and swimming pool represented an expansion of the conventional upper-class personifications inherent in the house. Architecturally, the recreation house exhibited an understanding of the rotational technique of modernist spatial organization in the way its flat roof slab oversailed the white-painted brick wall planes to shade the pavilion's openings, which gravitated to edges rather than

Straus House, detail of front door.

Straus House, living room as furnished by T. H. Robsjohn-Gibbings. Photograph by André Kertész. Courtesy Condé Nast.

Straus House, library as furnished by T. H. Robsjohn-Gibbings. Photograph by André Kertész. Courtesy Condé Nast.

centers. None of the wall planes was symmetrically composed. The pavilion's exposed brick interior wall, its sliding wood-framed window walls, the north-end interior wall, faced with rattan and incorporating a cocktail bar, and the rattan furniture materialized sophisticated relaxation *and* family recreation.[16]

These objects seemed to construct a modern elite identity that dispensed with classical compositional precepts and hierarchical differentiation for a functionalist approach to spatial organization. The recreation house, its cocktail bar, "Oriental" furniture, and the swimming pool suggest Los Angeles (or, as it was apt to be coded in Houston during the 1940s, "Hollywood") as the source of the sophisticated, informal, outdoor-oriented subject positions being constructed here.[17] *River Oaks* magazine characterized the Straus House and Recreation House in an illustrated feature entitled "Contemporary Classic," as antitheses: "The playroom . . . is as . . . informal as the main house is formal."[18] Staub negotiated modern identity through a hierarchy of representations that spatially concealed the most modern (with its subject positions liberated from hierarchy) with a more nuanced equilibration of modernity and tradition still based on the mechanics of hierarchy.

The recreation house would not have been mistaken for the work of the influential Los Angeles modern architect Richard Neutra, an Austrian immigrant, but it could have been the work of the Arkansas-born New York modernist Edward Durell Stone or of the Swiss-born New York architect William Lescaze. In 1936, Lescaze, at the suggestion of the Dallas merchant Stanley Marcus, was commissioned by the Magnolia Petroleum Company to design the Magnolia Lounge, a visitors' pavilion at the Texas Centennial Exposition in Dallas.[19] The next year, a compact, two-story country house was built outside Brownsville by George Kraigher, a pilot for Pan American Airways, to the designs of Richard Neutra.[20] These two small buildings introduced European rationalism (or, as it was more commonly known in the United States, the International Style of modern architecture)

Straus Recreation House, 1939, John F. Staub, architect. East elevation. Photograph by Elwood M. Payne, River Oaks Magazine *4 (Mar. 1940): 14.*

Straus Recreation House, interior. Photograph by Elwood M. Payne, River Oaks Magazine *4 (Mar. 1940): 14.*

to Texas. In 1937, the first modern architecture practice in Houston was begun by two architects educated at the University of Texas who obtained their initial professional experience in Chicago in the 1930s, Frederick J. MacKie and Karl Kamrath. Fred MacKie and Karl Kamrath came to Houston with only letters of introduction. By 1940 they had become the Houston architects whose buildings were most frequently published in the national architectural press.[21] During the first part of their career (both entered military service in 1942), MacKie and Kamrath produced traditional houses as well as buildings that reflected Kamrath's devotion to the Usonian architecture of Frank Lloyd Wright. MacKie and Kamrath's traditional houses (many of which were built in River Oaks) were uninspired. In contrast, their Usonian architecture was singular.[22] MacKie and Kamrath domesticated Wright's Usonian architecture in Houston by using the techniques Staub mastered in the 1920s. Geometric clarity in the organization and articulation of spaces, attentiveness to siting and orientation, and sensitivity to the nuances of scale, proportion, and materials detailing gave their small houses an inherent quality that represented modern architecture as eminently applicable to Houston.

By the time Karl Kamrath completed a two-story Usonian house for his family on Locke Lane in River Oaks in 1939, other modern houses had joined the Straus and Childress Houses in River Oaks.[23] The most spectacular was a two-story, flat-roofed, steel-framed house designed by Claude E. Hooton for Opal Woodley and J. R. Parten, which was built in Tall Timbers in 1939–41.[24] When construction of the house was announced in the *Houston Post* in February 1939, it was reported that the Parten House would have no operable windows since it was to be equipped with "summer and winter air-conditioning."[25] The Parten House, like the Straus and Kamrath Houses, identified modern architecture in River Oaks with subject positions that could be construed as progressive. Parten was an independent oil operator and a politically active liberal, Straus an air-conditioning contractor, Kamrath a modern architect. These houses linked modern architectural patronage to modern interior design and modern art in a chain of signification that set them and their occupants apart. Yet Hooton negotiated the Parten House's assertion of exceptional identity by materializing continuity with River Oaks through the medium of white-painted brick, as Staub did with the Straus House. Architecture in Houston during the New Deal period oscillated between a modernity that was rarely vanguard and a traditionalism streamlined of reactionary impulses.[26]

In 1937, Staub and Rather rehired a recent employee, Donald Barthelme, who worked with them until 1939 as a draftsman and designer. A Galvestonian, Barthelme studied architecture at the University of Pennsylvania, where he was a classmate of Louis I. Kahn's. After graduating from Penn in 1930, Barthelme worked in Philadelphia between 1931 and 1933, first for the professor of design at Penn's architecture school, the Franco-American classicist Paul Philippe Cret, then in the office of Zantzinger, Borie and Medary. Barthelme was involved in design revisions to the Camp House in Dallas after returning to Staub's office. Barthelme's initials appear on architectural drawings for two Staub houses that were not designed in the modern style: a country house in Galveston for Mary Margaret Guinard and William L. Moody III of 1937–38 and a country house in the Fort Worth suburb of Westover Hills, Texas, for Anne Burnett and James Goodwin Hall of 1938–39.[27] The houses were built on very different sites. The Moody House is set on a flat city block.

The Hall House (better known in Fort Worth as the Windfohr House after Anne Burnett's next husband, the lawyer and oil producer Robert F. Windfohr, whom she married in 1942) overlaps the edge of a small hill. Theses houses share long, linear floor plans hinged at a circular main stair in an L-plan configuration and incorporate service-garage wings. Visible in both is the process of spatial exploration, with rooms of differing volumes extended in thin lines to produce multiple exposures and orientations. Expansive loggias produced supplementary outdoor living space. Neither design seemed completely resolved, an unusual circumstance for Staub. The tentative social exploration that appeared to be in process was a search for subject positions liberated from 1920s conventions of bourgeois propriety. Yet because both houses were invested in maintaining the distinctions such propriety entailed, the awkwardness in their spatial organization reflects the tension between affirming and rejecting identity and subject positions spatially framing an upper class. Anne Burnett Windfohr's house, with its octagonal dining room, party loggia, and swan stair rail indicated her preference for the strong form, stylish, patrician alternative. Barthelme's name also appears on the drawings for the Winston House. The design of the Winston House displays none of the tension perceptible in the Moody and Windfohr Houses but also none of the departures from convention attempted in these two houses.

Staub's office produced several houses in the early 1940s that forecast postwar domestic architectural trends. A one-story shingle-surfaced house facing Galveston Bay, built for Rosalie Hutcheson and Lawrence S. Bosworth in 1941 on the grounds of the Texas Corinthian Yacht Club outside Kemah, Texas, was designed by Staub. The other two houses were designed by Tom Rather, a one-story house for Don Riddle, the former advertising director of the River Oaks Corporation, of 1942, which was quite similar to the Bosworth Cottage, and an expansive one- and two-story country house for Rather and his wife on Blalock Road, four miles west of Memorial Park, in what is now the suburban town of Piney Point Village. These three houses could be interpreted as examples of the California ranch house, a suburban house type introduced to Houston in the mid-1930s that became the dominant middle-income house type of the postwar period throughout the United States.[28] The postwar, middle-income, suburban ranch house rarely retained the idyllic sensations the Bosworth Bay Cottage still evokes (the Riddle and Rather Houses have been demolished). This weekend waterfront cottage also suggests the appeal of "contemporary" domestic architecture in its relaxed avoidance of what tended to be construed as the invidious formality of traditional identity and the impersonal regimentation of modern identity.

The ranch house represented the postwar, U.S., suburban, middle-class social consensus. Like the bungalow of the Progressive era, it was an anti-snob house type. In Houston, the ranch-type house—single story, built on a concrete slab foundation at grade level and incorporating a closed garage (or open carport) in the body of the house, often facing the street—was built in profusion in new residential subdivisions developed in the second half of the 1930s, the best-known being Garden Oaks, which was opened in 1937. As early as 1926 a model house designed by the staff architect of W. T. Carter Jr.'s Garden Villas development corporation, Edward Wilkinson, was described in a Houston newspaper real estate report as a "ranch house type . . . home," the earliest known use of the term "ranch house" in Houston

W. L. Moody III House, Galveston, 1937–38, John F. Staub, architect. Detail of entrance portal.

Anne Burnett Windfohr House, Westover Hills, Texas, 1938–39, John F. Staub, architect. Entrance front.

to describe a one-story, detached, suburban house.[29] Like the bungalow, the ranch house emphasized social identity positions implicitly critical of the hierarchies embodied in the country house. Organizing all spaces in a single story, eliminating the entrance hall, combining living and dining in a single space, and incorporating parked cars in the body of the house stressed practical convenience, family-centered domesticity rather than formal entertaining, and the rejection of elitist spatial layering. Like the country house, the ranch house was set at grade level and opened outward to its site. This was the social consensus that Staub confronted as he returned to his architectural practice from two and a half years of military service in 1944.

The mid-century point in Houston was marked by architectural trends that seemed at the time very disconnected. Karl Kamrath, in a brief essay on Houston architecture published in the limited-edition book, *Houston: Text by Houstonians* of 1949, wrote " . . . most of our important work (meaning large, the only way most Houstonians measure values) is comparatively dull and copied." The New York architect Philip Johnson, when asked by a reporter for the *Houston Chronicle* in January 1950 about local architecture, responded: "Must we talk about architecture in Houston? It's so dull." Yet despite these pessimistic assessments, the profile of modern architecture in Houston was rising.[30]

Within modern ranks there were antithetical tensions. The Usonian modernism of MacKie and Kamrath dominated Tiel Way, the next-to-the-last subdivision developed in River Oaks, where Kamrath built a house for his family in 1953. MacKie and Kamrath's seven houses on Tiel Way spatially shaped subject positions keyed to their Usonian identity. These involved enlightened, middle-class, family-oriented life ways that seemed less invidious and more relaxed than those of Staub's houses and embraced modernist culture. Kamrath was another one of the incorporators of the Contemporary Arts Association; MacKie and Kamrath designed the first Contemporary Arts Museum in 1949.[31] In 1952, the Contemporary Arts Association began the Modern House Tour of new, architect-designed houses in Houston. Conducted annually until 1965, the tour was, as the architectural historian Ben Koush discerned, Houston's parallel to the Case Study House program sponsored by the Los Angeles–based magazine *Arts and Architecture*.[32] Like the Case Study House program (or the Azalea Trail), the Modern House Tour functioned as an instrument in the formation of a public. The Modern House Tour sought to construct consensus on the compatibility of modern material culture with everyday life in Houston by exhibiting the range and adaptability of modern identity positions and demonstrating how modern subjectivity could be integrated with middle- and upper-middle-income suburban family life. What this effort to construct consensus repressed was acknowledgment of the conflict among advocates of modernism in Houston over which identity position (and corresponding architectural trend) to promote. To those unconvinced by its claim to be an architecture of democracy, Usonian architecture could seem oppressive in its totalizing compulsion. The contemporary alternative in modern architecture, if less insistent than the Usonian, often lacked rigor. A third alternative was a trend that emerged in 1950 and became the high style of mid-century modernism in Houston, the architecture of Ludwig Mies van der Rohe, the German modern architect who left Berlin to move to Chicago in 1938. Embedded in this intra-modernist conflict over identity (which tended to be articulated in terms of style) was an intense conflict over modern subjectivity, a conflict that generated continuing tension among members of the Contemporary Arts Association in the second half of the 1950s.[33]

The anti-Usonian, anti-contemporary faction was identified with the French émigrés, Dominique Schlumberger and John de Menil.[34] Dominique and John de Menil introduced Miesian modern practices to Houston when they commissioned Philip Johnson to design their house in the subdivision of Briarwood in 1948. Completed in 1951, the Menil House was a one-story, flat-roofed, pavilion-type house with internal garden courtyards and wall panels of brick or of floor-to-ceiling glass.[35] Dominique and John de Menil dismayed Philip Johnson when they asked the New York couturier Charles James to assist them in furnishing the house. James combined antique European and American Victorian furniture with surreal upholstered pieces he designed, and installed colored fabrics on the walls of many of the house's secondary spaces.[36] This was the backdrop for the collection of modern art Mr. and Mrs. de Menil began to acquire in the mid-1940s after they came to the United States from Paris.[37]

Dominique and John de Menil infused Miesian modernism with associations specific to Houston. Its material and spatial economy, its volumetric clarity and regularity, and its expansive proportions distinguished it from Usonian and contemporary alternatives and produced, in the context of modern architecture, some of the perceptible sensations experienced in a country house by Staub. Miesian architecture became an instrument in the formation of a public in Houston as the consensus style of the faction of Houston's modern elite that identified with Dominique and John de Menil. As Colin Rowe, who taught at the University of Texas at Austin from 1954 to 1956 and at the University of Houston in 1957–58, observed in 1956, the consensus being constructed around Miesian architectural practices in the early 1950s was coded as "classical" and "Palladian" to legitimize its identity as the patrician form of modern architecture.[38]

(opposite) Windfohr House, detail of stair rail.

Hugo Neuhaus's eldest son, Hugo V. Neuhaus Jr., studied architecture at the Harvard Graduate School of Design between 1939 and 1942, overlapping Philip Johnson, who had enrolled at the Graduate School of Design in 1940. Although Neuhaus and his partner, C. Herbert Cowell, were modern architects, their earliest houses and commercial buildings exhibited a decidedly contemporary interpretation of modern design.[39] Philip Johnson asked Hugo Neuhaus to administer construction of the Menil House. This experience exposed Neuhaus to Miesian building practices for the first time. In 1949–50 Neuhaus built a modern house on Lazy Lane in the Homewoods section of River Oaks for his family.[40] The glass-walled, flat-roofed pavilion he designed for his wife and stepson internalized the discipline of Mies and confirmed the role of the Menil House in identifying Miesian modern architecture as the patrician form of Houston modernism. The early work of Howard Barnstone, a graduate of Yale University who came to teach at the University of Houston in 1948, and his partner, Preston M. Bolton, with whom Barnstone began a practice in 1952, exhibited a similar transition from contemporary to Miesian practices by 1954, as did the buildings of Burdette Keeland and Anderson Todd, the latter a graduate of Princeton University who came to Houston to teach at Rice in 1949.[41] Colin Rowe's fascination with the class-consciousness sublimated in "Palladian"-ized Miesian modern architecture by the mid-1950s indicated the extent to which Palladian became a code word for upper class in the cultural politics of mid-century American modern architecture.[42]

When in 1953 Nina J. Cullinan, the elder sister of Margaret Cullinan Wray, for whom Cowell and Neuhaus had designed an exquisite Miesian courtyard house, made a gift to the Museum of Fine Arts to enable it to build a new gallery for traveling exhibitions, she specified that an architect "of outstanding reputation and wide experience with the type of construction here in mind" be commissioned.[43] An ad-hoc committee was constituted by the museum's board of trustees to recommend architects. Hugo Neuhaus, Preston Bolton, and Anderson Todd were the three committee members who were architects. In February 1954, the committee recommended Mies van der Rohe. His design of Cullinan Hall, completed in 1958, opened a new era for the museum.[44] Staub played a role in this episode. In 1955, Mies asked Staub to serve as the associate architect for Cullinan Hall.[45] Staub, Rather and Howze prepared construction documents for the addition and were responsible for construction administration as well as remodeling the 1920s section of the museum. Anderson Todd remembered the qualifications Mies cited when explaining to the building committee why he chose Staub rather than one of Houston's modern architects: "Here is an architect who clearly felt the need for beautiful and generous spaces, who fully understood the expressive possibilities of rich materials, and who, because he was an eclectic architect, would respect the work of another architect."[46]

The contradictory triumph of Miesian modernism as a sign of superiority in a democratic polity confirmed Staub's professional marginalization because he failed to conform to this consensus.[47] When Howard Barnstone produced his book *The Architecture of John F. Staub*, he excluded almost all of Staub's postwar contemporary houses from the catalogue section of the book, relegating them to the list of works in an appendix. Barnstone articulated his objections to these houses in stylistic terms. Yet what confounded him was Staub's seeming inability to comprehend the inferior social status of the contemporary ranch-type house and the identity positions associated with it when viewed from the perspective of Philip Johnson's discourse on the "classicism" of Mies.[48]

A two-story house that Staub and Rather designed in 1947 in River Oaks for Margaret Wiess and James A. Elkins Jr. exemplified the dilemma Staub confronted in seeking to find points of continuity between his accustomed practices and the changing state of American domestic architecture. Elkins was vice president of the City National Bank, in which his father owned controlling interest; Mrs. Elkins was the youngest daughter of Olga and Harry Wiess. The street front of the Elkins House is notable for its lack of windows, an indication that it was equipped with central air-conditioning. Staub incorporated subtle volumetric recessions and projections as well as variations in the bonding pattern of its sandstruck buff brick facing to animate the planar street front of the house and balance horizontal extension with vertical thrust. A low-pitched hipped roof, with clipped eaves on the north-facing street front and wider overhangs on the other faces of the house, confirmed the house's horizontal planarity. Awning windows, which Staub and Rather used frequently in the late 1940s, were aligned with brick courses. The low-set, cast-iron decorative panel in front of the undivided plate-glass stair window and above the recessed front door contained a pattern of rectangles and squares that were reiterated in differing formats in the paneled front door and the wood-framed screened door. A strategically placed hedge screened a street-facing double-car garage, which Staub dropped down to street level, introducing a subtle split-level sectional shift in the ground floor of the house.

The Elkins House has an L-plan configuration. The living room, signified by the location of the chimney stack, looks out to the backyard through sliding panels of plate glass and a roofed loggia. The entrance and stair hall alongside the living room terminates on axis with the entrance to the dining room, which fills out the rear arm of the L, framing one side of the loggia and its patio extension. The dining room has exposure to the south- and east-facing backyard on two sides through windows of undivided plate glass. The back

James A. Elkins Jr. House, River Oaks, Houston, 1947–48, Staub and Rather, architects. Street elevation.

arm of the L is thicker than the living room arm, since it also contains the rear-facing kitchen and a breakfast room. The ground-floor plan of the Elkins House is two rooms deep, with a closet-lined cross-corridor (a lateral spatial continuation of the rear loggia) projected through the middle of the house between the street-facing garage and the rear-facing kitchen and breakfast room. Staub slotted an informal family room–play room (Mr. and Mrs. Elkins would have three children) in between the front entrance hall and the garage, lit only by a north-facing window. This room, although accessible from the entrance hall, belonged to the domestic part of the house (garage-kitchen-cross-corridor) rather than to the reception rooms (entrance–living room–dining room).

The Elkins House, built for clients who were the age of Staub's children, demonstrated his effort to respond to postwar expectations by giving increased emphasis to family life and decreasing the sense of separation between reception and serving spaces as well as decreasing dependence on historical models. The presence of the family room–play room and the closet-lined cross-corridor, and incorporation of the garage not in a wing but in the house's principal volume, reflect an awareness of trends in the planning economy and efficient management of domestic space that became part of the discourse of American modern architecture in the 1930s.[49] Staub's details represent his interest in developing forms of modern material expression, especially the fireplace opening in the living room wall of exposed brick, framed with thin slivers of slate, and the streamlined detailing of the stair and stair rail.

The rear loggia, screened on the east with one-story-high pivoting vertical louvers and incorporating an extension of the patio that intersects the rear lawn with a whiplash curve, suggests subject positions related to private, family-centered backyard living, Southern California style, rather than the formal social rituals of garden parties or Azalea Trail visitations. Staub's streamlined use of Chinoiserie references in detailing the cast-iron panel, front door and screened door, and the wood gate in the brick wall extending from the front of the house around the side-street line of the backyard distance the Elkins House from postwar modern identity. Frank Lloyd Wright never rejected architectural ornament, and the Finnish American architect Eliel Saarinen, who was at the height of his influence in the postwar 1940s, made material ornament an important component of the buildings he produced in the United States, especially at the Cranbrook Academy of Art outside Detroit, where Saarinen was director of architecture and urban design.[50] Yet neither Wright nor Saarinen would have countenanced ornament based on historic precedent. As innocuous as these details were in the Elkins House, they would have stood out as suspect, even in the context of the contemporary houses Cowell and Neuhaus and Howard Barnstone were designing at the end of the 1940s.

Elkins House, detail of living room fireplace surround.

(opposite)
Elkins House, detail of entrance bay.

Elkins House, detail of stair rail.

The first ranch-type house built to Staub and Rather's design was located on the 110,000-acre El Piloncillo Ranch in Dimmit County, Texas, 275 miles southwest of Houston near the Texas-Coahuila border. Designed in 1948 and built for Mary Alice Finch and Dan Harrison Jr. of Houston, it represented an application of the planning strategies of the Moody House in Galveston to a sprawling, one-story house in which guests needed to be accommodated, especially for hunting parties, in an isolated, scrub desert landscape.[51] Staub worked with the ranch house type through the 1950s in suburban houses built in Houston, Beaumont, and Shreveport. What marks them as examples of the ranch-house type is their single-story organization and compositional horizontality. One Houston example was the house Staub, Rather and Howze designed in 1952 for Mr. and Mrs. Robert P. Gregory, completed in 1953 by the contractor Edward A. Miller on a lot on Memorial Drive in the subdivision of Pinewood Estates.[52]

A fundamental principle of Staub's practice had been balanced composition. Like other second- and third-generation country house architects, Staub emphasized horizontality in composing the wall planes of his country houses. Yet through the countervailing articulation of verticality he sought the proportioned equilibrium inculcated by classical practice to ensure perceptions of decorum, dignity, and repose. Because the Gregory House and Staub's other ranch-type houses tended to be low-set and built on flat sites, they lacked the space-shaping and space-framing capacity of two-story houses. Unlike Staub's suburban houses of the 1920s and 1930s, the one-story postwar ranch houses were not capable of modulating suburban space by volumetrically displacing flatness. On large, flat sites, they simply reinforced the depressing sensation of formless sprawl that became an identifying feature of Houston's postwar suburban landscape. The symmetry of the street front of the Gregory House is constructed volumetrically but with projecting wings whose eaves lines were dropped even lower than the central portion of the house. The recessed entrance, framed by twin picture windows (fixed plates of glass flanked by operable sash), achieved what would not have seemed possible in the context of Staub's interwar country houses. The Gregory House was indistinguishable from the pair of long, very low-set ranch-type houses that flanked it. The suppression of balanced composition in favor of unmitigated horizontal extension and the systematic lowering of architectural horizons resulted in houses that sacrificed the sense of proportioned distinction and hierarchically graded scale that had been essential to the construction of identity in Staub's country houses. Also absent was the dialectical tension (the thesis-antithesis-synthesis dynamic) that had animated Staub's

Robert Gregory House, Pinewood Estates, Houston, 1952–53. Staub, Rather and Howze, architects. Demolished.

adaptation of historical models. The ordinariness of these houses is what disturbed Barnstone. To him they seemed to register capitulation to the dispiriting conformity that was the subject of so much criticism of American middle-class culture in the postwar period.[53]

Staub corrected this course with the house Staub, Rather and Howze designed in the Homewoods section of River Oaks for Mr. and Mrs. Harris Masterson III between 1952 and 1954.[54] Built by the Thad Dederick Construction Company, the house cost $323,896.

Ralph Ellis Gunn was the landscape architect. Rienzi, as Harris Masterson called the house, became the model for a one-story suburban house type in which Staub embedded the contemporary ranch house in a Palladian pavilion. In 1999, two years after Harris Masterson's death and five years after Mrs. Masterson's death, Rienzi was opened to the public as the European decorative arts collection of the Museum of Fine Arts, Houston.[55] Katherine S. Howe, curator of decorative arts at the museum and director of Rienzi, found in the papers of Harris Masterson three sketches he sent Staub in 1952 showing a floor plan, a front elevation, and the rear elevation of a one-story house. Masterson drew a long rectangular living room at the back of the house, which would look north toward Buffalo Bayou through a wall of glass. Masterson's sketch of the rear elevation showed this glass prism projected forward on structural columns above the downslope of the site, with the indication of a driveway to one side, suggesting that it conveyed cars down to a lower-level garage.

Masterson's front elevation showed a one-story, symmetrical block flanked by recessed wings, the parapet of the symmetrical block studded with what appear to be statues. Katherine Howe found Staub's reply to the correspondence containing the sketches in which he told Masterson " . . . the plan and interiors you have outlined are extremely attractive, and the desired combination of Palladian with Contemporary offers an interesting challenge."[56] Treating the Palladian and the contemporary as dialectical antitheses, Staub synthesized a house type that enabled him to recover the patrician identity positions of the country house, conserving and sustaining them in a disguised ranch house conforming to the contemporary consensus on how his postwar clients wanted to live, whether these clients were twenty or more years younger than Staub (as were Carroll and Harry Masterson) or were Staub's age and commissioning him to design retirement or resort houses.

Staub achieved this synthesis by expanding the plan diagram of Masterson's sketch to accommodate parallel bands of rooms: family rooms facing north toward the bayou, reception rooms facing south toward a paved motor court entered from Kirby Drive. As in other postwar houses by

Rienzi, Homewoods, River Oaks, Houston, 1952–54, Staub, Rather and Howze, architects. Entrance (south) elevation.

1406

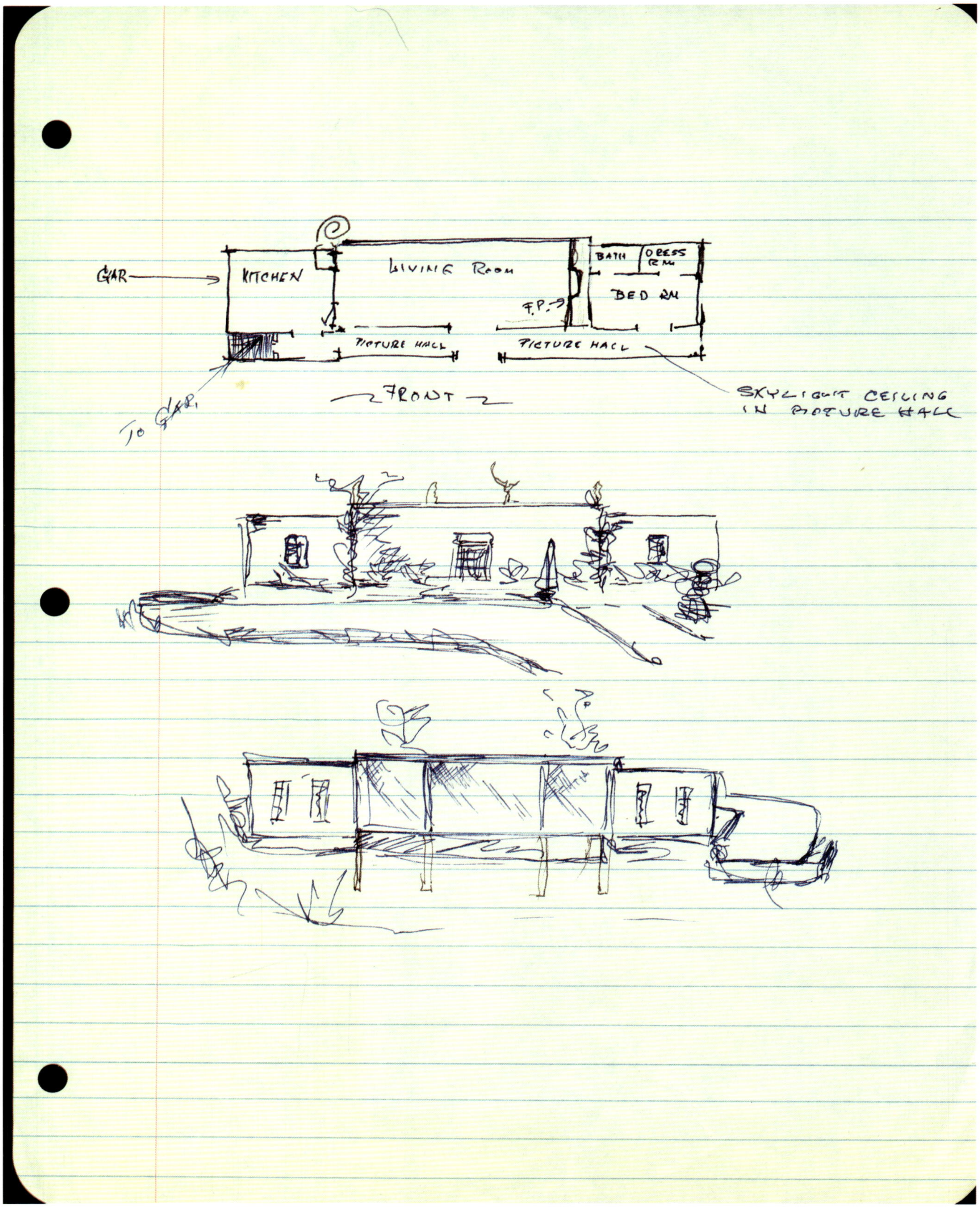

Three sketches by Harris Masterson describing his conception of his house, undated, c. March 1952. Masterson Family Collection, Woodson Research Center, Fondren Library, Rice University.

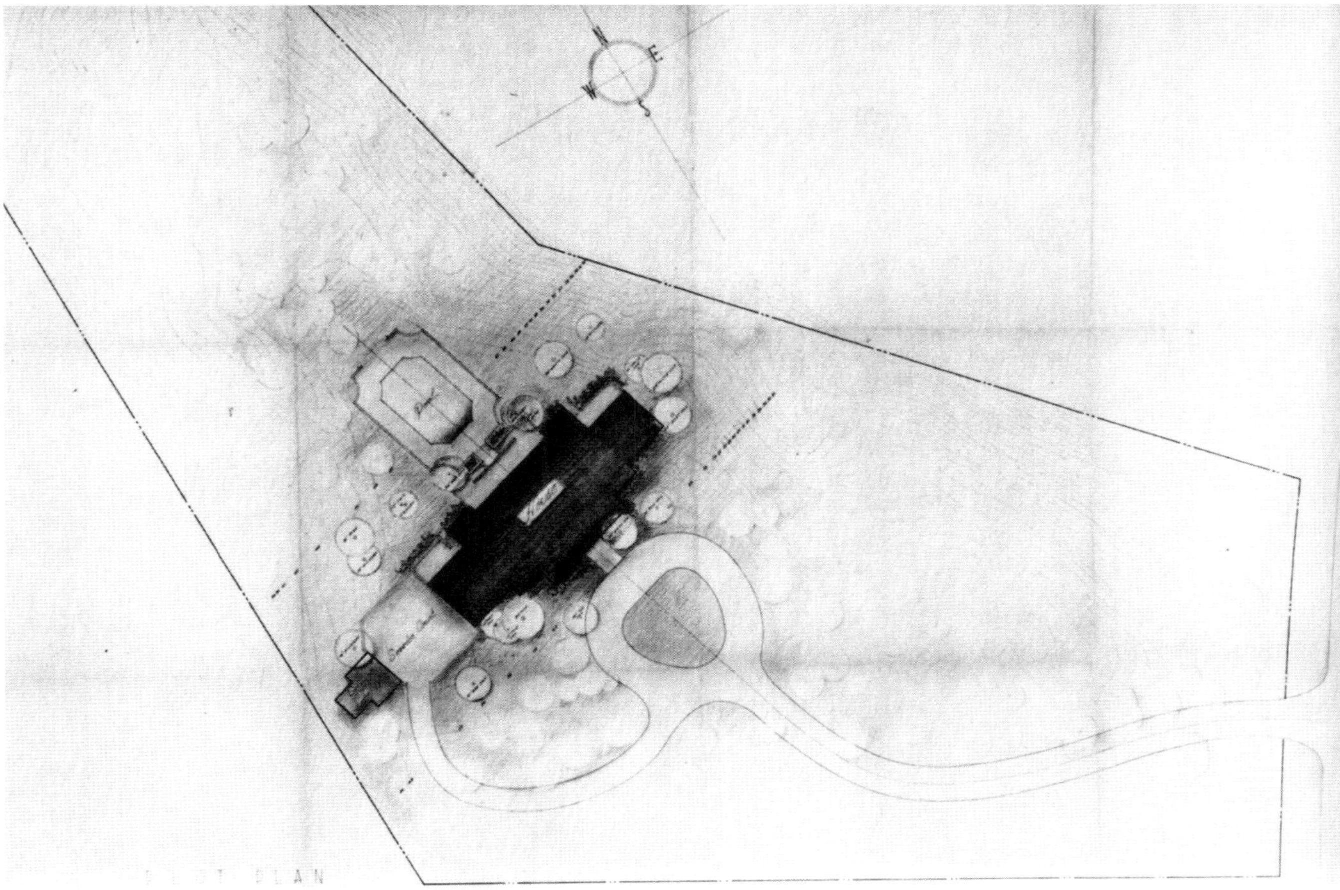

Rienzi, preliminary site plan. Masterson Family Collection, Woodson Research Center, Fondren Library, Rice University.

Staub, central air-conditioning made it feasible to double-stack rooms in plan. According to Katherine Howe, Masterson discovered a majestic southern magnolia tree on the downhill slope of the four-and-one-third-acre site. This tree became the fixed point around which the house site took shape.[57] Staub and the landscape architect, Ralph Ellis Gunn, had the property graded to regularize the topography, resulting in a two-tiered shelf on which the house and its terraces were built. A full story below the house is a paved, balustraded terrace containing a swimming pool. Below this terrace is a glade (where the magnolia tree stood) that extends northward into bayou woodland. Staub and Gunn used axes and cross axes to integrate the house and its setting. Ravines along the side property lines frame the house and provided access to the basement-level garage on the west.

The interiors of the Masterson House continue the exchange between the contemporary and the traditional. To either side of the marble-paved, skylit octagonal entrance hall are the formal living room (labeled "drawing room" on the plans and dining room. The two are equally sized: eighteen feet wide, twenty-eight feet long, and fourteen feet high. In comparison to the size of reception rooms in many of Staub's interwar country houses, these rooms seem small except for their tall ceilings. Yet Staub manipulated the perception of proportion so masterfully in both rooms that the drawing room feels like a miniature saloon—the long gallery of an English country house—and the dining room is quite grand, with an apsidal niche centered on one end wall and gilded Ionic pilasters framing symmetrically aligned openings and supporting a dentiled and modillioned cornice. Staub achieved his characteristic sensation of intimate monumentality in the reception rooms of the Masterson House. Although furnished with eighteenth-century English furniture, they felt like rooms in a house rather than museum installations. The central hall steps down on axis at the split between levels to intersect a cork-floored, skylit cross-corridor that connects all the rooms in the house yet, like the cross-corridor in the Elkins House, is spatially invisible. The cross-corridor is the line of demarcation between the reception and family rooms. Staub pushed the family bedrooms to either end of this corridor: Mr. and Mrs. Masterson's suite of rooms on the west and two bedrooms and associated bathrooms for Mrs. Masterson's son and daughter on the east end.

Staub paired the living room and library in the central north-facing bay of the house. The living room, at twenty-eight feet by twenty feet, is slightly larger than the drawing

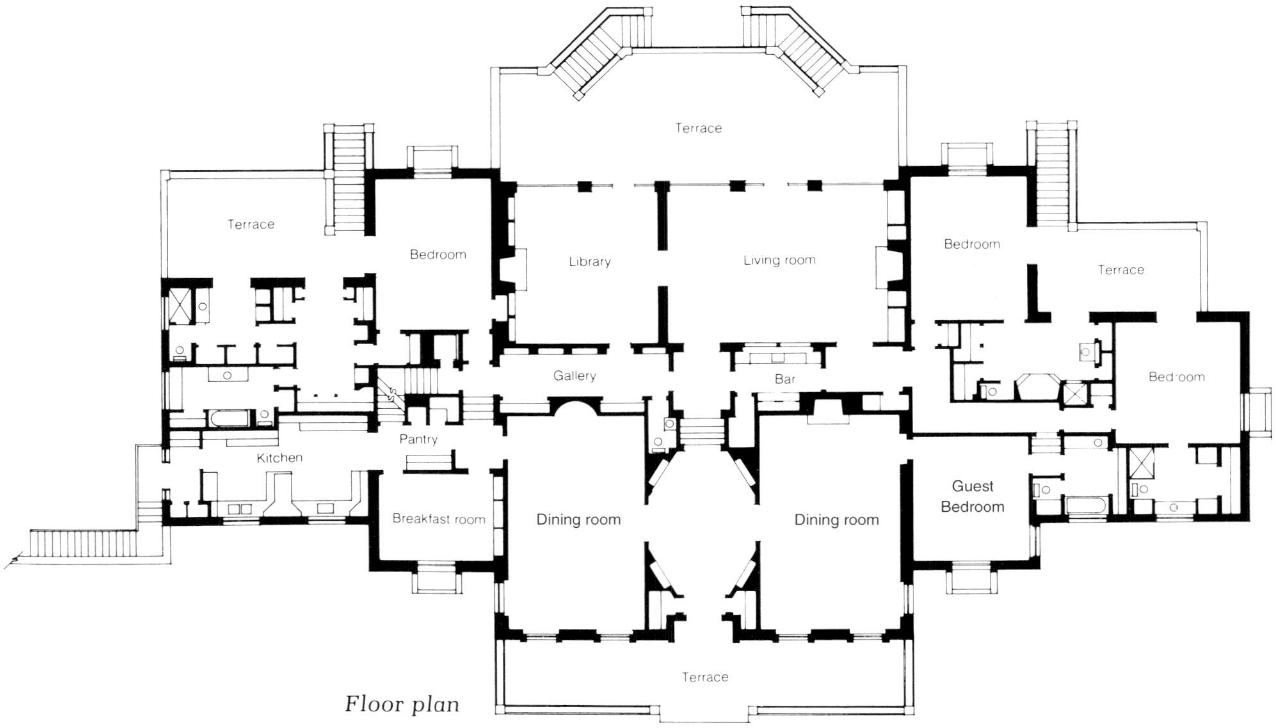

Floor plan

Rienzi.

room; the library is an eighteen-foot, six-inch square. Both rooms have eleven-foot-high ceilings. Illuminated by reflected north light, neither feels as big or spatially buoyant as the drawing and dining rooms. The end wall of the library was paneled in straight-grained clear American walnut. An eighteenth-century-style carved mantle front and a band of fretwork just below the cornice animate the dark-toned space. The living room originally had a fireplace opening centered on its end wall on axis with the library fireplace. It was flanked by cabinets concealed behind doors faced with Philippine mahogany plywood. The cabinets contained a television set, hi-fi record player, and radio. Centered on the long interior wall of the living room, in the depth of the cross-corridor, was a substantial cocktail bar that spatially conveyed a sense of convivial hospitality.

In the living room, contemporary subjectivity overrides the minuet rhythms of the other reception and family rooms. Opening to the back terrace and overlooking the swimming pool, the living room revealed the Masterson House's submerged identity as a 1950s suburban ranch house. One other room that performed this identity without inhibition was Mrs. Masterson's daughter's bathroom. Centered on a sunken bathtub set in a mirrored niche, the small room was paved with flamboyant Norwegian rose marble and sported a crystal chandelier. Somewhat more circumspect in registering contemporary subjectivity was the wall of storage cabinets lining the cross-corridor between the central hall and Mr. and Mrs. Masterson's bedroom. Internally illuminated,

(opposite) Rienzi, entrance hall.

EXIT

Rienzi, bathroom.

(previous page) Rienzi, looking from bar across living room to north-facing terrace.

the cabinets were fitted out as vitrines to display the substantial collection of porcelain Harris Masterson would acquire.

Rienzi reflects the personalities and proclivities of its owners. Harris Masterson was the descendant of a Brazoria County planter family. His grandfather and his grandfather's brothers had moved to Houston in the 1880s and 1890s.[58] Harris Masterson's parents built one of William Ward Watkin's grandest houses in the early 1920s.[59] But the dissolution of his father's inheritance and his parents' marriage in the mid-1920s cast Harry Masterson into the world of necessity. After a variety of sales positions in Houston and service in the U.S. Army during World War II (where, according to Katherine Howe, he discovered country houses, furniture, and porcelain while stationed in England), Masterson opened an antiques shop in the River Oaks Shopping Center in the late 1940s.[60] In 1951, he married Carroll Sterling, the only daughter of Isla Carroll and Frank Prior Sterling and the niece of Ross S. Sterling. Ross Sterling had sold his Humble Oil stock when he left the Humble Oil and Refining Company in the mid-1920s for new careers as a newspaper publisher, banker, and real estate developer, all businesses he lost in the Depression. Frank Sterling retained his position as an officer and director of Humble Oil and his investment in it. In the early 1930s, Carroll Sterling married Bert F. Winston, who was from a Fort Bend County planter family. Their marriage ended in divorce in the early 1940s after the birth of two children. Carroll Sterling then married John Cowan, who died in an airplane accident. She and her children returned to Houston in 1950 and early the next year she married Harry Masterson at Christ Church.[61] Carroll Sterling had the resources that permitted Harris Masterson to build a house that precisely shaped an identity position sustaining his self-invention as an Anglo-Southern aristocrat.

Masterson used material culture to advance a cultural agenda. His house was a technology of self-fashioning that constructed him as an arbiter of taste and style. What stands out in this context is the extent to which Staub's architecture spatially structured and sustained Masterson's cultural project, imbuing it with purpose, coherence, and form. The challenge of synthesizing the Palladian and the contemporary retrieved Staub's sense of formal assurance, as the entrance elevation of the house demonstrates. Although the five-bay-wide central block is long and low, Staub returned to the modulated proportions characteristic of his interwar country houses to compose the symmetrical elevation, invoking a Palladian identity to construct the house as a pavilion rather than as the rustic lodge trope favored by advocates of both Usonian architecture and the contemporary ranch house. Cast stone balustrades bounding the motor court, elliptical insets faced with cast-iron grilles that rhythmically punctuate the drawing room and dining room windows, and cast stone obelisks stationed on the parapet and balustrades frame the otherwise simple, planar house front, imparting identity and scale gradation with such delicacy and restraint that the forecourt did not look incongruous when filled with big-finned Cadillacs, which prevailed until Harris Masterson came to favor Rolls-Royces instead.[62]

Like Staub's interwar country houses, the Masterson House is double-fronted. The garden elevation registers the house's internal sectional variations. Staub applied symmetry in organizing the house and its terraces to impose spatial discipline on the contemporary house but not at the expense of the uses to which interior spaces were assigned or the family-centered subject positions these spaces supported. Staub's ability to negotiate Masterson's aristocratic aspirations with imagination and tact is especially perceptible in the drawing room and dining room. The miniaturization of grandness perceptible in these rooms animates them and sustains their dignity and decorum. Rienzi comes as close as any of Staub's houses to treating the construction of upper-class-ness as an explicit design requirement. Given its counter-cyclical timing and the strength of the modernist competition in Houston in the early 1950s, the architecture of the Masterson House makes a case for the relevance of "traditional" hierarchical identity. Staub succeeded because he exploited the contradictions of Harris Masterson's charge—merging the Palladian and the contemporary, rather than suppressing one or the other term—to make architecture out of them. The presence of contemporary subjectivity gave the house its sense of reality just as Staub's systematic integration of house and site grounded identity and constructed belonging spatially.

The double-stacked plan of the Masterson House reappeared on many of the houses Staub, Rather and Howze designed in the mid- and late 1950s. Houses for Mr. and Mrs. William L. Walker in Wilmington, North Carolina, of 1953–54, Mr. and Mrs. Harry E. Brants in the Ridglea section of Fort Worth of 1955–56, Mr. and Mrs. George A. Peterkin in River Oaks of 1957, and Mr. and Mrs. Hugh Brinkley in Memphis, Tennessee, of 1960–61 represent variations of this plan for couples who were contemporaries of Staub's and wanted manageably sized houses that would accommodate entertaining and visiting children and grandchildren.[63] Staub, Rather and Howze produced a more expansive version of this type for Mary Greenwood and Ben M. Anderson and their two daughters, Burdine and Mary, in the Tall Timbers section of River Oaks between 1956 and 1958.

As the house of a family (rather than a retirement house for a couple), the Anderson House demonstrated how, after Rienzi, Staub negotiated the Palladian-contemporary dialectic in one-story houses to sustain their owners' patrician identities while planning them in conformance with

Rienzi, garden (north) elevation and terraces seen from bayou glade.

the postwar consensus on family-centered domesticity. The street front of the Anderson House represents the transposition of composition and details from the contemporary ranch-type Gregory House to Staub's evolved Palladian ranch-house type.

The one-story house was built on a deep lot that slopes down to Buffalo Bayou from a circular cul-de-sac stubbed into what had originally been two large lots facing Willowick Road. Staub composed the street front as a symmetrical, five-bay-wide façade centered on a recessed entrance capped by an elliptical fanlight. Rectangular vent panels faced with decorative cast-iron screens are stationed above each opening, reproducing the compositional rhythm of the Masterson House.

The side-gabled central block is flanked by low-parapeted, flat-roofed wings advanced forward to frame the center. Were it not for the three-part sash windows centered in each wing, they might be mistaken for garden walls rather than wings of the house. They serve to minimize the lateral expanse of the front elevation by implying that they are secondary spaces (the parents' dressing rooms are behind the left-hand bay; the daughters' dressing room is behind the right-hand bay) and prevent the one-story house from sprawling as Staub's ranch-type houses do. Practically invisible are a pair of diagonally aligned screen walls that frame the façade and the paved motor court in front of it. The wall to the left is a garden wall, but behind the right-hand wall is a three-car garage.

The interior of the house is structured on a T-plan hall. The central stem leads on axis from the four-foot-wide front door, framed by sidelights and the elliptical fanlight, to the rear-facing living room. The crosspieces of the hall lead to the master bedroom wing on the left and past the dining room and daughters' rooms on the right to the kitchen and an expansive family sitting room, which is spatially continuous with the kitchen. Service spaces and the garage angle off the family room end of the house. The architectural decor, proportions, and finishes of the reception spaces proclaim the owners' patrician identity. The entrance hall is twelve feet wide and eleven feet high. It spatially conveys a sensation of generous hospitality. The hall is paved with black and white cement tiles and finished with scenic wallpaper. The living room is nineteen feet, four inches wide and twenty-three feet long; its ceiling is twelve feet high.

The dining room is nineteen feet, four inches long and seventeen and a half feet wide, with a ceiling as tall as the living room's. The living room is finished with raised, fielded paneling and a modillion cornice. The floor is wood parquet with broad diagonal runners. The dining room is finished with reflective silver Chinese tea-chest paper. Its floor is composed of wide polished wood planks. Unusual for a Staub house, the two rooms, although side-by-side, do not open into each other. Each must be entered from the hall or the rear loggia. A drawing of the floor plan might suggest that the two rooms are strictly compartmented, but this perception is undercut because Staub faced the rear elevation of the central block with an aluminum-framed plate glass curtain wall, with operable sash inset in the gridded frame. Staub detailed this window wall assembly as though it were inserted in a pilaster screen, from which a generously dimensioned, flagstone-paved, rear-facing Tuscan loggia projects. What is not apparent on the street front of the house is that the ground plane slopes all the way across the site, so that the garden loggia is nearly five feet above grade. This made it possible for Staub to evoke the neoclassical portico of the Josiah Gorgas House in Tuscaloosa, Alabama, of 1819 by the architect William Nichols, condensing the contemporary with a Southern regional variant of the Palladian.[64]

The reception rooms of the Anderson House possess the noble proportions typical of Staub's interwar houses. Within this frame, Staub inscribed contemporary subjectivity. For instance, panels on the fireplace wall of the living room contain secret doors at each corner of the room permitting access to a hi-fi from the living room, the cross-hall, and the master bedroom in one corner, and revealing a passageway between the living room and the adjacent master bedroom in the other corner, so that when large numbers of people were entertained the master bedroom could be pressed into service as overflow social space. Although a departure from the formal hierarchies of the country house, the application of this practice in the Anderson House exhibited the appeal of contemporary life ways.[65] Staub adhered to the modernist discourse on the desirability of functional flexibility by designing the compact guest room next to the front door so that it could also be used as the cloakroom and its bathroom as the visitors' toilet when Mr. and Mrs. Anderson entertained. The biggest departure from the spatial practices embedded in Staub's interwar houses involved subjectivity and the kitchen. Because Mary Anderson liked to cook, the kitchen was designed for her use. It was domesticated rather than treated as service space that performed economy and efficiency. Opening up the kitchen with an island counter and a bay window broke down the hierarchical system of spatial layering through which kitchens were dialectically constructed as service space in the country house. Extending the kitchen to encompass a family sitting room entailed inclusion of such elements as a rustic, exposed-brick fireplace wall, an additional bay window, a window seat, pine paneling, wide plank floors, and a wood-beamed ceiling. Architectural components, spatial expansiveness, and surface finishes attested to the kitchen's elevation in social status. Staub articulated the distinction between the informal and formal living rooms of the Anderson House by characterizing the latter as a pavilion and the former as a lodge.[66]

Ben M. Anderson House, Tall Timbers, River Oaks, Houston, 1956–58, Staub, Rather and Howze, architects. Entrance (south) elevation.

Anderson House, detail of entrance portal.

Anderson House, detail of grill.

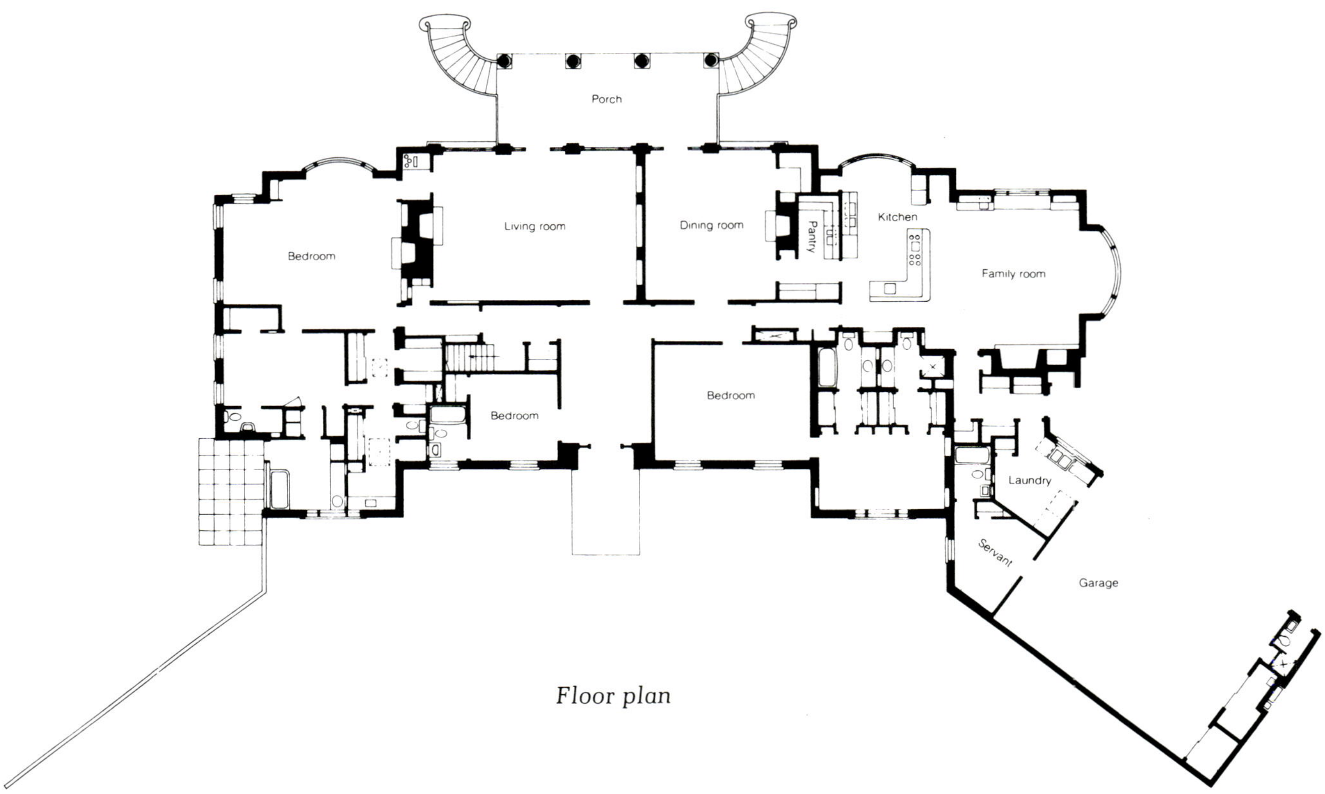

Floor plan

Anderson House.

Anderson House, living room.

Anderson House, rear (north).

In 1958, Margaret and James Elkins commissioned Staub, Rather and Howze to design a new house for them on an fifteen-acre site on Buffalo Bayou in the Bayou Woods subdivision, adjoining the west side of the Wiess Stables tract.[67] James Elkins had become president of the City National Bank in 1950. During the early 1950s, the City National Bank's performance relative to other Houston banks began to advance rapidly, moving ahead of one competitor after another year by year so that by 1955 it had become the second-largest bank in Houston. In 1956 the City National merged with the oldest and third-largest bank in Houston, the First National, surging far ahead of the city's other major banks in terms of deposits.[68] Planning began in 1958 to construct a new headquarters for the First City National Bank to replace both the First National's 1904 building in the old financial district near the foot of Main Street and the City National Bank's twenty-four-story building, which Judge Elkins, Jim Elkins's father, had completed in 1947, the first postwar skyscraper in Houston. The bank initially retained Wilson, Morris, Crain and Anderson of Houston to design its new building. First City's chief lender, Horace C. Flanigan, president of the Manufacturers' Trust Company of New York, expressed uncertainty about First City's choice of architect because Wilson, Morris, Crain and Anderson had not yet had a high-rise building built to its designs. According to Carol Herselle Krinsky, Flanigan advised Judge Elkins to hire the architectural firm that had designed Manufacturers' Trust's Fifth Avenue headquarters, Skidmore, Owings and Merrill.[69] Gordon Bunshaft of Skidmore, Owings and Merrill designed the First City complex on a full-block site on Main Street: a slender, thirty-two-story office slab alongside a free-standing, glass-walled banking pavilion, and behind the banking pavilion, a line of drive-in windows.[70] The First City National Bank confirmed the ascendancy of Miesian modern architecture in Houston. Upon its completion in 1961, it was highlighted in national news publications to advertise Texas' modern identity.[71] The First City complex seemed to legitimize the tendency of journalists in the 1960s to construct Houston as a "new" city.

Designed and built at the same time as the First City National Bank Building, Staub's house for Mr. and Mrs. Elkins was his most ambitious modern design. Unlike his ranch-type houses of the 1950s, it appeared to be a pavilion rather than a lodge. Howard Barnstone disliked this house as ardently as Staub's ranch houses and would have eliminated it from the book had not Staub insisted it be included so as not to slight his clients. Barnstone objected to Staub's construction of identity and subjectivity.[72] The north-facing front of the house bounds a formally landscaped motor court by Pat Fleming, who designed the landscape settings for the house. It consists of a planar wall surfaced with subtly toned gray, gray-blue, and pink Mexican adoquín paving stones. The wall is rimmed with ornamental iron stanchions and screens containing stacked and running bands of stylized Greek keys. The horizontal screens take up the void between the flat roof of the house (at the level of the top of the stone wall) and a secondary roof plane that spans the central portion of the house. Visitors enter by passing on axis through the stone wall plane into a recessed garden courtyard walled with plate glass set in gold-anodized aluminum frames. Double glass doors open into a wide cross-hall paved with polished terrazzo. At one end are a curving, cantilevered, open-riser stair down to the basement-level recreation room, set in a two-story well opening to the bayou landscape through a two-story-high window, and a set of steps leading down into the center of the large living room, which is a rectangle in plan with chamfered corners.

On the other end, the cross-hall leads past the dining room, recessed several steps below the level of the hall and framing one side of the entrance courtyard, to the family room–library. Occupying the L wing that unobtrusively bounds the west side of the motor court are the kitchen, a basement-level garage, and the children's bedrooms. Concealed behind the wall plane of the entrance hall is the master bedroom suite. It lies at the center of the house, yet its presence is undetected by guests. Staub's planning skill was evident in the deft way he provided for contemporary family subjectivity that would not conflict with large-scale formal entertaining yet kept Mr. and Mrs. Elkins at the center of the house. Taking advantage of the site's slope down to Buffalo Bayou, Staub inserted a recreation room in the exposed basement. This room opens through sliding glass doors onto a broad terrace containing a large swimming pool. The master bedroom suite is dramatically cantilevered out over the rear terrace above the recreation room.

Appearances notwithstanding, the house does not conform to the modern pavilion type. Barnstone admired the resourcefulness of Staub's planning but not the pretense of pavilion regularity when the house had an L-plan configuration. T. H. Robsjohn-Gibbings was the interior designer for the Elkins House (new interiors were installed in the 1970s by the Houston designer Winston Farbar to complement Mr. and Mrs. Elkins's growing collection of heroically scaled abstract expressionist and color field paintings). While Robsjohn-Gibbings's furniture had seemed modern in the 1930s and 1940s, his penchant for streamlining models from classical antiquity, toward which he inclined in the 1950s meant that he was no longer in the forefront of interior design associated with postwar modern architecture. Robsjohn-Gibbings lost no Texas clients over this circumstance. Staub's interpretation of modern "Palladian" architecture seemed much more attuned to Robsjohn-Gibbings than to

Elkins House, vista from entrance cross hall toward living room.

(previous page) James A. Elkins Jr. House, Houston, 1958–61, Staub, Rather and Howze, architects. Detail of entrance elevation.

Elkins House, staircase.

Elkins House, terrace beneath cantilevered bedroom wing.

Philip Johnson or Mies van der Rohe. The Elkins House represents Palladian modernism of the 1950s filtered through the aesthetic sensibility of a decorator. To Barnstone in the mid- and late 1970s, this combination was anathema. From Barnstone's perspective, Staub's misinterpretation of the modern Palladian pavilion affected the house's performance of its owners' social identity.[73]

The critical confusion over limits, authority, and legitimizing identity that the Elkins House provokes did not reflect just the crisis of eclectic architects, such as Staub, trying to assimilate to modernist practices but also a developing crisis among American modern architects as they sought to negotiate the contradictions that Palladianizing modern architecture entailed.[74] Staub's architectural choices and judgments seem inconsistent because they do not reinforce the economy of meaning that codes the Johnson-, Neuhaus-, and Barnstone-designed houses as both exemplars of high-style Miesian architecture and, more subtly, as upper class. It is the subjective perceptions and sensations that the Elkins House produces in visitors that legitimize Staub's architecture. Experiencing the choreography of movement through volumes—the open-air void of the entrance courtyard, the straightaway of the wide cross-hall, the well of the staircase, and the descent into the living room—enables visitors to feel the spatial vividness of this sequence, which the admission of daylight from different exposures animates further. The spiral stair (which for Barnstone evoked the open-riser spiral stairs that the Houston architect Bailey Swenson incorporated in his extravagant contemporary houses of the 1950s) is spatially lilting. Detailing the rails of the balustrades as unfurling ribbons converts ascent or descent into a rhythmic experience. Photographs of the cantilevered rear bedroom bay imply a science-fiction-like exaggeration in the extent of its projection, a perception reinforced by Staub's treatment of the walls above as solid stucco planes penetrated by awning windows that are centered and frame a picture window. Yet the experience of sitting beneath this overhang is elevating rather than threatening. The presence of shelter overhead combined with the absence of framing piers constructs this subjective sensation as quintessentially modern.

Staub encountered a problem in trying to condense Palladian modern identity and Palladian-contemporary subjectivity in the Elkins House. It is experienced as a modern house, although it belongs to a genre of modernism affiliated with interior designers and therefore marginalized in the discourses of mainstream mid-century modern American architecture.[75] Because its departures were materialized in the extensive use of gold anodized aluminum, for example, the house encountered problems with critical reception. It pained Barnstone that Staub seemed not to comprehend that it was déclassé to mix Philip Johnson with Bailey Swenson. For Barnstone, to incorporate an open-riser spiral stair with gold handrails was to materialize affiliation with Bailey Swenson. Bailey Swenson's clients for his most uninhibited contemporary houses in the first half of the 1950s were Jewish families in the Houston neighborhood of Riverside Terrace. Barnstone was Jewish. Formal decisions that, for Staub, may have seemed unrelated to broader chains of signification were, for Barnstone, inseparable from such associations. On coming to Houston, Barnstone identified with Dominique and John de Menil and their circle of partisans at the Contemporary Arts Museum rather than affiliating with Houston's Jewish upper middle class. His reactions to the problematic construction of modernity at the Elkins House touched on a complex of issues involving social class, ethnic and religious stereotypes, anxieties about belonging and exclusion, refinement and vulgarity, and superiority and inferiority all condensed into a critique of taste and style.[76] To Barnstone, the prospect of Staub forfeiting his social relevance as an architect not just by failing to elevate the class standing of his clients but also by exposing them to invidious judgment through an inability to perceive clearly and select accurately was demoralizing. That the formal issues involved the materialization of identity and subject positions that were personally problematic for Barnstone intensified his adverse response. Barnstone's criticisms disclose how modern architecture had been used in the 1950s to reconstruct in sublimated form the identity and subject positions exposed and dismantled in the modernist critique of the eclectic country house. Staub's "misunderstandings" reveal how consistently modern architecture had been spatially coded to support and legitimize assertions of class superiority in the competitive market of mid-century modernist positions in Houston.[77]

In contrast to the Elkins House, Staub, Rather and Howze materially coded class identity in one of Staub's last houses, a weekend cottage for Homoiselle Haden and Albert Bel Fay, with such restraint that it is almost imperceptible. Albert Fay, an independent oilman, investor, and cattle rancher, was a champion sailor with a special affinity for the Caribbean. A Republican and a conservationist, he served as U.S. ambassador to Trinidad and Tobago in the mid-1970s during the administration of Pres. Gerald Ford. Mrs. Fay (like her cousin and sister-in-law, Carolyn Grant Fay) was a Galvestonian.[78] The Fay Cottage was built in Kemah, Texas, on Galveston Bay twenty-five miles southeast of Houston and eight miles down shore from Bay Ridge. It is located a mile north of the Texas Corinthian Yacht Club, the sailing club that Albert and Ernest Fay and three other friends organized in 1938.[79]

The Fay Cottage beguiles because its formal economy is so exquisitely calibrated to its identity as a weekend cottage. It performs patrician propriety, continuity, and belonging so effortlessly that it seems oblivious of any expectation of performance. Constructed by the Kemah builder Joe Hogan in 1960–61, the house extends in a one-room-deep configuration along the ridge above the bayshore.[80] The linear plan of the Fay Cottage is interrupted by a cross axis of guest bedrooms that separates the social spaces of the house from the master bedroom at the south end.

Wide porches on the southeast-facing bay side of the house were intended for outdoor living. Interior finishes of vertical pine siding support its resort cottage identity. The closet-lined passage from the living room to the master bedroom and the compact bathrooms (one per bedroom) adhered to the modernist discourse on spatial economy and personal amenity. Wide wood plank floors subtly underscore patrician identity through their breadth of scale and spatial generosity. Staub's use of tray ceilings in the living room and master bedroom and of fireplace openings framed with pine molding and brick surrounds balanced intimations of expansiveness with rusticity. Staub had the living room papered with nautical maps to acknowledge Albert Fay's love of sailing and identify the house with the subjectivity of the sailor-adventurer.

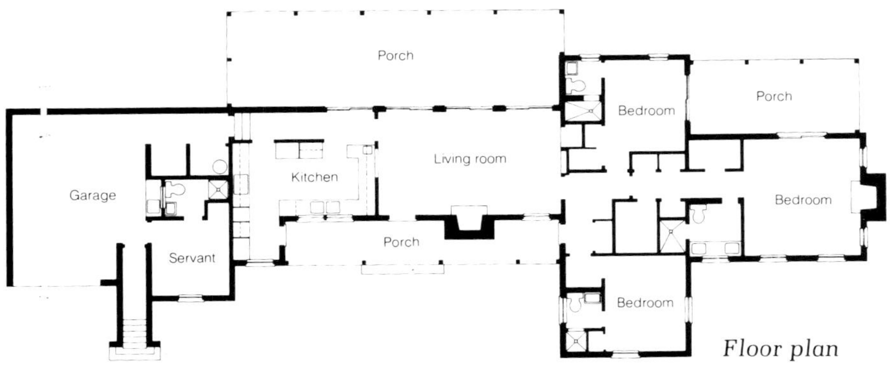

Floor plan

Albert Bel Fay Bay House, Kemah, Texas, 1960–61, Staub, Rather and Howze, architects.

Staub incorporated a pyramidally roofed tower and exterior stair on the landward front of the house, thickly sectioned, stepped-profiled chimney stacks, louvered shutters hinged from the top rather than the sides of window openings, stucco-finished walls, and thick white shingles to evoke the vernacular architecture of Bermuda, which was also the model for the country house Staub designed for Mr. and Mrs. Fay in Houston in 1939.[81] The perception of the Bermuda style at the bay house is more fluid than photographs might suggest, submerging and reemerging in an ambivalent figure-ground relationship with the ranch-house type. On Staub's contemporary ranch houses of the 1950s, such antitheses were not resolved with the same confidence that his Palladianized ranch houses exhibit. At the Fay Bay Cottage, this figure-ground/style-type ambiguity does not represent a failure to synthesize competing or contradictory tendencies but a subtle assertion of subjective authenticity. The ordinariness of the Fays' house naturalized their patrician status not as something unusual or requiring legitimizing performance but as unexceptional and inherent. The profile of the chimney against the gabled south end of the house condenses this ambiguity by composing and proportioning the scale relationship of house and landscape.

The implicit subjects this scene evokes—swimming pool, outdoor fireplace, and bayside porch in the foreground, framing the perspective of the bayshore sweeping out to Red Bluff Point in the background—combine familiarity with and an enjoyment of outdoor leisure activities with a sense of mastery that does not need to be asserted because it is just part of the picture, in the background perhaps but always in focus. The restraint, understatement, and ordinariness materialized in the Fay Bay Cottage worked to naturalize upper-class-ness in the context of a postwar social consensus that identified normality with more egalitarian representations of suburban, middle-class domesticity and stigmatized explicit acknowledgements of class distinction as a reactionary anachronism.

Fay Bay House, detail of outdoor chimney.

The houses Staub produced in the postwar period demonstrated his willingness to engage the changed circumstances affecting American architectural practice at the midpoint of the twentieth century. They also display the uncertainty and tension with which he negotiated changing attitudes about the representation of social class in the United States after World War II and the displacement of subject positions redolent of the 1920s—revised and streamlined in the 1930s—by less invidious personifications of class difference. Staub sought to merge with what he perceived to be the postwar architectural mainstream by adopting the type of the one-story ranch house as successor to the no longer socially sustainable country house. Both his choice of house type and of the contemporary tendency in architecture can be seen, in retrospect, to have represented a misjudgment, a lapse of acuity in the sort of critical discernment that in architectural discourse is customarily denoted by the word "taste." It is not that Staub was incapable of designing good ranch houses but that the egalitarian, family-centered domesticity with which they were identified in the postwar era conflicted with his facility for composing difference and constructing proportioned settings that framed and spatially sustained class distinction. Staub's formulation of a revised ranch-house type, the Palladianized ranch house, paralleled developments in modern architecture in the United States that were especially pertinent in Houston. By composing the difference in identity and subject positions between the ranch and the pavilion—the contemporary and the Palladian—Staub negotiated modernizing trends to recover a sense of formal assurance that sustained his practice in the aftermath of the country house era.

CHAPTER 10 : ARCHITECTURE, SOCIAL CONSTRUCTION, AND THE COUNTRY HOUSES OF JOHN F. STAUB

Bayou Bend, detail of stair.

As instruments in the formation of a public, the country houses of John F. Staub socially constructed identity positions that from the 1920s through the 1950s sought to legitimize and sustain an upper class in Houston. As technologies of self-fashioning, they constructed subject positions that sought to inspire and reward their occupants for internalizing practices, attitudes, and styles of representation that during the second quarter of the twentieth century identified an American upper class. Houston's entrepreneurial elite seems to have been most receptive to internalizing the subject positions of the patrician lady and gentleman in the 1920s. New elites emerging in the 1930s and 1940s, as the city's economy faltered then resumed an expansionary course, seemed less convinced of the social utility patrician identity and subject positions offered them.[1] By 1950, elite contingents in Houston began to appropriate modernist forms of identity to advance agendas for distinction that were antithetical to the patrician country house and its implied way of life.

American eclectic architects of Staub's generation were marginalized by the discourses of the modern movement in the 1940s just as the last generation of American Victorian architects had been marginalized by an earlier generation of eclectics around 1900 and as modernists would be in the 1970s. Such fluctuations in critical estimation might alert critics and historians to the existence of cycles of cultural transformation that tend to supplant regimes of practice at intervals, a process whose operation was clear by the end of the nineteenth century. Recognition of this process might temper uncritical acceptance of the polemical judgments that an out-faction uses to undermine the legitimacy of in-faction practices. Yet so compelling was the modernist consensus and so emotionally satisfying its fundamentalist conviction of moral certitude that even the postmodern critique of modernism in the 1970s failed to reposition eclectic architecture securely within the discourse of twentieth-century architectural history. It is this historiographical problem that the discourse of sociology and the rhetoric of social construction seek to circumvent. Analyzing what might be described as the social metaphysics of Staub's architecture is one way to make sense of it without debating style. Approaching Staub's architecture from the perspective of social construction also makes it possible to consider it alongside modern architecture in order to clarify the antithetical premises on which these two sets of practice were based as well as the ways that contradiction began to erode the premises of each (how beauty, propriety, and continuity masked an argument advancing the legitimacy of class hierarchy in the country house and how classical architectural metaphors surreptitiously reinserted class distinction into mid-twentieth-century American modern architecture). Architectural analysis based on social construction does not pretend to resolve contradictions but to externalize them and therefore clarify problematic social issues architects sought to frame through their practices. The country houses of Staub, his peers, and their antecedents addressed what Jackson Leers identified as the late-nineteenth- and early-twentieth-century "antimodern" American response to the instability that capitalist processes produced: they sought to "reconstruct a coherent sense of identity in a culture which was rendering all identities (and values) vaporous and unreal."[2] As Lears observed, "the common pattern of culture [characteristic of the antimodernizers] involved a denial of the conflicts in modern capitalist society, and affirmation of continuity, harmony, and progress."[3] Continuity and harmony were affects that were central to Staub's country houses, which used beauty as an instrument in the formation of a public to construct consensus around the myth of patrician superiority and the legitimacy of elite leadership.

Examining works of architecture in terms of social construction also highlights the ways that buildings are received in the communities where they are built. Staub's houses were deliberately integrated with their (often constructed) landscape settings and were so persuasively naturalized that they seem inseparable from these settings. Yet the conservative values embedded in Staub's architecture were inconsistent with the expansionary dynamic and entrepreneurial flow of Houston. In contrast to the myth of market man (summarized by Joel Warren Barna as "the prince brings prosperity"), Staub's houses spatialized arguments advanced on behalf of a counter-thesis of class superiority seeking to construct consensus on its virtues and benefits by making the attributes of its superior identity perceptible, tangible, and spatially inhabitable.[4] Authenticity, authority, belonging, continuity, decorum, legitimacy, permanence, propriety, refinement, stability, and wholeness were the virtues these houses sought to make real and immediate through their apparent perfection and integrity, their beauty. Their persuasive appeal intimated the possibility of transforming the identities of their subjects—the families who occupied them—by conferring on them the emotional rewards of inspiration, empowerment, and entitlement: grace, charm, and composure. Staub's techniques—composing difference; efficiently regulating typification and individuality; fusing intimacy and monumentality; framing and magnifying; and proportionally enlightening and levitating—sought to ensure the material and spatial credibility of these houses so that their qualities were experienced as intrinsic rather than merely ascribed. The geometric rigor, volumetric clarity, and rhythmic fluidity of the houses reflected the inclinations and skill of Staub the mathematician and dancer. His country houses were capable of producing subjective sensations that elevated and ennobled their subjects by subtly ritualizing the routines of daily family life. Architecture was used as an instrument to socially construct a representation of upper-class identity that would make the subject positions associated with it irresistible, both to its beneficiaries and those others who could be recruited into forming a supportive public. Its values—stability, permanence, wholeness—were "other" to the values of entrepreneurial capitalism, which relied on disequilibrium, sudden change, and fragmentation to maximize economic opportunities.

In the 1920s, the architectural "other" against which these houses were constructed was the preceding generation of elite houses of the 1900 to 1910 period with their raised foundations, heavy lidded eaves, bulky front porches, single-light plate-glass windows, dark-toned, oak-trimmed interiors, and notional representation of historical models. By the 1930s, this "other" had become the styling excesses of the picturesque historical models of the 1920s. In the Marx brothers' movies of the 1930s such houses were the counterparts of the subject position portrayed by the actress Margaret Dumont. Her Anglophile surnames, formal attire, erect carriage, and impeccable diction identified her with the popular cultural stereotype of the subject of 1920s country houses. In the postwar period, as eclectic architecture itself became modernism's "other," the dialectic shifted. The relevant movie parallel is Billy Wilder's *Sunset Boulevard* of 1950, with its uncomplicated, future-oriented (if, of necessity, opportunistic), modern subjects, portrayed by Nancy Olson and William Holden, dialectically opposed to the sinister, deluded, anachronistic subjects of 1920s hierarchical role-playing portrayed by Gloria Swanson and Erich von Stroheim. Wilder architecturally established the identity of the antagonists in *Sunset Boulevard* by ensconcing them in a gloomy, cavernous Spanish Mediterranean country house. The postwar dialectical inversion played out in *Sunset Boulevard* challenged Staub to construct new suburban residential typologies that synthesized the Palladian villa and the contemporary ranch house to accommodate revised elite identity and subject positions.[5]

C. Milby Dow House, detail of stair.

From the perspective of social class, the country house's "other" was (in Michael Hays's term) the "architecturalization" of lower-middle-class identity and subject positions.[6] The invidious identity projected onto this class—lack of discernment and subtlety and a tendency to exaggerate in futile efforts to overcompensate for deficient gentility, manifest in seeking to transform houses into "homes" or, even worse, "mansions"—was the mythic attribute against which the composure, decorum, and proprietary claims to belonging of the American country house discourse were constructed. Any anxiety or defensiveness inhering in this particular operation of elite social construction may well reflect the paradox

Penny Sparke observed, which was especially pertinent to Houston with its exceptional social fluidity: "the need to create a material environment intended . . . both to underscore and to disguise a social transition."[7] Staub's country houses functioned as talismans conferring the twentieth-century American equivalents of honor on the families who occupied them, signifying that they had successfully transcended the indignity, obscurity, and transience of a lower-middle-class identity.

The contradiction this counter-lower-middle-class identity entailed involved its grounding in the hierarchy of class distinction. The existence of an upper class is implicitly predicated on the existence of a lower class, against which upper-class representations—and authority—can be dialectically coordinated. The country house, its beauty and charm notwithstanding, was inescapably linked to a dialectics of hierarchical social class division subject to the politics of divisiveness. Hays's quotation of Theodor Adorno's deduction—"Art works . . . are form only in relation to what they need to eliminate. . . . Without this reminder, without contradiction and non-identity, harmony would be irrelevant aesthetically"—underscores the extent to which the architectural mechanics of class construction—the composing, proportioning, whole-making practices that gave the country house its radiant identity—are bound dialectically to social divisiveness.[8] Harmony, the classical technique for constructing unity by joining multiple elements, seeks to elide this contradiction by respecting the singularity of constituent parts. Yet as an examination of Staub's architecture makes clear, his skill in composing difference was one of the phenomena that makes his houses so compelling as works of spatial, and social, construction as, in Hays's words, " . . . a reflection of the myth of harmony."[9] Divisiveness in Staub's houses was architecturally sublimated and naturalized with conceptual precision, spatial economy, and imaginative wit because differentiation was at the emotional core of the identity and subject positions these houses materialized.

The discourses of twentieth-century modern architecture were premised on rejection of class hierarchy and classical composition. As was visible in Houston in the postwar period, the neo-Palladian movement taken up by some U.S. modern architects after Colin Rowe proposed parallels between the villas of Palladio and Le Corbusier in 1947 sought to encode modern architectural practices with hierarchical undertones.[10] This did not lead to the renewal of a reformed modernist country house as a symbol of elite hegemony, although such extraordinary individual examples as the house and garden complex by the architect Eero Saarinen, his associate Kevin Roche, the interior designer Alexander Girard, and the landscape architect Dan Kiley for Xenia Simons and J. Irwin Miller in Columbus, Indiana, completed in 1957, were built.[11] Instead under modernist dispensation, the country house as an instrument in the performance of narratives of enlightened and responsible authority migrated to the American corporate workplace: the suburban corporate campus. The architects Skidmore, Owings and Merrill and Eero Saarinen and Associates were especially associated with this trend.[12] Patrician in their avoidance of hierarchical spatial markers of administrative distinction and in their promotion of policies inviting public access and use, these corporate country houses functioned as instruments in the formation of a public prepared to support a consensus on the mid-century vision of the good community, where political conflict and spatial incoherence were absent, and modern technology, an enlightened (white-collar) populace, and suburban pastoral beauty were harmonized in a mythical world of nature conservation, generational managerial continuity, and progressive paternalism. By the early 1970s, the contradictions latent in the mythic constructs of American postwar corporate suburbia had surfaced.

The utopian ambitions of the discourses of modern architecture and urbanism made the aspirations to civic propriety of American eclectic architectural discourses of the first half of the twentieth century seem feeble by comparison. Yet in historical perspective the construction of civic propriety proved to be one of the enduring spatial virtues of the eclectic regime.[13] That Staub's architecture, consisting principally of freestanding, single-family, suburban houses, should exert the collective spatial presence it does in Houston attests to the strong-form, space-framing and -shaping capacities of his houses. Staub's houses spatially register claims to authenticity because they are systematically integrated with their landscapes. They materialize an elite version of community because Staub and his eclectic colleagues in Houston invested in practices that promoted spatial definition and coherence, using hierarchical gradation to give the monotonous natural landscape of Houston a sense of layered depth, composed order, and formal stability. Staub's houses do not restrict expression of their magic to their occupants only but extend their charms to those who pass by. As Michael Benedikt discerned, the words used to describe these houses—dignified, noble, hospitable, gracious, welcoming, serene—are subjective personal characterizations as much as they are architectural attributes.[14] They are words that contribute to the social construction of what Berger and Luckmann, using an architectural metaphor, call the "edifice of legitimations . . . built upon language," which continues to empower materialization of the myth of upper-class-ness in the 1920s suburbs of Houston.[15]

Staub's subtle proportioning practices, fusing intimacy and monumentality, contribute to the charm his architecture exerts. This phenomenon was a broadly shared characteristic

Rudolph C. Kuldell House, detail of stair.

of American eclectic architecture of the 1920s and 1930s. The buildings of Staub's peers—Philip Trammell Shutze in Atlanta, Richard Koch in New Orleans, H. B. Thomson in Dallas, John Gaw Meem in Santa Fe, Wallace Neff in Pasadena, George Washington Smith in Montecito, Arthur L. Loveless in Seattle, to name only a few—also exhibit this characteristic.[16] It imbues the houses and nondomestic buildings of these architects with an ambiguity that produces visceral sensations of delight. Spatially they assert the authority associated with monumental architecture. Yet simultaneously they envelope their occupants in diminutive settings that enchant because, rather than seeking to ingratiate through coyness and winsomeness, they retain their dignity and decorum. The dialectical subtlety with which these contrasting sensations are performed—and experienced—sustains constructions of upper-class identity and subjectivity that attract, compel, and persuade. The proportional appeal to subjective emotion embedded in this architecture functions instrumentally to recruit and reproduce subjects graced by its charisma. Nelson Aldrich, Richard Bushman, and Suzannah Lessard all use the word "grace" to suggest the presence of a spiritual dimension in the materialization of upper-class identity and subject positions.[17] In analyzing the ways that relations between subjects and objects can be mediated by the sensations of bodily pleasure induced by composition, proportion, materiality, and other tactics of spatial management, it is possible to discern how, through architecture, affect is produced and reproduced, bonding subjects and objects in the case of the country house by emotionally generating elation and enlightenment that subjects experience as inhering in objects. These are the seductive affects with which Staub and his contemporaries invested the country houses they designed in order to sustain mythic identity and subject positions that would look and feel (and even smell and acoustically resonate as) upper class.

The eventual transformation of eclectic architecture into modern architecture's "other" makes it possible to isolate another attribute through which the country house socially constructed patrician identity and subject positions. This involved the ethos of limits, which becomes evident once dialectically opposed to the antithetical modernist myth of limitlessness. Containment, measure, proportion, and restraint imply the presence of limits. Like harmony and hierarchy, the phenomenon of limits challenged eclectic architects to invent spatial experiences that worked with limits in order to construct sensations of imaginatively transcending them. Suzannah Lessard saw in the architectural sensibilities of her great-grandfather, Stanford White, and his son (her grandfather, Lawrence Grant White) a defining personal contrast between repeated pursuit of the dissolution of limits (Stanford White) and an affirmation of limits (Lawrence White) that she identifies with her grandfather's strong-form patrician subjectivity.[18] Aldrich likewise links the phenomenon of limitation to what he characterizes as "Old Money . . . representations of the social world," which he describes as "dense," "thick," and privileging cyclical repetition in the service of generational continuity over the antithesis he identifies with market man, "a lively sense of the individual self."[19] Joel Barna captures the aura of class solidarity infusing the patrician discourse on limits when he distinguishes between the subject positions identified with Texan entrepreneurial culture (and their instrumental, bottom-line, just-give-me-what-I-want attitudes toward architecture) and the attitudes of those "above the line," for whom "buildings are not simply things that individuals own and use. Instead [buildings] constitute an estate that owns and uses individuals in service to their social class."[20] Staub's dexterity and ingenuity in composing difference derive from a reverence for the limiting circumstances that distinguish gentlemanly conduct and deportment from alternatives identifying the subject positions of other social classes. He spatialized the phenomenon of limits in his country houses to underpin mythic representations of upper-class identity by performing patrician virtues—self-discipline, consideration for others, restraint, and responsibility—that legitimize upper-class claims to trustworthiness and leadership.

How, to what extent, and—crucially—whether or not country houses (and other building types) construct class identity and subject positions in a positivist sense are propositions that are (to invoke Jacques Derrida's use of the term) undecidable.[21] As Hays demonstrates in his analysis of the rationalist projects of Hannes Meyer and Ludwig Hilberseimer of the 1920s, architecture makes its appeals and seeks to construct consensus on its value and virtues not through operations of spatial determinism but by offering its products as technologies of self-fashioning, modeling what Derrida described as a consistent, internally unified way of life that can imaginatively fulfill inhabitants' expectations and aspirations.[22] It is in the make-believe world of imagination that myth operates most efficiently to invest the objects of architecture with identity and subject positions, to which the people who inhabit these objects do not have to conform slavishly (and perhaps not conform at all) in order to enjoy the advantages and affiliations such identity and subject positions advance. The incompatibility of fictions of class superiority with twentieth-century American ideologies of political egalitarianism and a liberated capitalist economy are elided with the least friction through recourse to symbolic representation. The country houses of John F. Staub constructed class identity and subjectivity in Houston from the 1920s through the 1950s by exquisitely balancing make-believe and phenomenal responsiveness. Staub made an

J. Robert Neal House, detail of stair.

architecture of class representation out of the materialization of responsiveness to practical circumstances and limiting conditions. He made this architecture credible because of the rigor, wit, and style that inhered in his design practices.

Under the dispensation of style an economy of meaning took form in early-twentieth-century American architecture in which the dialectical antitheses of antimodern representation and modern technique could be negotiated and coherent identity and subject positions constructed to credibly frame American economic elites as an upper class. Eclectic architects constructed consensus on the validity of using historical models as a critique of modernization while efficiently regulating the modernity of these models by submitting them to the discipline of Darwinian materialist discourse to ensure responsiveness to conditions of siting and use. Within this eclectic economy of meaning, style also functioned as a fetish, efficiently regulating architectural criticism of the social project of the country house by channeling debates about the legitimacy of social class into debates on stylistic representation.

Dialectically redressing what can easily seem like the layering of make-believe on willful deception in the discourses of American eclecticism is the reality of Staub's country houses. They continue to function as instruments in the formation of a public by captivating with their beauty, proportioned composure, and livability. They retain relevance in the Houston real estate market that preceding generations of elite houses did not. They continue to perform upper-class identity in Houston with a persuasiveness that no other elite housing type can match. Given their long-term performance record, it is tempting to characterize the appeal these houses exert as timeless. While the rigor, economy, and precision of Staub's planning have ensured that they continue to function flexibly and absorb changing expectations about how upper-income families should live, what is timeless about them is not their architecture but the identity and subject positions they materialize. Staub's houses construct class because, as Suzannah Lessard wrote of Stanford White, " . . . part of his calling was to teach the new rich how to be rich in style."[23] Yet their legitimacy and credibility ultimately derive from their groundedness, their civic propriety, their construction of continuity and belonging: architectural analogues of human virtues that Nelson Aldrich collectivized as character.[24] It is the internal dialectics spatially embedded in these houses, their deliberate negotiation of fine and folk, their systematic integration of decorum and generosity, and the energy that stems from regulating the contradiction between what Colin Rowe antithesized as character and composition that cause Staub's country houses to resonate with the mythical allure that Aldrich describes as the "celebrated . . . ability [of the upper classes] to bring others close to the healing touch of their own ineffable presence in the world."[25]

(opposite) Alex Camp House, detail of stair.

NOTES

CHAPTER 1. JOHN F. STAUB, HOUSTON, AND THE SOCIAL CONSTRUCTION OF UPPER-CLASS IDENTITY

1. Le Corbusier, *Towards a New Architecture*, trans. Frederick Etchells, 9.

2. On the phenomenon of "social construction" see Peter L. Berger and Thomas Luckmann, *The Social Construction of Reality: A Treatise in the Sociology of Knowledge*. On "identity" see Erik H. Erickson, *Identity: Youth and Crisis*, 9, 16–17, 20–23. On the "subject" and subjectivity see K. Michael Hays, *Modernism and the Posthumanist Subject: The Architecture of Hannes Meyer and Ludwig Hilberseimer*, 7–8. On the concept of the subject, Hays cites Theodor W. Adorno, "Subject and Object," in *The Essential Frankfurt School Reader*, ed. Andrew Arato and Eike Gebhardt, 497–98.

3. Alexander Tzonis and Liane Lefaivre observe that "Classical means related to the social order of the *classici*, the highest rank of the hierarchical social structure of ancient Rome, juxtaposed to that of the lowest, that of the *proletarii*. One could demonstrate in many other ways the relation between classical architecture and society, starting with classical architecture's obsession with rigorous quantification, exactitude, and detail." Tzonis and Lefaivre, *Classical Architecture: The Poetics of Order*, 1.

4. Nelson W. Aldrich Jr., *Old Money: The Mythology of America's Upper Class*, 36, 106–40.

5. Howard Barnstone, *Architecture of John F. Staub: Houston and the South*, 3–5. See also Ellis A. Davis and Edwin H. Grobe, comps. and eds., *The New Encyclopedia of Texas*, vol. 2, 1177; "Staub, John F.," *Who's Who in America*, vol. 24, 1946–47 (1946), 2247; "Staub, John F.," *Who's Who in America*, vol. 38, 1974–75 (1974), 2938; Michael Ennis, "The Man Who Built River Oaks," *Texas Monthly* 7 (Oct. 1979): 134–39; and Wendy Haskell Meyer, "John F. Staub: A New Book About Our City's Eclectic Architect," *Houston Home/Garden* 6 (Oct. 1979): 55–60.

6. On Staub's grandfather, Peter Staub, see Robert Parkinson, "Staub, Peter"; David Babelay, "Swiss Settlers, Knoxville"; and Claudette Stager, "Gruetli" at the *Tennessee Encyclopedia of History and Culture* website http://tennesseeencyclopedia.net; "Staub, Peter (Feb. 2, 1827–May 19, 1904)" in Knox County History Committee, East Tennessee Historical Society, *The French Broad-Holston Country: A History of Knox County, Tennessee*, ed. Mary U. Rothrock, 489–90. On Staub's Opera House, the enterprise for which the Staub family was best known in Knoxville, see Knoxville History Committee of the East Tennessee Historical Society, *Heart of the Valley: A History of Knoxville, Tennessee*, ed. Lucile Deadrick, 463–67.

7. John Thomas Rather Jr., "Charm in the Small House as Shown in 'Hopecote,' in Knoxville, Tennessee" *House Beautiful* 57 (Feb. 1925): 116. A biographical entry on Thomas Hope is included in *The French Broad-Holston Country*, 428–29. Four of Hope's buildings are profiled in William Ross McNabb, *Tradition, Innovation, and Romantic Images: The Architecture of Historic Knoxville*, 2–5, 56.

8. Anderson Todd referred to Staub's skill as a dancer in "Recollections: Comments from Colleagues of Staub," *Texas Architect* 29 (Nov.–Dec. 1979): 54.

9. Staub interview with David T. Courtwright, Houston Metropolitan Research Center, Oral Histories Collection, Houston Public Library, Interview No. 174, Mar. 20, 1975. Staub was awarded the Navy Cross, the U.S. Navy's third-highest ranked award, for bombing a German submarine in the North Sea.

10. A biographical profile of Harrie Thomas Lindeberg (1880–1959) appears in *The National Cyclopedia of American Biography*, vol. 47 (1965), 527. On Lindeberg's architecture the basic source is H. T. Lindeberg, *Domestic Architecture of H. T. Lindeberg*. See also Mark Alan Hewitt, *The Architect and the American Country House*, 53–57, 181–86; and Kim Coventry, Daniel Meyer, and Arthur H. Miller, *Classic Country Estates of Lake Forest: Architecture and Landscape Design, 1856–1940*, 211–17.

11. Alexandra Fatio, *Maurice Fatio Architect*, 14–21.

12. Lindeberg's biographical entry in *The National Cyclopedia of American Biography* identifies his father as a shipbuilder.

13. An entry in Leland M. Roth, *The Architecture of McKim, Mead and White, 1870–1920: A Building List* suggests that the Stillman House, Mondeanne, was initially a McKim, Mead and White commission. On the Stillman House see Harrie T. Lindeberg, "Thatched Roof Effect with Shingles," *The Brickbuilder* 18 (July 1909): 133–40; "A Thatched Palace: An Estate at Pocantico Hills, Albro and Lindeberg, Architects," *Architectural Record* 28 (Nov. 1910): 314–28; and Harrie T. Lindeberg, "The Design and Plan of the Country House," *The American Architect* 99 (Apr. 12, 1911): 133–37.

See also "Two Houses of Individuality Showing the Versatility of Architects Albro and Lindeberg," *Architectural Record* 30 (Oct. 1911): 368–73; A. H. Forbes, "The Work of Albro and Lindeberg," *Architecture* 26 (Nov. 15, 1912): 206–40; C. Matlack Price, "The Recent Work of Albro and Lindeberg," *Architecture* 31 (Jan. 1915): 1–39; C. Matlack Price, "Individuality in Country Houses," *House and Garden* 37 (Feb. 1920): 18–23, 25; Russell F. Whitehead, "Harrie T. Lindeberg's Contribution to American Domestic Architecture," *Architectural Record* 55 (Apr. 1924): 308–72.

14. Barnstone, *Architecture of John F. Staub*, 55.

15. Barnstone, *Architecture of John F. Staub*, 4. Barber and McMurry were extensively published in the 1920s. William Ross McNabb illustrates the Powell Smith House, the First Christian Church, the Calvin Holmes House, and the M. D. Arnold House in Knoxville by Charles Barber and Barber and McMurry in *Tradition, Innovation, and Romantic Images*, 29–35, 42–45, as well as the Church Street United Methodist Church, on which Barber and McMurry collaborated with John Russell Pope (pp. 50–51).

16. Richard L Bushman, *The Refinement of America: Persons, Houses, Cities*, xix.

17. "Picturesque Setting for River Oaks Structure." *Houston Post*, Oct. 21, 1923.

18. When Lindeberg sent Staub to Houston in 1921, Lindeberg's initial client, Hugo V. Neuhaus, found office space for him in the Union National Bank Building, where Neuhaus's office was located. The *Morrison and Fourmy's Houston City Directory, 1923* (hereafter cited as *Houston City Directory*) lists Staub's office address as room 207 in the Union National Bank Building. The *Houston City Directory, 1922* lists among the office tenants in the Union National Bank Building: Neuhaus and Company (rooms 201–206), the W. T. Carter Lumber and Building Company (room 208), Edward M. Armstrong, M.D. (rooms 713–14), Fred Rice Lummis, M.D. (rooms 819–20), J. J. Sweeney (rooms 911–12), and Joseph A. Tennant (rooms 1111–12). W. T. Carter Jr., Drs. Armstrong and Lummis, the manager of the Sweeney estate, J. J. Sweeney's grandson John S. Mellinger, and Tennant became Staub's clients, as did Hubert B. Finch, vice president of the bank.

On J. T. Rather Jr. (1896–1968), see the commemorative booklet "A Tribute in Memory of J. T. Rather, Jr., 1898–1968, From His Associates at Rice University," and "Rather, John Thomas, Jr.," *Who's Who in America*, vol. 35, 1968–69 (1968), 1790. The *American Architects Directory*, with editions published in 1956, 1962, and 1970, contains brief entries for John F. Staub (1956: 531, 1962: 670, and 1970: 873), John Thomas

Rather Jr. (1956: 452, 1962: 574), Donald Barthelme (1956: 28, 1962: 37, 1970: 47), Albert H. Howze (1956: 260, 1962: 330, 1970: 426), Charles H. Kiefner (1956: 298, 1962: 377), Milton B. McGinty (1956: 353, 1962: 447, 1970: 577), and Vance D. Phenix (1956: 433, 1962: 550). George S. Koyl, ed. (1956 and 1962), and John F. Gane (1970), ed., *American Architects Directory*.

19. The John F. Staub Collection (Mss 303) of the Houston Metropolitan Research Center's Architectural Component contains minimal drawings (primarily floor plans, assembled for the production of Howard Barnstone's book) for Ben M. Anderson House, Edward H. Andrews House, Harry E. Brants House in Fort Worth, Tex., Hugh Brinkley House in Memphis, Tenn., W. T. Carter Jr. Lodge, C. Milby Dow House, Irving M. Eisen House in Beaumont, Tex., Stephen P. Farish House, Albert B. Fay Bay House in Kemah, Tex., Edward Bel Fay Bay House in Kemah, Tex., Lamar Fleming Summer House near Hunt, Tex., Amy Staub Galyon House in Knoxville, Tenn., Alfred C. Glassell House in Shreveport, La., Dan J. Harrison House, George S. Heyer House, J. W. Parker House, Edward Randall III House, Josephine Abercrombie Robinson House outside Versailles, Ky., Seymour Sacks House, Tom Scurry House, Hugh Sprunt House in Memphis, Tenn., J. M. Tatton House in Victoria, Tex., William L. Walker House in Wilmington, N.C., Harry C. Wiess Stable, and the Andrew J. Wray House. Larger (but not complete) sets of drawings exist for the Hugo N. Dixon House in Memphis, Tenn., Claud B. Hamill House, Harris Masterson III House, Memorial Park Bath House and Pool, George A. Peterkin House, W. C. Richardson House in Beaumont, Tex., John F. Staub House, and the J. Cooke Wilson House in Beaumont, Tex. Complete drawing sets exist for the Hugh Roy Cullen House, the J. Robert Neal House, and the Ray M. O'Brien House in Shreveport, La. A complete set of drawings, including preliminary design drawings, exists for the Alex Camp House in Dallas. The Houston Metropolitan Research Center's Photographic Collections contain a set of snapshots of historic Texas buildings that David R. Williams gave to John Staub (Mss 114/404–453). The Oral Histories contain an interview with John Staub (Interview No. 174) conducted by David T. Courtwright on March 20, 1975. The Architectural Component's Howard Barnstone Collection contains the material Barnstone assembled to prepare his book on Staub.

20. Staub entered the U.S. Naval Reserve in 1942. He was appointed commanding officer of the U.S. Naval Auxiliary Air Station in Manteo Point, North Carolina, in 1943 and transferred to the Naval Auxiliary Air Station in Harvey Point, North Carolina, as commanding officer later that year, where he served until 1944. Staub and Rather also organized a war-time practice, Niven, Staub, Rather and Jenkins, with the Houston structural engineer Francis J. Niven and the architect and mechanical engineer Raymond L. Jenkins, to design airfields and camps for the U.S. Army Corps of Engineers. During Staub's absence, Rather additionally collaborated with Harvin C. Moore on the design of the U. S. Naval Hospital in Marlin, Texas, in 1945. In 1942, when Staub re-entered the navy, Tom Rather became a name partner in the firm of Staub and Rather. See the biographical entry "Staub, John F," in *Who's Who in America*, vol. 24, 1946–47, 2247.

21. Madeleine Staub was also a member of the Garden Club of Houston, a founding member of the River Oaks Garden Club, a member of the Junior League of Houston, and a member and president of the Assembly. From 1940 to 1945 she was a trustee of the Museum of Fine Arts.

22. Rick Gardner and Rob Muir are two of the three photographers for David B. Warren's book *Bayou Bend Gardens: A Southern Oasis*. David T. Courtwright is John A. Delaney Presidential Professor of History at the University of North Florida in Jacksonville, Florida. Jerome Iowa is the author of *Ageless Adobe: History and Preservation in Southwestern Architecture*.

23. See "Funeral Services Set for John F. Staub," *Houston Post*, Apr. 14, 1981, 9A and "Staub," 22C. On Madeleine Staub see "Staub," *Houston Post*, Oct. 26, 1981, 7E.

24. Lars Lerup's book *After the City* and Albert Pope's book *Ladders* meditate on the city that Houston became in the second half of the twentieth century. On the garden city alternative, see Robert A. M. Stern, ed., with John Montague Massengale, *The Anglo American Suburb*.

25. U.S. Bureau of the Census, *Fourteenth Census of the United States*, and *Sixteenth Census of the United States*.

26. David G. McComb, *Houston: The Bayou City*, 10–18.

27. Earl Wesley Fornell, *The Galveston Era: The Texas Crescent on the Eve of Secession*, 10, 158, 192.

28. Harold L. Platt, *City Building in the New South: The Growth of Public Services in Houston, Texas, 1830–1910*, 186; and Kenneth Lipartito and Joseph Pratt, *Baker and Botts in the Development of Modern Houston*, 47.

29. Platt, *City Building in the New South*, 157, 171, 175–77; Joe R. Feagin, *Free Enterprise City*, 51.

30. McComb, *Houston*, 113–14; Platt, *City Building in the New South*, 176; Feagin, *Free Enterprise City*, 53–54.

31. McComb, *Houston*, 116.

32. Marilyn McAdams Sibley, *The Port of Houston: A History*.

33. Walter Buenger and Joseph Pratt, *But Also Good Business: Texas Commerce Bank and the Financing of Houston and Texas*, 65–66; McComb, *Houston*, 7–8.

34. Buenger and Pratt, *But Also Good Business*, 73–78; McComb, *Houston*, 142.

35. Pamela G. Smart. "Sacred Modern: An Ethnography of an Art Museum," ii; Penny Sparke, "Always in Good Taste: The Enduring Legacy of Elsie de Wolfe," *Harvard Design Magazine* 11 (Summer 2000): 19.

36. Histories of these and other Houston organizations that socially framed local elites include Marguerite Johnston, *A Happy Worldly Abode: Christ Church Cathedral, 1839–1964*; Patrick J. Nicholson, *Houston Country Club Seventy-Fifth Anniversary, 1908–1983*; Jack Donahue, *The Finest in the Land: The Story of the Petroleum Club of Houston*; *The Texas Corinthian Yacht Club: The First Fifty Years, 1938–1988*; and Dorothy Knox Howe Houghton, *The Houston Club and Its City: One Hundred Years*.

37. On the Sealy House see Richard Guy Wilson, *McKim, Mead and White Architects*, 124–27, and Eleanor H. Gustafson, "'The Open Gates': The George Sealy House in Galveston," *Antiques* 108 (Sept. 1975): 508–14.

38. A number of these Houston buildings were published in the national architectural press: the Scanlan Building in A. N. Rebori, "The Work of Burnham and Root, D. H. Burnham, D. H. Burnham and Co., and Graham, Burnham and Co.," *Architectural Record* 38 (July 1915): 100; the Southern Pacific Building in "Southern Pacific Railway Building, Houston, Texas," *Western Architect* 20 (Sept. 1914): plate section; and the Texas Company Building in "The Texas Company Building, Houston, Texas," *Architectural Record* 55 (Mar. 1924): 261.

39. On Cram, Goodhue and Ferguson's work at the Rice Institute, see Montgomery Schuyler, "The Work of Cram, Goodhue and Ferguson," *Architectural Record* 29 (Jan. 1911): 30, 77–78, 86; "William M. Rice Institute, Houston, Texas," *American Architect* 102 (Dec. 11, 1912): 207–208 and plates; Franz Winkler, "The Administration Building of the Rice Institute, Houston, Texas," *The Brickbuilder* 21 (Dec. 1912): 321–24; "Rice Institute, Cram, Goodhue and Ferguson, Architects," *Western Architect* 19 (Feb. 1913): 20. See also Ralph Adams Cram, "Have I a 'Philosophy of Design'?" *Pencil Points* 13 (Nov. 1932): 731; Ralph Adams Cram, *My Life in Architecture*, 126; and Douglass Shand-Tucci, *Ralph Adams Cram: An Architect's Four Quests: Medieval, Modernist, American, Ecumenical*, 106–20.

40. Sadie Gwin Blackburn, "Evolution of the Domestic Landscape," in Dorothy Knox Howe Houghton, Barrie M. Scardino, Sadie Gwin Blackburn, and Katherine S. Howe, *Houston's Forgotten Heritage: Landscape, Houses, Interiors, 1824–1914*, 57–58.

41. J. S. Cullinan to R. Lee Blaffer, Apr. 7, 1916, J. S. Cullinan Collection, Houston Metropolitan Research Center, Houston Public Library.

42. Christopher Gray, "All the Best Places: Shadyside," *House and Garden* 155 (Aug. 1983): 46–47, and Mark Alan Hewitt, "Harrie T. Linde-

berg and Modern Domestic Architecture," in H. T. Lindeberg, *Domestic Architecture by H. T. Lindeberg*, xiii.

On Hugo Victor Neuhaus (1882–1947) see "Hugo Neuhaus, Well-Known Banker, Dies," *Houston Chronicle*, Oct. 11, 1947, 1; "Hugo Neuhaus Dead; Houston Banker, 65," *New York Times*, Oct. 12, 1947, 76; and Martin Neuhaus, "The History of the Neuhaus Family (To 1935)," trans. W. O. Neuhaus, Lillie Neuhaus, and Ilse Neuhaus Richardson, unpublished manuscript, collection of W. O. Neuhaus III, Houston, Texas.

On Kenneth E. Womack (1879–1946) see the biographical entry in *The New Encyclopedia of Texas*, vol. 1, 262, and S. Deane Wasson, *Houston Cotton Exchange and Board of Trade: Fifty Years a Cotton Market, 1874–1924*, 22.

On William Stamps Farish (1881–1942) see *The New Encyclopedia of Texas*, vol. 1, 310; "W. S. Farish Dies; Standard Oil Head," *New York Times*, Nov. 30, 1942, 23; Henrietta Larson and Kenneth Porter, *History of Humble Oil and Refining Company: A Study in Industrial Growth*, 23–24; and *National Cyclopedia of American Biography*, vol. 32 (1945), 325.

On D. D. Peden (1874–1958) see George Fuermann, *Peden 1965: Seventy-Five Years and Just a Beginning*.

On Harry Carrothers Wiess (1887–1948) see *The New Encyclopedia of Texas*, vol. 1, 653 and 984; Larson and Porter, *History of Humble Oil and Refining Company*, 26; and *National Cyclopedia of American Biography*, vol. 35 (1949), 76–77.

43. "Houston's Cradle of Culture and Environs," *Houston Gargoyle* 5 (May 1, 1932): 11.

44. The "country house" as a late-nineteenth- and early-twentieth-century American house type (rather than a house situated on a rural estate) can be functionally defined as a free-standing elite house type, usually two or three stories high, that relates to its site as though it were a house in the country. It is apt to be double fronted, with a formally composed entrance front as well as a formally composed garden front. The country house opens to its grounds through intermediate loggias, porches, and terraces, and the design of the house may be coordinated with the design of adjacent landscape settings to facilitate domestic occupation. Implicitly, the country house type, especially when built in cities, contrasted with older urban house types. These, especially if built prior to the 1830s, were likely to be row houses rather than free-standing, with priority of use of any associated outdoor space given to domestic services. Town houses were likely to be elevated above streets to ensure security and some measure of visual privacy and to have architectural décor concentrated on street fronts only. Because row housing was virtually unknown in any Texas city of Anglo-American origin, detached houses freestanding in landscaped grounds were the characteristic type of elite housing from the 1830s forward. What distinguished the "modern" country house type from these older freestanding houses was that the older houses tended not to make direct connections to their landscaped grounds (often because they were built on elevated foundations) and were architecturally composed only where visible from public thoroughfares.

45. Mark Alan Hewitt in *The Architect and the American Country House*, the authoritative source on the American country house, discusses these phases in chapters 4, 5, and 6. See Hewitt, *Architect and the American Country House*, 124–239. See also Clive Aslet, *The American Country House*.

46. Aldrich, *Old Money*, 36. Nelson W. Aldrich Jr., the most perceptive contemporary analyst of what he calls the "mythology" of an American upper class, uses the term "patrician" for what he deduces to be the exemplary subject position of this class. Aldrich demonstrates that upper classes in the United States have worked to retain their authority by affiliating with and supporting such institutions as preparatory schools and research universities, art museums, symphony orchestras, and nature conservation groups that absorb, filter, and refine newly accumulated wealth in order to conserve cultural and environmental patrimonies for the common good. He describes this as part of the upper class's "educational" mission: transforming entrepreneurs into patricians as well as keeping patricians patrician by retarding lapses into déclassé circumstances, what Aldrich, citing John Jay Chapman, an early-twentieth-century apologist for an American upper class, calls "a loss of social relevance." Domestic architecture contributes to this educational transformation by spatially structuring implied ways of life that instill and inspire in their occupants, both masters and servants, appropriate subject positions, personifying the ways upper-class-ness should be lived (and lived in proximity to) and how this experience is to be spatially distinguished from middle-class-ness, for instance. Domestic architecture also has the capacity to identify its occupants as upper class, an identity that facilitates upper-class subjects' recognition of each other and represents them collectively to members of other classes. Elite neighborhoods and their satellites (schools, churches, social clubs, and shops) expand this social geography into larger spatial collectives that reinforce subjectivity, identity, and class cohesion. Aldrich, *Old Money*, 37, 142.

47. Hewitt to author. Richard Longstreet, *On the Edge of the World*, 1–39.

48. Smart, "Sacred Modern," 209.

49. The construction of continuity, evident phenomenally in the park and parkway boulevard complex invented by the American landscape architect and urban planner Frederick Law Olmsted, was an important ideological value of the Progressive movement. Spatial continuity, historical continuity, and social continuity were themes stressed by Progressive-era reformers as they sought to formulate popular consensus on the social construction of unifying identities for American industrial cities and their tumultuous populations. William H. Wilson examines the city planning implications of this ideology in *The City Beautiful Movement*. Joseph M. Siry examines the social, economic, class, ethnic, and cultural conflicts that moved enlightened elites in late-nineteenth-century American cities toward a "progressive" consciousness in *The Chicago Auditorium Building: Adler and Sullivan's Architecture and the City*. Harold L. Platt examines the emergence of a Progressive consciousness among elements of Houston's elite in *City Building in the New South: The Growth of Public Services in Houston, Texas, 1830–1910*.

50. Tzonis and Lefaivre, *Classical Architecture*, 5.

51. Suzannah Lessard, writing about the Villard Houses in New York, designed by the firm of McKim, Mead and White, of which her great-grandfather Stanford White was a member, points to the ideological challenge that Staub and other elite architects confronted in constructing an architecture of patrician identity when she writes that "architecture built for the upper classes in democratic America is built upon unstable imaginative ground." Lessard's meditations on the Villard Houses address the mechanics of constructing elite identity in domestic architecture on this unstable ground. She discerns that the houses ". . . speak primarily of the high rank of their occupants. The architecture seeks to convince us of the legitimacy of the hegemony of the few." The houses enlist support for this assertion of power through multiple strategies of identification: appeals to vicarious projection (speaking of an especially grand interior, she observes that it "encourages us to imagine ourselves members of the nobility of an aristocratic culture . . ."), aesthetic seduction ("The beauty of the architecture remains persuasive and true"), and romantic narrative ("The architecture turns family into dynasty . . ."). Reflecting on the fate of the railroad speculator Henry Villard, who encountered financial reverses that led to a short tenure in his block of grand houses, Lessard contrasts the vagaries of historical circumstance with the mythic reality of the architecture: "The man goes down, but the false promise that drove him forward remains standing, absurdly perfect, an illusion that to this day has the power to enthrall us." Staub and his contemporaries negotiated a dialectics of reality and make-believe in constructing patrician identity through architecture that materially and socially grounded fancifulness, exuberance, and grandeur in local circumstance. They made stylistic fantasy credible and persuasive because of the skill, discretion, and restraint with which they integrated romantic imagery and daily life.

Suzannah Lessard, "Three Houses: From Mount Vernon to the McMansion," *Harvard Design Magazine* 11 (Summer 2000): 10, 12, 14, 15.

Ptolemy Dean, in his insightful analysis of the work of the English neoclassical architect John Soane, describes the subjective sensations produced by the spatialization of axial projection: "Inside, a sequence of rooms was laid out along the new east and north fronts, each one connected with opening doors forming an unbroken 'enfilade' through the structure. When all the doors are opened, particularly on the east front, a tremendous sense of depth and perspective is achieved, magnified by the effect of light streaming through the large windows that extend almost to ground-floor level. . . . A rhythm is achieved through the use of repeated arched openings, providing a vista of diminishing layers in perspective." Ptolemy Dean, *Sir John Soane and the Country Estate*, 44.

It is this subjective perceptual sensation of deep "power space" that the modern architect Philip Johnson called "processional" space in an essay published in 1965. See Philip Johnson, "Whence and Whither: The Processional Element in Architecture," in *Philip Johnson: The Glass House*, ed. David Whitney and Jeffrey Kipnis, 26–32.

52. Howard Barnstone, "Rediscovering John F. Staub: The Great Eclectic of Houston's Elite," *Texas Architect* 29 (Nov.–Dec. 1979): 53.

53. Suzannah Lessard, *The Architect of Desire: Beauty and Desire in the Stanford White Family*, 117.

54. Lessard, *Architect of Desire*, 85 and 65; Aldrich, *Old Money*, 266.

55. The cultural historian Richard L. Bushman, in *The Refinement of America*, his panoramic work on the chains of signification (as Michael Hays calls them) linking material culture, "lifestyle," and power, examines how investment in beauty, grace, and art legitimized wealth, class, and authority in eighteenth- and nineteenth-century America. Bushman notes three characteristics of the social life associated with grand houses: exclusivity, beauty, and theatricality, all pertaining to formal entertainment, which he deduces was the primary programmatic activity around which such houses took shape. Ceremonious forms of living, refined of impurity, were, as Bushman observes, "performed" in grand houses that appeared in turn to perform for public approval the superiority and honor imputed to their owners. Bushman, 25, 48–52, and xiv.

56. "Individuality," a term drawn from the discourse of social Darwinism, gained currency in American architectural criticism in the 1910s. Especially with respect to domestic architecture, "individuality" seems to have encoded the notion of managing a variety of subject positions without exceeding the limits of upper-class identity. Herbert Croly, the early-twentieth-century American architecture and social critic, made the notion of management ("efficient regulation") central to his political treatise *The Promise of American Life* of 1909 as a device for balancing the contradictory forces associated with privately accumulated industrial wealth (and the political power that stemmed from such concentrations) and a democratic polity. See, for example, Herbert D. Croly, "The Farm House 'De-Luxe': Country Seat of Robert J. Collier, Esq., John Russell Pope, Architect," *Architectural Record* 31 (June 1912): 561, and Herbert Croly, *The Promise of American Life*, 23. The resonance of Croly's title and his prominence as an architectural editor and critic are reflected in the title of an article by the Boston architect Ralph Adams Cram, "The Promise of American House Building," *House and Garden* 29 (Jan. 1915): 8–12.

57. The phenomenon of "typification"—organizing experience in conformance with some master model—is addressed by Berger and Luckmann, *The Social Construction of Reality*, 72, and by Tzonis and Lefaivre, *Classical Architecture*, 152, 278.

58. Staub, in the words of Michael Hardt and Antonio Negri, "historicize[d] the past in order to put it to work." See Hardt and Negri, *Empire*, 126. Also Mitchell Schwartzer, "Myths of Permanence and Transience in the Discourse on Historic Preservation in the United States," *Journal of Architectural Education* 48 (Sept. 1994): 2–11. And Mark Crinson, *Empire Building: Orientalism and Victorian Architecture*, 151, where Crinson writes of a church designed by an English architect for an exotic locale: "A myth is being created here of a distinct, traditional way of life contained by and in harmony with the proposed church. . . . But more importantly, this linkage was also a way of negating differences, assuming equality, and absorbing oriental architecture into the British scheme."

59. Lewis Mumford, *Sticks and Stones: A Study of American Architecture and Civilization*, 28.

60. Aldrich, *Old Money*, 37; Tzonis and Lefaivre, *Classical Architecture*, 5.

61. Bushman links gentility, "beautification," and the assertion of social authority (Bushman, *Refinement of America*, xiv, 404). Aldrich isolates composure as an identifying patrician characteristic (Aldrich, *Old Money*, 83).

CHAPTER 2. BROADACRES

1. On Broadacres see Anne S. Bohnn, "Broadacres Historic District." The Broadacres Historic District is listed in the National Register of Historic Places; the application is at the Texas Historic Sites Atlas <http://atlas.thc.state.tx.us/shell-kword.htm> under "Broadacres," "Harris County," and "National Register Properties."

On James A. Baker Jr. (1892–1973), see J. H. Freeman, *The People of Baker Botts*, 92–93; and Joseph Pratt, "8F and Many More: Business and Civic Leadership in Modern Houston," *Houston Review of History and Culture* 1 (summer 2004): 4. James A. Baker Jr. and his wife, Bonner Means, were the parents of James A. Baker III, chief of staff during the first term of Pres. Ronald Reagan, secretary of the treasury during Reagan's second term, and secretary of state during the administration of Pres. George H. W. Bush. On Capt. James A. Baker (1857–1941), see Buenger and Pratt, *But Also Good Business*, 81–82; Lipartito and Pratt, *Baker and Botts in the Development of Modern Houston*, 49–51,53–56, 58–60; Freeman, *People of Baker Botts*, 33–43; Fredericka Meiners, *A History of Rice University: The Institute Years, 1907–1963*, 14–15; and Pratt, "8F and Many More," 4.

In 1923 Alice Graham and James A. Baker bought the Oaks, the country house of Baker's former partner E. B. Parker, where Baker lived until his death. About 1925 they commissioned Staub to carry out interior alterations to the Sanguinet and Staats–designed house. A photograph of Staub's paneled library was published in Dorothy Dawes Chillman's article "Books and Their Shelves," in *Civics for Houston* 1 (Apr. 1928): 8.

2. The "Plat of Broadacres, An Addition to the City of Houston" was filed in February 1923. H. A. Kipp was the consulting engineer. Watkin's original plat called for only two entrances, on the southeast from Bissonnet and on the northeast from the neighboring N. P. Turner Addition, with the three boulevards completely insulated from subdivisions to the west. The city of Houston refused to accept the plat unless North and South were continued westward to intersect Mandell Street. No drawing of this original layout is known to survive. Bohnn, "Broadacres Historic District."

3. Dean, *Sir John Soane and the Country Estate*, 44, and Philip Johnson, "Whence and Whither: The Processional Element in Architecture," in *Philip Johnson*, ed. Whitney and Kipnis, 26–32.

4. Although Broadacres was never advertised, it was used by the Guardian Trust Company to promote sales in the adjoining Edgemont addition. See "Broadacres Is One of Houston's Most Attractive Sections" and the Guardian Trust Company's advertisement "Edgemont Adjoining Broadacres," *Houston Chronicle*, Nov. 16, 1924, 38, 39.

On Frank P. Sterling, a co-founder, director, and vice president in charge of production of the Humble Oil and Refining Company until his retirement in 1933, see *The New Encyclopedia of Texas*, vol. 2, 322. Sterling and his wife Isla Carroll were the adoptive parents of Carroll Sterling, who became Staub's client following her marriage to Harris Masterson III.

5. Freeman, *People of Baker Botts*, 3–18.

6. Ibid., 19–23.

7. Ibid., xii; Lipartito and Pratt, *Baker and Botts in the Development of Modern Houston*, 48–49.

8. Barnstone, *Architecture of John F. Staub*, 13.

9. On Palmer Hutcheson (1887–1966) see *The New Encyclopedia of Texas*, vol. 1, 420, 425; Freeman, *People of Baker Botts*, 85–87; Zarko Franks, "'Rights for All' Base of Attorney's Career," *Houston Chronicle*, Mar. 14, 1952, 8; and "Hutcheson, Leading City Attorney, Dies," *Houston Chronicle*, June 20, 1966, section 4, 21. Zarko Franks's profile quotes Hutcheson on the emotional attachment he felt to the city when looking down from his offices on the seventeenth floor of the Niels Esperson Building: "I can look out of certain windows in this building and see the houses where my father used to live, where my mother was born, where I was born, and where my first son was born."

10. On Mrs. Hutcheson's father, see John D. Thompson, "Thomson, Thaddeus Austin," *New Handbook of Texas*, vol. 6, 478; and on her great-grandfather, see Malcolm D. McLean, "Thomson, Alexander, Jr.," *New Handbook of Texas*, vol. 6, 478.

11. Bushman, *Refinement of America*, 27.

12. Copy of undated typescript from John F. Staub's office: "Client, Cost, Comp[letion] Date, Est[imated] Cost," c. 1940; and Barnstone, *Architecture of John F. Staub*, 74–76. On Christian J. Miller (1872–1954) see "Industry Mourns Death of Chris Miller," *AGC News Service*, Dec. 28, 1954, 1. Miller was a Danish-born carpenter who became a general contractor in 1914. His brother and sometime collaborator was Pete Miller. Staub told Barnstone he regarded Chris Miller as the best builder he worked with in Houston. Barnstone, *Architecture of John F. Staub*, 16.

13. Colin Rowe, "Character and Composition: Or Some Vicissitudes of Architectural Vocabulary in the Nineteenth Century," in Rowe, *The Mathematics of the Ideal Villa and Other Essays*, 74.

On the double fronts of country houses and the issues involved in translating these to nonrural settings, see "Bellefontaine at Lenox, Massachusetts, Designed by Carrère and Hastings, Architects," *House and Garden* 2 (Jan. 1902): 1–9, which discusses the difference between the arrival front and garden front of a country house in the country (p. 1) and the importance of indoor-outdoor connections (p. 9). It is intriguing to note that when Charles Platt installed a kitchen behind the ceremonious street façade of the Frank Cheney House in South Manchester, Connecticut, he was criticized rather than congratulated by an unnamed critic in *House and Garden* for violating the ethic of honest expression; see "A House in the Suburbs of Hartford Being the Residence of Frank Cheney, Esq., at South Manchester, Designed by Charles A. Platt, Architect," *House and Garden* 6 (Sept. 1904): 151–55. By the mid 1910s critical attitudes had changed, as can be seen from a pair of articles published in *House and Garden* in 1916: Rollin Lynde Hartt, "Houses with Their Backs to the Street: A Serious Dissertation in the Interests of Privacy," *House and Garden* 29 (Apr. 1916): 16–17; and Ernest Irving Freese, "How Do Your Rooms Face? If You Build by the Compass You Can Have Sunlight and Shade as You Wish," *House and Garden* 30 (July 1916): 15. By 1921, the practice of endowing suburban houses with garden elevations in addition to their street elevations was taken for granted. See "The Back of the House," *House and Garden* 40 (Nov. 1921): 27. Hester Scott, executive director of Will Hogg's Forum of Civics and editor of the Forum's monthly magazine, *Civics for Houston*, echoed this attitude in the article "The Front of the House: Few Know How Fair and Full of Grace are the Fronts away from the Highway," *Civics for Houston* 1 (May 1928): 10–11. Miss Scott came to Houston from Condé Nast, the publisher of *House and Garden*.

14. Aldrich, *Old Money*, 74. Aldrich observes of an upward-bound parvenu: "There he learned the rudiments of the great operating principal of the upper class aesthetic—sublimation."

15. Tzonis and Lefaivre, *Classical Architecture*, 5, 9.

16. Lindeberg, "The Design and Plan of the Country House," 137.

17. As Richard Bushman observed, "To elevate life to a higher level of beauty and grace required support from a beautiful environment." Bushman, *Refinement of America*, xviii.

18. Michael Benedikt, "Class Notes," *Harvard Design Magazine* 11 (Summer 2000): 8.

19. On William S. Cochran (1879–1951) see *The New Encyclopedic of Texas*, vol. 1, 294–95; the brochure *Houston Riding and Polo Club 1st Horseshow and Gymkhana, June 19th, 20th, 21st, 1925*. On Mrs. Cochran, see *Social Register of Houston*, 26 (subsequent volumes of this series are entitled *Social Directory of Houston* and are published by the Mount Vernon Publishing Company). Copy of undated typescript from John F. Staub's office: "Client, Cost, Comp. Date, Est. Cost"; Barnstone, *Architecture of John F. Staub*, 90–91, and "Contracts Awarded," *Texas General Contractors Association Monthly Bulletin* 7 (Feb. 1926): 32.

20. Copy of undated typescript from John F. Staub's office: "Client, Cost, Comp. Date, Est. Cost" and Barnstone, *Architecture of John F. Staub*, 103–105, 92–94.

21. On C. Milby Dow (1892–1961) see "City Benefactor Dow Dies in Car," *Houston Chronicle*, Apr. 19, 1961, section 5, 1; "Dow Was Major City Benefactor" and "C. Milby Dow Funeral Rites Set Friday," *Houston Chronicle*, Apr. 20, 1961, section 2, 4, and section 4, 19. *Morrison and Fourmy's Directory of the City of Houston, Texas*, 1900–1901 to 1927.

22. Surprisingly little published information is available on Joseph A. Tennant (1888–1948) despite his prominence as a consulting engineer. See the obituary notices "Joseph A. Tennant," *New York Times*, Dec. 16, 1948, 29, and "Joseph Allan Tennant, 60" in *Houston Post*, Dec. 16, 1948, section 4, 9. Tennant was first listed in the Houston city directory in 1917, with the offices of his consulting engineering practices located in the Union National Bank Building, where he remained until moving to the Niels Esperson Building when it opened in 1927.

23. On Mrs. Tennant's genealogy, see Hattie Borden Weld, *Historical and Genealogical Record of the Descendants as Far Known of Richard and Joan Borden* and Rachel Bluntzer Hébert, *The Forgotten Colony: San Patricio de Hibernia*, 316, 330.

24. "Famous Tennant Azalea Garden Charms Visitors with Perfect Unity of Design," *Houston Chronicle*, Feb. 20, 1938, 8A. After Joe Tennant's death, Mrs. Tennant married J. Allen Myers Jr.

25. Lessard, *Architect of Desire*, 117: "It was sensibility that put us a cut above the rest of the world: we were artists in a mode that somehow also made us socially superior. In this way the domineering aspect of class superiority was avoided. Yet the physical embodiments of that sensibility—the long drive, the Tapis Vert, the box garden, the house itself—though joyous and light nevertheless conveyed something more than sensibility. They conveyed dynasty, wealth, and power."

26. Staub told Barnstone that the elevation drawing of Tintinhull House, an early-eighteenth-century country house published in Horace Field and Michael Bunney's *English Domestic Architecture of the XVII and XVIII Centuries*, of 1905, was his source for the street elevation of the Tennant House. Barnstone, *Architecture of John F. Staub*, 92–93. The most famous of these pedimented American houses is the Hammond-Harwood House in Annapolis, Maryland, of 1774 by William Buckland.

The Tennant House did not perform as smoothly functionally as it did spatially and proportionally. A grandson of Mrs. Tennant's remembers that her daughter complained that in one bedroom, low window sills and the arrangement of doors meant there was no place beds could be stationed without creating awkward conflicts. Staub recalled that when he added a second-floor addition above the kitchen, his relationship with Mrs. Tennant became so tense that he delegated completion of the project to his associate, J. T. Rather Jr. Staub explained to Howard Barnstone that it was his practice not to center a fireplace on the short wall of a rectangular living room. The Tennant House is a rare instance from the 1920s and 1930s where Staub disregarded this practice. The eighteenth-century English marble mantle installed in the living room does complement the room's meticulously articulated composition and proportions. What the Tennant House accomplished with understated flair was to enliven typification with individuality, perform belonging with its front-back reversal and construct continuity between house and garden as well as house and community.

27. Aldrich, *Old Money*, 83; Berger and Luckmann, *The Social Construction of Reality*, 72. "Georgian Simplicity and Dignity for a Texas House," *House and Garden* 60 (Sept. 1931): 72–73.

28. Copy of undated typescript from John F. Staub's office: "Client, Cost, Comp. Date, Est. Cost"; Barnstone, *Architecture of John F. Staub*, 138–39.

29. Kemp Strother Dargan (1884–1954) is first listed in the 1912 edition of the *Houston City Directory* as a member of the fire, tornado, accident, and liability insurance firm of Cravens and Cage. The 1920–21 city directory is the first to identify the firm as Cravens, Dargan, and Roberts. It became Cravens, Dargan, and Company in 1925.

30. Smart, "Sacred Modern," 18; George E. Marcus, *Lives in Trust: The Fortunes of Dynastic Families in Late Twentieth-Century America*, 142.

31. Copy of undated typescript from John F. Staub's office: "Client, Cost, Comp. Date, Est. Cost"; Barnstone, *Architecture of John F. Staub*, 130–32.

32. On Rudolph Charles Kuldell (1889–1973) see Donald L. Bartlett and James B. Steele, *Empire: The Life, Legend, and Madness of Howard Hughes*, 80; the biographical entry on Howard R. Hughes in *The New Encyclopedia of Texas*, vol. 1, 404, 407; Leon Hale, "'Retired' General Kuldell Engineers Beef Farm," *Houston Post*, Dec. 5, 1948, section 5, 7; and *Who Was Who in America*, vol. 6, 1974–76, 236.

33. Barnstone, *Architecture of John F. Staub*, 26.

34. Hewitt, *Architect and the American Country House*, 118–23, and Aslet, *The American Country House*, 84–109.

35. See, for instance, Howard T. Fisher's critique of antiquarianism in *Architectural Record*'s annual country house issue for 1929, cited by Barnstone (p. 37): Fisher, "New Elements in House Design." *Architectural Record* 66 (Nov. 1929): 397.

36. The exceptional architectural consistency of Staub's Broadacres houses and their systematic integration with their setting resonates with the observation of the twentieth-century French sociologist Pierre Bourdieu that "Social identity lies in difference, and difference is asserted against what is closest, which represents the greatest threat." Quoted in Russell Hardin, "Identity: Social," *International Encyclopedia of the Social and Behavioural Sciences*, Neil J. Smelser and Paul B. Baltes, eds. in chief, vol. 11, 7167.

CHAPTER 3. RIVER OAKS

1. On River Oaks see Cheryl Caldwell Ferguson, "Upscale Suburban Architecture and Development in Dallas and Houston, Texas, 1890–1930"; Cheryl Caldwell Ferguson, "River Oaks: 1920s Suburban Planning and Development in Houston," *Southwestern Historical Quarterly* 104 (Oct. 2000): 190–228; Barry J. Kaplan and Charles Orson Cook, "Civic Elites and Urban Planning: Houston's River Oaks," in *Houston: A Twentieth-Century Urban Frontier*, ed. Francisco A. Rosales and Barry J. Kaplan, 22–33; "River Oaks," *The Anglo American Suburb*, ed. Robert A. M. Stern with John Montague Massengale, 83; "River Oaks Subdivision" in *Houston Architectural Survey*, vol. 3, 498–507; and Barnstone, *Architecture of John F. Staub*, 7–11. There is a reference to Country Club Estates prior to the Hoggs' involvement in the newspaper article "Country Club Home Section to Open Soon," *Houston Chronicle*, June 17, 1923, 47.

2. Barnstone, *Architecture of John F. Staub*, 28. David B. Warren, curator and subsequently director of the Bayou Bend Collection and Gardens of the Museum of Fine Arts, Houston, from 1965 until 2003, states that it was Staub, rather than Miss Hogg, who coined the term Latin Colonial. No documentation has yet surfaced to positively identify either Miss Hogg or Staub as the author of this evocative term. See "Introduction: Bayou Bend, the Collector, and the Collection" in David B. Warren, Michael K. Brown, Elizabeth Ann Coleman, Emily Ballew Neff, *American Decorative Arts and Paintings in the Bayou Bend Collection*, xvi; Kate Sayen Kirkland, "Envisioning a Progressive City: Hogg Family Philanthropy and the Urban Ideal in Houston, Texas, 1910–1975," 150–69; and David B. Warren, *Bayou Bend Gardens: A Southern Oasis*, 12–14.

3. On J. S. Hogg (1851–1906), see Robert C. Cotner, "Hogg, James Stephen," *New Handbook of Texas*, vol. 3, 652–53; Robert C. Cotner, *James Stephen Hogg: A Biography*; *National Cyclopedia of American Biography*, vol. 29 (1941), 106; Kirkland, "Envisioning a Progressive City," 50–67; and Warren, *Bayou Bend Gardens*, 4–8.

On William Clifford Hogg (1875–1930) see John A. Lomax, *Will Hogg, Texan*; Arthur J. Lefevre, "Hogg, William Clifford," in *New Handbook of Texas*, vol. 3, 654–55; Bruce J. Weber, "Will Hogg and the Business of Reform"; Bruce J. Weber and Charles Orson Cook, "Will Hogg and Civic Consciousness: Houston Style," *The Houston Review* 2 (winter 1980): 20–36; Emily Ballew Neff, "Will Hogg: Building Heritage in Texas," in Emily Ballew Neff with Wynne H. Phelan, *Frederic Remington: The Hogg Brothers Collection of the Museum of Fine Arts, Houston*, 2–37; and Kirkland, "Envisioning a Progressive City."

On Ima Hogg (1882–1975) see Virginia Bernhardt, *Ima Hogg: The Governor's Daughter*; David B. Warren, "Ima Hogg, Collector," *Antiques* 121 (Jan. 1982): 228–43; Virginia Bernhardt, "Hogg, Ima," *New Handbook of Texas*, vol. 3, 651–52; Kirkland, "Envisioning a Progressive City"; and Warren, *Bayou Bend Gardens*.

4. Daniel Yergin, *The Prize: The Epic Quest for Oil, Money, and Power*, 93; and James A. Clark and Michel T. Halbouty, *Spindletop*, 108–10.

5. John O. King, *Joseph Stephen Cullinan: A Study of Leadership in the Texas Petroleum Industry, 1897–1937*, 98–100.

6. Texas Parks and Wildlife Department Historic Sites and Restoration Branch, *Preservation Plan and Program for Varner-Hogg Plantation State Historical Park, Brazoria County, Texas*, 83–88. Also see Elizabeth Morford, "History in Houses: The Varner-Hogg Plantation in Texas," *Antiques* 76 (Aug. 1959): 126–29.

7. Bernhard, *Ima Hogg*, 48–49.

8. Lefevre, "Hogg, William Clifford," 654–55; King, *Joseph Stephen Cullinan*, 190, 193.

9. Mike Hogg (1885–1941) was a graduate of the Lawrenceville school and of the law school at the University of Texas. Tom Hogg left Lawrenceville in 1905 and never resumed his academic education. Kirkland, "Envisioning a Progressive City," 67–70, 316–18, 327–30, 332–336; Bernhard, *Ima Hogg*, 53–54, 57–58; and Hubert Roussel, *The Houston Symphony Orchestra, 1913–1971*, 19–27.

10. Texas Parks and Wildlife Department, *Preservation Plan and Program for Varner-Hogg Plantation State Historical Park*, 92–93.

11. Kate S. Kirkland gives a detailed account of Ima Hogg's illness in her essay "A Wholesome Life: Ima Hogg's Vision for Mental Health Care," *Southwestern Historical Quarterly* 104 (Jan. 2001): 424–27. See also Bernhard, *Ima Hogg*, 59–63; Kirkland, "Envisioning a Progressive City," 71–75; and Warren, *Bayou Bend Gardens*, 10.

12. Bernhard, *Ima Hogg*, 62–63; Warren, "Ima Hogg, Collector," 5; Neff, "Will Hogg: Building Heritage in Texas," 24–26; and Kirkland, "Envisioning a Progressive City," 445–448.

13. Will C. Hogg to J. S. Cullinan, Oct. 13, 1916; J. S. Cullinan to Will C. Hogg, Oct. 24, 1916; Will C. Hogg to J. S. Cullinan, Feb. 27, 1917; B. W. Ward to J. S. Cullinan, Feb. 28, 1917; J. S. Cullinan to Will C. Hogg, Mar. 19, 1918; J. S. Cullinan to H. A. Kipp, May 13, 1918; Will C. Hogg to B. W. Ward, Aug. 7, 1919; William S. Farish to H. A. Kipp, Sept. 9, 1919; H. A. Kipp to Will C. Hogg, Sept. 9, 1919; Will C. Hogg to J. S. Cullinan, Oct. 3, 1919; and J. S. Cullinan to H. A. Kipp, Oct. 17, 1919, Joseph Stephen Cullinan Collection, Houston Metropolitan Research Center, Houston Public Library. Warren, *Bayou Bend Gardens*, 10.

14. Texas Parks and Wildlife Department, *Preservation Plan and Program for Varner-Hogg*, 91, 93–94, 115–22; Neff, "Will Hogg: Building Heritage in Texas," 18–19; and Warren, *Bayou Bend Gardens*, 11–12. On Hogg's efforts with regard to the proposed subdivision of Community Place, see Will C. Hogg's letter to Mrs. O. S. Carlton, Nov. 20, 1919, in the William Clifford Hogg Collection, Center for American History, University of Texas at Austin.

15. See Ann Quin Wilson's National Register application for the Hogg Building at <http://atlas.thc.state.tx.us/shell-kword.htm> under "Hogg Building," "Harris County," and "National Register Properties"; also "Builds Home atop Big Office Building," *Houston Chronicle*, Feb. 6, 1921, 20. Norhill's opening was advertised in the *Houston Chronicle* on June 20, 1922, 25, offering "South End Facilities, North End Prices." The Varner Realty Company's plat of Colby Court is dated January 16, 1923. See "First Homes Started in Colby Court," *Houston Post-Dispatch*, Mar. 23, 1924, 8.

16. "Memorial Park Donation to City Explained," *Houston Chronicle*, Nov. 30, 1926, 10. This article quotes a lengthy statement issued by Henry W. Stude, vice president of the Varner Realty Company, establishing the chronology of the purchase of property that was then sold to the City of Houston to become Memorial Park. See also Sarah H. Emmott, *Memorial Park: A Priceless Legacy*, 23–27, and Kirkland, "Envisioning a Progressive City," 123–25.

17. Smart, "Sacred Modern," ii.

18. Bruce Weber and Orson Cook evaluate Hogg's conception of city planning and his performance as a civic visionary in their essay "Will Hogg and Civic Consciousness: Houston Style," 20–36.

19. "Memorial Park Donation to City Explained," *Houston Chronicle*, Nov. 30, 1926, 10.

20. See Allen V. Peden, "Presentations: Hugh Potter," *Houston Gargoyle* 1 (Apr. 10, 1928): 10–11, which contains Potter's account of his and Mike Hogg's decision to take over Country Club Estates. Hugh Potter (1888–1968) bought out the Hogg family's interest in the River Oaks Corporation in 1936 and operated it until he dissolved the corporation at the end of 1954. Potter was a cofounder of the Urban Land Institute, a member of its first board of trustees, served as its president in 1943 and 1944, and cofounded with J. C. Nichols its Community Builder's Council, of which he became chairman after Nichols's death in 1950. He was president of the Houston Chamber of Commerce in 1933, president of the National Association of Real Estate Boards in 1934, and chair of the Houston City Planning Commission after it was reconstituted by Mayor Holcombe in the second half of the 1930s. See Garnett Laidlaw Eskew with John R. MacDonald, *Of Land and Men: The Birth and Growth of an Idea*, 97–112, 168, 200; "River Oaks Creator Hugh Potter Dies," *Houston Chronicle*, Mar. 30, 1968, section 2, 21; and "Developer, H. Potter, Dead at 79," *Houston Post*, Mar. 30, 1968, section 4, 8. Overshadowed by Will Hogg and Ima Hogg, Potter was the disciplined force behind the long-term success of River Oaks.

21. Drawings in the Hare and Hare Collection, Houston Metropolitan Research Center, Houston Public Library.

22. Hare and Hare's appointment as planning consultants to Country Club Estates, Inc., was announced in the article "Expert to Beautify Country Club Estates," *Houston Post-Dispatch*, Aug. 25, 1924, 5. Kipp's appointment was announced one year later: "Engineer Is Elected Vice President of Country Club Estates," *Houston Chronicle*, Aug. 1, 1925, 3; Sam Keeper, "River Oaks Upkeep in New Hands," *Houston Chronicle*, Dec. 1, 1954, section G, 1.

23. "Engineering," *River Oaks Magazine*, Oct. 1939, 6–7. Kipp (1883–1968) came to Houston in 1912 as a drainage specialist. He was consulting engineer to the Houston Board of Park Commissioners from 1915 to 1917. In addition to his work for the River Oaks Corporation, he had been consulting engineer for the platting of Shadyside, Broadacres, Edgemont, and Southampton. He also planned Briarwood, a small subdivision surrounded by River Oaks, developed by the developer-builder George T. Broun. See "20-Acre Briarwood Is Being Improved at Cost of $35,000," *Houston Post*, Nov. 8, 1936. Kipp also laid out the Texas Medical Center. See "Herbert Kipp Rites to Be at 3 Today," *Houston Post*, Sept. 16, 1968, section 1, 13.

When comparing Hare and Hare's master plan studies of 1924 with the layout Kipp carried out, the simplicity of Kipp's plan stands out. What Kipp's plan lacked by comparison was the reservation of bayou frontage as park space. Following Kipp's plans, all the real estate frontage in River Oaks on Buffalo Bayou was developed as house sites. Kipp installed oval community parks, around which streets divided, at widely spaced intervals (usually one per section). He took advantage of a ravine to create Pine Valley Court and in 1935 platted the River Oaks Courts, which dealt resourcefully with problematic house sites that would otherwise have faced the busy thoroughfare streets of South Shepherd Drive and San Felipe Road. Section Eight of 1938 even contains a small public park, River Oaks Park, with frontage on (although no access from) Westheimer Road. Whether Potter and the Hoggs determined that the Hare and Hare proposal reserved too much real estate for public use that could be sold instead or had doubts about installing open space amenities that might invite outsiders to make themselves at home in River Oaks, Kipp's more economical distribution of open space and his less-labored curving geometry were preferred.

The post–World War II sections of River Oaks are Block 12 (Tiel Way), for which the plat map is dated August 1, 1946, and Block 26, an alley-like private drive that is connected to South Shepherd Drive between Kirby Drive and Chilton Drive. The plat is dated Oct. 14, 1947.

24. The River Oaks Corporation did not make these planning choices a topic of its advertising. Support for interpreting the planning practices of the River Oaks Corporation as constructing suburban space as the antithesis of Broadacres, Shadyside, and Courtlandt Place can be deduced from Don Riddle's article, "Homes to Last for All Time: The Story of River Oaks," *National Real Estate Journal* (Mar. 4, 1929): 21–28, in which he wrote, "In order to reduce traffic hazards and to preserve the sweeping appearances—the wide vistas—of rights-of-way, no trees are planted or left standing in curves or esplanades. Most of the trees necessary to the development are planted on the actual homesites" (p. 23). There is an echo of this description in a terse summary of River Oaks's characteristics in an article on planned residential developments in the United States published in *Architectural Forum* in 1935: "No trees or shrubs planted in the curb space on a theory that it improves vistas to confine such improvements to the properties themselves." See "River Oaks, Houston, Texas, River Oaks Corporation," *Architectural Forum* 62 (May 1935): 473.

Potter, Kipp, and their landscape consultants spatially constructed community identity through River Oaks's landscaping. As with the curving street grid and the range of lot sizes they incorporated, they also constructed distinctiveness dialectically in terms of landscape. In concert with unusually deep front setback lines that the corporation imposed consistently through its deed restrictions (even in sections with the narrowest lots), River Oaks feels very different spatially from North and South Boulevards. A deed restriction requiring two-story construction in most subdivisions (some one-story houses were constructed south of San Felipe) meant that openness, which can be problematic in the flat landscape of the Gulf coastal plain, was counterbalanced by house fronts that framed collective space volumetrically and front lawns that were terraced up from the sidewalk toward the house to mitigate a sensation of oppressive flatness. Because trees were not planted in rows, Southern magnolia trees and live oak trees stood out on front lawns, achieving full-bodied, symmetrical canopies and—especially the oak trees—dramatic branching patterns that made each an embodiment of River Oaks's icon, the live oak tree. Kipp and the corporation's first two landscape architects, Mason Coney until 1927 and the English landscape architect Henry Hutchinson from 1927 to 1929, spatialized River Oaks's natural asset, topographical variation. The terrain closest to Buffalo Bayou was cut through by shallow ravines, declivities through which the coastal plain naturally drained into the bayou channel. Rather than filling in the ravines, the River Oaks Corporation used them to construct the suggestion of hilliness, most effectively near the east entrance to River Oaks on Kirby Drive. Henry Hutchinson used a part of this ravine system to install the River Oaks Rock Garden and Troon Falls in 1927, identifying River Oaks, as its advertising constantly suggested, as a magical landscape set apart from the mundane world of Houston. Lack of the sort of spatial closure associated with the tree-lined Main Boulevard, Rice University, and Broadacres identified River Oaks as a landscape characterized by breadth, openness, and accessibility without, however, being undefined. In contrast to the "urban" Main Boulevard landscapes, River Oaks was constructed as suburban. Topographic variation was highlighted to confirm its special standing in comparison to the unqualified flatness of other elite Houston neighborhoods.

Landscape was deliberately externalized as a constituent of community identity in River Oaks, in part because Will Hogg seems to have understood its potential to shape perception and affect attitudes. His correspondence reveals his enthusiasm for constructing southernness by emphasizing certain types of trees and shrubs. He was entranced by what he described to Mason Coney in 1927 as a "Magnolia garden" he visited in Charleston, South Carolina. With characteristic impulsiveness, Hogg decided River Oaks must have one too along with "oodles of azaleas, which I assume do well here [Houston], though I am not sure." Henry Hutchinson was responsible for planting a "magnolia walk" along South Shepherd Drive on River Oaks's eastern border in 1929 that is still in evidence. See Will Hogg to Mason Coney, Apr. 16, 1927, William Clifford Hogg Papers, Center for American History, University of Texas at Austin; "Houston Will Have Its Magnolia Walk," *Houston Press*, Jan. 19, 1929; and Riddle, "Homes to Last for All Time," 25.

25. Arthur C. Comey's city planning document, *Houston: Tentative Plans for Its Development* of 1913, contains two pages of cross-sections of standardized street types. One, "Proposed Cross-Sections for Highways and Parkways," illustrates a "Bayou Parkw ay" condition in which the bayou channel, landscaping, and parkway drives flanking the channel are systematically integrated. Hare and Hare, in the *Report of the City Planning Commission, Houston, Texas* of 1929, also include a page of standard street sections illustrating a "'Typical Bayou Parkway." See Arthur Coleman Comey, *Houston: Tentative Plans for Its Development*, 47; and *Report of the City Planning Commission, Houston, Texas*, 38.

26. The rendering was published in the brochure "Low Price Pre-Development Sale in River Oaks," Apr. 1927, River Oaks Scrapbooks, vol. 5A, Houston Metropolitan Research Center, Houston Public Library.

27. Neff, "Will Hogg: Building Heritage in Texas," 4–5, 13. Rem Koolhaas in *Delirious New York: A Retroactive Manifesto for Manhattan*, 6, described the parkway systems of Robert Moses as a "utopian fragment."

28. Barnstone, *Architecture of John F. Staub*, 8.

29. Hugh Potter to Edward Andrews, July 1, 1924, River Oaks Scrapbooks, vol. 1, Houston Metropolitan Research Center, Houston Public Library. The letterhead lists Will Hogg, Womack, Montieth, Clayton, the cotton exporter Edwin L. Neville, Mike Hogg, and Hugh Potter as directors.

30. "Picturesque Setting for River Oaks Structure," *Houston Post*, Oct. 21, 1923; copy of undated typescript from John F. Staub's office: "Client, Cost, Comp. Date, Est. Cost."

31. Letter from Kenneth E. Womack, president of the River Oaks Country Club, and W. E. Montieth, vice president, June 5, 1924, to club members seeking authorization to sell members' stock shares to Country Club Estates, Inc., for $125,000, and an additional sum that will cancel the club members' outstanding debts of $75,000 for construction of the clubhouse, $25,000 for its furniture and equipment, $90,000 for construction of the golf course, $87,000 for the cost of the two-hundred-acre site, and $50,000 in related improvements, River Oaks Scrapbooks, vol. 1, Houston Metropolitan Research Center, Houston Public Library; and "River Oaks to Spend $175,000 before Spring," *Houston Chronicle*, Dec. 21, 1924, announcing the second phase of construction at the country club including a ballroom, a dining room, a swimming pool and bathhouse, and a sprinkler system for the fairways.

32. Marcus, *Lives in Trust*, 80; Benedikt, "Class Notes," 6.

33. An advertisement, "Country Club Estates," *Houston Post*, Nov. 6, 1924, lists Staub as consulting architect and Hare and Hare as landscape architects. By January 1925 both names had been dropped from Country Club Estates, Inc., advertising. Clippings of the November 1924 advertisement and others from November and December are mounted in the River Oaks Scrapbooks, vol. 1. They do not appear in the microfilms of the *Post* and the *Chronicle* for these dates. This is one of a number of examples of such discrepancies, suggesting that when both newspapers were microfilmed, advertising pages were not consistently microfilmed.

34. Northrop designed the first house to be completed, a two-story, five-bay-wide, American Georgian house at 3352 Del Monte Drive of 1925, and the two smallest houses, both built south of San Felipe, 3215 Avalon of 1925 and 3232 Huntingdon Place of 1926, both described as Dutch Colonial. Briscoe and Dixon designed the Redbird House at 3237 Inwood of 1926. Staub designed the Latin Colonial House at 3374 Chevy Chase, completed in 1925, and the Early Republic House at 3260 Chevy Chase Drive of 1926. During the 1990s, all of these houses except the Redbird House and the Early Republic House were demolished.

35. The Redbird House (the name derives from the figure of a redbird centered in decorative iron guardrail panels affixed to French doors on the street front of the house) was described as being in the "French Colonial" style while it was under construction: "Campbell Buys French Colonial Home," *Houston Chronicle*, Oct. 11, 1925, 37. When R. M. Luster's soft-focus photograph of one of these French doors was published in Don Q. Riddle, *River Oaks: A Pictorial Presentation of Houston's Residential Park*, the house was described as being in the Latin Colonial style. Barnstone, *Architecture of John F. Staub*, 28.

36. Cram and Ferguson's architectural drawings of the Sewall House, including Mrs. Sewall's sketches for the two alternative designs, are deposited in the Woodson Research Center, Fondren Library, Rice University. The house is illustrated in Cram and Ferguson, *The Work of Cram and Ferguson, Architects, Including the Work of Cram, Goodhue and Ferguson*, 336–37; "Gardens at Houston and River Oaks, Texas, Visited by the Garden Club of America in February 1939," *Landscape Architecture* 29 (July 1939): 187; and "The Home of Mrs. Cleveland Sewall," *Antiques* 53 (June 1948): 435. The article "River Oaks to Spend $175,000 before Spring," *Houston Chronicle*, Dec. 21, 1924, 15, mentions the impending construction of a $140,000 house designed by Cram and Ferguson. The River Oaks pictorial supplement to the April 11, 1926, edition of the *Houston Chronicle* has a photograph of the Sewall House under construction on page 9. The National Register application (which contains many inaccuracies) is at <http://atlas.thc.state.tx.us/shell-kword.htm> under "Harris County," "Sewall," and "National Register Properties." Blanche Harding Sewall (1889–1973) was self-effacing; her obituary disclosed little about her artistic interests and philanthropic activities: "Sewall," *Houston Chronicle*, May 29, 1973, section 3, 32. Mrs. Sewall was cocompiler of the first *A Garden Book for Houston* of 1929.

37. Staub remembered that Mrs. Sewall had retained Mildred Stapley and Arthur Byne as her collecting consultants.

38. "Clayton Builds Beautiful Home," *Houston Chronicle*, Aug. 24, 1924, 41; "W. L. Clayton Home Erected in Three Units Near Club," *Houston Chronicle*, Sept. 21, 1924, 29; "House of W. L. Clayton, Esq., Houston, Texas," *Architectural Forum* 49 (Sept. 1928): 337–38; "House of W. L. Clayton, Esq., Houston, Texas," *Southern Architect and Building News* 55 (Jan. 1929): 51–53; "An Historic Colonnade in Texas," *House and Garden* 55 (Apr. 1929): 136; and Marguerite Johnston. *Houston: The Unknown City*, 227–28. Peter Flagg Maxson's National Register application for the Clayton Summer House is at <http://atlas.thc.state.tx.us/shell-kword.htm> under "Harris County," "Clayton Summer," and "National Register Properties." On Susan Vaughan Clayton (1881–1960), see "Mrs. W. L. Clayton Dies after Illness." *Houston Post*, Jan. 8, 1960, 1, and Ellen Clayton Garwood, *Will Clayton: A Short Biography*. On William L. Clayton (1880–1966) and Anderson, Clayton and Company see Ellen Clayton Garwood, *Will Clayton: A Short Biography*; William L. Garwood Jr., *Will Clayton: Economic Statesman*; James A. Tinsley, "Clayton, William Lockhart," *New Handbook of Texas*, vol. 2, 149–50; Thomas D. Anderson, "Anderson, Monroe Dunaway," *New Handbook of Texas*, vol. 1, 167;

Thomas D. Anderson, "Anderson, Clayton and Company," *New Handbook of Texas*, vol. 1, 170–71; Fredrick J. Dobney, ed., *Selected Papers of William L. Clayton*.

39. Hewitt, *Architect and the American Country House*, 234.

40. "New River Oaks Home," *Houston Chronicle*, May 18, 1925, 11.

41. Staub to author.

42. "Antique Iron Rescued for River Oaks," *Houston Chronicle*, June 28, 1925, 18; "New Orleans Gates are Reclaimed for Homes in Houston," *Houston Post-Dispatch*, June 28, 1925, 4.

43. John F. Staub, "Latin Colonial Architecture in the Southwest," *Civics for Houston* 1 (Feb. 1928): 6–7; and "Latin Colonial Architecture," *Southern Architect and Building News* 56 (Aug. 1930): 33–35. As Barnstone observes, portions of the text were copied from an article by the New Orleans architect Nathaniel C. Curtis, "Architectural Traditions in New Orleans," *Journal of the American Institute of Architects* 13 (Aug. 1925): 279–86.

44. Copy of undated typescript from John F. Staub's office: "Client, Cost, Comp. Date, Est. Cost"; Barnstone, *Architecture of John F. Staub*, 106–13; the National Register application for Bayou Bend at <http://atlas.thc.state.tx.us/shell-kword.htm> under "Harris County," "Bayou Bend," and "National Register Properties"; "Bayou Bend," *New Handbook of Texas*, vol. 1, 431; "Son of 'Father of Tree Surgery' Explains Method of Saving Giant Basswood," *Houston Chronicle*, Apr. 27, 1927, 3; "Houston Builders Figure Hogg Home," *Houston Post-Dispatch*, May 15, 1927, Real Estate and Building section, 6; "Chris J. Miller Is Given Hogg Home," *Houston Post-Dispatch*, June 12, 1927, Real Estate and Building section, 1; "Hogg Residence Millwork Awarded," *Houston Post-Dispatch*, July 3, 1927, Real Estate and Building section, 2; "First Pictures of Miss Ima Hogg's House in River Oaks," *Houston Post-Dispatch*, Aug. 26, 1928, Real Estate and Building section, 1; "'Bayou Bend'—A Georgian Residence in Texas," *House and Garden* 59 (Mar. 1931): 61, 63–65; "Nineteenth Century Tradition Reflected in This Distinguished Southern House," *Southern Architect and Building News* 57 (Nov. 1931): 14–20; "Gardens at Houston and River Oaks, Texas," 184–85, 191; "The Home of Miss Ima Hogg," *Antiques* 53 (June 1948): 428; "Americana at Its Finest: Ima Hogg's Bayou Bend," *Interiors* 123 (Nov. 1963): 78–83; Mac Griswold and Eleanor Weller, *The Golden Age of American Gardens: Proud Owners, Private Estates, 1890–1940*, 241–42; Hewitt, *Architect and the American Country House*, 234, 236; Bernhard, *Ima Hogg*, 75–92; Kirkland, "Envisioning a Progressive City," 435–45; and Warren, *Bayou Bend Gardens*, 15–22.

Staub told Barnstone that he and Birdsall Briscoe were simultaneously commissioned as collaborating architects to design country houses on adjoining sites for the Hogg siblings and Judge and Mrs. Frederick C. Proctor. They agreed between them that Staub would design Bayou Bend and Briscoe the Proctor House. Each always listed the other as associate architect. Barnstone, *Architecture of John F. Staub*, 57.

David Warren gives the cost of constructing Bayou Bend as \$294,771.15 based on the Hoggs' accounting. He notes that the sum included the cost of a "dark blue Ford sports car" for John Staub. David B. Warren, "The Reopening of Bayou Bend in Houston, Texas," *Antiques* 144 (Sept. 1993): 336.

45. "Mike Hogg, Oil Operator and Realtor, Dies," *Houston Chronicle*, Oct. 11, 1941, section 1, 1; "Mike Hogg Wed at Galveston," *Houston Press*, July 22, 1929. Barnstone, *Architecture of John F. Staub*, 10.

Alice and Mike Hogg lived in the house designed by Charles W. Oliver at 2007 River Oaks Boulevard until 1931, when they bought the house built in 1927–28 next door to Bayou Bend by Judge and Mrs. Frederick C. Proctor at 2950 Lazy Lane; see "Hogg Buys Property," *Houston Press*, Mar. 3, 1931. Mike Hogg lived at what the Hoggs called Dogwoods until his death in 1941. His widow, who subsequently married Staub's widowed client, Harry C. Hanszen, sold the house in 1954 to Mr. and Mrs. Thomas McDermott. William Taylor, "Mike Hogg Mansion in River Oaks Sold," *Houston Press*, Dec. 16, 1954; and Derro Evans, "Houston: Dogwoods in Bloom," *Texas Homes* 8 (Feb. 1984): 56–63.

46. Bernhard, *Ima Hogg*, 83–85; "Hogg's Remains Due Wednesday," *Houston Press*, Sept. 23, 1930. A subsequent news story, "Steamer to Bring Back Hogg's Auto," *Houston Press*, Oct. 17, 1930, reported that the North German Lloyd Line's *Seydlitz* was transporting Will Hogg's Hispano-Suiza to Houston from Germany.

47. David Warren notes that the Hoggs called the property "Bayou Banks" when the house was being planned, although by 1929 the name Bayou Bend had been settled on. Warren cites a letter Miss Hogg wrote to her friend Julia Ideson, city librarian of Houston, in 1925 in which "Bayou Banks" is mentioned as a name redolent of "quiet, contentment, country" (Warren, Brown, Coleman, and Neff, *American Decorative Arts and Paintings*, xvi). Will Hogg's fascination with the poetic power of names was also evident in the choice of a name for the River Oaks subdivision where Bayou Bend was built. When platted in 1926, it was called Homewoods. Will Hogg's papers show that this was chosen in preference to the Neighbors, Contentment, and Colony Court, all under consideration in 1925. The name of Homewoods's only street, Lazy Lane, reflects Hogg's sense of humor. See David B. Warren, "Bayou Bend: A Southern Garden," (2000), 8; and Box 6, William Clifford Hogg Collection, Center for American History, University of Texas at Austin. Also see Warren, *Bayou Bend Gardens*, 15, 66. David Warren cites a letter from Will Hogg to his sister that gave her responsibility for overseeing the planning of the Homewoods subdivision.

48. Thomas E. Hogg (1887–1949) seems to have been the most persistently emotionally troubled of the four siblings. In 1913 and again in 1916 he and his wife Marie lived briefly at Varner in West Columbia. In 1923–24, Marie and Tom Hogg built an important Spanish Mediterranean–style house at 202 Bushnell Avenue in Laurel Heights Place in San Antonio, the first in a series of distinctive Spanish-style houses designed by the San Antonio architects Atlee B. and Robert M. Ayres. See Bernhard, *Ima Hogg*, 56, 65–67; "The House of Thomas E. Hogg, San Antonio, Texas," *American Architect* 134 (Aug. 20, 1928): 237–39; John C. Ferguson, "The Country Houses of Atlee B. and Robert M. Ayres," *Cite: The Architecture and Design Review of Houston* (Spring 1986): 18–20; Donald E. Everett, *San Antonio's Monte Vista: Architecture and Society in a Gilded Age, 1890–1930*, 121–23; and Robert James Coote, *The Eclectic Odyssey of Atlee B. Ayres, Architect*, 104–107.

49. Mac Griswold, "Introduction," in Warren, *Bayou Bend Gardens*, xi–xii. David Warren's article on Ima Hogg's career as a collector describes the range and sequence of her acquisitions. In 1929 and 1930 she acquired a collection of works on paper by Paul Cézanne, Lyonel Feininger, Paul Klee, Emil Nolde, Pablo Picasso, and Diego Rivera. Emily Neff indicates that Ima Hogg tried to interest Will Hogg in modern art but he resisted her encouragement. In 1939 Miss Hogg gave her modern collection to the Museum of Fine Arts, one of its first important accessions of twentieth-century modern art. See David B. Warren, "Ima Hogg, Collector," 230–32; *A Permanent Legacy: 150 Works from the Collection of the Museum of Fine Arts, Houston*, 14–15; Neff, "Will Hogg: Building Heritage in Texas," 30–31; and Kirkland, "Envisioning a Progressive City," 414–17.

50. "Court Order Is Sought in Hogg Home Dispute," *Houston Post* Oct. 4, 1957, section 1, 2; Marshall Verniaud, "Judge Upholds Miss Hogg's Right to Give Home Away," *Houston Post*, Dec. 17, 1957, section 1, 1; "Looking Ahead for the Museum of Fine Arts of Houston: Collections," *The Museum of Fine Arts of Houston Bulletin* 20 (1958): unpaginated.

51. "Symphony Workers Assemble for Meeting at Bayou Bend," *Houston Post*, Feb. 13, 1938, section 3, 3; "Women 'Spearhead' Orchestra," *Houston* 16 (July 1944): 8; Kirkland, "Envisioning a Progressive City," 215–16, 355–56.

52. Mrs. Allen B. Hannay, "Houston Is Garden City," *Houston* 7 (Apr. 1936): 20–21; Mrs. Frances Hannay, "Houston Gardens Attract Nation-Wide Attention," *Houston* 8 (Mar. 1937): 21; Frances Hannay, "Houston's Own Azalea Trail," *Houston* 9 (Feb. 1938): 11; "12,000 See Gardens," *Houston* 9 (Mar. 1938): 28; "Local Azalea Trail Viewed by Thousands," *Houston* 10 (Mar. 1939): 30; Mrs. Birdsall P. Briscoe, "Trails and Trails," *Houston* 12 (Feb. 1941): 26; and Mrs. L. A. Stevenson, "Seventh Annual Azalea Trail," *Houston* 13 (Feb. 1942): 36.

The Azalea Trail seems to have been the River Oaks Garden Club's response to an annual spring garden tour that the slightly older Garden Club of Houston began in the early 1930s. See "Three Gardens of the 13 to be Shown April 22, 23, and 24 by the Garden Club of Houston," *Houston Gargoyle* 5 (Apr. 17, 1932): 9. Barrie Scardino and Minnette B. Boesel's research indicates that in 1932 the River Oaks Garden Club sponsored a competition to recognize well-designed local gardens. In 1934, it held its first garden "pilgrimage," the forerunner of the Azalea Trail. See the National Register of Historic Places nomination application for the River Oaks Garden Club Forum of Civics at <http://atlas.thc.state.tx.us/shell-kword.htm> under "Harris County," "River Oaks Garden Club," and "National Register Properties."

53. "Gardens at Houston and River Oaks, Texas," 183–91.

In his meticulous research on the evolution of the gardens of Bayou Bend, David Warren determined that azaleas were not planted at Bayou Bend until 1931. It was Ima Hogg who popularized this flowering East Asian evergreen shrub in Houston, a plant associated with Charleston, Savannah, and Mobile, and therefore, like the Southern magnolia (which is native to Houston), an icon of southernness (Warren, *Bayou Bend Gardens*, 32–33). By the 1950s, azaleas had become the identifying flower of elite Houston gardens. Mac Griswold and Eleanor Weller in their book, *The Golden Age of American Gardens*, remarked on Ima Hogg's influence, noting that "[t]oday, broadleaf gardens in a woodland setting seem uninventive, but in the twenties and thirties they were something new in Texas. Just like the white columns, camellias and azaleas stood for Southern conservatism, for the antebellum Southern tradition revived and revised to fit the large suburban estate lot. . . . Bayou Bend . . . consecrated and popularized the formula for hundreds of later gardens." Houston's domestic landscapes give clear evidence of the Hoggs' skill in appealing to perception and imagination to invent new identities socially constructed as "traditional" and "southern." Griswold and Weller, *Golden Age of American Gardens*, 242.

Will Hogg sought to systematize and institutionalize forms of gardening in Houston, which he accomplished through externalization and publicity. During its year-long publication run, the Forum of Civics' monthly magazine *Civics for Houston* produced a regular gardening page. In 1929 the forum published *A Garden Book for Houston*, prepared under Will Hogg's sponsorship by Blanche Sewall and Mary Malone Elliott with the nurseryman Edward C. Teas, which the River Oaks Garden Club continues to keep in publication. In 1929 the River Oaks Corporation also issued an illustrated hardcover book, *River Oaks: A Pictorial Presentation of Houston's Residential Park*, edited by Don Riddle and with photographs by R. M. Luster, to document the community's first five years of development. The consistency with which the River Oaks Corporation asserted superiority through its spatial activities, and then projected this superior identity through media, attests to the Hoggs' and Potter's understanding of their task as one of instructing Houstonians through the construction of new, and what they considered superior, models of domestic and civic life. As the River Oaks Corporation's spatial practices, rhetoric, and imagery made clear, the identity and subject positions these models entailed were based on the premise of patrician superiority.

54. The chronology of the development of the gardens at Bayou Bend is presented in Sally Robert Banttari, "The Evolution of the Bayou Bend Gardens, Houston, Texas (1926–1989)," and in Jon Emerson and Associates, "A Plan for the Preservation, Management, and Interpretation of Bayou Bend Gardens, Houston, Texas, a Property of the Museum of Fine Arts, Houston," 1994, figure 4. I am grateful to Jane Anderson Curtis for making a copy available to me. See also David B. Warren, "Albert Sheppard Remembers Bayou Bend," *Cite 37: The Architecture and Design Review of Houston* (spring 1997): 24–25; Jane Anderson Curtis, "Bayou Bend Gardens," *Cite 37: The Architecture and Design Review of Houston* (spring 1997): 20–23; Kirkland, "Envisioning a Progressive City," 454–56; and Warren, *Bayou Bend Gardens*, 41–45. On the Houston landscape architect C. C. Pat Fleming (1909–96), see Paige Allred Phillips, "C. C. Pat Fleming, Houston, Texas, Landscape Architect."

55. Emerson, "A Plan for the Preservation, Management, and Interpretation of Bayou Bend Gardens," figures 11 and 12; Kirkland, "Envisioning a Progressive City," 452–53; and Warren, *Bayou Bend Gardens*, 33–39. On the Houston landscape architect Ruth London (1892–1966) see Kelly McCaughey Allegrezza, "Ruth London (1892–1966), Houston Landscape Architect."

56. Stanley Tigerman observed the spatial implications of entering a room near one of its corners, emphasizing its three-dimensional volume, versus the planar sensation that entering a room on its central axis produces. Entering from the corner was a practice of the twentieth-century Philadelphia architect Louis I. Kahn.

57. Tebbs and Knell's photograph of the now-demolished tap room were published in two articles about Bayou Bend: "'Bayou Bend'—A Georgian Residence in Texas," 65, and "Nineteenth Century Tradition Reflected in This Distinguished Southern House," 19. In June 1948 *Antiques* magazine produced an entire issue devoted to Texas that contains several photographs of Miss Hogg's Texian and Mexican War collections installed in the tap room. See "A Texas Collection" and "The Mexican War" in *Antiques* 53 (June 1948): 420, 444–45. The tap room was replaced in 1958–59 by the Murphy Room, a Connecticut-colonial-style interior designed by Staub, Rather and Howze and the first museum room Miss Hogg built at Bayou Bend. See Warren, "Ima Hogg, Collector," 234. Staub, Rather and Howze were architects for the conversion of Bayou Bend to a house museum, which primarily entailed the replacement of millwork and wall finishes in bedrooms to complement the furniture installations Miss Hogg made there. The spaces now known as the Pennsylvania German Hall, the Texas Room, and the Newport Room, all located on the second floor of the bachelors' wing, entailed the most extensive installation of new architectural detail and (in the case of the Texas Room) spatial reorganization. Staub, Rather and Howze reused the beaded vertical pine paneling from the tap room in the Pennsylvania German Hall. After the museum opened in 1966, Miss Hogg and David Warren collaborated on two additional installations that entailed reorganization of existing spaces and replacement of architectural decoration, the Chillman Rooms of 1969 on the ground floor of the service wing and the Belter Parlor of 1971 in what had been the ground-floor passageway, cloakroom, and guest toilet in the main block next to the dining room. Langwith, Wilson, and King designed these alterations. See David B. Warren, "The Empire Style at Bayou Bend: New Period Rooms in Houston," *Antiques* 97 (Dec. 1970): 122–27.

58. "Americana at Its Finest," 80.

59. Howard Barnstone was fascinated by the capacity of Staub's houses to seem both small and expansive simultaneously. In 1976, while writing *Architecture of John F. Staub*, Barnstone bought Staub's Copley House of 1926–27 at 17 Shadowlawn Circle. He was enthralled with the Copley House because it seemed to transcend the contradiction between being reassuring and imposing.

60. Barnstone, "Rediscovering John F. Staub," 53.

61. Staub, "Latin Colonial Architecture in the Southwest," 6. David Warren noted that as part of the restoration of Bayou Bend, completed in 1993, the architectural conservator Martin E. Weaver performed a chemical analysis of the stucco. This disclosed that mortar had interacted with the powdered rose quartz and powdered garnet used to integrally color the stucco, causing the graying effect that prompted painting of the exterior in the 1970s. David B. Warren, "The Reopening of Bayou Bend in Houston, Texas," 337.

62. Warren, "Bayou Bend: A Southern Garden," 3.

63. Barnstone, *Architecture of John F. Staub*, 107. On Homewood see John Martin Hammond, "Homewood, Baltimore, Maryland," *Architectural Record* 41 (May 1917): 435–47, and 41 (June 1917): 525–35; and Catherine Rogers Arthur and Cindy Kelly, *Homewood House*.

64. Barbara SoRelle Bacot, "New Orleans after the Fires," in *Louisiana Buildings 1720–1940: The Historic American Buildings Survey*, ed. Jessie Poesch and Barbara SoRelle Bacot, 37–69. As evidence of interest in the Creole architecture of New Orleans in the 1920s see Arnold Gen-

the, "Grilles and Galleries of Old New Orleans," *House and Garden* 46 (Aug. 1924): 53–55. On the Lyons House by Armstrong and Koch, the first example of neo-Creole architecture in New Orleans to be widely published, see Lyle Saxon, "A Breath from the Vieux Carré," *House and Garden* 44 (Nov. 1923): 72–73.

65. In his first book, *Modern Architecture: Romanticism and Reintegration*, Henry-Russell Hitchcock noted, beginning in the late nineteenth century, "the development in America . . . of a domestic architecture of craftsmanship," which he linked to the anti-eclectic practices that he called the New Tradition. However, Hitchcock judged this architecture of craftsmanship to be "of importance as a transitional manifestation . . . . Today it is probably too late to look for a further real development. For America has became conscious of foreign 'modernism,' and original creation is now all but impossible along these lines for that reason and because the day of the New Tradition is probably coming to a close." Harrie T. Lindeberg was one of the two contemporary American country house architects Hitchcock identified by name. Hitchcock, *Modern Architecture*, 102–103.

66. Barnstone, *Architecture of John F. Staub*, 109–10; Ridley W. Wills II, *The History of Belle Meade: Mansion, Plantation, and Studies*.

67. Bernhard, *Ima Hogg*, 28; Michael J. Kross, National Historic Landmark nomination application for Bayou Bend, 2003; Warren, *Bayou Bend Gardens*, 16–17.

68. "A Georgian Bay in High Relief," *House and Garden* 59 (Mar. 1931): 61.

69. Warren, *Bayou Bend Gardens*, 3; Barnstone, *Architecture of John F. Staub*, 110.

70. David B. Warren, *Bayou Bend: American Furniture, Paintings, and Silver from the Bayou Bend Collection*, 38, 2, 22, 21.

71. Marcus, *Lives in Trust*, 80.

72. Lessard, "Three Houses," 37; Tzonis and Lefaivre, *Classical Architecture*, 278.

73. Tzonis and Lefaivre, *Classical Architecture*, 5; Aldrich, *Old Money*, 36, 37; Schwartzer, "Myths of Permanence and Transience," 2.

74. Edward W. Wolner's analysis of the phenomenon of the "city-within-the-city" as a model of mixed-use, high-rise, urban development in Cleveland, Cincinnati, Columbus, and Detroit addresses the ideology of American architectural eclecticism in the 1920s and reveals provocative parallels with Bayou Bend, despite obvious differences in size, scale, and use between the Hogg country house and the skyscraper projects Wolner examines. Wolner is attentive to what he describes as the "conflations of tradition and modernity" evident in the Midwestern skyscraper complexes and "the various ways in which their roles mixed traditional and modern worlds" by affirming "the timeless values of classicism and the dynamic character of a skyborne future." The efforts of the builders of these complexes to construct "an idealized equilibrium between the relative intimacy and stability of community life in a town or small city on the one hand, and the instrumental rationality, large-scale enterprise and dynamic change of the metropolis on the other" was based on the presumption that there was no contradiction between history and modernity. In concluding that "[t]hrough compelling representations of aspects of a small-town or frontier past, and of those associated with a machine-efficient future, each skyscraper patron in his mixed-use development merged a romance of tradition with another about modernity," Wolner touches on the emotional core of these building projects, which seemed to their builders to magically reconcile the contradictions between past and present. See Edward W. Wolner, "The City-within-a-City and Skyscraper Patronage in the 1920s," *JAE: Journal of Architectural Education* 42 (Winter 1989): 10–23.

75. Lorenzo J. Greene's report on the circumstances in which Houston's African American middle class lived spoke to the realities of racial and class difference in the segregated South that Bayou Bend so serenely transcended. Greene interviewed Dr. B. J. Covington, one of Houston's leading black physicians, who lived in the grandest house on Dowling Street in Third Ward. Dr. Covington's recitation of the indignities to which he was subject is a bitter reminder of the realities of racial injustice experienced by even the African American elite in a Southern city. Lorenzo J. Greene, "Sidelights on Houston Negroes as Seen by an Associate of Dr. Carter G. Woodson in 1930," *Black Dixie: Afro-Texan History and Culture in Ho* eth and Cary D. Wintz, 143–45. Kate Kirkland examines what later generations would judge to be the shortcomings of the Hoggs' progressive vision in "Envisioning a Progressive City," 166–67.

76. George Lipsitz, *The Possessive Investment in Whiteness: How White People Profit from Identity Politics*, 142.; and Schwartzer, "Myths of Permanence and Transience," 2.

77. Sparke, "Always in Good Taste," 19.

78. Smart, "Sacred Modern," 12.

79. The River Oaks Community Center claimed place culturally in its extrapolation of a French Quarter patio garden entered through a portal that echoed Staub's gate piers at the south end of River Oaks Boulevard. This garden courtyard typology was an unusual sort of space in Houston retail architecture of the 1920s, which conformed to the paradigm of the downtown, sidewalk-oriented storefront building, even in the suburbs. The community center acknowledged modernity in the expansive aprons of car parking space along River Oaks Boulevard and Westheimer Road and in the segregation of service access from customer access. Had the center been expanded along River Oaks's Westheimer frontage in a pair of bars flanking River Oaks Boulevard, as described in newspaper reports when the first (and only) phase was built, it would have constructed a spatially harmonious, multiblock retail arcade that set an architectural standard for urbane suburban development that was simultaneously modern and traditional. See "River Oaks Corporation Plans Shop Center, Home for Offices," *Houston Post-Dispatch*, June 24, 1927, 9; "Store Group Is Under Way at River Oaks," *Houston Chronicle*, Aug. 21, 1927, Real Estate and Building section, 2; "River Oaks Corporation Moves into New Offices." *Houston Post-Dispatch*, Oct. 16, 1927, Real Estate and Building section, 3; and Katherine Pollard, "Houston Provides for Shopping on Wheels," *Civics for Houston* 1 (Jan. 1929): 6–7.

80. Copy of undated typescript from John F. Staub's office: "Client, Cost, Comp. Date, Est. Cost"; Barnstone, *Architecture of John F. Staub*, 140–41; "Junior League Building Will Cost $35,000 Net," *Houston Post-Dispatch*, Aug. 25, 1929, Real Estate and Building section, 1; "Through the Lorgnon," *Houston Gargoyle* 2 (Nov. 17, 1929): 11.

81. Ruth West, "Junior League at Home," *Houston Gargoyle* 2 (June 2, 1929): 13.

82. Copy of undated typescript from John F. Staub's office: "Client, Cost, Comp. Date, Est. Cost"; Barnstone, *Architecture of John F. Staub*, 79–80; "Plans New Home," *Houston Post-Dispatch*, Mar. 29, 1925, 51; "In August," *Houston Chronicle*, Aug. 9, 1925, 33.

83. Copy of undated typescript from John F. Staub's office: "Client, Cost, Comp. Date, Est. Cost"; Barnstone, *Architecture of John F. Staub*, 99–102; "Thirteen Homes Being Constructed in River Oaks," *Houston Chronicle*, Mar. 27, 1927, Real Estate and Building section, 1; "Colonial Home of Handmade Brick," *Houston Chronicle*, Apr. 24, 1927, Real Estate and Building section, 2; "Colonial Home Is Complete," *Houston Press*, Apr. 23, 1927.

84. John Thomas Rather Jr., "Porches and Porticoes," *Civics for Houston* 1 (Apr. 1928): 10–11; and Lambert Landscape Company, *Lambert Gardens* (brochure), two photographs of the William A. Smith garden.

85. Copy of undated typescript from John F. Staub's office: "Client, Cost, Comp. Date, Est. Cost"; Barnstone, *Architecture of John F. Staub*, 156–57.

86. Betsie Bolger, "River Oaks Heirloom," *Texas Homes* 9 (Mar. 1985): 72–79.

87. Allegrezza, "Ruth London (1892–1966)," 67–70.

88. Marcus, *Lives in Trust*, 142; Berger and Luckmann, *The Social Construction of Reality*, 72.

89. On Joseph H. Chew, see Davis and Grobe, *The New Encyclopedia of Texas*, vol. 1, 262.

90. Hubert B. Finch is first listed in the 1906–1907 edition of the *Houston City Directory* as a clerk at the Merchants National Bank. By the 1910–11 edition (by which time, the Merchants National Bank had been absorbed by the Union National Bank), he was listed as assistant cashier. In the 1913 edition, he was additionally listed as manager of the Houston Clearing House Association. In the 1919 directory, Finch was listed as cashier of the Union National Bank. In the 1923–24 edition, he was also listed as a director of the bank.

91. On the Mellinger family, see the biographical entry for George J. Mellinger in Davis and Grobe, *The New Encyclopedia of Texas*, vol. 2, 1996.

92. Aldrich, *Old Money*, 67–68.

93. Sparke, "Always in Good Taste," 19.

CHAPTER 4. SMALL HOUSES

1. Inez Rather Lasell to author, 1995.

2. Bushman, *Refinement of America*, xiv.

3. Sinclair Lewis in his novel *Babbitt* uses the term "bungalow" to establish the cultural context in which his subject, the residential real estate broker George Babbitt, operates. Sinclair Lewis, *Babbitt*, 31, 37.

4. Alan Gowans, *The Comfortable House: North American Suburban Architecture, 1890–1930*, 84–89.

5. On the bungalow in Houston see William F. Stern, "The Lure of the Bungalow," *Cite: The Architecture and Design Review of Houston* (Winter 1986): 8–11, and Margaret Culbertson, *Texas Houses Built by the Book: The Use of Published Designs, 1850–1925*, 68–75, 81–86.

6. "Six Small Houses of Brick, Stucco, and Wood: A House in Houston, Texas, John F. Staub, Architect," *House Beautiful* 61 (May 1927): 640.

7. *House Beautiful*'s brief description of the Latin Colonial House focused on its surface finishes and coloration: ". . . walls of a pink apricot stucco . . . a roof of copper-clad shingles of green, blue, and russet colors . . . blinds are painted a copper blue-green . . . exterior woodwork is vermilion glazed with umber and purple." "Six Small Houses of Brick, Stucco, and Wood," 640.

8. The *Texas General Contractors Association Monthly Bulletin* contains a section called "Recent Contracts Awarded" that reported on the awarding of new construction contracts in Texas towns and cities. Comparing entries for River Oaks, Southampton, and the Turner addition between January 1925 and July 1926 indicates the extent to which the earliest houses built in River Oaks were consistently more expensive than those in the other two middle-income neighborhoods. The lowest contract awarded during this period for a house in River Oaks was for nine thousand dollars (these were for two of the Northrop-designed houses built by the River Oaks Corporation). Contract prices ranging between six thousand dollars and ten thousand dollars were the norm in Southampton and the Turner addition during this interval, although more expensive houses were built in each as well.

9. "Lumber Man Buys Home of Early American Type," *Houston Chronicle*, May 16, 1925, 62.

10. "Model Home to Be Built in River Oaks," *Houston Post-Dispatch*, July 5, 1925, Real Estate section, 3; "Newest Home in River Oaks Opens Today," *Houston Chronicle*, Feb. 14, 1926, 20; "Hugh Potter Buys River Oaks Home," *Houston Chronicle*, Oct. 3, 1926, 58.

11. "New River Oaks Home," *Houston Chronicle*, May 18, 1925, 11; "Second Home in Country Club Estates Finished" and the accompanying ad "A New Home with an Ancient Balcony," *Houston Chronicle*, Aug. 16, 1925, 48. The house was opened to the public again near the end of 1926: "Latin Colonial Is Open in River Oaks," *Houston Post-Dispatch*, Nov. 28, 1926, Real Estate and Building section, 1. See the biographical entry on David M. Picton Jr. (1888–1951) in the *National Cyclopedia of American Biography*, vol. 40 (1955), 330–31.

12. Martha Nance and David Picton are listed in the 1923–24 edition of the *Houston City Directory* as living at 4503 Mount Vernon Street in Rossmoyne. Their back yard abutted the back yard of the house at 4410 Rossmoyne Boulevard, where Ima, Will, and Mike Hogg lived from 1918 until they moved into Bayou Bend in 1928. In the same issue of the city directory, Hugh Potter was listed as living at 4119 Yoakum Boulevard in Montrose, three blocks north of the Hogg family house. (Rossmoyne Boulevard is an extension of Yoakum Boulevard.)

13. William T. Campbell Jr., the son of one of J. S. Hogg's partners in the Hogg-Swayne syndicate, bought Briscoe and Dixon's Redbird House while it was under construction in October 1925. Judge and Mrs. Frederick C. Proctor built their house next door to, and in tandem with, Bayou Bend. Judge Proctor, the retired general counsel for the Gulf Oil Corporation in Texas, had been a partner in the foremost corporate law firm in Victoria, Texas, before joining L. A. Carlton, a Hogg family friend, in a Beaumont law practice in 1905 that specialized in oil-related matters, which led to Proctor's association with Gulf. See John L. Sims, "Proctor, Frederick Cocke," in *New Handbook of Texas*, vol. 5, 345–46; "New Residence Is Started on Site in River Oaks," *Houston Chronicle*, Aug. 7, 1927, Real Estate and Building section, 3; "Gleaming White Home in Midst of Trees," *Houston Chronicle*, May 13, 1928, Real Estate and Building section, 3; and Evans, "Houston: Dogwoods in Bloom," 56–63. The Hare and Hare Collection in the Houston Metropolitan Research Center, Houston Public Library, contains a series of plans dated from October 1927 to January 1928 for the Proctor estate. These were for what became the oldest designed gardens in River Oaks by the time they and the house were demolished, along with the house, in May 2005. As Barnstone points out, Staub's first two privately commissioned houses in River Oaks, the Joseph H. Chew House of 1925 and the small Kemerton Dean House of 1925, were built for associates of Kenneth Womack's cotton firm, Sanders and Company.

14. Dorothy Dawes Chillman, "A Blending of Periods in Harmonious Design," *Civics for Houston* 1 (Feb. 1928): 8–9. Dorothy Dawes graduated from Parsons in 1920 then taught there until 1923, when she married James Chillman Jr. and moved to Houston. After Mrs. Chillman's death in 1968, Ima Hogg dedicated the installation of Empire furniture at Bayou Bend to her memory. See "Something New at Bayou Bend," *Houston Chronicle*, Mar. 25, 1969, section 4, 3, and Warren, "The Empire Style at Bayou Bend," 122–27. Dorothy and James Chillman's daughter, Helen Dawes Chillman, became Visual Resources librarian at Yale University.

15. Christopher Hight, "Inertia and Interiority: 24 as a Case Study of the Televisual Metropolis," *Journal of Architecture* 9 (Autumn 2004): 373.

16. Bushman, *Refinement of America*, xviii.

17. Barnstone, *Architecture of John F. Staub*, 8–10, 84.

18. "Work on Staub's New Home Begins," *Houston Post-Dispatch*, Sept. 27, 1925, Automotive section, 4.

19. Barnstone, *Architecture of John F. Staub*, 84.

20. Birdsall Briscoe performed a similar maneuver in the house he and Sam H. Dixon Jr. designed for Mr. and Mrs. Henry Stude in Shadyside of 1924. The compact house is outflanked by the garage to expand the house's street frontage. See "House of Henry Stude, Esq., Houston, Texas," *Architectural Forum* 44 (Mar. 1926): 49–50, and Birdsall P. Briscoe, "The Private Garage," *Civics for Houston* 1 (Mar. 1928): 6–7. Briscoe's article on harmonizing the design of the residential garage-apartment building with that of the country house illustrates the Stude garage as one of several examples by various Houston architects.

21. "Neighborhood News in River Oaks," *Homes for All Times* 2 (Sept. 1931): unpaginated. This report notes construction of the addition to the Staub house.

22. Ray Holcombe, "Architecture and the Small House," *Southern Architect and Building News* 54 (Mar. 1928): 36–40.

23. Charles O. Cornelius, "Transplanting the Eastern Tradition," *House Beautiful* 63 (Jan. 1928): 24–28, 41–44.

24. Cornelius had recently written *Early American Furniture* and published with R. T. H. Halsey, the same year his article on the Staub House appeared, *A Handbook of the American Wing*.

25. Barnstone, *Architecture of John F. Staub*, 72; Rather, "Charm in the Small House," 112–16; and "'Hopecote' House, Mr. Albert Guinn Hope, Knoxville, Tenn.," *The Architect* 4 (June 1925): plates 57–61.

26. Salisbury's tributes to the Staub House are located at 3443 Inwood Drive (1930), 2003 Bellmeade Road (1931), and 1936 Larchmont Road (1936).

27. "Brick, Shingles Vary Texture of Texas House," *Architectural Record* 88 (Dec. 1940): 62–63.

28. "Bright Outlook for 1933 Construction," *Houston* 3 (Jan. 1933): 9, and *Houston Architectural Survey*, 524–26.

29. On the Hardison House see Anchorage Foundation of Texas, *Braeswood: An Architectural History*, 13–14. On the Hill House see "Gillette Hill, Esq., Houston, Tex., Moore and Lloyd, Architects: 24," *House and Garden* 70 (Sept. 1936): 135.

30. A photograph of the Ballinger Mills Jr. House appears in Ellen Beasley and Stephen Fox, *Galveston Architecture Guidebook*, 185.

31. Rather, "Porches and Porticoes," 10–11, which includes a photo of the Lindsey House.

32. "House of H. Q. Hickman, Houston, Texas, Hiram A. Salisbury, Architect," *American Architect* 133 (Jan. 5, 1928): 62.

33. "The Honeymoon Cottage Competition," *Pencil Points* 9 (July 1928): 444–49.

34. Kevin Phillips, *Wealth and Democracy: A Political History of the American Rich*, 133.

35. Copy of undated typescript from John F. Staub's office: "Client, Cost, Comp. Date, Est. Cost"; Barnstone, *Architecture of John F. Staub*, 124–25.

36. Staub employed this Soane-like cornice detail frequently. Unfortunately, it is not one of the attributes discussed by Ptolemy Dean in his insightful analysis of the architectonics of Soane's houses.

37. Barnstone, *Architecture of John F. Staub*, 124.

38. David G. McComb, *Galveston: A History*, 150–51, 174, 189.

39. Copy of undated typescript from John F. Staub's office: "Client, Cost, Comp. Date, Est. Cost"; Barnstone, *Architecture of John F. Staub*, 126–29.

40. Hays, *Modernism and the Posthumanist Subject*, 86.

41. On Dr. Edward Randall Jr. (1891–1971) see William Manning Morgan, *Trinity Protestant Episcopal Church, Galveston, Texas, 1841–1953: A Memorial History*, 364–65; University of Texas Medical Branch at Galveston Faculty and Staff, *The University of Texas Medical Branch at Galveston: A Seventy-Five Year History*, 142; and *Who's Who in America*, vol. 33, 1964–65 (1964), 1640. Howard Barnstone credited Katherine and Edward Randall with introducing him, Dominique, and John de Menil to the Victorian architecture of Galveston in the 1950s. This led Barnstone, under John de Menil's sponsorship , to write *The Galveston That Was*, published in 1966, with its photographs by Ezra Stoller and Henri Cartier-Bresson.

42. Bushman, *Refinement of America*, 402.

43. I am indebted to Olive Duncan Hershey for clarifying the social significance of niceness in the discourse of River Oaks.

44. In Houston's hinterland it is possible to see houses built between the 1920s and the 1950s, many designed by Houston architects, that perform the distinction between country house sophistication and small-town domesticity in order to signify the patrician identity of their residents. The Morrison-McNeill House at 310 S. 6th Street and Salisbury and McHale's Walter Shult House of 1957 at 500 Hillcrest Drive in Richmond, Texas, exemplify this contrast, as do the Wintermann House at 307 E. Lake Avenue in Eagle Lake by Robert C. Smallwood of Houston, the Leon Abovitz House of 1933 at 212 N. Resident Street in Wharton by the Houston architect Lenard Gabert, the Meta Hawkins and James C. Lewis House of 1932 at 2517 Avenue G in Bay City by Joseph W. Northrop Jr., and the Jack F. Hutchins House of 1948 at 706 Heights Avenue in El Campo by Birdsall P. Briscoe. Staub, Rather and Howze contributed to this phenomenon with their house for Mr. and Mrs. William N. Lehrer of 1953–54 in Garwood near Wharton, El Campo, and Eagle Lake.

CHAPTER 5. GRAND HOUSES

1. Among the most notable of these country houses are, in Austin, the Charles T. Rather House at 606 Rathervue Place (1910; now part of the Episcopal Seminary of the Southwest) by the Boston architects Brigham, Coveney and Bisbee and Mr. and Mrs. Walter W. Fischer's house at 3417 Hampton Road (1935) by the Chicago architect Harry Howe Bentley. In Bryan, Texas, the country house that the retired diplomat William S. Howell Jr. built at the intersection of Boonville Road and Osborn Street (1939), designed by the New York architects Delano and Aldrich, their only work in Texas, was destroyed by fire. In Dallas, the Florence Patton and Pio Crespi House at 5555 Walnut Hill (1941) was a late work of the New York and Palm Beach architects Treanor and Fatio. See Derro Evans, "Dallas: Villa Fiorenza." *Texas Homes* 9 (Sept. 1985): 64–71. El Paso's grandest country house is the James G. McNary House at 4601 Hastings (1917; now the Franciscan Fathers Seminary) by the Pasadena architect Myron C. Hunt, one of his largest houses. In addition to the Adler and Staub–designed country houses in Fort Worth, there is the Helen and Lloyd H. McKee House of 1927 at 23 Westover Road in Westover Hills by the St. Louis architects Jamieson and Spearls. In San Antonio there are the Stella Cook and Robert W. Maverick House at 401 Torcido Drive in Alamo Heights (1929) by the Montecito architect George Washington Smith and the J. B. Robertson House at 303 Devine Road in Olmos Park (1929) by the New York architect William McK. Bowman. On the Robertson House, see "A Venetian Villa in Our Southwest," *House and Garden* 57 (Feb. 1930): 71, 102–105, and Edmund B. Gilchrist, "A Venetian Villa in Texas," *Architectural Forum* 52 (Apr. 1930): 537–69.

2. Aldrich, *Old Money*, 36.

3. Copy of undated typescript from John F. Staub's office: "Client, Cost. Comp. Date, Est. Cost"; Barnstone, *Architecture of John F. Staub*, 117–18.

4. On Edwin Elmore Bewley (1881–1946) see *History of Texas: Fort Worth and the Texas Northwest*, ed. Captain B. B. Paddock, vol. 3, 3–6 and 66–67; *Who Was Who in America*, vol. 2, 61.

5. Stephen M. Salny, *The Country Houses of David Adler*, 197.

6. Ibid., 34–35.

7. Page, Anderson and Turnbull, *Tarrant County Historic Resources Survey: Fort Worth: Near North Side and West Side and Westover Hills*, 96, 100–101, and 109.

8. Ibid., 183, 186.

9. One notes similarities to Lutyens's alterations and additions to Abbotswood of 1901 and the detailing of the terrace balustrades at the Deanery Garden of 1902. See Gavin Stamp, *Edwin Lutyens: Country Houses from the Archives of Country Life*, frontispiece, 28, 85. A Tebbs and Knell photograph of the china cabinet in the dining room of the Beweley House was published in "Lacquered Red, Yellow and Gold Enrich This Cabinet in a Texas Dining Room," *House and Garden* 60 (Sept. 1931): 49.

10. Aldrich, *Old Money*, 37.

11. Copy of undated typescript from John F. Staub's office: "Client, Cost, Comp. Date, Est. Cost"; Barnstone, *Architecture of John F. Staub*, 122–23. Also "The Value of Good Detail," *House and Garden* 58 (Dec. 1930): 55; and "House of John P. King, Fort Worth, Texas, John F. Staub, Architect," *Southern Architect and Building News* 57 (Aug. 1931): 19–20.

12. Copy of undated typescript from John F. Staub's office: "Client, Cost, Comp. Date, Est. Cost"; Barnstone, *Architecture of John F. Staub*, 142–44.

13. Barnstone, *Architecture of John F. Staub*, 143–44.

14. Among country house architects of Staub's generation, the Atlanta architect Philip Trammell Shutze stood out for of his use of Italian Baroque models that, by the restrained standards around which consensus formed in the 1920s, registered as flamboyant. See, for example, Shutze's two best-known houses, Hentz, Reid and Adler's country house for Mary Trigg and Andrew Calhoun of 1922–24 and Hentz, Adler and Shutze's Swan House for Emily MacDougald and Edward H. Inman of 1926–28, both in Atlanta and illustrated in Elizabeth Merrill Dowling, *American Classicist: The Architecture of Philip Trammell Shutze*, 62–77, 89–115. Also Henry Hope Reed, "America's Greatest Living Classical Architect: Philip Trammell Shutze of

Atlanta, Georgia," in *Classical America IV*, ed. William A. Coles, 5–46; and Griswold and Weller, *Golden Age of American Gardens*, 215–17.

15. On John P. King see *History of Texas*, 17–18.

16. On Herman Gartner see *History of Texas*, 84–85.

17. Ibid., 81–84.

18. Ibid., 58.

19. Barnstone, *Architecture of John F. Staub*, 34–35.

20. On Amon G. Carter (1879–1955) see *National Cyclopedia of American Biography*, vol. 43 (1961), 486–87, and Ben H. Procter, "Carter, Amon G.," *New Handbook of Texas*, vol. 1, 998–99.

21. Barrick, Nolan E., *Texas Tech: The Unobserved Heritage*.

22. Barnstone, *Architecture of John F. Staub*, 34–35.

23. Ibid., 34.

24. On J. Robert Neal (1894–1939) see "J. Robert Neal Dies in Boston," *Houston Post*, Nov. 27, 1939, 1; "Robert Neal Dies Suddenly in Boston," *Houston* 20 (Dec. 1939): 10; and the biographical entry on his son J. Robert Neal Jr. in Joseph Lynn Clark and Elton M. Scott, *The Texas Gulf Coast: Its History and Development*, 521.

25. See the biographical entry on J. W. Neal in *The New Encyclopedia of Texas*, vol. 1, 212.

26. "J. Robert Neal Dies in Boston," *Houston Post*, Nov. 27, 1939, 1; Johnston, *Happy Worldly Abode*, 149; *The New Encyclopedia of Texas*, vol. 1, 212.

27. Lila Gordon, "Mrs. J. W. Neal Is Generous and 'Young,'" *Houston Chronicle*, May 24, 1954, section D, 1.

28. "Second National Bank Control Interest Is Sold," *Houston Chronicle*, Nov. 20, 1943, section 1, 1. Biographical file entry for Mrs. J. W. Neal in *Houston Chronicle* biographical clippings microfiche file, Texas and Local History Component, Houston Metropolitan Research Center, Houston Public Library.

29. Barnstone, *Architecture of John F. Staub*, 165.

30. Copy of undated typescript from John F. Staub's office: "Client, Cost, Comp. Date, Est. Cost"; Barnstone, *Architecture of John F. Staub*, 164–70.

31. The development of the Neal landscape was documented by landscape historian Suzanne Turner's historic landscape report "J. Robert Neal Residence, Houston, Texas: Overview of Historic Landscape Issues" in consultation with Curtis and Windham, Architects, Feb. 1998. Thanks to William Curtis for making a copy of this report available.

32. See "Gardens: A Portfolio of Paintings by George Stonehill with Notes on the 1933 Scene," *Fortune* 8 (Aug. 1933): 70; and "Gardens at Houston and River Oaks, Texas," 186. Also Emerson, "A Plan for the Preservation, Management, and Interpretation of Bayou Bend Gardens," 40–41 and figures 11 and 12.

Suzanne Turner's report on the Neal garden contains a digest of correspondence from the Olmsted Brothers files deposited at the Frederick Law Olmsted National Historic Site in Brookline, Massachusetts, which is administered by the National Park Service. This digest mentions other landscape professionals working in Houston—Vera Baker Chinn, a landscape architect who in August 1931 had left Staub's office to move to New York; a rather flustered letter from Estelle B. Sharp on behalf of her Houston Studio Gardens landscape service (with which Vera Chinn had been associated and for which the landscape architect Ruth London worked) offering their services as horticultural consultants; and J. Allen Myers Jr., a Harvard landscape architecture school and Olmsted Brothers alumnus who was returning to Bryan, Texas, in December 1932 after closing his office in Birmingham, Alabama.

J. F. Dawson noted in a letter to J. R. Neal in October 1932 the difficulty of finding azaleas that could cope with Houston's soil conditions, suggesting that azaleas were not yet common in Houston. Letters from December 1932, as planting was being installed, communicated Dawson's frustration that Mr. and Mrs. Neal were heeding the advice of the Houston nurseryman Edward C. Teas rather than Olmsted Brothers' planting plan because the Neals wanted bigger plants.

The digest does not contain reference to a lawsuit that Neal instigated against his neighbor, John E. Green, general counsel of the Gulf Oil Corporation in Texas, in September 1933 because the garage of Green's newly planned country house was positioned so that its car stalls were visible from the forecourt of Neal's house. Neal lost the suit since Green's building plans did not violate the setback requirements of Homewoods's restrictive covenants. See "Diagram in Garage Injunction Trial," *Houston Post*, Sept. 10, 1933, 4.

The design and construction of the Neal House paralleled another grand, Depression-era country house, Cheekwood, built outside Nashville by Mabel Wood and Leslie Cheek, the daughter-in-law and son of Joel Cheek's cousin, who had run the Cheek-Neal wholesale grocery business so that Cheek and Neal could concentrate on the coffee company. Completed late in 1932, the Cheekwood house and gardens occupy a one-hundred-acre estate and were designed by the Ithaca, New York, landscape architect Bryant Fleming. The sale of the Cheek-Neal Coffee Company fourteen months before the stock market crash of October 1929 prompted the construction of these country houses, which affirm upper-class identity and subject positions on a scale that the economic crisis of the early 1930s might have seemed to render ill-advised. They attest to the mythic power of the country house discourse and its implied promise to confer superiority and distinction on its subjects. On Cheekwood see Parke Rouse Jr., *Living by Design: Leslie Cheek and the Arts*, 30, 38, 39–43. See also Griswold and Weller, *Golden Age of American Gardens*, 203, 206, and Garden Study Club of Nashville, *History of Homes and Gardens of Tennessee*, ed. Roberta Seawell Brandau, 390–95.

33. Barnstone, *Architecture of John F. Staub*, 166, 168. Suzanne Turner's digest of the correspondence in the Olmsted Brothers archive indicates that in November 1931 Dawson was making inquiries of his other clients in an effort to recommend an interior designer to Neal, who seems to have not wanted for Staub to be involved with the house's interiors. Turner, "J. Robert Neal Residence," 48.

34. Turner, "J. Robert Neal Residence," 50.

35. Milton McGinty, "Recollections: A Perfectionist," *Texas Architect* 29 (Nov.–Dec. 1979): 54.

36. Turner, "J. Robert Neal Residence," 48, 50, 53.

37. Staub to author. Ed Arrants, who was admired by his peers for his talent, was killed in an automobile accident while working for Staub.

38. "Robert Neal Dies Suddenly in Boston," *Houston* 20 (Dec. 1939): 10.

39. "Elizabeth Neal Dies; Hospital Benefactor," *Houston Chronicle*, Mar. 8, 1970, section 4, 5.

40. Mary Frazer, "Neal Mansion Being Sold—$325,000: Mecom May Buy Fabulous Residence," *Houston Press*, Jan. 13, 1954.

41. Copy of undated typescript from John F. Staub's office: "Client, Cost, Comp. Date, Est. Cost"; Barnstone, *Architecture of John F. Staub*, 171–79.

42. On Hugh Roy Cullen (1881–1957) see the authorized biography by Ed Kilman and Theon Wright, *Hugh Roy Cullen: A Story of American Opportunity*; *National Cyclopedia of American Biography*, vol. 47 (1965), 42–44; and *Who Was Who in America*, vol. 3, 200.

43. Kilman and Wright, *Hugh Roy Cullen*, 39–41, 77.

44. Ibid., 42.

45. Ibid., 77, 103, 107–108.

46. Ibid., 126–28.

47. Ibid., 137, 145, 132–33.

48. Ibid., 153–56, 159, 173, 176–81.

49. Ibid., 176–81; Larson and Porter, *History of Humble Oil and Refining Company*, 410.

50. Kilman and Wright, *Hugh Roy Cullen*, 165–66.

51. Barnstone, *Architecture of John F. Staub*, 172.

52. Barnstone, *Architecture of John F. Staub*, 172.

53. Mrs. Allen B. Hannay, "Houston Is Garden City," *Houston* 7 (Apr. 1936): 20–21; Mrs. Frances Hannay, "Houston Gardens Attract Nation-Wide Attention," *Houston* 8 (Mar. 1937): 21; Frances Hannay, "Houston's Own Azalea Trail," *Houston* 9 (Feb. 1938): 11; "12,000 See Gardens," 28; "Local Azalea Trail Viewed by Thousands," 30; Briscoe,

"Trails and Trails," 26; Stevenson, "Seventh Annual Azalea Trail," 36; Kilman and Wright, *Hugh Roy Cullen*, 207–208. Marguerite Johnston's book, *Houston: The Unknown City*, contains a photograph on page 364 taken at a meeting of symphony staff and board members in the garden of the Cullen House. Participants are sitting in what appears to be Sheraton-style metal garden furniture.

54. Kilman and Wright, *Hugh Roy Cullen*, 188–89.

55. Ibid., 228–31, 248–50. The William M. Rice Institute and the Hermann Hospital Estate were the beneficiaries of the bulk of their donor's bequests. The M. D. Anderson Foundation (organized in 1936 by William L. Clayton's partner M. D. Anderson) and Houston Endowment (organized by Jesse H. Jones in 1937) did not become major philanthropies until after the deaths of their donors.

56. Kilman and Wright cite Cullen's antipathy to policies advocated by Jones and Clayton and proposals he thought might benefit them (Kilman and Wright, *Hugh Roy Cullen*, 241–44, 246–47). See also the brief report "Businessmen in the News," *Fortune* 48 (Oct. 1953): 87, on a political confrontation between Jones and Cullen relating to an Anderson, Clayton and Company property.

57. Charles J. V. Murphy, "Texas Businessmen and McCarthy," *Fortune* 49 (May 1954): 100–101, 208, 211. Murphy's detailed article reported that some of McCarthy's richest and most ardent Texan supporters were beginning to distance themselves from the senator in the wake of the U.S. Army hearings in fall 1953 but that Cullen "has been a vigorous tub thumper for the McCarthy cause. . . . Just a few weeks ago he called the Senator 'the greatest man in America'" (p. 100). Kilman and Wright's authorized biography of Cullen, published in 1954, never mentions McCarthy. See also Don E. Carleton, *Red Scare! Right Wing Hysteria, Fifties Fanaticism, and Their Legacy in Texas*, 267–77.

58. In the postwar period, Cullen and the Dallas oilman H. L. Hunt became subject types of the right-wing Texan oilman in the national news media. The two identified with very different subject positions, however, as Hunt declined the role of civic philanthropist that Cullen embraced so enthusiastically.

59. Hitchcock, *Modern Architecture*, 19–22, 155, 219.

60. "J. H. Kirby Home to Be One of City's Finest," *Houston Post-Dispatch*, June 27, 1926, Real Estate and Building section, 5; architectural drawings for the Sterling Bay Cottage are deposited in the Alfred C. Finn Collection, Houston Metropolitan Research Center, Houston Public Library; "Estate of J. M. West on Clear Lake," *Houston Post-Dispatch*, Jan. 27, 1929, Real Estate and Building section, 2; Dorothy Hoskins, "An Italian Villa of Today: The Clear Lake Home of Mr. and Mrs. James Marion West," *Houston Gargoyle* 3 (May 11, 1930): 10–11.

61. Copy of undated typescript from John F. Staub's office: "Client, Cost, Comp. Date, Est. Cost"; Barnstone, *Architecture of John F. Staub*, 184–90.

62. On Stephen P. Farish (1891–1962) see *The New Encyclopedia of Texas*, vol. 1, 310–11; Clark and Scott, *Texas Gulf Coast*, 602–603; and the obituary notice "Farish," *Houston Chronicle*, Sept. 1, 1962, section 1, 22.

63. Johnston, *Houston: The Unknown City*, 247; Frederick Leon Webster, "Art in the Little Theater: Talented Houstonians Combine Their Efforts for a Finer Drama," *Civics for Houston* 1 (Oct. 1928): 16.

64. Clark and Scott, *Texas Gulf Coast*, 603.

65. Copy of undated typescript from John F. Staub's office: "Client, Cost, Comp. Date, Est. Cost"; Barnstone, *Architecture of John F. Staub*, 191–94.

66. Judith Walker Linsley and Ellen Walker Rienstra, *Beaumont: A Chronicle of Promise*, 73–83.

67. Linsley and Rienstra, *Beaumont*, 91–93; Robert Wooster, "Yount, Miles Frank," *The New Handbook of Texas*, vol. 6, 1133; and Judith Linsley and Ellen Rienstra, "McLean, Marrs," *The New Handbook of Texas*, vol. 4, 426–27.

68. Fred McKinley and Greg Riley, *Black Gold to Bluegrass: From the Oilfields of Texas to Spindletop Farm of Kentucky*.

69. *Texas General Contractors Association Monthly Bulletin* 9 (Dec. 1928): 20.

70. Bradley Brooks, "Owen J. T. Southwell, Architect, and the John Henry Phelan House," *Texas Gulf Historical and Biographical Record* 35 (Nov. 1999): 3–17; Dorothy M. Hoskins, "'A Hundred Thousand Welcomes': The Home of Mr. and Mrs. John Henry Phelan in Beaumont," *Houston Gargoyle* 3 (Nov. 2, 1930): 17–18; and *Texas General Contractors Association Monthly Bulletin* 9 (Aug. 1928): 13.

71. On James Cooke Wilson (1879–1944) see *The New Encyclopedia of Texas*, vol. 1, 1046; T. C. Richardson, *East Texas: Its History and Its Makers*, ed. Dabney White, vol. 4, 28–29; *The National Cyclopedia of American Biography*, vol. 33 (1947), 394; and Barnstone, *Architecture of John F. Staub*, 192. Mrs. Wilson bequeathed the house to the Art Museum of Southeast Texas, which used it as an art museum until 1987. Faced with the need for more space, the museum wisely decided to build a purpose-designed building at another site instead of adding to the house. The house reverted to other beneficiaries designated by Mrs. Wilson, who sold it. It is once again a single-family residence.

72. Barnstone, *Architecture of John F. Staub*, 214–15. The architectural drawings for the Camp House in the John F. Staub Collection of the Houston Public Library's Houston Metropolitan Research Center comprise the most complete set in the collection. This is the only house for which drawings document the entire design process. The collection contains preliminary drawings, alternative design sketches, and prints of shop drawings from various manufacturers in addition to the working drawings and detail drawings. It also includes a blueprint (dated November 1933) of interior elevations of the living room and an adjoining porch of the house at 1902 Bennett Avenue, where the Camps were first listed as living in the 1908 issue of the Dallas city directory. The print is labeled as measured by the Dallas architect Ralph Bryan and drawn by O'Neil Ford.

73. Barnstone, *Architecture of John F. Staub*, 215.

74. James Chillman Jr., "The Architect and House: 7—John F. Staub of Houston, Texas," *Pencil Points* 22 (Jan. 1942): 16–18; copy of undated typescript from John F. Staub's office: "Client, Cost, Comp. Date, Est. Cost"; "Contracts Awarded," *Texas General Contractors Association Monthly Bulletin* 18 (Feb. 1937): 13; and Patsy Swank, "Should the City Save the De Golyer Estate?" *D: The Magazine of Dallas* 3 (Apr. 1976): 65–67.

In 1976 the City of Dallas acquired the forty-four-acre Rancho Encinal, the country house of Mr. and Mrs. E. L. De Golyer, on the south shore of White Rock Lake and in 1978 bought the adjacent Camp property, combining their grounds to become the Dallas Arboretum and Botanical Garden, which opened in 1982. The De Golyer House functions as a house museum. The Camp House is rented for social events and contains the staff offices of the Arboretum.

75. Harry Hurt III, *Texas Rich: The Hunt Dynasty from the Early Oil Days through the Silver Crash*, 122–23; and Lisa Ruffin, "Dallas: Mount Vernon—The Hilltop Mansion of Legendary Oilman H. L. Hunt," *Texas Homes* 9 (Feb. 1985): 64–71.

76. Alex Camp House drawings, John F. Staub Collection, Houston Metropolitan Research Center, Houston Public Library. The earliest preliminary sketches are from July and August 1936. Despite subsequent changes, the spatial organization and appearance of the Camp House were fixed by September 1936. Working drawings are dated February 1, 1937. The last dated drawing in the collection, for replacement of the stair rail, is from January 19, 1939, and is signed by Barthelme. It shows the rail in its present configuration. A written note on the drawing instructs the contractor to install a cardboard mockup for Mrs. Camp's approval before proceeding. Alex Camp died on April 28, 1939; Mrs. Camp occupied the house until her death in 1970.

Staub did not indicate to Barnstone that he considered Mrs. Camp difficult or arbitrary; his anecdote about his quip at her dinner party was how he remembered her. Evaluating the completed house as the product of negotiation makes one realize that the indecisiveness imputed to Mrs. Camp in Barnstone's text might instead have been a keen sense of perception, which she could perhaps not articulate but about which she was very certain.

77. "$100,000 Home to be Erected by J. O. Winston, Jr.," *Houston Post*, Nov. 6, 1938, section 4, 8; copy of undated typescript from John F. Staub's office: "Client, Cost, Comp. Date, Est. Cost"; Barnstone, *Architecture of John F. Staub*, 246–49; Chillman, "The Architect and House: 7," 23–24.

78. On James O. Winston Jr. (1902–93), see Clark and Scott, *Texas Gulf Coast*, 229–30.

79. Aldrich, *Old Money*, 91.

CHAPTER 6. COUNTRY RETREATS

1. The city of Port Arthur, Texas, platted in 1894, developed as an industrial city after the discovery of oil at Spindletop in 1901 rather than the lakefront winter resort for Midwestern millionaires that its founders Arthur Stilwell and John W. Gates envisioned as one of its potential futures. The nineteenth-century bayfront settlements of Fulton and Rockport, Texas (next door to each other on Aransas Bay, up the coast from Corpus Christi), and Port Isabel, Texas (originally Point Isabel, near Brownsville on the Laguna Madre), were reinvented as waterfront resort towns in the early twentieth century after they lost their earlier economic functions as beef production and shipping ports. La Porte, Texas (next door to Bay Ridge), was a railroad-era resort on Galveston Bay founded in 1890, the same time period in which San Leon (originally called North Galveston) farther south along Galveston Bay was developed. Port Aransas (c. 1890) on the northern tip of Mustang Island at Aransas Pass, across Corpus Christi Bay from Corpus Christi, was founded as part of an ambitious economic and infrastructure development scheme. The effects of the Panic of 1893 inhibited bayfront resort development along the Texas coast until the turn of the twentieth century. Seabrook (1900) and Bayview (c. 1902) on Galveston Bay; Bayside (1908) on Cópano Bay near Fulton, Rockport, and Port Aransas; Palacios (1902) and Collegeport (1908) on Tres Palacios Bay; and Port O'Connor (1909) on Lavaca Bay near Port Lavaca and Victoria were railroad-related resort town developments. Bacliff on Galveston Bay and Shoreacres, a resort community developed around the Houston Yacht Club on Galveston Bay, just south of La Porte, in 1926 were developments of the 1920s.

2. See Peter Flagg Maxson's nomination application of the Morgan's Point Historic District to the National Register of Historic Places of 1994 at <http://atlas.thc.state.tx.us/shell-kword.htm> under "Morgan's Point," "Harris County," and "National Register Properties."

3. "Peden Clubhouse on Bay Ridge Sold at $36,000 Cash," *Houston Post-Dispatch*, Dec. 18, 1927, Real Estate section, 2; Barnstone, *Architecture of John F. Staub*, 119–20.

4. The Sterling Bay House is listed in the National Register of Historic Places; see <http://atlas.thc.state.tx.us/shell-kword.htm> under "R. S. Sterling," "Harris County," and "National Register Properties." Architectural and landscape architectural drawings for the house are in the Alfred C. Finn Collection and the Hare and Hare Collection, Houston Metropolitan Research Center, Houston Public Library.

5. Charles Platt, *The Architecture of Charles A. Platt*, 23–41.

6. "W. H. Irvin's $35,000 Home on Bay," *Houston Post-Dispatch*, Dec. 11, 1927, Real Estate and Building section, 3.

7. The nineteenth-century Galveston architect N. J. Clayton frequently used the Lone Star, the icon of Texas, as a decorative device on his public buildings. See Barrie Scardino and Drexel Turner, *Clayton's Galveston: The Architecture of Nicholas J. Clayton and His Galveston Contemporaries*.

8. The cottage of the A. A. Bath family at 119 Bay Ridge Road exemplifies the La Porte builders' vernacular. See also "A Summer Play Ground on the Bay Shore," *The Houstonian* 1 (July 28, 1917): 9; and Gordon Wittenberg, "On Tour: Morgan's Point: Once Bustling Bay Ridge Survives," *Cite: The Architecture and Design Review of Houston* (Aug. 1982): 16–17.

9. Maxson, Morgan's Point National Register Historic District nomination application.

10. "Down on the Bay," *Houston Gargoyle* 4 (July 19, 1931): 13. See also "Along the Waterfront," *Houston Gargoyle* 3 (Aug. 10, 1930): 15; "Lorgnon," *Houston Gargoyle* 3 (Aug. 17, 1930): 15; and "Through the Lorgnon," *Houston Gargoyle* 4 (July 26, 1931): 13.

11. The Randolph Stable was of wood construction. After it burned, Mr. and Mrs. Randolph sold the property to Mr. and Mrs. Seymour Sacks, who had Staub design a house for them in 1950–51. The Sacks House was demolished in the late 1990s. See Ann Crawford Fears, *Frankie: Mrs. R. D. Randolph and Texas Liberal Politics*, 14.

In their architectural and landscape history of Lake Forest, Illinois, Kim Coventry, Daniel Meyer, and Arthur H. Miller discern a generational shift during the 1890s in the way that the children and grandchildren of Lake Forest's founding families conceived their own identity and subject positions. This transformation in conception and social style mirrored the town's transition from a country place community centered around members of Chicago's Second Presbyterian Church and the college they founded at Lake Forest in the 1850s to one centered on the Onwentsia Country Club and its promotion of such high-status sports as golf, polo, and fox hunting. Coventry, Meyer, and Miller, *Classic Country Estates of Lake Forest*, 63–69.

When Frederick Law Olmsted, still a journalist and not yet a landscape architect, traveled through east and south Texas in 1854–55, he visited Houston. Olmsted rode into Houston from the northwest and remarked with approval on the pine forest through which he passed, an unusual ecological zone in the grasslands of the coastal plain. Frederick Law Olmsted, *A Journey through Texas: Or, a Saddle-Trip on the Southwestern Frontier*, 61.

12. "Carter Builds $40,000 Club on 100-Acre Tract." *Houston Post-Dispatch*, May 5, 1929, Real Estate and Building section, 1; copy of undated typescript from John F. Staub's office: "Client, Cost, Comp. Date, Est. Cost"; Barnstone, *Architecture of John F. Staub*, 133–37; "The House of W. T. Carter, Jr., in Houston, John F. Staub, Architect," *House Beautiful* 71 (June 1932): 434, 439–41.

13. On William T. Carter Jr. (1887–1957), see *The New Encyclopedia of Texas*, vol. 1, 408, 425; and J. Lester Jones, *Centennial 1876–1976: W. T. Carter and Bro.*, 44.

14. Writers' Program of the Works Projects Administration in the State of Texas, *Houston: A History and Guide*, 148–49.

15. The Subdivision Collection of the Houston Metropolitan Research Center's Texas and Local History component at the Houston Public Library contains two sales brochures for Garden Villas: *The Garden City of Houston: Garden Villas* (undated) and *Garden Villas: Where Nature Greets You* (undated). Garden Villas had a staff architect prior to the Great Depression, Edward Wilkinson, an Englishman who studied architecture at the Rice Institute. However, the wood houses built there in the 1920s were not architecturally distinctive or remarkable. See "Office Opened by Edward Wilkinson," *Houston Post*, Nov. 27, 1938, section 2, 18.

16. See the advertisement in the Real Estate section of the *Houston Post-Dispatch*, July 12, 1925, 2, in which the community is described as "laid out on a carefully designed Garden City plan. . . ." See the articles "Suburban Place Is Given Name," *Houston Post-Dispatch*, Apr. 19, 1925, 21, and "Garden Villas Is Popular Addition," *Houston Post-Dispatch*, May 17, 1925, Real estate section, 1.

17. *The New Encyclopedia of Texas*, vol. 1, 425.

18. Neuhaus, "The History of the Neuhaus Family (To 1935)."

19. Copy of undated typescript from John F. Staub's office: "Client, Cost, Comp. Date, Est. Cost"; Barnstone, *Architecture of John F. Staub*, 152–55.

20. Staub to Barnstone, interview of July 17, 1977.

21. "Elegant Home to be Built at Beaumont," *Houston Post*, July 23, 1911, 37.

22. *Brochure of the Work of William Ward Watkin*; architectural drawings for the Wiess House are deposited in the Woodson Research Center, Fondren Library, Rice University.

23. Dorothy Hoskins, "Grace, Beauty in the Southern Home of Mr. and Mrs. Harry Carothers Wiess (Shadyside)," *Houston Gargoyle* 3 (Jan. 19, 1930): 17. These photographs show the house following Lindeberg's alterations and additions. Also see "Gardens at Houston and River Oaks, Texas," 190.

24. See R. M. Luster's photograph of Mrs. Wiess and her friends on horseback in front of the Stables: "Saddle, Boot and Spur," *Houston Gargoyle* 4 (Mar. 22, 1931): 17. Also the chapter "Polo, Anyone?" in Johnston, *Houston: The Unknown City, 1836–1946*, 317–20.

25. Peter Carl's insightful meditation on the role of "background" is contained in his essay "The Godless Temple, 'Organon of the Infinite,'" *Journal of Architecture* 10 (Feb. 2005): 77, 82: "The background [as, for example, in an early Renaissance devotional painting] is not simply a stage-set, but, as background in any profound sense, embodies that which is common-to-all, like ethics or like Heidegger's 'earth' *(physis)* as receptacle of culture. . . . Architecture qualifies the richness, conflicts, history, and structure of this background, from whose excess of meaning all creativity of finitude takes its measure."

26. Frank A. Watts, "Houston Resumes 'Remodeling' Her Skyline," *Houston* 15 (May 1934): 15. See also the advertisement "'Freon' Air-Conditioning Was Installed in This Building after It Was Built," *Architectural Forum* 62 (May 1935): 1, illustrating the original Humble Building of 1919 and its equipment with a York Ice Machinery Corporation central air-conditioning system. A photograph of Staub's no-longer-extant super-service station prototype for the Humble Oil and Refining Company of 1938 was published in the article "Buildings for Selling Services Offer Unique Design Opportunities," *Architectural Record* 90 (July 1941): 85, without identification or architectural attribution, which was highly unusual. The photograph was reproduced again in the October 1941 issue of *Architectural Record*, page 69, also without attribution. Staub told Barnstone that Donald Barthelme produced this design. Barnstone, *Architecture of John F. Staub*, 50.

27. See the National Register of Historic Places nomination for the Edward Albert Palmer Memorial Chapel and Autry House at <http://atlas.thc.state.tx.us/shell-kword.htm> under "Palmer Memorial," "Harris County," and "National Register Properties."

28. Lon Tinkle, *Mr. De: A Biography of Everette Lee De Golyer*, 33; Larson and Porter, *History of Humble Oil and Refining Company*, 271.

29. See the entry on John F. Grant in Emory E. Bailey, ed., *Who's Who in Texas*, 62.

30. "Building Permits for Week Near $500,000; 1925 Total $17,000,000," *Houston Post-Dispatch*, Aug. 30, 1925, Real Estate section, 1.

31. See the entry on Ernest Bel Fay's father, Charles S. Fay, in Bailey, *Who's Who in Texas*, 32.

32. Carolyn Grant Fay, "The House," typescript memoir, Spring 1987. I am grateful to Marie Fay Evnochides for a copy of her mother's memoir. "Plans for $35,000 Fay Home Spur Interest in Country Estates Area," *Houston Post*, Nov. 7, 1937, section 3, 1. On the Sharp House see "Texas Takes to Modern," *House and Garden* 77 (May 1940–II): 32–33. The Sharp House of 1937 was designed by Stayton Nunn-Milton McGinty with interiors by Joseph Mullen. It was demolished by the Houstonian in 2004.

33. Copy of undated typescript from John F. Staub's office: "Client, Cost, Comp. Date, Est. Cost"; Barnstone, *Architecture of John F. Staub*, 220–22; and Chillman, "The Architect and House: 7," 19–20.

34. Fay, "The House," 1.

35. Ibid., 2.

36. The objectivity of the Fay House corresponds to Aldrich's insight into the forms toward which patrician identity gravitates: ". . . contained and reasonable," "well-protected, comfortable, and aesthetically agreeable. . . ." Writing about social class and architecture, Benedikt described this implied dialectical confrontation with neediness in terms of power, denial, and virtue to suggest the appeal typification may have exercised in the latter half of the 1930s as an emblem of class superiority. See Aldrich, *Old Money*, 36, and Benedikt, "Class Notes," 8. See also the website of the Jung Educational Center of Houston: <http://www.cgjunghouston.org/aboutus.htm>.

37. Hugh Best in *Debrett's Texas Peerage*, 163–64, reproduces a list of the charter members of the Bayou Club.

38. "Houston Riding and Polo Club to Erect Club House," *Houston Post*, Dec. 4, 1938, section 6, 4; "Construction on Bayou Clubhouse Gets Under Way," *Houston Post*, May 17, 1940, section 1, 4.

39. Copy of undated typescript from John F. Staub's office: "Client, Cost, Comp. Date, Est. Cost"; Barnstone. *Architecture of John F. Staub*, 250–52; and Chillman, "The Architect and House: 7," 25.

40. Marcus, *Lives in Trust*, 79, 145.

41. "Memorial Park Estates to Be New Addition," *Houston Post*, Dec. 1, 1935, Real Estate and Building section, 2.

42. Johnston, *Houston: The Unknown City*, 282. I am grateful to David H. Knapp, Mrs. Robert Pullen, Mrs. Robert Straus, Mrs. David Underwood, and Mrs. Paul Wise for their recollections of Briar Hollow. Between 1966 and 1983, Briar Hollow was transformed from a country place neighborhood into a mixed-use district of office and apartment buildings and parking garages, some of mid- and high-rise construction. The first house to be demolished so its property could be commercially redeveloped was Staub's house for Dr. and Mrs. Allen McMurrey (1941–42) at 22 Briar Hollow Road and Briar Hollow Place.

43. "New Residential Project on Post Oak Revealed as Gillette Buys 20 Acres," *Houston Post*, Apr. 3, 1938, section 2, 11. West Oaks was developed in two sections: North and South West Oak Drives west of South Post Oak Lane, and North and South Wynden Drives and Huntley, east of South Post Oak Lane. Since the late 1980s, almost all of the houses built there between the late 1930s and early 1950s have been replaced by gated subdivisions, with each subdivision occupying what had once been a single residential lot.

44. "Farish Pays $147,900 Cash for 174-Acre Estate along Buffalo Bayou, West of City," *Houston Post-Dispatch*, Nov. 18, 1928, Real Estate and Building section, 1. The article "Country Homes on Post Oak Prove Popular," *Houston Post*, Nov. 17, 1935, of the Real Estate and Building section, 1, contains a useful map identifying property ownership along Post Oak Road (now South and North Post Oak Lane), north and south of Buffalo Bayou, and Memorial Drive.

The section of Bayou Woods developed by Stephen P. Farish (lying north of Memorial Drive) was platted July 12, 1940, and planned by the architect (and, as he identified himself on the plat map, "city planner") Harold H. Denney. Section 2 of Bayou Woods, south of Memorial Drive, was platted December 30, 1941; Fleming and Sheppard were the planners, William S. Farish the developer. Sherwood Forest was developed in sections, two of which were platted in 1945.

CHAPTER 7. TYPIFICATION, CONSENSUS, AND THE RIVER OAKS HOUSE

1. Of the twenty-two Staub houses built in River Oaks between 1930 and 1941, those not discussed in this chapter are the houses of Elaine Smith and Clarence M. Frost at 2110 River Oaks Boulevard (1933–34); Mary Fredrica Gross and Ray L. Dudley at 3371 Chevy Chase Drive (1936–37); Charlotte Padgitt and George V. Rotan at 2300 Pine Valley Drive (1936–37); Marian Mellinger and James L. Britton at 1824 Larchmont Road (1936–37); Katherine McGowan and Lewis Randolph Bryan Jr. at 3315 Ella Lee Lane (1937–38; designed by Tom Rather); Marie Garrett and Claud B. Hamill at 2124 River Oaks Boulevard (1938–39; next door to the Frost House); and Gladys Madigan and Edward House Andrews at 3637 Inwood Drive (1940–41; demolished in the late 1990s).

Two Staub-designed houses were built in the subdivision of Riverside Terrace for Katherine and J. Coulter Means Jr. at 3904 South MacGregor Way (1936–37; extensively altered) and for Loretta Grim and Sellers J. Thomas at 3302 South MacGregor Way (1937–38).

2. "Texas," *Fortune* 20 (Dec. 1939): 87.

3. McComb, *Houston*, 142, 168.

4. Buenger and Pratt, *But Also Good Business*, 107.

5. Ibid., 97–107. Jones and two other businessmen involved in these negotiations were Staub's clients, Capt. James A. Baker and Harry C. Wiess. Barnstone, *Architecture of John F. Staub*, 114–16, 318.

6. Larson and Porter, *History of Humble Oil and Refining Company*, 395; Julia Cauble Smith, "East Texas Oilfield," *New Handbook of Texas*, vol. 5, 409–10; David F. Prindle, "Railroad Commission," *New Handbook of Texas*, vol. 2, 772–74; Larson and Porter, *History of Humble Oil and Refining Company*, 424–63; Yergin, *The Prize*, 254.

7. Larson and Porter, *History of Humble Oil and Refining Company*, 266, 459, 475, 479, 483–86; Don E. Carleton, *A Breed So Rare: The Life of J. R. Parten, Liberal Texas Oil Man, 1896–1992*, 76, 82, 84, 97, 124–27, 257; Yergin, *The Prize*, 254–59.

8. Larson and Porter, *History of Humble Oil and Refining Company*, 330.

9. Carleton, *A Breed So Rare*, 87. The house was designed about 1931. According to the *Tarrant County Historic Resources Survey*, Roeser and his wife instead bought the McKee House in Westover Hills in 1935. Page, Anderson and Turnbull, *Tarrant County Historic Resources Survey*, 143, 202.

10. Carleton, *A Breed So Rare*, 97, 110, 116.

11. Kilman and Wright, *Hugh Roy Cullen*, 206. Kilman and Wright indirectly acknowledged Cullen's acquiescence in the matter of prorationing: "Roy Cullen's attack was not against 'government control,' however. Like most oil operators, he recognized the need for industrial regulation . . . but not control that destroyed the right of private ownership."

Lon Tinkle cited the observation of the geologist Everette L. De Golyer in 1939 that "prospecting for oil in the United States has always been a highly competitive cooperative effort" to clarify the paradoxical nature of the consensus that had been effected by the mid-1930s. The independents and the majors had a reciprocal economic relationship that persisted even in the midst of ideological conflict, as Cullen's lucrative deals with the Humble Oil and Refining Company in the early 1930s demonstrate. See Tinkle, *Mr. De*, 186, and Larson and Porter, *History of Humble Oil and Refining Company*, 400, 410.

12. Harold M. Hyman, *Craftsmanship and Character: A History of the Vinson and Elkins Law Firm of Houston, 1917–1997*, 118. Hyman observed that Judge Elkins and such friends as Herman and George Brown and Gus Wortham drank, swore, gambled, and " . . . peppered conversations and letters unembarrassedly with regional colloquialisms . . ." (p. 58). Hyman tied the rise to power of this contingent not only to their wealth-producing activities but also to the construction of consensus institutionalized informally in socializing that occurred in a suite in Jesse Jones's Lamar Hotel, Suite 8-F. Suite 8-F was rented by Herman Brown, a paving and infrastructure contractor based in Austin who sent his younger brother and business partner (and Tom Rather's client), George R. Brown, to Houston in 1926. The Suite 8-F contingent consisted of people like Elkins, from towns in central Texas, usually from middle-class backgrounds, who had studied at Texas universities or colleges and were intelligent, ambitious, hardworking, and eager to increase their wealth and power. Joseph Pratt and Christopher Castañeda identified the core participants as Herman and George Brown (from Belton and Temple, Texas); Judge Elkins; James Abercrombie (also from Huntsville); Gus Wortham, founder of the American General Life Insurance Company (from Mexia, Texas); former governor William P. Hobby, a newspaper man by profession whom Ross Sterling had made editor of the *Houston Post-Dispatch*, which Hobby and his wife bought out of bankruptcy along with Radio KPRC with the assistance of Jesse Jones; Hobby's wife, Oveta Culp Hobby (who was from Killeen, Texas, near Temple); the independent oilman R. E. Smith; and William A. Smith, who, like the Brown brothers, was an infrastructure contractor. Hyman observed that Jesse Jones's protracted absence from Houston during the Depression and World War II made it possible for Judge Elkins, the Brown brothers, and their compatriots to achieve positions of economic and political authority that might otherwise have been claimed. See Pratt, "8F and Many More," 7, 31–34; Joseph A. Pratt and Christopher J. Castañeda, *Builders: Herman and George Brown*, 158–72; Hyman, *Craftsmanship and Character*, 89.

Margarett Root and Herman Brown bought Staub's Chew-Weems House, next door to Rather's house for Alice and George Brown, on Inwood Drive in 1946. Governor and Mrs. Hobby had Staub and Rather remodel J. S. Cullinan's house in Shadyside in 1947, which they bought from the Cullinan estate. In 1952, Mr. and Mrs. R. E. Bob Smith had Staub, Rather and Howze remodel the Moore and Lloyd–designed house they bought at 3208 Chevy Chase Drive. Mr. and Mrs. William A. Smith bought Staub's Finch House on Inwood Drive after H. B. Finch's death in 1935. Bill Smith lived there until his death in 1991. For Josephine Abercrombie and her husband, H. B. Robinson, Staub, Rather and Howze designed a country house outside Versailles, Kentucky, in 1958. The Abercrombie House is illustrated in Barnstone, *Architecture of John F. Staub*, 294–97.

There are biographical profiles in *The New Handbook of Texas* for Herman Brown (1892–1962), vol. 1, 761–62; George Rufus Brown (1898–1983), vol. 1, 760–61; James Anderson Elkins (1879–1972), vol. 2, 825; James Smither Abercrombie (1891–1975), vol. 1, 5–6; Gus Sessions Wortham (1891–1976), vol. 6, 1085; William Pettus Hobby (1878–1964), vol. 3, 640; Oveta Culp Hobby (1905–95), vol. 6, 637–40; Robert Everett Smith (1894–1973), vol. 5, 1108; and Leopold L. Meyer (1892–1982), vol. 4, 700–701. There is a very brief profile of William A. Smith in Clark and Scott, *Texas Gulf Coast*, 204. There is a biography of J. S. Abercrombie in Patrick J. Nicholson, *Mr. Jim: The Biography of James Smither Abercrombie*.

In his book *Houston: Land of the Big Rich*, the journalist George Fuermann identified the business and civic leaders whom he called the "Rulers." They were Jesse Jones, Judge Elkins, Glenn H. McCarthy, Mayor Oscar F. Holcombe, Hugh Roy Cullen, William L. Clayton, Herman and George Brown, and Oveta Culp and William P. Hobby. George Fuermann, *Houston: Land of the Big Rich*, 78–86.

13. "Contracts Awarded," *Texas General Contractors Association Monthly Bulletin* 14 (July 1933): 15; copy of undated typescript from John F. Staub's office: "Client, Cost, Comp. Date, Est. Cost."

14. Personal and professional information on David D. Bruton comes from city directory listings beginning with the 1930–31 issue (the first in which Mr. and Mrs. Bruton were listed), continuing forward to 1948 (the last year for which Harriett M. Bruton is listed), and concluding in 1951, the year Bruton and his second wife, Laura, sold the house.

15. During the late 1950s, vignettes from the Bruton-Francis House were published in *House and Garden*. See *House and Garden* 112 (Oct. 1957), in which the living room is illustrated on the front cover, and "You Can Frame Old Fireplaces with New Mantles," *House and Garden* 114 (Dec. 1958): 102, highlighting the interior design work of Winston Farber. On William H. Francis Jr. (1914–58), see Clark and Scott, *Texas Gulf Coast*, 426–27; and *Who Was Who in America*, vol. 3, 298. From 1938 to 1941 and from 1945 to 1949, Francis was associated with and became a name partner in the law firm of Vinson, Elkins, Weems and Francis. He withdrew from the firm in 1949, three years after his marriage to Caroline Wiess, to pursue independent practice and oversee his oil investments. From 1957 until his death in May 1958, Francis served in the Dwight D. Eisenhower administration as an assistant secretary of the Department of Defense.

16. "Bowles Builds $35,000 Home," *Houston Post*, Sept. 8, 1935, 11. Copy of undated typescript from John F. Staub's office: "Client, Cost, Comp. Date, Est. Cost." Ethel and Robert Bowles are first listed in the 1932–33 issue of the Houston City Directory and are last listed in the 1941 issue. The Standard Oil Company of Kansas is first listed with offices in Houston in the 1932–33 *Houston City Directory*. The president of the company was Charles B. Wrightsman, whose parents, Edna Lawing and Charles J. Wrightsman, bought Staub's Gartner House in Fort Worth in 1938 and lived there until Charles J. Wrightsman's death

in 1959. Although Charles B. Wrightsman maintained his office in Houston, he never seems to have had his primary residence there. He was, however, a founding member of the Bayou Club. Wrightsman is best known for the collection of eighteenth-century European furniture he assembled and gave to the Metropolitan Museum of Art. See "The Gartner-Wrightsman-Young House and Its Architect," *Historic Fort Worth Presents 2002 Designer Showcase*, tour brochure printed by Historic Fort Worth, 2002, 5; and James Parker, "The Wrightsman Rooms at the Metropolitan Museum of Art," *Antiques* 97 (Jan. 1970): 102–108.

17. Barnstone, *Architecture of John F. Staub*, 198; Elizabeth and Patrick R. Rutherford are first listed as living in the Bowles House in the 1942–43 issue of the Houston City Directory.

18. Anne Schlumberger Bohnn, Edwin A. Eubanks, and Stephen Fox, "An Interview with C. C. Pat Fleming," *Cite 29: The Architecture and Design Review of Houston* (fall 1992–winter 1993): 34–35.

19. Frank D. Yturria and Lee Govatos to author. A third house that architecturally and chronologically suggests the influence of the Bowles House is in Victoria, Texas (midway along the Gulf coast between Beaumont and Brownsville), designed by the San Antonio architect Bartlett Cocke for Dr. and Mrs. Rawley W. Ward at 902 West Stayton Avenue of 1936–37. The Ward-Braman House lies three blocks west of Staub's Monterey-type house for Mr. and Mrs. J. Meredith Tatton at 601 West North Avenue of 1936–37.

20. See the biographical entry on George Heyer's father, George W. Heyer, in *The New Encyclopedia of Texas*, vol. 2, 1474, 1477. The 1927 Houston city directory listed Ella S. Heyer, widow of George Heyer, as having died in November 1926. The names of her son George Heyer and his wife, Jane, first appear in the 1928 Houston city directory, with Heyer listed as affiliated with the Harmand Teplow Company with offices in the Cotton Exchange Building. The 1929–30 city directory listed Heyer as manager of the Cranfill-Reynolds Company and of the Union Exploration Company. Cranfill-Reynolds was acquired by the Moody-Seagraves Interests and Heyer became president. In the 1930–31 city directory, O. R. Seagraves was listed as chairman of the board and W.L. Moody III as vice president and treasurer of Cranfill-Reynolds, with Heyer listed as president.

21. On T. W. Gregory see Anders, Evan, "Gregory, Thomas Watt," *New Handbook of Texas*, vol. 3, 331.

22. Moody-Seagraves Interests underwent Houston's most spectacular corporate bankruptcy during the Depression. Heyer's oil company survived and, with participation from W. L. Moody's brother, Shearn Moody, became the General Crude Oil Company, of which George Heyer was president. On W. L. Moody III and his association with O. R. Seagraves see Arthur M. Louis, "It's Moody vs. Moody in the Struggle for American National," *Fortune* 83 (Mar. 1971): 110–12. In 1937–38 Staub designed a house in Galveston for Moody and his wife, Mary Margaret Guinard. On the Moody-Seagraves bankruptcy see Buenger and Pratt, *But Also Good Business*, 96, 102. George Heyer died in 1944; his widow Jane Gregory Heyer (subsequently Marechal) occupied the house until her death in 1991.

23. Barnstone, *Architecture of John F. Staub*, 201; copy of undated typescript from John F. Staub's office: "Client, Cost, Comp. Date, Est. Cost"; "George Heyer to Build Home," *Houston Post*, Jan. 26, 1936, Real Estate and Building section, 2.

24. Barnstone, *Architecture of John F. Staub*, 201.

25. Staub to author.

26. Aldrich, *Old Money*, 91.

27. Barnstone, *Architecture of John F. Staub*, 200.

28. Ibid., 161–63, 145–51; copy of undated typescript from John F. Staub's office: "Client, Cost, Comp. Date, Est. Cost." The Hill House survives in good condition. The Hanszen House was doubled in size and suffered the loss of all of Staub's interiors in 1979–81.

29. Barnstone, *Architecture of John F. Staub*, 161–63, 145–51; copy of undated typescript from John F. Staub's office: "Client, Cost, Comp. Date, Est. Cost"; "No Castle in Spain: Home of Mr. and Mrs. William J. Crabb, 2416 Pine Valley Drive," *River Oaks Magazine*, Mar. 1939, 11–13; Sandy Sheehy, "River Oaks Latin Classic," *Texas Homes* 3 (Sept.–Oct. 1979): 96–103.

In 1969, the Pratt House became the first Staub house in River Oaks to be demolished. Demolition of the Crabb House in May 1985 occasioned a protest demonstration in River Oaks organized by Carolyn Farb in which the historian Dorothy Knox Howe Houghton, architectural historian Barrie Scardino, and neighbors Gayle F. Bentsen and Judy P. Meyer (the wife of Peter Staub Meyer) participated. See John Kaliski, "Hindcite: Crabbing about Preservation," *Cite: The Architecture and Design Review of Houston* (summer 1985): 26.

On George A. Hill Jr. (1892–1949) see *The New Encyclopedia of Texas*, vol. 2, 323; Clark and Scott, *Texas Gulf Coast*, 715–17, which also contains entries on Hill's father (pp. 714–15), his son Raymond M. Hill (pp. 717–18), and the Houston Oil Company of Texas (pp. 718–20); the *National Cyclopedia of American Biography*, vol. 39 (1954), 47–48; *Who Was Who in America*, vol. 2, 253; and the entry "Hill, George Alfred, Jr." in the *New Handbook of Texas*, vol. 3, 611. Hill was president of the board of trustees of the Museum of Fine Arts from 1934 to 1938 and was president of the board of trustees of the San Jacinto Museum of History from 1938 until his death. An ardent collector of Texana, he was the author of books and papers on issues relating to oil and gas as well as Texas history. He was a parishioner of Christ Church, a founding member of the Bayou Club, a member of the Tejas Club, and a member of the Texas Corinthian Yacht Club.

On Harry Clay Hanszen (1884–1950) see the J. T. McCants Collection in the Woodson Research Center, Fondren Library, Rice University, on members of the board of trustees and board of governors of Rice University. Hanszen was born in Jefferson County, Missouri. He was admitted to the University of Chicago in 1904 but dropped out in 1906 to seek his fortune in the Oklahoma oil fields. He became a scout for the Gypsy Oil Company of Tulsa, which was acquired by the Gulf Oil Corporation. Hanszen worked for Gulf in Texas, Louisiana, and Mexico and became a vice president of Gulf before resigning in 1921 to become an independent oil operator. Hanszen organized the Calcasieu Oil Company in Lake Charles, Louisiana, in 1926 but moved its headquarters to Houston. He was married twice, first to Katherine Bel, widow of James W. Gardiner, in 1929 and, following her death in 1942, to Alice Nicholson, the widow of Mike Hogg, in 1948. Hanszen was elected a trustee of the Rice Institute in 1942 and chairman of the board of trustees in 1946. He was a parishioner of Christ Church and a member of the Bayou Club, the Tejas Club, and the Eagle Lake Rod and Gun Club. Hanszen College at Rice University is named for him.

On Wallace E. Pratt (1885–1981) see *The New Encyclopedia of Texas*, vol. 1, 522; *Who Was Who in America*, vol. 7, 1977–81, 462; Larson and Porter, *History of Humble Oil and Refining Company*, 64–65, 88–89, 114–18, 335, 397–402; and Martin Donell Kohut, "Pratt, Wallace Everette," *New Handbook of Texas*, vol. 5, 318–19.

On Dolores Welder's family see Mrs. Patrick H. Welder's entries in the *New Handbook of Texas* on "Power, James," vol. 5, 306, and "Welder, James Francis," vol. 6, 874. Also Bill and Majorie K. Walraven, *Empresario's Children: The Welders of Texas*.

CHAPTER 8. REGIONALISM

1. Chillman, "The Architect and House: 7," 15–26. The other articles in this series were: Leon Keach, "The Architect and the House: 1—Royal Barry Wills, Small House Specialist," *Pencil Points* 18 (Feb. 1937): 65–80; Kenneth Reid, "The Architect and the House: 2—Randolph Evans of New York," *Pencil Points* 18 (Apr. 1937): 197–212; Kenneth Reid, "The Architect and the House: 3—William Wilson Wurster of California," *Pencil Points* 19 (Aug. 1938): 469–86; Paul R. Hunter, "The Architect and the House: 4—Roland E. Coate of Los Angeles," *Pencil Points* 20 (Oct. 1939): 625–40; S. B. Zisman, "The Architect and the House: 5—O'Neil Ford of Dallas, Texas," *Pencil Points* 21 (Apr. 1940): 195–210; Don Hatch, "The Architect and the House: 6—Don Hatch of New York," *Pencil Points*

22 (Oct. 1941): 617–32; Talbot F. Hamlin, "The Architect and the House: 8—Alden B. Dow of Michigan," *Pencil Points* 23 (Apr. 1942): 269–86.

2. On regionalism in architecture, see Vincent B. Canizaro, *Architectural Regionalism: Collected Writings on Place, Identity, Modernity, and Tradition.*

3. On David R. Williams (1890–1962) see Muriel Quest McCarthy, *David R. Williams: Pioneer Architect;* Michael Glen Wade, "David Reichard Williams: Avant-Garde Architect and Community Planner, 1890–1962"; and Wayne Gard, "Williams, David Reichard," *New Handbook of Texas,* vol. 6, 980. On Williams's most programmatically consistent regionalist house, the Elbert Williams House of 1932–33 in the Dallas suburb of University Park, Texas, see Violet Richardson, "Rambling Texas Home of Elbert Williams," *American Home* 13 (Jan. 1935): 70–72, and Wayne Gard, "The Ranch-House Goes to Town," *Better Homes and Gardens* 15 (June 1937): 32–33. Of his writings, see David R. Williams, "An Indigenous Architecture: Some Texas Colonial Houses," *Southwest Review* 14 (Oct. 1928): 60–74, and "Toward a Southwestern Architecture," *Southwest Review* 16 (Apr. 1931): 301–13.

4. Staub donated this collection of 130 snapshots to the Houston Metropolitan Research Center of the Houston Public Library. It is part of the Houston Metropolitan Research Center Photography Collection, Mss 114/404–534.

5. Peter C. Papademetriou, "Texas Transitions: Eclecticism, Regionalism, Modernism," paper presented at the Thirty-second Annual Meeting of the Society of Architectural Historians, 1979, 11, 13. On O'Neil Ford (1905–82), see Sam Zisman's profile in *Pencil Points*'s "The Architect and House" series (Apr. 1940) as well as Mary Carolyn Hollers George, *O'Neil Ford, Architect;* Mary Carolyn Hollers George, "Ford, O'Neil," *New Handbook of Texas,* vol. 2, 1074–75; and David Dillon, *The Architecture of O'Neil Ford: Celebrating Place.*

6. See Kenneth B. Ragsdale, *The Year America Discovered Texas: Centennial '36.* See also Paul Goeldner, *Texas Catalog: Historic American Buildings Survey,* 1–12; and on Dallas as a center of regionalist cultural ferment, Rick Stewart, *Lone Star Regionalism: The Dallas Nine and Their Circle, 1928–1945.*

7. The descriptive term "Texas farm house" was used in two reports on the construction of Staub's J. Coulter Means House: "Opening of Bids on Means Home Set for April 14," *Houston Post,* Apr. 5, 1936, section 1, 20; "Means Home Contract Let to Bertelsen," *Houston Post,* Apr. 19, 1936, section 4, 6. "Tom Scurry Builds $25,000 Residence," *Houston Post,* Aug. 2, 1936, section 1, 12. The Scurry House was described in the *Post*'s building report as being an example of "Early American architecture." Copy of undated typescript from John F. Staub's office: "Client, Cost, Comp. Date, Est. Cost."

8. On Tom Scurry (1898–1944) see Freeman, *People of Baker Botts,* 137, and Sam H. Acheson, Herbert P. Gambrell, Mary Carter Toomey and Alex M. Acheson Jr., eds., *Texan Who's Who: A Biographical Dictionary of the State of Texas,* vol. 1, 411.

9. On Scurry's father, see Claudia Hazlewood, "Scurry, Thomas," *Handbook of Texas,* vol. 5, 945–46; on his paternal grandfather, see L. W. Kemp, "Scurry, Richardson A.," *Handbook of Texas,* vol. 5, 945; and on his paternal grandfather's brother, for whom Scurry County was named, see Thomas W. Cutrer, "Scurry, William Read," *Handbook of Texas,* vol. 5, 946.

10. Barnstone, *Architecture of John F. Staub,* 206–207.

11. Goeldner, *Texas Catalog,* 121–22.

12. Barnstone, *Architecture of John F. Staub,* 207.

13. Copy of undated typescript from John F. Staub's office: "Client, Cost, Comp. Date, Est. Cost"; "Mr. and Mrs. J. M. Jennings' Home," *Houston Post,* June 26, 1938, section 2, 5. Mr. and Mrs. Jennings are first listed in the 1934 issue of the Houston City Directory. Jennings was district manager of the Bishop Oil Company, which was also first listed in 1934. Its offices were initially in the Niels Esperson Building, although by the time Mr. and Mrs. Jennings built their house, the company's offices had been moved to the Second National Bank Building.

14. Barnstone, *Architecture of John F. Staub,* 223–24.

15. For a succession of interpretations of the Larkin House, see Harold Kirker, *California's Architectural Frontier: Style and Tradition in the Nineteenth Century,* 16–22, and Mark L. Brack, "Domestic Architecture in Hispanic California: The Monterey Style Reconsidered," in *Perspectives in Vernacular Architecture IV,* ed. Thomas Carter and Bernard L. Herman, 163–73. Two early published examples of the twentieth-century neo-Monterey-type suburban country house were "Residence of Mr. and Mrs. Carlton B. Swift, Pasadena, California, Donald D. McMurry," *Architectural Record* 64 (Nov. 1928): 382–84, and "Where a Picketed Gateway Guards the Dooryard Path," *House and Garden* 57 (Jan. 1930): 67, illustrating the Cotton House in Montecito by Roland E. Coate, who became especially identified with the Monterey type. Coate designed two houses in Houston, both for Ben Clayton, W. L. Clayton's brother and business partner in Anderson, Clayton and Company.

16. On Lamar Fleming Jr. (1892–1964) see *Who Was Who in America,* vol. 4, 1961–68, 316; Lamar Fleming Jr., *Growth of the Business of Anderson, Clayton and Company,* ed. James A. Tinsley, vol. 10; and Douglas K. Fleming, *Thoughts of a Cotton Man: From Lamar Fleming's Collected Papers.*

17. Fleming, *Thoughts of a Cotton Man,* v.

18. Copy of undated typescript from John F. Staub's office: "Client, Cost, Comp. Date, Est. Cost"; and Barnstone, *Architecture of John F. Staub,* 210–11. In the Barnstone book, the year given for the design of the Fleming Summer House is incorrect.

19. Mark Odintz, "Kerr County" *New Handbook of Texas,* vol. 3, 1077–79.

20. Family members see the Mexican and immigrant British cultural influences of the area reflected in their parents' house. They especially remember the influence of the Gallagher Ranch Complex near Helotes, Texas, on their mother.

On Fredericksburg and its distinctive Texas-German vernacular architecture, see Samuel Gideon, "A Little German Town in the Lone Star State," *American Architect* 139 (Apr. 1931): 44–47. See also John Rutherford Bryant, "The European-Texan Buildings: Indigenous Building Traditions among the Nineteenth-Century European Immigrants to Texas." Of Fredericksburg, Bryant asserts: "Not only did the German-Texans continue traditional house types and adopt Anglo house types, but in the vicinity of Fredericksburg, Gillespie County, they developed an indigenous house type. This house type, the Sunday house, grew out of the changing patterns of living in the community of Fredericksburg" (p. 127).

21. Bryant observes the "shelves of rock" in the Hill Country landscape that are a prominent feature of the Fleming landscape (p. 45), as well as the predilection for "coursed ashlar limestone" construction (p. 111), and the "German-Texan story-and-a-half stone masonry house" (p. 115) in the areas where German immigrants established communities in the Hill Country. Bryant has entries on two houses that strongly recall aspects of the Fleming House's spatial organization, the Johannes Reugner House in Fredericksburg, which he dates to the mid-1850s (p. 100) and the Heinrich Hinmann House in New Braunfels, which he dates to about 1860 (pp. 121–25).

22. Staub to author.

23. Copy of undated typescript from John F. Staub's office: "Client, Cost, Comp. Date, Est. Cost"; Barnstone, *Architecture of John F. Staub,* 229–32; "Harrisons Plan Home on Lazy Lane," *Houston Post,* Mar. 6, 1938, section 5, 1; "$150,000 Home for Dan Harrison Is Nearing Completion," *Houston Post,* Aug. 13, 1939, section 2, 14; and Chillman, "The Architect and House: 7," 15.

24. Barnstone, *Architecture of John F. Staub,* 229, 231–32.

25. Nicholson, *Mr. Jim,* 256–58. On Daniel Jefferson Harrison (1879–1974) see Ellis Arthur Davis, ed., *Historical Encyclopedia of Texas,* vol. 1, 256.

26. Larson and Porter, *History of Humble Oil and Refining Company,* 402–403. Humble Oil's acquisition of an out-of-control well that Harrison and Abercrombie drilled in the Conroe oil field north of Houston

for $300,000 in 1932 was legendary; it demonstrated what set the wildcatters, who were prepared to take whatever advantage they could find, even in disaster, apart from the vertically integrated corporations, whose business was threatened by the uncontrolled pumping, whether this was done intentionally or as the result of an accident. On Old Ocean, see Nicholson, *Mr. Jim*, 269–72; Tinkle, *Mr. De*, 223; and Larson and Porter, *History of Humble Oil and Refining Company*, 410–11.

27. Nicholson, *Mr. Jim*, 273, 293–96.

28. Ibid., 296–301. Based on interviews with associates of Jim Abercrombie's, Patrick Nicholson characterized Harrison as honest and deliberate, aggressive in his business practices, yet respected for his trustworthiness and knowledge. Don Carleton indicated in his biography of J. R. Parten that Harrison was extremely conservative. He was one of the independent oilmen who supported Parten's efforts to defeat or at least moderate prorationing practices. He and Parten had very different attitudes—and operating styles—when it came to their service as regents of the University of Texas, to which both were dedicated, in the 1930s. See Nicholson, *Mr. Jim*, 256–57, and Carleton, *A Breed So Rare*, 110, 116, 242–49.

29. *Social Register of Houston* 1950, 58. Nicholson remarked that Mr. and Mrs. Harrison were supporters of the Houston Symphony Orchestra. Nicholson, *Mr. Jim*, 296.

30. Mary Uhrbrock, "A Natural Legacy," *Houston Home and Garden* 12 (Nov. 1985): 84–89.

31. Mrs. Birdsall P. Briscoe, "Trails and Trails," 26; Stevenson, "Seventh Annual Azalea Trail," 36; "Beautiful Gardens of Houston Opened to Public in Early March," *Houston* 18 (Feb. 1946): 6–7.

32. Barnstone, *Architecture of John F. Staub*, 269.

33. Copy of undated typescript from John F. Staub's office: "Client, Cost, Comp. Date, Est. Cost"; and Barnstone, *Architecture of John F. Staub*, 233–36; "Wray Residence," *Houston Post*, Apr.10, 1938, section 2, 12; "Contract Awarded for 12-Room House," *Houston Post* Apr. 24, 1938, section 2, 9; and Chillman, "The Architect and House: 7," 26.

34. See the biographical entry on Wray in Ann Hitchcock Holmes, *Joy Unconfined: Robert Joy in Houston: A Portrait of Fifty Years*, 142; "Insurance 'Pedlar' Andrew J. Wray Dies," *Houston Post*, Mar. 22, 1981, D6; and "Deaths: Margaret Cullinan Wray," *Houston Post*, Sept. 23, 1985, B5. Johnston, *Houston: The Unknown City*, 225.

35. The June 1948 issue of *Antiques* magazine was devoted to Texas. The editor, Alice Winchester, constructed a detailed historical narrative of Texas history materialized in prints, drawings, paintings, and photographs of buildings, furniture, and other artifacts that captures the New Deal–era Regionalist vision in a very imaginative way. See the sequence of sections in *Antiques* 53 (June 1948): 436–72.

CHAPTER 9. THE CONTEMPORARY AND THE PALLADIAN

1. Barnstone, *Architecture of John F. Staub*, 48.

2. In defining the postwar contemporary architectural trend and distinguishing it from modern, Barnstone quotes a line of advice from *House+Home*, a magazine published for the house-building industry: "'Modern' usually means something bad to homebuyers. If they like a modern house, they probably call it 'Contemporary'"; "18 Ways to Get Marketable Design: Advice Number 7, Don't Believe What Your Buyers Say about Style," *House+Home* 12 (Sept. 1957): 109. The term "contemporary" was broadly applied. What tended to set contemporary houses in Houston apart from modern architecture was the application of "contemporary" design themes as decoration rather than as a tectonic discipline.

Two expansive contemporary houses in Houston designed by southern Californian architects were publicized locally. One was the house of the Swiss immigrants Liesel and Gerhard Herzog in Braeswood, completed in 1952 and designed by the Beverly Hills architect Paul László. See Mary Ellen Preusser, "West Coast Architect Designs Special Home for Houstonians," *Houston Post*, Mar. 15, 1953, section 6, 1. The other was a weekend house, completed in 1959 in what is now the Quail Valley subdivision in Missouri City, Texas, for Patricia Welder and Hampton C. Robinson. It was designed by the Palm Springs architect William F. Cody. See "Houstonians Live in Desert Style," *Houston Post* Sept. 18, 1960, section 7, 1.

See also John Kaliski, "The Wright Stuff: Houston's Natural House," *Cite: The Architecture and Design Review of Houston* (fall 1984): 16–18.

3. "Prospective Work," *Texas General Contractors Association Monthly Bulletin* 17 (July 1936): 10; Michael E. Wilson, ed., *Harvin C. Moore, Houston Architect: A Catalogue of Drawings by Harvin C. Moore in the Houston Public Library/Houston Metropolitan Research Center*, 18, 24

4. Barnstone, *Architecture of John F. Staub*, 216–19; copy of undated typescript from John F. Staub's office: "Client, Cost, Comp. Date, Est. Cost"; "Recently Completed Straus Home," *Houston Post*, Nov. 28, 1937, section 3, 1; "Contemporary Classic," *River Oaks Magazine*, Mar. 1940, 12–15; "Houses with Two Bedrooms: House Fronts on Garden," *Architectural Record* 87 (May 1940): 60–61.

5. Diane Stafford, "Design in Retrospect: Harking Back to the Good Old Days of Design in Houston," *Houston Home and Garden* 14 (Oct. 1987): 77; "Residential Details: Recreational: 1. John F. Staub, Architect," *Architectural Record* 89 (Apr. 1941): 65.

6. "On the Periphery of Houston, People Lead Leisured, Charming Lives," *House and Garden* 97 (Mar. 1950): 96–99.

7. "Large Home Is Planned in Briar Hollow," *Houston Post*, Sept. 24, 1950, section 2, 2; Mrs. Straus to author.

8. R. D. Straus, "Industry's Pioneer Air Conditioner," *Houston* 6 (June 1935): 7; "Modernize Your Business with Carrier Weathermakers," *Houston* 5 (July 1934): 10; and "Manufactured Weather," *Houston* 4 (Aug. 1933): 12. On Robert D. Straus (1907–82) see the brief obituary notice "Straus," *Houston Post*, Sept. 18, 1982, 39E.

Straus stood out in one other respect: he was one of a handful of Jewish residents of River Oaks before the 1960s. In addition to Straus, I. H. Kempner Jr., Lillie Frank Abercrombie, and Maurice Hirsch lived in River Oaks; each was Jewish but married to a spouse who was not. George S. Cohen, president of Houston's major department store, Foley Brothers, lived in Montrose but owned two large adjoining lots on Inwood Drive backing up to the country club. Cohen never sold the lots but never built on them either, because, it is presumed, he was concerned about retaliation against Foley's. In the memorandums that Hugh Potter sent Will Hogg, he noted in May 1927 a conflict with George Cohen, which Potter attributed to Cohen's resentment over a slight he received at the River Oaks Country Club (Cohen was a charter member). One of Cohen's lots was not built on until the 1980s, the other until the early 2000s. Hugh Potter to Will C. Hogg, May 15, 1927, William Clifford Hogg Papers, Center for American History, University of Texas at Austin. William S. Worley notes that the issues of who, and how, to exclude was one that elite community developers discussed among themselves. Discrimination against Jewish property purchasers was widely practiced. Worley, *J. C. Nichols and the Shaping of Kansas City*, 148–53.

9. The air-conditioning issues of *Houston* magazine from the early 1930s contained lists of installations in Houston. The Hugh Roy Cullen House was the only Staub-designed house to be identified as air-conditioned (with a system by the York Air Cooling Division of the York Ice Machinery Corporation). See the York ad and list in *Houston* 5 (Aug. 1934): 2. Staub's alterations and additions to the Wiess House, which included installation of central air-conditioning, do not appear in these lists. Precisely when air-conditioning became available is difficult to detect from nationally circulated publications. A three-page advertisement for the Carrier-Lyle Corporation in *House and Garden* in 1930 uses the term "air-conditioning" but seems to mean central heating, noting that a "cooling unit [is] now under development." See "And Now They're Making Weather in Homes," *House and Garden* 57 (Jan. 1930): 27–29. An advertisement for the Carrier Weathermaker system (61 [Jan. 1932]: 77) implied that it was a heating system exclusively. Not until 1935 was an

article called "House and Garden Presents Air-Conditioning" published (8 [Aug. 1935]: 57–62).

10. Cheryl A. Brutvan with Marti Mayo and Linda L. Cathcart, *In Our Time: Houston's Contemporary Arts Museum, 1948–1982*, 9, 11. Both Carol and Bob Straus served on the first board of trustees of the Contemporary Arts Association; Mrs. Straus was instrumental in recruiting John de Menil as a trustee.

11. The Straus House is similar in conception to Lindeberg's Mrs. R. Boyer Miller House in Grosse Pointe, Michigan, of 1935, which does not seem to have been published until 1940, when it was illustrated in *Domestic Architecture by H. T. Lindeberg*, 31–36. The entrance front of the Miller House is very abstract, but the garden elevation is conventionally neo-Georgian.

12. The photograph of the Straus House published in the real estate section of the *Houston Post* on November 28, 1937, shows that shrubs had been planted to screen the garage doors but that they were not yet thick enough to do so.

13. Barnstone, *Architecture of John F. Staub*, 218.

14. "On the Periphery of Houston," 99.

15. Photographs of the house published in *River Oaks Magazine* in 1940 show the dining room with its English Sheraton table and chairs but no other interiors and no Robsjohn-Gibbings furniture. Kertész's photographs in *House and Garden*, published ten years later, show the same table and chairs in the dining room. The *House and Garden* article credits Robsjohn-Gibbings with the design of the living room and library. On T. H. Robsjohn-Gibbings (1905–76) see "Robsjohn-Gibbings: Twenty-Five Years of His Work," *Interiors* 32 (May 1961): 122–31, and "T. H. Robsjohn-Gibbings, 1905–1976," *Interiors* 136 (Jan. 1977): 6.

16. The recreation house was published in both "Contemporary Classic," 12–15, and "Residential Details: Recreational," *Architectural Record* 89 (Apr. 1941): 65.

17. The major U.S. architectural magazines during the 1930s—*American Architect*, *Architectural Forum*, *Architectural Record*, and *Pencil Points*—implicitly constructed new models of upper-income domesticity that, in contrast to the 1920s, could be dialectically framed as "casual." Coverage of new residential construction in Miami Beach (which had not figured prominently in the national architectural press in the 1920s, despite the building boom of the first half of the 1920s) and Miami, as well as the Bel-Air and Brentwood districts in Los Angeles, codified an upper-income alternative to the Georgian and American Colonial historical models that were also popular in the 1930s. See especially Jean-François Lejeune and Allan T. Shulman, *The Making of Miami Beach, 1933–1942: The Architecture of Lawrence Murray Dixon*.

18. "Contemporary Classic," 14.

19. "Thirteen Years of Fair-Building Reviewed in Current Exhibit," *Architectural Record* 80 (July 1936): 3.

20. "Open Planned, Window-Walled House in the Southwest," *Architectural Record* 85 (May 1939): 111.

21. "MacKie and Kamrath Open Office Here," *Houston Post*, Jan. 24, 1937, section 2, 6; Scott Reagan Miller, "The Architecture of MacKie and Kamrath"; Nory Miller, "Lone Stars—Howard Barnstone and Karl Kamrath," *Inland Architect* 21 (June 1977): 16–17; Gary McKay, "Karl Kamrath: Shaping the City's Character," *Houston Home and Garden* 8 (Jan. 1982): 18–24; Steven R. Strom, ed., *MacKie and Kamrath Architects: Guide to the Architectural Collection*. On Frederick James MacKie Jr. (1905–84) and Karl Kamrath (1911–88) see "Kamrath, Karl Fred," *New Handbook of Texas*, vol. 3, 1028, and Gerald Moorhead, "MacKie and Kamrath," *Texas Architect* 39 (Nov.–Dec. 1989): 62–63.

22. "Portfolio—Houses in Controlled Developments: Texas, River Oaks, Houston, MacKie and Kamrath, Architects," *Architectural Record* 88 (Nov. 1940): 60–61; "House for Jesse R. Stone, Houston, Texas, MacKie and Kamrath, Architects," *Architectural Forum* 73 (Dec. 1940): 520; "Fire Alarm Building," *Architectural Forum* 73 (Dec. 1940): 521–22; "Printing Plant," *Architectural Record* 90 (July 1941): 52–53; "War Needs—Housing: Houston, Texas," *Architectural Record* 91 (Apr. 1942): 47–50; "Project Center Building," *Architectural Record* 91 (May 1942): 52–53; "House for an Unusual Lot in Houston, MacKie and Kamrath, Architects," *Architectural Record* 92 (Nov. 1942): 50–51; "House in Houston, Texas, MacKie and Kamrath, Architects," *Architectural Forum* 78 (Feb. 1943): 61; "Good Sight-Lines in 960-Seat Theater," *Architectural Record* 95 (June 1944): 100; "Dental Clinic for a Hot Climate," *Architectural Record* 96 (July 1944): 78–80; "Efficiency Units for Texas" and "Industrial Housing for Texas," *Architectural Record* 99 (May 1946): 86–87.

23. "Three Dimensional Freedom," *River Oaks Magazine*, Nov. 1939, 14–16; "House for Karl Kamrath, Houston, Texas, MacKie and Kamrath, Architects," *Architectural Forum* 73 (Dec. 1940): 518–19.

24. "Ultra Modern Home Planned by Major J. R. Parten," *Houston Post*, Feb. 19, 1939, section 2, 8. The Parten House was demolished in 1988.

25. "Parten House," in Writers' Program of the Works Projects Administration in the State of Texas, *Houston: A History and Guide*, illustrations: section 2, following p. 52; James Ford and Katherine Morrow Ford, *Designs of Modern Interiors*, 32, 61, 83; Carleton, *A Breed So Rare*, 106–108, 146. Carleton does not mention construction of the Tall Timbers house in his biography of Parten.

26. "With Record Readers: Houston Citizens Vote on Recent Buildings," *Architectural Record* 86 (Nov. 1939): 12, 14. Between August 1939 and April 1941, *Architectural Record* conducted polls of "leading citizens" in seventeen U.S. cities to identify the most highly regarded new buildings in each city. In Houston, the eight buildings that received the greatest number of votes from the twenty-four jurors were modern in the sense that none was based on historical models. Most would now be categorized as modernistic rather than modernist, with the exception of MacKie and Kamrath's City of Houston Fire Alarm Building. Staub and Franzheim's Lamar Senior High School ranked fourth among the eight buildings selected. No houses were chosen by the Houston panel except as honorable mentions, and these were not illustrated. Staub's Hamill and Harrison Houses received honorable mentions, as did other examples of Houston architecture based on historical models.

27. Barnstone, *Architecture of John F. Staub*, 225–28, 324; copy of undated typescript from John F. Staub's office: "Client, Cost, Comp. Date, Est. Cost." On Donald Barthelme (1907–96) see Ben Koush, *Donald Barthelme: A Modernism Suitable for Everyday Use, 1939–1945*; Stephen James, "Donald Barthelme: Architecture and the Road to La Mancha," *Arris: Journal of the Southeast Chapter of the Society of Architectural Historians* 16 (2005): 56–68; Frederick Bartheme and Steven Barthelme, *Double Down: Reflections on Gambling and Loss*; Jan M. O'Brien and Stephen Fox, "Participants in Architecture: A Donald Barthelme Sampler," *Cite 35: The Architecture and Design Review of Houston* (Fall 1996): 8–11; Yolita Schmidt, "Donald Barthelme," *Texas Architect* 39 (Nov.–Dec. 1989): 44; and George S. Koyl, ed., *American Architects Directory*, 28 (1956); 37 (1962); and John F. Gane, ed., *American Architects Directory*, 47 (1970). The Donald Barthelme Papers are deposited in the Special Collections of the University of Houston Library.

28. The Bosworth Bay Cottage does not appear in the list of buildings Staub compiled around 1940 although L. S. Bosworth's name is included in an alphabetical typescript labeled "List of Clients" on which the date 9-28-38 is handwritten. Mr. and Mrs. Bosworth's grandson, W. Oscar Neuhaus III, is the source for its attribution to Staub, as is *The Texas Corinthian Yacht Club* (p. 99), which describes the house as being patterned on a capitol building of the Republic of Texas. This was probably the provisional capitol constructed in Austin in 1839. A one-story shingled clubhouse Staub designed for the Houston Riding and Polo Club (built in 1925 and now demolished) and Rather's house for Mr. and Mrs. Don Riddle of 1942 (also demolished) were quite similar to the Bosworth Bay Cottage. On the Austin capitol building see Seymour V. Connor, James M. Day, Billy Mac Jones, Dayton Kelley, W. C. Nunn, Ben Procter, and Dorman H. Winfrey, *Capitols of Texas*, 84–86. On the Riddle

House, see "4: If You Have No Maid, Gear Your House to a Well-Defined Routine," *House and Garden* 100 (Aug. 1951): 32.

On J. T. Rather's house see "In This House, Ventilating Equipment Fans up a Breeze," *House and Garden* 99 (May 1951): 134–35.

On the "ranch house" house type see Alan Hess, *The Ranch House;* Katherine Ann Samon, *Ranch House Style;* and Virginia McAlester and Lee McAlester, *A Field Guide to American Houses*, 474–80. In his article on David Williams's Elbert Williams House in *Better Homes and Gardens* in 1937, Wayne Gard included a list of ranch-type houses in Dallas, with addresses and architects. Gard, "The Ranch House Goes to Town," 67. *River Oaks Magazine* published an illustrated feature on a one-story house that it characterized as a "California" house rather than a "ranch house." See "Sweet and Low," *River Oaks Magazine* 2 (Apr. 1939): 16–17.

29. "E. L. Crain Announces Opening of Large New Subdivision," *Houston Post*, June 27, 1937, section 4, 6; "Welcome to Garden Oaks," photographic brochure complied by the Garden Oaks Company, c. 1940, unpaginated. I am grateful to Ben Koush for supplying me with a copy of this brochure.

"Garden Villas Has Ranch House Type Furnished Home," *Houston Post*, Aug. 8, 1926, Real Estate and Building section, 2. The opening paragraphs of the article characterized this new type:

> The Garden Villas furnished home is an unusual type, inasmuch as the living room runs clear through the center portion of the house, the living quarters being on the west side and the sleeping rooms on the east.
>
> However, this type of house traces its beginning to some of the oldest architectural types in the state. It is merely an improved and modernized version of the old ranch houses which were built primarily for comfort, convenience, and ventilation. These log houses were usually built with two rooms, a kitchen and a sleeping room—each the length of a log. These were joined in the center by a porch which served for the protection of the saddles and bridles. Later this porch became a living room.
>
> This type of house, facing the breeze, forms today one of the most practical houses for the Texas climate. It is closely allied with many Spanish plans. In fact, practically every warm zone has a variation of this type of house.

The photograph of the Garden Villas demonstration house accompanying the article illustrated a U-plan house (as it faced the street) with steeply pitched roofs and minimal Craftsman detailing. The long dimension of the house paralleled the street. Rather than the Houston bungalow arrangement of two parallel files of rooms, this house interposed a central living room with exposure at the front and back between the two files of rooms, which the article likened to the dogtrot of a double-pen log house. This diagram reappeared in the one-story Garden Oaks houses of the late 1930s and early 1940s, although the Garden Oaks houses typically incorporated a one-car garage or carport in one of the flanking files of rooms.

30. The Houston journalist George Fuermann, in his book *Houston: Land of the Big Rich*, published in 1951, wrote, "Architecturally, the Shamrock's exterior has one thing in common with too much Houston architecture: it is about as exciting as watching a blade of grass grow," Fuermann, *Houston: Land of the Big Rich*, 77. Karl Kamrath, "Architectural Impressions," in *Houston: Text by Houstonians*, 10; Kathleen Bland, "Glass House Builder Expounds on Ideas," *Houston Post*, Jan. 11, 1950, section 2, 1.

31. Brutvan, *In Our Time*, 6, 9–11; "Triangular Steel Framework," *Architectural Forum* 93 (Sept. 1950): 137.

32. Brutvan, *In Our Time*, 84; Ben Koush, "Houston Lives the Life: Modern Houses in the Suburbs, 1952–1962," 85–86. Koush points out that the CAA's Modern House Tour was paralleled by the Houston Home Builders Association's annual Parade of Homes, beginning in 1955. On the Case Study program, see *Blueprints for Modern Living: History and Legacy of the Case Study Houses*, organized by Elizabeth A. T. Smith.

33. The Menils' "disruptive" challenge (the term is Pamela Smart's) to the modernist status quo in Houston was first played out in the internal politics of the Contemporary Arts Association over the issue of whether it should be operated cooperatively by members or directed by a professional curator (the latter being the Menil preference). See Brutvan, *In Our Time*, 14, 22–23, 26–28.

34. On Dominique Schlumberger (1908–97) and John de Menil (1904–73) see Smart, "Sacred Modern"; Calvin Tomkins, "The Benefactor," *New Yorker* 74 (June 8, 1998): 52–67; Howard Barnstone, "Obit: John de Menil," *Architecture Plus* 1 (Aug. 1973): 71; "De Menil, John," *Who's Who in America*, vol. 38, 1974–75, 773; Linda Peterson, "Menil, John de," *New Handbook of Texas*, vol. 5, 621; Jon Kutner Jr., "Schlumberger," *New Handbook of Texas*, vol. 5, 921–22; "De Menil, Dominique," *Who's Who in America*, vol. 38–1, 1974–75, 773; Ann Holmes, "Dominique de Menil: From Jeune Fille to 'Renaissance Woman,'" *Art News* 82 (Jan. 1983): 80–85; Dominique Browning, "What I Admire, I Must Possess," *Texas Monthly* 11 (Apr. 1983): 140–47; Grace Glueck, "The De Menil Family: The Medici of Modern Art," *New York Times Magazine*, May 18, 1986, 28–46; William A. Camfield, "Dominique de Menil, 1908–1997," *Cite 40: The Architecture and Design Review of Houston* (winter 1997–98): 10–11.

35. "Imported Tile Floors for De Menil Home," *Houston Post*, June 26, 1949, section 2, 3; "Bids Taken for Large 1-Story Home," *Houston Post*, July 17, 1949, section 2, 13; "Art Collection and Home of the John de Menils in Houston's River Oaks," *Interiors* 123 (Nov. 1963): 84–91; James Johnson Sweeney, "Collectors' Home: In the John de Menil House A Great Ranging Art Collection," *Vogue* 147 (Apr. 1, 1966): 184–91; Mark Hewitt, "Neoclassicism and Modern Architecture, Houston Style: Or the Domestication of Mies," *Cite: The Architecture and Design Review of Houston* (Fall 1984): 12; Pilar Viladas, "They Did It Their Way," *New York Times Magazine*, Oct. 10, 1999, 85–94; Stover Jenkins and David Mohney, *The Houses of Philip Johnson*, 56–57; Richard Payne, *The Architecture of Philip Johnson*, 46–47; William Middleton, "A House that Rattled Texas Windows," *New York Times*, June 3, 2004, F1. Frank D. Welch, *Philip Johnson and Texas*, 34–60.

36. On Charles James and his contributions to the design of the Menil House, see Elizabeth Ann Coleman, *The Genius of Charles James* "Art Collection and Home of the John de Menils in Houston's River Oaks," 84–91; Viladas, "They Did It Their Way," 85–94; and Middleton, "A House that Rattled Texas Windows."

37. On the Menil's formation as collectors see Smart, "Sacred Modern," 38–166, and Tomkins, "The Benefactor," 56, 58.

38. Colin Rowe, "Neo-'Classicism' and Modern Architecture I," in *Mathematics of the Ideal Villa*, 120. Rowe had been pivotal in introducing Palladio into the discourse of postwar modern architecture with the essay from which this collection takes its title, written in 1947.

39. On Hugo Victor Neuhaus Jr., (1915–87) see Anderson Todd, "Hugo V. Neuhaus, Jr., 1915–1987," *Cite: The Architecture and Design Review of Houston* (Winter 1987): 19–20; "Neuhaus, Hugo Victor, Jr.," *New Handbook of Texas*, vol. 4, 982; Welch, *Philip Johnson and Texas*, 47, 51; and George S. Koyl, ed., *American Architects Directory*, 403 (1956); 512 (1962); and John F. Gane, ed., *American Architects Directory*, 663 (1970).

40. "Residence for Mr. and Mrs. Neuhaus," *Houston Post*, Feb. 12, 1950, section 2, 4; Marguerite Johnston, "The Home on Lazy Lane," *Houston Post*, Mar. 30, 1952. "Texas Living" supplement, 5–7; "Roman House," *House+Home* 2 (July 1952): 67–73; "In Texas, an Air-Conditioned Villa," *House and Garden* 105 (Feb. 1954): 50–53; and Hewitt, "Neoclassicism and Modern Architecture," 12–15.

41. On Barnstone, see Stephen Fox, "Howard Barnstone, 1923–1987," *Cite: The Architecture and Design Review of Houston* (Fall 1987): 18–21; "Barnstone, Howard," *New Handbook of Texas*, vol. 1, 388–89; George S. Koyl, ed., *American Architects Directory*, 27 (1956), 35 (1962); and Welch

Philip Johnson and Texas, 51–52. On Burdette Keeland (1926–2000) see Joe Mashburn, "Burdette Keeland Remembered," *Cite 48: The Architecture and Design Review of Houston* (summer 2000): 9; and Welch, *Philip Johnson and Texas*, 54–55, 61. On Anderson Todd see George S. Koyl, ed., *American Architects Directory*, 707 (1962); John F. Gane, ed., *American Architects Directory*, 921 (1970); *Who's Who in America*, vol. 2, 1992–93, 3361; and Welch, *Philip Johnson and Texas*, 52.

42. Rowe, "Neo-'Classicism' and Modern Architecture I," 120–21, 124–25, 134.

43. "Forecast '58," *House and Garden* 113 (Jan. 1958): 29, 37.

44. *The Museum of Fine Arts, Houston: An Architectural History, 1924–1986*, 66. On Nina Cullinan (1896–1983) see Carol Brown, "Cullinan, Nina J.," *New Handbook of Texas*, vol. 2, 440; and Anderson Todd, "Nina J. Cullinan, 1896–1983," *Cite: The Architecture and Design Review of Houston* (Spring 1983): 3.

45. *The Museum of Fine Arts, Houston*, 66, 68, 90–96, 100–103; Dore Ashton, "Sweeney Revisited," *Studio International* 845 166 (Sept. 1963): 110–13; Dore Ashton, "Commentary from Houston and New York," *Studio International* 873 17 (Jan. 1966): 40–42; "Two Ways of Looking at Art in Houston: I. The Museum of Fine Arts," *Interiors* 123 (Nov. 1963): 92–95; and Lynn M. Herbert, "Seeing Was Believing: Installations of Jermayne MacAgy and James Johnson Sweeney," *Cite 40: The Architecture and Design Review of Houston* (winter 1997–98): 30–33.

46. *The Museum of Fine Arts, Houston*, 76, 83–84. Anderson Todd, "Recollections: Reasons for the Choice," *Texas Architect* 29 (Nov.–Dec. 1979): 54.

47. Rowe begins his essay with the observation: "The Miesian and the Palladian: for some time in certain circles these epithets have been almost synonymous, and now that we are no longer shocked by their juxtaposition; and no longer even shocked by our lack of shock, one might well ask what larger issues are subtended by this little semantic revolution. . . ." Rowe, "Neo-'Classicism' and Modern Architecture I," 120.

48. Philip Johnson's explication of the formal sources for the design of his Glass House and Guest House in New Canaan, Connecticut, of 1949—written in 1950—pairs Mies and classicism. Examples: "The site relation of my house is pure Neo-Classic Romantic. . . ." "The guest house, with Baroque plan central corridor and three symmetrically placed rooms, was derived from Mies' designs. The three round windows in the rear of the façade are a Renaissance approach to a Miesian motif." "The guest house with central door and severely axial plan is jointly descended from the Baroque and from designs by Mies." Philip Johnson, "House at New Canaan, Connecticut," in *Philip Johnson*, ed. Whitney and Kipnis, 11, 12, 14.

In his introduction to the catalogue of the Contemporary Arts Museum's exhibition *Ten Years of Houston Architecture*, organized by Howard Barnstone and Burdette Keeland and displayed in March–April 1959, Henry-Russell Hitchcock wrote: "Mies's new wing of the Museum of Fine Arts, completed like the first units of the University of St. Thomas last year, brings up again the word 'classic.' . . . As everyone is aware the 'classic' easily becomes the 'academic' and in some hands the Miesian has already shown the signs of becoming the latter. But in the new portion of the museum Mies himself, while reverting to the symmetry and axiality usually associated with the academic—as, for example, in the older building of the museum here—has by the means of the directness of his structural expression . . . and in the elegance of his proportions continued the classicism of all his late work." Henry-Russell Hitchcock, "Introduction," *Ten Years of Houston Architecture*.

49. Frank Lloyd Wright's Usonian house type, formulated in the early 1930s, is the best-known American modernist house type that sought to provide a sense of spaciousness in a compact house by rigorously rationalizing interior planning, especially with respect to the kitchen, the corridor, the bathroom, and closets.

50. See the exhibition catalogue *Design in America: The Cranbrook Vision, 1925–1950*, especially the essays by Robert Judson Clark, "Cranbrook and the Search for Twentieth-Century Form," 20–33; David De Long, "Eliel Saarinen and the Cranbrook Tradition in Architecture and Urban Design," 46–89; and R. Craig Miller, "Interior Design and Furniture," 90–143.

51. Barnstone, *Architecture of John F. Staub*, 269–71.

52. "Residence 1207 Bids Due," *AGC News Service*, Sept. 16, 1952, 8; "Miller Awarded Residence 1207," *AGC News Service*, Nov. 11, 1952, 3.

53. Examining American cultural criticism of the 1950s, Jackson Lears observed, "A preoccupation with taste spread across the political spectrum; sometimes it seemed as if the chief issue dividing the 'Left' and 'Right' was whether all those concert goers really liked Verdi or not—whether refined aesthetic perceptions were trickling down among the mass of the population or whether the media's least-common-denominator approach was mixing 'the sacred and the profane, the genuine and the specious,' into 'a single slushy compost.' Even the sharpest critics seemed to define dissent in terms of taste. For Marcuse, by the 1960s, the sole escape from 'one-dimensional society' was *The Aesthetic Dimension*—the title of a book he published in 1968." Jackson Lears, "A Matter of Taste: Corporate Cultural Hegemony in a Mass-Consumption Society," in *Recasting America: Culture and Politics in the Age of Cold War*, ed. Lary May, 48.

54. Barnstone, *Architecture of John F. Staub*, 274–77; "Living with Antiques: The House of Mr. and Mrs. Harris Masterson, Houston, Texas," *Antiques* 109 (Apr. 1976): 742–49.

55. *Rienzi: The Museum of Fine Arts, Houston*.

56. John F. Staub to Harris Masterson, Mar. 18, 1952, Harris Masterson III Papers 1892–1980, Woodson Research Center, Fondren Library, Rice University.

57. The website of the Museum of Fine Arts, Houston, contains Katherine Howe's history of the property at <http://www.mfah.org/rienzi/main.asp?target=about&par1=2>.

58. *Who's Who in the South and Southwest*, vol. 9 (1965), 598; *Masterson and Allied Families: A Genealogical Study with Biographical Notes*, compiled by the American Historical Company.

59. Brochure of the Work of William Ward Watkin.

60. Harris Masterson was first listed in the 1930–31 issue of the Houston City Directory, when he was sixteen years old. He was first listed as employed in the 1936 edition, when he was a junior customer salesman for A. E. Pierce and Company, stock and bond brokers. He was first listed in the 1947 city directory after returning from military service as a representative of the American General Insurance Company. In the 1949 directory, he was listed as owner of an antiques store in the River Oaks Shopping Center.

61. *Masterson and Allied Families*, 25; Johnston, *Happy Worldly Abode*, 206. During the Korean Conflict, Masterson served in the U.S. Army at the rank of captain and was stationed at the Army General School in Fort Riley, Kansas. Much of the correspondence between Masterson and Staub in the Harris Masterson III Papers is addressed to Masterson at Fort Riley.

62. The photograph of the front elevation of Rienzi by F. Wilbur Seiders published in *Architecture of John F. Staub* shows one of Masterson's early 1950s Cadillacs parked outside the dining room window.

63. Barnstone, *Architecture of John F. Staub*, 284–85, 292–93, 309–11.

64. Ibid., 289–91.

65. In 1948 MacKie and Kamrath designed the "House of Expanding Rooms," a demonstration house constructed by the Revere Quality House Institute in Frank W. Sharp's Oak Forest subdivision, that spatialized the middle-income-family subject positions constructed in the immediate postwar period as "modern," "American," and "suburban." The emphasis on spatial flexibility on which MacKie and Kamrath's design was premised was not lost on the builders of much larger houses. See "Houses: Architect-Builder Team Shows Houston How to Design and Build a Good House for under $15,000," *Architectural Forum* 89 (Sept. 1948): 125–27. By the mid-1950s, *Fortune* magazine noted in an article titled "The $250,000 House" a trend in the opposite direction: "Rich Americans have begun to build big expensive houses once again. Dur-

ing all the years of the great depression and the war that followed, very few people could afford either to build or live as they had in the twenties." Admitting that an expensive house of the 1950s did not begin to compare in size or cost to the grand country houses of the Stately Home era, the *Fortune* article observed the popularity of what it described as "modern or contemporary design" for such houses. The examples illustrated included Staub and Rather's River Oaks house for Mr. and Mrs. Dunbar N. Chambers of 1949–50 (a Rather design), Wiley Vale's contemporary extravaganza for Lois Plummer and Herbert Townsend in River Oaks, Ted Weiner's modern house in the Ridglea section of Fort Worth by the New York architect Edward L. Barnes (highlighting a site-specific sculpture installation by Mary Callery), a house in Dallas by the architect-decorator Earl Hart Miller, and the radical remodeling of a house in Lake Forest by David Adler for the Texan-descended Mrs. Clive Runnells. "The $250,000 House," *Fortune* 52 (Oct. 1955): 133–42.

66. The inclusion of a second living room, the family room, in new Houston houses became an increasingly standard feature during the course of the 1950s. *House&Home* magazine frequently reported on Houston suburban development and the Houston housing market in the 1950s. *House&Home*'s report on the annual Parade of Homes noted as a trend that family rooms in Houston houses built for the 1958 Parade of Homes had become larger than living rooms. "Just Looking? No, They're Buying, Too," *House&Home* 14 (July 1958): 123.

67. "Elkins Residence Contract Awarded," *AGC News Service*, Aug.12, 1958, 8.

68. On James A. Elkins Jr. (1919–2006) see "James Anderson Elkins, Jr." *Houston Chronicle*, Feb. 23, 2006, 5B; Clark and Scott, *Texas Gulf Coast*, 8; *Who's Who in America*, vol. 1, 1982–83 (1982), 942; Buenger and Pratt, *But Also Good Business*, 174–75, 188–89, 193; and Pratt and Castañeda, *Builders*, 162–63.

69. Nicholas Lemann, "The Architects," *Texas Monthly* 10 (Apr. 1982): 219–20; Carol Herselle Krinsky, *Gordon Bunshaft of Skidmore, Owings and Merrill*, 70–72.

70. "Tripartite Scheme for Bank, Office Building, and Garage," *Architectural Record* 129 (Apr. 1961): 155–64; Skidmore, Owings and Merrill, *The Architecture of Skidmore, Owings and Merrill, 1950–1962*, 152–57; and Kevin Alter, "SOM in Houston," *Cite 40: The Architecture and Design Review of Houston* (Winter 1997–98): 34–37.

71. "Building: The New Face of Texas," *Fortune* 64 (Oct. 1961): 131. The unsigned article, probably by Walter McQuade, was effusive in its praise of the modern architecture being built in Texas. "If the quality of what men build on the face of the earth is an index to their civilization, then Texans are fast becoming the most civilized people in the U.S. For the new architecture of Texas is one of the most remarkable features in a great, statewide renaissance that takes in such other phenomena as first-rate theater, first-rate symphony orchestras, and magnificent and courageous collections of avant-garde painting and sculpture" (p. 30). On Houston as a "new" city, see "Houston: Boomingest Town in the U.S.," *Newsweek*, June 11, 1962, 78–80; "The Air-Conditioned Metropolis," *Time*, Apr. 12, 1963, 26–27; and "Houston Wins Its Big City Spurs," *Business Week*, Nov. 19, 1966, 130–34.

72. Barnstone, *Architecture of John F. Staub*, 52, 298–99.

73. Aldrich, *Old Money*, 83.

74. These were the contradictions that Rowe externalized in his pair of essays "Neo-'Classicism' and Modern Architecture" I and II. The second of the two is also published in *The Mathematics of the Ideal Villa and Other Essays*, 140–58. Neither was published until 1973.

75. As with the links between Surrealism and architecture and interior design, so the links between interior decoration and architecture have not been explored, in part, one suspects, because architects tend not to respect the contributions of interior designers to design projects in which the professional role of the decorator is not clearly subordinated to that of the architect. During the 1930s and 1940s, a segment of Los Angeles's architecture profession was composed of decorator-architects, such as J. E. Dolena and William Haines (Haines carried out a number of additions to Staub's Windfohr House in Fort Worth in the 1950s). Dallas, more so than Houston, possessed a decorator-architect contingent, its best-known exponent being John Astin Perkins. In Houston, Robert H. Wilson, who began practice in the 1950s, was a rare example of this professional subtype. In terms of identity, decorator-architects were stereotyped as investing more in ephemeral design (fabrics, furniture, finishes) than in construction. In terms of subjectivity, they were stereotyped as effeminate if not homosexual. Thanks to Paul W. Schieffer, Jeffrey Karl Ochsner, and Juan Ignacio Barragán Villarreal for their insights into the phenomenon of the decorator-architect.

76. Barnstone's complex response to issues of personal and collective identity is the subject of reflections by Phillip Lopate in "Elegy for Houston," *Texas Observer*, May 29, 1987, 10, and by Barnstone's brother, the poet and translator Willis Barnstone, in *We Jews and Blacks: Memoir with Poems*, 215–22.

77. Vincent Scully's critique of American modernist formalism of the late 1950s and 1960s is presented in his *American Architecture and Urbanism*, 191–200.

78. Mary Smith Fay, "Fay, Albert Bel," *New Handbook of Texas*, vol. 2, 968.

79. Johnston, *Houston: The Unknown City*, 324–25. Marguerite Johnston identified the other three founders as Dudley Sharp, William S. Farish Jr., and W. McIver Streetman. See *The Texas Corinthian Yacht Club*, 1–5. Of the club's original forty-six members, eleven were clients of Staub's.

80. I am grateful to the current owner, William E. King, for the information that his grandfather, Joe Hogan, built the Fay brothers' houses in Kemah.

81. Barnstone, *Architecture of John F. Staub*, 253–55; Chillman, "The Architect and House: 7," 21; Betty Dillard, "Houston: Ode to the Tropics," *Texas Homes* 7 (Sept. 1983): 64–71. The Albert B. Fay House in Houston was demolished in 1996.

CHAPTER 10. ARCHITECTURE, SOCIAL CONSTRUCTION, AND THE COUNTRY HOUSES OF JOHN F. STAUB

1. Harold Hyman makes this point when describing Judge James A. Elkins's aggressive business development practices on behalf of the City National Bank, which distinguished the City National from the more "gentlemanly" style of operation associated with such established Houston banks as the First National, the South Texas Commercial National, and the Union Nation. See Hyman, *Craftsmanship and Character*, 69.

2. T. J. Jackson Lears, *No Place of Grace: Antimodernism and the Transformation of American Culture, 1880–1920*, 56.

3. Ibid., 17.

4. Barna, *The See-Through Years*, 19–21.

5. Other architects of Staub's generation accommodated the postwar shift in styles of class representation by Palladianizing the ranch house. William Robert Mitchell Jr. illustrates a number of one-story, classically detailed ranch-type suburban houses that the Atlanta architect Lewis Edmund Crook Jr. produced in the 1950s in William Robert Mitchell Jr., *Lewis Edmund Crook, Jr., 1898–1967: A Twentieth-Century Traditionalist in the Deep South*, 65–71.

6. Hays, *Modernism and the Posthumanist Subject*, 86.

7. Sparke, "Always in Good Taste," 19.

8. Hays, *Modernism and the Posthumanist Subject*, 87.

9. Ibid., 90.

10. Colin Rowe, "The Mathematics of the Ideal Villa," in *Mathematics of the Ideal Villa*, 1–27.

11. On the Miller House and Garden see Gary R. Hilderbrand, *The Miller Garden: Icon of Modernism*.

12. A mature example—Skidmore, Owings and Merrill's headquarters building for the Weyerhaeuser Company between Tacoma and Seattle, Washington, of 1971, with its landscape designed by Peter Walker of Sasaki Walker Associates of San Francisco—exemplifies

the transformation of the eclectic country house into the modernist corporate campus. The Weyerhaeuser building seamlessly merges the identifying practices of modern architecture (tectonic constitution, spatial liberation, visual transparency, and responsiveness to nature) with those of the country house (systematic integration with the landscape, double fronts, hierarchical disposition of such supporting services and spaces as parking lots, and expansively proportioned interior spaces) to produce identity and subject positions that privilege white-collar employees and discreetly absorb blue-collar employees into the scenery. See Skidmore, Owings and Merrill, *The Architecture of Skidmore, Owings and Merrill, 1963–1973*, 94–105.

13. In the 1980s and 1990s the Miami architect Andrés Duany, the Pasadena architect Stephanos Polyzoides, and exponents of the New Urbanism both praised and carefully analyzed the urban-suburban planning of such city planning figures of the 1920s as John Nolen.

14. Benedikt, "Class Notes," 8.

15. Berger and Luckmann, *The Social Construction of Reality*, 64.

16. Shutze's architecture is the subject of Dowling, *American Classicist*. John Gaw Meem's work is documented and analyzed in a pair of books: Bainbridge Bunting, *John Gaw Meem: Southwestern Architect* and Chris Wilson, *Facing Southwest: The Life and Houses of John Gaw Meem*. George Washington Smith is the subject of three books: Patricia Gebhard, *George Washington Smith: Architect of the Spanish Colonial Revival*; George Washington Smith, *George Washington Smith: An Architect's Scrapbook*, ed. and with an introduction by Marc Appleton; and David Gebhard, *George Washington Smith, 1876–1930: The Spanish Colonial Revival in Southern California*. See the entry "Arthur L. Loveless" by Thomas Veith in *Shaping Seattle Architecture: A Historical Guide to the Architects*, ed. Jeffrey Karl Ochsner, 150–55. No books yet exist on the architecture of Richard Koch and H. B. Thomson.

17. Aldrich, *Old Money*, 105; Bushman, *Refinement of America*, xii; Lessard, *Architect of Desire*, 309.

18. Lessard, *Architect of Desire*, 85 and 65.

19. Aldrich, *Old Money*, 266.

20. Barna, *The See-Through Years*, 238.

21. See the entry on Derrida at http://en.wikipedia.org/wiki/Jacques_Derrida.

22. Hays, *Modernism and the Posthumanist Subject*, 241.

23. Lessard, *Architect of Desire*, 118.

24. Aldrich, *Old Money*, 91.

25. Rowe, "Character and Composition," 59–87; Aldrich, *Old Money*, 85.

BIBLIOGRAPHY

Acheson, Sam H., Herbert P. Gambrell, Mary Carter Toomey and Alex M. Acheson Jr., eds. *Texan Who's Who: A Biographical Dictionary of the State of Texas.* Dallas: The Texian Company, 1937.

Adorno, Theodor W., "Subject and Object." In *The Essential Frankfurt School Reader.* Edited by Andrew Arato and Eike Gebhardt, 497–98. New York: Urizen, 1978.

AGC News Service. Deposited in the office of the Houston Chapter of the Associated General Contractors of America.

Aldrich, Nelson W., Jr. *Old Money: The Mythology of America's Upper Class.* New York: Vintage Books, 1988.

Allegrezza, Kelly McCaughey. "Ruth London (1892–1966), Houston Landscape Architect." Master's thesis, Louisiana State University, 1999.

"Along the Waterfront." *Houston Gargoyle* 3 (August 10, 1930): 15.

Alter, Kevin. "SOM in Houston." *Cite 40: The Architecture and Design Review of Houston* (Winter 1997–98): 34–37.

"Americana at Its Finest: Ima Hogg's Bayou Bend." *Interiors* 123 (November 1963): 78–83.

Anchorage Foundation of Texas. *Braeswood: An Architectural History.* Houston: Old Braeswood Civic Club, 1988.

"And Now They're Making Weather in Homes." *House and Garden* 57 (January 1930): 27–29.

Andrée, Herb, Noel Young, and Patricia Halloran. *Santa Barbara Architecture: From Spanish Colonial to Modern.* Photography by Wayne McCall. Introduction by David Gebhard. Santa Barbara, Calif.: Capra Press, 1995 (first published 1975).

"Art Collection and Home of the John de Menils in Houston's River Oaks." *Interiors* 123 (November 1963): 84–91.

Arthur, Catherine Rogers, and Cindy Kelly. *Homewood House.* Baltimore: Johns Hopkins University Press, 2004.

The Art-Work of Houston, Texas. Chicago: Gravure Illustration Company, 1904.

Ashton, Dore. "Commentary from Houston and New York." *Studio International* 873 17 (January 1966): 40–42.

———. "Sweeney Revisited." *Studio International* 845 166 (September 1963): 110–13.

Aslet, Clive. *The American Country House.* New Haven: Yale University Press, 1990.

———"The Back of the House." *House and Garden* 40 (November 1921): 27.

Baker, Paul R. *Richard Morris Hunt.* Cambridge: MIT Press, 1980.

Banttari, Sally Robert. "The Evolution of the Bayou Bend Gardens, Houston, Texas (1926–1989)," Master's thesis, Louisiana State University, 1989.

Barna, Joel Warren. *The See-Through Years: Creation and Destruction in Texas Architecture and Real Estate, 1981–1991.* Houston: Rice University Press, 1992.

Barnstone, Howard. *The Architecture of John F. Staub: Houston and the South.* Austin: University of Texas Press, 1979.

———. "Obit: John de Menil." *Architecture Plus* 1 (August 1973): 71.

———. "Rediscovering John F. Staub: The Great Eclectic of Houston's Elite." *Texas Architect* 29 (November–December 1979): 49–54.

Barnstone, Willis. *We Jews and Blacks: Memoir with Poems.* Bloomington: Indiana University Press, 2004

Barrick, Nolan E. *Texas Tech: The Unobserved Heritage.* Lubbock: Texas Tech Press, 1985.

Barthelme, Frederic, and Steven Barthelme. *Double Down: Reflections on Gambling and Loss.* Boston: Houghton Mifflin, 1999.

Bartlett, Donald L., and James B. Steele. *Empire: The Life, Legend, and Madness of Howard Hughes.* New York: Norton, 1979.

"'Bayou Bend'—A Georgian Residence in Texas Designed after the Nineteenth Century Houses of Louisiana." *House and Garden* 59 (March 1931): 61, 63–65.

Beasley, Ellen, and Stephen Fox. *Galveston Architecture Guidebook.* Houston: Rice University Press and Galveston Historical Foundation, 1996.

Beeth, Howard, and Cary D. Wintz, eds. *Black Dixie: Afro-Texan History and Culture in Houston.* College Station: Texas A&M University Press, 1992.

Benedikt, Michael. "Class Notes." *Harvard Design Magazine* 11 (Summer 2000): 5–9.

Berger, Peter L., and Thomas Luckmann. *The Social Construction of Reality: A Treatise in the Sociology of Knowledge.* Garden City, N.Y.: Anchor Books, Doubleday, 1967 (first published 1966).

Bernhard, Virginia. *Ima Hogg: The Governor's Daughter.* Austin: Texas Monthly Press, 1984.

Best, Hugh. *Debrett's Texas Peerage.* New York: Coward-McCann, 1983.

Blueprints for Modern Living: History and Legacy of the Case Study Houses. Exhibition organized by Elizabeth A. T. Smith. Los Angeles: Museum of Contemporary Art; Cambridge: MIT Press, 1989.

Bohnn, Anne S. "Broadacres Historic District," Bachelor's thesis, University of Houston, 1979.

Bohnn, Anne Schlumberger, Edwin A. Eubanks, and Stephen Fox. "An Interview with C. C. Pat Fleming." *Cite 29: The Architecture and Design Review of Houston* (Fall 1992–Winter 1993): 32–36.

Bolger, Betsie. "River Oaks Heirloom." *Texas Homes* 9 (March 1985): 72–79.

Boughton, William Hart. "The Reason for Specifying Stucco." *House and Garden* 32 (July 1917): 11–13.

Boyd, John Taylor, Jr. "The Flintridge Country Club, Flintridge near Pasadena, California, Myron Hunt, Architect." *Architectural Record* 50 (July 1921): 93–101.

Brack, Mark L. "Domestic Architecture in Hispanic California: The Monterey Style Reconsidered." In *Perspectives in Vernacular Architecture IV,* edited by Thomas Carter and Bernard L. Herman, 163–73. Columbia: University of Missouri Press, 1991.

"Brick, Shingles Vary Texture of Texas House." *Architectural Record* 88 (December 1940): 62–63.

"Bright Outlook for 1933 Construction." *Houston* 3 (January 1933): [illegible].

Briscoe, Birdsall P. "The Private Garage." *Civics for Houston* 1 (March 1928): 6–7

Briscoe, Mrs. Birdsall P. "Trails and Trails." *Houston* 12 (February 1941): 26.

Brochure of the Work of William Ward Watkin. Privately printed, undated (c. 1925). Woodson Research Center, Fondren Library, Rice University.

Brooks, Bradley. "Owen J. T. Southwell, Architect, and the John Henry Phelan House." *Texas Gulf Historical and Biographical Record* 35 (November 1999): 3–17.

Brown, Frank Choteau. "Boston Suburban Architecture," *Architectural Record* 21 (April 1907): 245–80.

Brown, Peter Harry, and Pat H. Broeske. *Howard Hughes: The Untold Story.* New York: Penguin Group, 1996.

Browning, Dominique. "What I Admire, I Must Possess." *Texas Monthly*, April 1983, 140–47.

Brutvan, Cheryl A., with Marti Mayo and Linda L. Cathcart. *In Our Time: Houston's Contemporary Arts Museum, 1948–1982*. Houston: Contemporary Arts Museum, 1982.

Bryan, John Morrill. *Maine Cottages: Fred L. Savage and the Architecture of Mount Desert*. Photographs by Richard Cheek. New York: Princeton Architectural Press, 2005.

Bryant, John Rutherford. "The European-Texan Buildings: Indigenous Building Traditions among the Nineteenth-Century European Immigrants to Texas." Master's thesis, University of Texas at Arlington, 1987.

Buenger, Walter, and Joseph Pratt. *But Also Good Business: Texas Commerce Bank and the Financing of Houston and Texas*. College Station: Texas A&M University Press, 1986.

"Building: The New Face of Texas." *Fortune*, October 1961, 128–35.

"Buildings for Selling Services Offer Unique Design Opportunities." *Architectural Record* 90 (July 1941): 85.

Bunting, Bainbridge. *John Gaw Meem: Southwestern Architect*. Foreword by Paul Horgan. Albuquerque: University of New Mexico Press.

Bushman, Richard L. *The Refinement of America: Persons, Houses, Cities*. New York: Vintage Books, 1993 (first published 1992).

"Businessmen in the News." *Fortune*, October 1953, 87.

Camfield, William A. "Dominique de Menil, 1908–1997." *Cite 40: The Architecture and Design Review of Houston* (Winter 1997–98): 10–11.

Canizaro, Vincent B. *Architectural Regionalism: Collected Writings on Place, Identity, Modernity, and Tradition*. New York: Princeton Architectural Press, 2006.

Carl, Peter. "The Godless Temple, 'Organon of the Infinite.'" *Journal of Architecture* 10 (February 2005): 63–90.

Carleton, Don E. *A Breed So Rare: The Life of J. R. Parten, Liberal Texas Oil Man, 1896–1992*. Austin: Texas State Historical Association and the Center for American History, the University of Texas at Austin, 1998.

———. *Red Scare! Right Wing Hysteria, Fifties Fanaticism, and Their Legacy in Texas*. Austin: Texas Monthly Press, 1985.

Carson, Chris, and Frank D. Welch. "Conversation: O'Neil Ford in the Details." *Texas Architect* 54 (July–August 2004): 18–19.

Chillman, Dorothy Dawes. "A Blending of Periods in Harmonious Design." *Civics for Houston* 1 (February 1928): 8–9.

———. "Books and Their Shelves." *Civics for Houston* 1 (April 1928): 8–9.

Chillman, James, Jr. "The Architect and House: 7—John F. Staub of Houston, Texas." *Pencil Points* 22 (January 1942): 15–26.

Clark, James A., and Michel T. Halbouty. *Spindletop*. Houston: Gulf Publishing Company, 1980 (first published 1952).

Clark, Joseph Lynn, and Elton M. Scott. *The Texas Gulf Coast: Its History and Development*. Volume 3. New York: Lewis Historical Publishing Company, 1955.

Coleman, Elizabeth Ann. *The Genius of Charles James*. Brooklyn and New York: Brooklyn Museum and Holt, Rinehart and Winston, 1982.

Comey, Arthur C. *Houston: Tentative Plans for Its Development: Report to the Houston Park Commission*. Boston: Press of George H. Ellis Company, 1913.

Connor, Seymour N., James M. Day, Billy Mac Jones, Dayton Kelley, W. C. Nunn, Ben Procter, and Dorman H. Winfrey. *Capitols of Texas*. Waco: Texian Press, 1970.

"Contemporary Classic." *River Oaks Magazine*, March 1940, 12–15.

"The Cool Contents of Summer," *House and Garden* 118 (July 1960): 48–53.

Coote, Robert James. *The Eclectic Odyssey of Atlee B. Ayres, Architect*. Color photographs by W. Eugene George. College Station: Texas A&M University Press, 2001.

Cornelius, Charles O. *Early American Furniture*. New York: The Century Co., 1926.

———. "Transplanting the Eastern Tradition." *House Beautiful* 63 (January 1928): 24–28, 41–44.

Cotner, Robert C. *James Stephen Hogg: A Biography*. Austin: University of Texas Press, 1959.

Coventry, Kim, Daniel Meyer, and Arthur H. Miller. *Classic Country Estates of Lake Forest: Architecture and Landscape Design, 1856–1940*. New York: Norton, 2003.

Cram, Ralph Adams. "Have I a 'Philosophy of Design'?" *Pencil Points* 13 (November 1932): 729–34.

———. *My Life in Architecture*. Boston: Little, Brown, 1936.

———: "The Promise of American House Building." *House and Garden* 29 (January 1915): 8–12.

Cram and Ferguson. *The Work of Cram and Ferguson, Architects, Including the Work of Cram, Goodhue and Ferguson*. Introduction by Charles D. Maginnis. New York: Pencil Points Press, 1929.

Crinson, Mark. *Empire Building: Orientalism and Victorian Architecture*. London and New York: Routledge, 1996.

Croly, Herbert. "The Farm House 'De-Luxe:' Country Seat of Robert J. Collier, Esq., John Russell Pope, Architect." *Architectural Record* 31 (June 1912): 560–74.

Croly, Herbert D., and C. Matlack Price. "The Recent Work of Howard Shaw." 33 (April 1913): 284–331.

Culbertson, Margaret. *Texas Houses Built by the Book: The Use of Published Designs, 1850–1925*. College Station: Texas A&M University Press, 1999.

Curtis, Jane Anderson. "Bayou Bend Gardens." *Cite 37: The Architecture and Design Review of Houston* (Spring 1997): 20–23.

Curtis, Nathaniel C. "Architectural Traditions in New Orleans." *Journal of the American Institute of Architects* 13 (August 1925): 279–86.

Davis, Ellis Arthur, ed. *Historical Encyclopedia of Texas*. Dallas: Texas Historical Society, no date (c. 1935).

Davis, Ellis A., and Edwin H. Grobe, comp. and ed. *The New Encyclopedia of Texas*. Dallas: Texas Development Bureau, undated (c. 1925).

Dean, Ptolemy. *Sir John Soane and the Country Estate*. Aldershot: Ashgate Publishing Ltd., 1999.

"Dental Clinic for a Hot Climate." *Architectural Record* 96 (July 1944): 78–80.

Design in America: The Cranbrook Vision, 1925–1950 (exhibition catalog). Text by Robert Judson Clark and others. New York: Abrams, in association with the Detroit Institute of Arts and the Metropolitan Museum of Art, 1983.

Dillard, Betty. "Houston: Ode to the Tropics." *Texas Homes* 7 (September 1983): 64–71.

Dillon, David. *The Architecture of O'Neil Ford: Celebrating Place*. Austin: University of Texas Press, 1999.

Dobney, Fredrick J. editor. *Selected Papers of William L. Clayton*. Baltimore: The Johns Hopkins Press, 1971.

Donahue, Jack. *The Finest in the Land: The Story of the Petroleum Club of Houston*. Houston: Gulf Publishing Company, 1984.

Dowling, Elizabeth Merrill. *American Classicist: The Architecture of Philip Trammell Shutze*. Preface by Henry Hope Reed. Introduction by Vincent Scully. Photography by Timothy Hursley. New York: Rizzoli International Publications, 1989.

"Down on the Bay." *Houston Gargoyle* 4 (July 19, 1931): 13.

Eberlein, Harold Donaldson. "Examples of the Work of Mellor and Meigs." *Architectural Record* 39 (March 1916): 212–46.

———. "Five Phases of the American Country House." *Architectural Record* 36 (October 1914): 272–82.

"Efficiency Units for Texas" and "Industrial Housing for Texas." *Architectural Record* 99 (May 1946): 86–87.

Emerson, Jon, and Associates. "A Plan for the Preservation, Management, and Interpretation of Bayou Bend Gardens, Houston, Texas, a Property of The Museum of Fine Arts, Houston," 1994.

Emmott, Sarah H. *Memorial Park: A Priceless Legacy*. Houston: Herring Press, 1992.

"Engineering" *River Oaks Magazine*. October 1939, 6–7.

Ennis, Michael. "The Man Who Built River Oaks." *Texas Monthly* 7 (October 1979): 134–39.

Erickson, Erik H. *Identity: Youth and Crisis*. New York: Norton, 1968.

Eskew, Garnett Laidlaw with John R. MacDonald. *Of Land and Men: The Birth and Growth of an Idea*. Washington, D.C.: Urban Land Institute, 1959.

Evans, Derro. "Dallas: Villa Fiorenza." *Texas Homes* 9 (September 1985): 64–71.

———. "Houston: Dogwoods in Bloom." *Texas Homes* 8 (February 1984): 56–63.

Everett, Donald E. *San Antonio's Monte Vista: Architecture and Society in a Gilded Age, 1890–1930*. San Antonio: Maverick Publishing Company, 1999.

Fatio, Alexandra, comp. and ed. *Maurice Fatio: Architect*. New York: A. Fatio, 1992.

Fay, Carolyn Grant. "The House." Typescript memoir, Spring 1987. Collection of Marie Fay Evnochides.

Feagin, Joe R. *Free Enterprise City: Houston in Political and Economic Perspective*. New Brunswick: Rutgers University Press, 1988.

Fears, Ann Crawford. *Frankie: Mrs. R. D. Randolph and Texas Liberal Politics*. Austin: Eakin Press, 1999.

Ferguson, Cheryl Caldwell. "River Oaks: 1920s Suburban Planning and Development in Houston." *Southwestern Historical Quarterly* 104 (October 2000): 190–228.

———. "Upscale Suburban Architecture and Development in Dallas and Houston, Texas, 1890–1930." Ph.D. diss., University of Delaware, 2004.

Ferguson, John C. "The Country Houses of Atlee B. and Robert M. Ayres." *Cite: The Architecture and Design Review of Houston* (spring 1986): 18–20.

"Fire Alarm Building." *Architectural Forum* 73 (December 1940): 521–22.

Fisher, Howard T. "New Elements in House Design." *Architectural Record* 66 (November 1929): 395–405.

Fleming, Douglas K. *Thoughts of a Cotton Man: From Lamar Fleming's Collected Papers*. Foreword by James A. Tinsley. Privately printed, 1994.

Fleming, Lamar, Jr. *Growth of the Business of Anderson, Clayton and Company*. Edited by James A. Tinsley. Volume 10. Houston: Texas Gulf Coast Historical Association, 1966.

Forbes, A. H. "The Work of Albro and Lindeberg." *Architecture* 26 (November 15, 1912): 206–40.

Ford, James, and Katherine Morrow Ford. *Designs of Modern Interiors*. New York: Architectural Book Publishing Company, 1942.

"Forecast '58." *House and Garden* 113 (January 1958): 22–37.

Fornell, Earl Wesley. *The Galveston Era: The Texas Crescent on the Eve of Secession*. Austin: University of Texas Press, 1961.

Fox, Stephen. "Howard Barnstone, 1923–1987." *Cite: The Architecture and Design Review of Houston* (Fall 1987): 18–21.

———. "Sanguinet and Staats in Houston, 1903–1926," *Perspective: Society of Architectural Historians/Texas Chapter* 12 (Spring 1983): 2–11.

———. *Spanish Mediterranean Houses in Houston*. Houston: Rice Design Alliance, 1992.

———. "The Splendid Houses of Birdsall Briscoe." *Houston Home and Garden* 7 (May 1981): 36–37.

Freeman, J. H. *The People of Baker Botts*. Houston: Baker and Botts, 1992.

Freese, Ernest Irving. "How Do Your Rooms Face? If You Build by the Compass You Can Have Sunlight and Shade as You Wish." *House and Garden* 30 (July 1916): 15.

"The Front of the House: Few Know How Fair and Full of Grace are the Fronts away from the Highway." *Civics for Houston* 1 (May 1928): 10–11.

Fuermann, George. *Houston: Land of the Big Rich*. Illustrated by Lowell Collins. Garden City, N.Y.: Doubleday, 1951.

———. *Peden 1965: Seventy-Five Years and Just a Beginning*. Houston: Premier Printing Company, 1965.

Gane, John F., ed. *American Architects Directory*. New York: W. W. Bowker, 1970.

Gard, Wayne. "The Ranch-House Goes to Town." *Better Homes and Gardens* 15 (June 1937): 32–33.

A Garden Book for Houston. Houston: Forum of Civics, 1929.

The Garden City of Houston: Garden Villas. Texas and Local History Division of the Houston Metropolitan Research Center, Houston Public Library, undated.

"Gardens: A Portfolio of Paintings by George Stonehill with Notes on the 1933 Scene." *Fortune* 8 (August 1933): 70.

"Gardens at Houston and River Oaks, Texas, Visited by the Garden Club of America in February 1939." *Landscape Architecture* 29 (July 1939): 183–91.

Garden Study Club of Nashville. *History of Homes and Gardens of Tennessee*. Edited by Roberta Seawell Brandau. Nashville: Garden Study Club of Nashville and Parthenon Press, 1964.

Garden Villas: Where Nature Greets You. Texas and Local History Division of the Houston Metropolitan Research Center, Houston Public Library, undated.

"The Gartner-Wrightsman-Young House and Its Architect." *Historic Fort Worth Presents 2002 Designer Showcase*. Tour brochure printed by Historic Fort Worth, 2002.

Garwood, Ellen Clayton. *Will Clayton: A Short Biography*. Austin: University of Texas Press, 1958.

Garwood, William L., Jr. *Will Clayton: Economic Statesman*. Washington, D.C.: American Studies Center, 1981.

Gebhard, David. *George Washington Smith, 1876–1930: The Spanish Colonial Revival in Southern California*. Santa Barbara: Art Gallery of the University of California, Santa Barbara, 1964.

Gebhard, Patricia. *George Washington Smith: Architect of the Spanish Colonial Revival*. Salt Lake City: Gibbs Smith, 2005.

Genthe, Arnold. "Grilles and Galleries of Old New Orleans." *House and Garden* 46 (August 1924): 53–55.

"Georgian Simplicity and Dignity for a Texas House." *House and Garden* 60 (September 1931): 72–73.

George, Mary Carolyn Hollers. *O'Neil Ford, Architect*. College Station: Texas A&M University Press, 1992.

Gideon, Samuel. "A Little German Town in the Lone Star State." *American Architect* 139 (April 1931): 44–47.

Gilchrist, Edmund B. "A Venetian Villa in Texas." *Architectural Forum* 52 (April 1930): 537–69.

"Gillette Hill, Esq., Houston, Tex., Moore and Lloyd, Architects: 24" *House and Garden* 70 (September 1936): 135.

Glueck, Grace. "The De Menil Family: The Medici of Modern Art." *New York Times Magazine*, May 18, 1986, 28–46.

Goeldner, Paul. *Texas Catalog: Historic American Buildings Survey*. Edited by Lucy Pope Wheeler and S. Allen Chambers Jr. San Antonio: Trinity University Press, 1974.

Goldhagen, Sarah Williams. "Something to Talk About: Modernism, Discourse, Style." *Journal of the Society of Architectural Historians* 64 (June 2005): 144–67.

"Good Sight-Lines in 960-Seat Theater." *Architectural Record* 95 (June 1944): 100.

Gowans, Alan. *The Comfortable House: North American Suburban Architecture, 1890–1930*. Bibliography by Lamia Doumato. Cambridge: MIT Press, 1986.

Gray, Christopher. "All the Best Places: Shadyside: An Oasis Carved out of Houston's Bald Prairie." *House and Garden* 155 (August 1983): 46–47.

Greene, Virginia A. *The Architecture of Howard Van Doren Shaw*. Foreword by Stuart Cohen. Chicago: Chicago Review Press, 1998.

Griswold, Mac, and Eleanor Weller. *The Golden Age of American Gardens: Proud Owners, Private Estates, 1890–1940*. New York: Harry N. Abrams and the Garden Club of America, 1991.

Gustafson, Eleanor H. "'The Open Gates': The George Sealy House in Galveston." *Antiques* 108 (September 1975): 508–14.

Halsey, R. T. H., and Charles O. Cornelius. *A Handbook of the American Wing*. New York: The Metropolitan Museum of Art, 1928.

Hamlin, Talbot F. "The Architect and the House: 8—Alden B. Dow of Michigan." *Pencil Points* 23 (April 1942): 269–86.

Hannay, Mrs. Allen B. "Houston Is Garden City." *Houston* 7 (April 1936): 20–21.

Hannay, Mrs. Frances. "Houston Gardens Attract Nation-Wide Attention." *Houston* 8 (March 1937): 21.

Hannay, Frances. "Houston's Own Azalea Trail." *Houston* 9 (February 1938): 11.

Hardt, Michael, and Antonio Negri. *Empire*. Cambridge: Harvard University Press, 2000.

Hartt, Rollin Lynde. "Houses with Their Backs to the Street: A Serious Dissertation in the Interests of Privacy." *House and Garden* 29 (April 1916): 16–17.

Hatch, Don. "The Architect and the House: 6—Don Hatch of New York." *Pencil Points* 22 (October 1941): 617–32.

Hays, K. Michael. *Modernism and the Posthumanist Subject: The Architecture of Hannes Meyer and Ludwig Hilberseimer*. Cambridge: MIT Press, 1992.

Hébert, Rachel Bluntzer. *The Forgotten Colony: San Patricio de Hibernia*. Burnet: Eakin Press, 1981.

Herbert, Lynn M. "Seeing Was Believing: Installations of Jermayne MacAgy and James Johnson Sweeney." *Cite 40: The Architecture and Design Review of Houston* (Winter 1997–98): 30–33.

Hess, Alan. *The Ranch House*. Photography by Noah Sheldon. New York: Harry N. Abrams, 2004.

Hewitt, Mark Alan. *The Architect and the American Country House*. Photographs by Richard Cheek. New Haven: Yale University Press, 1990.

Hewitt, Mark. "Neoclassicism and Modern Architecture, Houston Style, Or the Domestication of Mies." *Cite: The Architecture and Design Review of Houston* (Fall 1984): 12–15.

Hight, Christopher. "Inertia and Interiority: 24 as a Case Study of the Televisual Metropolis." *Journal of Architecture* 9 (Autumn 2004): 369–83.

Hilderbrand, Gary R. *The Miller Garden: Icon of Modernism*. Introduction by David Dillon. Photography by Ezra Stoller and Alan Ward. Washington, D.C.: Spacemaker Press, 1999.

"An Historic Colonnade in Texas." *House and Garden* 55 (April 1929): 136.

Hitchcock, Henry-Russell. "Introduction." *Ten Years of Houston Architecture* (exhibition catalog).Chaired and co-chaired by Howard Barnstone and Burdette Keeland Jr. Houston: Contemporary Arts Museum, 1959.

———. *Modern Architecture: Romanticism and Reintegration*. New York: Payson and Clarke, Ltd., 1929.

Holcombe, Ray. "Architecture and the Small House." *Southern Architect and Building News* 54 (March 1928): 36–40.

Holmes, Ann. "Dominique de Menil: From Jeune Fille to 'Renaissance Woman.'" *Art News* 82 (January 1983): 80–85.

———. *Joy Unconfined: Robert Joy in Houston: A Portrait of Fifty Years*. Houston: San Jacinto Museum of History Association, 1986.

"The Home of Miss Ima Hogg." *Antiques* 53 (June 1948): 428.

"The Home of Mrs. Cleveland Sewall." *Antiques* 53 (June 1948): 435.

"Homewood, Baltimore, Maryland." *Architectural Record* 41 (May 1917): 435–47, and 41 (June 1917): 525–35.

"The Honeymoon Cottage Competition." *Pencil Points* 9 (July 1928): 444–49.

"'Hopecote' House, Mr. Albert Guinn Hope, Knoxville, Tenn." *The Architect* 4 (June 1925): plates 57–61.

Hoskins, Dorothy M. "Grace, Beauty in the Southern Home of Mr. and Mrs. Harry Carothers Wiess (Shadyside)." *Houston Gargoyle* 3 (January 19, 1930): 17.

———. "'A Hundred Thousand Welcomes': The Home of Mr. and Mrs. John Henry Phelan in Beaumont." *Houston Gargoyle* 3 (November 2, 1930): 17–18.

———. "An Italian Villa of Today: The Clear Lake Home of Mr. and Mrs. James Marion West." *Houston Gargoyle* 3 (May 11, 1930): 10–11.

Houghton, Dorothy Knox Howe. *The Houston Club and Its City: One Hundred Years*. Houston: Houston Club, 1994.

Houghton, Dorothy Knox Howe, Barrie Scardino, Sadie Gwin Blackburn, and Katherine S. Howe. *Houston's Forgotten Heritage: Landscape, Houses, Interiors, 1824–1914*. Houston: Rice University Press, 1991.

"House and Garden Presents Air-Conditioning" *House and Garden* 68 (August 1935): 57–62.

"House for an Unusual Lot in Houston, MacKie and Kamrath, Architects." *Architectural Record* 92 (November 1942): 50–51.

"House for Jesse R. Stone, Houston, Texas, MacKie and Kamrath, Architects." *Architectural Forum* 73 (December 1940): 520.

"House for Karl Kamrath, Houston, Texas, MacKie and Kamrath, Architects." *Architectural Forum* 73 (December 1940): 518–19.

"House in Houston, Texas, MacKie and Kamrath, Architects." *Architectural Forum* 78 (February 1943): 61.

"A House in the Suburbs of Hartford Being the Residence of Frank Cheney, Esq., at South Manchester, Designed by Charles A. Platt, Architect." *House and Garden* 6 (September 1904): 151–55.

"House of Henry Stude, Esq., Houston, Texas," *Architectural Forum* 44 (March 1926): 49–50.

"House of H. Q. Hickman, Houston, Texas, Hiram A. Salisbury, Architect." *American Architect* 133 (January 5, 1928): 62.

"House of John P. King, Fort Worth, Texas, John F. Staub, Architect." *Southern Architect and Building News* 57 (August 1931): 19–20.

"The House of Thomas E. Hogg, San Antonio, Texas," *American Architect* 134 (August 20, 1928): 237–39.

"House of W. L. Clayton, Esq., Houston, Texas." *Architectural Forum* 49 (September 1928): 337–38.

"House of W. L. Clayton, Esq., Houston, Texas." *Southern Architect and Building News* 55 (January 1929): 51–53.

"The House of W. T. Carter, Jr., in Houston, John F. Staub, Architect." *House Beautiful* 71 (June 1932): 434, 439–41.

"Houses: Architect-Builder Team Shows Houston How to Design and Build a Good House for under $15,000." *Architectural Forum* 89 (September 1948): 125–27.

"Houses with Two Bedrooms: House Fronts on Garden." *Architectural Record* 87 (May 1940): 60–61.

Houston Architectural Survey. Houston: Southwest Center for Urban Research, 1980.

The Houston Blue Book: A Society Directory. Houston: J. R. Wheat Publishers, 1896.

"Houstonians Live in Desert Style." *Houston Post*, September 18, 1960, section 7, 1.

Houston Riding and Polo Club 1st Horseshow and Gymkhana, June 19th, 20th, 21st, 1925. River Oaks Scrapbooks, Volume 2, River Oaks Collection, Texas and Local History Division of the Houston Metropolitan Research Center, Houston Public Library.

Houston: Text by Houstonians. Drawings by Michel Cadoret. Photographs by Sibylle de l'Epine. Marrero: Hope Haven Press, 1949.

Hunter, Paul R. "The Architect and the House: 4—Roland E. Coate of Los Angeles." *Pencil Points* 20 (October 1939): 625–640.

Hurt, Harry, III. *Texas Rich: The Hunt Dynasty from the Early Oil Days through the Silver Crash*. New York: Norton, 1981.

Hyman, Harold M. *Craftsmanship and Character: A History of the Vinson and Elkins Law Firm of Houston, 1917–1997*. Athens: University of Georgia Press, 1998.

Illustrated City Book of Houston, 1915. Houston: City of Houston, 1915.

"Individualism in Architecture: A House at Orange, New Jersey, Wilson Eyre, Architect." *Architectural Record* 32 (October 1912): 275–79.

"In Texas, an Air-Conditioned Villa." *House and Garden* 105 (February 1954): 50–53.

"In This House, Ventilating Equipment Fans Up a Breeze." *House and Garden* 99 (May 1951): 134–35.

James, Stephen. "Donald Barthelme: Architecture and the Road to La Mancha." *Arris: Journal of the Southeast Chapter of the Society of Architectural Historians* 16 (2005): 56–68.

Jenkins, Stover, and David Mohney. *The Houses of Philip Johnson.* Afterword by Neil Levine. Photographs by Steven Brooke. New York: Abbeville Press Publishers, 2001.

Johnson, Philip. *Philip Johnson: The Glass House.* Edited by David Whitney and Jeffrey Kipnis. New York: Pantheon Books, 1993.

Johnston, Marguerite. *A Happy Worldly Abode: Christ Church Cathedral, 1839–1964.* Houston: Cathedral Press, 1964.

———. *Houston: The Unknown City, 1836–1946.* College Station: Texas A&M University Press, 1991.

Jones, J. Lester. *Centennial 1876–1976: W. T. Carter & Bro.* Revised edition. privately printed, 1978.

"Just Looking? No, They're Buying, Too." *House+Home* 14 (July 1958): 120–25.

Kaliski, John. "Hindcite: Crabbing about Preservation." *Cite: The Architecture and Design Review of Houston* (Summer 1985): 26.

———. "The Wright Stuff: Houston's Natural House." *Cite: The Architecture and Design Review of Houston* (F all 1984): 16–18.

Kaplan, Barry J., and Charles Orson Cook. "Civic Elites and Urban Planning: Houston's River Oaks." In *Houston: A Twentieth-Century Urban Frontier,* edited by Francisco A. Rosales and Barry J. Kaplan, 22–33. Port Washington, N.Y.: Associated Faculty Press, 1983.

Keach, Leon. "The Architect and the House: 1—Royal Barry Wills, Small House Specialist." *Pencil Points* 18 (February 1937): 65–80.

Kilman, Ed, and Theon Wright. *Hugh Roy Cullen: A Story of American Opportunity.* New York: Prentice-Hall, 1954.

King, John O. *Joseph Stephen Cullinan: A Study of Leadership in the Texas Petroleum Industry, 1897–1937.* Nashville: Vanderbilt University Press and the Texas Gulf Coast Historical Association, 1970.

Kirker, Harold. *California's Architectural Frontier: Style and Tradition in the Nineteenth Century.* Santa Barbara: Peregrine Smith, 1973 (first published 1960).

Kirkland, Kate Sayen. "Envisioning a Progressive City: Hogg Family Philanthropy and the Urban Ideal in Houston, Texas, 1910–1975." Ph.D. diss. , Rice University, 2004.

———. "A Wholesome Life: Ima Hogg's Vision for Mental Health Care." *Southwestern Historical Quarterly* 104 (January 2001): 416–47.

Knox County History Committee, East Tennessee Historical Society. *The French Broad-Holston Country: A History of Knox County, Tennessee.* Edited by Mary U. Rothrock. Knoxville: East Tennessee Historical Society, 1946.

Knoxville History Committee of the East Tennessee Historical Society. *Heart of the Valley: A History of Knoxville, Tennessee.* Edited by Lucile Deadrick. Knoxville. East Tennessee Historical Society, 1976.

Koolhaas, Rem. *Delirious New York: A Retroactive Manifesto for Manhattan.* New York: Oxford University Press, 1978.

Koush, Ben. *Donald Barthelme: A Modernism Suitable for Everyday Use, 1939–1945.* Houston: Houston Mod, 2005.

Koush, Ben. "Houston Lives the Life: Modern Houses in the Suburbs, 1952–1962." Master's thesis, Rice University, 2002.

Koyl, George S., ed. *American Architects Directory.* New York: W. W. Bowker Company, 1956 and 1962.

Krinsky, Carol Herselle. *Gordon Bunshaft of Skidmore, Owings and Merrill.* New York and Cambridge: The Architectural History Foundation and MIT Press, 1988.

"Lacquered Red, Yellow and Gold Enrich This Cabinet in a Texas Dining Room." *House and Garden* 60 (September 1931): 49.

Lambert Landscape Company. *Lambert Gardens.* Houston, 1938.

Larson, Henrietta, and Kenneth Porter. *History of Humble Oil and Refining Company: A Study in Industrial Growth.* New York: Harper and Brothers, 1959.

Lears, Jackson. "A Matter of Taste: Corporate Cultural Hegemony in a Mass-Consumption Society." In *Recasting America: Culture and Politics in the Age of Cold War,* edited by Lary May, 38–57. Chicago: University of Chicago Press, 1989.

Lears, T. J. Jackson. *No Place of Grace: Antimodernism and the Transformation of American Culture, 1880–1920.* Chicago: University of Chicago Press, 1981.

Le Corbusier. *Towards a New Architecture.* Translated by Frederick Etchells. London: Architectural Press, 1946 (first edition 1923).

Lejeune, Jean-François, and Allan T. Shulman. *The Making of Miami Beach, 1933–1942: The Architecture of Lawrence Murray Dixon.* Miami Beach and New York: Bass Museum of Art and Rizzoli, 2000.

Lemann, Nicholas. "The Architects." *Texas Monthly* 10 (April 1982): 142–51.

Lerup, Lars. *After the City.* Cambridge: MIT Press, 2000.

Lessard, Suzannah. *The Architect of Desire: Beauty and Danger in the Stanford White Family.* New York: Dial Press, 1996.

———. "Three Houses: From Mount Vernon to the McMansion." *Harvard Design Magazine* 11 (Summer 2000): 10–15.

Lewis, Sinclair. *Babbitt.* New York: Harcourt, Brace, 1922.

Lindeberg, Harrie T. "The Design and Plan of the Country House." *The American Architect* 99 (April 12, 1911): 133–37.

———. *Domestic Architecture of H. T. Lindeberg.* Introduction by Royal Cortissoz. New introduction by Mark Alan Hewitt. New York: Acanthus Press, 1996 (first published 1940).

———. "Thatched Roof Effect with Shingles." *The Brickbuilder.* 18 (July 1909): 133–40.

Linsley, Judith Walker, and Ellen Walker Rienstra. *Beaumont: A Chronicle of Promise.* Woodland Hills: Windsor Publications, 1982.

Lipartito, Kenneth, and Joseph Pratt. *Baker and Botts in the Development of Modern Houston.* Austin: University of Texas Press, 1991.

Lipsitz, George. *The Possessive Investment in Whiteness: How White People Profit from Identity Politics.* Philadelphia: Temple University Press, 1998.

"Living with Antiques: The House of Mr. and Mrs. Harris Masterson, Houston, Texas." *Antiques* 109 (April 1976): 742–49.

"Local Azalea Trail Viewed by Thousands." *Houston* 10 (March 1939): 30.

Lomax, John A. *Will Hogg, Texan.* Austin: University of Texas Press and the Hogg Foundation for Mental Health. 1968 (first published 1940).

Longstreth, Richard. *On the Edge of the World: Four Architects in San Francisco at the Turn of the Century.* New York and Cambridge: The Architectural History Foundation and the MIT Press, 1983.

Lopate, Phillip. "Elegy for Houston." *Texas Observer,* May 29, 1987, 10.

"Lorgnon." *Houston Gargoyle* 3 (August 17, 1930): 15.

Louis, Arthur M. "It's Moody vs. Moody in the Struggle for American National." *Fortune* 83 (March 1971): 110–12.

Marcus, George E., with Peter Dobbins Hall. *Lives in Trust: The Fortunes of Dynastic Families in Late Twentieth-Century America.* Boulder: Westview Press, 1992.

Mashburn, Joe. "Burdette Keeland Remembered." *Cite 48: The Architecture and Design Review of Houston* (Summer 2000): 9.

Masterson and Allied Families: A Genealogical Study with Biographical Notes. Compiled by the American Historical Company. Privately printed 1965.

McAlester, Virginia and Lee. *A Field Guide to American Houses.* Drawings by Lauren Jarrett and Juan Rodríguez-Alaniz. New York: Knopf, 1984.

McCarthy, Muriel Quest. *David R. Williams: Pioneer Architect.* Dallas: Southern Methodist University Press, 1984.

McComb, David G. *Galveston: A History.* Austin: University of Texas Press, 1986,.

———. *Houston: The Bayou City.* Austin: University of Texas Press, 1969.

McGinty, Milton. "Recollections: A Perfectionist." *Texas Architect* 29 (November–December 1979): 54.

McKay, Gary. "Karl Kamrath: Shaping the City's Character." *Houston Home and Garden* 8 (January 1982): 18–24.

McKinley, Fred, and Greg Riley. *Black Gold to Bluegrass: From the Oilfields of Texas to Spindletop Farm of Kentucky.* Austin: Eakin Press, 2005.

McNabb, William Ross. *Tradition, Innovation, and Romantic Images: The Architecture of Historic Knoxville.* Knoxville: Frank H. McClung Museum, University of Tennessee, Knoxville, 1991.

Meiners, Fredericka. *A History of Rice University: The Institute Years, 1907–1963.* Houston: Rice University and the Rice University Historical Commission, 1982.

Meyer, Wendy Haskell. "John F. Staub: A New Book about Our City's Eclectic Architect." *Houston Home/Garden* 6 (October 1979): 55–60.

Miller, Nory. "Lone Stars—Howard Barnstone and Karl Kamrath." *Inland Architect* 21 (June 1977): 16–17.

Miller, Scott Reagan. "The Architecture of MacKie and Kamrath." Master's thesis, Rice University, 1993.

———. "The School of Frank Lloyd Wright." *Cite 40: The Architecture and Design Review of Houston* (Winter 1997–98): 25–26.

"Mirabeau B. Lamar Senior High School, Houston, Texas, John F. Staub, Kenneth Franzheim, Lamar Q. Cato, Harry D. Payne, Louis A. Glover, Architects." *Architectural Forum* 70 (May 1939): 364–66.

Mitchell, William R., Jr. *Lewis Edmund Crook, Jr., 1898–1967: A Twentieth-Century Traditionalist in the Deep South.* Atlanta: The History Business, 1984.

"Modernize Your Business with Carrier Weathermakers." *Houston* 5 (July 1934): 10.

Morford, Elizabeth. "History in Houses: The Varner-Hogg Plantation in Texas." *Antiques* 76 (August 1959): 126–29.

Morgan, William Manning. *Trinity Protestant Episcopal Church, Galveston, Texas, 1841–1953: A Memorial History.* Houston: Anson Jones Press, 1954.

Morrison and Fourmy's Houston City Directory. Houston: Morrison and Fourmy Directory Company. Various years.

Mumford, Lewis. *Sticks and Stones: A Study of American Architecture and Civilization.* Second revised edition. New York: Dover Publications, 1955 (first published 1924).

Murphy, Charles J. V. "Texas Businessmen and McCarthy." *Fortune* 49 (May 1954): 100–101.

The Museum of Fine Arts, Houston: An Architectural History, 1924–1986. Celeste Marie Adams, ed. Museum of Fine Arts Bulletin, Houston: Vol. 15, 1-2, 1992.

The National Cyclopedia of American Biography. New York: James T. White, various years.

Neff, Emily Ballew, with Wynne H. Phelan. *Frederic Remington: The Hogg Brothers Collection of the Museum of Fine Arts, Houston.* Princeton: Princeton University Press and the Museum of Fine Arts, Houston, 2000.

Neuhaus, Martin. "The History of the Neuhaus Family (To 1935)." Translated by W. O. Neuhaus, Lillie Neuhaus, and Ilse Neuhaus Richardson. Unpublished manuscript. Collection of W. O. Neuhaus III, Houston, Texas.

Nicholson, Patrick J. *Houston Country Club Seventy-Fifth Anniversary, 1908–1983.* Houston: Houston Country Club, 1984.

———. *Mr Jim: The Biography of James Smither Abercrombie.* Houston: Gulf Publishing Company, 1983.

Ochsner, Jeffrey Karl, ed. *Shaping Seattle Architecture: A Historical Guide to the Architects.* Seattle: University of Washington Press, 1994.

Olmsted, Frederick Law. *A Journey through Texas: Or, a Saddle-Trip on the Southwestern Frontier.* Foreword by Larry McMurtry. Austin: University of Texas Press, 1978 (first published 1857).

O'Neal, William B., and Christopher Weeks. *The Work of William Lawrence Bottomley in Richmond.* Foreword by Jaquelin T. Robertson, photography by Richard Cheek. Charlottesville: University Press of Virginia, 1985.

"On the Periphery of Houston, People Lead Leisured, Charming Lives." *House and Garden* 97 (March 1950): 96–99.

"Open Planned, Window-Walled House in the Southwest." *Architectural Record* 85 (May 1939): 111.

Page, Anderson and Turnbull. *Tarrant County Historic Resources Survey: Fort Worth: Near North Side and West Side and Westover Hills.* Fort Worth: Historic Preservation Council for Tarrant County, Texas, 1988.

Papademetriou, Peter C. "Doldrums in the 'Forties: Houston Building Design in Transition." *Texas Architect* 29 (November–December 1979): 28–35.

———. "Texas Transitions: Eclecticism, Regionalism, Modernism." Paper presented at the Thirty-second Annual Meeting of the Society of Architectural Historians, San Antonio, Texas, 1979.

Parker, James. "The Wrightsman Rooms at the Metropolitan Museum of Art." *Antiques* 97 (January 1970): 102–108.

Payne, Richard. *The Architecture of Philip Johnson.* Foreword by Philip Johnson, essay by Hillary Lewis. Boston: Bulfinch Press, 2002.

Peden, Allen V. "Presentations: Hugh Potter." *Houston Gargoyle* 1 (April 10, 1928): 10–11.

A Permanent Legacy: 150 Works from the Collection of The Museum of Fine Arts, Houston. Introduction by Peter C. Marzio. New York: Hudson Hills Press and the Museum of Fine Arts, Houston, 1989.

Phillips, Kevin. *Wealth and Democracy: A Political History of the American Rich.* New York: Broadway Books, 2002.

Phillips, Paige Allred. "C. C. Pat Fleming, Houston, Texas, Landscape Architect." Master's thesis, Louisiana State University, 2003.

Platt, Charles A. *The Architecture of Charles A. Platt.* Introduction by Royal Cortissoz. New introduction by Charles D. Warren. Foreword by Robert A. M. Stern. New York: Acanthus Press, 1998.

Platt, Harold L. *City Building in the New South: The Growth of Public Services in Houston, Texas, 1830–1910.* Philadelphia: Temple University Press, 1983.

Poesch, Jessie, and Barbara SoRelle Bacot, eds. *Louisiana Buildings 1720–1940: The Historic American Buildings Survey.* Baton Rouge: Louisiana State University Press, 1997.

Pollard, Katherine. "Houston Provides for Shopping on Wheels." *Civics for Houston* 1 (January 1929): 6–7.

Pope, Albert. *Ladders.* New York: Princeton Architectural Press, 1996.

"Portfolio—Houses in Controlled Developments: Texas, River Oaks, Houston, MacKie and Kamrath, Architects." *Architectural Record* 88 (November 1940): 60–61.

Potter, Hugh. "When You Buy Real Estate." *House and Garden* 71 (February 1937): 126–28.

Pratt, Joseph. "8F and Many More: Business and Civic Leadership in Modern Houston." *Houston Review of History and Culture* 1 (Summer 2004): 2–7.

Pratt, Joseph A., and Christopher J. Castañeda. *Builders: Herman and George Brown.* College Station: Texas A&M University Press, 1999.

Preusser, Mary Ellen. "West Coast Architect Designs Special Home for Houstonians." *Houston Post,* March 15, 1953, section 6, 1.

Price, C. Matlack. "Individuality in Country Houses." *House and Garden* 37 (February 1920): 18–23, 25.

———. "The Recent Work of Albro and Lindeberg." *Architecture* 31 (January 1915): 1–39.

"Printing Plant." *Architectural Record* 90 (July 1941): 52–53.

"Project Center Building." *Architectural Record* 91 (May 1942): 52–53.

Ragsdale, Kenneth B. *The Year America Discovered Texas: Centennial '36.* Foreword by Stanley Marcus. College Station: Texas A&M University Press, 1987.

Rather, John Thomas, Jr. "Charm in the Small House as Shown in 'Hopecote,' in Knoxville, Tennessee." *House Beautiful* 57 (February 1925): 112–16.

———. "Porches and Porticoes." *Civics for Houston* 1 (April 1928): 10–11.

Rebori, A. N. "The Work of Burnham and Root, D. H. Burnham, D. H. Burnham and Co., and Graham, Burnham and Co." *Architectural Record* 38 (July 1915): 8–168.

Reed, Henry Hope. "America's Greatest Living Classical Architect: Philip Trammel Shutze of Atlanta, Georgia." In *Classical America IV*, edited by William A. Coles, 5–46. New York: Norton, 1977.

Reed, Roger G. *A Delight to All Who Knew It: The Maine Summer Architecture of William R. Emerson*. Photographs by Richard Cheek. Portland: Maine Citizens for Historic Preservation, 1995.

Reid, Kenneth. "The Architect and the House: 2—Randolph Evans of New York." *Pencil Points* 18 (April 1937): 197–212.

———. "The Architect and the House: 3—William Wilson Wurster of California." *Pencil Points* 19 (August 1938): 469–86.

Report of the City Planning Commission, Houston, Texas. Houston: Forum of Civics, 1929.

"Residence of Mr. and Mrs. Carlton B. Swift, Pasadena, California, Donald D. McMurry." *Architectural Record* 64 (November 1928): 382–84.

"Residential Details—Recreational: 1. John F. Staub, Architect." *Architectural Record* 89 (April 1941): 65.

"Rice Institute, Cram, Goodhue and Ferguson, Architects." *Western Architect* 19 (February 1913): 20–22.

Richardson, C. F. "Houston's Colored Citizens: Activities and Conditions Among the Negro Population." *Civics for Houston* 1 (August 1928): 5.

Richardson, T. C. *East Texas: Its History and Its Makers*. Edited by Dabney White. New York: Lewis Historical Publishing Company, 1940.

Richardson, Violet. "Rambling Texas Home of Elbert Williams." *American Home* 13 (January 1935): 70–72.

Riddle, Don. "Homes to Last for All Time: The Story of River Oaks." *National Real Estate Journal* (March 4, 1929): 21–28.

———. *River Oaks: A Pictorial Presentation of Houston's Residential Park*. Houston: River Oaks Corporation, 1929.

Rienzi: The Museum of Fine Arts, Houston. Houston: Museum of Fine Arts, Houston, 1999.

"River Oaks, Houston, Texas, River Oaks Corporation." *Architectural Forum* 62 (May 1935): 472–73.

"Robsjohn-Gibbings: Twenty-Five Years of His Work." *Interiors* 32 (May 1961): 122–31.

"Roman House." *House&Home* 2 (July 1952): 67–73.

Roth, Leland M. *The Architecture of McKim, Mead and White, 1870–1920: A Building List*. New York: Garland Publishers, 1978.

Rouse, Parke, Jr. *Living by Design: Leslie Cheek and the Arts*. Foreword by John Walker. Afterword by John Canaday. Design by Raymond Geary. Williamsburg: The Society of the Alumni of William and Mary, 1985.

Roussel, Hubert. *The Houston Symphony Orchestra, 1913–1971*. Austin: University of Texas Press, 1972.

Rowe, Colin. *The Mathematics of the Ideal Villa and Other Essays*. Cambridge: MIT Press, 1977.

Ruffin, Lisa. "Dallas: Mount Vernon—The Hilltop Mansion of Legendary Oilman H. L. Hunt." *Texas Homes* 9 (February 1985): 64–71.

"Saddle, Boot and Spur." *Houston Gargoyle* 4 (March 22, 1931): 17.

Salny, Stephen M. *The Country Houses of David Adler*. Introduction by Franz Schulze. New York: Norton, 2001.

Samon, Katherine Ann. *Ranch House Style*. Photographs by Edmund Barr. New York: Clarkson Potter Publishers, 2003.

Saxon, Lyle. "A Breath from the Vieux Carré." *House and Garden* 44 (November 1923): 72–73.

Scardino, Barrie, and Drexel Turner. *Clayton's Galveston: The Architecture of Nicholas J. Clayton and His Galveston Contemporaries*. Foreword by Peter Brink. College Station: Texas A&M University Press, 2000.

Schmidt, Yolita. "Donald Barthelme." *Texas Architect* 39 (November–December 1989): 44.

Schuyler, Montgomery. "The Work of Cram, Goodhue and Ferguson." *Architectural Record* 29 (January 1911): entire issue.

Schwartzer, Mitchell. "Myths of Permanence and Transience in the Discourse on Historic Preservation in the United States." *Journal of Architectural Education* 48 (September 1994): 2–11.

Scully, Vincent. *American Architecture and Urbanism*. New York: Henry Holt and Company, 1988 (first published 1969).

Shand-Tucci, Douglass. *Ralph Adams Cram: An Architect's Four Quests: Medieval, Modernist, American, Ecumenical*. Amherst: University of Massachusetts Press, 2005.

Sheehy, Sandy. "River Oaks Latin Classic." *Texas Homes* 3 (September–October 1979): 96–103.

Sibley, Marilyn McAdams. *The Port of Houston: A History*. Austin: University of Texas Press, 1968.

Siry, Joseph M. *The Chicago Auditorium Building: Adler and Sullivan's Architecture and the City*. Chicago: University of Chicago Press, 2002.

"Six Small Houses of Brick, Stucco, and Wood: A House in Houston, Texas, John F. Staub, Architect." *House Beautiful* 61 (May 1927): 640.

Skidmore, Owings and Merrill. *The Architecture of Skidmore, Owings and Merrill, 1950–1962*. Introduction by Henry-Russell Hitchcock. Text by Ernst Danz. Translation by Ernst van Haagen and Antje Pehnt. New York: Praeger Publishers, 1963.

———. *The Architecture of Skidmore, Owings and Merrill, 1963–1973*. Introduction by Arthur Drexler. Text by Axel Menges. New York: Architectural Book Publishing Company, 1974.

Smart, Pamela G. "Sacred Modern: An Ethnography of an Art Museum." Ph.D. diss., Rice University, 1997.

Smelser, Neil J., and Paul B. Baltes, editors-in-chief. *International Encyclopedia of the Social and Behavioural Sciences*. Oxford: Elsevier Science Ltd., 2001.

Smith, George Washington. *George Washington Smith: An Architect's Scrapbook*. Edited and with an introduction by Marc Appleton. Los Angeles: Tailwater Press, 2001.

Social Register of Houston 1950. Houston: The Social Register of Houston, 1950 (subsequent volumes, published in odd-numbered years, are entitled the *Social Directory of Houston*).

"Southern Pacific Railway Building, Houston, Texas," *Western Architect* 20 (September 1914): plate section.

Sparke, Penny. "Always in Good Taste: The Enduring Legacy of Elsie de Wolfe." *Harvard Design Magazine* 11 (Summer 2000): 16–20.

Stafford, Diane. "Design in Retrospect: Harking Back to the Good Old Days of Design in Houston." *Houston Home and Garden* 14 (October 1987): 70–71.

Stamp, Gavin. *Edwin Lutyens: Country Houses from the Archives of Country Life*. New York: The Monacelli Press, 2001.

Staub, John F. "Latin Colonial Architecture." *Southern Architect and Building News* 56 (August 1930): 33–35.

———. "Latin Colonial Architecture in the Southwest." *Civics for Houston* 1 (February 1928): 6–7.

Stern, Robert A. M., ed., with John Montague Massengale. *The Anglo American Suburb*. London: Architectural Design, 1981.

Stern, William F. "The Lure of the Bungalow." *Cite: The Architecture and Design Review of Houston* (Winter 1986): 8–11.

Stevenson, Mrs. L. A. "Seventh Annual Azalea Trail." *Houston* 13 (February 1942): 36.

Stewart, Rick. *Lone Star Regionalism: The Dallas Nine and Their Circle, 1928–1945*. Austin: Texas Monthly Press and the Dallas Museum of Art, 1985.

Straus, R. D. "Industry's Pioneer Air Conditioner." *Houston* 6 (June 1935): 7.

Strom, Steven R., ed. *Mac Kie and Kamrath Architects: Guide to the Architectural Collection*. Houston: Houston Public Library, 2000.

"A Summer Play Ground on the Bay Shore." *The Houstonian* 1 (July 28, 1917): 9.

Swank, Patsy. "Should the City Save the DeGolyer Estate?" *D: The Magazine of Dallas* 3 (April 1976): 65–67.

Sweeney, James Johnson. "Collectors' Home: In the John de Menil House a Great Ranging Art Collection." *Vogue* 147 (April 1, 1966): 184–91.

"Sweet and Low." *River Oaks* 2 (April 1939): 16–17.

"Texas." *Fortune* 20 (December 1939): 80–91.

The Texas Corinthian Yacht Club: The First Fifty Years, 1938–1988. Houston: privately printed, 1988.

Texas General Contractors Association Monthly Bulletin. Various issues, 1922–37. Texas and Local History Division of the Houston Metropolitan Research Center, Houston Public Library.

Texas Parks and Wildlife Department Historic Sites and Restoration Branch. *Preservation Plan and Program for Varner-Hogg Plantation State Historical Park, Brazoria County, Texas.* Volume 2. Austin: Texas Parks and Wildlife Department, 1983.

"Texas Takes to Modern." *House and Garden* 77, no. 2 (May 1940): 32–33.

"A Thatched Palace: An Estate at Pocantico Hills, Albro and Lindeberg, Architects." *Architectural Record* 28 (November 1910): 314–28.

"Thirteen Years of Fair-Building Reviewed in Current Exhibit." *Architectural Record* 80 (July 1936): 3.

"Three Dimensional Freedom." *River Oaks Magazine* 2 (November 1939): 14–16.

"T. H. Robsjohn-Gibbings, 1905–1976." *Interiors* 136 (January 1977): 6.

"Through the Lorgnon." *Houston Gargoyle* 4 (July 26, 1931): 13.

Tinkle, Lon. *Mr. De: A Biography of Everette Lee De Golyer.* Foreword by Norman Cousins. Boston: Little, Brown, 1970.

Todd, Anderson. "Hugo V. Neuhaus, Jr., 1915–1987." *Cite: The Architecture and Design Review of Houston* (Winter 1987): 19–20.

———. "Nina J. Cullinan, 1896–1983." *Cite: The Architecture and Design Review of Houston* (Spring 1983): 3.

———. "Recollections: Reasons for the Choice." *Texas Architect* 29 (November–December 1979): 54.

Tomkins, Calvin. "The Benefactor." *New Yorker* 74 (June 8, 1998): 52–67.

"Triangular Steel Framework." *Architectural Forum* 93 (September 1950): 137.

"A Tribute in Memory of J. T. Rather, Jr., 1898–1968, from His Associates at Rice University." Unpublished booklet deposited in the Woodson Research Center, Fondren Library, Rice University.

"Tripartite Scheme for Bank, Office Building, and Garage." *Architectural Record* 129 (April 1961): 155–64.

Turner, Suzanne. "J. Robert Neal Residence, Houston, Texas: Overview of Historic Landscape Issues." Unpublished report in consultation with Curtis and Windham, Architects, February 1998.

"12,000 See Gardens." *Houston* 9 (March 1938): 28.

"Two Houses of Individuality Showing the Versatility of Architects Albro and Lindeberg." *Architectural Record* 30 (October 1911): 368–73.

"The $250,000 House." *Fortune* 52 (October 1955): 133–42.

"Two Ways of Looking at Art in Houston." *Interiors* 123 (November 1963): 92–98.

Tyler, Ron, ed. *The New Handbook of Texas.* 6 volumes. Austin: Texas State Historical Association, 1996. http://www.tsha.utexas.edu/handbook/online/

Tzonis, Alexander, and Liane Lefaivre. *Classical Architecture: The Poetics of Order.* Cambridge: MIT Press, 1986.

Uhrbrock, Mary. "A Natural Legacy." *Houston Home and Garden* 12 (November 1985): 84–89.

University of Texas Medical Branch at Galveston Faculty and Staff. *The University of Texas Medical Branch at Galveston: A Seventy-Five Year History.* Austin: University of Texas Press, 1967.

U.S. Bureau of the Census. *Fourteenth Census of the United States.* Washington, D.C.: GPO, 1924.

———. *Sixteenth Census of the United States.* Washington, D.C.: GPO, 1942.

"The Value of Good Detail." *House and Garden* 58 (December 1930): 55.

Wade, Michael Glen. "David Reichard Williams: Avant-Garde Architect and Community Planner, 1890–1962," Ph.D. dissertation, University of Louisiana at Lafayette, 1978.

Walraven, Bill, and Marjorie K. Walraven. *Empresario's Children: The Welders of Texas.* Sinton: Rob and Bessie Welder Wildlife Foundation. Corpus Christi: Javelina Press, 2000.

"War Needs—Housing: Houston, Texas" *Architectural Record* 91 (April 1942): 47–50.

Warren, David B. "Albert Sheppard Remembers Bayou Bend." *Cite 37: The Architecture and Design Review of Houston* (spring 1997): 24–25.

———. *Bayou Bend: American Furniture, Paintings, and Silver from the Bayou Bend Collection.* Foreword by Ima Hogg. Houston: Museum of Fine Arts, Houston, 1975.

———. "Bayou Bend: A Southern Garden." *Antiques America* (2000).

———. *Bayou Bend Gardens: A Southern Oasis.* Introduction by Mac Griswold. Photographs by Rick Gardner, Don Glentzer, and Rob Muir. London and Houston: Scala Publishers and the Museum of Fine Arts, Houston, 2006.

———. "The Empire Style at Bayou Bend: New Period Rooms in Houston." *Antiques* 97 (December 1970): 122–27.

———. "Ima Hogg, Collector." *Antiques* 121 (January 1982): 228–43.

———. "The Reopening of Bayou Bend in Houston, Texas." *Antiques* 144 (September 1993): 328–37.

Warren, David B., Michael K. Brown, Elizabeth Ann Coleman, and Emily Ballew Neff. *American Decorative Arts and Paintings in the Bayou Bend Collection.* Houston and Princeton: The Museum of Fine Arts, Houston, and Princeton University Press, 1998.

Wasson, S. Deane. *Houston Cotton Exchange and Board of Trade: Fifty Years a Cotton Market, 1874–1924.* Houston: Rein Printing Company, 1924.

Watts, Frank A. "Houston Resumes 'Remodeling' Her Skyline." *Houston* 15 (May 1934): 15.

Weber, Bruce J. "Will Hogg and the Business of Reform." Ph.D. diss., University of Houston, 1979.

Weber, Bruce J., and Charles Orson Cook. "Will Hogg and Civic Consciousness: Houston Style." *The Houston Review* 2 (Winter 1980): 20–36.

Webster, Frederick Leon. "Art in the Little Theater." *Civics for Houston* 1 (October 1928): 16.

Welch, Frank D. *Philip Johnson and Texas.* Foreword by Philip Johnson. Photographs by Paul Hester. Austin: University of Texas Press, 2000.

"Welcome to Garden Oaks." Photographic brochure complied by the Garden Oaks Company, c. 1940.

Weld, Hattie Borden. *Historical and Genealogical Record of the Descendants as Far Known of Richard and Joan Borden.* Los Angeles: privately printed, 1899.

West, Ruth. "Junior League at Home." *Houston Gargoyle* 2 (June 2, 1929): 13.

"Where a Picketed Gateway Guards the Dooryard Path." *House and Garden* 57 (January 1930): 67.

Whitehead, Russell F. "Harrie T. Lindeberg's Contribution to American Domestic Architecture." *Architectural Record* 55 (April 1924): 308–72.

Who Was Who in America. Chicago: The A. N. Marquis Company, various volumes.

Who's Who in America. Chicago: A. N. Marquis, Inc., various volumes.

Who's Who in Texas. Edited by Emory E. Bailey and a Staff of Selected Writers. Dallas: Who's Who Publishing Company, 1931.

Who's Who in the South and Southwest. Chicago: Marquis Who's Who, various volumes.

"William M. Rice Institute, Houston, Texas." *American Architect* 102 (December 11, 1912): 207–208 and plates.

Williams, David R. "An Indigenous Architecture: Some Texas Colonial Houses." *Southwest Review* 14 (October 1928): 60–74.

Wills, Ridley W., II. *The History of Belle Meade: Mansion, Plantation, and Studies.* Nashville: Vanderbilt University Press, 1991.

Wilson, Charles Reagan, and William Ferris, eds. *Encyclopedia of Southern Culture.* Chapel Hill: University of North Carolina Press, 1989.

Wilson, Chris. *Facing Southwest: The Life and Houses of John Gaw Meem*. New York: Norton, 2001.
Wilson, Michael E., ed. *Harvin C. Moore, Houston Architect: A Catalogue of Drawings by Harvin C. Moore in the Houston Public Library/Houston Metropolitan Research Center*. Editorial consultation by Nancy Hadley. Houston: Houston Public Library, 1987.
Wilson, Richard Guy. *McKim, Mead and White, Architects*. New York: Rizzoli International Publications, 1983.
Wilson, William H. *The City Beautiful Movement*. Baltimore: Johns Hopkins University Press, 1989.
Winkler, Franz (pseudo. Montgomery Schuyler). "The Administration Building of the Rice Institute, Houston, Texas." *Brickbuilder* 21 (December 1912): 321–24.
"With Record Readers: Houston Citizens Vote on Recent Buildings." *Architectural Record* 86 (November 1939): 12, 14.
Wittenberg, Gordon. "On Tour: Morgan's Point: Once Bustling Bay Ridge Survives." *Cite: The Architecture and Design Review of Houston* (August 1982) 16–17.
Wolner, Edward W. "The City-within-a-City and Skyscraper Patronage in the 1920s." *JAE: Journal of Architectural Education* 42 (winter 1989): 10–23.
Worley, William S. *J. C. Nichols and the Shaping of Kansas City: Innovation in Planned Residential Communities*. Columbia: University of Missouri Press, 1990.
Writers' Program of the Works Projects Administration in the State of Texas. *Houston: A History and Guide*. Houston: The Anson Jones Press, 1942.
Yergin, Daniel. *The Prize: The Epic Quest for Oil, Money, and Power*. New York: Simon and Schuster, 1991.
"You Can Frame Old Fireplaces with New Mantles." *House and Garden* 114 (December 1958): 102.
Zisman, S. B. "The Architect and the House: 5—O'Neil Ford of Dallas, Texas." *Pencil Points* 21 (April 1940): 195–210.

INDEX

Adams, B. B., 145
Adler, David, 136, 138, 144, 151
advertising for neighborhoods, 4, 6, 68, 73
air-conditioning, 169, 290–91, 297, 302, 311
Aldrich, Nelson W., Jr., 2, 340, 343, 347n 46
Allen, A. C., 6
Allen, J. K., 6
Allen Parkway, 70, 73
Anderson, Ben M., 317
Anderson, Clayton and Company, 263, 265
Anderson, Mary (née Greenwood), 317
Anderson House, Fort Worth, 138
Anderson House, River Oaks, 317, 319–24
architecture: classical, 301, 345n 3; and continuity, 99, 288, 340; nature vs. history as basis for, 114; social construction role of, 7, 9–15, 31, 66, 111, 338
The Architecture of John F. Staub (Barnstone), 4–5
Arrants, Edward B., 162
austerity, 30, 31, 192, 210
Austin, Carol (Mrs. R. D. Straus), 290
authenticity, 99, 217, 232
Azalea Trail, 78, 165, 287, 354n 52

Bain, Lorena (Mrs. J. P. King), 144
Baker, Botts, Andrews and Wharton, 20, 262
Baker, Botts, Baker and Lovett, 20
Baker, Botts, Parker and Garwood, 18, 20
Baker, Capt. James, 20
Baker, James A., Jr., 18
Baker, Judge James A., 20
Barber and McMurry, 2
Barna, Joel, 340
Barnstone, Howard: on divine float in Staub's houses, 15; and Staub's first book, 4; on Staub's post-1935 suburban houses, 246, 302, 308, 325, 330–31
Barthelme, Donald, 197, 297
Bayou Bend: architectural profile, 80–99, *100*, *335*; gardens, 78, 80, 85, 87, 94, 354n 53; house museum conversion, 353–54n 57; influence of, 99; origin of name, 353n 47; overview, 3; social function, 78–80
Bayou Club, 239–44
Bayou Woods, Houston, 244, 325–31, 361n 43
Bay Ridge Park, Texas, 212–17
Beaumont, Texas, 183–92
belonging: Broadacres houses, 21, 28, 30, 31, 50, 52; and continuity in modern designs, 293; country retreats, 214, 217, 233; Fay Cottage, 331; grand houses, 200, 201; and Staub's style, 15. *See also* naturalization
Benedikt, Michael, 26, 338
Berger, Peter L., 338
Berney House, 138, 151
Bertelsen, A. A., 104, 179, 281
Bewley, Edwin E., 136
Bewley, Martha (née Jennings), 136
Bewley House, 136–44, 210
Bewley Mills, 136
Blaffer, R. Lee, 7
Blanton, Elizabeth (Mrs. P. S. Wareing), 5
Bolton, Preston M., 302
Borden, Lucile (Mrs. J. A. Tennant), 31, 35
Bosworth, Lawrence S., 297
Bosworth, Rosalie (née Hutcheson), 297
Bosworth Bay Cottage, 297, 367n 28
Bowles House, 250–52
Braeswood, Houston, 124
Briar Hollow, Houston, 244
Briarwood, Houston, 301
Briscoe, Birdsall P., 7, 68, 73, 76, 78
Briscoe and Dixon, 75, 76, 77
Broadacres, Houston: Cochran House, 26, 28–31; Dargan House, 42–44, 46–51; Dow House, 31–35, *337*; Hutcheson House, 21–25, 27, 31, 129, 247–48; Kuldell House, 30, 44, 50, 52–65, 66, *339*; map, **18**; overview, 3; Palmer Hutcheson House, 24, 27; site planning, 18–20; and social construction of identity, 19–20, 21, 23, 31, 35, 65–66; Staub's consistency in, 350n 36; Tennant House, 35–45
Brown, Alice (née Pratt), 124
Brown, George R., 124
Bruton, David D., 248
Bruton, Harriet M., 248, 254
Bruton House, 248–50, 254
Buenger, Walter, 246
Buffalo Bayou: Allen Parkway, 70, 73, 74; country retreats on, 230, 234, 237–44; Elkins House, 325–31; Memorial area, 69, 220–30, 243, 244, 306
Bullock, Frank N., 212
Bullock, Laura, 212
Bullock Bay Cottage, *213*, 214–17
bungalow house type, 113–14, 115, 117
Burnett, Anne (Mrs. R. F. Windfohr), 297
Burnham, D. H., 7
Burton, Nenetta (Mrs. A G. Carter), 153
Bushman, Richard L., 3, 21
Byrne Thomas S., 136

Callery, Caroline (née Staub) (daughter), 5
Callery, Nancy Staub (granddaughter), 5
Camp, Alex S., 192
Camp, Roberta (née Coke), 192, 197
Camp House, 192–98, 342, 359n 72, 360n 76
Carleton, Don E., 247
Carter, Amon G., 153
Carter, Frankie (Mrs. R. D. Randolph), 217
Carter, Lillie (née Neuhaus), 165, 217
Carter, Nenetta (née Burton), 153
Carter, William T., Jr., 165, 217, 220, 244
Carter Lodge, 217–20, 221, 230
centrality: Bayou Club, 237; Broadacres houses, 65; country retreats, 225; grand houses, 169, 194, 196, 200; and regionalism, 287, 288; River Oaks houses, 80, 87, 104
ceremoniousness: Bayou Club, 239; Broadacres houses, 25; continuity with service, 139, 144; as form of living, 347n 55; grand houses, 185; small country houses, 119, 129
Chambers, Sarah (Mrs. Tom Scurry), 262
Cheek, Joel O., 153
Cheek-Neal Coffee Company, 153

Chew, Joseph H., 100, 111
Chew, Rebecca (née Donelson), 100
Chew, William B., 111
Chew House, 100, 102–3, 104
Childress, Doris, 290
Childress, Virgil, 290
Chillman, Dorothy (née Dawes), 117, 356n 14
Chillman, James, Jr., 117, 124, 262
Christian, Jane, 156
City National Bank, 247, 302, 325
civic virtue: architectural reflection of, 99; and emergent elites, 165; Hoggs as exemplars of, 69, 73, 78, 80; modern vs. eclectic visions of, 338; and River Oaks community identity, 68, 73, 111
Clark Hardison House, 124, 126
classical architecture, 301, 345n 3
class system: architectural expression of, 262, 340; Bayou Bend's masking of, 99; capitalism's complications for, 336–38; country houses as statements of, 338, 340, 343; democratic contradictions for, 3, 9, 15, 69–70, 162, 168, 340, 347n 51; grand houses as confirmation of, 210; modernist ambivalence toward, 177, 290, 297, 301, 334, 338, 369n 65–66; ranch house as challenge to, 297, 301; and small country houses, 129. *See also* middle class; social construction of upper-class identity
Clayton, Sue (née Vaughan), 76
Clayton, William L., 7, 73, 76, 168
Clayton Summer House, 76, 77
climatic responsiveness: air-conditioning's impact on, 169, 290–91, 297, 302, 311; Broadacres houses, 21, 23, 26, 28, 35, 52, 59; country retreats, 217, 234; grand houses, 138, 162; and regionalism, 262, 263, 274, 278, 287; River Oaks houses, 94; small country houses, 114, 119; Staub's talent for, 12, 21, 343
Cochran, Annie (née Martin), 26, 111
Cochran, Mary Alice (Mrs. H. B. Finch), 104
Cochran, O. L., 26
Cochran, William S., 26
Cochran House, 26, 28–31
Coke, Roberta (Mrs. Alex Camp), 192, 197
Colby Court, Houston, 69
community and social status: architectural role in promoting, 1, 104; Bayou Club, 239–44; continuity in design, 21, 69, 287; country houses, 338, 340, 343; country retreats, 217; grand houses, 182; and Hoggs, 99; River Oaks identity, 7, 68, 69, 70, 73, 99, 104, 111, 246–47, 355n 79
contemporary genre. *See* modernism
contemporary-Palladian dialectic. *See* Palladian-contemporary dialectic
continuity: Broadacres houses, 43, 50, 52; of class through architecture, 99, 288, 340; and community identity, 21, 69, 287; country retreats, 214; grand houses, 136, 138–39, 144, 159, 192, 194, 196, 200, 201; house-to-site plan, 31; landscape's contribution, 12, 20, 116; modern houses, 77, 291, 293, 297, 319, 331; and Progressivism, 347n 49; River Oaks houses, 69, 87; small houses, 116, 136; and stability of social identity, 336
Cornelius, Charles O., 122, 124
Country Club Estates Company, 68, 70, 73
Country Club Estates House. *See* Latin Colonial House; Redbird House
country houses: architectural criticism of, 262; as critique of modernism, 9, 66; definition of type, 347n 44; exterior themes, 21; and historical eclecticism, 9; modernist challenge to, 4, 290; Palladian-contemporary revival, 308; as social construction, 1–2, 19; as statements of class distinction, 338, 340, 343; and Staub, 2, 3, 28. *See also* Broadacres; River Oaks; small country houses
country retreats: Bayou Club, 239–44; Bullock Bay Cottage, 213, 214–17; Carter Lodge, 217–20, 221, 230; Fay House, 233–39; Goodrich House, 230–33; introduction, 212; overview of, 3–4; and social construction of identity, 214, 217, 220, 222, 227, 233, 243–44; vs. suburban homes, 233; Wiess Stables, 211, 220–30, 325
Courtland Place, Houston, 3, 220
Courtwright, David T., 4
Cowell, C. Herbert, 302
Crabb, Dolores (née Welder), 259
Crabb, William J., 259
Craftsman movement, 113, 212
Cram, Ralph Adams, 20, 73, 76
Cramer, Ethelyn (Mrs. R. C. Kuldell), 44, 50
Cranfill-Reynolds Company, 252
Cranz, Lillie (Mrs. H. R. Cullen), 164–65, 168
Cravens, Dargan and Company, 42, 288
Cravens, James R., 42
Crawford, E. B., 255
Cullen, Hugh Roy, 164, 165, 168, 247
Cullen, Lillie (née Cranz), 164–65, 168
Cullen, Roy Gustav, 165
Cullen House, 164–79
Cullinan, J. S., 7, 68
Cullinan, Margaret (Mrs. A. J. Wray), 287, 288
Cullinan, Nina J., 302
Cullinan Hall, 302
Cunningham, Johanna (Mrs. J. H. Phelan), 183

Dallas, Texas, Camp House, 192–98
Dargan, Estelle W. (née White), 42
Dargan, Kemp S., 42
Dargan House, 42–44, 46–51
Darwinian discourse, 9, 77–78, 99, 274, 293
Dawes, Dorothy (Mrs. J. Chillman), 117, 356n 14
Dawson, James F., 159, 162
Dean, Ptolemy, 348n 51
Delabarre, Madeleine Louise (wife). *See* Staub, Madeleine Louise
democratic society, negotiating upper-class identity in, 3, 9, 15, 69–70, 162, 168, 340, 347n 51
Depression, Great, 3, 246–47
divine float in Staub's houses, 15, 94
Dixon, Sam H., Jr., 73
Donelson, Rebecca (Mrs. J. H. Chew), 100
Donoghue, T. J., 7
Dow, Charles Milby, 31–32
Dow House, 31–35, 337
Dow Motor Company, 35

Eagle Petroleum Company, 212
Early Republic House, 116–17, 118, 129, 133
eclecticism, historical: and country houses, 9; mid-20th century decline of, 290; vs. modernism, 4, 9, 66, 76, 290, 336, 340, 343; and regionalism, 262; and respect for other architects, 302; simplification trend, 246; and social construction of identity, 9, 31, 338; Staub/Hogg partnership in, 73, 76; Staub's contribution to, 1, 288; value for Houston, 99
elites, entrepreneurial: adoption of patrician subjectivity, 78, 165, 336, 347n 46; architecture's contribution to, 111; consensus-building, 246–47, 362n 12; Hoggs' influence on, 78; landscape's role in, 19; and Progressivism, 7; and race and ethnicity, 15; social framework for, 1. *See also* class system; emergent elites; established elites
Elkins, James A., Jr., 247, 302, 325
Elkins, Margaret (née Wiess), 227, 302, 325
Elkins houses: Bayou Woods, 325–31; River Oaks, 289, 302–5, 306
El Piloncillo Ranch, Dimmit County, 306
emergent elites: architectural legitimization of, 111; and country house as status symbol, 338; in Fort Worth, 153; in Houston, 6, 35, 68, 70,

99, 164–65, 179; and oil industry, 7, 20, 179, 198, 247, 365n 26; and Staub's changing clientele, 260
established elites: in Fort Worth, 136, 151, 153; in Galveston, 113; in Houston, 20, 26, 31–32, 42, 153, 165; oil industry barons as, 7; and Staub's early projects, 6–7
ethnicity. *See* race and ethnicity
European influences on Staub, 153
European rationalism, 288, 295–96
evolutionary rhetoric, 9, 77–78, 99, 274, 293
exurban houses, 230. *See also* country retreats

Fairchild, Cameron, 124
family-centered subjectivity, 305, 317, 319, 325, 369n 66
Fanz, Anna Cornelia (Mrs. F. Staub) (mother), 2
Fanz, Emma (Mrs. A. G. Hope) (aunt), 2
Farish, Lottie (née Rice), 179
Farish, Stephen Power, 179, 198, 244
Farish, William S., 7, 179, 244, 247
Farish houses: Ravenna, 179–87, 259–60, 287; in Shadyside, 7, 10
Fatio, Alexandra, 2
Fatio, Maurice, 2
Fay, Albert Bel, 331
Fay, Carolyn (née Grant), 233, 235
Fay, Ernest Bel, 233
Fay, Homoiselle (née Haden), 331
Fay Cottage, 331–33, 361n 36
Fay House, 233–39
Finch, Hubert B., 104, 111
Finch, Mary Alice (Mrs. D. J. Harrison, Jr.), 287, 306
Finch, Mary Alice (née Cochran), 104, 111
Finch House, 104–7, 111
Finn, Alfred C., 7
First City National Bank, 325
First National Bank, 26
Fleming, C. C. Pat, 183, 185, 248, 250, 254, 325. *See also* Fleming and Sheppard
Fleming, Clare (née Knowles), 263
Fleming, Lamar, Jr., 263, 265
Fleming and Sheppard, 85, 94, 237, 254, 287, 290
Fleming Summer House, 263, 265, 268–78
Fondren Library, Rice University, 227
Ford, O'Neil, 262
Fort Worth, Texas, 136–53, 210, 297–300
Fort Worth Club Building, 153
Fort Worth National Bank, 136
Francis, Caroline (née Wiess), 4, 248
Francis, William H., Jr., 248
Franzheim, Kenneth, 227
Frazer, Alice Nicholson (Mrs. M. Hogg), 78
Frederick, Anthony, 104
F-W-C Royalty Company, 179

Galveston, Texas: and Houston, 6; Latin Colonial style in, 124, 126; modern houses in, 297, 298; small country houses in, 113, 129–34
Galveston Bay area, 212–17
Garden Oaks, Houston, 297
Garden Villas, Houston, 220, 367n 29
Gardner, Rick, 4
Gartner, Elizabeth (née Reynolds), 145, 151
Gartner, Herman, 145, 151
Gartner House, 145, 148–50, 151, 152, 153
gate piers, River Oaks, 67, 99, 101, 248
General Crude Oil Company, 252
German-Texan families, 165
Gerner, Charles J., 117
Goodrich, Esther (née Whinery), 230
Goodrich, Raymond, 230, 232
Goodrich House, 230–33
Gowans, Alan, 114
grand houses: Bewley House, 136–44, 210; Camp House, 192–98; Cullen House, 164–79; Farish House, 179–87, 259–60, 287; Gartner House, 145, 148–50, 151, 152, 153; influence on suburban homes, 252; introduction, 136; King House, 144–47; Neal House, 155, 153–64, 169, 177, 210, 341, 358n 32; River Crest, Fort Worth, 138–51; and social construction of identity, 136, 151, 156, 162, 168, 169, 177, 192, 198, 201, 210; Wilson House, 183, 188–92, 359n 71; Winston House, 198–209
Grant, Carolyn (Mrs. E. B. Fay), 233, 235
Great Depression, 3, 246–47
Greenwood, Mary (Mrs. E. M. Anderson), 317
Gregory, Jane (Mrs. G. S. Heyer), 252, 306
Gregory, Julia (née Nalle), 252
Gregory, Thomas Watt, 252
Gregory House, 306–8
Griswold House, 124, 125
Guadalupe River, Fleming Summer House, 263, 265, 268–78
Gunn, Ralph Ellis, 308, 311

Haden, Homoiselle (Mrs. A. B. Fay), 331
Hanszen House, 255, 258
Harding, Blanche (Mrs. C. Sewall), 73, 76
Hare and Hare, 70, 214
Harrison, Dan J., Jr., 278, 281, 287, 306, 365n 26–28
Harrison, Ethel (née Hedeman), 278, 281
Harrison, Mary Alice (née Finch), 287, 306
Harrison House, 261, 278–81, 287
Harrison Oil Company, 281
Hays, K. Michael, 340
Hedeman, Ethel (Mrs. D. J. Harrison), 278, 281
Helmbrecht, Marie, 129
Helmbrecht, William C., 113, 129
Helmbrecht House, 113, 129–34
Hermann Park, 7, 8
Hewitt, Mark Alan, 9, 76
Heyer, George S., 252, 306
Heyer, Jane (née Gregory), 252, 306
Heyer House, 245, 252–57
Hickman House, 124, 127, 129
Highland Park, Dallas, 192
Hill, George A., Jr., 255
Hill, Mary (née Vandenberge), 255
Historical Buildings Survey, 263
historic models: and country house type, 9; grand houses, 182; Latin Colonial fusion in Houston, 77; overview, 1; and regionalism, 262–63; Staub's attachment to, 305; value of, 308. *See also* eclecticism, historical; vernacular buildings
Historic American Buildings Survey, 262
historic preservation, Houston's lack of, 5
Hogan, Joe, 331
Hogg, Alice Frazer (née Nicholson), 78
Hogg, Ima: and Bayou Bend, 78, 87, 99; as collector, 353–54n 49; and Latin Colonial style, 68, 73, 76; photo, 69; and River Oaks development, 68; and Staub, 3; and upper-class identity, 7, 121
Hogg, James S., 68
Hogg, Mike, 3, 68, 69, 70, 78, 247
Hogg, Sallie (née Stinson), 68
Hogg, Tom, 68, 78, 353n 48

Hogg, Will C.: and Bayou Bend, 78, 99; gardening leadership of, 354n 53; and River Oaks development, 68–69; and Staub, 3; and upper-class identity, 7, 73, 111
Hogg Brothers, 68, 69, 70, 73
Hogg-Swayne syndicate, 68
Homewoods, River Oaks: Hanszen House, 255, *258*; Pratt House, 255, 259, 363n 29; Rienzi, 290, 308–17, *318*. *See also* Inwood Drive; Lazy Lane
Honeymoon Cottage competition, 124, 129
Hooton, Claude E., 296, 297
Hope, Albert G. (uncle), 2
Hope, Emma (née Fanz) (aunt), 2, 124
Hopper, Thomas T., 104
house museums, 5. *See also* Bayou Bend; Camp House; Rienzi
Houston, Texas: architectural contribution to myth of, 100; Bayou Woods, 361n 44; country retreats as misfits in, 244; cultural politics in mid-20th century, 290; Depression's impact on, 246; downtown view, *74*; and fluidity of class identity, 3; historical sketch, 5–9; modernism's influence on, 295–301, 325; small country houses in, 133; Staub's arrival, 2; value of historical eclecticism for, 99. *See also individual neighborhoods*
The Houston Gargoyle, 9, *11*, *13–14*, 100, *101*, *112*
Houston National Bank, 246
Houston Riding and Polo Club, 244
Houston Ship Channel, 6
Houston Symphony Orchestra, 68, *80*
Howe, Katherine S., 308, 311
Howze, Albert, 4
Hughes, Howard R., 50
Hughes Tool Company, 44
Humble Oil and Refining Company, 20, 165, 179, 192, 227, 230
Humble Tower, 227
Hunt, Jarvis, 7
Hunt, Texas, Fleming Summer House, 263, 265, 268–78
Hutcheson, Eleanor (née Thomson), 20
Hutcheson, Joseph C., 20
Hutcheson, Joseph C., Jr., 20
Hutcheson, Palmer, 20
Hutcheson, Rosalie (Mrs. L. S. Bosworth), 297
Hutcheson House, 21–26, *27*, 31, 129, 247–48
Hyman, Harold M., 247

individuality: Broadacres houses, 21, 26, 30, 31, 35, 43; grand houses, 169, 183, 196, 201; and Houston clients, 100; origins of architectural, 348n 56; and regionalism, 287; River Oaks houses, 104; Staub's talent in projecting, 230; and typification, 30–31, 246, 248, 250, 254, 255, 259–60
instruments in public formation: Azalea Trail, 78, 165, 287, 354n 52; beauty as, 336; definition, 7; Modern House Tour, 301; and small country houses, 113, 117, 129
integration: Bayou Bend, 85; downtown and River Oaks, 73, 74; of established and emergent elites, 65–66; in home design, 23; Staub's talent for, 21, 31, 317; and Tennant House, 35
interior design: architects' lack of respect for, 369n 75; Elkins House, 325, 330; Menil House, 301; Neal House, 156; Straus House, 290, 293, *295*; tradition and modernity, 169
International Style, 295–96
intimacy, 43–44, 268, 278. *See also* monumentality and intimacy
Inwood Drive, River Oaks: Bowles House, 250–52; Bruton House, 248–50, 254; Chew House, 100, *102–3*, 104; Clayton House, 76; Cullen House, 164–79; Finch House, 104–7, 111; Heyer House, *245*, 252–57; Sewall House, 76
Iowa, Jerome, 4
Irwin, W. H., 214
Irwin Bay Cottage, 214, 217

J. J. Sweeney Jewelry Company, 111
James, Charles, 301
Jamieson, James P., 7
Jennings, Anna G., 263
Jennings, John M., 263
Jennings, Martha (Mrs. E. E. Bewley), 136
Jennings House, 263, *268*
Jensen, Thomas, 265
Jewish ethnicity in Houston, 331, 365n 8
John F. Grant Lumber Company, 234
Johnson, Philip, 301, 302
Jones, Jesse H., 7, 168, 177, 246
Junior League of Houston, clubhouse, 100, 244

Kamrath, Karl, 296, 301
Keeland, Berdette, 302
Keith, Olga (Mrs. H. C. Wiess), 220
Kellum-Noble House, 263, *265*
Kemah, Texas, 297, 331–33, 367n 28
Kessler, Hattie (Mrs. W. W. Neuhaus), 165
Kilman, Ed, 164–65
King, John P., 144, 151
King, Lorena (née Bain), 144
King House, 144–47
Kipp, Herbert A., 70, 351n 23
Kirby Drive, River Oaks, 70, 290, 308–17, *318*
Knowles, Clare (Mrs. L Fleming, Jr.), 263
Knoxville, Tennessee, 2
Kraigher, George, 295
Krinsky Carol Herselle, 325
Kuldell, Ethelyn (née Cramer), 44, 50
Kuldell, Rudolph C., 44, 50
Kuldell House, 30, 44, 50, 52–65, 66, *339*

Lambert Landscape Company, 104
land development in Houston, 5, 20, 68, 69, 73, 114. *See also* site planning; suburban development
landscape. *See* naturalization
landscaping: and Bayou Bend, 78, 80, 85, *87*, 94, 354n 53; Bayou Club, 239; Broadacres houses, 18–20, 28, 35; building continuity with, 12, 20, 116; grand houses, 156, 159, 162, 169, 183, 185; and Gulf Coast topography, 7, 21; integration of downtown to River Oaks, 73; live oak avenues, 7, 9, 19, 20, 31; modern houses, 290, 293, 325; and regionalism, 287; River Oaks houses, 70, 104; spatial buoyancy of, 12; and typification, 248, 250, 254
Larchmont Road, River Oaks, 104, *108–10*, 111, 117, 263, 290–95
Larkin House, 263
Lasell, Inez (née Rather), 113, 129
Latin Colonial House, River Oaks, 75, 77, 114–17, *119*, 124
Latin Colonial style: and Bayou Bend, 95; Bowles House, 252; in Galveston, 124, *126*; Ima Hogg's role in, 68, 73, 76; influences and development, 73, 75–78, 99–100, 350n 2; local media coverage of, 79, 117; Picton House, 114–17, *119*; Redbird House, 73, *75*; and regionalism, 262; rural version, 235; Wray House, 287
Law, Caroline (née Wiess), 4, 248
layering of space: Broadacres houses, 26, 28, 35; country retreats, 235; grand houses, 159, 185, 192, 194, 198; and Gulf Coast topography, 70; and ranch house type, 301, 306; and regionalism, 278, 287; River Oaks houses, 80, 100; and site planning, 9; small country houses, 116; and typification, 248, 250
Lazy Lane, River Oaks: Cullen House, 164–79; Farish House, 179–87, 259–60, 287; Harrison House, *261*, 278–81, 287; Neal House, *135*, 153–64, 169, 177, 210, *341*, 358n 32. *See also* Bayou Bend

Lee, Mabel (Mrs. T. F. Rothwell), 183
Leers, Jackson, 336
Leonard, Margaret, 124
Lescaze, William, 295
Lessard, Suzannah, 340, 347n 51
Lindeberg, Harrie T., 2, 7, 222
Lindsey, John H., 4
Lipartito, Kenneth, 20
live oak avenues, 7, 9, 19, 20, 31
Lloyd, Hermon, 124, 290
London, Ruth, 85, 104, 156
Lovett, Edgar Odell, 7
Luckmann, Thomas, 338
Lutyens, Edwin L., 28, 139

Mackay, William, 87
MacKie, Frederick J., 296
Magnolia Lounge, 295
Magnolia Petroleum Company, 183, 295
Main Boulevard, Houston, 7, 8, 73
Main Street, Houston, 7
Maragliotti, Vincent, 12
Marcus, George E., 73
Martin, Annie (Mrs. W. S. Cochran), 26, 111
Massachusetts Institute of Technology (MIT), 2
Masterson, Carroll (née Sterling), 317
Masterson, Harris III, 308, 310, 311, 317
Masterson House (Rienzi), 290, 308–17, 318
Mauran, Russell and Crowell, 7
Maxson, Peter Flagg, 212, 217
Maxwell House coffee, 153
McComb, David G., 246
McGinty, Milton, 156
McKim, Mead and White, 2, 7
Meachum, Marguerite (Mrs. J. S. Mellinger), 104
Mecom, John W., 162
Mecom, Mary Elizabeth (née Withers), 162
Mellinger, George J., 111
Mellinger, John Sweeney, 104, 111
Mellinger, Marguerite (née Meachum), 104
Mellinger House, 104, 108–10, 111
Memorial area, Houston, 69, 220–30, 243, 244, 306
Memorial Park, 69
Memorial Park Estates, Houston, 244
Menil, Dominique de (née Schlumberger), 301–2
Menil, John de, 301–2
Menil House, 301, 302
middle class: and Bayou Bend experience, 78, 80; Garden Villas subdivision, 220; Jewish, 331; and modernism, 301, 369n 65–66; and ranch house type, 297, 301; small country houses for, 113, 134; and stigmatizing of bungalow, 114; suburban encroachment on country retreats, 244; upper-class construction of, 337–38
Miesian architectural practices, 301–2, 325
Mies van der Rohe, Ludwig, 301, 302
Milby and Dow, 31
Miller, Christian J., 21, 26, 78
Miller, Pete, 198, 248, 250, 290
Miller, Robert P., 306
Mills, Ballinger Jr., 124
Mitchell, Elizabeth (Mrs. J. W. Neal), 153, 162
MIT (Massachusetts Institute of Technology), 2
Modern Houston (Maragliotti), 12
modernism: ambivalence toward class system, 177, 290, 297, 301, 334, 338, 369n 65–66; Anderson House, 317, 319–24; architectural leaders, 295–97, 301, 302; and Camp House, 197; and continuity, 77, 291, 293, 297, 319, 331; vs. eclecticism, 4, 9, 66, 76, 290, 336 340, 343; Elkins houses, 289, 302–5, 306, 325–31; Fay Cottage, 331–33, 361n 36; functionalism, 295, 319; Hoggs' construction of, 78; influence on Houston, 295–301, 325; Miesian architectural practices, 301–2; and ranch house type, 290, 297, 301, 306–8; vs. regionalism, 288; Rienzi, 290, 308–17, 318; Staub's struggle with, 290, 297, 306–8; Straus House, 196, 290–95
modernization and River Oaks, 69–70, 73
Monteith, Walter E., 73
monumentality and intimacy: Bayou Club, 239; Broadacres houses, 25; country retreats, 222, 225; grand houses, 139, 145, 151, 169, 182, 201; modern houses, 311; and regionalism, 287; River Oaks houses, 94; Staub's talent for combining, 338, 340; and typification, 250, 254
Moody House, 297, 298
Moore, Harvin C., 124, 290
Morgan, W. B., 290
Morgan-Bouiffle Company, 262
Morgan's Point area, 212–17
movement in architectural space. *See* spatial organization
Muir, Rob, 4
Mulvey, Carl, 124
Murray, Thomas M., 31, 44
Myers, J. Allen Jr., 35

Nalle, Julia (Mrs. T. W. Gregory), 252
Nance, Martha (Mrs. D. M. Picton), 117
naturalization: Broadacres houses, 59; country retreats, 214, 217, 232, 233–34, 235; grand houses, 138, 145, 162, 200; modern houses, 332; and proportionality, 139; and regionalism, 268, 274; and social construction of identity, 247; Staub's talent for, 12, 336, 338, 343. *See also* climatic responsiveness; topography
nature vs. history as basis for architecture, 114
Navarro Oil Company, 179, 198
Neal, Elizabeth (née Mitchell), 153, 162
Neal, James Robert, 153, 156
Neal, John W., 153
Neal, Marian Holt (née Seward), 153, 162
Neal House: architectural profile, 153–64, 169; and Cheekwood House, Nashville, 358n 32; vs. Cullen House, 177; entrance portal, 135; and social construction of identity, 169, 210; stair detail, 341
Neff, Emily (née Ballew), 73
neighborhoods and social geography, 347n 46. *See also individual neighborhoods*
Nelson, Pete L., 217
Neuhaus, Hugo V., 7
Neuhaus, Hugo V., Jr., 302
Neuhaus, Lillie (Mrs. W. T. Carter, Jr.), 165, 217
Neutra, Richard, 295–96
New Orleans influences, 76–77, 94, 99, 100
Nichols, William, 319
North Boulevard, Broadacres, 21–26, 31–35, 42–44, 46–51
Northrop, Joseph W., Jr., 68, 73, 114, 117
Nunn, Stayton, 124

oil industry: Bruton, 248; consensus in, 362n 11; and country retreats, 232; Cullen, 164–65; and emergent elites, 7, 20, 179, 198, 247, 355n 26; and grand houses, 183, 192; Harrison, 281; Hoggs' investment in, 68; and Houston's development, 6, 7; prorationing debate, 246–47; Wiess, 227
Oliver, Charles W., 100
Olmsted, Frederick Law, 347n 49, 360n 11
Olmsted Brothers, 156

Palladian-contemporary dialectic: Anderson House, 317, 319–24; and class system paradox, 334; Elkins House, 325–31; Fay Cottage, 332; introduction, 4, 301–2; Rienzi, 290, 308–17, *318*; and Staub's response to modernism, 337
Palmer Memorial Church, 227
Park Realty and Investment Company, 212
Parten, Jubal R., 247, 296–97
Parten, Opal (née Woodley), 296–97
Parten House, 297
patrician subjectivity: advertising for, 70; architecture's contribution to, 12, 15, 66, 111; Bayou Club, 239; Broadacres houses, 30, 31, 65; and Broadacres pedigrees, 20; and community solidarity, 217; country retreats, 225, 227; definition, 2; grand houses, 136, 192, 198; and historic modeling, 9, 263; Houston elites' adoption of, 78, 165, 336, 347n 46; and layering of space, 26; and modernism, 297, 302, 319; multiple aspects of, 230; and New Orleans influence, 77; and Palladian-contemporary dialectic, 317, 319; and regionalism, 278; River Oaks houses, 96, 99; small country houses, 114, 117, 124; Staub's role in, 1, 2–3, 15, 336–37; and typification, 248, 252; and virtues of limitation, 340. *See also* social construction of upper-class identity
Patton House, 69
Patton plantation, 68
Peden, D. D., 7
Peden House, *10*, 227
Peden Iron and Steel Company, 212
Pencil Points, 4, 128, 262
Phelan, Johanna (née Cunningham), 183
Phelan, John Henry, 183
Phelan House, 183
Phenix, Vance D., 124, 156
Phillips, Kevin, 129
Picton, David M., Jr., 117
Picton, Martha (née Nance), 117
Picton House, 114–17, *119*
picturesqueness: Broadacres houses, 26, 28, 50, 52, 59, 65; River Oaks houses, 96, 104
Pinewood Estates, Houston, 306
Piney Point Village, Texas, 297, 367n 28
postmodern critique of modernism, 336
Potter, Hugh, 3, 68, 70, 111, 117, 244
Pratt, Alice (Mrs. G. . R. Brown), 124
Pratt, Joseph, 6, 20, 246
Pratt, Pearl (née Stuckey), 255, 259
Pratt, Wallace E., 255, 259
Pratt House, 255, 259, 363n 29
Progressivism, 7, 12, 73, 113–14, 347n 49
proportionality: Bayou Club, 237; Broadacres houses, 59; grand houses, 182, 194; modern houses, 306, 308, 311, 317; and naturalization, 139; and regionalism, 278, 287; River Oaks houses, 94; small country houses, 113, 114, 115, 117, 119; Staub's liberatory style, 15, 25; and typification, 250. *See also* monumentality and intimacy
proprietary land development, 20

Quintana Petroleum Company, 165

race and ethnicity: Bayou Bend's masking of, 99; Jewish community in Houston, 331, 365n 8; and proprietary land development, 20; segregation as given, 15, 26
ranch house type: and Fay Cottage, 332; Gregory House, 306–8; middle-class coding of, 297, 301; Staub's style, 290, 306, 334
Randall, Edward, Jr., 133
Randall House, 133–34
Randolph, Frankie (née Carter), 217
Randolph, Mary (Mrs. J. C. Wilson), 183, 192, 359n 71
Randolph, Robert D., 217
Randolph Stable, 217
Rather, Inez, 113, 129
Rather, John Thomas, Jr., 3, 4, 124, 297
Ravenna (Farish House), 179–87, 259–60, 287
Reconstruction Finance Corporation, 246
Redbird House, 73, *75*
Reed Roller Bit Company, 179
regionalism: Fleming Summer House, 263, 265, 268–78; Harrison House, 261, 278–81, 287; introduction, 262; and Palladian style, 319; Scurry House, 262–63, *264*, *266–67*; and social construction of identity, 287–88; Staub's expression of, 262, 274; Wray House, 282–88
Renfert, Heinrich, 113
repetition, 246. *See also* typification
resort settings. *See* country retreats
restraint: Fay Cottage, 331, 332; and limits on display of class, 201, 210, 340; and typification, 247, 250, 255
Reynolds, Elizabeth (Mrs. H. Gartner), 145, 151
Rice, Ella (Mrs. J. O. Winston, Jr.), 198
Rice, Lottie (Mrs. S. P. Farish), 179
Rice Institute (Rice University), 7, 8, 20, 227
Rienzi (Masterson House), 290, 308–17, *318*
River Crest, Fort Worth, 136, 138–53
River Oaks Boulevard, 70, 72, 164
River Oaks Community Center, 99, *101*, 355n 79
River Oaks Corporation, 68, 70, 73, 124, 129
River Oaks Country Club, 3, 7, 68, 73, 74, 244
River Oaks Country Club Estates, Houston: advertising for, 4, 351n 24; and city vs. country environs, 70; Elkins House, 289, 302–5, *306*; gate piers, 67, 99, *101*, 248; historical development, 68–73, 74, 351–52n 23–24; introduction, 3; and Latin Colonial style, 73–78, 99–100, 114–17, *119*, 124; Mellinger House, 104, *108–10*, 111; modernism's impact on, *196*, 290–95, 296–97, 301, 302; regionalist houses in, 262–63; small houses in, 114–24, *125*, *127*, 129, 133; and social construction of identity, 7, 68, 69, 70, 73, 78, 96, 99, 104, 111, 246–47, 355n 79; Tall Timbers, 70, 244, 297, 317, 319–24; Welder House, 259, *260*, 363n 29. *See also* Bayou Bend; Homewoods
River Oaks Garden Club, 78, 354n 52
Robsjohn-Gibbings, T. H., 290, 293, 325
Roeser, Charles F., 151, 247
Rothwell, Mabel (née Lee), 183
Rothwell, Talbott F., 183
Rowe, Colin, 21, 301, 302, 338, 343
Rowles, Winston and Company, 198
Russell Brown Company, 183

Saarinen, Eero, 338
Saarinen, Eliel, 305
Salisbury, Hiram A., 124, 129
Sanders and Company, 111
Sanguinet, Staats and Hedrick, 153
scale and proportionality. *See* proportionality
Schiwetz, E. M., 124
Schlumberger, Dominique (Mrs. J. de Menil), 301
Schwartzer, Mitchell, 99
Scurry, Sarah (née Chambers), 262
Scurry, Tom, 262
Scurry House, 262–63, *264*, *266–67*
Sealy, George, 7
Second National Bank, 153
self-effacement theme, 235, 239, 246, 260
service station prototype design, 227

Sewall, Blanche (née Harding), 73, 76
Sewall, Cleveland, 76
Sewall House, 76
Seward, Marian Holt (Mrs. J. R. Neal), 153, 162
Shadyside, Houston: vs. country retreat setting, 222; early development of, 9; Farish House, 7, 10; Peden House, 10, 227; Wray House, 282–88
Shepherd, Benjamin A., 26, 111
Sherwood Forest, Houston, 244
ship channel project, 6
Sims Bayou, Garden Villas, 220
site planning: Broadacres, 18–20; country retreats, 234; integration with house, 21, 31, 317; live oak avenues, 7, 9, 19, 20, 31; and regionalism, 262; spatial layering in, 9; and typification, 246, 248
Skidmore, Owings and Merrill, 338
small country houses: architectural competition, 124–33; definition of, 113; introduction, 113–14; Picton House, 114–17, 119; and social construction of identity, 113, 117, 129, 133–34; Staub House, 117–18, 120–24
Smallwood, Robert, 214
Smart, Pamela G., 7, 9, 70
Smith, Elizabeth (née Wiess), 227
Smith, Madeline (née Welder), 104
Smith, William A., 104
Soane, John, 44, 129, 169
social construction of upper-class identity: architecture's role in, 7, 9–15, 31, 66, 111, 338; Broadacres, 19–20, 21, 23, 31, 35, 65–66; consensus through architecture, 246–47, 362*n* 12; country houses' role in, 1–2, 19; country retreats, 214, 217, 220, 222, 227, 233, 243–44; in democratic society, 3, 9, 15, 69–70, 162, 168, 340, 347*n* 51; grand houses, 136, 151, 156, 162, 168, 169, 177, 192, 198, 201, 210; and historical eclecticism, 9, 31; and Hoggs siblings' civic role, 7, 69, 73, 111; and immigrant assimilation, 165; internal limits on, 201, 210, 340; and modernism, 290, 293, 295, 301, 312, 317, 331; and proprietary land development, 20; and regionalism, 287–88; in River Oaks, 7, 68, 69, 70, 73, 78, 96, 99, 104, 111, 246–47, 355*n* 79; small country houses, 113, 117, 129, 133–34; Staub's contribution to, 1–3, 15, 136, 230, 262, 335–43; and typification, 247, 255, 259–60. *See also* elites, entrepreneurial; patrician subjectivity; virtues, upper-class
South Boulevard, Broadacres, 26–31
South Post Oak Lane, Houston, 217, 230, 244
Southwell, Owen J., 183
Sparke, Penny, 7, 338
spatial organization: Broadacres houses, 23, 25–26; grand houses, 136; hierarchical, 87, 104, 129; and Houston's lack of zoning, 5; and landscaping, 12; modern houses, 330–31; River Oaks houses, 85, 87, 94, 104; small country houses, 113, 117; and social construction of identity, 1, 9, 15; Staub's principles of, 12, 21, 23, 26. *See also* continuity; integration; layering of space; topography
speculative land development, 68, 73, 114
The Stables (Wiess Stables), 211, 220–30, 325
Staub, Alice (née York) (daughter-in-law), 5
Staub, Anna Cornelia (née Fanz) (mother), 2
Staub, Caroline (Mrs. C. Callery) (daughter), 5
Staub, Fritz (father), 2
Staub, John Delabarre (son), 5, 117
Staub, John F.: antiques interest, 122, 124; and Barnstone, 4, 15; biographical sketch, 2–5, 346*n* 20; client relationships, 136, 177, 197, 212, 278; contribution to historical eclecticism, 1, 288; critical assessment of, 262; elements of social style, 217; European influences on, 153; and Hoggs, 3, 73; integration of house and site, 21, 31, 317; on Latin Colonial style, 77–78; as master of balance, 227; Mies van der Rohe on, 302; and Palladian-contemporary dialectic, 337; photo, 1; practical problem-solving talent, 120; principles of design, 12, 15, 21, 23, 25, 26, 136, 230, 336, 338, 340, 343; rarity of grand houses for, 136; and regionalism, 262, 274; as small country house inspiration, 124; and social construction of identity, 1–3, 15, 136, 230, 262, 335–43, 336–37; struggle with modernism, 290, 297, 306–8
Staub, Madeleine Louise (née Delabarre) (wife): antiques interest, 122, 124; background of, 2; and client relations, 3, 20; death of, 5; memberships, 346*n* 21
Staub, Nancy (Mrs. W. Wareing, Jr.) (daughter), 4, 117
Staub, Peter (grandfather), 2
Staub, Rather and Howe, 4
Staub House, 117–18, 120–24
Stedman, Wilfred H., 73
Steele, D. F., 192
Sterling, Carroll (Mrs. H. Masterson III), 317
Sterling, Frank Prior, 20, 317
Sterling, Ross S., 214, 247, 317
Sterling Bay Cottage, 214, 217
Stinson, Sallie (Mrs. J. S. Hogg), 68
Stone, Edward Durell, 295
Straus, Carol (née Austin), 290
Straus, Robert D., 290, 291, 365*n* 8
Straus-Frank Company, 290
Straus House, 196, 290–95
Straus Recreation House, 293, 295, 296
Stuckey, Pearl (Mrs. W. E. Pratt), 255, 259
Stude, Henry W., 69
subdivisions. *See* land development; *individual neighborhoods*
suburban development: architecture of, 76; encroachment on country retreats, 244; enlightened, 73; post-WWII architectural shifts, 4; and resort areas, 214; small country houses, 113
sustainability. *See* climatic responsiveness
Swank, Arch B., 262
Swenson, Bailey, 331
symmetry: Bayou Club, 237, 239; Broadacres houses, 21, 31, 35, 42–43, 65; country retreats, 222, 225, 233; grand houses, 169, 194; modern houses, 293, 317; and regionalism, 287; River Oaks houses, 82, 85, 87, 91, 104; small country houses, 114, 115, 116, 119; and typification, 248, 250
systematic integration. *See* integration

Tall Timbers, River Oaks, 70, 244, 297, 317, 319–24
technology of self-fashioning: and antique collecting, 124; architecture as, 340; and Bayou Bend imagery, 78; definition, 7; Masterson House, 317; Staub's houses as, 336
Tennant, Joseph A., 31, 35
Tennant, Lucile (née Borden), 31, 35
Tennant House, 35–45, 349*n* 26
Texas Centennial, 262, 295
Texas Company, 68
Texas Corinthian Yacht Club, 297, 331–33
Texas Railroad Commission, 68, 247
Thad Dederick Construction Company, 308
Thompson, George, Jr., 151
Thomson, Eleanor (Mrs. P. Hutcheson), 20
Thomson, H. B., 20
Todd, Anderson, 302
topography: compensation for flat, 12, 70, 100, 183, 185, 343; and landscape design, 7, 21; River Crest context, 138
typification: Bayou Club, 243; Bowles House, 250–52; Bruton House, 248–50, 254; and country retreats, 233; Harrison and Farish houses, 287; Heyer House, 245, 252–57; and individuality, 30–31, 246, 248, 250, 254, 255, 259–60; in modern houses, 291; origins of concept,

typification (*cont.*)
348n 57; and regionalism, 278; and social construction of identity, 247, 255, 259–60; and spread of Staub's ideas, 252. *See also* country houses; ranch house type

upper-class identity. *See* social construction of upper-class identity
Usonian modernism, 290, 296, 301, 368n 49

Vandenberge, Mary (Mrs. G. A. Hill, Jr.), 255
Varner Company, 117
Varner Plantation, 68, 69
Varner Realty Company, 69
Vaughan, Sue (Mrs. W. L. Clayton), 76
ventilation considerations. *See* climatic responsiveness
vernacular buildings: and Bayou Bend, 94, 95, 96; Bermuda, 332; Creole planters house, 234, 237, 281; New Orleans influences, 76–77, 94, 99, 100
Vinson and Elkins, 247
virtues, upper-class: architectural expression of, 1, 15, 99, 343; Broadacres houses, 30, 44, 66; interior design, 124; and limitation, 201, 210, 340; and small country houses, 129. *See also* civic virtue
volumetric qualities. *See* proportionality

W. T. Carter Lumber and Building Company, 217
Wareing, Elizabeth (née Blanton), 5
Wareing, Nancy (née Staub) (daughter), 4, 117
Wareing, Peter Staub (grandson), 5
Wareing, William A. III (grandson), 4
Wareing, William A., Jr. (son-in-law), 4
Warren and Wetmore, 7
Watkin, William Ward, 7, 18, 19, 114, 153, 222
Welder, Dolores (Mrs. W. J. Crabb), 259
Welder, Madeline (Mrs. W. A. Smith), 104
Welder House, 259, 260, 363n 29
West, Ruth, 100
West and Jensen, 153, 164
West Oaks, Houston, 244
Westover Hills, Texas, 297
Whinery, Esther (Mrs. R. Goodrich), 230
White, Estelle (Mrs. K. S. Dargan), 42
White, Stanford, 340
Wiess, Caroline (Mrs. W. H. Francis, Jr., Mrs. T. N. Law), 4, 248
Wiess, Elizabeth (Mrs. L. H. Smith), 227
Wiess, Harry C., 7, 220, 227, 230
Wiess, Margaret (Mrs. J. A. Elkins, Jr.), 227, 302, 325
Wiess, Olga (née Keith), 220
Wiess Stables, 211, 220–30, 325
Wilkinson, Edward, 297
Williams, David R., 262
Wilson, J. Cooke, 183, 192
Wilson, Mary (née Randolph), 183, 192, 359n 71
Wilson, Morris, Crain and Anderson, 325
Wilson House, 183, 188–92, 359n 71
Windfohr, Anne (née Burnett), 297
Windfohr, Robert F., 297
Windfohr House, 297–300
Windham, Russell, 136
Winston, Ella (née Rice), 198
Winston, James O., 198
Winston House, 198–209
Withers, Mary Elizabeth (Mrs. J. W. Mecom), 162
Womack, Kenneth E., 7, 73
Woodley, Opal (Mrs. J. R. Parten), 296
World War I, 2, 6
World War II, 4
Wray, Andrew Jackson, 287, 288
Wray, Couch and Elder, 288
Wray, Margaret (née Cullinan), 287, 288
Wray House, 282–88
Wright, Frank Lloyd, 290, 305, 368n 49
Wright, Theon, 164–65

Yergin, Daniel, 68
York, Alice (Mrs. J. D. Staub) (daughter-in-law), 5

ISMAEL

I believe in the body

IVO

IMPULSTANZ
Vienna International Dance Festival

ISMAEL

I believe in the body

Edited by Johannes Odenthal
With photographs by Anno Wilms
and Dieter Blum

Spector Books

IVO

Table of contents

INTRODUCTION Ismael Ivo. The unfinished reconstruction of a lifework—Johannes Odenthal and Karl Regensburger [4]

CHAPTER A

A visionary of the body: On Ismael Ivo's early solo productions—Johannes Odenthal [14] "We were not afraid to link all these different influences". Percussionist and composer Dudu Tucci in conversation with Johannes Odenthal [34] "It was fascinating to see him dance in my notations! The magic of an enchanted time". Choreographer and performer Mara Borba in conversation with Petra Schaeber [42] Santa Thereza. Marcel Kaskeline on the Black activist Thereza Santos [51] "We firmly believed that it is very important for people to see Ismael's work". Karl Regensburger, Director of ImPulsTanz Vienna, on the beginning of a unique collaboration [54] "An existential pain was inscribed in his body". Andrée Valentin, first manager and companion, remembers Ismael Ivo [66] On the difficulty of continuing with the development of Expressive Dance. Dancer, journalist, and movement explorer Irene Sieben recalls Ismael Ivo's artistic arrival in Berlin [74] "We are both very much into Black empowerment". Francesca Harper, artistic director of Ailey II, in conversation with Petra Schaeber [82] "I'm interested in the magical aspect of movement". Johannes Odenthal in conversation with Ismael Ivo (2004) [90] Dance as trance-action. A homage by dance scholar Gabriele Brandstetter [102]

CHAPTER B

Artaud, Genet, and Müller: How Ismael Ivo links radical theatrical modernism with postcolonialism—Johannes Odenthal [106] The emergence of images from images —remembering *Francis Bacon*. Artist Penelope Wehrli on space and the body in choreographic theater [122] "Is the body still a taboo?". A conversation with Ismael Ivo on the occasion of the new production of *Othello* (1995) [130] "Ismael was always aware that his exhibiting the naked Black body for a predominantly white audience would be seen as a provocation". Werner Schretzmeier, co-founder and director of the Theaterhaus Stuttgart, in conversation with Johannes Odenthal [138] The art of George Tabori. Marcel Kaskeline on the origins of an artistic friendship [147] "There was a veritable fan club that would wait for Ismael after the performances". Dancer Riccarda Herre in conversation with Johannes Odenthal on the time in Weimar [150] "A brother from the same origins". Choreographer and dancer Koffi Kôkô on Ismael Ivo [158] "Intuition is memory pointed toward the future". Ismael Ivo in conversation with Johannes Odenthal (2004) [162] "Ismael was an artistic synthesis, a total work of art". Visual artist Gottfried Helnwein in conversation with Johannes Odenthal [170] "A change in perception is the basis for a change in reality". Ismael Ivo in conversation with Johannes Odenthal (2013) [178]

APPENDIX Image credits [280] Acknowledgements [283] Biographies [284] Colophon [288]

CHAPTER C

Life as a dance and the world as a play. Dance scholar and researcher in movement Cássia Navas in conversation with Petra Schaeber [186] "How can space inspire movement and movement inspire space?". Marcel Kaskeline in conversation with Johannes Odenthal [202] Mapplethorpe. Marcel Kaskeline on the importance of Robert Mapplethorpe for Ismael Ivo [214] A river of ideas. Dance curator Rino Achille de Pace on working with Ismael Ivo in Venice [218] "There it was, what he wanted the whole time: intensity!". Dancer Fernanda Bueno in conversation with Petra Schaeber [226] On working with Ismael. Choreographic assistants Franca Pagliasotto, Valentina Schisa, and Elisabetta Violante on their collaboration with Ismael Ivo [234] The cannibal of the opera house. Ismael Ivo on the challenges of a new Brazilian art of dance—in conversation with Johannes Odenthal (2017) [242] A living library of gestures. Danilo Santos de Miranda, regional director, SESC São Paulo, on European-Brazilian collaborations [246]

CHAPTER D

Catalogue raisonné and biography—Marcel Kaskeline [257]

This book has two parallel levels: in the rhythm of the double pages, photo series alternate with contributions by the authors. The photo series on the double pages 4/5 through to 112/113 is by Anno Wilms, the pictures were taken between 1982 and 1991 in Berlin and New York. The photo series on the double pages 116/117 through to 254/255 is by Dieter Blum. The pictures were taken between 1993 and 2012 on the stage and in the studio and on a journey he took with Ismael Ivo to Brazil.

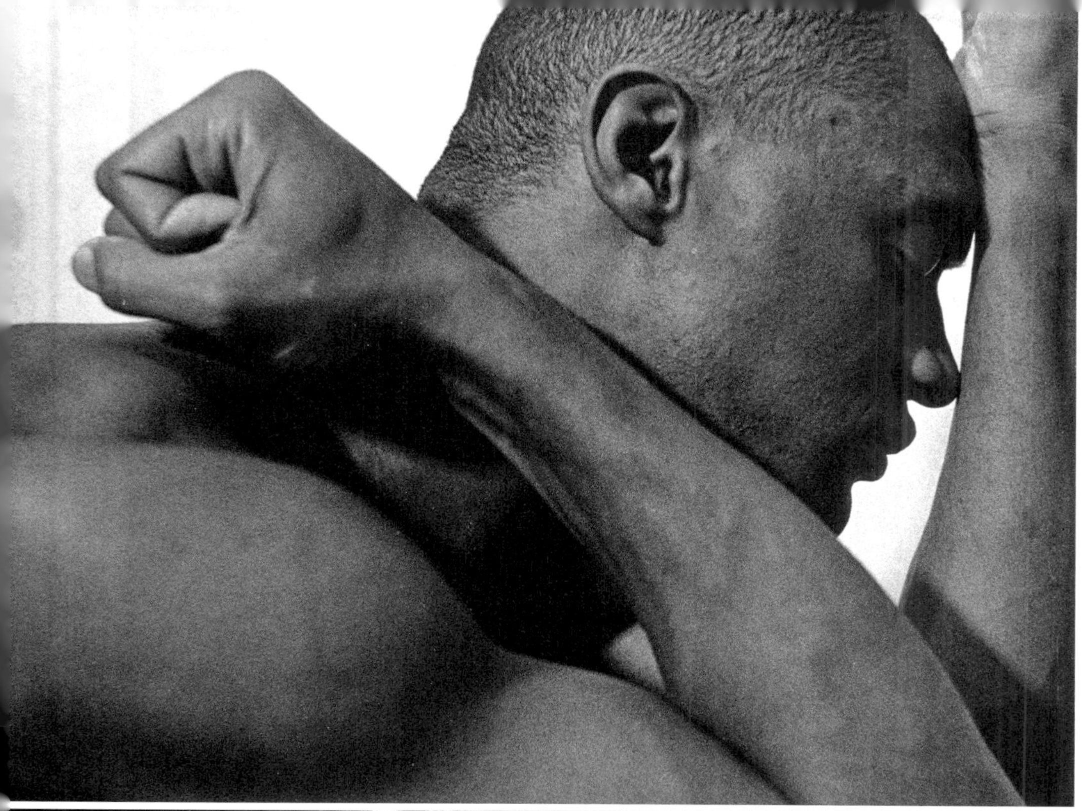

Ismael Ivo

The unfinished reconstruction of a lifework

This book is a tribute to Ismael Ivo. The Afro-Brazilian performer, choreographer, teacher, initiator of festivals and educational programs, and director of dance companies did not just leave behind an oeuvre of more than 100 choreographies; his vision of dance as a way of emancipation from social injustice and resistance with the means of contemporary art points far beyond his untimely death in April 2021.

This book gives voice to a wide range of contemporary witnesses to his artistic biography. Ismael Ivo's legacy is essentially immaterial, passed on solely in the memories of his overwhelming presence on stage, in photographs, films and video documentations, in interviews, in the impulses for movement that he set in countless workshops and conversations. For us, this project raised the fundamental question of how a personality whose work was radically based on the transformation and mediation of the body can be portrayed in a book.

Apart from dance itself, Ismael Ivo's life's work unfolded on a primarily oral level. In interviews, he has spoken about the processes of embodiment, of taking up political, social, artistic or cultural causes—the concrete manifestation of an aesthetic metabolism. He repeatedly refers to the first cultural manifesto of Brazilian modernism, to *Antropofagia*, a work by a group of writers around Oswald de Andrade who emancipated themselves from European colonization. In doing so, Ismael Ivo placed the performative possibilities of the body at the center of his work: as a means of expression, as translation, as an assertion of one's own space, as resistance, and also as a militant message.

The creation of this book posed challenges not only over how to engage with Ismael Ivo's immense body of work, but how to devise a suitable form for it at the same time. In collaboration with the publisher and the graphic designer, we have chosen a path that functions on two levels: that of physical expression in the photo series by Anno Wilms and Dieter Blum, and that of verbal, above all oral, mediation in the interviews with Ismael Ivo and his companions. It is an attempt at a contemporary archaeological "excavation" that allows us to experience Ismael Ivo's work from as many different perspectives as possible.

On a more general level, it is also an attempt to counter the immateriality of contemporary dance with a journalistic work of memory charged with the present. The result is an assemblage of

recollections approaching a key performative oeuvre of the last fifty years, in the spirit of Walter Benjamin's *Arcades Project*—unfinished and based on the personal encounters of the artists and companions involved.
It shows that it is above all through the connection with his biography as an Afro-Brazilian that the work of Ismael Ivo will have an impact on future developments in the performing arts. The themes of racism, identity, post- and neo-colonial dislocation are deeply rooted in his work. The fact that Ismael Ivo's path has taken him from São Paulo via New York, Berlin, Vienna, Stuttgart, Weimar, and Venice back to São Paulo—with excursions all over the world—is part of the unique profile of this exceptional artist.
The publication is organized into four sections:

CHAPTER A
focuses on the early solos of the 1980s, in which Ismael Ivo, drawing on the potential of African-American rituals, developed his individual language and his own presence—with incredibly successful solo productions such as *Ritual of a Body in Moon*, *Phoenix*, *Under Skin*, or *Delirium of a Childhood*. At the same time, he began working with Karl Regensburger to establish the Vienna Dance Weeks, later to become the ImPulsTanz festival.

CHAPTER B
is dedicated to the intensive collaboration with Ushio Amagatsu, Hans Kresnik, Márcia Haydée, Koffi Kôkô, and George Tabori in productions of the 1990s such as *Apocalypse*, *Francis Bacon*, *Othello*, or *The Maids* after Jean Genet, produced in close cooperation with ImPulsTanz, the Theaterhaus Stuttgart, the Weimar National Theater and the Haus der Kulturen der Welt, Berlin.

CHAPTER C
summarizes the period of major choreographic production for companies worldwide, but especially in Venice and in São Paulo, where he was ballet director.

CHAPTER D
includes the first complete *catalogue raisonné* of Ismael Ivo's work, compiled by Marcel Kaskeline.

Johannes Odenthal and Karl Regensburger

A visionary of the body
On Ismael Ivo's early solo productions
Johannes Odenthal

The solo production *Phoenix*, created in 1985, is one of Ismael Ivo's key works. It is his first major stage production in Europe. After its premiere at the Schaubühne am Lehniner Platz, *Phoenix* plays for one week in Berlin. In Hamburg, the piece is seen by more than 20,000 people in four weeks. It establishes Ismael Ivo as a performer and lays the foundation for his artistic and personal path in Europe. In nine movement images, the mythical bird Phoenix, a symbol of rebirth, becomes the template for a radical self-invention in the pervasion and transformation of his own body's history. Ismael Ivo dances his way of resistance against foreign determination as a Black man and as a dancer. Like a mighty bird, he can spread his arms as wings, developing a driving dynamic of motion in stomping sequences of steps that are marked by lightning-fast switches between body concepts of ballet, modern dance, or ritualistic movement sequences from Candomblé. Images of imprisonment, oppression, and existential desolation alternate with expansive extroverted explosions of his power to dominate the stage. Ballet poses instantly spiral into ecstatic head and shoulder movements that charge the body with energies of transgression.

In a ten-minute movement sequence with a white parasol, Ismael Ivo embodies layers of meaning from the rituals of Candomblé as well as the racist structures of Brazilian society, which abolished slavery only at the end of the nineteenth century, the last in the Western world to do so. The parasol is not only a symbol of colonial influences but also an integral part of the great rituals of African American religions. For Ismael, the umbrella becomes an extension of the body wherein the social and spiritual energies of his own history are concentrated. It is impressive to witness a transformation process taking place within the movements, within the posture, from externally determined restriction to a physical liberation from those constraints through the construction of a new self. To become master of one's own body, to assert one's own space: this is the message that Ismael Ivo celebrates in

Phoenix. It is also the exposure of the naked body as a radical surrender to such a public process of redefinition. Ismael Ivo thereby touches on an existential level the yearning for a confrontation of collective and individual traumas and entrenched societal injustices that can affect every human being. It is this search for a shared history and for a shared future that constitutes the utopian core of his solo performances. In the colonial metaphor of the umbrella, Ismael Ivo condenses the process of social transformation. In the 1985 program booklet he writes:

> Let us try to open the gateways to the fountainhead of creative powe r. Pan-African art is grounded in an intellectual history strongly focused on ethical and social concerns. Past, present, and future memories of one's roots or of a nationality are components that every artist carries within themselves. And so the deep connection to their own roots comes alive within them, too, and they embody—whether we realize it or not—the bridge to a past that is common to us all.

This shared past is not always comfortable: "It doesn't bother me. I invoke, I cry, I fight, I scream." For him, the memory of what we have in common is a web of conflicts that he accepts as a challenge and puts on stage in the image of the *Phoenix*. He names growing up in São Paulo, one of the largest urban centers on earth, as a lesson of life.

> ... persistent racial conflicts hiding behind a false image of democracy, constant presence of devastating poverty, yet also the persistence of human brotherhood, the persistence of a hidden love that feeds on its cultural roots. African roots, Brazilian roots, the heritage of Indigenous cultures almost completely annihilated and isolated, and their blending with the culture of immigrants.
>
> If we take a closer look at the country, we see big cities, daring modernity, and industrial audacity, coupled with violence, poverty, and prostitution at all levels, immorality, and corruption in all social classes. Following the ostensible liberation from slavery, the African American diaspora has settled as a 'sub-existence' around the big cities.

Ismael Ivo takes a combative stance both in his performance and in his texts. To him, the criticism of a racist and unjust society is

just as important as the recourse to one's own cultural origins, I
to the knowledge of African intellectual and physical history. The West African dancer and choreographer Koffi Kôkô, one of Ismael Ivo's closest artistic companions since the 1990s, describes this equally nostalgic and traumatic aspect of his friend's quest. Between Koffi Kôkô's socialization in Benin and Ismael Ivo's in São Paulo stands the Black Atlantic, the history of three centuries of slavery.

I remember: in my childhood, on Sundays we attended church with the family, but on Fridays we attended African rituals. The celebrants were always dressed in white, and they engaged in spiritual consultations with the ancestors. There was one special day: this was dedicated to the magic cult of 'preto velho', the spirit of the elderly slaves of African descent who worked and died in Brazil. The 'pretos velhos', highly respected for their austerity and honesty, still remembered the old Africa; they told of their sufferings, and they gave us advice and hope for the future. They were old and tired; as soon as they arrived, they always demanded a 'chair'. There were long pauses in their speech, silences, stares into the void, meditative concentration, sometimes disrupted by sudden twitches and tremors, an uncanny physical intensity of life, timeless expressions. They have always fascinated me. This was my first contact with the history of my roots, with the origins of the African diaspora. It was the beginning of my reflection on life, death, rebirth, and eternity.

What Ismael Ivo describes here in reference to *Phoenix*, the vigorous quest for his own roots as the starting point for a redefinition and self-discovery of his personal and artistic position in the present, is a powerful catalyst for his performative practice, for his radical artistic position in the history of European dance. Central works in the 1980s such as *Under Skin* (1987) and *Delirium of a Childhood* (1989) follow in this *Phoenix* tradition.

Ismael Ivo was a personality who repeatedly turned his own biography into a utopian perspective. It was not only the critique

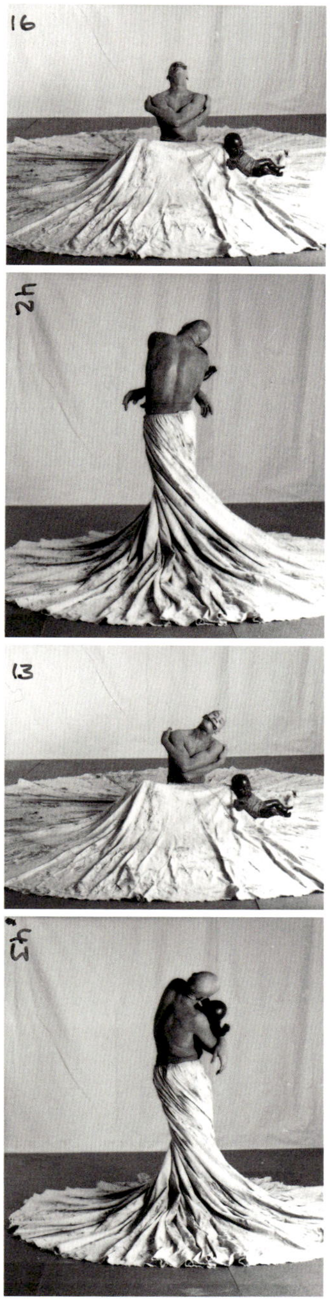

II

of an actual situation that was at the center of his solo productions, but above all the possibility of transformation. This links him to the most recent approaches of postcolonial thinkers such as Felwine Sarr, Nikita Dhawan, or Achille Mbembe, who, parallel to the massive critique of hegemonic white knowledge structures, also place the future of a planetary perspective for all of humanity at the center of their thinking and acting. I see Ismael Ivo as an artist whose work, as early as the 1980s, embodied these contemporary approaches more than almost anyone else, a pioneer who combined his message with an outstanding presence on stage in a way that few other performers have managed in the postwar period. In fact, Ismael Ivo connects to a visionary force of modern dance like that realized by a Mary Wigman or a Josephine Baker at the beginning of the twentieth century. In his solo performances, he combined a radical critique of society and culture with a deep longing for a humanist perspective. With this, he reached hundreds of thousands of people not only in Europe but around the world.

Phoenix was not the first production along this path. Ismael Ivo's international career began with his congenial musical partner Dudu Tucci at the end of the 1970s. In 1982, *Ritual of a Body in Moon* was the first of many successful productions in Berlin. In this piece, too, the body is initially concealed, this time in a wide hooded cape from which the dancer's foot emerges in an impressive sequence of movements. A magical space unfolds on stage in the manner of an evocation of spirits. Ismael Ivo is finally able to free himself from the invisibility of the cloak, only his head remains entangled in the fabric, from which the dancer twists a mighty rope that holds him captive. Only with the disentanglement from this restraint does the body gain its space. A bull's horn becomes a cultic wind instrument, the body emancipates itself by way of a movement ritual, lying on the floor, gyrating.

In *Phoenix*, there is a net suspended above the stage; here it is a 16-foot high ladder, from the top of which Ismael Ivo, hanging by

III

IV

his feet, lowers himself headfirst. In the progressive absorption of Afro-Brazilian ritual movements, the body finds its freedom. *Ritual of a Body in Moon* evolves between Brazil and Europe, drawing directly on Afro-Brazilian rituals, especially through Dudu Tucci's instrumentalization, while simultaneously opening the space for its own modern performance art.

For Ismael Ivo, the body was the starting point for his artistic work: the body as an infinite potential for individual transformation, for crossing boundaries, but also for a social perspective. This particular quality was fed from a variety of sources. Crucially, Ismael Ivo brought with him unique resources of physical potential, to which he was systematically devoted throughout his life with the utmost discipline. In turn, the central source of his artistic contextualization was the political Black Liberation Movement, which challenged the racist structures in Brazilian society. The close connection between performative forms of expression and political activism shaped Ismael Ivo's artistic approaches in the 1970s and continued in modified form throughout his entire oeuvre.

A second source was the Afro-Brazilian rituals of Candomblé, the experience of crossing physical boundaries, but above all the connection to African ancestors and spiritual roots.

A third source was the engagement with radical positions of modernism and contemporary art. From Antonin Artaud to Marina Abramović, the body as a medium of liberation and social transformation became a frame of reference that Ismael continued to explore systematically. Christianity and the history of civilization have shaped a hostility toward the body. Overcoming this as the starting point for revolutionary artistic action serves as a leitmotif throughout Ismael Ivo's work. His performances have frequently blended all three of these movements together.

The Return of the Body

In 1982, Suhrkamp Verlag published the anthology *Die Wiederkehr des Körpers* (The Return of the Body), edited by Dietmar Kamper and Christoph Wulf. This publication looks into a set of themes that have systematically preoccupied both science and art over the last forty years. It is about the question of how the human body can assert itself or find an active role within an increasingly independent dynamic of rationalism. The body seemed to have dropped off the ongoing process of enlightenment. This has fundamentally changed over the course of the twentieth century. From today's perspective, I would describe it in such a way that the human body as a repository of knowledge, as a medium of cognition, as a political actor, as the social base of our existence has become indispensable for the shaping of individual and collective futures. Today, the body has become a central focus especially in the humanities and artistic practice, but also for the epistemological processes in natural sciences.

On an aesthetic level, this debate took place in the performance art of the 1960s and 1970s, in the unconditional inclusion of the viewer's own presence as part of the creative process in the work of artists such as Joseph Beuys, Marina Abramović, Carolee Schneemann, or Joan Jonas, or the protagonists of Viennese Actionism. The performative body was centered around political themes such as the construction and deconstruction of identities, the breaking down of social prejudices, and the emancipation from heteronomy. The body has become a political platform for the negotiation and reinvention of identity. This corresponds to the new departure of a dance scene that frees itself from the conventional body images of ballet or modern dance. German dance

theater, Japanese Butoh, and American postmodern dance are the decisive impulses for a new dawn in the dance scene, where the stage once again becomes a space for critique and transformation. At the same time, these developments correspond with a broader public discourse. In the 1980s, new independent venues emerged that gave space to these changes, such as the Theaterhaus in Stuttgart, the Tanzfabrik and TanzTangente in Berlin, the ImPulsTanz festival in Vienna, the Werkstatt in Düsseldorf or Kampnagel in Hamburg. The new artistic developments are also reflected in the organization of workshops and new dance studios, in an explosion of body research, from Feldenkrais to Body Mind Centering, in the founding of new journals and the establishment of new scientific disciplines. Independent dance companies emerge and distinguish themselves outside the established theatrical landscape with alternative forms of production and content.

I believe it is very important to explain this situation of a fresh start in order to emphasize the context in which Ismael Ivo's performances took place. In Europe, Ivo encountered a dance, performance, and cultural scene for which his concept of the body as a form of expression and resistance, as a possibility for social emancipation and change, was an excellent fit. In this sense, the first major solo productions mentioned above, such as *Ritual of a Body in Moon* or *Phoenix*, were the artistic response to a fundamental change in the discourse of Western thought resulting from the intrusion of the body into the hitherto dominant rational worldview.

v

And yet Ismael Ivo himself was closely associated with the first Brazilian modernism of the 1920s, as he says in an interview, with Oswald de Andrade's *Manifesto Antropófago* and the literary character Macunaíma, the hero without any qualities, created by Mário de Andrade. Absorbing other cultures into one's own body, digesting them and spitting them out, in other words the idea of a physical processing of the most diverse cultural influences in Brazilian society and culture as a counter-proposal to European post-colonial dominance: Ismael Ivo was already grappling with this in the late 1970s in São Paulo—a cultural cannibalism as a provocation of European cultural dominance. From this perspective, Ismael Ivo quite naturally sought further connections on his artistic path, e.g. toward German expressive dance and dance theater: he studied Harald Kreutzberg and Mary Wigman, and established a continuous exchange with the protagonists of dance theater, above all with Hans Kresnik, but also with Susanne Linke, Reinhild Hoffmann, and Pina Bausch. Through the Japanese-Brazilian director and dancer Takao Kusuno, he was also already closely connected with Butoh while still in Brazil. In 1980 he created *As Galinhas*, directed by Kusuno, which featured the clipped feathers of chickens as a metaphor for dictatorship. Ten years later, Ismael Ivo renewed this direct contact with Butoh in his collaboration with Ushio Amagatsu. Intensive encounters with Kazuo and Yoshito Ohno followed. His search for new sources knew no bounds. Since the 1970s, he has repeatedly explored literature, systematically investigating radical approaches in theater and performance art. Ismael Ivo himself became a mediator of a tradition of radical modernism, as it is preserved in the work of Federico García Lorca, Antonin Artaud, Pier Paolo Pasolini, Jean Genet, or Heiner Müller.

VI

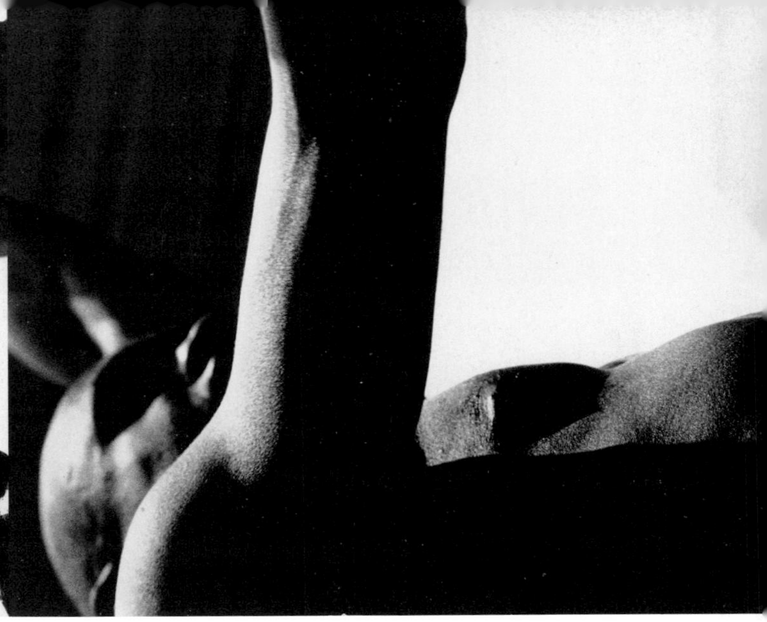

In these traditions, the human body was revealed as a memory space, as a living library, as the locus of trauma, but above all as a medium of transformation. As a result, the body became a political actor at the center of the arts. Ismael Ivo has helped to shape this transformation process, he embodied it and made it effective like few others.

I	Ismael Ivo with activists at a demonstration, 1981, Salvador de Bahia, photographer: Juca Martins/Olhar Imagem
II, VI	*Delirium of a Childhood*, 1989, photographer: Uwe Boek, Berlin
III	*Delirium of a Childhood*, 1988, photographer: Michael K. Epstein
IV	*Ritual of a Body in Moon*, 1984, photographer: George Ross
V	*Poetry Moves* in preparation for *Under Skin*, Literaturhaus Berlin, photographer: Othman Seehauser

"We were not afraid to link all these different influences"
Percussionist and composer Dudu Tucci in conversation with Johannes Odenthal

DUDU TUCCI When I met Ismael, he became my icon, the person to whom I could dedicate my music, to whom I dedicated myself artistically. That was in 1977, we were both twenty-two years old. I worked with him until 1985.

ODENTHAL Why was Ismael the ideal partner for your music?

TUCCI I come from an operatic family. My father was a singer, a soloist, my mother sang in the choir. Music was my heritage, my life. At college, I studied experimental music, John Cage, David Tudor, but also Schoenberg, Varèse, Bartók, Puccini, and of course Arrigo Barnabé. I was especially impressed by John Cage and his collaboration with Merce Cunningham. I wanted to create something comparable with Ismael.

At the same time, the rhythms of Umbanda, the Afro-Brazilian religion, also played an important role. At the age of eleven, I participated in the rituals of the Umbanda, at thirteen I was initiated, and I learned the rhythms of all the deities. I was familiar with these energies and their translation into music. Ismael was a person who could combine all those influences of the avant-garde and the tradition, just as I did. I came into contact with the avant-garde while I was at university. Back then, I was influenced by the Brazilian tradition. The Tropicalismo of Gilberto Gil or Caetano Veloso belonged to my generation. But our method was the *Antropofagia* movement. I did Cage à la Dudu, adapted Schoenberg, and combined both with the berimbau. My music incorporates Bartok as much as it does John Cage or Steve Reich.

We lived in a dictatorship that began in 1964 and ended only in 1985. *Ritual of a Body in Moon* was partly a response to this dictatorship. It was conceived as a theater production, using the means of physical expression in dialogue with the music. What we did was absolutely unusual, provocative. But we were not afraid to combine the most diverse influences. That was the essence of our artistic rapport.

In 1981, Ismael was able to establish contacts in various Brazilian cities for the presentation of *Ritual of a Body in Moon*. We traveled without management, overland by bus, from São Paulo to Rio, to Salvador, and all the way to the north, and we were completely broke by the end.

It was in Salvador that Ismael got to know Alvin Ailey. The dancer Zula Lemos, who also lives in Berlin today, had met Ailey on the beach. Zula approached him, and because I was the only one who could speak English, I translated. We asked if he was Alvin Ailey. *Sometimes*, he replied. Zula invited Ailey to see our production. And Ailey thought right away that Ismael should get a scholarship to New York.

What was fascinating about Ismael's presence was that he could express our pain with his physical expression. He possessed unparalleled body control. I wasn't part of the dance scene, which was very small. I actually wanted to become a writer and make music to go with it. Ismael was for me a bridge toward expression, and he also drew inspiration from literature, theater, activists.

ODENTHAL Were you successful?

TUCCI You can't compare it with today. The dance and art scene recognized our work, but beyond that, we didn't find a public. In 1982, we had our first guest performance in Europe. The composer and musician Arrigo Barnabé was invited to the Jazz Festival in Berlin with his program *Clara Crocodilo*. I was his percussionist. I was able to convince Barnabé that Ismael had to be there as well. The plane ticket was paid for by my father because Ismael was not part of the group. It was a huge surprise for Ismael that we could fuse the approaches of Arrigo Barnabé and *Ritual of a Body in Moon* for the guest performance in Berlin. We were in the city for five days in early November and played at the Philharmonie. I stayed behind in Berlin at that time for personal reasons, and I was supported by Friedemann Graef, Leanore Ickstadt, and Niko Schäuble, who kindly put me up.

Later we invited Ismael to Berlin and showed our work at Tanztangente Berlin and with Christine Hasting in Munich. We also went to Vienna, to the Schmelz, for a workshop festival that was organized by Carter Collins and went bankrupt. Karl Regensburger then took it over and developed it into the Wiener Sommertanzwochen and ImPulsTanz.

Later Karl took over Ismael's management, and we performed *Ritual of a Body in Moon* at the Schaubühne, at the Alte Oper Frankfurt, and in Vienna. We also played at La MaMa Theater in New York and lost a lot of money there. That was in 1984, the performances were not very well attended. What was a huge success in Europe—at Kampnagel we were sold out for a week—flopped in New York. Karl had to bring us back to Europe on a roundabout route via Romania because we didn't have the money to pay for all the excess baggage.

ODENTHAL You were initiated into the rituals of Umbanda, Ismael had his contacts with Candomblé. The crossing of borders and trance played an important role.

TUCCI Without this experience, the performance would have been something completely different. Transcending energies was crucial for both of us. We both brought our respective inner worlds with us. I was an artistic medium as much as Ismael. We bonded over a great intuition, which I applied to the music as Ismael did to the dance. I am a drummer through whom the others play. I have never moved away from that. This is a reality for me.

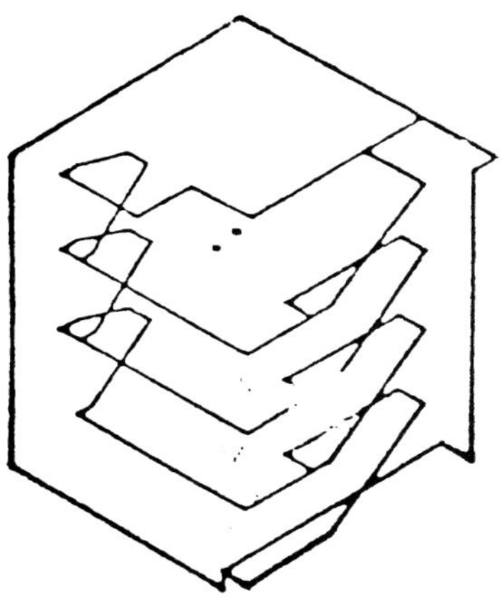

I

ODENTHAL Ismael went to Europe in 1984 and had a unique career as a dancer.

TUCCI He could never have had a career in Brazil. The audience for dance and performance was just too small. And then there is this structural, historical racism. Our artistic dreams came true because we were able to work in Europe. But then again, I don't know of any other Black artist who has been as successful outside of Brazil as was Ismael. Brazil is a very brutal place, a racist country where slavery still lives as a mental structure. Ismael could find his way with his charisma, but not in Brazil.

II

III

IV

V

I	Letterhead Salão da Discoteca, 1981
II	*Ritual of a Body in Moon*, 1981, Ismael Ivo and Dudu Tucci, photographer: Gudrun Stockinger
III–VII	Program: *Creatures of the Night*, 1984, Vienna

VI

VII

"It was fascinating to see him dance my notations! The magic of an enchanted time"

Choreographer and performer Mara Borba in conversation with Petra Schaeber

PETRA SCHAEBER You are one of the people who met Ismael when he was still very young, at the beginning of his career in the 1970s. How did that come about?

MARA BORBA I met Ismael in 1974 at a project that was very influential in the dance scene of São Paulo in the 1970s. Teatro Galpão was an important place for the alternative dance and theater scene. It offered free courses with renowned artists from the fields of dance and theater. It was aimed at young talents who explored new forms of expression outside the conventional patterns of classical dance or theater. This diversity and experimentation resulted in creations and pieces, produced by new performers, including Ismael and myself.

Ismael came from amateur theater, I have a degree in plastic arts. We were both looking for creative references in dance. Since we first met back then, we have developed many projects together as choreographers and performers and continued to evolve artistically. We never parted again, we were soul mates. For a long time, our emotional and artistic connection was a shared journey, with much learning, with many affinities and conflicts —all very rich and strong.

I

Rather than limiting ourselves to the rehearsal room, we were expressive performers with the stage vibrating in our veins. We started to dance at the age of twenty, trying out techniques and mixing tools. This gave us a freedom that was guided by a particular aesthetic that broke with conventions. The stage was the reinforcing element that supported the scenic results of our proposals. The dramatization of the choreographic expression became our dramatic language in the universe of dance. We lived with the question: this is neither dance nor theater —what is it then? We made dance theater without knowing what it was.

SCHAEBER Can you tell us a little about how you perceived Ismael?

BORBA Ismael was a gentle person, with an open smile, a charismatic manner, and a very special energy. He had a subtle sense of humor, laughed a lot, even at trifles, and was pleasant to be around. He had a sense of artistic depth, and his magnetism gave his movements and his presence a personal touch. In those days we did not have any specific, representative commitment, neither in the social nor in the political field. During the dictatorship, we participated in public protest actions, against censorship. We were artists and that was it.

I remember an experience in Salvador during the Bahia Dance Festival in the late 1970s and early 1980s. We were walking together and were approached by a group of local artists who invited Ismael to a party and made a point of emphasizing how important his presence would be. They ignored me. He asked, "What about Mara?" and the response was, "Not the white one!" Ismael said, "If she doesn't go, I won't go. She is an artist and like a sister to me." I will never forget that. We didn't talk about it again, but for me, it was an example of a greatness, of an authenticity of being. Ismael saw human and artistic values on a universalist level.

SCHAEBER How did your artistic relationship evolve after the first phase?

BORBA The Grupo Experimental de Dança was founded in 1982 by Klauss Vianna, then director of the Balé da Cidade de São Paulo. It was a daring act to hire artists from the São Paulo dance scene to interact with the company's trained classical dancers. Ismael and I were among those invited. During that time we participated in bold creations and exciting projects. Ismael, however, left Grupo Experimental before I did. He performed his own solo at a Festival de Dança da Bahia in Salvador. It was there that he received an invitation from Alvin Ailey to come to New York to perfect his technique. Before he left, he bid me farewell and said, "Mara, I'm going, but you're going too!"

And so it came to pass. Ismael brought me to Europe several times. I was invited to more than fifteen seasons of the Wiener Tanzwochen and taught a wide variety of courses there. I directed, choreographed, and worked as a creative interpreter on various projects, including *Francis Bacon* in 1995, which was a very important stage in our career. Later we met again in Weimar at the German National Theater from 1996 to 2000, he as a director and I as a creative artist. After that, our paths and interests diverged. I returned to Brazil, Ismael stayed in Europe.

SCHAEBER You were closely involved with *Phoenix*, a piece that shaped Ismael's path in Europe. Can you tell us a little bit about it?

BORBA There were many creations and artistic associations that shaped us, but I think *Phoenix* was not only the big turning point in Ismael's international career but also of special importance for our artistic relationship. *Phoenix* was Ismael's first major production on German soil. It is what he started out with, and he performed the piece for three years on major stages all over the world. The solo piece premiered at the Schaubühne am Lehniner Platz in Berlin. We shared the title of "choreographer," and I was responsible for directing the show.

The invitation to direct *Phoenix* was a demonstration of trust, recognition, and affection. Ismael believed in my talent and courage. I still have the written and drawn script and choreography notes. A personalized archive full of memories. Ismael loved to look at the drawings. He curiously followed the notes and deftly deciphered the inserted codes. These drawings formed the basis for the choreographic interpretation. It was fascinating to see him dance my notes! The magic of an enchanted time.

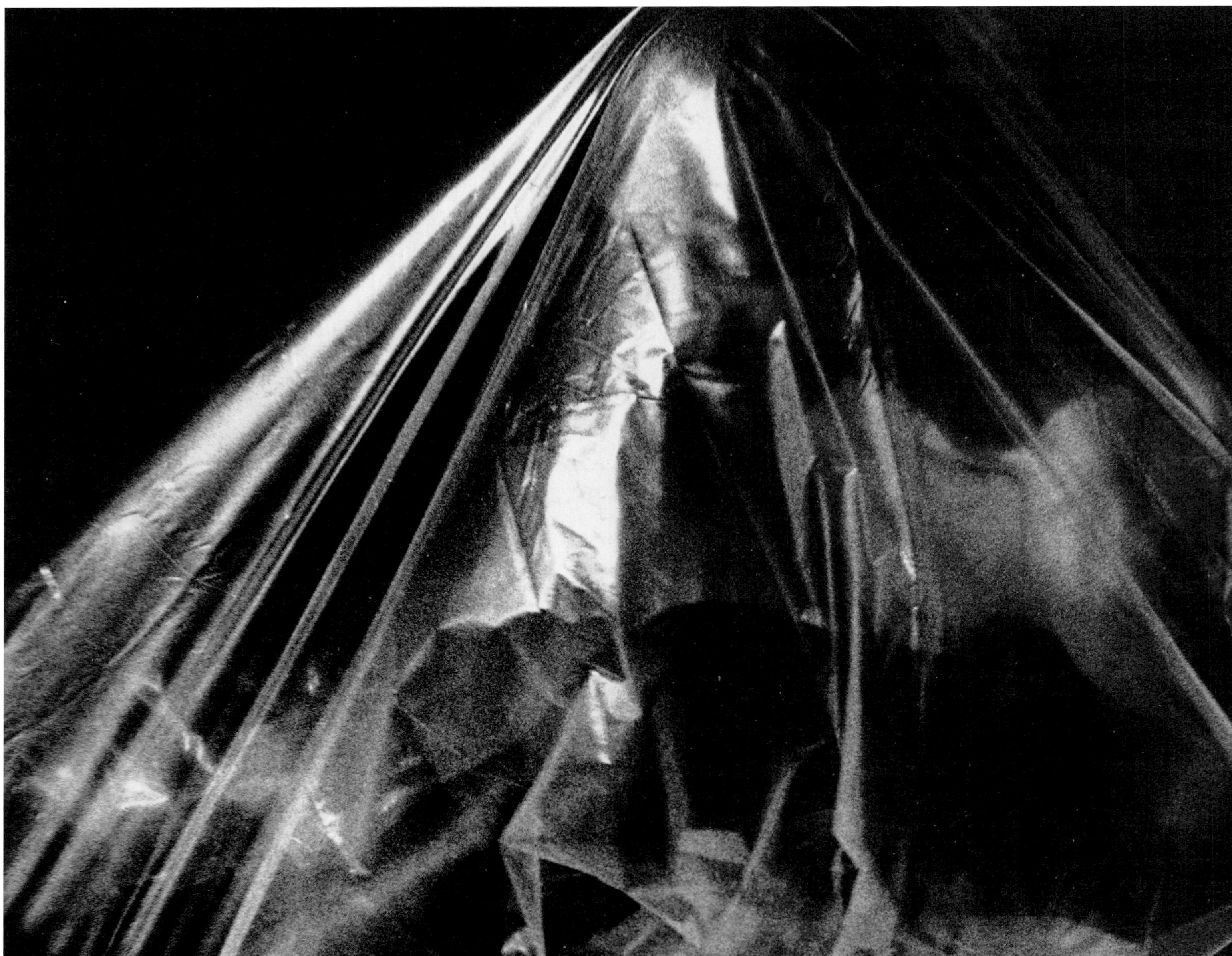

SCHAEBER It took many years for Ismael to return to Brazil. Did you notice any changes in Ismael's work and in his discourse?

BORBA In Vienna and Venice, Ismael broadened his horizons and consolidated his relevance as an international artist. This is his own achievement, no doubt. He had a talent for these things, he knew the rules, was a good strategist, and won a lot of recognition. But success has a price. Media interest and his career in Brazil became more and more linked to the importance of his success. To see him in that context, with a statement crafted for a new audience, bothered me. After all, we grew up without boundaries. There was light, a lightness, and a broad human view of life. We belonged to each other and at the same time, we knew that we were not the only ones.

II

Ismael had his relevance and will always have it. That is undeniable. It was significant that he was the first Black director of the Balé da Cidade de São Paulo. But that is not why his work was different. He had triumphs and made mistakes, as did all his predecessors. There were conflicts and discontents, something that is enriching and part of the journey.

The last time we saw each other was by chance at the Balé headquarters. As always, our meeting was tender and full of emotion. We sat down in a room, talked, and laughed. I was very critical of Ismael at times, but our affection overcame our differences. When Ismael died, I felt that a part of him had left some time ago, but the best part of him lives on in me.

III

IV

V

I, IV, V — *Sagra Beroh*, 1979, Teatro Maria Della Costa, São Paulo, Mara Borba and Calú Ramos, photographer: Thereza Pinheiro

II — *Francis Bacon*, 1993, Theaterhaus Stuttgart, Ismael Ivo and Mara Borba, photographer: Christian Brachwitz

III — Notations by Mara Borba

I

Santa Thereza

Marcel Kaskeline on the Black activist Thereza Santos

The award ceremony for the Ordem do Merito Cultural was scheduled to take place on December 2, 2010, at Rio de Janeiro's Theatro Municipal, the magnificent historic opera house lavishly decorated in gold and marble. For Ismael, it was clear from the start that Thereza Santos had to be present at the awards ceremony.

II

Thereza was born in Rio de Janeiro and had lived mostly in São Paulo after her return from exile. In old age, she moved back to Rio, where she had a cousin, and lived in a nursing home in the Grajaú neighborhood. The nursing home is a nondescript, freestanding building on a tree-lined residential street.

Thereza was a shadow of her former self. On their last vacation together in Salvador da Bahia, she had still been the energetic person we always knew—even though she was constantly coughing due to a heavy cigarette habit. At the Feira de São Joãquim, the turbulent wholesale market of Salvador, she had still haggled over a sack of dried shrimp, with enthusiasm and full use of her theatrical talents, posing in front of the merchant with her imposing physique and wild, black mane.

Persecuted as a member of the Communist Party during the military dictatorship, Thereza had fled to Africa. Legend has it that she arrived at the Angola airport barefoot and with nothing but the clothes on her back. Thereza helped to develop the educational system in Angola and Guinea. Machine gun in hand, she made sure the children could reach their school safely.

Back in Brazil, Thereza became an early mentor and lifelong friend to Ismael. She supported his first artistic steps and sharpened his eye for the weaknesses of the "Democracia Racial". "Dona Leni is my biological mother," Ismael used to say, "and Thereza Santos is my spiritual mother."

Now Thereza sat gaunt and hunched over on the bed of her darkened room. In the nursing home, she was considered somewhat confused, albeit sharp-tongued, so none of the other residents liked to share the room with her. Upon entering, she looked at us incredulously. It seemed to me as if she never had any visitors.

When Ismael took her in his arms, Thereza slowly came to life, as if she were waking up from a deep sleep. "Come, let's go have some lunch," Ismael suggested. The nurses got her ready and from then on we picked her up for lunch every day. At first, we would just go to Lanchonete, two blocks away, but as time went on, our trips became longer each day. At one point we drove all the way to Santa Teresa, one of Rio's historic neighborhoods. This is where Thereza Santos was born. Her parents named her Jaci, an Indian name because they wanted her to be special. Thereza found this name inappropriate for a Black woman and hid it from the world. Instead, she named herself after the part of town where she was born.

The day of the ceremony arrived. In the evening, limousines pulled up in front of the grandly illuminated theater with its golden and green domes. The interior was chilled down so that the society ladies could wear their mink stoles. The audience waited anxiously for three-quarters of an hour late because the plane carrying the President of the Republic had been delayed. When Luiz Inácio Lula da Silva entered the stage, the audience rose as one. Only Thereza remained seated: "Just because he's president, he doesn't have to keep us waiting."

I Thereza Santos and Ismael Ivo, 2004, Rio de Janeiro, photographer: Dieter Blum
II Ismael Ivo and Luiz Inácio Lula da Silva at the award ceremony for the Ordem do Merito Cultural do Brasil, 2010,
A 50 Theatro Municipal de Rio de Janeiro

In Berlin, we always met at Café Einstein; it reminded us a bit of Vienna. I had a hard time digesting the rough charm of Berlin. I will tell you how I came to the Schaubühne am Lehniner Platz to organize a guest performance for Ismael. When I greeted the porter at the stage door with the Austrian "Grüss Gott" or "God bless you", he replied: "Well, if you run into him." When we took over the management of Ismael, I was twenty-eight years old. We were trying to present *Ritual of a Body in Moon* in an important theater.
After the exchange with the porter, I was somehow let through to the two directors. They were Jürgen Schitthelm and Klaus Weiffenbach. I told them that they had such a fantastic Black dancer here in Berlin. He absolutely had to perform at the Schaubühne. They looked at me agape. The Schaubühne stood for directors like Peter Stein or Luc Bondy. But they kind of liked my audacity, and they gave me two stages that could be combined because they themselves were going on a tour to Andrzej Wajda in Poland. "If you have the courage, then do it, you keep 70 percent of the door money, we get 30 percent." We didn't have to pay rent. We made it happen a few months later, and it turned out to be a real triumph. The marvelous photos of Anno Wilms in the display cases on Kurfürstendamm certainly contributed to the success. There was a run on the tickets, you just can't imagine. And this led to the Schaubühne secretly co-producing the next production, *Phoenix*. They built the entire stage set in their workshops. And we were allowed to perform in their theater again for an entire week. And with that we had this seal of approval: we were high culture. Pina Bausch in Wuppertal became possible, the Cologne Opera—suddenly all these doors opened. We were able to go to many places, which was important.
In Hamburg, we were at Kampnagel with *Phoenix*, scheduled for a week. The negotiations took place in an elevator, first floor to fourth floor, which was all the time Peter Zadek gave me. He asked if we really thought we could do it, fill 800 seats. I said that

I

I didn't see any problem with that. All right, he said, 70/30! And on the way out I said to him: 80/20 would help. And he said: that's fine. In the end, we played not just one week, but four or five night each week. And there were not 800, but 1,000 visitors each time. And that was without complimentary tickets. These tours ultimately saved the festival in Vienna, because we were able to pay off the oppressive debt we had accumulated. There was one lucky break after another. Or friends turned up who asked if they could help us. Poppy Wechsberg, for example, was so impressed by the Dance Weeks and Ismael that she sold a house in the 14th district, put two million shillings on the table, and told us we could give it back whenever we were able too.

In 1983 I organized workshops with Ismael and Dudu at Tanzforum Wien, which were a huge success. Those were the most beautiful studios in Vienna. But the whole thing was more like a hobby for the wife of a wealthy entrepreneur. When we became more and more successful, with Ismael, with Cristina Caprioli, and others, the owner summoned me to explain that the studios were intended to be a loss-making venture and that he did not want such success. It was clear to us that we had to change our direction. We looked for a neutral location and found the Sports University on the Schmelz, which we were able to rent in the summer of 1984 with the help of Hilde Hawlicek, the Minister of Culture at the time. This naiveté of our early days proved very useful in other situations as well. It's how I met Pina Bausch, for example. I drove from Berlin to Wuppertal in my old Passat and went straight to the porter at the theater. I simply asked for Pina Bausch, who was on her lunch break. "Where is she?", I asked him, along the lines of I have an important appointment with her. And he really gave me her private address. I drove there, rang the bell, and Pina Bausch opened the door wearing an apron. "I have a fantastic dancer for you," I said, and she backed away a few steps at first. She thought, here comes a madman. Her partner, Rolf Borzik, quickly led me into the salon, mainly to get me away from Pina. So I could tell

II

him all about it. And a few months later we played in Wuppertal. And if you played with Pina Bausch, you had it easier all over Europe. Today I wouldn't dare to do that. We firmly believed that it is very important for people to see Ismael's work. That gave us strength. And everyone felt that we were passionate about what we were doing.

What has bound me to dance all my life? I was very attached to the subject of the body. And more than anywhere I found it in dance. Vienna was very hostile to the body at the time. Everything that had to do with dance was lumped in with the Free Dance Movement of the 1930s and then very quickly associated with physical education under National Socialism. In Ismael's case, it was obvious that there could be no connection whatsoever. But dance and movement were marked by societal rejection. And when we started the festival in the early 1980s, we had the good fortune that the way the body was looked at was changing all over the world. Until then, dance in Vienna had been synonymous with the waltz, with ballet. Naturally, Ismael expanded my interest in dance exponentially. We had a deep trust in one another. That also gave us a lot of strength. But it doesn't mean that we did not have our quarrels, which at times we fought out very loudly. Ismael was in Vienna every year, maybe with one or two exceptions. We were very close friends until the end. That went far beyond professional matters.

What united us was our shared passion for the body. Ismael's presence on stage was incomparable, whether in front of a group of students in a studio or in front of 3,000 people in the Vienna Stadthalle. Ismael was always there one hundred percent and tried to take the people with him. That fascinated me incredibly. When Ismael entered a room, it would fall quiet.

When we met Harry Belafonte, I felt the same thing. Ismael was like his younger brother. They had transcended determination by others on the ground of their skin color, they were free, even if the structures of racism were completely conscious to them.

III

IV, V

But I also experienced Ismael as a fighter. That must have been around 1983. He had a very nice apartment in Vienna Josefstadt. And there was a commotion in the house because a Black man had moved in. Ismael was deeply indignant. I tried to calm him down. Ismael took it very personally. He felt strongly about that. When you are attacked, you have to stand up to it. But Ismael never pushed this issue in public. He was the same with the issue of homosexuality.

Ismael was the face of the festival. He was also the one who invited the international teachers. In the 1990s, the invitation policy passed more into my hands, but Ismael remained my advisor throughout. What I appreciated a lot about him was the fact that he would not flinch at inviting choreographers who behaved arrogantly toward him. Even though Ismael knew of their dislike, he kept an open mind toward everyone.

There was an election campaign with Helmut Zilk for mayor in the late 1980s, Ursula Pasterk represented culture. Sixty posters were put up at the time. And Ismael was the face of culture. The Johann Strauss monument and Ismael's famous leap. I was not very comfortable with it. We did it anyway. Somehow it also showed that politics had noticed us, that there was a movement going on that was being recognized politically. Today, the festival is no longer put into question. But it remains a very hard process. I had to resign from the management of Ismael in the early 1990s because the festival had become so big. The Theaterhaus Stuttgart and the National Theater in Weimar helped overcome this dependence on touring, followed later by the Venice Biennale or the appointment in São Paulo.

What made Ismael stand out, especially in direct collaboration with artists, was his resilience, his capacity to deflect. The early rehearsals with Hans Kresnik were brutal, ruthless, and hurtful. Ismael took it, broke the ice, and a new friendship was born, grounded in mutual respect. In the choreography of *Apocalypse*, Ushio Amagatsu forced Ismael to bend one arm for an hour. It was always a matter of restraining this exuberant power and expression, of creating physical resistance to the performance. Ismael went along with everything, he was always looking for a radical challenge. This opened the way for incredibly fruitful collaborations with artists such as Ushio Amagatsu, Hans Kresnik, Heiner Müller, Márcia Haydée, and Marina Abramović.

VI, VII

VIII

I Internationale Sommertanzwochen Wien (today: ImPulsTanz – Vienna International Dance Festival), photographer: Christa Niels
II ImPulsTanz – Vienna International Dance Festival, 2019, Vienna, Ismael Ivo and Karl Regensburger, photographer: Karolina Miernik
III ImPulsTanz – Vienna International Dance Festival, 2002, Arsenal, Vienna
IV, V 1985, photographer: Idris Kolodziej, Berlin
VI, VII Workshop ImPulsTanz – Vienna International Dance Festival
VIII "Goldenes Verdienstzeichen des Landes Wien", 2005, Burgtheater Wien, photographer: Simon Rainsborough

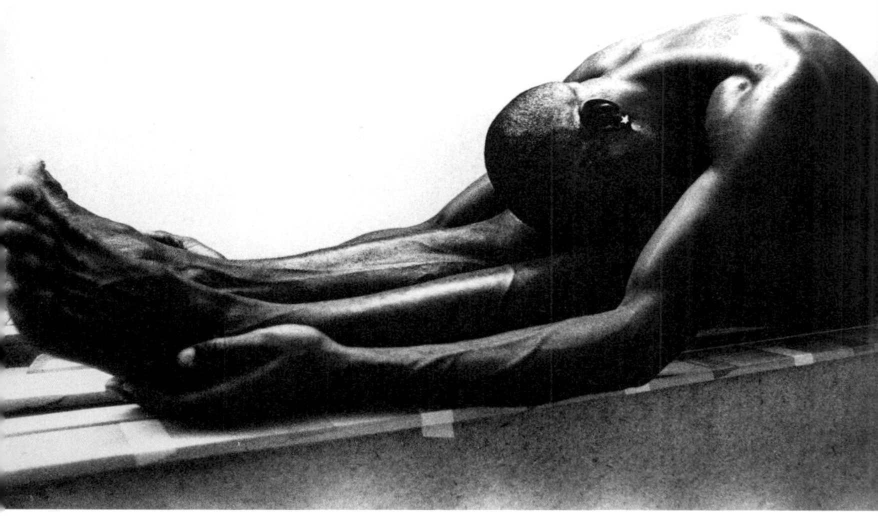

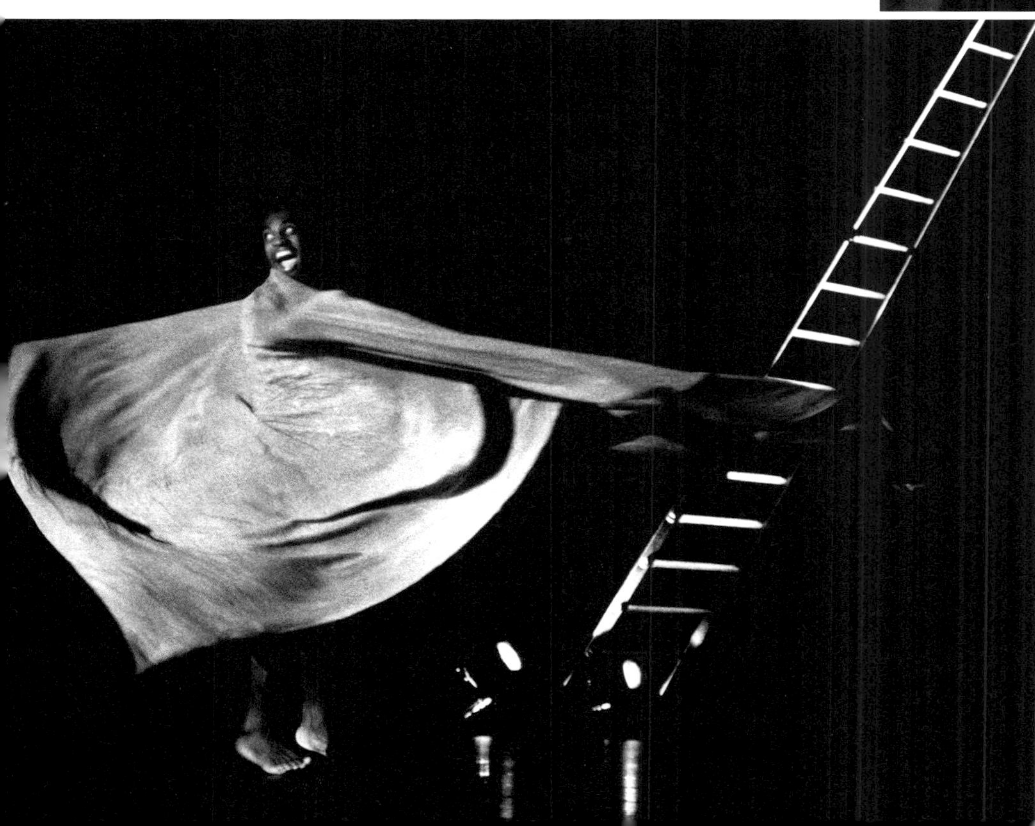

"An existential pain was inscribed in his body"

Andrée Valentin, first manager and companion, remembers Ismael Ivo

Meeting Ismael has had a defining impact on my life. He led me to dance, then later to Vienna. In 1986 Ismael, Karl Regensburger and I set up the production and management company Pegasos GmbH. We drew the spirit for our work from the 1970s, from a quest for social transformation. The 1980s brought about a new dawn with countless projects that dealt with the body and new forms of dance. Our first encounter took place in a vegetarian restaurant on Ku'damm called Zorba the Buddha, a reference to the Sannyasins' successful combination of life-affirmation and contemplation. I worked there on weekends.

One day, a strikingly handsome man entered the place. An unusual appearance with incredible charisma. Tall in stature, with perfect posture. He wore a flowing coat and was very elegant. This must surely be a model, I wondered. My first thought: I would like to be friends with this man. Later, when I walked over to the disco Zorba the Buddha—Far Out, opposite the Schaubühne, I spotted the photos of this very man in the showcases, in white pants and bare-chested. He seemed to be a dancer.

Ismael visited the restaurant again. Again he exuded the same friendliness, this affection for other people. A friend of mine suggested that in order to get to know him, I should do an interview with him for the *Osho Times*. And so I went to his table and asked him. He greeted me as if I were a *New York Times* journalist, openly and warmly. Two weeks later, we met again. He asked me if I wanted to see his production *Phoenix*. A solo about the cycle of death and rebirth, a subject that has always fascinated me. *Phoenix* was a revelation. I had never seen that kind of dance before. Dance was not high on my list of interests at the time.

Our encounter was a happy coincidence. I had previously worked in film production in Munich with Schlöndorff, von Trotta, and Hauff, I had formed "the women's offensive" with the women of Trikont-Verlag, the first German publishing house for women's literature, and was one of its managing directors. Meanwhile, in keeping with the spirit of the times, I was drawn to India in search of meaning. It was on this level of self-discovery and transcendence that I connected with Ismael. An existential pain was inscribed in his body, and he wanted to express this pain with his body in all facets. It was about the *Biblioteca do Corpo*, as Ismael would later call his project in Venice, Vienna, and São Paulo.

Working with Ismael was extremely stimulating, very creative, but also challenging. He was very demanding in his artistic process of creation. He had an incredibly strong will and was highly disciplined. He was confident in everything he did and would subject himself to extreme situations on stage. In 1988, for example, after a serious car accident in which several vertebrae in his upper back were fractured, he was back on stage with *Phoenix* after only four months. Even though his entire upper body was in a plaster cast, he had been exercising his legs every day, under severe pain. Watching him dance again brought tears to my eyes. He was literally the phoenix rising from the ashes.

His incredible presence, charisma, and vision drew people into his spell. He was able to recognize their strengths and encouraged these. Needless to say, he did enjoy the focus of attention on his person. He was not free from seeking approval. It happened again and again that hopes and expectations were projected onto him, that he could not live up to. Ismael went his own way, consistently. He was very loyal to those who were close to him. That was the "Famiglia", Karl, me, later Marcel. In his relationships, he also had a hidden, very private side, of which I knew nothing.

I, II

Ismael was what we call a stage hog. It was incredibly difficult to hold your own next to him. He required strong artistic partners like Ushio Amagatsu. In the rehearsals in Tokyo for *Apocalypse*, which I attended, Amagatsu worked with Ismael primarily on movements that came from within. In order to do this, he drastically restricted Ismael's range of motion. Ismael was to develop movement from the inner core, to reduce the obvious. He was to dispense with the ballet poses

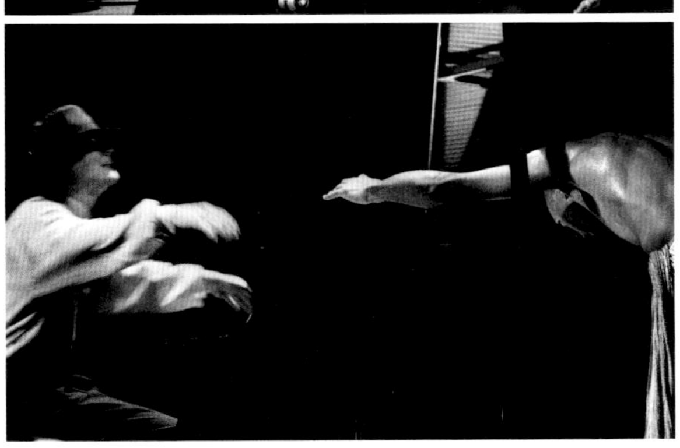

III

and to limit the dramatic movements of the Horton technique. Along with the German expressive dancers, the Japanese Butoh masters were the closest to Ismael. I still remember the encounter with Kazuo Ohno, who invited us to his home in a Tokyo suburb after the premiere of *Apocalypse* (1989). After a meal lovingly prepared by Ms. Ohno, we went with his son Yoshito Ohno to the very modest garden studio. The son respectfully dressed his father, the sensei, in one of the costumes, and the then 82-year-old Kazuo Ohno, the legend of Butoh, danced for us. Rain was drumming on the corrugated metal roof. I hold this deeply moving moment full of magic with gratitude to this day. In the same year, Kazuo Ohno was also a guest at ImPulsTanz.

In addition to Amagatsu, it was above all Hans Kresnik who was of great importance to Ismael. When working with such personalities, he could be like a student. He was completely at the service of a project. One could almost speak of humility when he was truly convinced of the other. Kresnik challenged him, he worked very figuratively, he pushed him to his limits. That's what Ismael wanted, he appreciated him very much. George Tabori, on the other hand, was like a father to Ismael. Their collaboration and friendship meant a lot to him.

No other European city has given Ismael Ivo as much recognition as Vienna. Vienna adopted him artistically. I was very touched by the fact that after the news of his death, the flags at the theaters in Vienna were set at half-mast. It is hard to say just how much Ismael gave to the city. Together with Karl, he helped shape the art scene. With the workshops, he wanted to open up dance to young people in particular. From the beginning, we wanted an open festival that would showcase the diversity of dance. Not everyone liked that. Although we were very reflective, we were not conceptual thinkers. Our vision was emotional, driven by a love of dance. We wanted to reach a large audience. Internationally, Vienna is now a dance capital, especially in summer.

Within the festival, Ismael considered himself a teacher, someone who always set new impulses, initiated projects—research projects, coaching for dancers, collaborations with other artistic disciplines. In addition, he always paid attention to who would be invited as teachers. Because in teaching, as in performing, quality had the highest priority. Together with Karl, he developed strategies for the further development of the festival and for its promotion. In addition, his role as artistic representative of the festival to the political institutions was very important.
But the success of ImPulsTanz is mainly based on the personal touch, the attention to the artists. Karl is characterized by a rare generosity. A grandezza. There was always an abundance, even if money was sometimes very tight. It was all about the appreciation of artists, and they felt it. That's why it's tragic that Ismael was deprived for so long of the recognition he wanted so much from his native Brazil. It was only with his appointment at the Theatro Municipal in São Paulo that this wound seemed to begin to heal.
Ismael truly enriched my life. I miss him very much, his Homeric laughter, his humor, his enthusiasm and curiosity, and his affection.

I, II *Apokalypse*, 1989, Takashi Kako and Ismael Ivo, photographer: Bernd Uhlig
III *Apocalypse* (restaging), 2006, Theaterhaus Stuttgart, Ismael Ivo and Takashi Kako, photographer: Davide Berger

On the difficulty of continuing with the development of Expressive Dance

Dancer, journalist, and movement explorer Irene Sieben recalls Ismael Ivo's artistic arrival in Berlin

On November 7, 1982, he was first seen on European soil: at the Jazzfest Berlin in the Philharmonie. Festival director George Gruntz had inserted the project of the Brazilian pianist Arrigo Barnabé with fifteen musicians and a dancer into his program as a performative supplement. As a critic wrote, Ismael Ivo, twenty-seven years young, appeared "ready to pounce like a tamed big cat". The Afro-Brazilian had won the award for best solo dancer in his hometown of São Paulo, where he had been immersed in a dance and theater scene that reflected urban life with all of its social conflicts. While he had a close encounter with American modern dance in Alvin Ailey's company in New York, he chose to follow a different vision.

That he rang the doorbell of TanzTangente in Berlin-Steglitz a short time later, hoping to be able to show his solo *Ritual of a Body in Moon* on our small studio stage—his first solo outside of Brazil—was connected to a utopian vision. Ismael Ivo was on the trail of the history of expressionist dance. The pioneering Brazilian percussionist Dudu Tucci, who accompanied him that day, and the Berlin saxophonist Friedemann Graef had played together in Barnabé's band. Graef also played music in the choreographic projects of Leanore Ickstadt, the dancer who had brought me on board in 1981 when she founded TanzTangente. So it was Graef who was the catalyst. He had sent Ivo and Tucci to Steglitz.

Leanore and I knew each other from Mary Wigman. As students in her studio in Berlin-Dahlem, we experienced the last flushes of a once-revolutionary dance that had roused the ballet world and confronted it with a gesture of liberation.

We belonged to those in the Wigman Studio who wanted to free ourselves from the pathos of the master. It was mostly thanks to our technique teacher, the phenomenal dancer Manja Chmièl, that we were inspired by a highly complex body language that felt abstract, but not cool, equivalent to the contemporary arts. We became involved in a fresh current that was embodied in 1962 in the studio group Motion. Around the same time, the group Neuer Tanz Berlin (New Dance Berlin) was formed, which finally helped Chmièl to break away from Wigman and establish a training studio of her own.

Ismael Ivo perceived this period, which led to the emergence of dance theater in Germany, as a "revival" and a belated appreciation of this important innovation in dance. He had come to Germany in search of the tradition of German expressive dance. Meanwhile, the "survivors" of the Wigman tradition, dancers in the multimedia Group Motion, had emigrated to Philadelphia in the United States after Wigman's studio had closed. Dore Hoyer, who had considered herself the "last flag bearer of expressive dance," chose suicide. She saw no future for herself and her art form. It was not until the generation of returnees from the USA —dancers from the Group Motion and its breakaway offshoot Zero Movings Compagnie—established a new field with Tanzfabrik Berlin in 1978, where this tradition may not have been seamlessly continued, but where "contemporary" dance, as we call it today, came into being.

In her projects with the Berlin Musicians and Dancers Company —"Bermuda" for short—Leanore Ickstadt had frequently brought colleagues from the USA to Steglitz. In 1982, Bill T. Jones and Arnie Zane, two choreographers already firmly established in New York, gave a lecture demonstration (though it must be said that Bill T. Jones, as a Black man, belonged more to those dancers who had advanced American Modern Dance). Did Ismael know of Leanore's and my expressive dance backgrounds, or was he simply following his instincts? We can only guess. He said, "I immediately felt at home in Berlin—I think I have been an expressive dancer from the start!" He had dedicated his first major solo, *Ritual of a Body in Moon*, accompanied by Dudu Tucci on percussion, to Alvin Ailey, whose company had introduced itself to

Berlin dance audiences with a very impressive guest performance at the Akademie der Künste's "Pantomime-Music-Dance-Theater" festival.

"Alvin Ailey discovered me in Brazil, he supported me, brought me to his school, to his company in New York. And he had the greatness to let me go because he saw that I had to follow a vision, to look for the essence of my own expressiveness in the revival of German expressive dance. It was not until I came to Germany that I realized how I had always been an expressive dancer." That's what Ivo told me when I interviewed him. That meant he could expect a full presence from the audience, sympathy, and intelligence. "I don't want to feed them something that yet again simply pleases them. I want to share a moment of truthfulness." What connected him to Mary Wigman was not her rather more sublimated physical language of gliding, spinning, whirling, vibrating and jumping, but her ability to own the space, her transparency in the process of giving and taking, an ethereal connection between the one who sees and the one who is seen. Ismael Ivo was sure that embodied two different things if he left behind dance styles and rhetoric: the dreamer and the dream. Just as the universal gesture of outstretched hands implies both: giving and taking, merging outside and inside.

Ritual of a Body in Moon drew one hundred people to TanzTangente on September 1, 1983. The hall was absolutely packed. There was no barrier, no ramp, no distance between the exuberant magic of transformation on a stage barely larger than 24 × 26 feet, and a euphoric audience. The room was on fire. The tension was high, the atmosphere intense. An almost naked black body of immense power symbolized the uncovering of civilizational shells and thus something existential, wild. Ivo asked himself: Why is the body still a taboo? While Susanne Linke, the Wigman and Folkwang student, rose above her body and searched for the spiritual essence, Ivo consciously focused on the physical, on flesh, bones, skin, and sweat, thus confronting his audience with the transcendence of

I

a ritual process and thus with death and survival, or life. But also with ecstasy, and joy. No trace of minimalism. His physicality had a vigor similar to Wigman's very early *Witch Dance*, in which she wore a mask, showed her claws, and stomped before losing herself in mythological figures.

What Ismael Ivo called his "new spatial order" was also strongly shaped by Dudu Tucci's rhythmic tapestry. He was, after all, considered a pioneer in Europe who was largely responsible for the boom in Brazilian music. In the workshops that Ismael Ivo gave at TanzTangente, Tucci's congas played an important role. And even on March 15, 1989, when Tucci and Ivo had already gone their separate ways, his music underpinned Leanore Ickstadt's first choreography—*Exu*—for her state-sponsored, professional dance company Dance Berlin, which caused a furor at the time.

II

I Workshop at TanzTangente Berlin, 1983, photographer: Irene Sieben

II *Ritual of a Body in Moon*, TanzTangente Berlin, 1983, photographer: Irene Sieben

"We are both very much into Black empowerment"

Francesca Harper, artistic director of Ailey II, in conversation with Petra Schaeber

PETRA SCHAEBER How was your first meeting with Ismael in New York, almost forty years ago?

FRANCESCA HARPER I was a girl studying at the Alvin Ailey School. I remember there was a wonderful moment in *Memoria*, a piece that the students are allowed to perform with the main company. Ismael was the person leading everyone out from the wings onto the stage with more than forty dancers following him. I remember just being so impressed. *Memoria* was choreographed by Alvin Ailey. It's a piece for the second company, the company I run now. The school performs this piece every year at City Center as a part of their Season.

SCHAEBER Do you remember his working schedule?

HARPER He was intense, always very intense, focused, and serious about this work. It was undeniable. He was passionate. I think he really maximized every opportunity. I always felt the importance of having been chosen by Alvin, the way he was made him take his work very seriously and it was always apparent to us.

SCHAEBER Ismael stayed for almost two years. How had he developed?

HARPER I will say one thing, I think when Ismael told us that he was going to start ImPulsTanz, move to Europe, and begin his journey as a curator, we were excited. But, honestly, I think some of us hoped that he would dance with Alvin Ailey. He had star quality and he was so special as a performer. We know now, years later, that it was Ismael's calling in life to become what he became, from starting ImPulsTanz to developing *Biblioteca do Corpo*, to serving as Artistic Director of Balé da Cidade de São Paulo. His artistic journey was an intuitive one. He felt his calling and manifested his dreams. And, thank goodness he listened to himself.

SCHAEBER How do I have to imagine the group? Were there other Brazilians?

HARPER There were hundreds of dancers in the school. Alvin Ailey is one of the biggest organizations and schools in the world, and even then, it was very robust with an international presence. Alvin's mission for inclusivity has always been admirable and palpable. I think the Alvin Ailey organization is one of the only organizations that offer classes for all people. That was also part of Alvin's dream, to open his arms to international students, and the student body reflected that.

SCHAEBER And what would you describe as the main characteristic of Ismael's work in New York and later in Europe?

HARPER Again, intensity. He did a lot of dance theater work that was very provocative, work that would push the boundaries and have the audience not only look at beauty but also at the intense and painful sides of our human existence.

SCHAEBER Did you come to Brazil later? How was your experience?

HARPER I was the first choreographer he invited when he was appointed director of the dance company Balé da Cidade de São Paulo in Brazil. I felt honored. He had just inherited the company. The dancers were so strong and so wonderful. Not only was the dance on the highest level, but to have the support of the theater and the orchestra, I had a full live orchestra and even got to experiment with aerial work. Ismael encouraged me to utilize my wildest imagination. That support was unlike any other experience I ever had.

SCHAEBER Is there still a memory of Ismael in New York? Do your younger students have any idea of who he was, what he did?

HARPER Yes. The second memory I had of Ismael was when my mother brought him back to New York from Vienna. I think she and he had done some work together in Korea judging dance competitions. He came to New York, and I was working with my company, The Francesca Harper Project, at the time. When Ismael came, my mother asked him to come to a rehearsal. That was the beginning of everything. After he saw that rehearsal, he invited my company to the Venice Biennale. As time passes, naturally information sometimes gets lost. Of course, my generation knows Ismael, but doing this book or having more exposure through the documentary is so important, especially with the Internet. We really have an opportunity for people to understand his legacy and the stories, especially for people of color.

SCHAEBER How did you experience Ismael's consciousness as a Black Brazilian? Was he having a strong dialogue, a strong consciousness of being Black, or was he feeling more Brazilian? What was your impression during your time in New York?

HARPER We were connected because we are both very much into Black empowerment. That was the essence of who he was, and he was very much aware of that. I think that transcends where you're from, even your origin. I was from New York City and Ismael was from Brazil, but we were very close, we called each other brother and sister. Empowerment was important for us as curators, directors, and educators. We were proactive and very aware that we were creating opportunities for other people of color because there are just so few that are given with unconscious bias operating so strongly in our world and even just in the abuse of power that operates within racial discrimination. Promoting empowerment for people of color was something that bonded us.

The one thing I would want people to know was how fearless Ismael was in understanding his value. He walked around the world unapologetically. In ways, he understood this even more so than I did. He constantly reminded me. He was aware of the importance of empowering himself, in understanding the importance of being courageous and the powerful impact it had on others. I think his selflessness was a trait I admired so much. He really was doing it for others, from the heart. It was not only his generosity but the fact that he was living his life unapologetically. I think that's something that I hope people will be inspired by as we move forward and for the next generation.

"I'm interested in the magical aspect of movement"
Johannes Odenthal in conversation with Ismael Ivo (2004)

JOHANNES ODENTHAL When did you first think of becoming a dancer?

ISMAEL IVO Whenever I'm asked this question, I go back to images from my childhood. There's this joy of being able to move freely. This feeling, for example, of spinning around my own axis until I lose my balance. Those are my first images of the pleasure of movement. This feeling of flying away with my body, of transcending ordinary consciousness.

ODENTHAL But you didn't think about dance yet.

IVO That came much later. It started in high school when my teacher in literature encouraged me to write little poems and rehearse choral texts with our theater group. Those were my first experiences of performing something on stage in front of an audience. I then began to perform in a theater group on the weekends.

ODENTHAL So it wasn't the carnival club where you had your first experience as a samba dancer or the rituals of Candomblé. That's how we imagine the beginning of a dancer's career in Brazil.

IVO No, no. Although I did start observing the rituals at a very early age, I was caught up in this fascination. I was fascinated by transgression, by what we call trance or transcendence. That made me very curious. We could perceive other realities. It was a mixture of fear and fascination. I come from a Catholic family, like almost all other Brazilians. That meant attending a Catholic school and Mass every Sunday. But during the week, we all went to the different rituals. For us, that wasn't a contradiction.

ODENTHAL So you're not initiated into the rituals. It was more the spiritual idea that you experienced in those rituals, an idea of movement that goes beyond the purely aesthetic.

IVO I became very familiar with the rituals, so I was quickly ascribed a role as a mediator between the initiates and the community. I don't want to say that I became a medium, but I was given an exposed position in the rituals very early on.

ODENTHAL Did these experiences help shape your idea of dance? The African American rituals as the background of a specific understanding of dance?

IVO Perhaps these experiences expanded my capacity to analyze and comprehend movement. That's about knowing how to enter a stage and how to transform the space with the audience. If you're asking about the capacity to be able to transform a space or an atmosphere energetically through visible movement, that's a point that is central to me. But that is a modern tradition and doesn't relate to the rituals of African American religions. I'm interested in the magical aspect of movement. The transformational power of the dancer entering a stage: that to me is the ritual dimension of contemporary dance. You enter the arena.

ODENTHAL Ritual, but especially trance, is described as an altered state of consciousness. Is that a level at which we can better understand the ritual aspect of the performance?

IVO That's what I mean by the magical power of performance. You create a way for the audience to fly, to reach a different level of consciousness. To become breathless. Finding that moment of communication is what I try to do with every performance. I think that's a central mission of theater.

ODENTHAL How did you start doing theater on a professional level? Was there a modern dance movement in São Paulo?

IVO No. There was a ballet company, there were some ethnic groups dedicated to the African American dance tradition. There were also some teachers who taught the techniques of José Limón, Martha Graham, or Louis Falco. But being contemporary in the arts primarily meant trying out ideas. You were free to use whatever movement vocabularies were available. In São Paulo, the truly contemporary was defined by inventiveness.

ODENTHAL In what atmosphere did this contemporary art unfold? We are talking about the late 1970s, early 1980s. The phase of *modernismo* was over. The concept of anthropophagy, of cultural cannibalism, emerged in the 1920s, a concept that is still effective today. Perhaps you can describe the intellectual and artistic situation in São Paulo when you were developing your own forms of expression with your first solo works.

IVO Our approach was determined by the choice of how and in what context something was presented to the public. There were no barriers. You could do anything. You could be inspired by the visual arts or start from literature to create body images. The first choreography I developed myself, a solo of fifteen minutes, I did without music, starting from two poems by Federico García Lorca, "Grito hacia Roma" and "El rey de Harlem." By translating the concept of anthropophagy into performance, I developed a kind of basic model for many of my later works. I eat the words and translate them into movement. Lorca's poems challenged me to develop particular movements. In the Harlem poem, the king cries and cries and cries. That moved me to jump in the air, over and over, speaking the poem. That was the central moment of the performance.

There was a great freedom to combine ideas and images with movement. It was less about contemporary dance and more about performance. From the beginning, the social aspect played a role, as did the political commitment. I was and am committed against racism, against oppression, against social injustice. It was the time of the Black civil rights movement in Brazil. I worked with Thereza Santos, for example, whose commitment was a major influence on me.

On the other hand, it was essential for me to find a form of expression for myself. The contemporary art movements at that time were all based on the search for freedom. And for that I had to find a personal route. I was less interested in aesthetic forms than in ideas. Along the way, I met Takao Kusuno, who came from Japan. He knew Hijikata and Kazuo Ohno, the founders of Butoh. We were influenced by this slowing down of movement. In Brazil, Kusuno worked intensively with the Indigenous people from the Amazon. He never talked to me about Butoh, but he showed me how to find movements in a very different way than in modern dance. We started from images or from conditions. And he slowed me down completely, from a hundred to zero, to find a different momentum in the performance. The first production we did together in 1980 was called *As Galinhas* [Eng: The Chickens]. He chose me, a young Black dancer, and a seventy-year-old French woman, Renée Gumiel. We worked with poems by Marcel Proust. The chickens, they were the animals that were the most oppressed. They are being manipulated, their wings clipped, to be exploited to the fullest. Kusuno used this image to translate a social problem into a performance.*

I was born an expressive dancer. To this day, I have ideas or images first, and then I find movements.

ODENTHAL Even if the context for your work is completely different today, this constellation, as you described it for São Paulo and Brazil, still determines your approach to artistic or political themes. An important step in your development was the encounter with Alvin Ailey, who saw you in Brazil and invited you to New York. In 1983 you left Brazil and went to New York, to the center of the avant-garde. Did this change your idea of dance?

IVO Totally. São Paulo is a wild city, living there was a real life lesson for me. New York on the other hand was more of a school for me. I had two classes of ballet every day. In total, I took five daily classes. I lived exclusively for dance. I received a ballet scholarship for classes with a venerable ballet teacher, Gabriela Darvash, every weekend. I showed my own work, which I never gave up at any point, at La MaMa Theatre, starting with my solo *Pegasus Celebration*. New York, that was an opportunity for me to develop my technique as a dancer.

ODENTHAL How did you find your place in Alvin Ailey's company?

IVO After three months I was invited to learn the repertoire. For the first time in my life, I had a class with forty Black American dancers, with people who shared my story. After five months, I was part of the first company. It was a very hard school that I went through. It was a wonderful moment. Ailey was still alive. The rehearsals for *Memoria* were directed by his assistants. I remember very clearly the day Ailey came into the studio. By chance, I was the first to come on stage in a long line of young dancers. We had to do a sweeping port de bras movement, a kind of calling out with our arms. After three or four movements, Ailey said: "Stop!" Oh my God, I thought, my career is over now. I'm ruined. Ailey came to me and said, "What do you mean by these movements? A port de bras is not just a port de bras. You're calling generations of people, of Africa, of Brazil, with these movements. The piece is called *Memoria!*" And then we started from the beginning. It was a very fruitful culture shock.

ODENTHAL You focused a lot on solo work. Few other dancers have put the solo at the center of their work as much as you have.

* *As Galinhas* was re-performed at the Haus der Kulturen der Welt, Berlin, at the IN TRANSIT 2006 festival, with the original cast from 1980.

IVO Maybe the solo is a response to the social and existential condition of my life. From the very beginning, I saw it as a weapon. I wanted to find a place, my place in society. That wasn't easy for me as a Black man. It was easier when you went back to folklore. Then you could find your place.

That continuous stomping as Pegasos was an existential voice for me, the desire to break through that wall. And when you see later productions like *Othello*, *Mephisto*, or *Francis Bacon*, you'll realize: I've always pursued a personal relationship with these subjects. Mephisto, that's always the Other in society. I knew from the beginning that I could never become the prince in a ballet company. With *Othello*, my personal question was directed at the actors in blackface. I take a very intuitive approach to choosing my subjects. But the intuition springs from my perception, from social and racial experiences.

ODENTHAL In Germany, you are very far removed from all this history, unlike in New York, which is the center of a Black American cultural history. In Germany, there is no real awareness of the *Middle Passage*, the enslavement of millions of Africans, and their exploitation in the Americas. In a way, you're coming into an exotic environment. This is where German expressive dance brought you. You wanted to learn more about this tradition. But you also came to a country that has a completely different perceptual horizon with regard to Black culture.

IVO Today, dance researchers, especially in the United States, are beginning to decipher this ethnic, exotic perspective. Thus, there is a heightened awareness when young African dancers are expected to act in an African way. The West still demands something African that does not correspond with the notion of the contemporary. The central object of Western exoticism is the body. This is where the taboos are located. But for me as a dancer, the body is not taboo. I am at home in it. I go to the extreme in order to exhibit this body, constantly overstepping boundaries. I provoke. There is no other way for me. Yet I have survived on this path until today.

Very often I would feel misunderstood in Germany. Not so much by the audience, but by the critics. However, today things have changed. The naked body on stage has become a big thing. As a dancer today, I am seen in a completely different context. In the early 1990s, people were still shocked when I offensively presented the naked body on stage in *Francis Bacon*.

ODENTHAL What is your vision of dance?

IVO I believe in dance as an art form, as a unique way of expression. And to me, dance seems to be a form that can be used to communicate between cultures. With dance, I have always been able to move from one culture to another. It was possible for me to work for months in Japan with Kazuo Ohno or Ushio Amagatsu.

ODENTHAL And the point of departure for the dance section of the Venice Biennale, which you directed for the first time in 2005?

IVO For the Bienniale, I'm revisiting a theme we first developed back in the mid-1990s: Body Utopias. I have found the right place here to connect to this theme. The Biennale is a kind of window to the most important ideas in the world. That's why I didn't want to invent just another dance festival, but to take up themes from the visual arts. The starting point was the body, the body as a medium. That's why I didn't call the festival the Dance Biennale, but the Body Biennale. I was not interested in the destruction of the body, but in its exploration as a medium, and also as an aspiration in our society today. International terrorism has changed our social and existential conditions. People have entered a different space. The body has become the target of attacks. And that is a reflection of social and economic changes that are linked to the overcoming of colonialism. Economy and finance are the primary means of oppression. But there is always a counter-reaction. In Europe, new walls are being built. How do bodies respond to this situation? I consider the body to be a document of our time. How can this archive be given a form?

Documentary dance theater, that's a form that interests me. What do choreographers come up with that can change our perception? For example, I use the story The Incredible and Sad Tale of Innocent Eréndira and Her Heartless Grandmother by Gabriel García Márquez. It is a text in which a grandmother leads her own granddaughter into prostitution. Prostitution is a huge problem in Brazil, but also in Europe: the girls who come to the West from Eastern Europe and are enslaved here. I want to make a video where the dancers do interviews with the young prostitutes in the streets of São Paulo. Dancers have also been selling themselves all the time. I would like to interview the dancers about their feelings. A second idea is to focus on the biographies of the disappeared girls of the city of Venice, to follow their traces. That's still the Márquez idea. But there is a context of topicality. Just as Helena Waldmann worked with young Iranian actresses in her *Letters from Tentland*, trying to translate the ban on dance in that country into a unique language of movement.

ODENTHAL Here we touch on the problem of victim art. Aren't these examples of using the stories of victims to find new artistic ways of expression? Of course, it's important for art to touch on these issues. But people need their own voice. You solved that in *Olhos D'Agua* by letting three great women tell their own stories. They are the living memory, unbroken in their stature, without accusation, masters of life.

IVO I would like to develop this approach further. I am not interested in victims and perpetrators, as in *The Maids* after Genet. I am interested in what can be seen in the darkest crevices of the human soul, as part of our own psyche.

ODENTHAL Yoshi Oida has referred to Christianity in relation to Jean Genet's concept of the body. Christianity seeks the path to spirituality through punishment of the body, through purification, through negation of sexuality. From this point of view, Genet places the body in what the West considers an immoral position. The desire of the body is accepted in all its forms. Genet places himself, as it were, in the desire of the body. He is not the Christian priest who beats the body, he moves through the cruel body of the flesh to spirituality, to freedom, to freedom in death.

IVO Genet designed his perspective on life from the vantage point of death. This is the perspective of the oppressed, the underdog, the outcast. From this perspective, he was not seeking to destroy the body, but to expose another reality, the reality of social power structures, of oppression. Genet's view of the body is similar to that of Frantz Fanon, who describes the Black person's body in its double-consciousness, in their own perception of themselves on the one hand, and in their external determination through the white gaze on the Other.

ODENTHAL You produced *The Maids* after Jean Genet, directed by Yoshi Oida and in cooperation with Koffi Kôkô. In it, you refer to a fifteen-minute film, *Un Chant d'Amour*, that Jean Genet directed himself. It shows two prisoners in adjacent cells. The only connection is a straw that can reach the neighboring cell through a crack in the wall, through which one prisoner breathes the smoke of a cigarette to the other.

IVO What connects me to Genet is the radicality toward one's own existence. This is in line with Pasolini, Artaud, Bacon, and Müller. Like Genet, I am interested in the margins of existence. In the unreserved exposure of social and individual structures and conditions, the immersion in the madness of the depths of human existence as well as in visions of utopian freedom.

ODENTHAL You talk about this magical moment on stage. Can you try to describe it in more detail?

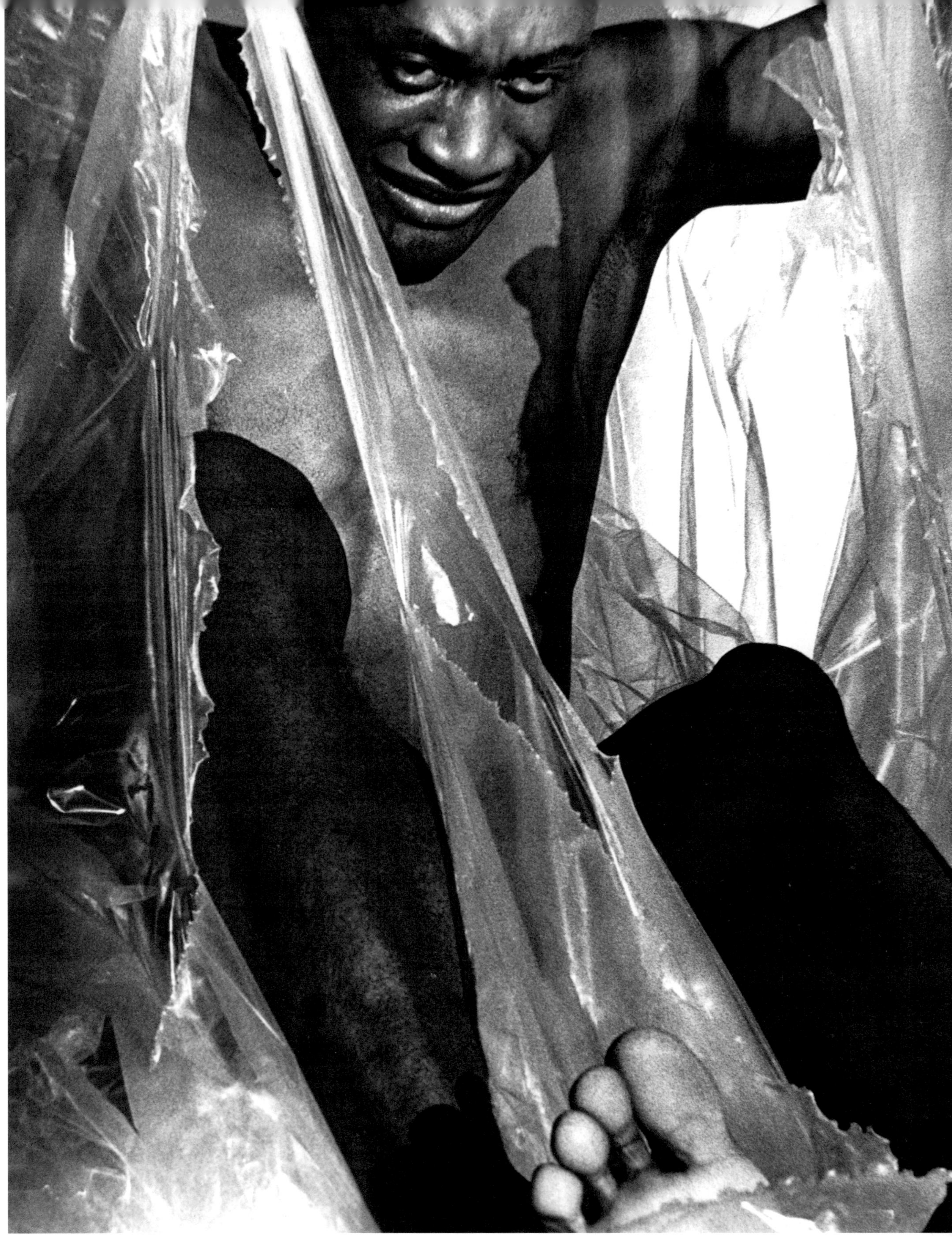

IVO I try to reach the animal in the human, the point where every moment constitutes expression. In other words, I try to capture the moment in its entirety, in all its potential, to make it as intense as possible. The next moment comes almost by accident. The next step is an explosion. Any one moment could render the following impossible. You arrive at a movement, a form. But what leads you to that form? Before you do anything: what happens inside of you? There is an impulse, an order. But before the impulse, before the order? I go back behind the impulse, to the experience that gave me the impulse. I try to get in front of the impulse with my dance, to invent my own life through the dance, as it were. The tension in the moment when the dancer starts a movement in front of the audience, this tension creates the magic. Even with the smallest movement, the audience feels it. And in this instant an incredible amount of information is exchanged, consciously and unconsciously.

ODENTHAL You have been dealing with poetry right from the beginning of your artistic development. How do you see this relationship between body and text, between dance and literature? Does dance represent a response to poetry for you?

IVO What has fascinated me from the beginning is the possibility of taking poetry into the body, of bringing it back, as it were. When I realize that dancers or people I talk to don't understand one hundred percent of what I'm saying with words, I take the words back into my mouth, close it, and show what I wanted to say in movements. I believe that the real meaning of what we want to say is always stored in our bodies. We may think that we are not moving, but we are: We move. Even when we talk. There are thousands of movements. There's an infinite number of things happening inside you. And even when you write: There's always movement. And poetry for me is the challenge to bring back the words, to connect them with the body through movement, and to communicate. But what we're really talking about here is consciousness. I try every day to become more aware of my body and myself. I try to touch new parts of my body all the time that haven't been touched before. You ask someone: What does your foot look like, but don't look! They don't know. People too often do not touch their own body and do not know their proportions. In short, they have not developed an awareness of themselves. Physical experience must always be mental experience as well if you want to open up new spaces in the body. But the point here is not rationalization. The key is to develop an awareness of what you are doing, the experience that you can change. We need to embody our experiences, to express them with the body.

Technique, in turn, is a code, a way through which you can understand the physical possibilities of the body. Technique is a means to understand, to order, to comprehend its functions. But technique can also be a prison. You can kill your body through technique. Dance is the celebration of what it is to be human. Dance is conscious communication. For that, we have to prepare the body, and for that, technique is an important prerequisite. But I have to digest all the information, incorporate it, make it my own. This is a stage of perception and expression that is very far from rationalization. It requires total awareness. In doing so, you always also touch a realm that we call trance.

ODENTHAL Alongside your artistic work on stage, you have a great commitment in the pedagogical field. You were instrumental in founding the Vienna Dance Weeks with Karl Regensburger and helped develop it into the largest European dance platform.

IVO The International Dance Weeks sprang from the same motivation as my artistic work. It's about the exchange of ideas. Although hundreds of workshops take place all over Europe, Vienna remains the central meeting point. All artists are invited to stay for several weeks. It's about an exchange between dancers, between teachers, and students. That was the initial idea, plain and simple.

First publication: *Ismael Ivo di Johannes Odenthal*, in the series "dance for word / dance forward: Interviste sulla coreografia contemporanea" edited by Susanne Franco, Palermo: A 94 L'Epos 2005, pp. 11ff.

A homage by dance scholar Gabriele Brandstetter

Ismael Ivo was one of the most important artists in dance, performance, and theater who embodied "interweavings" of different dance and physical cultures like no other dancer. He was a fellow at the IRC "Interweaving Performance Cultures" in 2016/17 and enriched our research discussions with the impressive spectrum of his activities, with the intensity and passion of his dance, and with the abundance of ideas in his artistic research.

Ivo spent time in Berlin on and off since the 1980s, as a dancer and guest in projects at the Haus der Kulturen der Welt and other theaters and cultural institutions. Both here and in other European venues he encountered diverse dance and performance scenes. He was extremely intrigued by different artistic concepts and artists. But he never forgot that he was a Brazilian artist with African roots and that he was a citizen of the post-colonial society in Brazil, with its fusion of ethnicities. For him, it was not a contradiction to act both with his Brazilian roots of ritual and the heterogeneous influences of dance concepts like ballet, modern dance, and Tanztheater. His approach to contemporary dance was imbued with his awareness that it was important to respond as a Black dancer. He absorbed such disparate influences as the European theater concepts of Antonin Artaud and Jerzy Grotowski, the dialogue with Japanese Butoh and Noh, the dramatic works of Heiner Müller, the photography of Robert Mapplethorpe, the borderline experience in Francis Bacon's paintings, the expressive and extreme Tanztheater of Hans Kresnik. For Ivo, the body was like a passport of our time that allowed him to mirror the multiple social and individual layers of our existence across different cultures.

He took up myths and tragic material to interpret them in new and unconventional ways as a dancer and choreographer in *Othello* (1996), *Francis Bacon* (1994), or, as a duo with the Stuttgart-based fellow Brazilian prima ballerina Márcia Haydée in *Tristan and Isolde* (1999) or in the interpretation of Jean Genet's *The Maids* (2001) together with Koffi Kôkô, under the direction of Yoshi Oida.

What distinguished these artistic works was their obsessive urgency, artistic passion, and physical expression which often went to extremes. Ivo's artistic existence and his appeal to his audience was the crossing of boundaries. Again and again, he returned to the rituals and myths of his Brazilian roots. Oswald de Andrade's concept of modernism in Brazil, published in 1928 as the *Manifesto Antropófago*, was formative for his creative work. The manifesto espoused the idea of cultural, artistic cannibalism, which eats up all foreign influences to digest and excrete them as a newly transformed work of art. In Ismael Ivo's own words: "It is not easy to deal with the chaotic mess of the world! It is not easy to accept the human response to it! Eat me up! I vomit in a cascade of movements." This statement reveals Ivos's extreme embodiment of the idea of cultural and social entanglements that pass through the body. He coined the image of a *Biblioteca do Corpo*, which is both a dance and a political concept. In his play *Delirium of a Childhood* (1989), Ivo worked with this idea. He interwove his own childhood experiences in a poor neighborhood in São Paulo, with African lullabies and the expression of mourning in Gustav Mahler's *Kindertotenlieder*. Long before the Black Lives Matter movement, Ivo dealt with his experiences with the image of the Black body in the Western world and was committed to the fight against racism and oppression. When he returned to São Paulo in 2017, he saw it as a fresh start to work even harder for equal opportunities, to resist racism, and to start an educational dance program for children from the poorest neighborhoods.

Abridged version of an obituary published online at www.geisteswissenschaften.fu-berlin.de/en/v/interweaving-performance-cultures/_inhaltselemente-rd/obituary_ismael_ivo_text.html

Artaud, Genet, and Müller: How Ismael Ivo links radical theatrical modernism with postcolonialism

Johannes Odenthal

Antonin Artaud and Jerzy Grotowski, Jean Genet and Heiner Müller, Pier Paolo Pasolini and Marina Abramović, and other protagonists of radical modernism were artistic reference points for Ismael Ivo on his path as a performer and choreographer. Artaud in particular, the theater revolutionary who wrote his important theoretical works in the early 1930s, was an early guide for Ismael Ivo in his own understanding of performance. Thus *Artaud, Artaud!* was created as early as 1980 in New York, and premiered at the Alvin Ailey American Dance Center.

In his theater manifestos, Artaud calls for a clean break with the masterpieces of the past. He seeks impulses to free himself from the canon of a bourgeois cultural hegemony, to disrupt the violence that flows from this entrenched cultural dominance. It is about an unearthing of the sublime, an elemental, magical notion of a theater that evokes states of trance, as in the dance of the whirling dervishes: a "theater of cruelty" that is an expression of life, of existential borderline experiences that transcend artistic practice, with the stage as a ritual space for self-discovery, revolt, and expanded perceptions of reality. Artaud's exclamation reverberates throughout the twentieth century, especially in the theatrical and life art of Jerzy Grotowski, in the productions of Peter Brook, and the theater anthropology of Eugenio Barba and Richard Schechner.

Ismael Ivo took up this impulse artistically in Brazil as early as the 1970s, based on the experience of his own activist endeavors toward a Black resistance movement against social and cultural injustice. Here, radical modernism's artistic gesture of liberation corresponds impressively with the stirrings of a postcolonial critique. The combative tone in the texts of Aimé Césaire (*On Colonialism*, 1950) or Frantz Fanon (*The Wretched of the Earth*, 1961 with a foreword by Jean-Paul Sartre) charges the revolutionary artistic manifestos of the first half of the century with new content and critical energy of the colonized. In this context, Ismael Ivo embodies a Brazilian perspective wherein the fault

I

lines between colonialism and its inherent racist structures, the erasure of Indigenous cultures and knowledge, and the traumatic collective memories of slavery are deeply inscribed in social reality. Antropofagia, the Brazilian modernity of the 1920s, had been an early attempt at emancipation from European cultural domination: a two-fold process of decolonization, externally as a reaction to Europe and internally as the processing of a society made up of oppressors and oppressed.

From a contemporary point of view, Ismael Ivo the performer has chosen to use his own body to encounter these complex stratifications and to shape them for his own experiential horizon. The position he assumes in doing so is always artistic, never discursive. For the dance scene in Germany and Europe, he attains a key role that cannot be valued highly enough against the background of a broad cultural-scientific and activist revision of colonialism.

In Germany, Ismael Ivo continues to systematically pursue his relationship with radical theater modernism. He pursued a collaboration with Heiner Müller, who contributed a text fragment for the joint theater project with Hans Kresnik and Gottfried Helnwein in the early 1990s, under the working title "*Fremd im eigenen Körper: Auswanderungen*" ("Foreign in One's Own Body: Emigrations"). It was not produced until 1997, however, after Heiner Müller's death, when a dance theater performance was created in Weimar.

In this work, Heiner Müller describes Artaud's concept of theater as an attempt to break out of the Christian and especially Catholic culture's hostility toward the physical body.

> Artaud had a French Catholic upbringing that alienated him from his own sexuality, his body—the body was evil, it was sin, and its natural impulses must be condemned and suppressed [...] The body is tied up, shackled, kept in a coma-like state.

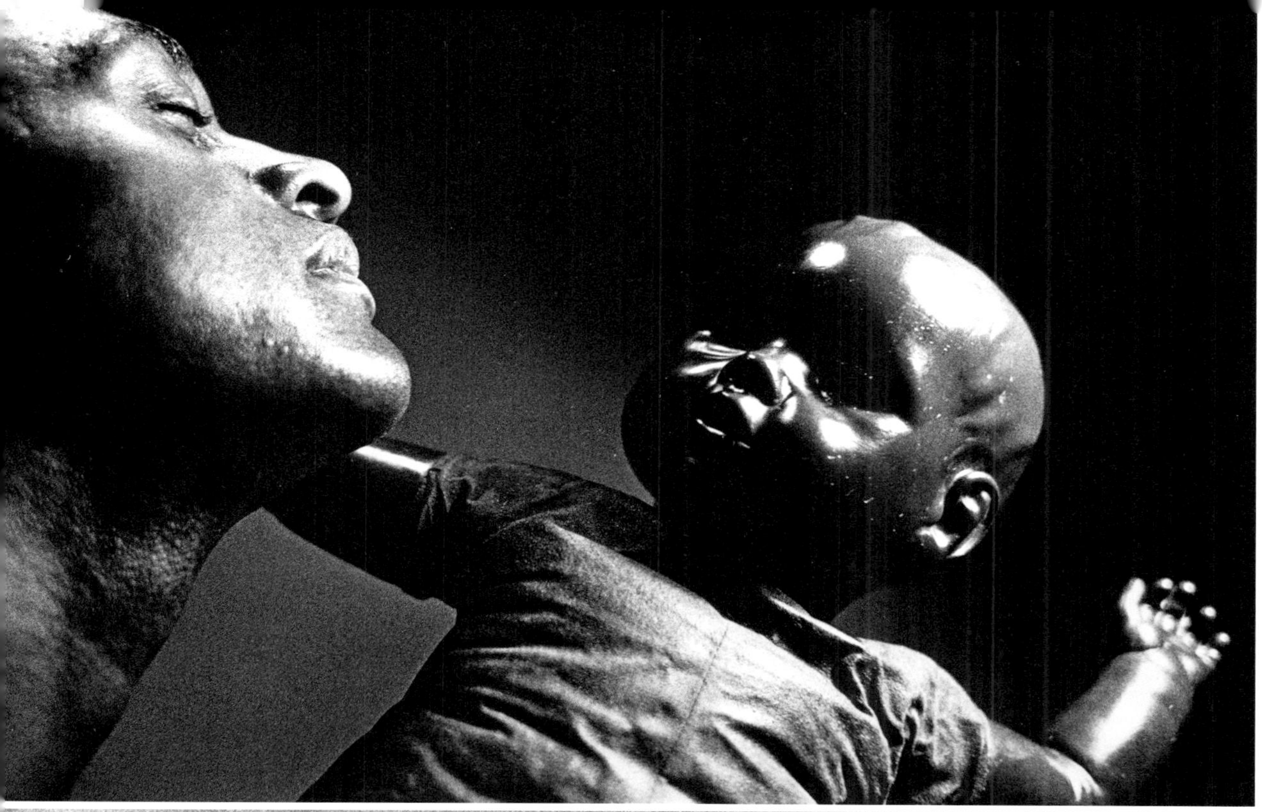

The attempt to free his body leads Artaud to Mexico and Latin America, like many other revolutionaries. "He decides to become an Indian, takes part in ritual ceremonies, and indulges in drug experimentation." But his attempt to overcome his European identity in America proves to be an illusion. "His alternatives: art or madness." Müller writes that art could not be a way out for Artaud, as it was always fraught with tradition. For Ismael Ivo, on the other hand, art was the only way out.

In his text fragment, Müller differentiates between a civilization of economy, of complete exploitation—with Auschwitz as the endpoint—and a civilization of waste, which is always oriented toward possibility, toward potentiality. He views Ismael Ivo as a person who carries both civilizations within him, and concludes with the aspect of the colonial perspective:

The black dancer who wants to break the boundaries of his body and skin (color). Boundaries imposed by racism—and breaking them as a prerequisite for humanity/(EITHER NO ONE OR EVERYONE)

Ismael Ivo reverses the gaze, he does not focus it on the utopia of the New World, which Artaud and numerous other artists and intellectuals were looking for in Latin America, but takes the path from the tropics to the center of dance modernism. This blew up the dance scene in a double way: projection and counter-projection led to an aesthetic explosion.

The piece *Francis Bacon* (1993), which Ismael Ivo produced with Hans Kresnik and stage designer Penelope Wehrli at Theaterhaus Stuttgart, is also in this vein. Here, the motif of the political body brings together Kresnik's approach to dance theater with Ismael Ivo's emancipatory and rebellious body image. Francis Bacon is perhaps the most important representative of figurative painting in the second half of the twentieth century. His exploration of the body in large triptychs, in his portraits of the Pope, but also in his attempts to visualize the spiritual dimension of the corporeal correspond with Artaud's questions as well as those of Hans Kresnik and Ismael Ivo.

At the very beginning of *Francis Bacon*, Ismael Ivo is alone on the narrow, stifling stage triangle exposed directly to the audience. He is struggling with an asthma attack. Clinical space, flickering neon light, completely naked, at the mercy of the space and the audience. Like a wounded prey, the dancer writhes, head against the wall, spinning on its axis. Then enters Tero Saarinen, who is hardly second to Ivo in his physical presence. Both go to their limits, the force between both bodies evokes images of desire, violence, and sexuality, while the stage design intensifies this feeling of being at the mercy of others. As in Vaslav Nijinsky's *L'après midi d'une faune*, the spectators' accustomed view of the spatial perspective of the stage is cut off; the unconditional physicality of the performers meets the unprotected gaze of the viewers, at the same time depriving them of any possibility of distance. In the congenial combination of Kresnik's staging, the dancer's presence, and the reinforcement by the stage design, *Francis Bacon* becomes one of Ismael Ivo's most successful productions ever.

In a duet in which Tero Saarinen and Ismael Ivo bite into a piece of raw meat, the stage becomes a place of dissolution and transgression of boundaries. A place of insanity, where Mara Borba, an important companion of Ismael Ivo since his beginnings in São Paulo, later turns into the incarnation of a Frida Kahlo, with amputated legs, bare-breasted, with a knife in her hand. On the narrow triangle that opens to the front of the stage, the three performers dance their exuberant physical search for connection to the world, penetrating deeply into the visual realms of Francis Bacon. Their approaches to radical performance art combine with the nightmares of a master painter.

Another key production for Ivo's overall oeuvre is the dance adaptation of Jean Genet's *The Maids* from 2001, a production by Haus der Kulturen der Welt in Berlin and Theaterhaus Stuttgart. A hallmark of his work is his collaborative approach with his West African dance partner Koffi Kôkô, theater master Yoshi Oida (director), composer and musician João de Bruçó, and set

designer Kazuko Watanabe. Jean Genet describes the prison of dependencies of the servants, the only way out of which, in the final analysis, is through a mythically exalted space of the transgression of the body. Genet used a real event as a model for his play, the ritual murder perpetrated by the Papin sisters, two maids who massacred their mistress in 1933.

The fact that the roles of the white servants are danced by two Black dancers projects the dimension of domination and rebellion into the context of a colonial upheaval. Genet—and also Sartre—is familiar with this dimension of the revolution of the oppressed, which is also physical and violent. In the period following the scandal-ridden premiere of *The Maids* in 1947, the brutal war of liberation in Algeria links the artistic and literary intelligentsia to the wars of liberation in all colonies. In this context, the metaphor of freedom takes on a central meaning for the dynamics of contemporary art. The living space of the maids in Jean Genet's play becomes an unbearable prison, reflecting the modes of social oppression. Their liberation is only possible through the ritual transgression of the set power structures.

One of Ismael Ivo's sources of inspiration was the short film *Un Chant d'Amour*, in which Genet describes the situation of two prisoners in adjacent prison cells who have no visual contact with each other and can only live out their love by using a straw to pierce the mortar of the separating wall and, through this connection, send the breath or cigarette smoke from the mouth of one to the body of the other. An intimate connection that can be read as a metaphor for violent physical separation and its transcendence. It is the alternative to the brutal humiliation by the prison guard who imposes physical intimacy by force. This imprisonment in one's own body and the overcoming of socially constructed walls and projections is a key theme for Jean Genet just as it is for Ismael Ivo.

This subject becomes clear in all its force with reference to the colonial construction of race, as formulated by Frantz Fanon, another intellectual companion for Ismael Ivo, in *Black Skin, White Masks* (1952) and then later in *The Wretched of the Earth* (1961) as a pamphlet. Fanon, a French citizen who had to radically experience foreign domination through the colonial gaze as a Black man, described the aspect of the exercise of violence from a psychoanalytic perspective. This theoretical approach has become a performative practice for Ismael Ivo. What attracted him to the works of Frantz Fanon, Jean Genet, or Heiner Müller was their revolutionary force, which he also found in Nijinsky and Artaud. In their works, theater is charged with social energy, with the potential for change. For Ismael Ivo, the rebellious and utopian body is at the center of this.

This central theme of Ismael Ivo's life runs like a thread through his choreographies. In *Delirium of a Childhood* (1989), he translates the experience of existential poverty, hunger, and death into a scenic ritual. In *Apocalypse* (1989), it is the collaboration with Ushio Amagatsu, the radical choreographer of the Butoh company Sankai Juku, and the pianist Takashi Kako that takes the performer to the limits of physical possibilities.

With *Mapplethorpe* (2002), Ismael Ivo not only works through his encounter with the American photographer in the 1980s in New York, whose uncompromising depiction of the naked male Black body exposes the ambivalent structures of desire and power. Ismael Ivo expresses the violence of this colonial framework right from the opening image of the performance. In the set design, developed with his stage designer and life partner Marcel Kaskeline, he is clamped naked between two massive panes of glass that stand vertically on the stage and then topple toward the audience to hit the stage floor with violent force.

In 2004, the Haus der Kulturen der Welt produced two major works with Ismael Ivo on the theme of the Black Atlantic. In the dance theater project *Olhos d'Agua*, which takes its starting point in a memory of his great-grandmother, who was still born a slave, Ismael Ivo addresses the role of women as bearers of cultural

memory, liberation, and survival. In another project, his idea of a *Black Atlantic City Bus Tour. Poetry of the Invisible* was also visionary. For the first time, it explored the traces of Black History in Berlin. Above all, the combination of education and performance, for example at the Tempelhof memorial to the handful of German soldiers who had died in the genocide against the Herero and Nama people at the beginning of the twentieth century in what is today Namibia, at the venue on Kurfürstendamm where Josephine Baker performed in the 1920s, or at the street signs in Wedding bearing the names of brutal colonial masters, brought the invisible subject of German colonialism and racism to the attention of a German public for the first time using the means of dance and performance.
Here we see an example of Ismael Ivo bringing together two major cultural-political themes and making them effective for a broad audience: the continuation of a critical and rebellious modernism of theater and art that is newly charged with the concepts of the postcolonial perspective. With his work, Ismael Ivo is perhaps the most outstanding protagonist of these themes in Europe between 1980 and 2005. It is only the younger generation of dancers and performers from African and Latin American countries that follow in his footsteps, assisted by a reorientation in the field of Cultural Studies.

I

Audition for the *Runway* production, 2008, micadanses Paris, with Ismael Ivo, Marina Abramović, Riccardo Tisci, photographer: Marco Anelli

Ismael Ivo. An elegant appearance. Then this broad smile. On stage concentrated force, a body with very long arms that can take sculptural forms.
...I remember a cold, wet day. Matthias Lilienthal guides us through the dilapidated Hackesche Höfe with its crumbling plaster. Somewhere in the attic, Hans Kresnik and I are supposed to view rehearsal rooms. When we get there, there is a photo session in progress. It was my first encounter with Ismael Ivo.
We then worked on three pieces in quick succession. First *Mars* after Fritz Zorn, in 1993 at Schauspiel Basel. Ismael Ivo dances Death in wild pas de deux with the actor Bernhard Schütz. This is followed by *Francis Bacon* in 1994 and one year later by *Othello* with an all-male cast. Both were produced at the Theaterhaus Stuttgart.
I have a photo from *Francis Bacon* in front of me. Ismael Ivo and Tero Saarinen. Both are in a steep slanting position, falling toward each other. Their feet look as if they were glued to the floor. Bare legs, strained muscles. Their upper bodies are in gray felt-like suit jackets. Behind them, at a slight angle, stands a cold metal wall with strange technical contraptions. The room has hardly any depth. The area in the right of the picture is in the dark. This is of course a snapshot, and I know that in the next second, the two dancers will pounce on each other like wild beasts. The civilizational restraints are suspended.
At the beginning of the piece, the right wall is lined with a dull black skin, below which is light blue with delicately drawn horizontal lines, as in Eadweard Muybridge's motion studies, which were an important influence for *Francis Bacon*. Horizontal rows of fluorescent tube lamps can flood the room with very bright, flickering light. They magnify the finer grid, burning it into our eyes. On the long metal wall, three beds can be folded down, they have the appearance of narrow dissection tables and reveal three equally narrow openings—a triptych in changing colors. The floor, bright orange, marks a triangular playing field.

Everything here serves to frame the three dancers, the steely pale Tero Saarinen, the sharply chiseled Mara Borba, and Ismael Ivo. They are a fighting trio and equal opponents. Their bodies are in matching suits, gray as if covered with dust. The three could be multiple aspects of one single being, male and female, night-black and misty pale, whole and amputated, sinewy tough and soft torn flesh, victim and perpetrator in equal measure, and all of it always close to the animal. The outbursts are also directed at themselves. And a constant sizing up, a constant shifting of the balance of power.

And yet Mara Borba also plays the feminine side, flowers in her hair, bare breasts proudly on display like a sphinx. She dances on knee stumps with herself and a huge knife as a crutch. And Tero dances a tenderly cautious waltz with the legless one. Then she is a bundle of flesh, suspended in a leather pouch, a speech bubble with a gruff voice. Everything is exaggerated. Just like it is in the paintings of Francis Bacon.

The rehearsals for this production took place on the premises of a disused slaughterhouse. A fitting place. And yet a beam of sunlight streams into the room. There was a lightness to everything. A small team, highly concentrated. Dense, probing rehearsals at the limits of the bearable, but also of the feasible.

The dedicated staff at the Theaterhaus give us the necessary support in these processes—whether it concerns the dissection tables, which have to be very versatile, or a fine gold paper, or whether raw liver is to be sewn up, which Tero will tear from Ismael's shackle like a dog.

A journey into the paintings of Francis Bacon. All of us are affected, we all seem to have a special connection to these pictures. Maybe because the physicality of the figures in them seems so tangible. Maybe because they convey an impulsive momentum—the bags of paint that Bacon threw at the paintings he had just finished. In the original they strike me as very spatial, they have a sculptural quality to them. I had seen the big retrospective in London

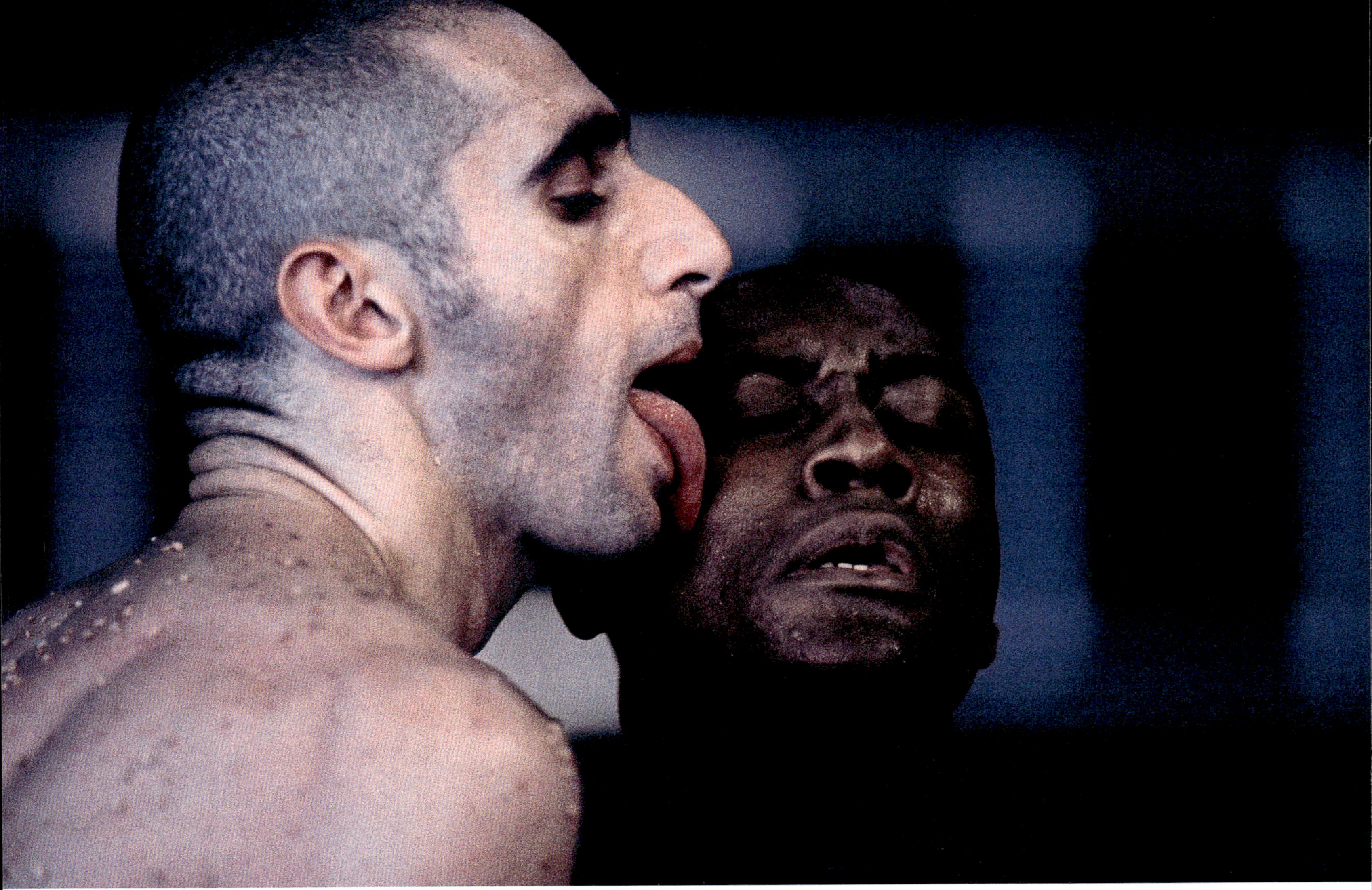

in 1985, a special privilege to have had such an immediate experience of the paintings' colorfulness and the tactility of the figures. The bizarre contortions of the bodies, the frozen cries and cocooned desires. And always framings for the bodies and the faces, in windows, in doors, on beds. Fight scenes and lovemaking. Violence and observant reticence all at once. The disfigured sitters observe the painter while painting.

These images are the foundation and inspiration for this work. In the rehearsals they transform, get into motion, and the movements become stories. We "think beyond" the condensed moments captured in the paintings.

The impulse to pick Bacon's art as the source material for a piece came from Ismael Ivo. And Kresnik was completely in tune with the expression of the clustered corporeality and the brutality visible and palpable therein. Kresnik and Ivo are congenial partners. Kresnik bundles Ivo's sprawling powers. He hones them, sharpens them. That the movements are forced into a space that is far too narrow turns it up another notch. And the choral music by Paulo Chagas, which spills out into ever new soundscapes and can become completely blurred, opens up these framings and bundlings once more.

Here everything seems to coalesce. The newly emerging images are escalations and yet they remain open and ever-changing. I have to decide for myself how to read them.

Ivo's glaring eyeballs shine out from behind a bouquet of flowers. He tiptoes carefully like a sweating clown-like bird in the misty orange sodium vapor light that swallows all depth.

With Ivo, everything is concentration. Every sinew seems conscious. He is completely present, everything seems to feel. From the outside, this often moves close to the affected. But it is the deeply cultivated attention to every single nerve.

Kresnik hacks away at it. Everything sleek and pretty is suspect to him. He turns it into something grotesque and into something that is painful to watch.

Where does the character begin, where is the self? Where is the director and where is the dancer? Where does one body end and another begin? One leg stretches and creates space. Everything is connected, intertwined.

I

II

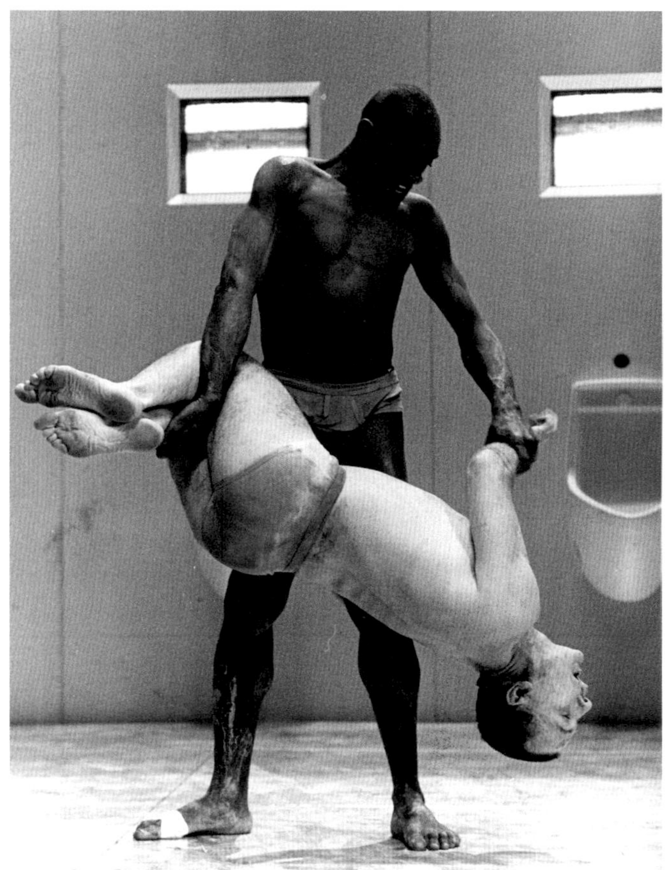

I, II *Mars*, 1993, Theater Basel, Ismael Ivo and Bernhard Schütz, photographer: Bettina Müller

"Is the body still a taboo?"
A conversation with Ismael Ivo on the occasion of the new production *Othello* (1995)

JOHANNES ODENTHAL With *Othello*, you have chosen a literary theme. What made you pick a classical theatrical subject, which belongs to a completely different tradition than your ritual dance productions?

ISMAEL IVO There are of course different sides and dimensions to my choice of *Othello*. I can say that it is a subject that I have always dreamed of bringing to life. As a teenager, when I saw the first productions, at the opera, at the theater, what concerned me most was the fact that there was always a white man with his face painted black. It wasn't so much the racist aspect that bothered me, although that is of course also there, but the question of whether this man in black face paint could really express what a Black man would feel in that situation. That was the main question for me at that time. Now the time has come to take up this question again. Of course, there are many other questions that exist today. There is the role of Othello, the function of the stranger in society. Othello knows his function and plays with it. There is Iago, who questions social morality, or the character of Desdemona, a woman who seeks adventure with a stranger like Othello, who tries to live through him what was closed to her, the path to the unknown. She tries to use him as a doorway that leads out of her own environment. She tells Othello that she herself does not see his color. It was also a utopian love. My question on stage is how to portray this Othello. He creates an important position for himself, so he knows how to take advantage of his strangeness. And at the same time, the whole of society knows that it is also dependent on him. Othello pushes this game very far until he draws his last card. If they allow him to marry Desdemona, then he would be king. And they allow it. The only honest reaction is from Desdemona's father, who says no: how can my daughter marry this Black stranger? But society silences him. Othello's love for Desdemona is a fiction. It is an idealization, it is not concrete. It seems to me that from one moment to the next, everyone is aware of what is going on. And from a certain point, Othello cedes the initiative to the others. I have to find out why. Because Othello is a sensitive, intelligent man. Why does he let Iago spin his intrigue? At a certain point, Desdemona also goes to her death without resistance. I don't know if that's the deep necessity of tragedy: although we know how things are going to turn out, we do not stop them from happening.

It also has a lot to do with the time we live in today. Just take the situation of O. J. Simpson. He's an Othello of our age. One of the first ideas of the new production is that no one leaves the stage. So everyone witnesses their own destiny. No one escapes their destiny.

ODENTHAL I have the impression that you're creating a kind of story ballet. Are there characters on stage that are acted out by the dancers?

IVO Yes. That's a challenge, that everyone fills a specific character. I also want to go further into the realm of theater, I'm interested in the power of drama. How do we revive drama, update it? And how do we bring it back into the body? Shakespeare still had that power of dialogue. I want to find the same in the body.

ODENTHAL You've already referred to your biographical interest in Othello. In the past few years, you have dealt with mythological figures from ancient Greece. Is there such a thing as a cultural identity for you at all? Do you have a nationality? Or do you belong to the migrants, to the nomads of a world culture?

IVO Even in Brazil I felt connected to a symbolic or rather mythological level of movement. And from the very beginning, I tried to understand life and reinterpret it in my dance. A mythical figure like Phoenix touches the level of immolation and rebirth, Pegasos has the experience of flying. These figures were very significant in relation to my roots. From Brazil, I went to New York to study with Alvin Ailey. I immersed my body in the education of modern dance. With Ailey, we had Horton and Graham. I always approached this material with great curiosity. It wasn't that my body was being molded. Rather, my body was experimenting the forms to its limits. In other words, I didn't train myself in a technique in that sense but rather allowed my body to explore the technique. And that also relates to my actual life in my body.

These experiences led me to Europe and to expressive dance. I found expressionism, which was completely unknown to me until then. For me, this is a constant dialogue, as Frantz Fanon described it in *The Wretched of the Earth*, this aspect that cultural roots are not something fixed. We have to understand them as development, as evolving in their universal connection. In this book, Fanon shows how European theater traces its roots to Greek tragedy, which in turn has its origins in Egyptian culture. For me, what is important is that while we need to point out the differences, we should also, more than anything else, strengthen the connections. What are the roots of Philip Glass' music, where does postmodern dance come from, where does minimalism come from? On this level, I have a dialogue with expressionism. This is where my curiosity about dance theater is articulated. This is also the level on which I work with Hans Kresnik. We have a conversation, even without words. I enter into his ideas as far as I can.

I bring my own existence into play, my own self. In the processes of work and discovery, I know no economy. From the first moment, I give myself completely. I can still reduce later. When I enter the studio, I remember nothing of what I have intellectually prepared. I let the movements in me have their own life. I don't know from which foot, which hand, from where the movement comes. I make my body available so that the ideas and movements can take over. It is then that I have returned to my roots. It's like being in a trance. I surrender my body to the idea and let the idea work in me without trying to pin anything down beforehand. You go down to the river every day. And the river is never the same. So you have to bring along your life energy anew every time. That's my relationship with Kresnik and with dance theater. One aspect of it is the reflection of the individual and society, and for me, the individual, the body itself, has to be totally in play. The dancer has to commit their own life.

ODENTHAL I must insist on the differences between cultures. You are talking about a universal culture, which is an anthropological level. But at the same time, the cultural backgrounds remain very different. For example, the culture in Germany puts you in a certain position. And *Othello* is also a play on that.

IVO I represent the opposite of a purist position. Roots are there. And we can learn a lot from them. But I'm striving for a fusion. For the connection and against the rediscovery. Dance is an existential thing for me. Dance is the experience of life in you, the invocation of adversity and possibility. It's always confrontation.

ODENTHAL Do you have a religious background? You are certainly not an animist! But you have a message, a belief that is related to your dance. I can remember your serious accident, which you only barely survived. The important thing for you was to be able to dance again.

IVO I am an expressionist! I am very close to my Brazilian roots without practicing them. What keeps me dancing is the question of existence. That magical moment on stage. I often leave the stage with a knowledge that something has happened, and I can't tell you how that communication between the audience and me came about. Sometimes I find that in literature, for example in Márquez. In South America, there is a magical sense of reality. Perhaps the sense of reality is broader. Borges constantly asked: What is real? It depends on your point of view. Go a little further to the right and maybe what you see is not so real. That's what fascinates me.

Why am I dancing? If it weren't for that magic moment when you feel that you're crossing a certain line, that you're really addressing people without lecturing them, if it weren't for that moment, there would be no continuity in dance.

ODENTHAL You describe yourself as an existentialist. What does existence mean to you?

IVO Existence, as I see it, is a fiction. Existence is a utopia. There is a belief in life in the sense of transforming the moment and thereby constantly opening up new possibilities. That is what I believe in. I believe in the body, not only in the soul. It is the house that I have at this moment in time. And I can try to explore and sensitize it more and more. I try to find a new spatial order, a spatial order from body to body, from dancer to audience. I ask the question of how I can fill this order with content. What are the possibilities of communication? The body is an open house of possibilities. It is so complex that I am constantly in dialogue with it without ever fully understanding it.

ODENTHAL Today we say that culture and society are symbolic systems. And human existence is always defined by this symbolic system. We are born into a particular context and look at the world from a particular perspective. When we move to another culture, we can shift that a little bit. But the symbols, the systems always remain. Ismael, you come from a different culture than the European one. Do you think that this common level of communication really exists?

IVO Not one hundred percent. And yet I know many moments when people said, "Oh my God, that's not him, that's me. That's me!"

ODENTHAL Does that happen to you?

IVO Yes, for example, when I deal with a subject that I was not familiar with before, like *Francis Bacon*. Discovering this pleasure in destruction, the pleasure in dominance, the cruelty that we all have, but rarely relate to.

ODENTHAL You show your work within the German theater system. Is that the appropriate place?

IVO Of course, it's the place I work for. I've always felt myself to be someone who infiltrates—myself and, by consequence, my surroundings. And because of this infiltration, the result is not part of my culture, but rather the consequence of a confrontation. But then it's not mine. It's ours. It becomes a third thing that ultimately belongs to all of us.

ODENTHAL Categories like colonialism and imperialism or the emancipation of the "Third World" no longer play a role for you?

IVO No. I am a long way away from that. I believe that we have cultural treasures that we all own. If we're smart, we'll explore them all and learn from them. When I hear the phrase "my culture," I respond with "our culture." Differences are welcome, but not in the sense of separation, but in the sense of communication. Because this is the only way you can make progress within humanism. This is an existential dream. In this respect, I am a believer. Because I trust in the possibilities of the human being.

ODENTHAL That seems to me fundamentally important for the discussion of a multicultural society. The problem is that curators and organizers think that foreign culture can only ever be presented in a European context. You are indeed talking about another possibility, that of dialogue.

IVO When I brought *Delirium of a Childhood* to Brazil, that is, a production that is connected to the roots but also takes a completely different form as dance theater, people reacted as if they had rediscovered something that had been lost. Distance from one's roots does not mean abandoning them. For me, it was very important to take the intellectual ideas to their essence. And that was the body. Only then do you have the possibility to transform. I immersed myself again in the writings of Grotowski. He's very important to my exploration of dancers. That already started with *Francis Bacon*. While I do have a company, I don't choreograph in a traditional sense. I want to give very clear guidelines, but of course, above all open up the possibilities of dialogue with the dancers' bodies. In my work, I start from a theatrical concept. I need a dramaturgy, I look for a direction. That is the prerequisite for achieving a choreographic result that is authentic.

ODENTHAL What do you mean by authenticity?

IVO When you create a piece in which you don't just reproduce, but participate with all your possibilities, then something like authenticity comes into being. You are not just a dancer, but a person who uses dance as a means of communication. Only when I create a dialogical structure between the dancers can it develop in the audience as well. I discover theater through dance. I explore the power of the dramatic because that's where I find existential questions that support the presence of the dancer. That's one of my starting points. That's why I'm so fascinated by mythology because it directly confronts us with a force that remains potent and powerful to this day. Like a mirror image of our society. With this approach to a theatrical language, I don't mean *physical theater*—of course, my work can also be called dance theater or choreographic theater—rather, I am looking very specifically for the dramatic force. In *Bacon*, I surrendered myself more radically than ever before. When you become aware of your own limitations, you will find an energy that is very closely related to the creative. Then a real dialogue can begin in which I am directly involved. I question myself, not some role. That, for me, is the resource of art. This utopia of the body and communication. That's also what I want to convey to my dancers as a possibility. So my choreographic structure is related to Artaud and Grotowski. And it's very similar to the vitality of Hans Kresnik's directing. He belongs to the kind of directors who have the ability to explore boundaries. We work together in that sense.

ODENTHAL Do you want to please an audience?

IVO Never!

ODENTHAL Do you want to shock?

IVO Not necessarily.

ODENTHAL Do you want to be loved?

IVO Not necessarily. For example, *Francis Bacon*: I didn't expect it to be such a success.

ODENTHAL Critics of your work accuse you of narcissism. What do you think about this accusation?

IVO Every critic is responsible for their own work. I don't understand it. *Francis Bacon* is a dirty performance. I expose the body in its violence, its dark recesses.

It has to do with what we just described as symbolic systems. A naked, Black body has a certain meaning within Western civilization. Then there's an important motif that you restage in every performance: the undressing of the body, that is, the uncovering of the thin layer of civilization, if you will. You associate a wild, primitive side of the human being, a kind of nature.

Why is the body still taboo? That's my first question. In my performance, I try to break down these barriers. And specifically in *Francis Bacon*, I've gone to the extreme. When I show what Bacon says: a body is nothing but flesh and bones. That's all there is to it. That shakes people up. There's that moment when I'm hanging like I'm in a slaughterhouse, or the beginning: I'm naked on stage and I have an asthma attack. That's not very nice. That's a confrontation with death. How can you call that narcissism? My idea is to open up and expose the body to confront something that is very deep and very serious, that is also taboo, that is death.

Delirium of a Childhood is a piece about hunger and childhood. For me, it goes far beyond the body. It's very emotional. The body of a child looking for food. What's narcissistic about that? If I put virtuosity on stage, if I want to show what I can do, I could understand that. I do exactly the opposite. I always work with an idea that challenges me. The essence of dance is the way toward the body and not its abstraction. You can fly, but only from the level of matter. You have to go through the material first and then you can take off.

First publication:
"'Is the body still a taboo?' Conversation with Ismael Ivo about the new production 'Othello,'" *Ballett international / Tanz aktuell* 7 (1995), pp. 26–29; reprinted in the essay collection *Tanz Körper Politik*, Recherchen 27, Theater der Zeit, 2005, second edition 2012.

"Ismael was always aware that his exhibiting the naked Black body for a predominantly white audience would be seen as a provocation"

Werner Schretzmeier, co-founder and director of Theaterhaus Stuttgart, in conversation with Johannes Odenthal

JOHANNES ODENTHAL Between 1991 and 2006, the Theaterhaus Stuttgart became the central production venue for Ismael Ivo. There was even talk of a permanent ensemble. The Theaterhaus was not really a dance institution, but you wanted to establish a dance division for and with Ismael Ivo that would also create an alternative to the all-dominant ballet. How did the close cooperation with Ismael come about? What was it about his artistic approach that convinced you?

WERNER SCHRETZMEIER The period of cooperation between Ismael Ivo and the Theaterhaus began as early as 1987 with the guest performance of *Under Skin*. In the same year, *Phoenix* ran for two weeks at the Theaterhaus to sold-out houses. In 1991 followed a production of *The Night of Dionysus*, and in 1993 came *Labyrinthos*. The collaboration with Ismael continued for almost twenty years, until 2006, when the new version of *Apocalypse* was created, a collaboration with ImPulsTanz. On the one hand, my motivation was the overpowering presence of ballet in Stuttgart, in terms of form and content. I wanted to counter this conventional form of dance with something new—with Ismael Ivo, who asserted a new body image with an unbelievable consistency, even provocation, and who, for me, was able to stand up to the predominance of tradition. That was a key factor. It was also clear to me that as a theater we could not close ourselves off to the dynamics of the European dance scene. And Ismael was someone who instantly highlighted the potential of contemporary dance to me. He also reached a large audience. We played his productions for weeks. And Ismael understood that he had a special audience in Stuttgart. In addition, we got along very well from the beginning.

I

ODENTHAL It was a stroke of luck for the Theaterhaus and the city that the collaboration of Márcia Haydée, the great white ballerina of the Stuttgart Ballet, and Ismael as her Black Brazilian counterpart came about. It was a unique constellation.

SCHRETZMEIER This went to the point that the then prime minister of the State of Baden-Württemberg, Lothar Späth, who never came to the Theaterhaus, visited us twice. It was also the perfect bridge between establishment and suburbia, between the municipal theater and the independent scene, if you will. On top of that, the success was a real statement for Márcia. She had been harshly criticized for the artistic direction of the ballet and felt that she had been removed from the court. The collaboration with Ismael was like rehabilitation for her. Right off the bat, they hit it big with *Tristan and Isolde*. And this congenial collaboration lasted for three or four years, until *Oedipus*, Tabori's last production, which came out at the Berliner Ensemble. It was an amazing story for us. Márcia was able to go back on stage with her head held high. She did just that, to the highest of standards. Both of them mixed up the city quite a bit with their abilities.

ODENTHAL Being able to produce at the Theaterhaus was incredibly important to Ismael. The success of *Francis Bacon*, *Othello*, or *The Maids* was also made possible by the liberal production conditions with a development and rehearsal time of at least eight weeks. The independent scene also saw itself as an alternative to the municipal theaters. We almost had an Ismael Ivo Dance Company at the Theaterhaus.

SCHRETZMEIER We had extremely little money. Support from the city and state amounted to about 600,000 DM a year out of a total budget of 4.5 million. I had the experience of *Phoenix* and *Under Skin*, and the experience of the other guest performances, which all went very, very well. I had to raise production funds for each new work, let's say from 50,000 DM upwards, spread over 14 to 20 performances. When they were sold out, we recouped the funds. That was the only way to do it. With his personality and artistic quality, Ismael captured the audience to such a degree that we could always take the risk. Eventually, we were talking about six-figure sums that we had to bring in for *Francis Bacon*. Then Claudia Bauer and Meinrad Huber came into play with their dance agency ecotopia. They organized the guest performances throughout Europe and later worldwide. All of this put together made it possible to stage these productions without having to depend on outside funding.

We were able to produce in-house. Hall 3, with about 100 square meters, was available as a rehearsal stage for several weeks. And the final rehearsals took place in the theater itself, in Hall 1.

ODENTHAL The reception from the audience was fantastic. How did the critics and politicians react?

SCHRETZMEIER Horst Koegler was the one who had criticized the ballet the most. But there were also critics like Angela Reinhardt who were not very gracious with Ismael. There were accusations of narcissism, exoticism, machismo. The collaboration with Márcia changed a lot of things.

Ismael expressed the freedom of the body like virtually no one else in the 1980s. The period was marked by a desire for new images, for what had not yet been seen. The uncompromizing nature of Ismael's work, his radicalism was also a political statement. We often talked about sociopolitical issues. Ismael was always aware that his exhibiting the naked Black body for a predominantly white audience would be seen as a provocation that he was consciously playing with. And it was always clear that this only works if it is completely under control. And that's exactly what he delivered. That's also what made him so important because he opened up the blinkered perspectives of many members of the audience. For contemporary dance, he emptied numerous boxes: all the historical garbage, the prejudices. He never became conformist. And that was what we expected of him. He was in an artistic environment where anything else would have tended to create confusion. He never had to settle, and never made any compromises artistically.

For us, it was important that Ismael could work from his center, and for that we all joined forces. This was never written down because we had a natural agreement that was the basis for the long period of our collaboration. That's why it's tragic that we couldn't make the idea of a company happen.

In the mid-1990s, after the great successes of *Francis Bacon* and *Othello*, we were on the verge of launching an Ismael Ivo Dance Company. The state of Baden-Württemberg had already allocated 300,000 DM. The city of Stuttgart, however, did not follow suit. The Theaterhaus was very dynamic with Ismael Ivo, while the ballet was artistically stagnant. Apparently, this was not acceptable. The entire national and international dance press attended the premieres of *Francis Bacon* and *Othello*. And yet the city did not want to go along with a further expansion of contemporary dance. With another 600,000 DM, a company could have been established.

II

Günther Beelitz then brought Ismael to Weimar because we just didn't get our act together in Stuttgart. We kept in touch with Ismael through regular guest performances, but the big idea of an independent company had failed.

ODENTHAL What did the collaboration look like artistically? Did the Theaterhaus provide a kind of dramaturgy, a conceptual direction?

SCHRETZMEIER The ideas always came from Ismael. He actually always had three to four ideas for us so we could bring one of them to fruition. We discussed them together. I was responsible for the entire theater and could rely completely on Ismael artistically. I saw my task as enabling the basic conditions for dance, for example, for ambitious sets that we constructed in-house or had produced outside.

The mode of operation at the Theaterhaus did without hierarchies. We were all generalists, everybody did everything. It was like a well-functioning artists' commune. We established the Theaterhaus in 1984 and opened it in March 1985. There were three of us, my wife Gudrun, Peter Grohmann, and I. The former factory site was remodeled in three-quarters of a year. That's how it was in the 1980s. Most of the independent projects were formed during that period. We were locking for something different in culture than what was offered at the opera houses and municipal theaters. And Ismael was a perfect fit for that. There was, as it were, a logic of its own. Ismael was very freedom-loving. But he also needed structures in order to progress artistically, to be able to implement his aesthetics. The last years of our collaboration were marked by Ismael's work for ImPulsTanz in Vienna and his work for the Venice Biennale. Our contact began to dissolve. Maybe both sides wanted something new and couldn't tell each other.

III

IV

V

The art of George Tabori

Marcel Kaskeline on the origins of an artistic friendship

The first time George Tabori and Ismael worked together was when Tabori was directing Arnold Schoenberg's opera fragment *Moses and Aron* at the Leipzig Opera House. The piece has three major protagonists: Moses, a speaking role, Aron, a tenor, and the chorus. Aron and Moses showed off all their dramatic talent. The chorus, on the other hand, stood rigid and stiff. George was not satisfied and enlisted the help of Ismael to choreograph its performance.

I

Ismael moved the actors. They stood or sat, facing front and back on chairs, stacked chairs, destroyed the stacks, lay on the floor, circled the stage. George and Ismael explored the possibilities to give the scenes a greater poignancy. It became too much for the chorus, and after a few days, one of the actors came to George: "One day we have to do this, the next day we have to do that, and the third day we have to do something completely different. Every day we have to do something different. We don't see any concept here".
George took Ismael by the hand, went onto the stage, and stood in front of the chorus, "I will explain the concept. The concept is to make mistakes. We make mistakes today and we make mistakes tomorrow. And the day after tomorrow, we may make fewer mistakes. But we always make mistakes. Because without mistakes, there is no art." George and Ismael sat down, the discussion was over, and rehearsals continued until the opening night.

I George Tabori, Ismael Ivo at ImPulsTanz – Vienna International Dance Festival, 1994, Volkstheater Wien, photographer: Claudia Herschberger

“There was a veritable fan club that would wait for Ismael after the performances”
Dancer Riccarda Herre in conversation with Johannes Odenthal on the time in Weimar

JOHANNES ODENTHAL When did you first meet Ismael Ivo?

RICCARDA HERRE It was in 1984, I was still at the ballet school of the Hamburg State Opera. Ismael Ivo was performing his solo production *Ritual of a Body in Moon* at Kampnagel. Our modern dance teacher at the time had encouraged us to see the work. After the performance, I was deeply impressed by his incredibly strong presence on stage. And then Ismael was actually invited to our class. We had our Graham lesson, the door opened, he walked in, elegantly dressed, with his signature long coat, and immediately attracted everyone’s attention. There was a part in the piece where Ismael improvised movements with his feet and our teacher couldn’t think of anything better than to ask us to do the same. There we were, with our bun and our leotards with pink tights, desperately trying to emulate him. You can imagine the result. Ismael was nevertheless very kind, gave us a few corrections along the way, and I thought to myself, someday you want to work with this dancer. For me, that was a certainty.

And it just so happened that Ismael organized an audition for a project company in Vienna at the very moment when I had completed my training in Hamburg in 1988. I auditioned, and got the part. Ismael had choreographed *Le Sacre du Printemps* as the third work in a three-part evening with Sonia Mota and Joe Alegado. I danced the role of the sacrificial virgin. Ismael himself was not on stage. When the company disbanded after a few months, he said to me, “No matter what else I do, as soon as I have a company, you’re in. We’ll work together again.” That’s what happened because he was incredibly reliable in that regard. When he started in Weimar in 1997, Mara Borba and other Brazilian artists were there, and I was there, too.

ODENTHAL Ismael was an outstanding soloist. From your perspective, what was the decisive factor in wanting to work with him?

HERRE For me, coming from ballet, which had to function in the group within a very clear aesthetic framework, he was impressive as a dancer, or better yet, as a performer. Especially in his solo pieces, he managed to captivate the audience. To be on stage together with such an artist, or better still to exist next to him and to find a common body language, was an exciting challenge for me. It wasn't always easy, and sometimes unpredictable, because an artist who sees himself primarily as a soloist doesn't necessarily stick to all the arrangements on stage. Therefore, in a way, it was also new and exciting every time, because you never knew exactly what was going to happen, you often had to react spontaneously.

ODENTHAL What was the decisive factor in your collaboration? You've worked closely together on almost ten productions.

HERRE For me as a dancer who explicitly never wanted to be a choreographer myself, it was always interesting to work with choreographers or directors who didn't prescribe a rigid choreography. As a dancer, having the opportunity to experiment with the given movement material, to change it and make it my own, was always what I was looking for. Ismael approved of this and gave me a great deal of freedom. We developed ideas together in dialogue because we had great appreciation for each other.

ODENTHAL Ismael always had a team for direction, choreography, and dramaturgy at his side.

HERRE There was always a corrective factor from the outside, through directing, choreographic assistance, or dramaturgy. The rule was that he was always on stage with us. That's why it was important for him to have someone he trusted, who gave him feedback, but also to us dancers.

ODENTHAL Then, in 1999, *Ariadne* was created, a solo evening for you.

HERRE That was also a promise he had made to me when I started in Weimar: "... and I plan to choreograph a solo evening for you." This was the first production in my career in which I was to perform ninety minutes alone on stage, accompanied by a string quartet. Ismael wanted to give me the space to work exclusively with him. That was a challenge for me. The piece came together very quickly. It was up to me to continue working with the material he gave me, to find the right rhythm, the timing. I've always been a soloist, I danced all the main parts, but I'd never been on stage alone for an entire evening.

ODENTHAL You talked about the Brazilian team that Ismael surrounded himself with in Weimar. Mara Borba, Gerald Thomas, Márcio Aurélio. With *Kuss im Rinnstein*, Ismael performed the Brazilian author Nelson Rodrigues, and that was at the National Theater in Weimar. That was certainly quite a statement. And at the same time, he worked on Heiner Müller's *Fremd im eigenen Körper* ("Foreign in One's Own Body: Emigrations"), dealt with *Faust*, brought Fassbinder onto the stage. German history. Was that a conflict?

HERRE You have to imagine it like this: There was the German National Theater with the statue of Schiller and Goethe on the forecourt. But the neo-Nazis were also sitting there on the benches in their combat boots. That was Weimar at that time: Goethe's Garden House, the day-trippers who strolled through the city with their cameras, the students of the Bauhaus University, a squat, but also neo-Nazis who gave the Hitler salute while the police looked the other way. In this situation, it was pure provocation when Ismael walked across the Theaterplatz. The Brazilian artist community was an antithesis to the public demonstration of a "German ethos" in front of the theater. For the artistic director Günther Beelitz, hiring Ismael was certainly also a political statement. As a company, however, we were perceived by the audience in more of an exotic sense.

ODENTHAL There were sold-out performances and a very positive reaction from the audience.

HERRE I think that the work of Joachim Schlömer, who was a choreographer at the National Theater before us, was somehow more stuffy and less accessible to the season ticket audience at the time. The pieces we showed were different. There is no denying that Ismael's presence on stage created a tremendous fascination with the audience. He won the audience over with this presence. It became almost something like a star cult; there was a veritable fan club that would wait for Ismael after the performances.

But it was also in Weimar where Ismael was immersed in the German municipal theater system for the first time. The whole apparatus with orchestra, workshops, complicated schedules. It was a great challenge for the entire Brazilian community, for example, to deal with these constraints of rehearsal times. Guest performance opportunities conflicted with a system that you had to fit into.

Then in 1999/2000, there was the change of artistic director from Beelitz to Märki. Savings had to be made, and, as is often the case in Germany, the dance division bore the brunt. I then went to Kresnik in Berlin.

ODENTHAL You worked intensively with both Ismael and Hans Kresnik. What was the difference?

HERRE Quite banal: With one choreographer I was on stage at the premiere, and the other sat in the cafeteria. With the premiere, Hans Kresnik handed the piece over to the dancers. That was also a kind of freedom. With Ismael, there was no handover. Ismael always remained present. With Hans, moreover, it was always his drawings that were the basis for our work. It was not the quality of movement that stood at the beginning, but the image that was to be transported. The dancers became part of the image, and movements were created as a result. With Ismael, the impulse and the emotion came directly from the body, that was up front, and an image then emerged from that.

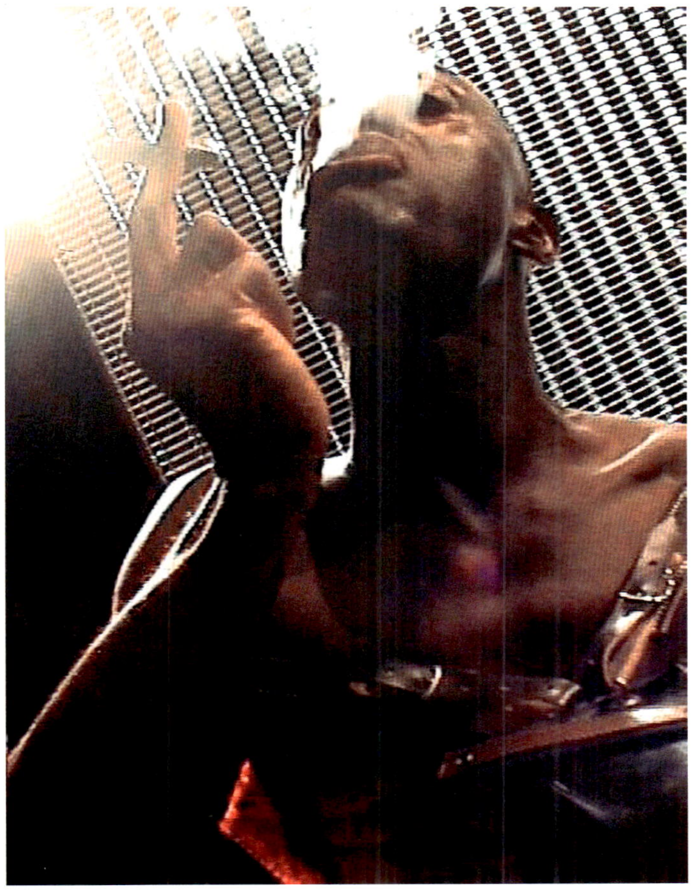

I

I *Mephisto*, 1999, Deutsches Nationaltheater Weimar, photographer: Christian Brachwitz

“A brother from the same origins”
Choreographer and dancer Koffi Kôkô on Ismael Ivo

Ismael Ivo is a brother to me in two different ways: a brother by virtue of sharing the same origins, and a brother in artistic encounter and confrontation. Ismael Ivo is not only a great dancer but also a personality of enormous presence. Someone who completely dominates a stage: an incredible presence that many dancers would love to achieve. Above all, Ismael is a person of great spiritual beauty.

One of the things that had driven him throughout his life was the return to his origins, to his sources. I can say without any presumption that it was through me that he learned to perceive Africa differently. The reason for this is quite simple: I come from my sources, and I embody this origin through the path I chose. With this background I continue to go forward, I never gave up on it, no matter how far I went.

Ismael was very nostalgic about his sources. But in the end, it is the path we take in life that makes us who we are. And because Ismael left Brazil, his journey was, as it were, predetermined, a journey that led him to modern dance, to modern art. At the same time, there was a conflict in this, because he was drifting away from his background. As an Afro-Brazilian, you always remain connected to the source of your origin.

In Jean Genet’s *The Maids*, we had a very deep encounter. There was never conflict, but there was a confrontation. And we wanted to go all the way to the end of this confrontation. The ritualistic side, which Yoshi Oida had developed as director, suited me very well. It felt like home to me. Ismael was forced to explore his innermost being in search of his origins. It was out of this confrontation that this piece became so deep and strong. The ritual created a bond between us. The power of two people who appreciated each other so much, wo respected each other completely, led us to learn an enormous amount from each other along the way.

I

II

Productions like *Delirium of a Childhood* were very close to the power of ritual. Ismael sought this inner power, a power that comes from the deep source of your heritage. At the same time, he was seeking modernity. And when he went back to Brazil, he most likely took this inner search even deeper.
Ritual means communicating with the energies within you, but also with those that surround you. For Ismael, this was strongly linked to the laws of the stage. But, to repeat: Ismael had a great longing, a nostalgia about these origins. The crucial point is that on stage you are radically forced to be yourself. You have got to be, you can't just want to be.
It was his soul that made him so great, along with his mental strength. Along the way, he thought that it was primarily the body that defined the dance. But in reality, it is defined by the inner work and the dialogue with the energies that surround us. They create the dance.
Ismael had a visionary perspective. Everything he did, everything he knew, he used to connect people and change society. There was a deep discontent in him, out of which he developed an incredible power that he always shared with us. Ismael was one of the greats, a great human being.

I *The Maids*, 2001, Theaterhaus Stuttgart, Kofi Kôkô and Ismael Ivo, photographer: Daniela Incoronato
II Ismael Ivo and Koffi Kôkô at the German premiere of *Mapplethorpe*, 2003, Haus der Kulturen der Welt, Berlin

"Intuition is memory pointed toward the future"
Ismael Ivo in conversation with Johannes Odenthal (2004)

JOHANNES ODENTHAL You have repeatedly polarized audiences with your dance productions. Some celebrate the works with standing ovations, others accuse you of narcissism. The focus is on how we deal with the body, the naked Black body on stage. Most recently, you directed *Mapplethorpe*, a play about the taboo of the Black male body in a white society.

ISMAEL IVO When you start looking at Mapplethorpe, you will automatically get to the stereotypes of the Black male erotic body. Mapplethorpe intended it that way. As an artist, he exhibited this taboo, these hidden fantasies of many people, in a very open way. That's incredibly exciting: as soon as you pull a taboo out from under the table and expose it, people start to engage with it, whether they like it or not, whether they're shocked or not. That's why it's a demythification of taboos. And Mapplethorpe managed to do that.

ODENTHAL But what exactly is the taboo here? Is it repressed desire? Forbidden sexuality?

IVO The taboo was the fantasy of the Black erotic man. It may be rooted in a colonialist concept. The Black population was there to be used and abused. This is where these erotic fantasies have their perverse origin. The Black body is locked into the existential situation of disempowerment. This is the condition of enslavement under colonial rule. And that is why this desire has not been a free one. In this sense, Mapplethorpe has changed a perspective by taking a point of view to a radical extreme. In doing so, colonial desire lost some of its strength. He reversed a situation. Normally you could say that something is pornography. Yet here you could not because as photography it mastered the situation. But at the same time, another phenomenon unfolded that comes very close to Jean Genet. One takes something from the underground and then describes this underground, which one is also personally connected to, in a truthfulness that unravels the "dirty," and reveals the beauty of this world. What Genet did in his literature, the description of the underground and its transformation into a "sacred" situation, Mapplethorpe did with photography.

ODENTHAL When I try to put your productions of the last few years into context, I always notice political positions that find expression in the choreographies. There is the theme of apartheid, the theme of emancipation, and also the confrontation with the European canon, such as in *Othello* or later in *The Maids* after Jean Genet. In addition to the artistic, content-related themes, you address the conditions of postcolonial existence and play with political subtexts in these productions. *The Maids*, interpreted by two Black dancers, enter the labyrinth of desire, power, and oppression.

IVO That's why it hurts me when critics are determined to see nothing but narcissism in my work. *Delirium of a Childhood*, for example, is a solo about hunger. I had researched hunger in the world and also interpreted memories from my own childhood, things I saw in my immediate environment. But I never changed my path, against all odds. I never gave up my original idea, that I would develop pieces. Like in *Francis Bacon*, where I start with a ten-minute solo naked. The nudity is part of the content. And thus it was clear to me what was going to happen in the critique of *Mapplethorpe*. "Here comes the Black Narcissus." Maybe in a Central European majority-white society, you are immediately stigmatized if you present yourself with this consistency, as I do. I am sure that a white dancer in a European story like *Bacon* would be viewed differently. The white naked body corresponds to the European concept of the self. I always define myself as an existentialist dancer. I interrogate existence, the body, the Black male body, and thus my own language, my context. When I see *Mapplethorpe* against that background, I also have to ask about what is the social, the actual situation of Black men today? That's part of my context when I put a Black male body on stage.

Research on the social conditions of Black people is part of my project. I learned that there are a striking number of Black youths under the age of 20 in prison in the U.S., quite a few of them on death row. My original idea was for me to be in the electric chair in the first scene. To me, that's still *Mapplethorpe*. We eventually changed that, but I am still in an extreme situation, locked between two panes of glass, where I can hardly move. It is the prison of the Black body, but also of the body in general. I try to break free from this glass box. In the process, the gigantic glass case collapses onto the stage. It's as if I'm being ejected into the real world. Into the world of photographers.

ODENTHAL Let's move on to your latest work, which explicitly deals with the *Black Atlantic*, with the idea of an imaginary space of communicative networks that has a concrete historical starting point in the European slave trade. The theme of memory, of memory through the body, is central here. Your own great-grandmother was born a slave, but in your memory, she is above all the ruler of the family and of history; for you, she is living memory and the center of your own identity. So your new project, *Olhos d'Agua* [Engl: Eyes of Water], unfolds around three outstanding women. Who are these personalities? And how do you get to the heart of this gigantic theme of memories with the tools of theater?

IVO As a performer, I wasn't thinking exclusively of a historically oriented project. Nor did I want to speak about colonialism yet again. So my point was not to take a moralizing view. Rather, I was looking for an image, an artistic idea that could engage with the history of the slave trade, a history that concerns me directly, because I am a part of it, as a dancer, an artist, a choreographer, and a human being. I carry this heritage in me, as a person, and so I didn't want to reiterate the historical facts in the production. From a certain point, the fact of crossing the ocean became the central theme for me. I believe that memories became irrevocably engraved in bodies at the moment when the displacement across the Atlantic began. Water became a metaphor for transformation and, as the defining motif for displacement, transformation, and dissolution, the main element of the entire production. But this moment of departure, when the coast of Africa is left behind, and a process sets in among those who want to survive, I try to find this moment in the body, on a symbolic level. I could call these "the hidden memories." It's something that you sometimes feel inside but cannot trace back to its underlying cause by way of logic. I don't know if it is something spiritual, something genetic, or something physical. And I am convinced that these people, who were trapped below deck on the ships, developed a special kind of resistance from the very first moment, in order not to forget their own roots, their own history, their own knowledge and paradigms.

But let's return to the artistic concept. I was looking for personalities who would, through their bodies, or let's say better, their whole lives, help to tell the story of the *Black Atlantic*. What motivates these personalities to resist oppression, to resist racism, despite all the hardships? What drove these women to sustain their resistance and keep going? I wanted to break down the broad theme of the *Black Atlantic* into individual exemplary biographies. For me, the theme of the ocean is condensed into the personal flow of individual lives.

After reaching this decision, it was clear to me that I needed to find a person who embodied a ritual legacy. After a lengthy search in Brazil, I finally met Mãe Beata, who had moved from Salvador de Bahia to Rio de Janeiro. She is a priestess and a central figure in the context of Afro-Brazilian rituals. I was interested in her personal memories, her family history, her initiation, all the information inscribed in her life, her memory, and her body as significant moments. We talked about her childhood memories. Who told her what about her origins? I tried to follow and understand the process of collective memory on a biographical and symbolic level, through real points of reference and ideas.

I already knew Thereza Santos, an extraordinary person who escaped the military dictatorship in Brazil to participate in the war of liberation in Angola. Back in Brazil, after several terms in prison, she became a leader in the Black Brazilian civil rights movement. Among other things, she founded the first Black women's rights association in Brazil. What interested me most about her was this power of survival. How was she able time and again to maintain inner resistance in situations that were extremely difficult politically, and to continue the fight for emancipation and equal rights? Like Gilberto Gil, she was under arrest. For Thereza Santos, there is this need to keep reinventing herself and to keep transforming her own history through political and social activities. For me, this urgency to act, to interfere, to create is the spirit that makes up the whole history of the *Black Atlantic*. This power of rebirth on both sides of the ocean.

And finally, Othella Dallas, the artistic personality. She was a student of the legendary Katherine Dunham. That was extremely interesting for me. My personal connection came from Alvin Ailey, who discovered me in Brazil and took me into his dance center in New York. Othella Dallas had her own school, based on the Dunham technique, on Dunham's vision of translating original dances, cultural traces, and roots of the whole African-Caribbean-Brazilian heritage into a contemporary dance language. Katherine Dunham was an anthropologist, she gave lectures, and she developed a scientific approach to the tradition of African dance forms. She, like Alvin Ailey, built her own center and had her own company. This is the school Othella Dallas was in, along with Eartha Kitt and others. Othella Dallas made it her life's work to explore and share these

unique materials, and the images and thoughts that emerge from them, through her body. Her life itself is a kind of exercise of rediscovery, of memory.

To me, these three older women, with the stories of their bodies and lives, formed the core of the *Black Atlantic* idea. It is their everyday practice, but also their official positions and activities, that translate the memory of the *Black Atlantic* into the present. They carry within themselves the history of Black resistance. It is not only about what we remember, but more importantly, how we remember. The production works like a jigsaw puzzle, it does not follow a discernible logic. It does not tell one story, but many. It is not about the reappraisal of historical or logical facts, but about people, about their way of life, and how they have mastered resistance, memory, and existence with their lives.

ODENTHAL This brings us back to the subject of the body. How and what does the body remember? And how can a historical topic be brought to life on the level of a dance theater production? I believe that here lies a more crucial reason for the successful development of ever new Black art forms. Do performers and musicians keep reinventing themselves based on memories and traditions?

IVO I've always wondered why certain movements appeal to me more than others. There is something on the level of the body that is very difficult to discover. It works very much through intuition. And I want to say that memory is more than the facts that we can recall. With the help of intuition, we develop a connection with these memories. When you delve into memory with your body, you bring that level to life, it's connected to a current reality. You reinvent it. Maybe that's the center for artistic creation by Black people in music or in dance. It's a way of recreating the present. At the same time, tradition is not something static: it is in motion, like one's own life. This kind of body memory, of lively tradition—that's what I'm interested in. Not the coagulation of the past, but the development of new solutions for social, political, and existential questions—using one's own vision, one's own intuition. As it were, intuition is memory pointed toward the future. And so I try to understand the motivations, the memories of these three great women and translate them into my own body, into the bodies of the performers.

Body-memory is based on body-perception. Perception determines our understanding of reality. As Borges put it, reality depends on the eye of the beholder. Thus, our work on memory is ultimately and finally a project of perception about hearing an emotional statement in order to pick up that emotion and respond with the body in motion. What we dancers learn from the three narrators we absorb, each of us with our own intuitive body experience, and then respond to it. As soon as you react, you create a new life for these facts. So I am neither here nor there. I want to give a response from the performative body-memory, between both sides. That is the motivation for my choreographic work.

First published in:
Der Black Atlantic, Haus der Kulturen der Welt in cooperation with Tina Campt and Paul Gilroy, Berlin: Haus der Kulturen der Welt 2004, p. 319–323.

"Ismael was an artistic synthesis, a total work of art"
Visual artist Gottfried Helnwein in conversation with Johannes Odenthal

JOHANNES ODENTHAL Your first collaboration with Ismael Ivo was the unfinished project on Antonin Artaud, in collaboration with Heiner Müller and Hans Kresnik. Heiner Müller had already written a concept note in which he described the Christian subordination of the sexualized body in relation to Artaud's theatrical revolt.

GOTTFRIED HELNWEIN Unfortunately, the project remained a fragment. Heiner Müller, Hans Kresnik, Ismael Ivo, and I, we met at Schloss Burgbrohl in the Eifel region of Germany to plan and develop the project. A first concept emerged. We were all interested in the subject of pain, the Occidental violence against the body. Artaud's theater was our starting point, and we wanted to interrogate it for the present. That has also been a basic objective of my work. When we were about to leave for the rehearsals in Los Angeles, Hans discovered at Frankfurt airport that he didn't have a passport. We had to postpone the project and then never got together again.

For me, the meeting of Ismael and Hans was a tremendous stroke of luck. The physical expressiveness of Ismael on the one hand, and the choreographic talent of Hans on the other. Ismael was like a primal force in his physicality. Everything he did was physical. He immediately embodied and implemented every cue, every instruction from Hans. Ismael was a total work of art. The artistic relationship between the two was like a love affair. The intelligence of the body in Ismael, who was ready for anything, to the point of excess. And the relentlessness in Hans, who wanted to get close to the brute elemental force of the human condition. This combination was aesthetically very appealing to both of them.

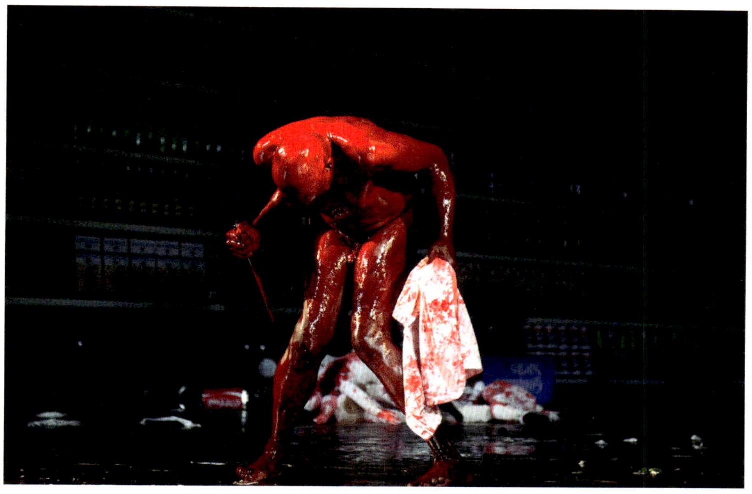

I

ODENTHAL Hans Kresnik thought up the scenes on stage as images. You can see this in his sketchbooks. Whereas Ismael Ivo acted out of images of the body. Both shared a political purpose. Hans Kresnik was the decisive political choreographer for German Tanztheater in the post-war period, who liberated dance from an aesthetic innocence, but who also always threw the dancers' bodies into "the fray".

HELNWEIN With his Marxist approach, Hans harbored a rage, a rebellion against every form of human oppression. But for him, it was clear that the struggle would continue on stage with aesthetic means. That's what drew me to him. What moved Hans was always related to the body. He used to say to me, use your images. And through Ismael, we discovered the power of physical expression. As a visual artist, I hadn't known that in this way. I was very grateful to be able to work with both of them, most recently in *The 120 Days of Sodom* after Pasolini at the Volksbühne in Berlin. We improvised a lot in the rehearsals. It was also a critical examination of the insanity of fascism. I inserted this Hitler quote, for example: "The Jew brings the Negro to the Rhine." This bullshit. Ismael wanted to use this sentence on stage. But his German wasn't good enough to carry it off. We dealt with the grotesque nature of right-wing violence, for example in *Pasolini—Das Testament des Körpers*.

Ever since the advent of expressionism, modernism has been interested in African art, in the preservation of this energy, which we associate with the elemental force of being human. For me, it's about the energies that are also inherent in the child as a potentially ideal condition: this unlimited power of imagination. In a way, growing up also implies violence toward this freedom. Ismael was like a child in the best sense, and so was Hans. It was liberating to be able to say whatever you want. And we were unscrupulous in what we said and did. The collective guilt, the sanctioning, the setting of boundaries—on stage, Ismael and Hans were able to free themselves from all that to a certain degree. They didn't censor themselves in what they were trying to do. This uncensored, this unrestrained element in the expression of the body and in the images of the stage, that's what connected us.

ODENTHAL In Vienna, Ismael Ivo found recognition like in no other city. Karl Regensburger says that Vienna had adopted Ismael artistically. There has been a close collaboration with Hans Kresnik and you in terms of content. Do you see an aesthetic line of tradition that connects all that?

HELNWEIN There is an Austrian cultural history that has prepared the ground for this. As early as the Baroque period, a flood of images emerged as a response to the Reformation. This spirit, these transgressions of the bodily sphere continue to have an effect in Egon Schiele, in Franz Xaver Messerschmidt, in Viennese Actionism. The expression of pain, performed on the body, has contributed to this Viennese ecosystem that connects us.

And in Vienna, above all, the audience has this passion for the protagonists of the stage, especially in the performing arts. Once you have won over the Viennese audience, you will be emotionally sustained by it.

II

III

The 120 Days of Sodom, 2015, Volksbühne am Rosa-Luxemburg-Platz, Berlin

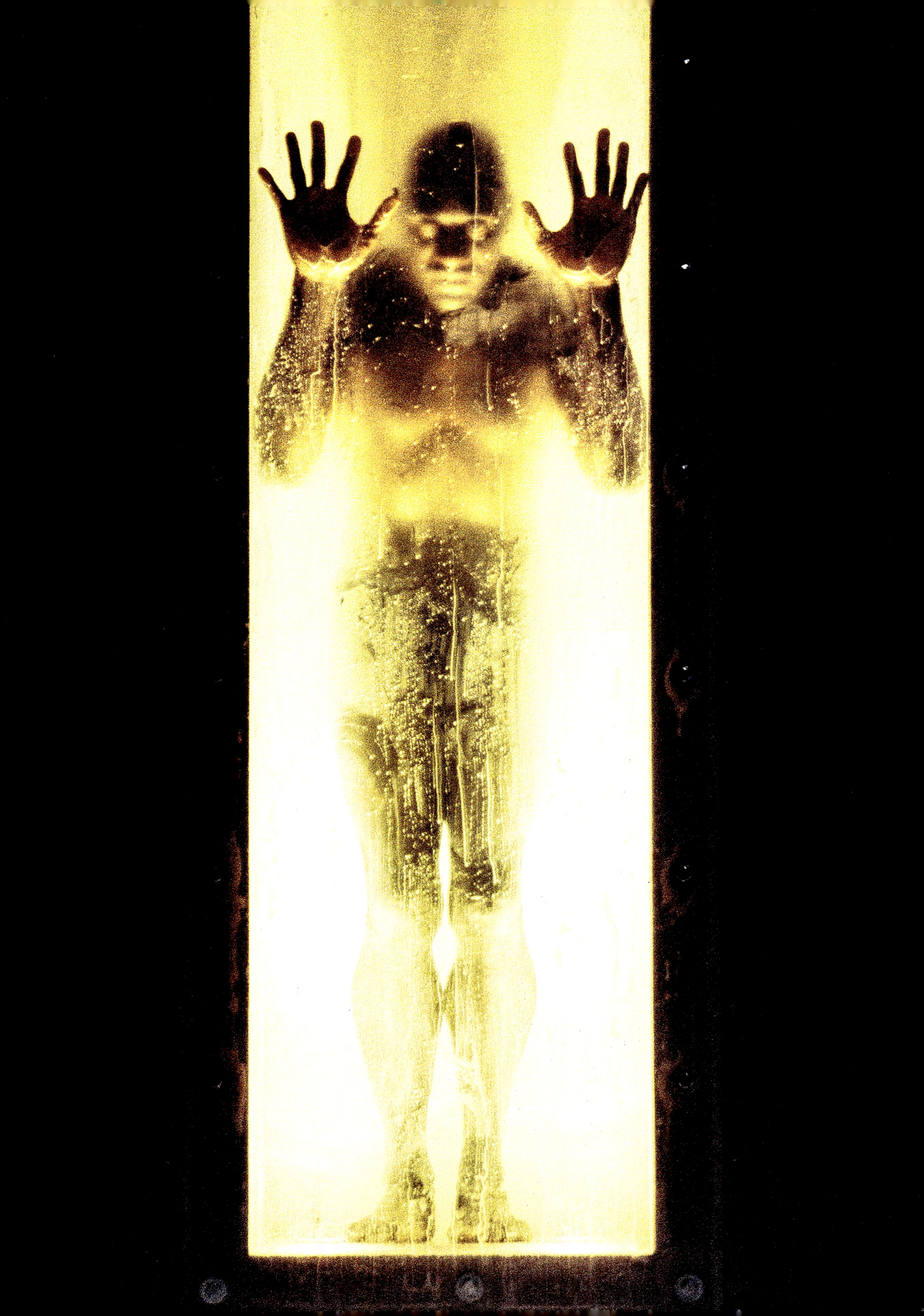

"A change in perception is the basis for a change in reality"
Ismael Ivo in conversation with Johannes Odenthal (2013)

ISMAEL IVO My roots, that's the New World. My heritage is based on a melting pot of Indigenous culture, colonialism, and African traditions that resulted from the slave trade. But as an Afro-Brazilian, I am no more or less Brazilian than the Indigenous people or the second, third, fourth, or fifth generation of Germans, Italians, or Portuguese living in Brazil; or the Japanese and Arabs who have made Brazil their home. And that's how I grew up. We all saw ourselves as Brazilians, no matter what our background was.

It was always about reinventing things, but also reinventing yourself because you were curious to discover alternative forms of expression. That's what has been my engine, my drive. Sometimes this has annoyed people because I have always tried to escape being labeled, even with the label of "Brazil". When critics have tried to categorize me in some—let's say—exotic or folkloric sense as "Brazilian", I simply did Shakespeare, or dealt with Francis Bacon, with ancient mythology, or the Apocalypse. I don't allow myself to be defined or cataloged within a fixed framework.

JOHANNES ODENTHAL Of course, from the perspective of numerous European critics, a *framing* took place, comparable to the photographs of Robert Mapplethorpe: the wonderful Black body as an object of desire. Let me compare this with the solos of Susanne Linke. They uphold the tradition of dance theater but don't focus on the body of a white woman. Although you see yourself in the tradition of German expressive dance and dance theater, you were never accepted into this tradition. As much as you pushed the body to its limits on stage, the Eurocentric gaze remained a challenge to your work.

IVO Maybe you're right. You talk about Robert Mapplethorpe as a metaphor for ambivalence. Desire as a dynamic between object and subject. But let's consider cultural intelligence: you can start from the culture you were born into in order to understand other cultures from there and use them for your own development process. That is exactly what I do with my work. I seek dialogue with the other, I don't try to copy it, but to develop something new, a third thing.

But let me come back to the point you make in relation to Mapplethorpe. Where do I stand as a Black male Brazilian who, by chance, meets the photographer Robert Mapplethorpe and is confronted with the contents of his particular provocative way of working? Mapplethorpe deliberately opened this field of stereotypes related to the Black body, sexuality, and racism. I tried to respond to it with the means I have as a performer. In the tradition of Frantz Fanon, Mapplethorpe emphasizes the relationship between the white and the Black body with all its connotations of sexuality and power and translates this colonial pattern into a contemporary artistic language. When I decided in 2002 to choreograph a solo piece around Mapplethorpe, I made my body the object of these ideas. Of course, I wondered why I was doing this to myself, especially since many would see the work yet again from the perspective of physical beauty. In a way, I was confronting my own *framing*. Right from the start, this work is very violent. I am sandwiched between two panes of glass that fall onto the stage with force. Later, I threaten the audience with a knife. I always remember this scene in particular, when I saw the fear in the eyes of the crowd: I felt like Oedipus in front of the Sphinx. Here you have the naked Black body. So how do you deal with it when I have a knife in my hand with which I could kill you? What sort of notion do you have in your head when you're confronted with the Black body on stage in an artistic context. These are questions that I consciously tried to trigger with my solo. When I met and worked with Robert Mapplethorpe in New York in the 1980s, it was also about my point of view as an Afro-Brazilian. That meant something completely different to being African American or positioning yourself as an African artist in Europe, like Isaac Julien, for example. But you always have to apply your cultural intelligence to put yourself in certain contexts, even to the extent of exposing yourself to cultural situations while having to provide the translation.

ODENTHAL In other words, in the U.S. you learned what made your Afro-Brazilian heritage so special, in comparison to the Afro-American culture. And this experience is further substantiated in Europe, in Germany, or Italy.

IVO Yes, the longer I live here, the more I feel Brazilian in my artistic drive. It's this distinctive way of dealing with the other culture, this curiosity, and creativity, of absorbing the other, digesting and advancing it in the reinvention of yourself. I clearly see this special quality when I look back at my work of the last twenty years, and it reminds me of my cultural DNA.

ODENTHAL And that's because Black culture in Brazil didn't have to assert itself against a majority culture as it did in the U.S. or the U.K., where a Protestant white dominant culture clearly defines a bogeyman. Despite open social discrimination, a Black Panther movement never emerged in Brazil.

IVO During the 1930s, Brazil saw the birth of the idea of a *democracia racial*, where differences of origin and skin color would have no social or political impact. Obviously, you have to look at that with great caution, because it became the cultural argument of a small white elite. But in Brazil, unlike in the U.S. of the 1960s, and of course very differently from Germany or Italy, you are immediately confronted with the diversity of cultures and ethnicities. Brazil is a melting pot, somehow blurred along the lines of one (single) cultural identity. As a Brazilian, I always had the feeling that I could discover the other, that I could cross any kind of border. More than anything else, this has driven my artistic search. I always compare myself to Macunaíma, the hero without a character in Mário de Andrade's 1928 novel of the same name. *Macunaíma* is the founding myth of modern Brazil. You are always searching for an identity, you operate with all kinds of tricks, and you experience the most diverse worlds, also on the level of your own body. To this day I ask myself, what is the utopia of a body. What does a body represent, and how do you reinvent yourself with your own body. With your body, you absorb the present and thus become a document of your time, which you experience and express artistically. In the process, the body itself becomes time. For me, the body is always this laboratory, and not only on the level of techniques but on a cultural level. I always try to address the bodies of others as well, all these other laboratories that are not static in their culture. I welcome the most diverse body concepts within me. As a Brazilian, I see myself in the tradition of cultural cannibalism, as established in Brazilian modernism by Oswald de Andrade in his *Manifesto Antropófago*. Starting from my Afro-Brazilian roots, I have absorbed and processed all the cultural and artistic currents of the present. In the eight years I was director of the dance section of the Venice Biennale I did the same. Like a thematic thread, the body runs through the festivals as a form of expression, as an archive of both memory and the present, as a political, social, emotional, or cultural platform for experience and transformation. On stage, I have always made my body available for these processes—as a gift, not as an answer to any questions, but as an offer of open exchange. In Brazil, cultural identity is always about reinvention. And it is not possible to focus your search on one single field of scientific inquiry. For example, the text on which I developed my first performance was a text by Federico García Lorca in Spanish, *El rey de Harlem,* in which he deals with the culture of Black people in Harlem. I not only recited this poem but also expressed it with my body. And it went on and on like that. I studied ballet with Alvin Ailey in New York, I took modern dance classes. When you've grown up in difficult economic conditions, you reach for everything you can achieve. But you do have to be able to integrate it into your own path. In Europe, for example, I produced *Othello* with Hans Kresnik, which is to say Shakespeare, German dance theater, and a Brazilian dancer interpreting *Othello* as a Black man. The piece begins with an Afro-Brazilian ritual. I was aware that this is literary history, this is the tradition of German dance theater. But for me, *Othello* doesn't just exist at the court in Venice, he must have roots. I start the piece in the audience, I conquer their space, before I arrive at Shakespeare. I had to define and incorporate the source of my existence and my interpretation in the Shakespeare context. When I had the great fortune to work with Heiner Müller, he wrote this text for me called *Fremder im eigenen Körper* ("Foreign in One's Own Body: Emigrations"). With every project I start, I have to redefine, rediscover, and reinterpret my body anew, as if I were forever starting from scratch.

ODENTHAL And yet I see you in the tradition of modernism, as indicated by the names of the artists with whom you have collaborated or whose work you explored. Antonin Artaud, Heiner Müller, Hans Kresnik, Francis Bacon, Robert Mapplethorpe, Sankai Juku, and numerous others stand for this line of tradition of a contemporary radical concept of theater and art. That's why I find it very interesting that you talk about your Brazilian method of cultural appropriation here in Europe, about your roots.

IVO Yes, it seems strange. When I was awarded Brazil's highest cultural medal by President Lula, it surprised me because I had left Brazil for Europe via New York to pursue my career there. But I think it's important to understand my Brazilian cultural experiences as a method. From my experience, you don't spend a lot of time asking questions, you start in a very concrete way to unlock spaces for yourself and to reinvent your own life all the time. My spaces—I'm talking about geographical and mental territories—don't exist *a priori*, I've always had to fight for them. That's how I unlocked my space in Alvin Ailey's company, in Sankai Juku's company, or through Hans Kresnik in German dance theater. I know of few Brazilians who have taken such a path. That's why I'm hard to pin down into categories of styles or schools. I always manage to escape from any identity, even from that as a Brazilian.

As for my preoccupation with extreme artist personalities such as Bacon, Mishima, Borges, Artaud, or Pasolini, this is again related to my preoccupation with the body. I'm always looking for the radical side of art as a way to affirm my presence, my being there. Of course, my Afro-Brazilian origins also play a role here, the issue of race, of dealing with prejudice. As a Black dancer, I may have connected with these radical positions in my search for an answer to my questions about discrimination.

ODENTHAL The works of the artists you mention are always about boundaries, boundaries of experience, boundaries of identity, boundaries of perception of reality. They are positions of an avant-garde that always questioned the existing orders.

IVO I see myself as someone who wants to survive. I am a survivor. I am a survivor from a non-privileged family. Many of my school friends have ended up in oblivion. They are in jail or already dead. I found this narrow path out of a difficult and hopeless situation. And I have often processed these experiences in my dance pieces, for example the experience of existential hunger in our neighborhood in *Delirium of a Childhood*. By placing myself within an international canon of works, I had to constantly reassert myself, in a field where I was not welcome. What attracted me to the works of Lorca or Müller was their revolutionary power. Nijinsky or Artaud were also revolutionaries.

ODENTHAL This revolutionary approach permeates your work. For you, dance has a transformative meaning for the self-determination of the individual in society. Parallel to the festivals in Vienna and Venice, you also invested in the training of dancers.

IVO Ever since I was a child, I had this dream of changing the world. And as a Black man, I always had the idea of changing people's perceptions. Changing perceptions is the basis for changing reality.

About thirty years ago, I introduced the concept of coaching for dancers and developed it into a continuing education program in Vienna during ImPulsTanz. For me, this means progressive continuing education for aspiring dancers. I believe that with our tools as artists—in my case, with dance—we can also influence social and political conditions. Art and culture are engines of development. There are amazing projects here, especially in Brazil, like the one by Lia Rodrigues in a favela in Rio de Janeiro, for example.

Together with the SESC São Paulo Cultural Center and the Secretariat for Culture, we are now rolling out the European coaching project to Brazil. We are jointly awarding ten scholarships to Brazilian dancers, and later thirty dancers will be invited to São Paulo. We have the chance to develop a new Brazilian, Latin American platform.

ODENTHAL One of the main theses about the *Black Atlantic*, the *Middle Passage*, the deportation of four million Africans to the two Americas, is that the cultural resistance of Black people has always given rise to new countercultures like jazz, reggae, or rap. Does the samba have a comparable significance in Brazil?

IVO I see a certain danger there. From the beginning, I tried to become the author of my own body, to develop my own vocabulary. With the samba, that wasn't really possible. It was always important to me to avoid this territory. From today's point of view, I would also call myself a post-exotic artist. Too many dancers have carried the flag of happiness in front of them and channeled all the energy into that one week of Carnival. All year long you live in very limited, if not to say miserable, conditions. And then you feast on five days of dancing a fantasy king. And it was precisely this fake, this inversion of social reality, that I wanted to avoid. It was clear to me that this could not be a path for me. But it was also about a commercialization of the image of Brazilian dance.

ODENTHAL I would like to conclude by talking about Brazilian modernism. After the concept of Antropofagia, it was Neoconcretismo in the 1960s and Tropicalismo in the 1970s that led Brazil toward its own modernity. Did these movements have any relevance for you? Or were they art movements of a white modernism that did not correspond with the concerns of Afro-Brazilians?

IVO That's true to some extent. I could always relate more to the 1920s because back then it was about very existential questions. From my perspective, the 1960s and 1970s were primarily about aesthetic issues. Tropicalismo as a reaction to the dictatorship had no meaning for me at that time, because back then I was directly invested in the issue of racism. And in those days, that was no laughing matter. I worked together with activists and artists like the director Thereza Santos. I was in Salvador de Bahia many times, connected with the Black Young Writers Movement, and we established a lecture series on Black culture in Brazil. That was tremendously important for me because it was only through that exposure that I realized how involved I was in that history. Although Gilberto Gil or Caetano Veloso were critical artists who went into exile, they didn't really organize a political resistance. I, however, was part of a group of young artists who understood their African American history as a political movement. But we also knew that under this mantle of *democracia racial*, everyday racism was not on the table, it was not being negotiated. This movement of the Black community in Brazil gives me strength to this day and remains a motivating force for me.

First publication: Positionen 6: *Zeitgenössische Künstler aus Brasilien* (Contemporary artists from Brazil). Ed. Alfons Hug, Göttingen: Steidl 2013.

I

II

I As Galinhas (The chickens), 1980, Teatro de Dança Galpão, São Paulo, with Takao Kusuno, Renée Gumiel, Ismael Ivo, Dorothy Lenner, Felicia Ogawa, photographer: Roberto Okumura

II As Galinhas (The chickens, restaging), 2006, Haus der Kulturen der Welt, Berlin, with Ismael Ivo, Renée Gumiel, Dorothy Lenner

Life as a dance and the world as a play

Dance scholar and movement researcher Cássia Navas in conversation with Petra Schaeber

PETRA SCHAEBER You are one of the most important scholars of the Brazilian dance scene. What was your first meeting with Ismael Ivo like?

CÁSSIA NAVAS I remember seeing Ismael on the Rua 13 de Maio. At that time, there were some well-known private dance schools and theaters on that street, as well as restaurants and bars. The street is in a very busy neighborhood called Bixiga, a place of Italian restaurants, but also of jazz, samba, African roots.

Ismael was associated with Espaço Infinito, a theater with an art and photography gallery owned by a woman named Sulamita. It was a building with large windows. Ismael was performing a solo in one of the upper windows, against the light. From the street, at first, we could only make out his silhouette. Then he came down, beat a drum, and began to dance on the steep street. This was already the *Rito do Corpo em Lua*, the *Ritual of a Body in Moon*, which he would later perform at a theater in São Paulo. It was very impressive: a large group of people followed him up the street—and yet we could still see him. He had the wingspan of an eagle; Ismael was a Black Eagle.

SCHAEBER Can you describe what the dance scene was like in Brazil?

NAVAS Ismael started here in São Paulo, a place where there was what we called independent dance. Unlike Rio de Janeiro, São Paulo didn't have a strong classical ballet tradition. In the late 1970s and early 1980s, the independent dance scene in the city was very vibrant. There were some established dance groups and teachers, including Ruth Rachau and the French dancer Renée Gumiel, whom I call the "mothers of modernism." Under the direction of Klauss Vianna, the Balé da Cidade de São Paulo was already in a phase of modernization.

There was a culture of experimentation. Despite the dictatorship, there was room for a counterculture. One of these places was the Teatro Galpão de Dança, which specialized in dance and provided all kinds of classes. Ismael's career began at Teatro Galpão de Dança, where he met Mara Borba and had classes with Ruth Rachau.

SCHAEBER What was special about Ismael Ivo as a dancer at the beginning of his career in Brazil?

NAVAS I think he was already a solo dancer then—he stuck to that throughout his career outside of Brazil. Ismael was an exceptional soloist because he was so present and strong on stage. It showed not only on stage, but also outside, in class, on the street, in cafes, and in restaurants. There was a power that emanated from him, a kind of "dance before the dance." In addition, there was the courage and the will to succeed that distinguished him. Ismael conquered worlds that would have been unthinkable for many dance soloists.

He was so striking that he was invited by the then director of the Municipal Ballet, Klauss Vianna, one of our great masters, to join the experimental group of the Balé da Cidade de São Paulo. Klauss had expanded the existing ensemble with a group called Experimental, composed of soloists from São Paulo's independent dance scene. This experimental group was causing quite a stir in the ballet scene.

So what did this mean for the beginning of his career? Because Ismael performed at Balé as a soloist, he was often invited along with people who came from other important schools, such as what is now EDASP—Escola de Dança de São Paulo, a municipal dance school. Ismael was the only Black member in this group, which shaped the dance scene of São Paulo. Experimental dance, that meant a difference for everyone, but even more so for a Black, homosexual, young man from the periphery.

In São Paulo, Ismael also met Takao Kusuno, a Japanese artist who belonged to the second generation of Butoh in Japan. To this day, we are the city with the largest Japanese population outside of Japan, and we have a very active Japanese Cultural Foundation.

SCHAEBER Did you ever talk to Ismael Ivo about the origin of his dance, his inspiration?

NAVAS Ismael has always been very curious and open to sharing. In an interview, I once asked him when was the first time in his life he had a memory of a movement. He thought for a moment and said, "My mother used to do a lot of laundry, mostly outdoors. For that, she had some washing bowls in our garden. I was small. I would lie down in a bowl, spin around, and watch the world turn in circles." This is what Ismael told me during a seminar at the Oficina Cultural Oswald de Andrade. So there was something, a physical training that was closely linked to movement in childhood. A love, an openness, the perception of a world in motion. A small child who fits into a bowl, spins around and sees how the trees turn. Life as a dance and the world as a spectacle.

Ismael came to the arts because he initially wanted to be in theater after seeing plays and telenovelas on TV Cultura, the state television network. Ismael recounted, "Although Sergio Cardoso, who played Uncle Tom, only wore black makeup in *Uncle Tom's Cabin*, there were also some well-known Black actors like Otelo." With that, he had a hypothesis about himself: that he would be an artist because he could be an artist.

In addition, there was his great talent—in terms of the body and its potential, but also his perseverance, his willingness to take risks, stubbornness, and curiosity. Qualities that he retained until the end of his life.

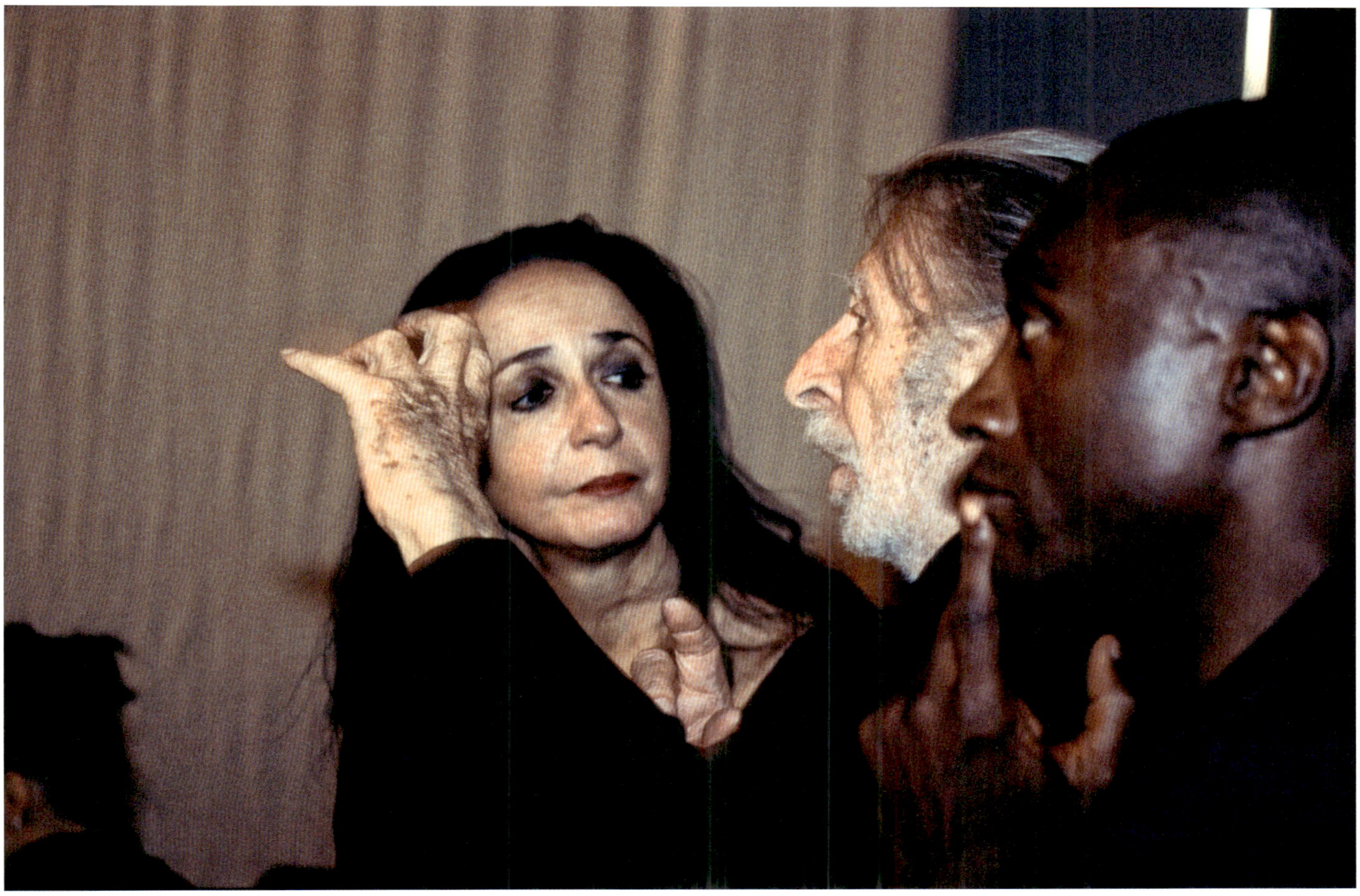

Ismael chose dance as a form of expression, but he crossed the continent of performing arts, of opera, of theater. Even before he left Brazil, his work was not about dance detached from any context, but about a need to produce and interpret knowledge through the body. This was one of his characteristic features. Ismael told stories. He is one of the inventors of our dance theater. He created his own style of acting, a scenic performance that is very much connected to his physicality. But he wanted more than that, so he used theatrical texts, or sometimes other texts in a verbal matrix within the pieces. That caught the attention of theater directors, actors, filmmakers.

SCHAEBER Can you tell us something about whether and how Ismael's work abroad was followed in Brazil?

NAVAS When Ismael returned to Brazil with his work, he was very well received, not only in the dance scene but also by film and theater people who recognized that he was something special.

At some point, Ismael started spending more time in Brazil again. First, there was the *Biblioteca do Corpo* project, which had started in Venice at the Arsenale and was implemented at the SESC São Paulo and with the Secretary of State for Culture and Creative Industries in São Paulo. Since 2011, I participated in the selection of Brazilian dancers for the project, which was then still called the *Arsenale de la Danza*. It was known that Ismael was head of the Venice Biennale. He invited me there for a workshop for the dancers of the program.

As curator of the Plataforma Internacional Estado da Dança, organized in 2012 by Teatro Sergio Cardoso and the Secretary of State for Culture, I had invited Ismael to bring *Francis Bacon* to São Paulo. It was a large-scale undertaking, with an audio description for the Deaf and a program printed in braille. The performances were sold out every night—just like other plays at SESC Pompéia, Teatro Sérgio Cardoso or SESC Santos.

We had already heard about ImPulsTanz in Vienna, but we were not aware of its dimensions. It was when Ismael invited me in 2013 that I got to know the festival, and became aware of its size and dimension.

His work abroad became more noticed the more he invited people from Brazil to collaborate with him, for example, the theater director Márcio Aurélio, Umberto da Silva, the dancers and choreographers Iracity Cardoso, Ana Mondini, and Mara Borba.

On the other hand, groups were always organizing themselves to travel to Europe, for example, the ballet of Teatro Castro Alves, which performed at the Venice Biennale. Also, Ismael was invited to Salvador to perform a piece by the director Jorge Vermelho.

SCHAEBER You accompanied Ismael Ivo on the *Qualificação em Dança* projects, which will be held for the eighth time in 2022. What did you experience there?

NAVAS In 2014, Ismael was invited by Aldo Valentim, the Secretary of Culture of the State of São Paulo, to become curator of the Qualificação em Dança program. The goal was to help dance groups and collectives in the interior of the state to qualify. Since Ismael had been living in Germany for thirty years, I was asked to act as an advisor. This program was meant to create opportunities for talent, for people with talent. Artists are everywhere, but sometimes they don't have the opportunity to develop.

We were in many places, Presidente Prudente, Assis, Campinas, Indaiatuba, Piracicaba, Santos and several times in Caraguatatuba. Sometimes we went by car. He always had to sit in the front because he was so tall, and I squeezed into the back. The most interesting thing was that we were in places where there was almost no cultural infrastructure. We would talk to the people in charge there—and it was a shock. There were people who had no idea who we were. So we had to say: look, I work on dance at the Universidade Estadual de Campinas—UNICAMP. And this is Ismael, he's great. He worked in Vienna, with Pina Bausch, and he danced with Márcia Haydée. I'm a dance scholar and I'm accompanying him because, like Ismael, I'm from São Paulo. He hasn't lived here for a long time, but it's his home. He often repeated the phrase "We travel across the country with a bag of fertilizer and a bag of seeds." That was his way of talking, of spotting and nurturing talent.

Ismael had faith in dance. He believed in what he was doing. I was with him in several situations where a superstar, which is what he was regarded as, would not go to work like that. He would have thousands of assistants. But Ismael just rolled up his pants and went to the young people, and danced with them. That was a great quality.

Often we would pick up Ismael at the airport and head straight off. He was always very tired then and often slept in the car. One day we almost had a serious accident on a road from São Paulo to Assis, when a storm came up. The cars were sliding on the road because of all the water, but the driver was very skillful. When we arrived in Assis, the whole city was dark. There were no lights at the hotel, so we filled out the hotel form using our cell phones. We looked for a restaurant for dinner, but everything was closed. Finally, we found a place by a fishery that was open because it had a generator. The place was full of fans watching TV because there was a soccer match in Brazil, an international championship. We couldn't talk because there was so much cheering. It was all very funny because at that moment someone was sent to formally welcome us, people from City Hall. The only thing missing was for them to raise the flag and sing the national anthem.

Ismael was a great traveling companion. He was a celebrity, we knew that. He brought a perspective of respect and discipline to working with these groups, and a belief in the future. I said, "Ismael, this library of the body, this qualification in dance, you would have liked to have had it when you were young, right?" And he answered, "I created the *Biblioteca do Corpo* because I would have liked to have had it".

SCHAEBER You have studied dance from a theoretical point of view. Ismael Ivo has performed on stage. What was your relationship with him like?

NAVAS In the beginning, we talked a lot. Ismael was a person of great intelligence and a good observer, not only of the world but also of people and what they said.

Talking to him was like watching a dance or thinking about art. I look at rehearsals and performances as if they were books, sometimes small articles, sometimes encyclopedias. But it's something else to sit down and see the dance out of itself and in all its contexts. All this is the result of a long career in dance.

Ismael had great respect for what people thought, for theoretical knowledge. This is also part of his peculiarity as a dancer, as an artist. We worked very closely together. Ismael was still living in Berlin. Sometimes he couldn't travel from Germany because he was busy with his commitments. So I visited the groups and gave him reports.

SCHAEBER How do you assess Ismael Ivo's importance for dance in Brazil?

NAVAS When Ismael became director of the Balé da Cidade de São Paulo in January 2017, it was a milestone. Never before had a Black person been in charge of the country's most important ballet company. Without wanting to diminish their value you can say that he was different from the previous directors. People from other populations and the Black movement began to pay more attention to the Balé da Cidade.

Ismael may also have been the director with the most substantial international career.

When Ismael returned to Brazil, he was already famous. I remember friends of mine talking about seeing his photo on posters on the London Underground and at Vienna airport.

I

With this, he gave the Balé da Cidade de São Paulo a very high place in the institutional landscape. At a theater like the Theatro Municipal, there is opera, drama, music, and sometimes even different musical groups. He fought hard for dance in the theater, he fought for funding, for visibility, for an agenda, for a place in the sun. He spoke on equal terms with the artistic directors of the institution. Ismael wanted to give dance a prominent place within the structures. And yet, by decision of the institution, he departed before the end of his term. It was not he who had asked to leave.

SCHAEBER Ismael Ivo knew how to recognize and train talent, talent in the plural. How was the contact with the dancers? What was your impression?

NAVAS The dancers had chosen him from a list of three names. In the beginning, they were very enthusiastic, but mistakes and misunderstandings crept in. Ismael was strongly questioned because he was "almost like a foreigner." He didn't know the hierarchical codes and sometimes one had to translate what he was saying. There were communication gaps. Dancers are difficult to direct but good at execution. The hierarchical system here is different from that in Germany. He was appointed to head the city ballet at the invitation of André Sturm, then Minister of Culture, a filmmaker who supported and respected him. That's part of the political, republican game.

SCHAEBER What would you highlight about Ismael Ivo's work as director of the Balé da Cidade?

NAVAS Ismael managed to move the ballet company from a temporary building to the cultural complex behind the Theatro Municipal. For years, the ballet was housed in rented premises on Rua João Passalaqua, originally a chandelier factory. Today it is located at Praça das Artes, a fantastic complex located on Avenida São João. It includes the historic building of the first public conservatory, founded by Mário de Andrade, one of the leaders of the *Semana de Arte Moderna* of 1922 The new building was built around the historic complex, but it is not fully occupied to this day.

When Ismael wanted to move the ballet company to Praça das Artes, the building was practically still under construction. He went to the city's mayor, with whom he had a good rapport. Finally, the minister in charge was instructed to fit out one or two floors for the ballet.

II

III

IV

A second significant change was that all dancers were employed under the labor law. Before, they had temporary contracts, and Ismael finally managed to change this situation. That was the first thing he did. So these are very important political and ethical milestones.

And there was one more thing that was very different: Even as a director, Ismael was in the spotlight. He took the microphone, went on stage, and addressed the audience. That may be common in some places in Europe, but here it caused some consternation. The director of the São Paulo Municipal Ballet on stage before the curtain opened—I had never experienced anything like it.

Ismael opened the Theatro Municipal to a whole different set of people. He invited people from transsexual groups, as well as women from the favelas, and encouraged young talent. This had been tried before, but only Ismael had the charisma to bring these plans to fruition. He reached out to people and he was combative.

Ismael's origins became more important. When he became director of the Municipal Ballet, the mayor at the time, João Dória, not only quickly recognized the qualities Ismael had but sensed the opportunities an artist like him could provide for the government.

Representing Black identity came to the fore in his new role as director of the Balé da Cidade de São Paulo—unlike in 2011, when he arrived in Brazil with the *Biblioteca do Corpo*. Was he now in a position where he was expected to speak about this issue in a certain way? For sure, yes. It was a place where this issue came to the fore. He did this through numerous actions, including the celebration of the 50th anniversary of the ballet company, a date that was honored by the publication of the book *Balé da Cidade de São Paulo, 50 anos*, published by the Fundação Theatro Municipal de São Paulo—a coffee-table volume with beautiful photographs, but also a brochure with my text in a Portuguese-English edition.

During the 2018 election campaign, Ismael often wore pink suits—his way of protest. At the time, the current Minister for Women, Family, and Human Rights had said in a speech that girls should wear pink and boys should wear blue. So there was something very symbolic about the pink suits.

SCHAEBER At the time of the *Biblioteca do Corpo*, was the question of identity not yet so present?

NAVAS Even though Ismael took up very sensitive subjects, it was not a priority. First, there was *Babilônia—il terzo paradiso* in 2011, which deals with environmental issues. In *Biblioteca do Corpo* he explored the question of the body, the imprinting of the social body, the political body. Then he made *Sacre du Printemps*, which was about sexuality, about life, and death. Then *Erendira*, an almost theatrical piece on innocence and cruelty. Finally, *Das Tripas ... Coração*, which addressed the organ trade. These are all strong themes, very topical. The talk was about the man and the woman, and not necessarily about the cause or the Black person.

I think that once Ismael arrived in Brazil, to head the ballet of the city of São Paulo, he was overwhelmed by different discourses, including a political discourse. A political discourse beyond classical aesthetic discourses. He even joined a political party, which many thought was a bold move. I believe that by approaching the issue of Black identity, he was taking a stance. Joining the party was another stance. I'm sure his desire to belong played a role in that. It was not so much a party-political option, but rather a matter of fitting into the state structures, into a context that he must have considered important. In Brazil, he tried to create socio-political contexts, for example, with his desire to create a dance school or to continue with the *Biblioteca do Corpo* and invent the future.

Ismael always had a political mindset, but it was a political mindset in art, a hypothesis, almost a blind belief in the potential of Brazilian dance.

Ismael died during the pandemic, it came as a shock. No one expects a Black Eagle to say goodbye like that. How would he be today, in this world that is gradually opening up to dance and its connections? We don't know, but he definitely wouldn't lack generosity and courage to face the new challenges. I could not say goodbye to Ismael, I could only send him white flowers and a Thank you: Thank you for so much art!

We will go on talking about Ismael for a long time. Many voices need to be heard, especially in the structures that are not as immediate as the elaboration of choreography or the creation of a piece. Such processes take a long time, sometimes a whole generation.

Teachers are beacons. Artists like Ismael have touched us through their works, words, and attitudes. He remains here with us in our memory to proclaim his legacy, to share it with us, with the artists, the public, the partners of art, and a professionalism filled with panache and pride. Evoé, Ismael.

I, III, IV Ismeal Ivo at the Escola de Artes Visuais do Parque Lage, Rio de Janeiro, 1987, photographer: Ricardo Tupper
II Ismeal Ivo at the Escola de Artes Visuais do Parque Lage, Rio de Janeiro, 1987

"How can space inspire movement and movement inspire space?"
Marcel Kaskeline in conversation with Johannes Odenthal

JOHANNES ODENTHAL You have developed 35 full-length pieces together with Ismael. From *Tristan und Isolde*, which premiered in October 1999, to the major productions at the Theatro Municipal in São Paulo, you were a crucial artistic partner. At the same time, you took on the duties of a personal assistant and Ismael Ivo's management. How would you describe working with Ismael? What were the creative processes like?

MARCEL KASKELINE Preparation for the pieces we did together was very intensive; we both undertook wide-ranging research on the themes. But when it came to the actual implementation, the work was very much associative in nature. We always tried to relate all the ideas back to the main theme. The projects came about in an exchange, in the space between us, so to speak. As a team, we developed a common horizon for the productions.

I

Ismael and I met in the realm of spatial imagination. He recognized a potential in me that I had not been aware of myself before. And with *Tristan und Isolde*, it became very concrete: I designed my first stage space, inspired by Mark Rothko's paintings. Since this piece was so successful, we wanted to continue working with the same team. Márcio Aurélio as director, Helge-Björn Meyer as dramaturg, Gabriele Frauendorf as costume designer, and me for the stage. So I was set for the two subsequent productions, *Aura—Homage to Miles Davis and Alvin Ailey* and *Floresta do Amazonas*, which premiered in Rio de Janeiro and Vienna respectively in the year 2000. And then I had to make a decision. I quit my job and devoted myself entirely to artistic work with Ismael.

ODENTHAL In 2002, *Mapplethorpe* was probably Ismael's last major solo work. You had a crucial part in the production with the impressive spaces you created. Could you use this example to describe how performative ideas and stage design came together?

II

KASKELINE We started with the encounter between Ismael Ivo and Robert Mapplethorpe in 1983 in New York. In a second step, we explored Mapplethorpe's photographic work. Mapplethorpe had his own way of combining social themes with his personal desires and passions. In doing so, he always forced taboos into the open, he never avoided them, even in relation to himself. He was part of his own criticism. The *Black Book* was not just about the Black body; it was about the male body at a time when people were used to only depicting the naked female body in photography. Mapplethorpe depicted the male body as an object, sexualized in a way that had not been done before in the public sphere.

For Ismael, it was important to understand that the issue of racism in the U.S. is different from that in Brazil. We discussed the fact that in North America it is mainly Black men who are in prison and that the death penalty is almost exclusively carried out for Black people. Our collaboration consisted of an intense exchange about these issues and finding images for them. Ismael had the idea to start with an image of the electric chair. We then found a more abstract format to represent societal constriction. Ismael's body was enclosed in an opening in a monumental metal wall, wedged between two panes of glass, the Black male body pressed together, an image of being confined as if between two huge microscope slides, placed vertically on the stage. And then this enormous wall tips forward in free fall, Ismael's body is thrust into the social sphere. On the back of the toppled wall, now lying flat, a field of lilies opens up, again referring to Mapplethorpe's photographs. In the following image, Ismael dances with a mirror. Inner and outer perception alternate or interfuse. This also informs the interaction with the audience, when Ismael turns the knife against them. In addition, the names of the prisoners who were on death row at that moment are projected. I sketched a dozen sets before we arrived at these motifs.

ODENTHAL Could Ismael's choreographic approach be described as a sequence of movement images? Or is it not the dance elements that lead from one scene to the next, but rather images, objects, and scenic spaces?

KASKELINE Ismael referred to *Mapplethorpe* as a dance installation because there was this close interplay between performative and spatial situations. The early solos didn't have a stage set in that sense, only set pieces, like a net or a ladder. Ismael also immersed himself in photographic motifs by Mapplethorpe. The image with the knife, the naked body on the pedestal, or the calla.

ODENTHAL Did you have to work against Ismael's exuberant energy and dominance on stage? How did the set and the choreography come together?

III

KASKELINE No, I didn't work against Ismael. As choreographer, he always had the final say. But the choreographies required a defined space. It was a constructive merging of different creative methods. I worked mainly with models which Ismael also used in the rehearsal room. He created his choreographic images within them. Inside the models, he was able to imagine the choreographies.

Ismael always talked a lot about using objects. He did the same when he was teaching, by the way. And stage design, that's also an object that the dancers can deal with. I designed the spaces in such a way that the dancers' movements always played a decisive role. How can spaces inspire movement and movement inspire spaces?

ODENTHAL That's a very important point. Ismael has practiced this close contact with objects on stage like an extension of the body even in his earliest productions. That was bound to shape your collaboration. To invent objects or spaces that challenge dance and movement and vice versa.

KASKELINE We were both deeply fascinated by magical realism. The possibility that objects can transform, the back-and-forth between different forms of matter. That played a big role for *Biblioteca del Corpo* at the Venice Biennale in 2012, for example. The dancers are stuck in cabinet boxes, but they can break free from them by pushing out the glass doors. The dance materializes on the shards of transformation.

The starting point was a literary model, *The Library of Babel* by Jorge Luis Borges. On the one hand, the body is a library of its time. On the other hand, there is the library of bodies. The piece also has this societal level. There is the wall, the social framework from which the individual breaks free in order to find an individual language. At the same time, every individual is a library.

ODENTHAL You produced *Biblioteca del Corpo* in Venice in 2012 and restaged it at the Theatro Municipal in São Paulo in 2019. It was, after all, more than a piece, it was like a program for Ismael's life's work.

IV

KASKELINE It's a key position, for sure. These two sides of the body, the individual and social responsibility. After the piece came out, the training program that had been established by Ismael between SESC São Paulo, ImPulsTanz Vienna, and La Biennale di Venezia was also renamed. In the beginning it was called *Arsenale della Danza*, later *Biblioteca do Corpo*.

ODENTHAL Ismael's outstanding quality was his stage presence, his performance. You mentioned the term dance installation for *Mapplethorpe*. I would like to come back to that because it formulates the connection to the visual arts. How did he manage to transmit this individual quality to a dance company? After all, you had to convey his movement images to a group of up to forty dancers.

KASKELINE I first saw Ismael on stage in *Othello*. In that production, the process of finding images and movements with the dancers was central. That wasn't always the case in the later productions which were sometimes considerably larger. If there were only a few weeks for the rehearsal phase, he had to be more prescriptive. Quite simply because he didn't have the right conditions for a different kind of production. Ismael motivated and encouraged the dancers to develop their own movement material. But at the same time, he brought a lot to the choreographic structure, he always thought from his own body. So he was always able to dance everything for the dancers. Even with forty dancers, he was aware of every single one. That's why he needed several assistants because he came to the rehearsals with unbelievably differentiated material of movement and literally poured it out. The assistants had the task of systematically developing this material with the dancers.

ODENTHAL With *Mapplethorpe*, you can go so far as to say that the objects that are on stage cannot be separated from the choreography or the performance. Is that still the case with *Biblioteca del Corpo*?

V

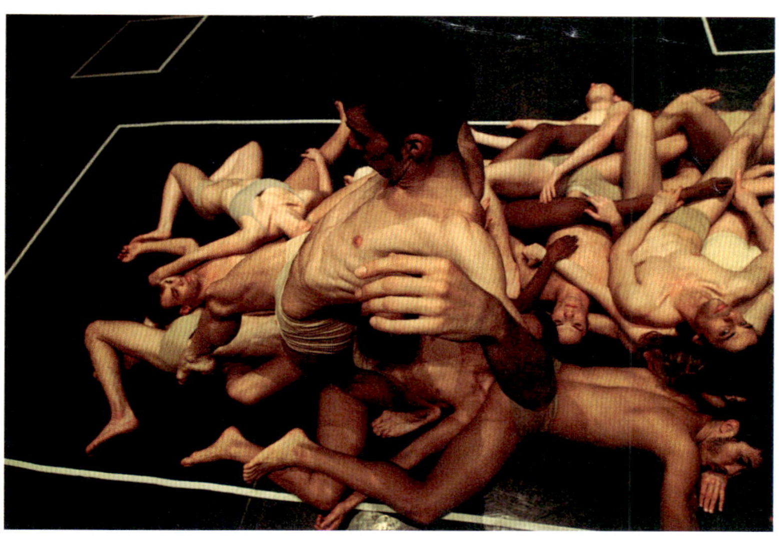

VI

KASKELINE Absolutely. I'll give you another example. *Le Sacre du Printemps* started from a very different kind of space design. I'm talking about the one at Napoli Teatro Festival Italia 2010. For Ismael, *Sacre* was about the destruction of nature. The societal processes surrounding this issue could only be expressed through a dialogue between space and dance. The choreography begins on an empty stage. When Stravinsky's music begins, a shower of rose petals commences, which lasts for the full forty minutes. What begins poetically ends in a torrential catastrophe. By the end, the dancers are stomping through the inch-high layer of petals, reducing their range of motion more and more. There was no longer the one solitary victim, but there were no more seasons of the year either. The audience understood this image of destruction in exactly the same way. The stage is the content layer, the horizon on which the dance develops. Ismael later took over this production for his company in São Paulo.

ODENTHAL For many stage pieces, you did extensive research on very political, socially critical themes. I would like to mention examples such as the organ trade, prostitution, and, time and again, discrimination, of course.

KASKELINE There were also very personal themes that Ismael dealt with, such as the near-death experience after his car accident in 1988 in *Illuminata*. The stage is shaped by a rain of black sand in which the dancers leave their traces, which are then blurred and rewritten.

In *Mercato del Corpo*, Ismael projected the subject of prostitution onto the art scene. The production took place in a Venetian palazzo. The dancers had their own rooms there. In the large hall, they were introduced by a well-known Italian television presenter and then auctioned off. Those who had bid the most could go with the dancer to the respective room, where they were given a private performance. Those who did not get anything at the auction also became part of the performance because what might be going on in the rooms was playing out in their minds. It was about the representation of this web of power and art. How can the artist assert their own space? And what do they have to sell? Societal conditions have always played a big role in dance. *Erendira* is about the societal conditions for prostitution, a worldwide issue. The starting point here was a story by Gabriel García Márquez. We dealt with the issue of women being forced into prostitution by their families. This fatal combination of social coercion and ostracism, which we observed in India, for example.

Social injustice, exploitation, and oppression, these are the themes that have occupied Ismael again and again.

VII

VIII

I, III	*The Waste Land*, 2009, Teatro alle Tese, La Biennale di Venezia, with dancers of Arsenale della Danza, photographer: Alvise Nicoletti
II	Ismael Ivo and Marcel Kaskeline, Berlin, 2011
IV	*Erendira*, 2005, Teatro alle Tese, La Biennale di Venezia, photographer: Gabriele Frauendorf
V	Rehearsal for *The Waste Land*, 2009, Teatro alle Tese, La Biennale di Venezia, with dancers of Arsenale della Danza, photographer: Alvise Nicoletti
VI	*Mapplethorpe*, 2002, Teatro Piccolo Arsenale, La Biennale di Venezia, photographer: Guto Muniz
VII	*Aura*, 2000, Theatro Municipal, Rio de Janeiro, photographer: Gabriele Frauendorf
VIII	*Illuminata*, 2006, Teatro alle Tese, La Biennale di Venezia, photographer: Marcel Kaskeline

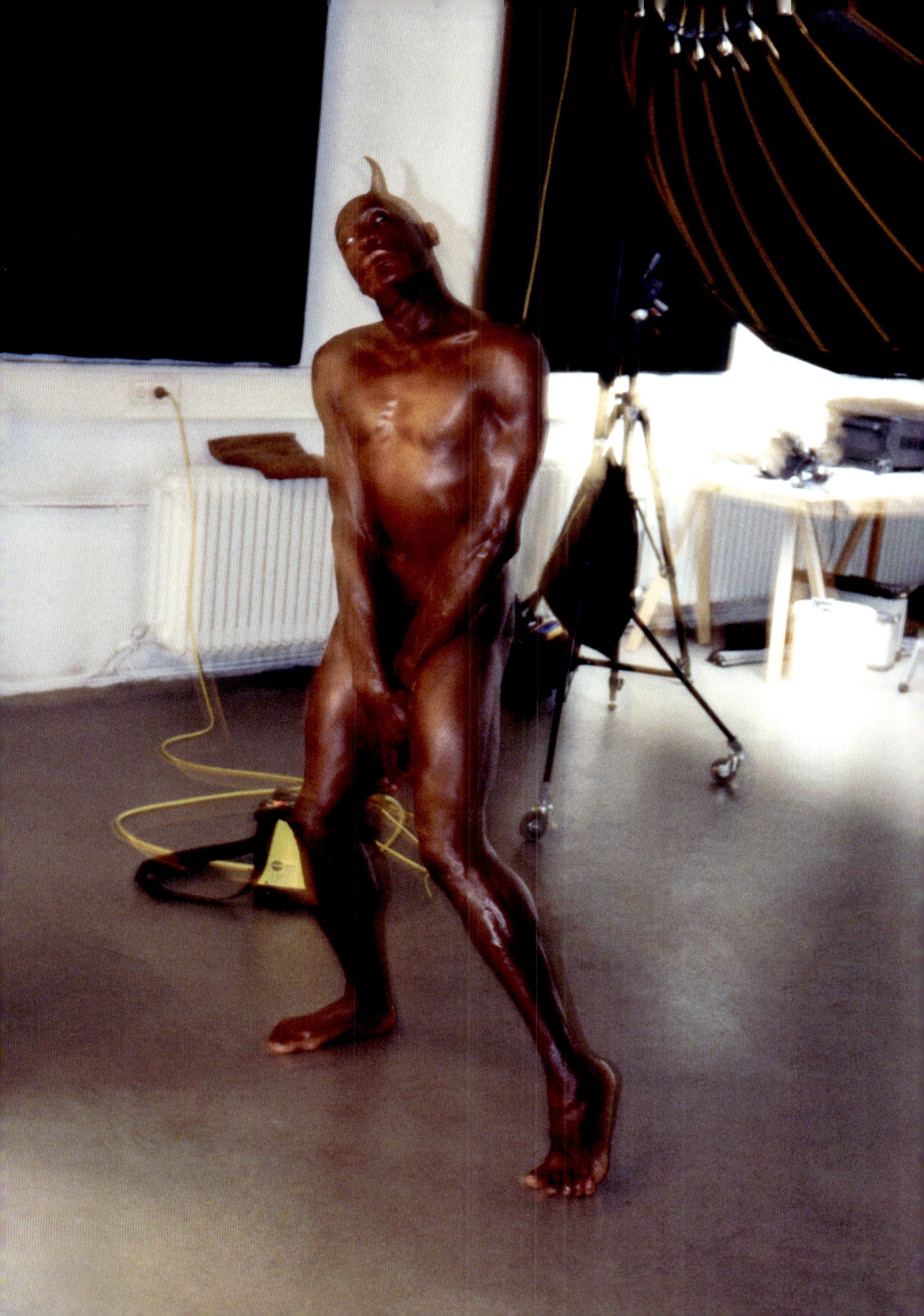

Mapplethorpe

Marcel Kaskeline on the importance of Robert Mapplethorpe for Ismael Ivo

On his first trip abroad, Ismael had met the journalist Gudrun Stockinger in Vienna. Gudrun knew that he had a scholarship with Alvin Ailey and when she was in New York on business, she contacted Ismael. Gudrun and Ismael arranged to meet for lunch, it must have been around 1983. "It's with a well-known photographer, Robert Mapplethorpe," she is believed to have said, "I thought you'd just tag along." Ismael had never heard the name, but was happy to accompany her to the loft where Robert lived and worked.

"While Gudrun interviewed Robert, I sat quietly on a sofa," Ismael recounted. "I tried not to draw attention to myself. Out of the corner of my eye, I looked at the photos that were standing everywhere and hanging on the walls: nude studies of Black men, Black men in obscene poses and performing sexual acts, Black penises hanging out of pants or staring at the viewer half-erect. I had just come from São Paulo and had never seen anything like it"

When Gudrun had finished with the interview, she is said to have told Robert, "To finish, I'd like to take a picture of you." "All right," Robert replied, "but only on one condition: that I get to take a picture of him." And he looked over at Ismael. "Robert saw my horror," Ismael recounted, "and added, 'Don't worry. All you have to do is take off your T-shirt.'"

I

"Robert worked exclusively with natural light. He placed me by the window of his studio. And gave instructions very calmly: 'Turn your head a little here. Look over there.' Like a choreographer. It was easy for me to work with that," Ismael said later. That's how Robert Mapplethorpe's portrait photo of Ismael came about. And Gudrun's photo of Robert working with Ismael.

Robert and Ismael kept in touch and became friends. "Robert was very respectful. A subtle, discreet, and educated man," Ismael later recalled. "Never once did he try to make sexual advances on me. I became a confidant to whom Robert could tell everything. He had many people around him who wanted to profit from his fame and often felt lonely. Robert knew that I was not interested in his fame as a photographer. I lived only for dance. Even after I left New York, we stayed in touch, talking regularly on the phone. Two days before Robert died, we had a long, intense phone conversation. It seems Robert already knew it was a farewell."

The *Mapplethorpe* piece was not intended as a biography. Their private friendship may have been the inspiration, but it was not the subject of our piece. It was meant to focus on Robert's artistic oeuvre, his treatment of the complex social taboos that he dragged into the light and his own obsession with the Black male body.

We researched the situation of Black men in the United States, which Ismael viewed differently from that in Brazil. In American prisons, death row inmates are almost exclusively young, Black men. The court sentences against them are disproportionately harsh. For decades, they have been the only ones on whom the death sentence is still carried out.

Initially, Ismael planned to begin the play sitting in an electric chair. I managed to get him to choose a more open image that alludes to a person's imprisonment in societal shackles and the limits of their own body.

I built dozens of set models and finally arrived at a solution in the form of a gigantic metal wall that took up the entire width of the stage—with a narrow, glass opening in its center. In the steamed-up air—it was specially made that way—of the tight glass case, Ismael's naked body was to move up and down until it touched the floor, pushed against his glass prison, and brought the entire wall crashing down toward the audience.

It was a private production, which we financed ourselves. The commission for the stage set went to the Holzart company, which had sufficiently large facilities in Berlin-Oberschöneweide. When we went to the workshop to inspect the stage set, which was finished down to the last detail, the workshop manager seemed visibly nervous. There it stood, the huge, impressive metal wall with the glass opening. For a demonstration, a technician took on the role of Ismael, pressing against the wall from inside the glass case. And it slowly crashed to the floor, creating a tremendous blast of air. The workshop manager was relieved: "Yesterday we did a test with a single section. It fragmented into a thousand pieces."

The back of the wall reveals a lava field with hundreds of white calla lilies, the flower most photographed by Mapplethorpe. To this day, it's still the most dramatic scene change I've been able to realize for a stage. After the glass case spat out its human contents, Ismael moved about in this unreal world. Behind him, a flat mirror projected his movements from the horizontal to the vertical. At various points, Ismael played with the audience's expectations. People actually seemed to feel threatened when Ismael played with a switchblade, inspired by one of Mapplethorpe's photographs. Elsewhere, he poured a jerrycan over himself, but instead of gasoline, it turned out to contain a powder that dyed Ismael white. We projected the names of those who were about to be executed in the United States onto the mirror, updating the list daily.

In the line of his solos, this one was the most technically complex. With its close interplay of space and body and the dimensions of an opera, this solo also represented something new for the entire dance world. Ismael called it a dance installation. For our collaboration, *Mapplethorpe* ushered in a new phase. Henceforth, my work was not limited to the space of the stage. We collaborated on the concept, did research together, discussed titles, and developed specific aesthetics for each piece. All subsequent, large-scale pieces were created in close consultation.

It quickly turned out that the premiere of *Mapplethorpe* in Venice was a resounding success not only with the audience but also with the festival itself. Ismael was invited to succeed Caroline Carlson as director, initially for two years. Rather than Dance Biennale, Ismael called his program Body Biennale.

Each year, he would choose a specific theme for the program of guest performances by international artists and companies. In addition, he set up an advanced training program for professional dancers, *Arsenale della Danza*, which later merged with his *Biblioteca do Corpo* project, in collaboration with partners from Hong Kong, Zurich, and Vienna as well as SESC São Paulo and the city's own cultural department. He was later to take up the ideas developed there for the SP Escola de Dança, the state dance academy in São Paulo, which ultimately became his legacy in Brazil.

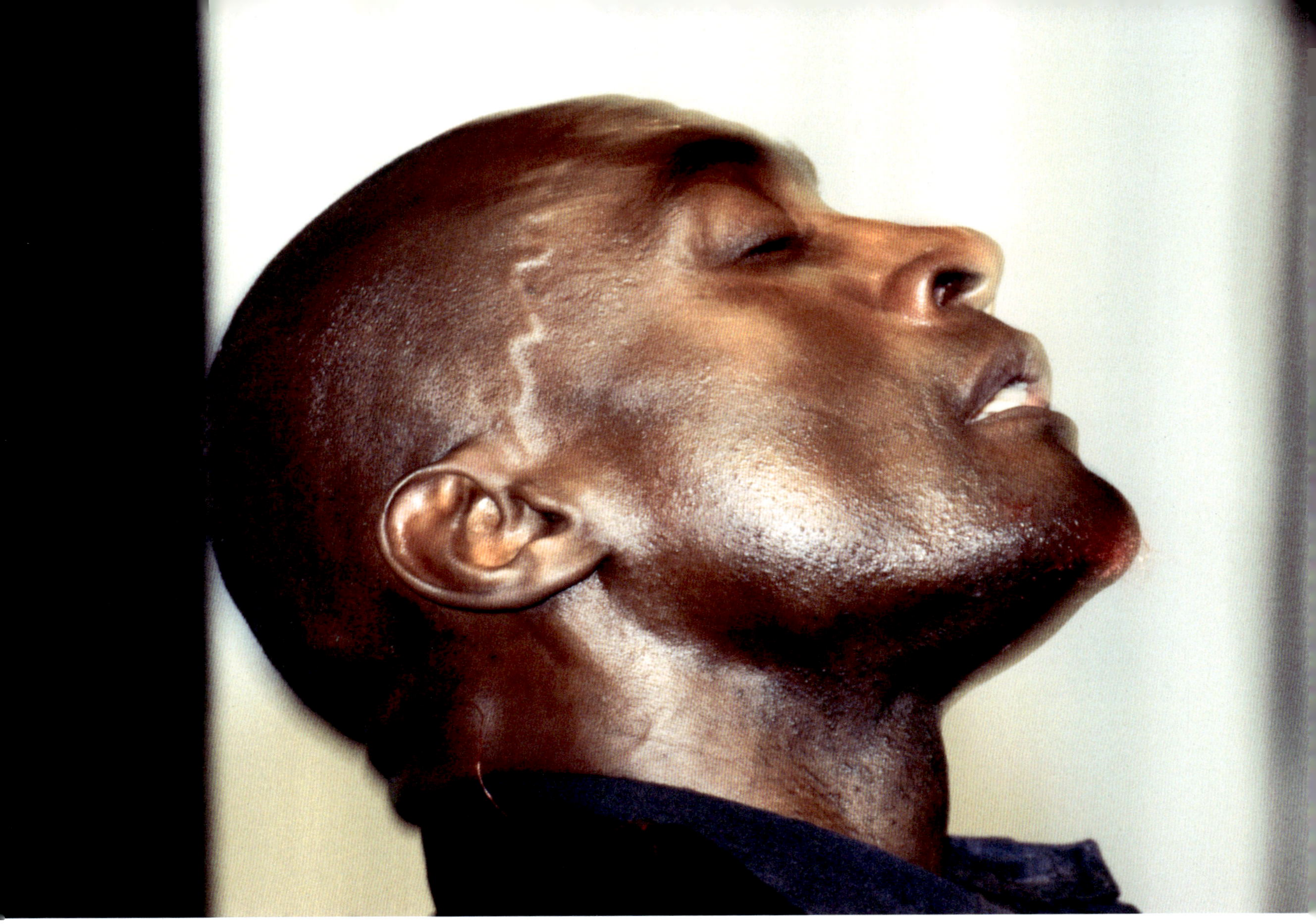

"A river of ideas"
Dance curator Rino Achille de Pace on working with Ismael Ivo in Venice

THE BODY IN THE MIDDLE

There are many—including many artists—who are still convinced that art can subtly transform our perception of the world. There are no groups that, like the constructivists or the surrealists, can vaguely recall their great enthusiasm for inventing and promoting a new vision of art. Our living conditions have of course changed radically but there is no doubt that our cultural perception must expand beyond borders that welcome new perspectives.

The world is moving at a fast pace and "the Body in the middle" tries to recompose itself, amidst miraculous new medical technologies, dissected by computer monitors, by genetic mapping, by the display of hibernating human models. We proceed into the era of metamorphosis, we recognize and physically feel the inevitable globalization of the body's vocabulary, expressions, reactions, and curiosity. Dance is one of the most particular answers and remains a mystery, an adventure. Always looking for a balance between inner perception and experience, adapting to external circumstances dance represents for us the door through which new stimuli enter and translates itself into a source of new ideas and inspiration.

Excerpt from the presentation that Ismael Ivo wrote for the Venice Biennale, Dance Festival, 2005.

In 2001 Carolyn Carlson, the director of the Dance Sector of the Venice Biennale of the time, gave me carte blanche to establish a section of the dance festival dedicated to male solos. In 1999 she had personally curated *SoloDonna*, a project devoted to female energy.

It was while I was working on that section of the festival, *SoloMen*, that I met Ismael Ivo for the first time.

I obviously knew his forays into an artistic dimension that went well beyond the sphere of dance, but while I was working with him I never ceased to be amazed at how much his creative energy could expand, not only to the dimension of Ismael as a performer, choreographer or director but also to the visionary flair of the artistic curator.

The passage through the lagoon with a work dedicated to Robert Mapplethorpe and its surprising impact on the city's public perhaps marked the furrow of what would have been Ismael's joyful destiny: an almost ten-year-long bond with the prestigious Biennale institution and above all with the city of Venice itself where he was immediately welcomed and loved. And he reciprocated this great love, by giving his art to everyone, with the generosity and elegance that had always distinguished him.

Ismael is a special human being. The first meetings with him, in planning what he wants to propose for Venice from 2005 onwards, have something magical and magnetic, and they involve our entire work group. There is no doubt that we will accompany this *Orixá* embodied in a beautiful man—Black, velvet eyes, deep voice, everlasting smile—with blind fidelity, on an uninterrupted journey of exploration.

These are truly bright years for contemporary dance, which is experiencing a sort of revival in a city crowded with fans from all over the world, year after year. *Body Attack*, *Under Skin*, *Ground Zero*, *Beauty*, festivals, and educational projects are born that become relevant pages in the cultural script of those years, in some cases taking on the weight of real media catalysts.

Nature has given Ismael what is most precious: beauty, inner wealth, and great humanity. Ismael is as glamorous as he is spiritual, attentive to listening to other, always outstanding in consideration, gratitude, and humility.

His ability to anchor contemporary dance in reality is remarkable. His shows, projects, and collaborations address thorny religious and social issues and propose performative actions related to neuroscience, ethnic minorities, gender conflicts, or very specific scientific insights, such as advances achieved in the field of cardiological rehabilitation and how much these owe to dance or music.

I

The 2006 festival closes with the LDP Company from Seoul. For them, Ismael has created *Fragments*, a choreography inspired by Heiner Müller's texts. This performance ends with a male and a female dancer who are, with great sensuality, about to devour an apple before it falls

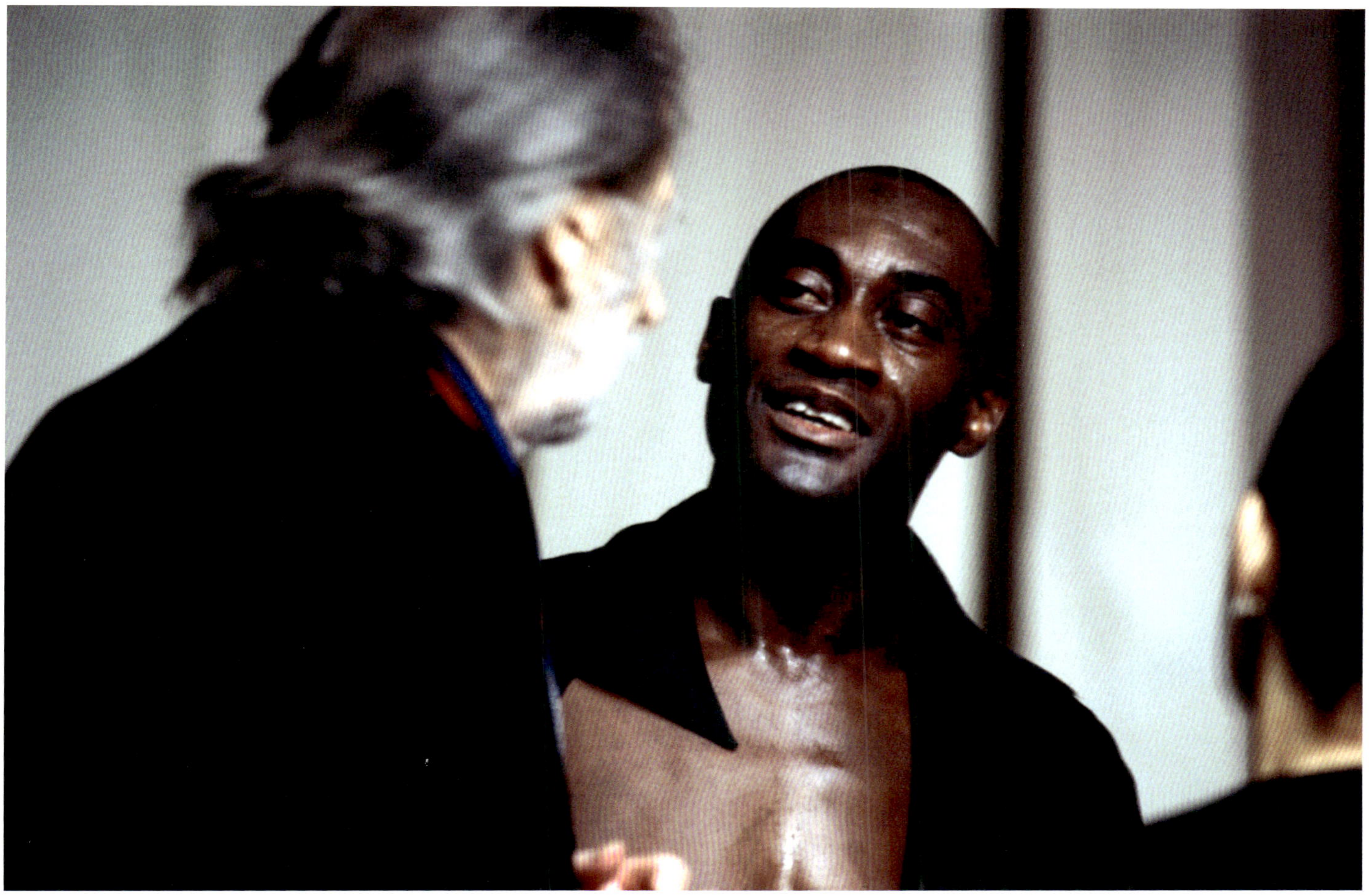

from them, leaving their mouths stuck together as they satisfy their hunger with an endless kiss.
It is the last evening, we stroll with Ismael from the Teatro alle Tese to the exit, a walk that allows us to exchange thoughts and reflect on the festival that has just come to an end. We are both still enchanted by what we have just seen, perhaps I more so than him, who had created that work. In a few minutes, that image generated within us a river of ideas from which next year's festival would flow. *Body & Eros*, as we instantly named it on that short summer stroll, was to become one of the most influential contemporary dance festivals of our time.

II

III

IV

V

I Arsenale della Danza, Teatro alle Tese, La Biennale di Venezia, photographer: Alvise Nicoletti
II Ismael Ivo and Paulo Baratta, Ca' Giustinian, La Biennale di Venezia
III Construction of stage set for *Erendira*, 2005, Teatro alle Tese, La Biennale di Venezia, photographer: Gabriele Frauendorf
IV Arsenale della Danza, Teatro alle Tese, La Biennale di Venezia
V Golden Lion for Lifetime Achievement of Pina Bausch, 2007, La Biennale di Venezia

592 ESPECIAL
HUMAITA

ILE OMIOJUARO
FUND. 20-04-85

"There it was, what he wanted all along: intensity!"
Dancer Fernanda Bueno in conversation with Petra Schaeber

PETRA SCHAEBER You are a dancer with the Balé da Cidade de São Paulo and played an important role in bringing Ismael back to São Paulo. Can you tell us something about that?

FERNANDA BUENO At the Balé da Cidade de São Paulo, of which I have been a member for fifteen years, it is customary for the dancers to make a list of three proposals when there is a political change. At the end of 2016 we had reached that point, the new mayor João Dória had been elected and was due to take office in January 2017.

For me, Ismael Ivo seemed like the right fit. I did not know him personally but had followed his career and projects here in Brazil. First, it was the *Biblioteca do Corpo* and then the project of the State of São Paulo, *Qualificação em Dança*, which brought him back to Brazil. A man who had left his country for so many years came back, bringing with him everything he had harvested and planted, everything he had created and developed.

I would have liked to have met and worked with him a few years earlier when he came to Brazil with *Biblioteca do Corpo*. But the project was designed for dancers who were at the beginning of their careers and there was an age limit for participation while I was already a trained dancer with the Municipal Ballet at the time. The *Biblioteca do Corpo* fascinated me because it corresponded to my artistic desires, the way I like to work, with different choreographers, and varied workshops, to then return to creative practice. So I reached out to Ismael to ask if he would be willing to take over the directorship of the ballet and be on our list. When I think back to that meeting, I get all emotional. We didn't know each other, but Ismael was extremely open-minded and generous. We talked a lot and at the end, he said with surprise, "Wow! I wouldn't have thought of this now, at this moment in my life. But I'm in!"

I presented Ismael Ivo to the company and when the vote was over, his name was on the list. The list was forwarded to the administration, the minister in charge of culture, André Sturm, approved the proposal and João Dória made Ismael the director of the Balé da Cidade de São Paulo.

At that time, we were still on holidays at the ballet. I was traveling in Europe when my phone rang unexpectedly. I answered it, and it was Ismael saying, "I'm not calling to tell you that I'm officially your director now. You may already know that. Fernanda, I'm calling to thank you. You made your way to me, and now I'm returning to Brazil." I was thrilled by this gesture of generosity and humility. A man like him, with everything he had already achieved, with everything he represents, calls to thank me. From that moment on, we built a very strong professional history, for which I am very grateful.

SCHAEBER How did you perceive Ismael's work at the head of the Municipal Ballet?

BUENO Ismael was a fantastic man, full of energy, creativity, and ideas. He wanted us to tell a story with our bodies, a story that was related to our lives. He didn't want a dancer to just lift their leg or do a few pirouettes. His suggestions were exactly what we needed as artists, performers, and creatives. Sometimes he would start the day full of indignation, "Have you seen what's in the headlines?" He challenged us to inform ourselves and take a stand, to look closely at our society, to look at what was happening in the world, and to "vomit it out" with the poetry of our bodies. This was our daily work with him. Not everyone has this dedication, this readiness.

One of the works he presented to the ballet was *O Risco* [meaning a risk, but also a scratch]. We got involved with it and immersed ourselves in an extensive research process from which the piece was born. It was a very brave project, as he was using his institution to address an issue that was problematic for the government, the painting over of the graffiti on Av. 23 de Maio, which had ignited a cultural-political conflict.

Many of the pieces Ismael proposed as part of the Balé da Cidade were works he had already choreographed, but would "set free" to see what we wanted to contribute to them. It was the same with another piece *Das Tripas ... Coração* [a pun on the phrase "getting everything out of yourself" and the problem of organ trafficking]. He introduced the piece to the group with a solo and then gave me the material saying, "I want you to give me something back." What now? How am I supposed to take a completed work and modify it? I studied, read, researched—and then changed the whole choreography, the solo, it became a different work—that was incredible.

For me, the time with Ismael was full-on, both personally and professionally. In the professional environment, we managed to build a relationship that I've never had at any point in my career. I've never had so much freedom, never had so much space to contribute, to create, to compose something together with such a creative mind as his. That was very nice for me—for my career and also for me personally, because through this collaboration we became good friends.

SCHAEBER I heard that Ismael attended your wedding—how did that happen?

BUENO Ismael and my future husband Kléber Pagú met during the celebrations of the 50th anniversary of the Balé da Cidade de São Paulo. In this context, we immersed ourselves in the universe of urban art, not only the graffiti scene but all the artistic languages that occupy public space. It was also during this time that I met Pagú. Pagú showed us another kind of stage and opened our eyes to the artistic forms throughout the city. Ismael became his great mentor. They became a fantastic duo, animated by equally creative and restless spirits.

We got along so well that Pagú and I got married, Ismael becoming the master of ceremonies at our wedding. Ismael used to joke, "The things we don't have to do in this life, even weddings are among them! Fernanda, can you believe it?"

I

SCHAEBER They also danced in *Le Sacre du Printemps*, which was created between Ismael Ivo and Marcel Kaskeline as set designer. The stage floor was gradually covered with flower petals during the performance. How did it feel to work on this piece?

BUENO Renewal! Reawakening! In this piece, there was a very special situation during one of the rehearsals. I fainted. Actually, it was part of the scene: before the final solo begins, there is the scream, fainting, and finally the solo to death. But during the rehearsal I really fainted, I hit my forehead and stayed motionless. When I came to, I heard the music in the background. The first thing I thought was, "Oh man, I'm late, the solo is over"—but I couldn't move. Then they realized something had happened, I heard Ismael ask to stop the music and everything went quiet. When I regained consciousness, he looked at me and asked if everything was okay. I could not answer. Then he smiled and said, "Have fun!" There it was, what he wanted all along. Intensity! Enjoy it and live. That's all we have.

SCHAEBER How would you describe Ismael's legacy for Balé da Cidade?

BUENO It was Ismael who made sure that the dancers were respected in the institution. It was he who got us out of a building where the municipal ballet was temporarily housed for fifty years. We moved to the building on Praça das Artes, near the Theatro Municipal. It was Ismael who made sure that the dancers got permanent contracts.

But it was much more than that. One scene stands out in my mind: In the building on Praça das Artes, there was a very long corridor. Once when I came to work, I could see Ismael down the hallway, no one else. There was only him, and he was walking as if he was going to heaven, as if he were in the clouds. When I entered the corridor, I stood silently watching this huge man walking, singing, and thinking. Then he made a turn and entered a room—the hallway was empty, but it was filled with this man who had walked here and left his ideas behind.

I believe that his legacy is in people's bodies, in those who were privileged to work with him, who had the opportunity and honor to be close to this spirit, this man, this human being. I hope that we can share these experiences so that other people get to know Ismael, that more films are made about him, that there are more conversations, and that there are more people who can give an account of having met him.

II

I Cover of magazine *veja São Paulo*: „The most loved“, issue May 8, 2019, photographer: Alexandre Battibugli
II *A Biblioteca de Babel*, 2019, Theatro Municipal, São Paulo, dancers of Balé da Cidade, photographer: Stig

On working with Ismael

Choreographic assistants Franca Pagliasotto, Valentina Schisa, and Elisabetta Violante on their collaboration with Ismael Ivo

Entering the rehearsal room with Ismael was exciting and scary at the same time: you never knew where his inspiration would lead him, what paths he would take to bring us to the quality of movement or into the dimension he had in mind.

Ismael chose the dancers very carefully, aesthetics and quality of movement were important, but the energy was fundamental. Even excellent dancers became uninteresting for him if they showed an unwilling and indifferent attitude toward improvisation and were not open to experimentation. Ismael was looking for "a sensitive body," those were his words.

The auditions would go on for a long time. In one instance the audition stretched over 15 days. After the first two days, he chose a group of dancers who worked closely with him for two weeks, not only on repertoire material but also on new dynamics. In that time he gave us so much material that practically half the piece could be filled with it. Those were hard, busy days that were also mentally exhausting. Ismael often used very intense meditation practices such as the Sufi technique, where you start with a small vibration and continue to feel the energy spreading everywhere, making the whole body vibrate, until a state close to unconsciousness is reached, where the body's movement is driven by an inner force that you didn't even know you had. This is how Ismael made us discover and overcome our limits.

Orbits, Yin Yang, and Sliding are just some of his themes in improvising and constructing the material. Ismael let us explore the material for hours. In the process, he watched us like a panther, observing carefully how we moved with each other, urging us to give more, leading us into another dimension, and making us use the body through dance in all its possibilities, all its dynamics. The days often ended in this intensity, and when he came back the next day, he opened his notebook in which he had jotted down what had come to his mind, mostly at night. From these improvisations, new choreographies, solos, and duets were born.

Ismael had a very close relationship with music, he loved composers like Philip Glass, and the great classics like Stravinsky and Vivaldi; but the rhythms of Koji Kondo or Les Tambours du Bronx were also very present in his pieces. It did not really matter what music he chose, he would leave the rest to us, and we would spend whole days counting the beat and exploring how his creations could be set to the music. When he moved, he was driven by the dynamics of the rhythm; this was another reason why his choreographies were so complex, because they were often not counted, but developed from the rhythms.

When we as his assistants noticed Ismael moving in his inspiration, we jumped from our chairs and had to follow him to memorize everything. Then he sat down, we reworked it, set it to music, and created the movement phrases that were to be transferred to the bodies of other dancers. It was an exhausting job because Ismael kept correcting them as they performed their parts. He was known to correct the choreography or change the music even on the day of the premiere if he was not yet satisfied.

When Ismael created choreographies, he drew inspiration from a variety of sources: a painting, a piece of music, a photograph, or simply our bodies moving even as we warmed up. He was there to watch us, and at any moment he could rise from his chair and say, "Do it again ... Show me again." He could start a whole choreography from a simple, tiny movement, but in the creative process, Ismael was a volcano. We made whole pieces in six weeks, masterpieces with thirty-five dancers that would have taken anyone else months to create. Everything was ready in his head when he came to the studio. He would put down his towel, warm up, start moving, ask me or Elisabetta to learn the movement phrases he was creating, and then he would tell us to teach them to the dancers. And while we were still doing that, he took two of them aside and put together a duet. When we reached the lunch break, we already had thirty minutes of material and we had to force him to take a break. Otherwise, he would just stay there and create another two hours of the performance. The movement phrases

jumped from one body to another until they found the one who could really bring them to life. Ismael gave great freedom to the dancers to modify the dynamics of the movement according to their physicality until the result had reached a sublime quality. His sensitivity to understanding precisely where to push the dancers was the key. He knew exactly in which role dancers would perform their best and gave all on stage the space to create their own "momentum". Everyone had to give one hundred percent, whether it was a walk across the stage or a grand duet—no excuses were accepted.

There were always special objects in Ismael's shows: cascades of petals in *Le Sacre du Printemps*; a huge basin of rice in *Mishima*; in *Francis Bacon*, there were so many objects behind the stage that there was someone whose only job it was to arrange and prepare them according to when they were needed in a scene. Whenever there was an object on stage, it had to serve a specific purpose. The way we touched it or used it was very important—Ismael worked on that for hours. Whether it was ropes, chairs, or tables, the furnishings of the plays were always very complex. It was not easy to work with such details that helped the dancers and restricted them at the same time, for example, when they were forced to reduce their movements—as in *Biblioteca del Corpo*, where the thirty-five dancers were enclosed in small cells like busy bees or books on a shelf. The piece began with movement phrases confined to a space of one meter by one meter. Movement seemed almost impossible here at first. But as it turned out, it was possible after all ...

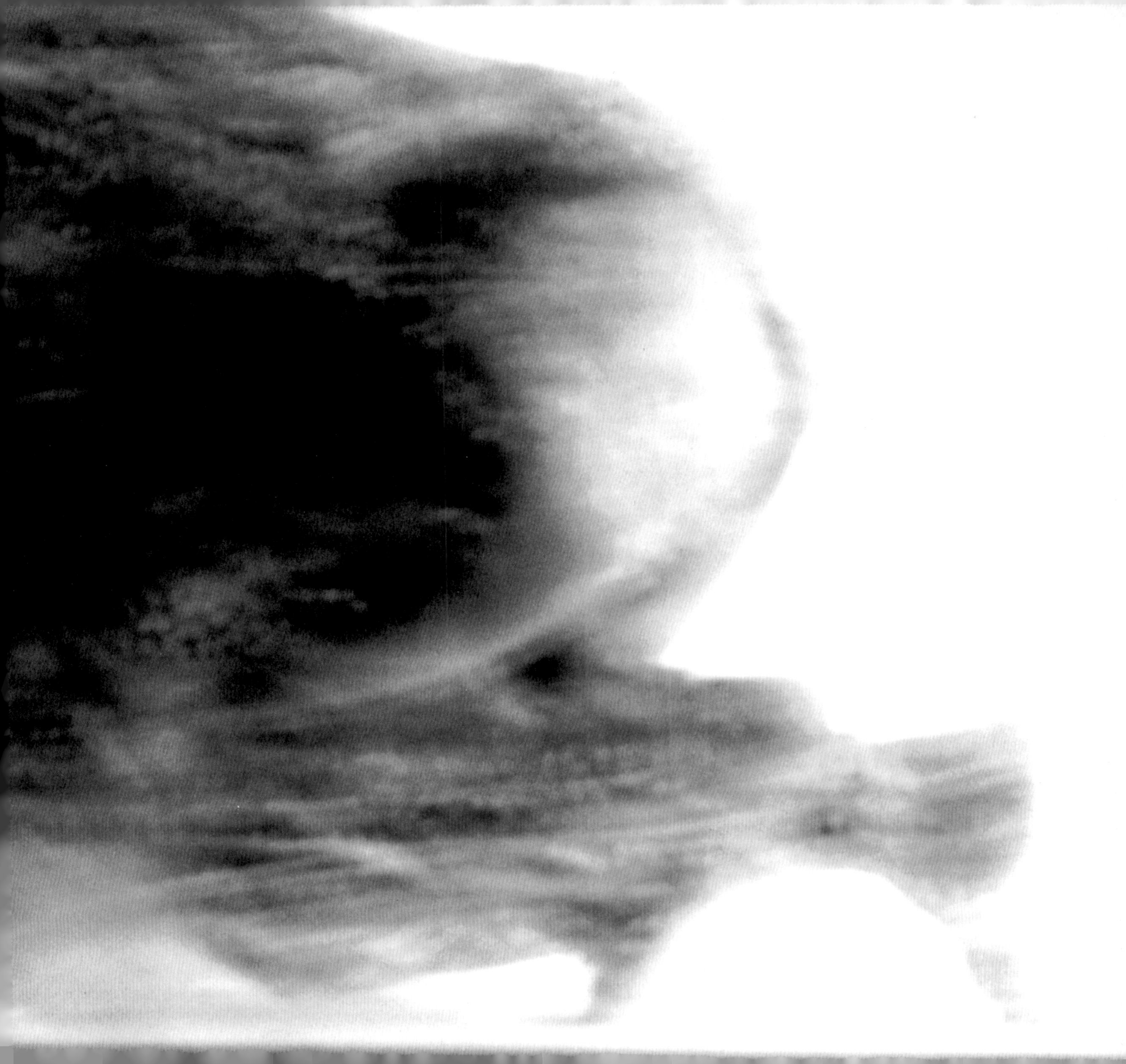

The cannibal of the opera house
Ismael Ivo on the challenges of a new Brazilian art of dance—in conversation with Johannes Odenthal (2017)

JOHANNES ODENTHAL You took over as artistic director of the Balé da Cidade de São Paulo at the Theatro Municipal earlier this year. This is the largest dance company in Latin America in one of the most impressive and important theaters of the country. You were appointed by Mayor João Dória Júnior, a Social Democrat who took office on January 1, 2017. This swift decision is an expression of a political sea change in Brazil that also touches on culture. The people of Brazil are facing a network of corruption of unimaginable dimensions. President Dilma Rousseff has been removed from office, and her successor Michel Temer is under investigation by the Office of the Public Prosecutor. The leadership tiers in cultural institutions have also been affected by this corruption scandal. How would you describe your appointment as the new artistic director in relation to this enormous political challenge?

ISMAEL IVO Toni Morrison once said that it is exactly in difficult times when the artists come to the fore to give hope and bring about change.

I was designated to take up a directorship of Göteborg Opera when I received the invitation of Mayor João Dória Júnior and Secretary of Culture André Sturm to join the company Balé da Cidade de São Paulo at São Paulo Opera House. In the end, I chose this position because it is the city where I was born and where I grew up, in the Zona Leste, one of the poorest and most densely populated neighborhoods. In the announcement of my appointment by the mayor, I said: "I was born a Black child in a poor neighborhood and grew up in very humble circumstances. But I had a dream and I saw dance as an opportunity. That's another reason why today I accept the directorship of Balé da Cidade at the Opera House." The country is in the midst of a major political upheaval. The level of corruption has reached historic dimensions, and the political system has lost all credibility. In this situation, São Paulo's new mayor—a businessman with no political past—has become a promising candidate for the presidency.

ODENTHAL As the tenth-largest economy in the world, Brazil is an unimaginably rich country. However, only a small elite and a somewhat larger middle class benefit from this wealth. There are few regions in the world where the conflicts between poverty and wealth are as extreme as in São Paulo. How do you describe your artistic concept for such a prominent venue in a megacity like São Paulo with such extreme social conflicts? On the one hand, it's about an aesthetic representation in a classical institution, and on the other hand, it's about reaching people who until then never had access to these artistic spaces. How can art be used to overcome this rift in society?

IVO São Paulo is one of the largest cities in the world. And it is precisely here that I see an opportunity. Any cultural act, even if it's just a drop in the ocean, can instantly reach millions of people. When I became a part of a powerful institution, the Opera House, I immediately developed an "open door" policy. In the last six months alone, more than 1,500 young people from favelas, ghettos, or social initiatives have visited the Opera House. For the first time in their lives, they saw an opera house from the inside, participated in rehearsals, saw performances, had discussions. It was an incredible inspiration for them, but also very moving for us in the institution. I have to say I have praised my predecessors from the day I started as artistic director because they had shaped the company as a platform for new ideas. But I have set a new focus with the programmatic title "*Corpo Cidade*" ("City-Body"). I started by creating an experimental company, a kind of laboratory that explores existential social and personal themes of the city. When a cultural-political conflict erupted in São Paulo over graffiti, we went with our dancers and took over the public space surrounding the graffiti. The dancers improvised on the themes of the graffiti and filmed and documented the street actions. The project was then transferred to the stage of the Opera House, where the documentation from the urban space communicated with the choreography on stage. The project is called *Risco*, taking a risk. Rise, crash, rise again, and survive. The battle over public space was ignited by the graffiti and was carried out with great passion in all the media and on the streets. We revealed the social tensions behind this and brought them onto the opera stage with this project.

ODENTHAL In addition to the Opera House, you also perform on a dozen smaller stages and 53 event spaces in libraries throughout the city. Were there any structures created in the past that you can use in a new way?

IVO We have organized the company in such a way that the dancers can also go to the various event spaces in the libraries. There we give seminars and workshops that are open to everyone without admission. It's the best way: to go out and meet the communities in their own neighborhoods. For me, it's a way of giving back to people. I was also inspired by the choreographer and dance educator Royston Maldoom, whose cooperation with the Berlin Philharmonic Orchestra sparked a whole movement of outreach work in Germany. In the next season, we will implement a project on a comparable scale. The dancers of the company will go to different parts of the city and work with adolescents in community centers. The seminars will be developed as part of a large performance. In the end, all the individual choreographies will come together in the Opera House, where they will be musically accompanied by the city's symphony orchestra. The families of the young people will be invited to the premiere. We need to occupy all possible spaces to promote coming together, communication, and dialogue.

ODENTHAL As a Black dancer and choreographer in Brazil, you have been confronted with hidden and open racism, and you have always taken a political, militant, activist position. Now you are a director in the biggest theater in the city. How is this story received in your hometown? How does the media react? And what can you do in this position to promote a rethink and a change in society?

IVO I was very surprised to see the media roll out a red carpet for me. Let's talk about those early days until now! The reception of my work was very positive. I was on the front page of the biggest daily newspaper in São Paulo four times. I am the first Black artist in Brazil to lead a major dance company. Last week, the city's cultural secretary named me artistic director of the company, independent of my position as director of ballet. I share this position with music director Roberto Minczuk. It is the first time in the history of the institution that dance is represented at the executive level. And, of course, it is the first time that a Black artist holds the position of artistic director.

This November, we celebrate the month of Civil Rights and "Black Self-Consciousness" in Brazil. In the past, this has not received much attention. But now I have prepared a special program. It starts on a big stage in front of the Opera House. It is a performance with the musicians of a samba school with large percussion groups and forty young people from the favela Paraisópolis. This prelude is followed by three Black DJs on the main stage of the Opera House, who enter into dialogue with the symphony orchestra. Then a young dance company called Sansacroma from the Capão Redondo district performs, followed by a documentary about Mercedes Batista, a pioneer of Afro-Brazilian dance and student of Katherine Dunham. And finally, I will show my choreography *Das Tripas ... Coração*, a work that deals with the international organ trade. This is an issue that affects Black youth in particular.

ODENTHAL What does your programming look like otherwise? The ensemble was a modern company with a broad aesthetic spectrum from modern ballet to dance theater. What artistic direction do you see for the ensemble in the next two years?

IVO As a director, I remain focused on the physical, artistic, and intellectual development of the dancers. I interpret my function as bringing new socio-political and artistic challenges to the ensemble. I see this as long-term change.

Sometimes when I walk down the corridors in the Theatro Municipal, I realize that I have arrived at the place where the first meetings for *Manifesto Antropófago* took place. That's incredible! Because this manifesto has always been a basis for how I see myself as an artist and as a person. I work in a building where Brazilian modernism was born, back in the 1920s, in an elite circle with revolutionary ideas. And today I have the opportunity to become *Macunaíma*, the "cannibal of the Opera House." I hope that this will be an inspiration for the future.

First published in:
Theater der Zeit 11
(November 2017),
pp. 35–37.

A living library of gestures

Danilo Santos de Miranda, Regional Director, SESC São Paulo, on European-Brazilian collaborations

In order to remain alive and intellectually vibrant, a library must continue to add new works to its archives. New arrivals intermingle with the pre-existing items on the shelves, creating communicating vessels that subdivide into a complex living being. With every immersion in its sections, aisles, bookcases, volumes, and pages, this universe is partially revealed, its intricacies unraveled. A chapter in a book from Section A can be linked to an article found in a magazine from Section B which, in turn, is reminiscent of an image seen while leafing through one of the manuals from Section C.

If things are this dynamic and volatile in a place this peaceful, with all the stillness and silence required in a space devoted exclusively to reading, what to say about a library dedicated to the body? To be more precise, a library dedicated to the breadth of its gestures. Is it possible to catalogue movements? Yes and no. 'No' because they exist in acts and presence, in the transience of now, mobilizing forms, intensities, rhythms, noise, etc. while at the same time affecting the environment and the circumstances in which they take place. Yes, because they last as the memory and the projection of bodies, they are continuously evoked and updated. They are the repository of the body's repertoire, acquired over time and continuously and simultaneously reprocessed and given new meaning by those who make them. Could the body be a library of gestures? If so, it is imperative that we scrutinize those that are already settled in as well as those that are gradually embodied. After all, we are talking about a living library.

Dance is the ideal medium for the intellect-body to perform its inventions. It is the perfect space for the creation of gestures: favorably permeable to the movements that inhabit the life going on inside the body and simultaneously willing to work them in plastic and expressive terms in an attempt to achieve aesthetic syntheses that can impact the senses and transcend the utilitarianism that saturates contemporary experiences—which so frequently subjugates the body. By contrast, the "post-everything" era we are living in allows us to move through the whole gamut of dance genres, breaking down hierarchies and experimenting with combinations and fusions of classic, modern and contemporary styles in a melting pot where ballet, hip hop, and vogue can be mixed and matched to create surprising gestural perspectives.

As noted in prior reflections about the legacy of Ismael Ivo, each one of us is an infinity of movements, which suggests that we live *in* our gestures, and not just through them. In the inestimable arc of movements that adds up to us, histories are compiled into waves, desires seek touch, fears prompt lapses, struggles conceive choreographies, and so on. Ismael Ivo was a skillful reader and translator of these and many other transpositions experienced by human corporality, much like an artificer of bold acts, bursting with power and pregnant with existential senses. A master in the art of revealing and inventing corporalities, his talent to engender poetics, activate spaces and subvert standards set him apart. A bibliographer of gestures, this Brazilian artist who belonged to the world and to posterity, kept channels open and staggeringly active through music, literature, painting, theatre, everyday life, ancestrality, spirituality, and philosophy. Hence, his library is transformed into a workshop of movements. Nothing could be more opportune than a comprehensive space for this "workshop", which revolves around expressive and poetic gestures that aim to extend Ismael Ivo's dancing and proposing body, which has itself embraced so many others.

This is where SESC comes in, an organization whose social and educational purposes are largely implemented through different art genres and based on the essential criteria of cultural diversity. Having reached a position of influence in the local and international contemporary dance scene over the last decade, SESC was where Ismael Ivo signed his first professional contract as a dancer in the 1980s. Since then and up to 2020, he was a permanent fixture in SESC's programs, the vigor of his choreographies and

I

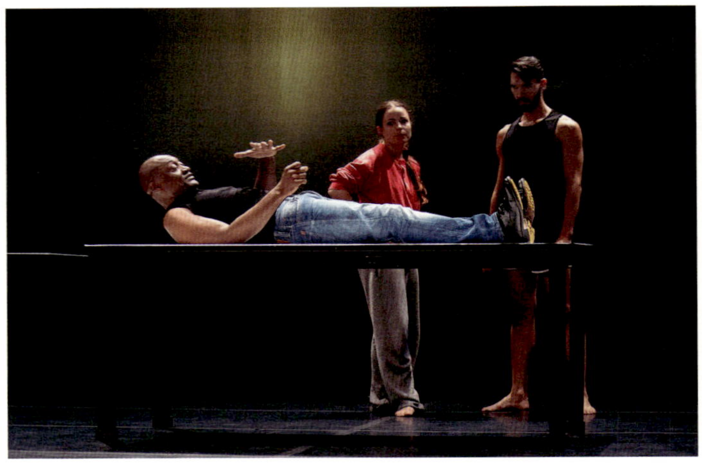

performances always a highlight. To this day the creative's presence can still be felt on SESC's stages.

Ismael Ivo started *Biblioteca do Corpo* in the 2010s; it was a far-reaching socio-cultural project for young professional dancers that stemmed from the Arsenale della Danza, an initiative linked to the Venice Biennale and SESC was its main partner in Brazil. Led by the dancer and professor, the project offers an original method for the guidance and preparation of dance performers at the outset of their careers that also includes social welfare initiatives. Conceived to help beginners with their artistic pursuits, *Biblioteca do Corpo* benefits from the wide-ranging experience accumulated, and constantly updated, by Ismael Ivo during his vast professional and personal life and gives participants an opportunity for professional and personal development. A frequent international traveler himself, the cosmopolitan creative saw his "library" as a "bridge" that connects places around the world and allows emerging dancers to travel around the globe to learn and perform. Ismael Ivo was committed to helping create an environment where new generations of dancers and choreographers could blossom.

A retrospective look at this trajectory through a lens that focuses on the close relationship between this exponent of contemporary dance and SESC helps to give it the dimension it deserves. With that in mind, the show *Babilônia—O Terceiro Paraíso* (Babylon, the Third Heaven) was presented at SESC venues across the state of São Paulo as early as 2011. Resulting from the first tentative steps toward a catalog of movement, the project featured artists who had attended workshops held the previous year in Venice. In 2012, the partnership between the group directed by Ismael Ivo, SESC, and the São Paulo State Secretariat for Culture led to the creation of *Biblioteca de Corpo, a library of the body*. Performed at SESC Pinheiros' emblematic Paulo Autran Theatre, it featured new dancers from the project by the same name, their bodies moving like living books, with pages made of limbs and movements.

II

III

In 2013, *Biblioteca de Corpo* moved to Vienna, Austria, but kept the connection with Brazil very much alive. That was when SESC, the ImPulsTanz Festival and the São Paulo State Secretariat for Culture joined forces and resources to help ten Brazilian dancers participate in the process that had started in the Austrian capital city, and which marked the beginning of a new chapter in the life of the "library-bridge". In the same year, the *No Sacre* show, also performed at SESC Pinheiros, brought together more than twenty dancers who, after an intense training immersion in Vienna, performed a piece resembling a ritual around the contrasts between instinct and reason.

In tune with the now regular joint process between *Biblioteca de Corpo* and the ImPulsTanz Festival, in 2014 Ismael Ivo chose a short story by Gabriel García Márquez as inspiration for the show *Erêndira,* to be performed first at the ImPulsTanz Festival and later at SESC. The choreography explores the relationship between fantastic narrative and sensitive social and existential issues in the twenty-first century.

This sample collection of gestures coordinated by institutions and artist collectives under Ismael Ivo's guidance was rounded off with a robust program catalyzed by the Body Library and ImPulsTanz in 2015. SESC is very proud of the partnership established with the Festival at the time, especially because it allowed initiatives under the program to be allocated between Vienna and São Paulo, leading to an enriching exchange for the contemporary dance scene in both countries. If the vitality of libraries depends on a combination of well-established and new titles and the surprising correlations that can be created among them, then Ismael Ivo's ingeniousness must be recognized: he was a creative in the broadest sense of the word, with facets that complemented each other—artist and educator—who tirelessly sought to build bridges between repertoires, people, institutions and places. Inspired by his example, it is not hard to imagine that the performers involved in these processes, even more so than the new contributions made

to the library created and fed by Ivo, will come to build their own Body Libraries.

To conclude this homage and as a way of putting it into perspective, it should be noted that the collaboration between Ismael Ivo and SESC is but one of the types of cultural initiatives that have been carried out through the institution's programs since at least the 1980s. The interaction with highly reputed professionals in their respective creative fields has been frequent and consistent since that time and, with SESC's encouragement and support, they have been sharing their creative processes with audiences who show an interest in advancing within different artistic genres while striking a balance between the education and social aspects.

Based on the institution's vast experience, it is clear that the benefits to those who take part in these immersions go well beyond professional artistic achievement, reaching other dimensions of existence, such as providing an opportunity to socialize, nurturing citizenship, improving the quality of life, and recognizing that anyone can be creative. If the intellect-body can be seen as a book and a library all at once, then it is up to institutions like SESC to create the right circumstances so that people—guided by artist-educators—feel encouraged to share them with one another, thereby weaving connections with each other and, as a consequence, among them.

Translated from the Portuguese by Patricia Pick

IV

V

I Rehearsals for *Das Tripas … Coração* (restaging), 2017, Theatro Municipal, São Paulo, with Ismael Ivo, Valentina Schisa, dancers of Balé da Cidade, photographer: Clarissa Lambert

II, III *Moving the City*, 2010, Arsenale della Danza, Venice

IV, V *Das Tripas … Coração*, 2015, Theatro Municipal, São Paulo, dancers of Balé da Cidade, photographer: Clarissa Lambert

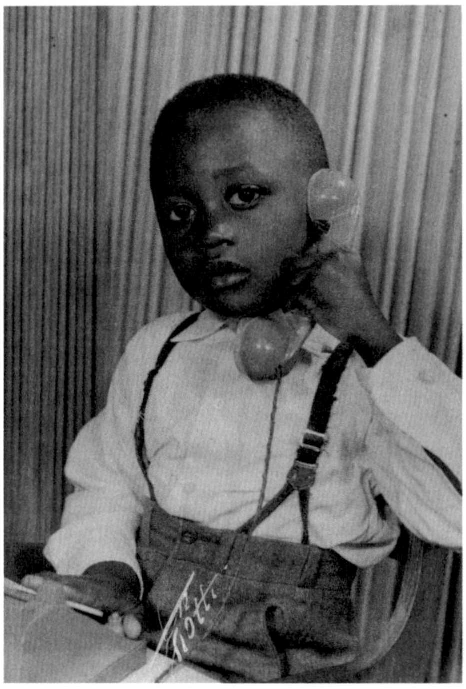

I

1955 born January 17, 1955, in the Vila Prudente district of São Paulo, Brazil (parents: Sebastião Ivo and Leni de Campos Ivo)

1959 purchase of parental home in Rua Gomes, Vila Ema Vila Prudente Zona Leste, São Paulo, Brazil

1963–1966 ZULEIKA FERREIRA DA COSTA AGUIAR
primary school
Vila Margarida, São Paulo, Brazil

Final certificate: December 14, 1966

1967–1971 GINÁSIO COLEGIO ESTADUAL DE VILA SANTA CLARA
secondary school
Vila Santa Clara, São Paulo, Brazil
graduation with final certificate

Ensino Fundamental II: January 10, 1972

1970 ESCOLA VALPARAISO
typewriting course
São Paulo, Brazil

His parents had planned an apprenticeship as a bank clerk for the young Ismael Ivo.

Certificate: July 30, 1970

1971 SCHEME
Teatro de Arena, São Paulo, Brazil

Director: Maria Goretti

1972–74 CORONEL BONIFÁCIO DE CARVALHO
Instituto De Educação Estadual
high school
Centro, São Paulo, Brazil

Final certificate Ensino Médio: November 26, 1974

1972 SHOW LUANDA 2000
Teatro de Arena, São Paulo, Brazil

Director: Maria Goretti

II

1973 ROAD TO SALVATION
Centre of Arts Educabas, Brazil

Director: Carlos Fisher

THE KISS ON THE ASPHALT
Centre of Arts Educabas, Brazil

Director: Amaury Alvarez & V. de Lucca

1974 DE CABRAL DE ISABEL
Teatro SESC Pompeia, São Paulo, Brazil

Director: Silney Siqueira

IN THE BEGINNING WAS THE CHAOS
Teatro SESC Pompeia, São Paulo, Brazil

Director: Silney Siqueira

1975–76 FACULDADE DE TURISMO DO MORUMBI
today: Universidade Anhembi Morumbi
undergraduate psychology course
São Paulo, Brazil

Immatriculation: February 24, 1975

1975 MOCKIMPOTT
Teatro Paiol, São Paulo, Brazil

Director: Jose Luis Gomes

PULSATIONS
Teatro Galpão de Dança, São Paulo, Brazil

Award "Best Play of the Year"

Director: Célia Gouvêa
Music: Saulo Wanderley
Performers: Students from the Teatro de Dança Galpão

During the military dictatorship, the Teatro de Dança Galpão 1974–1981 is a meeting place for the avant-garde of modern dance in Brazil. Here Ismael Ivo meets artists with whom he will later collaborate, including Marcio Aurelio, Mara Borba, Iracity Cardoso, Renée Gumiel, Takao Kusuno, Sônia Motta, and Ruth Rachou.

Premiere: November 20, 1975

1976–79 DANCE CENTER RUTH RACHOU
dance training
São Paulo, Brazil

1977 ODE PARA ROMA
Grupo de Teatro de Dança Galpão, São Paulo, Brazil

Director: Sônia Motta
Musical director: Marco Antônio Carvalho
Lighting: Gian Carlo Bortolotti
Choreography: Ismael Ivo
Performancer: Ismael Ivo
Text: Federico García Lorca: *Grito hacia Roma*
Premiere: January 28, 1977

1978 THE CARTAC AND THE JAZZ
Teatro Faap, Fundação Armando Álvares Penteado, São Paulo, Brazil

Choreography: Ismael Ivo & Sônia Motta

CARTAS PORTUGESAS
Teatro Municipal de São Paulo, Brazil

Director: Emilie Chamie
Choreographer: Ismael Ivo, Juliana Carneiro da Cunha
Dancers: Ismael Ivo, Juliana Carneiro da Cunha

PEGASUS CELEBRATION
Teatro Castro Alves, Salvador da Bahia, Brazil

Choreographer: Ismael Ivo
Dancer: Ismael Ivo
Stage design & costumes: Ismael Ivo
Music: Egberto Gismontis, Nana Vasconcleos
Restaging: 1984, Tanztangente, Berlin, Germany
Choreographer & dancer: Ismael Ivo
Musical accompaniment: Dudu Tucci (percussion)

POR UM BEIJO

SESC Pixinguinha, São Paulo

Performers: Ismael Ivo, Célia and others
Premiere: October 1978
São Paulo

III

IV

V

1979 SAGRA BEROH

Group Cena Oficina de Dança, Teatro Brasiliero de Comédia
Maria Della Costa, São Paulo

Concept & choreography: Mara Borba
Dancers: Ismael Ivo, Mara Borba, Calú Ramos, Ana Michaela
Stage & costumes: Mara Borba

YOUNG BLOOD

Teatro Castro Alves, Salvador da Bahia /
Teatro B. Comedia / Teatro Pinxinguinha, São Paulo, Brazil

Choreographer: Ismael Ivo
Dancer: Ismael Ivo
Costumes & props: Ismael Ivo

Award for best Solo Dancer of the National Festival

1980 AS GALINHAS

(The chickens)
Teatro Galpão de Dança, São Paulo, Brazil

Director: Takao Kusono
Dancer: Ismael Ivo
Actors: Renée Gumiel, Dorothy Lenner
Sound design: Flávia Calabi
Lighting: José Roberto Harbs
Premiere: 1980, São Paulo, Brazil
Duration: 60 minutes, no interval
Restaging: 2006, Haus der Kulturen der Welt, Berlin, Germany

THE VISITORS IN THE NIGHT

Theatro Municipal de São Paulo, Brazil

Choreographer: Stefan Dosse
Dancer: Ismael Ivo

1981 RITO DO CORPO EM LUA

later also: *Ritual of a Body in Moon*
Teatro Galpão São Paulo / Teatro Maria della Costa, Brazil
Idea & creation: Ismael Ivo & Dudu Tucci
Choreographer: Ismael Ivo
Dancer: Ismael Ivo
Stage design & costumes: Ismael Ivo
Live music: Dudu Tucci (percussion, composition, and arrangements)
Lighting: Takao Kusuno, Felicia Ogawa
Production manager: Ângela de Castro
Premiere: December 11, 1980
São Paulo, Brazil
Restaging: October 12, 1984
Schaubühne am Lehniner Platz, Berlin, Germany

TROFEU PIRANDELLO

Award as best solo dancer of São Paulos for
the performance *Rito do Corpo em Lua*
São Paulo, Brazil

PERSONAL INVITATION BY ALVIN AILEY TO NEW YORK

Ismael Ivo meets Alvin Ailey by chance during his guest performance of *Rito do Corpo em Lua* in Salvador da Bahia and is invited by him to the Alvin Ailey American Dance Center in New York.

1982 / 83 BALÉ DE CIDADE DE SÃO PAULO

Member of Grupo Experimental of the dance company of the Theatro Municipal, São Paulo

Director Balé da Cidade: Klauss Vianna

VI

I Ismael Ivo, 1959
II Ismael Ivo, January 22, 1973
III, VI, V *Por um Beijo*, Ismael Ivo, Célia Regina Cruz, SESC Pixinguinha, Sao Paulo, 1978
VI *Sagta Beroh*, Ismael Ivo, Calú Ramos, Ana Michaela, Teatro Maria Della Costa, São Paulo, 1979, photographer: Thereza Pinheiro

1982 **BOLERO**

Balé da Cidade de São Paulo / Grupo Experimental
São Paulo, Brazil

Director: Lia Robato
Dancers: Ismael Ivo and others

Awarded Best Play of the Year

CLARA CROCODILO

Teatro SESC Pompeia, São Paulo, Brazil

Ismael Ivo performed as a dancer together with Mara Borba in the jazz concert program *Clara Crocodilo*. At the instigation of the musician Dudu Tucci, Ismael Ivo was given the opportunity to participate in the guest performance at the jazz festival in the Berlin Philharmonic Hall in Germany. It was Ismael Ivo's first trip abroad. According to his own statement, it was then that he made the decision to live in Berlin.

Choreographer: Ismael Ivo
Dancers: Ismael Ivo & Mara Borba
Costumes: Ismael Ivo
Music: Arigo Barnabe (composer)
Live music: Dudu Tucci (percussion), and others
Restaging: as solo version
1982, Jazz Festival Berlin / Philharmonie Berlin, Germany
Dancer: Ismael Ivo

COMMERCIAL FOR GEORGE HENRI

model
apparel manufacturer George Henri, Rio de Janeiro, Brazil

TROFEU PIRANDELLO

awarded Best Solo Dancer of São Paulo for the dance part in *Clara Crocodilo*
São Paulo

1983 – 1985 **ALVIN AILEY AMERICAN DANCE CENTER**

scholarship from the Ford Foundation, Rio de Janeiro
New York City

Dance Center director: Dennis Jefferson

At the Alvin Ailey American Dance Center Ismael Ivo is introduced to the "Lester Horton Technique", among other things, which becomes a basis for his later pieces. An intensive connection develops with fellow student and daughter of Denise Jefferson, Francesca Harper. She will later become one of the most important teachers at Ismael Ivo's training projects Arsenale della Danza and Biblioteca do Corpo®.

1983 **BLUES SUITE**

New York City Theatre

Choreographer: Alvin Ailey
Dancers: Alvin Ailey's Workshop Company
Music: traditional, performed by Brother John Sellers

MEMORIA

New York City Theatre

Choreographer: Alvin Ailey
Dancers: Alvin Ailey's First Company
Music: Keith Jarrett: *Runes, Solara March*

1984 / 85 **ALVIN AILEY AMERICAN DANCE THEATER**

member of the Repertory-Workshop-Company
New York City

Director: Alvin Ailey

1984 **INTERNATIONALE TANZWOCHEN WIEN**

founding of Internationale Sommer- and Internationale Wintertanzwochen Wien
today ImPulsTanz – Vienna International Dance Festival
University Sports Center Schmelz, Vienna

Founding members: Karl Regensburger, Ismael Ivo
Artistic director: Ismael Ivo
Director: Karl Regensburger
Assistant directors: Andrée Valentin, Sylvia Scheidl

VII

VIII

1984 ff **IMPULSTANZ**
VIENNA INTERNATIONAL DANCE FESTIVAL

1984: Internationale Sommertanzwochen Wien
1985 – 1997: Internationale Wintertanzwochen Wien
since 1984: Workshop festival
1984 – 1999: University Sports Center Schmelz, Vienna, Austria
since 2000: Arsenal, Vienna, Austria
since 1988: Performance program
Volkstheater, Odeon, Theater Der Kreis / Schauspielhaus, Akademietheater, Burgtheater, Casino am Schwarzenbergplatz and others, Vienna, Austria

Founded by Ismael Ivo and Karl Regensburger, the festival continues to this day and is considered the largest European festival of contemporary dance art. It takes place annually from mid-July to mid-August. Every year Ismael Ivo personally facilitated several workshops, some of them for beginners and non-professionals.

Artistic director / later: artistic advisor: Ismael Ivo
Director / later: artistic director: Karl Regensburger
Assistant director / later: artistic coordination: Andrée Valentin
Artistic director workshop department: Rio Rutzinger and others

DISCORDS OF A WOMAN

Centro Latino-Americano, New York City, USA

Director: Ismael Ivo
Choreographer: Ismael Ivo
Dancers: Karin Elmore, N.N.
Costumes & props: Ismael Ivo
Music: William Tompson (composer & live music)
Restaging: 1988, Seoul Olympic International Modern Dance Festival, Seoul, Korea
Dancers: Mina Yoo & Ismael Ivo

ARTAUD, ARTAUD!

Studio theater at the Alvin Ailey American Dance Center, New York City, USA

Choreographer: Ismael Ivo
Props: Ismael Ivo

CREATURES OF THE NIGHT

Seperationstheater, Vienna, Austria

Choreographer: Ismael Ivo
Dancer: Ismael Ivo
Costumes: Clarissa Prath
Photography: Ralf Fröhlich
Production manager: Karl Regensburger
Producer: Internationale Tanzwochen Wien

Winding Ways

Music & arrangements: Dudu Tucci
Accompaniment: Tibau Lucas

Discords of a Woman (restaging)

Choreographer: Ismael Ivo
Dancers: Karin Haberl, Rose Stone Akras, Sebastian Prantl
Music: Dudu Tucci (composer), Tibau Lucas

Solitude

Choreographer: Ismael Ivo
Dancers: Marie-Elsa Roche, Zenta Haerter
Music: Dudu Tucci (composer), Tibau Lucas

Tutuguri

Choreographer: Ismael Ivo
Dancer: Ismael Ivo
Music: Dudu Tucci (composer), Tibau Lucas

Artaud, Artaud! (restaging)

Choreographer: Ismael Ivo
Dancers: Paolo Portanti, Rose Stone Akras, Karin Haberl, Zenta Haerter, Sebastian Prantl, Marie-Elsa Roche, Satoko Umeda
Music: Keith Jarrett (concerts at Lausanne and Köln)

Pegasus Celebration (restaging)

Choreographer: Ismael Ivo
Dancers: Ismael Ivo solo, Rose Stone Akras, Karin Haberl, Zenta Haerter, Sebastian Prantl, Paolo Portanti, Marie-Elsa Roche, Satoko Umeda
Music: Dudu Tucci (composer), Tibau Lucas

1985 PHOENIX

Schaubühne am Lehniner Platz, Berlin

Idea: Ismael Ivo
Choreographer: Ismael Ivo & Mara Borba
Director: Mara Borba
Dancer: Ismael Ivo
Lighting: Marie Christinie Brandy
Stage design: Slavek Debosz
Costumes: Ric Schachtebeck
Sound design: Fritz Veenstra
Assistent choreographer: Sergio Funari
Production manager: Karl Regensburger
Assistent producer: Andree Valentin
Producers: Karl Regensburger & Ismael Ivo
Musical director: Ulli Bariel
Percussion: Topo Gioia
Percussion: Samson Gassama
Electric violin: Ulli Bartel
Synthesizer tapes: Lars Stroschen since 1986 a.k.a. PROPELLER ISLAND
Premiere: October 5, 1985 Berlin
Duration: feature-length solo
Restaging: 1988, Schillertheater Berlin
Idea: Ismael Ivo
Choreographer: Ismael Ivo & Mara Borba
Director: Mara Borba
Co-director & Dramaturge: Johann Kresnik
Dancer: Ismael Ivo

Phoenix is Ismael Ivo's most frequently performed piece. The four-year tour through numerous cities in Germany and Europe, and to Tokyo and Osaka, with several weeks of guest performances in Berlin and Hamburg established Ismael Ivo's fame in Europe.

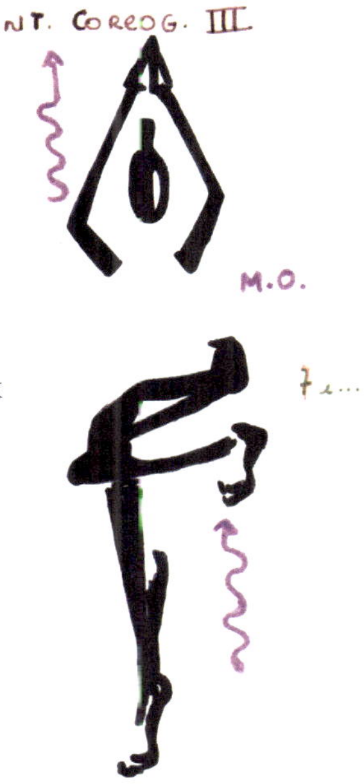

IX

1986 PEGASOS GMBH

founding
events management for contemporary art
Berlin

Associates: Ismael Ivo, Karl Regensburger
Registration: February 16, 1986

PHOENIX – Brazilian dancer Ismael Ivo presents his new program in Hamburg

TV feature

Author: Christiane Sträter
Editor: Christiane Sträter
Producer: dpy / e-te-s
Shooting: January 1986, Hamburg

1987 FRIO NO BARRIGA

short movie

Director: Nilson Villa Bóas, Brazil
Dancer: Ismael Ivo
Acting: Marina Mequita
Premiere: November 16, 1987 MIS, Jardim Europa, São Paulo

CAR ACCIDENT

The serious car accident was a drastic experience for Ismael Ivo, which he would later process artistically.

Date: March 29, 1987 Freeway near Nuremberg

UNDER SKIN

inspired by Federico García Lorca, Antonin Artaud, Winnie Mandela
Literaturhaus Berlin

Choreographer: Ismael Ivo
Dancer: Ismael Ivo
Lighting design: Marie-Christine Brandy
Sound & equipment: Michael Zengerling, Fritz Veenstra
Stage design: Marie-Christine Brandy, Gerald A. Mayerhofer
Makeup: Rossento Martins
Production manager: Karl Regensburger
Assistent producer: Andrée Valentin
Producer: Pegasos GmbH Berlin Karl Regensburger & Ismael Ivo
Musical accompaniment: Egberto Gismonti & Nana Vasconcelos: *Duas Voces*
Premiere: January 16, 1987 Berlin
Duration: feature-length solo

1988 SACRE DU PRINTEMPS

Theater of the French Cultural Center, Vienna

Choreographer: Ismael Ivo
Dancers: Riccarda Herre, Mina Yoo and others
Props: Ismael Ivo
Producer: Internationale Tanzwochen Wien
Music: Igor Stravinsky

VII Ismael Ivo, ImPulsTanz, Vienna, 2013, photographer: KarolinaMiernik
VIII Ismael Ivo und Koffi Kôkô, ImPulsTanz, Vienna, 2019
IX Notations by Mara Borba

VIENNA DANCE LABORATORY
Studio Moliére, Vienna, Austria

Choreographers: Sônia Mota (Brazil), Joe Alegado (USA), Ismael Ivo
Producer: 4th Internationale Wintertanzwochen Wien

DELIRIUM OF A CHILDHOOD
Schillertheater, Berlin

Concept: Ismael Ivo
Choreographer: Ismael Ivo
Dancer: Ismael Ivo
Lighting design: Heinze Baumann
Music selection: Ismael Ivo
Artistic advisor: Takao Kusono
Producer: Pegasos GmbH
Music (recordings): Gustav Mahler: *Symphony No. 9*, *Kindertotenlieder*, *Rückert-Lieder* (Christa Ludwig and the Berlin Philharmonics, directed by Herbert von Karajan)
Musiques de l'Afrique traditionnelle. Vol. 5: Une journée chez les Basssaris, Senegal
Premiere: July 3, 1988
Berlin
Restaging: 1997 ImPulsTanz, Vienna
1998, Deutsches Nationaltheater Weimar
Duration: 60 minutes, no interval

1989 KA-RU-MEN CARMEN
TV production
NHK TV production, Japan

Director: Akira Sugiura
Actors: Sayoko Yamaguchi, Ismael Ivo
Script: Makoto Sato
Music: Shinichiro Ikebe
Principal photography: June 5 – 17, 1989

APOCALYPSE
Spiral Hall, Tokyo, Japan

Concept: Takashi Kako, Ismael Ivo, Ushio Amagatsu
Artistic director: Ushio Amagatsu
Choreographer: Ismael Ivo
Dancer: Ismael Ivo
Live piano: Takashi Kako
Lighting: Tsutomu Yamago
Sound operator: Takahiro Ono
Costumes: Masako Hayashibe
Masaya Iizuka
Production manager: Nubuyuki Ozaki
Producer: Wacoal Art Center
Production manager: Karl Regensburger
Music: Takashi Kako composer
Premiere Japan: June 29, 1989
Spiral Hall, Tokyo
Premiere Europe: August 18, 1989
Odeon Theater, ImPulsTanz – Vienna International Dance Festival, Vienna
Duration: feature-length solo
Restaging: 2006, Theaterhaus Stuttgart and ImPulsTanz Festival, Vienna

1991 DIE KREISRUNDEN RUINEN
after a story by Jorge Luis Borges
Freie Volksbühne, Berlin
in cooperation with Internationale Tanzwochen Vienna, official contribution to Berlin's bid for the Olympic Games

Choreographer: Ismael Ivo
Dancer: Ismael Ivo
Director: Lothar Baumgarte
Stage design & costumes: Ismael Ivo
Production manager: Karl Regensburger
Composers: Pierre Noack, Jürgen Meyer
Premiere: 1991, Berlin
Duration: feature-length solo

AN ANGEL OR THE OLD DREAM OF FLYING
inspired by Gabriel García Marquez
Common Ground Dance Theatre, London

Choreographer: Ismael Ivo
Dancers: Company of Common Ground Dance Theatre, London
Director: Lothar Baumgarte
Premiere: 1991, London

1993 LABYRINTHOS
Theaterhaus Stuttgart

Idea: Ismael Ivo
Producer: Ismael Ivo
Choreographer: Ismael Ivo
Dancers: José Luis Sultan, Zula Lemes, Ismael Ivo
Lighting design: Ralph Köhler
Stage design & costumes: Rossento Martins
Production manager: Claudia Bauer, Meinrad Huber
Music: Marcelo Royo composer
Musicians: Jörg Schwickerath, Voker Rehn, Marcelo Royo
Premiere: 1993, Stuttgart
Duration: feature-length trio

X

MARS
by Fritz Zorn
in an adaptation by Johann Kresnik and Hansjörg Schertenleib
Theater Basel / Hamburger Schauspielhaus

Director & choreographer: Johann Kresnik
Co-choreographer: Ismael Ivo
Dancer: Ismael Ivo
Actors: Cast of Theater Basel or Hamburger Schauspielhauses respectively
Libretto: Johann Kresink, Hansjörg Schertenleib
Stage design & costumes: Penelope Wehrli
Lighting: Herrmann Münzer
Dramaturge: Hansjörg Schertenleib, Wilfried Schulz
Sound design / sound: Robert Hermann
Video editing: Daniel Schöneck
Assistent director: Jörn Klare, Annette Ramershoven
Poster: Gottfried Helnwein
Music: Serge Weber composer
Music director: Serge Weber
Musicians: The Contemporary Alphorn Orchestra, Patricia Draeger (accordion, flute, piccolo flute): *Mytha*
Premiere: May 15, 1993
Basel
November 5, 1994
Hamburg
Duration: 120 minutes, no interval

FRANCIS BACON
Theaterhaus Stuttgart

Director: Johann Kresnik
Choreographer: Mara Borba, Tero Saarinen, Ismael Ivo, Johann Kresnik
Dancers: Ismael Ivo, Mara Borba, Tero Saarinen
Libretto / dramaturge: Hansjörg Schertenleib
Stage design / costumes: Penelope Wehrli
Lighting design: Ralf Köhler
Assistent director: Nicola Egeler
Artistic director: Werner Schretzmeier
Music: Paulo Chagas composer
Music (recordings): Quadro Quartet string quartet, Michael Weilacher percussion, Anne Horbach soprano, Vincent Grégoire counter tenor, Pierre Baudson baritone, Celso Antunes conductor, Daniel Leon sound engineer
Premiere: December 18, 1993
Stuttgart, Germany
Restaging: September 25, 1996
Weimar
Duration: 70 minutes
Restaging: 2012, ImPulsTanz – Vienna International Dance Festival, Vienna

X *Labyrithos*, Theaterhaus Stuttgart, 1993, Ismael Ivo, Zula Lemes, Jose Luis Sultan

1994 MOSES AND ARON

Opera by Arnold Schönberg
Oper Leipzig in cooperation with Deutsches Nationaltheater Weimar

Music director: George Alexander Albrecht
Director: George Tabori
Choreographer: Ismael Ivo
Singers: Matteo de Monti Moses
Hans Aschenbach Aron and others
Design: Gottfried Pilz
Artistic directors: Udo Zimmermann Leipzig,
Günther Beelitz Weimar
Music: Arnold Schönberg composer
Musicians: Gewandhausorchester /
Staatskapelle Weimar
Choir: Choir of Oper Leipzig and Choir of Deutsches Nationaltheaters Weimar
Supernumeraries of Oper Leipzig
Premiere: November 26, 1994
Leipzig, Germany
Duration: 150 minutes, interval after first act

1995 – 1997 THEATERHAUS STUTTGART

associate member

1995 OTHELLO

Theaterhaus Stuttgart, Germany,
in coproduction with Steps '96, Zurich

Director: Johann Kresnik
Choreography: Ismael Ivo & Johann Kresnik
in cooperation with the theater cast
Dance: Ismael Ivo Othello,
José Luis Sultán Jago,
Daniel Chait Desdemona,
Esteban Hernández
Emilia, soldier etc.,
Alexander Fend Cassio, soldier etc.,
Rasmus Olme Rodrigo, soldier etc.,
Reinier Schimmel Bianca, soldier etc.,
Tamás Bakó Ludovico, soldier etc.
Set: Penelope Wehrli
Costumes: Claudia Rannow
Lighting: Heinze Baumann
Dramaturge: Hans-Jürgen Pullem
Expressionist coaching: Mara Borba
Assistant choreographer: Iracity Cardoso
Production management: Claudia Bauer, Meinrad Huber
Music: Livio Tragtenberg
Music (recordings): Silvia Ocougne
Premiere: July 1, 1995
Stuttgart
Duration: 85 minutes, no interval

1997 – 2000 DEUTSCHES NATIONALTHEATER WEIMAR

Head choreographer and director of the dance company at Deutsches Nationaltheater Weimar, Germany

1997 A BRIEF HISTORY OF HELL

Deutsches Nationaltheater Weimar

Choreography: Ismael Ivo in cooperation
with Mara Borba
Directors: Gerald Thomas, Mara Borba
Dance: Ismael Ivo, Rosa Costa,
Renato Jones Fernandes,
Riccarda Herre, Steffany Jockel,
Kiko Moreira, Livia Patrizi,
Virgis Puodziunas, Teresa Rotemberg,
Sven Seeger, Lukas Tiedje,
Rosalba Torres
Libretto & design: Gerald Thomas
Lighting: Alexander Gnadl
Makeup: Johannes Ohla
Assistant choreographer: Ana Mondini
Coach: Sônia Mota
General director: Günther Beelitz
Music director: Aleksandar Kalajdzie
Music: Heitor Villa-Lobos and improvisations by the percussion ensemble of the Staatskapelle Weimar
Musicians: Staatskapelle Weimar
Premiere: February 5, 1997
Weimar
Duration: 60 minutes

FREMD IM EIGENEN KÖRPER: AUSWANDERUNGEN ZU ANTONIN ARTAUD

after an idea by Heiner Müller
Deutsches Nationaltheater Weimar
in cooperation with Ludwigsburger Schlossfestspiele

Choreographer: Ismael Ivo
Director: Lothar Baumgarte
Dancers: Ismael Ivo, Mara Borba, Riccarda Herre,
Steffany Jockel, Kiko Moreira,
Christina Numa, Virgis Puodziunas,
Teresa Rotemberg, Sven Seeger,
Umberto da Silva
Design: Ric Schachtebeck
Lighting: Thomas Eggers
Dramaturge: Hans-Jürgen Pullem
Assistent choreographer: Ana Mondini
Assistent producer: Petra Janzen
Chief artistic director: Günther Beelitz
Music: Paulo Chagas
Premiere: November 27, 1997
Weimar
Duration: 70 minutes

MEDEA

with *Medeamaterial* by Heiner Müller
Studio stage of the Deutsches Nationaltheater Weimar

Choreographer & director: Ismael Ivo
in collaboration with dancers
and actors
Dancers: Steffany Jockel, Sônia Mota,
Teresa Rotemberg, Rosalba Torres
Actors: Katja Paryla Medea,
Steven Merting Jason
Stage design: Ismael Ivo
Costumes: Lars Betko, Mathias Werner
Dramaturge: Ralf Fiedler
Makeup: Hendrikje Lüttich
Assistent choreographer: Ana Mondini
Chief artistic director: Günther Beelitz
Premiere: October 18, 1996
Weimar
Duration: 60 minutes

1998 DIE BITTEREN TRÄNEN DER PETRA VON KANT

(The Bitter Tears of Petra von Kant)
after Rainer Werner Fassbinder
Studio stage of the Deutsches Nationaltheater Weimar

Choreographer & director: Ismael Ivo
Dancers: Rosemarie Deibel (Petra von Kant),
Teresa Rotemberg (Sidonie von Grasenabb),
Steffany Jockel (Gabriele von Kant),
Riccarda Herre (Karin Thimm),
Christina Numa (Marlene)
Design: Marie-Luise Lichtenthal
Dramaturge: Ralf Fiedler
Makeup: Johannes Ohla
Assistent choreographer: Ana Mondini
Lighting engineer: Thomas Eggers
Sound: Thomas Fischer, Olaf Remde
Props: Wilfried Meister
Chief artistic director: Günther Beelitz
Premiere: October 25, 1997
Weimar
Duration: 75 minutes, no interval

CALLAS
A PIECE FOR FOUR FEMALE DANCERS

Studio stage of the Deutsches Nationaltheater Weimar

Choreographer: Ismael Ivo
Dancers: Riccarda Herre, Christina Numa,
Teresa Rotemberg, Rosalba Torres
Premiere: 1998, Weimar
Duration: feature-length quartet

KUSS IM RINNSTEIN

(The Asphalt Kiss)
after the play by Nelson Rodrigues
Tanztheater by Marcio Aurelio and Ismael Ivo
Deutsches Nationaltheater Weimar, venue: Redoute

Choreography: Ismael Ivo
Director & libretto: Marcio Aurelio
Dancers: Ismael Ivo (Arandir), Riccarda Herre (Selminha), Umberto da Silva (Aprígo), Ricardo Viviani (Amado Ribeiro), Steffany Jockel (Dália), Lukas Tiedje (Chief Inspector Cunha / choir), Teresa Rotemberg (Dona Matilde / Dona Judith), Sven Seeger (Inspector Aruba / choir), Virgis Puodziunas (Sodré / choir), Eduardo Laranjeira (Werneck / choir), Esteban Hernandez (Pimentel / choir), Mara Borba (widow of the deceased / choir), Christina Numa (Death), Kiko Moreira (the deceased)
Actor: Thomas Koch
Design: Marie-Luise Lichtenthal
Dramaturge: Ralf Fiedler
Makeup: Johannes Ohla
Assistent choreographer: Ana Mondini
Assistant producer: Petra Janzen
Chief artistic director: Günther Beelitz
Music: Steve Shehan
Premiere: March 13, 1998
Weimar
Duration: 90 minutes, no interval

DER NACKTE MICHELANGELO

(Naked Michelangelo)
Schaubühne am Lehniner Platz, Berlin /
Deutsches Nationaltheater Weimar, venue: Redoute

Director: George Tabori & Ismael Ivo
Voice: Matteo de Monti (baritone)
Live piano: Tatjana Blome
Dance: Ismael Ivo, Mara Borba, Esteban Hernández, Riccarda Herre, Steffany Jockel, Kiko Moreira, Virgis Puodziunas, Umberto da Silva, Ricardo Viviani
Understudies: Eduardo Laranjeira, Sven Seeger,
Lukas Tiedje
Stage & costumes: Dietrich von Grebmer
Lighting: Alexander Koppelmann, Erich Schneider
Makeup: Johannes Ohla
Assistant director: Constanze Alber
Assistant choreographer: Ana Mondini
Assistant producer: Petra Janzen
Chief artistic director: Günther Beelitz, Weimar
Music: Dmitri Shostakovich: *Suite on Verses by Michelangelo Buonarroti, op. 145a*
(German by Jörg Morgener)
Premiere: June 18, 1998
Berlin
Duration: 75 minutes, no interval

1999 MEPHISTO

after Johann Wolfgang von Goethe's *Faust I* and *II*
Deutsches Nationaltheater Weimar
opening production for Weimar – European Capital of Culture 1999

Choreographer: Ismael Ivo
Script & director: Marcio Aurelio
Dancers: Ismael Ivo (Mephisto), Ricardo Viviani (Faust), Lukas Tiedje (Faust's shadow / Philemon / Euphorion), Andreas Weißert (Faust's vice), Riccarda Herre (Margarete / Sphinx), Mara Borba (Helena / Sphinx), Elisabeth Farr (angel), Aramis Klein (angel), Kiko Moreira (angel), Aleksandra Janeva (Baucis / Sphinx)
Stage & costumes: Marie-Luise Lichtenthal
Dramaturge: Ralf Fiedler
Makeup: Johannes Ohla
Assistant choreographer: Ana Mondini
Chief artistic director: Günther Beelitz
Music (recordings): Nicolas Lens: *Flamma Flamma. The fire requiem*, Arrigo Boito: *Mefistofele*, Diamanda Galas: *The Litanies of Satan*, George Crumb: *Black Angels*, Istvan Marta: *Doom, A Sigh*, Charles Ives: *They are there!*, Franz Schubert: *Wanderers Nachtlied*
Piano improvisation: Christian Weinreich
Premiere: March 27, 1999 Weimar
Duration: 90 minutes, no interval

SOLI BACH

Workshop stage of Deutsches Nationaltheaters Weimar

Choreographer: Ismael Ivo
Dancers: Steffany Jockel, Virgis Puodziunas, Eduardo Laranjeira, Ricardo Viviani
Live piano: Christian Weinreich
Costumes & design: Marie-Luise Lichtenthal
Assistant choreographer: Ana Mondini
Head of production : Steve Markusfeld
Chief artistic director: Günther Beelitz
Music: Johann Sebastian Bach: *The Well-Tempered Clavier*, Preludes and choral intro
Premiere: 1999, Weimar
Duration: feature-length quartet

ARIADNE

Workshop stage of the Deutschen Nationaltheater Weimar

Choreographer: Ismael Ivo
Dancer: Riccarda Herre
Design: Marie-Luise Lichtenthal
Libretto: Ralf Fiedler
Makeup: Karena Smolka
Assistant choreographer: Ana Mondini
Chief artistic director: Günther Beelitz
Music: Dmitri Shostakovich: *String Quartet No. 8, 9,10*
Musicians: Dehler-Quartett of the Staatskapelle Weimar
Premiere: May 22, 1999 Weimar
Duration: 60 minutes, no interval

DAS LEICHENBEGRÄBNIS DER GROSSEN MAMA

(Big Mama's Funeral)
based on short stories by Gabriel García Márquez
Workshop stage of the Deutschen Nationaltheaters Weimar

Choreographer: Ismael Ivo
Dancers: Steffany Jockel, Umberto da Silva, Aramis Raúl Klein, Lorenzo Homem, Esteban Hernández, Kiko Moreira, Virgis Puodziunas
Stage design: Dieter Lange
Costumes: Marie-Luise Lichtenthal
Idea & dramaturge: Helge-Björn Meyer
Makeup: Sabine Kreitel
Lighting: Thomas Eggers
Assistant choreographer: Ana Mondini
Chief artistic director: Günther Beelitz
Music: Alexander Balanescu: *Possessed* (recording with Balanescu Quartet), Wim Mertens: *4 Mains* (recording with Hans François and Wim Mertens)
Premiere: September 10, 1999 Weimar
Duration: 80 minutes, no interval

TRISTAN ISOLDE

after a motif from Richard Wagner's opera by the same name
Theaterhaus Stuttgart, in coproduction with the Haus der Kulturen der Welt, Berlin

Tristan Isolde is the starting point of an intense artistic partnership between Ismael Ivo and Marcel Kaskeline that will span 22 years and 38 productions.

Idea: Ismael Ivo
Choreographer: Ismael Ivo in cooperation with Márcia Haydée
Dancers: Márcia Haydée (Isolde), Ismael Ivo (Tristan)
Director: Marcio Aurelio
Stage design: Marcel Kaskeline
Dramaturge: Helge-Björn Meyer
Costumes Isolde: Gabriele Frauendorf
Costumes Tristan: Christine Lange
Lighting: Heinze Baumann
Producer: Theaterhaus Stuttgart in cooperation with the Haus der Kulturen der Welt, Berlin
Artistic director Stuttgart: Werner Schretzmeier
Artistic director Berlin: Johannes Odenthal
Music: Franz Liszt: *Isoldes Liebestod*, orchestra version of the Chicago Symphony Orchestra conducted by Sir Georg Solti; Richard Wagner: *Isoldes Liebestod*, orchestra version of the Radio Filharmonisch Orkest conducted by Edo de Waart, Richard Wagner: *Isoldes Liebestod* from *Tristan und Isolde* (recording with Margaret Price and the Staatskapelle Dresden conducted by Carlos Kleiber), *Isoldes Liebestod*, musical arrangement for string quartet by Hans-Peter Jahn
Premiere: October 1, 1999 Stuttgart
Duration: 75 minutes, no interval

DIONYSOS

Puchheimer Kulturcentrum, Munich

Concept: Ismael Ivo
Choreographer: Ismael Ivo
Dancer: Ismael Ivo
Stage design: Marcel Kaskeline
Costumes: Gabriele Frauendorf
Dramaturge: Helge-Björn Meyer
Music: Parana Bomfim (composer & live performer)
Premiere: 1999, Munich
Duration: feature-length solo

2000 AURA

homage to Miles Davis and Alvin Ailey
Theatro Municipal do Rio de Janeiro, Brazil

Concept: Ismael Ivo
Choreographer: Ismael Ivo
Co-choreographer: Márcia Haydée
Director: Marcio Aurelio
Soloists: Márcia Haydée, Ismael Ivo
Corps de ballet: Corps de ballet of the Theatro Municipal
Stage design: Marcel Kaskeline
Costumes: Gabriele Frauendorf
Lighting: Heinze Baumann
Dramaturge: Helge-Björn Meyer
Assistant choreographer: Hélio Bejani
Producer: Theatro Municipal do Rio de Janeiro
Artistic director: Dalal Achcar
Music: Miles Davis: *miscellaneous*
Nina Simone: *Bring me to the water, I'm going home!*
Premiere: October 19, 2000 Rio de Janeiro
Duration: 40 minutes

FLORESTA DO AMAZONAS

based on motifs from William Shakespeare's *The Tempest*
Wiener Stadthalle, Vienna

Concept: Ismael Ivo
Choreographer: Ismael Ivo
Co-choreographer: Márcia Haydée
Director: Marcio Aurelio
Dancers: Márcia Haydée (Prospero), Ismael Ivo (Caliban), Ziya Azazi (Ariel), Aida Leiner (Miranda), Ricardo Viviani (Ferdinand), Peter Beil, Lourenco Homem, Leon Muciz, Inn-Pang Ooi (male settlers), Andrea Bily, Adife Kaya, Ana Nele Riepl, Karen Schönemann, Chiara Tanesini (female settlers)
Dramaturge: Helge-Björn Meyer
Stage design: Marcel Kaskeline
Costumes: Gabriele Frauendorf
Lighting: Heinze Baumann
Technical coordination: Heinze Baumann
Makeup: Norbert Snoopy Suppan
Assistant choreographer: Carla Vannucchi
Training management: Carla Vannucchi
Head of production : Petra Wirth
Producer: Wiener Stadthalle
Managing director: Rudolf Krenn
Live music: Parana Bomfim, João de Bruço (the stage music quotes from the oratorio *Floresta do Amazonas* by Heitor Villa-Lobos)
Premiere: December 15, 2000 Vienna
Duration: 80 minutes, no interval

BABEL 2000

after a story by Jorge Luis Borges
Deutsches Nationaltheater Weimar

Choreographer: Ismael Ivo
Director: Marcio Aurelio
Dancers: Ismael Ivo, Esteban Hernández, Lorenzo Homem, Aramis Raúl Klein, Eduardo Laranjeira, Umberto da Silva, Ricardo Viviani, Elisabeth Farr, Riccarda Herre, Steffany Jockel
Narrator: Ismael Ivo extract from J. W. von Goethe's *Prometheus*
Stage design: Dieter Lange
Costumes: Marie-Luise Lichtenthal
Dramaturge: Helge-Björn Meyer
Lighting: Benjamin Schmidt
Makeup: Johannes Ohla
Assistant choreographer: Ana Mondini
Chief artistic director: Günther Beelitz
Music: Steve Shehan
Premiere: February 2000, Weimar
Duration: 70 minutes, no interval

2001 MEDEA

inspired by Heiner Müller's *Medeamaterial*
Ankara State Ballet, Turkey

Choreographer: Ismael Ivo
Choreographic collaboration: Márcia Haydée
Dancers: Márcia Haydée, Ismael Ivo, Arzu Dirin, Volkan Ersoy, Ayse Findanlik, Bahri Gürcan, Aysegül Aydemir, Armagan Davran, Elif Firat, Hakan Odabasi, Almula Özlem, Serkan Ceylan, Sanem Ergüler, Sehrhat Güdül and others
Guest actor: Nursen Girginkoc
Stage design: Marcel Kaskeline
Costumes: Gabriele Frauendorf
Lighting: Heinze Baumann
Assistant choreographer: Anjelik Uygan
Producer: Ankara State Opera and Ballet
Artistic director: Remzi Buharalı
Music: Urna Chahar-Tugchi, Arvo Pärt, Henryk Mikolaj Górecki, Kodō, Eitetsu Hayashi
Premiere: April 28, 2001 Ankara
Duration: 50 minutes

XI ÖDIPUS

after Sophocles
Berliner Ensemble, in coproduction with Theaterhaus Stuttgart

Director: George Tabori
Choreographer: Ismael Ivo
Dancers: Ismael Ivo (Oedipus), Márcia Haydée (Iokaste), Jonas Fürstenau (Laios, Teiresias), Cristina Perera (Sphinx, Antigone), Chiara Tanesini (The Plague)
Stage design: Marcel Kaskeline
Costumes: Margit Koppendorfer
Dramaturge: Henrik Adler
Assitant director: Inken Seltmann
Producer: Berliner Ensemble, Theaterhaus Stuttgart
Artistic director Berlin: Claus Peymann
Artistic director Stuttgart: Werner Schretzmeier
Music: Wolfgang Dauner, Arvo Pärt, Kodō, Christian Wolz, Bob Ostertag and Kronos Quartet
Premiere: September 28, 2001 Berlin
Duration: 75 minutes, no interval

DIE ZOFEN

after Jean Genet
Theaterhaus Stuttgart and Haus der Kulturen der Welt, Berlin in cooperation with Léonard de Vinci Opéra de Rouen, France; Teatro Comunale di Ferrara, Italy

Director: Yoshi Oida
Choreographers: Ismael Ivo, Koffi Kôkô
Dancers: Ismael Ivo, Koffi Kôkô, Ziya Aziza
Sprecher: Stefan Feddersen-Clausen
Stage design: Kazuko Watanabe
Costumes: Kazuko Watanabe
Lighting: Lutz Deppe
Assistant director: Jean Christophe Blondel
Head of production: Beatrice May Ritzen Stuttgart, Christiane Uekermann Berlin
Artistic director Stuttgart: Werner Schretzmeier
Artistic director of music, dance and theater at HKW: Johannes Odenthal
Live music: João de Bruço
Premiere: March 24, 2001 Stuttgart
April 3, 2001 Rouen
April 7, 2001 Berlin
December 14, 2001 Ferrara
Duration: 75 minutes, no interval

2002 MAPPLETHORPE

Teatro Piccolo Arsenale, Venice
"SoloMen"—Festival of the Biennale di Venezia

Director: Carolyn Carlson
Choreographer: Ismael Ivo
Dancer: Ismael Ivo
Stage design & costumes: Marcel Kaskeline
Lighting: Heinze Baumann
Sound Design: Fender Schrade
Video Susanne Reizlein
Dramaturge: Marcel Kaskeline
Stage manager: Heinze Baumann
Production management: Marcel Kaskeline
Producer: Ismael Ivo in cooperation with Marcel Kaskeline, Heinze Baumann and La Biennale di Venezia
Music (recordings): Patti Smith: *Wave*, Steve Reich: *Pulses / Section I, II, IIIa*, Zoku und Kôdô: *Leonard*, Egberto Gismonti und Nana Vasconcelcos: *Don Quixote*, Giacomo Puccini: *E lucevan le stelle* performed by Giuseppe di Stefano; Kronos Quartett / Bob Ostertag: *All the Rage*, Kronos Quartett / George Crumb: *Departure*, Patti Smith: *About a Boy*
Premiere: May 7, 2002 Venice
Duration: 75 minutes, no interval

6th SWISS INTERNATIONAL COACHING PROJECT FOR CHOREOGRAPHERS – SIWIC 2002

Tanzhaus Wasserwerk, Zurich

Artistic director: Ismael Ivo
Producer: Verein Profession Choreografie
Managing director & organization: Regina Christen
Artistic consultant: Richard Wherlock
Assistant artistic director: Teresa Rotemberg
Lighting & technical director: Heinze Baumann
Stage design: Marcel Kaskeline
Duration: June 28 – July 13, 2002 Zurich

XI *Floresta do Amazonas*, Wiener Stadthalle, Vienna, 2000, photographer: Gabriele Frauendorf

M. – WIE CALLAS

Theaterhaus Stuttgart

Idea: Ismael Ivo
Choreographer: Ismael Ivo
Dancers: Márcia Haydée & Ismael Ivo
Co-choreographer: Márcia Haydée
Stage design: Marcel Kaskeline
Costumes: Margit Koppendorfer
Lighting: Heinze Baumann
Music (recordings): Arias by Maria Callas: *Puccini* ("Vissi d'arte, vissi d'amore"), *Puccini* ("O mio babbino caro"), *Catalani* ("Ebben? Ne andró lontana"), *Bizet* ("Habanera"), *Bellini* ("Casta Diva")
Premiere: 2002, Stuttgart
Duration: feature-length duo

2003 FRAGMENTS

after motifs by Heiner Müller
LDP Laboratory Dance Project Seoul
The 23rd International Modern Dance Festival

Choreographer: Ismael Ivo
Artistic director LDP: Mina Yoo
Dancers: Jin-Yeob Cha, Pan Sun Kim and the Ensemble LDP
Premiere: May 2003, Seoul

MEDEAMATERIAL

by Heiner Müller
a project with students of the Scuola d'Arte Dramtica Paolo Grassi, Milano
Teatro Herberia, Rubiera, Italy

Text: Heiner Müller
Director: Ismael Ivo
Choreographer: Ismael Ivo
Dancers: students of the 3rd year of the Atelier di Teatrodanza, Milano
Stage design: Marcel Kaskeline
Costumes: Enza Bianchini
Lighting: Giovanni Garbo, Paolo Latini
Premiere: May 10, 2003
Rubiera, Italy

DURCH DIE NACHT MIT …
MARINA ABRAMOVIĆ UND ISMAEL IVO

(Through the night with … Marina Abramović and Ismael Ivo)
TV program ZDF / arte

Director: Edda Baumann-von Broen and Hanna Leissner
Protagonists: Marina Abramović & Ismael Ivo
Others: Vladislav Mamyshev-Monroe, Klaus Biesenbach
Camera: Boris Fromageot, Günther Uttendorfer, Frederic Doss
Editor ZDF / arte: Martin Pieper
First broadcast: November 14, 2003, arte
DVD release: October 2006, Zweitausendeins
Duration: 60 minutes
Award: Grand Premio 2004, Asolo Art Film Festival, Asolo, Italy

RÖMERQUELLE

TV commercial and poster campaign, Vienna

Choreographer: Ismael Ivo
Dancers: Ismael Ivo, Carla Oya, Karl Schreiner
Producer: Römerquelle
First broadcast: 2003, Vienna
Duration: 50 seconds

2004 NAKED HAMLET

after the drama *Hamlet* by William Shakespeare
CRR Dance Theatre Company, CRR Concert Hall, Istanbul

Choreographer: Ismael Ivo
Dancers: Tan Temel (Hamlet), Ismael Ivo (Horatio), Nurhan Nebioglu (Claudius), Cennet Erdogan (Gertrude), Ece Gözmen (Polonius), Gökmen Kasabali (Laertes), Ayrin Ersöz (Ophelia), Harika Onur (Rosencrantz / courtisan), Sernaz Demirel (Guildenstern / courtisan), Eylem Gülter Yazici (woman from the Seraglio / courtisan), Erdem Gündüz (ghost / man from the Seraglio)
Stage design: Marcel Kaskeline
Costumes: Marcel Kaskeline
Costumes Hamlet: Bahar Korçan
Lighting: Heinze Baumann
Production management: Feride Akpinar
Producer: CRR Dance Theatre Company
Leitung Dance Company: Geyvan McMillen
Music: Andreas Bick: *Windscapes*, Richard Strauss, John Cage, Alfred Schnittke, Shostakovich and Bob Ostertag (Kronos Quartet), Ludwig van Beethoven
Premiere: April 27, 2004
Istanbul
Duration: 75 minutes, no interval

OLHOS D'AGUA

commissioned work as part of the program series *Der Black Atlantic*, Haus der Kulturen der Welt, Berlin

Two major research trips are associated with the project, the first to Benin and the second to Salvador da Bahia and Rio de Janeiro.

Artistic director: Ismael Ivo
Director: Maria Thais Lima Santos
Choreographer: Ismael Ivo
Storytellers & protagonists: Mãe Beata, Othella Dallas, Thereza Santos
Dancers: Ismael Ivo, Cristina Perera, Catherine Womba Tolopu, Apolo Franca, Rafael Luiz Nunes, Edsell Scott, José Antonio Roque Toimil
Stage design & costumes: Marcel Kaskeline
Dramaturge: Hans Jürgen Pullem
Lighting & technical directors: Heinze Baumann, Hermann Volkery
Head of production : Christiane Uekermann
Assistant producer: Eva Maria Helfrich
Assistant director: André Bolouri
Assistant choreographer: Cristina Perera
Artistic director of music, dance and theater and project director of *Der Black Atlantic*: Johannes Odenthal
Music: Steve Shehan (composer & percussion)
Premiere: September 18, 2004
Berlin
Duration: 75 minutes, no interval

BLACK BERLIN CITY BUS TOUR
POETRY OF THE INVISIBLE

commissioned work as part of the program series
Der Black Atlantic
Haus der Kulturen der Welt, Berlin

Concept: Ismael Ivo & Marcel Kaskeline
Choreographer: Ismael Ivo
Dancers: Ismael Ivo, Cristina Perera, Catherine Womba Tolopu, Apolo Franca, Rafael Luiz Nunes, Edsel Scott, José Antonio Roque Toimil
Singer & MC: Twana Rhodes
Costumes: Marcel Kaskeline
Dramaturge: Hans Jürgen Pullem
Assistant choreographer: Cristina Perera
Assistant director: André Bolouri
Artistic director of music, dance and theater and project director of *Der Black Atlantic*: Johannes Odenthal
Premiere: September 6, 2004
Berlin
Duration: 120 minutes

XII

THE TEMPEST

based on the play by William Shakespeare
Benefit Dance Performance donated to The International Peace Foundation, UNICEF and CARE
Presented by Culture in Motion – Daimler-Chrysler and Goethe-Institut
Thailand Cultural Center, Bangkok

Choreographer: Ismael Ivo
Co-choreographer: Márcia Haydée
Dancers: Márcia Haydée (Prospero), Ismael Ivo (Caliban), Pichet Klunchun (Ariel), Vararom Pachimsawat (Miranda), Jitti Chompee (Ferdinand), Sirimongkol Natayakui (King of Milano), Leonhard Behrens (youth), Vararin Tavivordilok, Patreya Amornviriyakui, Pimoopan Pornpetrattanasiri, Patta Nuchnoi, Thitipan Dechurat (ghosts), Meunphun Amphunassang, Kelly Wadlegger, Nippon Wannamahin, May Yimsai, Michiko Ikeda, Thitipong Aobom, Sirithorn Srichalakom, Vimolporn Kriengkraikasem, Skuna Wongsaroj, Oranit Suwantap, Duangsamorn Yoenyong, Pitchayanund Chindahporn, Fasai Supnirund
Stage design: Marcel Kaskeline
Costumes: Marcel Kaskeline in cooperation with Vilaiporn Bunnang
Lighting: Heinze Baumann
Assistant choreographer: Cristina Perrera
Special training: Günter Schöberl
Head of production: Vararom Pachimsawat / Dance Center Bangkok
Producer: International Peace Foundation & Bridges
Managing director Bridges: Uwe Morawetz
Music: Steve Shehan composer
Premiere: January 14, 2004
Bangkok
Duration: 80 minutes, no interval

2005–2012 LA BIENNALE DANZA
INTERNATIONAL FESTIVAL OF CONTEMPORARY DANCE, VENICE

artistic director
La Biennale di Venezia, Venice

2005 BODY ATTACK

La Biennale Danza
3rd International Festival of Contemporary Dance, Venice
La Biennale di Venezia, Venice

Director of dance section: Ismael Ivo
President of the Venice Biennale: Davide Croff
Duration: May 29–July 2, 2005
Venice

XIII

ERENDIRA

based on the story by Gabriel García Márquez
La Biennale di Venezia 2005
Teatro delle Tese, Venice

Idea: Ismael Ivo
Choreographer: Ismael Ivo
Dancers: Arianna Belloli, Sylvia Parmeggiani, Caroline Baudouin Nehr, Ivo Banchiero, Pan Sum Kim, Pichet Klunchun, Stefano Mazzotta
Actor: Cleide Eunice Queiroz
Stage design: Marcel Kaskeline
Costumes: Gabriele Frauendorf
Lighting & sound editor: Peter Göhler
Dramaturge: Helge-Björn Meyer
Assistant choreographer: Franca Pagliassotto
Technical directors: Marciano Rizzo, Mascia Pavon, Carlo Pallieri
Head of production: Rino Achille de Pace (Venice); Cena Cultural Produções / Julia Gomes (São Paulo)
Producer: La Biennale di Venezia in cooperation with SESC Sao Paulo
Live music: Damiano Visentin (fisarmonica)
Music (recordings): Andreas Bick (composer): *Windscapes*, Apocalyptica
Premiere: June 8, 2005
Venice
Duration: 80 minutes, no interval

GERMAN NATURALIZATION

In 2005 Ismael Ivo takes German citizenship. It replaces the unlimited residence and work permit he has held for many years. He retains his Brazilian citizenship.

Issue date of passport: September 23, 2005
Berlin

GOLDENES VERDIENSTZEICHEN DES LANDES WIEN

Award ceremony: September 6, 2005
Vienna

2006–2010 ACCADEMIA NAZIONALE DI DANZA

visiting lecturer
Istituto superiore di studi coreutici University, Rome

2006–2007 ERNST BUSCH ACADEMY OF DRAMATIC ARTS

Visiting lecturer choreography course

2006 UNDER SKIN

La Biennale Danza
3rd International Festival of Contemporary Dance, Venice
La Biennale di Venezia, Venice

Director of dance section: Ismael Ivo
Organization management DMT: Renato Qualia
Assistant director: Rino Achille de Pace
Program coordination: Rino Achille de Pace, Stefania Lora, Alfredo Zanolla
Organization: Beppe Arone, Rosaria Crotone,
Office: Maya Romanelli, Andrea Bonadio
President of the Venice Biennale: Davide Croff
Board of directors: Massimo Cacciari
General director: Gaetano Guerci
Duration: June 8–25, 2006
Venice

SYMPOSIUM *UNDER SKIN*

Teatro Piccolo Arsenale, La Biennale di Venezia, Venice

Duration: June 9–11, 2006
Venice

LEONE D'ORO FOR THE LIFETIME ACHIEVEMENT OF CAROLYN CARLSON

eulogy by Ismael Ivo
La Biennale di Venezia, Venice

The Golden Lion award for a dance work was created by Ismael Ivo in 2006.

ILLUMINATA

Teatro delle Tese, La Biennale di Venezia, Venice

Idea: Ismael Ivo
Choreographer: Ismael Ivo
Dancers: Ismael Ivo, Adamo Dias, Marco delle Foglie, Orestes Hellewegen, Gregory Livingston
Soprano: Sylvia Nopper
Stage design: Marcel Kaskeline
Costumes: Gabriele Frauendorf
Lighting: Peter Göhler
Dramaturge: Helge-Björn Meyer
Assistant choreographers: Franca Pagliassotto, Mariana Duarte
Technical director: Marciano Rizzo with Macia Pavone
Production management: Rino Achille de Pace (Venice) Cena Cultural Produções / Julia Gomes (São Paulo)
Producer: La Biennale di Venezia and Fondazione Teatro Comunale di Bozano in cooperation with Cena Cultural Produções, Brazil
Festival director: Ismael Ivo
President of the Venice Biennale: Davide Croff
Music: Arnaldo de Felice (composer)
Musical director: Pierpaolo Mariuzzi
Musicians: Orchester Academia Neue Musik Bolzano: Machiko Takeshi (flute, alto flute, bass flute), Arnaldo de Felice (oboe, oboe d'amore), Roberto Gandler (clarinete, bass horn), Gianmaria Romanenghi (percussion)
Premiere: June 8, 2006
Venice
Duration: 85 minutes, no interval

XIV

XII *The Tempest*, Thailand Cultural Center, Bangkok, 2004
XIII *Erendira*, Teatro delle Tese, Venice, 2005, Cleide Eunice Queiroz, Arianna Belloli, Pan Sum Kim, photographer: Gabriele Frauendorf
XIV *Illuminata*, Teatro delle Tese, Venice, 2006, photographer: Piero Tauro

AS GALINHAS

(The chickens)
InTransit Festival / Copa da Cultura Brasil
Haus der Kulturen der Welt, Berlin

Director: Takao Kusuno
Choreographer: Ismael Ivo
Dancer: Ismael Ivo
Actors: Renée Gumiel, Dorothy Lenner
Coordination: Eva Maria Helfrich
Technical director: Hermann Volkery
Producer: Haus der Kulturen der Welt, Berlin
Director: Bernd M. Scherer
Artistic director of music, dance and theater: Johannes Odenthal
Premiere: 1980, São Paulo
Restaging: May 27, 2006, Berlin
Duration: 60 minutes, no interval

XV

APOLLO & HYACINTH

Opera by Wolfgang Amadeus Mozart
Bode-Museum, Museums-Insel Berlin

Idea: Christoph Hagel
General artistic direction: Christoph Hagel
Choreographer: Ismael Ivo
Dancers: Ismael Ivo (Apollo), Bettina Bölke / Yui Kawaguchi (Melia), Oren Lazovski (Hyacinth), Jeroen Mosselmann (Oebalus), Christian Schwaan (Zephyrus)
Singers: Katharina Göres, Uta Buchheiser, Natalia Farbi, Barbara Ehwald, Andreas Taubert, Kaspar Kröner, Deniz Yilmaz, Thomas Volle, Ingo Witzke, Gero Bublitz
Museum guides: Kristian Jarmuschek and Thomas F. Hoffmann
Stage design: Marcel Kaskeline
Costumes: Barbara Naujok with Sarah Rolke
Lighting: Jens Krüger
Assistant choreographer: Franca Pagliassotto
Production management: Mark Böse
Producer: TOCC Concept GmbH Berlin, in cooperation with Visitor Services of Staatliche Museen zu Berlin
Music: Wolfgang Amadeus Mozart (composer) *KV 38 Apollo et Hyacinthus*
Live orchestra: Berliner Symphoniker
Conductor: Christoph Hagel
Premiere: November 18, 2006, Berlin
Duration: 75 minutes with prologue, no interval

BRIEF AN MEINEN KÖRPER

(Letter to My Body)
Wilhelma-Theater, Stuttgart
Diploma project of the students of the State University of Music and the Performing Arts

Texts: Heiner Müller and personal ads from the internet
Director: Ismael Ivo
Choreographer: Ismael Ivo
Actors: Anne Düe, Sina Ebell, Carolin Elsner, Claudia Grottke, Jan Krauter, Konstantin Lindhorst, Sophie Lochmann, Andreas Schmid, Martin Weigel, Maria Weyand
Stage design: Gregor Scholz
Costumes: Viola Hülswitt
Audio-visual design: Fender Schrade
Dramaturge: Peter C. von Salis
Producer: Wilhelma Theater Stuttgart
Artistic director: Volker Canaris
Premiere: December 16, 2006, Stuttgart
Duration: 60 minutes, no interval

DOUBLES

Theaterlabor Bielefeld

Choreographer: Ismael Ivo
Performance: Theaterlabor Bielefeld
Premiere: 2006, Bielefeld

2007 PREMIO DANZA & DANZA

Award for the artistic direction of the 4th International Dance Festival of the Biennale di Venezia, *Under Skin*

Receipt of award: March 26, 2006

MATTHÄUS-PASSION

by Johann Sebastian Bach
Novo Teatro Comunale di Bolzano

Music: Johann Sebastian Bach, BWV 244
Idea: Ismael Ivo
Choreographer: Ismael Ivo
Musical director: Claudio Astronio
Soloists: Ismael Ivo, Sarah Greter, Franca Pagliassotto, Karl Schreiner
Corps de ballet: Dance company Fabula Saltica: Vito Alfarano, Roberto Costa Augusto, Massimo Cerruti, Federica Iacuzzi, Paola Maran
Singers: Makoto Sakurada (Evangelist), Sergio Foresti (Jesus), Christian Hilz (Judas, Petrus, Pontius Pilatus), Susanne Ryden (soprano), Max Mauthe von Degerfeld (alto)
Stage design & costumes: Hans-Martin Scholder
Video: Daniel Kohl
Lighting: Ingo Bracke
Assistant choreographers: Franca Pagliassotto, Karl Schreiner
Producer: Nuovo Teatro Comunale di Bolzano in coproduction with Teatro Sociale di Rovigo
Artistic director: Manfred Schweigkofler
Conductor: Claudio Astronio
Choirmaster: Andi Ellecosta
Choir & orchestra: Bozen Baroque
Premiere: April 1, 2007, Bolzano
Duration: 150 minutes

BODY AND EROS

La Biennale Danza
5th International Festival of Contemporary Dance, Venice
La Biennale di Venezia, Venice

Director of dance section: Ismael Ivo
Managing director DMT: Renato Qualia
Artistic collaboration: Rino Achille de Pace
Program coordination: Rino Achille de Pace, Stefania Lora
Organization: Beppe Arone, Rosaria Crotone, Alfredo Zanolla, Andrea Bonadio
Office: Maya Romanelli
President of the Venice Biennale: Davide Croff
Board of directors: Massimo Cacciari
General director: Gaetano Guerci
Duration: June 14–30, 2007, Venice

LEONE D'ORO FOR THE LIFETIME ACHIEVEMENT OF PINA BAUSCH

eulogy by Ismael Ivo
La Biennale di Venezia, Venice

Award ceremony: May 30, 2007, Venice, Italy

MERCATO DEL CORPO: VENDITA ALL'ASTA DI DANZATORI E DANZE

(Market of the body: auction of dancers and dances)
Palazzo Contarini della Porta di Ferro, La Biennale di Venezia, Venice

Idea: Ismael Ivo
Artistic director: Ismael Ivo
MC: Rosanna Cancellieri
Dancers: Ismael Ivo, Abeer Will, Yui Kawaguchi, Twana Rhodes, Sebastian Corsten, Miguelete, Michela Lucenti
Corpo frutta: Giulia Sartor
Artistic collaboration: Marcel Kaskeline
Casting: Marcel Kaskeline
Producer: La Biennale di Venezia with CSS Teatro Stabile di Innovazione del Friuli Venezia Giulia
Premiere: June 16, 2007, Venice
Duration: varies according to the course of the auction

XVI

XV *Illuminata*, Teatro delle Tese, Venice, 2006, photographer: Piero Tauro
XVI *Mercato del Corpo*, Venice, 2007

GOLDENE JOHANN-STRAUSS-MEDAILLE

Award of the Vienna Tourist Board

Receipt of merit: October 17, 2007
Vienna City Hall

2008 RUNWAY

working title, project
ImPulsTanz – Vienna International Dance Festival
Parliament building, Vienna, planned

After several preparatory meetings, extensive research, and auditions, the project cannot be continued due to the loss of sponsors, and will therefore not be performed.

Concept, idea, realisation: Marina Abramović, Ismael Ivo, Riccardo Tisci
Performer: Marina Abramović, Ismael Ivo, Riccardo Tisci, Courtney Love
Head of production : Karl Regensburger
Artistic coordination: Marcel Kaskeline
Assistant choreographers: Franca Pagliasotto, Karl Schreiner
Producer: ImPulsTanz – Vienna International Dance Festival
Auditions: March 1 & 2, 2008
Paris
Premiere: cancelled

XVII 

XVIII 

DIE NACHT DES DIONYSOS

(The Night of Dionysos)
Wilhelma Theater, Stuttgart

Idea: Ismael Ivo
Choreographer: Ismael Ivo
Dancer: Ismael Ivo
Stage design & costumes: Marcel Kaskeline
Audio-visual design: Fender Schrade
Video editing: Katrin Jedon
Head of production : Marcel Kaskeline
Producer: Ismael Ivo Management in cooperation with the State University of Music and the Performing Arts Stuttgart
Music (recordings): Rufus Wainwright: *Agnus Dei*, Paulo Chagas: *Birthing*, *Men's Love*, *Scotchtape*, *Film*, Kronos Quartet: Dmitri Shostakovich *Quartet No. 8*, Les Tambours du Bronx: *Requiem*
Premiere: March 13, 2008
Stuttgart
Duration: 70 minutes, no interval

ACCADEMIA NAZIONALE DI DANZA

Rome

Visiting lecturer: Ismael Ivo
Artistic director AND: Margarita Parrilla
President AND: Bruno Borghi
Block seminar: May 2008

BEAUTY

La Biennale Danza
6th International Festival of Contemporary Dance, Venice
La Biennale di Venezia, Venice

Director of dance section: Ismael Ivo
Managing director DMT: Massimo Ongaro
Artistic collaboration: Rino Achille de Pace
Program coordination: Rino Achille de Pace, Stefania Lora
Organization: Beppe Arone, Rosaria Crotone, Alfredo Zanolla, Andrea Bonadio
Office: Maya Romanelli
President of the Venice Biennale: Paolo Baratta
Board of directors: Massimo Cacciari
General director: Andrea Del Mercato
Duration: June 14–29, 2008
Venice

SYMPOSIUM *BEAUTY*

Corderie Arsenale, La Biennale di Venezia, Venice

Duration: June 14, 2008
Venice

LEONE D'ORO FOR THE LIFETIME ACHIEVEMENT OF JIRÍ KYLIÁN

eulogy by Ismael Ivo
La Biennale di Venezia, Venice

Award ceremony: June 17, 2008
Venice

 XIX

2009–2017 PROJECT FOR PROFESSIONAL EXCELLENCE IN DANCE

founder, director and trademark owner
Arsenale della Danza / Biblioteca do Corpo®

2009–2012 as "Arsenale della Danza" at La Biennale di Venezia, Italy
2013–2017 as "Biblioteca do Corpo" at ImPulsTanz – Vienna International Dance Festival
in collaboration with Tanzwerk101, Zurich (director Frank Rutishauser); The Hong Kong Academy for Performing Arts, Hongkong, (director Anita Donaldson); SESC São Paulo (director Danilo Miranda); SEC Secretaria de Estado da Cultura São Paulo, Brazil

2009 ACCADEMIA NAZIONALE DI DANZA

Rome

Visiting lecturer: Ismael Ivo
Artistic director AND: Margarita Parrilla
President AND: Bruno Borghi

Block seminars: January, February, November, and December 2009

GRADO ZERO

La Biennale Danza
7th International Festival of Contemporary Dance, Venice
La Biennale di Venezia, Venice

Director of dance section: Ismael Ivo
Production management DMT: Massimo Ongaro
Artistic collaboration: Rino Achille de Pace
President of the Venice Biennale: Paolo Baratta
Board of director: Massimo Cacciari
General director: Andrea del Mercato
Duration: March 30 – June 30, 2009
Venice

APOTEOSI

final of the opening event of the World Swimming Championships
part of a double bill with Wayne McGregor
Stadio dei Marmi, Rome

Idea & artistic director: Margherita Parrilla
Choreographer: Ismael Ivo
Video installation: Fabrizio Plessi
Dance solos: Sarah Grether, Marta Lastowska, Seeta Patel, Karl Schreiner, Pal Szepesi
Special appearance: Ismael Ivo
Dance ensemble: 100 students of the Accademia Nazionale di Danza
Assistant choreographer: Franca Pagliassotto
Head of production: Accademia Nazionale di Danza, Rome
Producer: Ministry of Culture and Sports, Italy
Music: Fabio Frizzi & Scanner
Performance: July 18, 2009
Rome

XVII Ismael Ivo and Marina Abramovic, Berlin, 2003
XVIII *Die Nacht des Dionysos*, Wilhelma Theater, Stuttgart 2008
XIX Ismael Ivo, Biblioteca do Corpo, 2013, photographer: Marta Lamovsek

XX

ATLAS

Cava del Casino Visconti, Ornavasso VB, Italy

Idea: Maddalena Calderoni
Concept: Andrea Longhi
Choreographer: Ismael Ivo
Dancer: Ismael Ivo
Singer: Maddalena Calderoni Sopran
Props: Marcel Kaskeline
Lighting: Nevio Cavina
Artistic director: Maddalena Calderoni
Production management: Maddalena Calderone, Riccardo del Togno
Producer: Tones of the Stones Festival
Music: Giaccomo Rossini, R. Ciammarughi, Björk
Premiere: July 25, 2009, Ornavasso VB, Italy
Duration: 35 minutes

THE WASTE LAND

Arsenale della Danza / La Biennale di Venezia Danza
Teatro della Tese, Venice

Concept: Ismael Ivo
Choreographer: Ismael Ivo
Dancers: Arsenale della Danza: Deniz Aygor, Beniamino Borghi, Monika Born, Ivelice Brown, Alessio Calciolari, Sara Catellani, Veronica Cornacchini, Eleonora Folegnani, Valeria Galluccio, Alice Guazzotti, Roberta Maffioletti, Simona Miraglia, Tomoko Ogawa, Reiko Okada, Stefano Roveda
Stage design & costumes: Marcel Kaskeline
Assistant choreographers: Franca Pagliassotto, Karl Schreiner
Assistant producer: Joseph Candeloro
Technical director: Carlo Paglieri
Producer: La Biennale di Venezia in collaboration with Goethe Institut Mailand
Music: Igor Stravinsky (composer): *Le sacre du printemps*, Andreas Bick (composer): *The Waste Land*
Premiere: June 20, 2009, Venice
Duration: feature-length piece

ARSENALE DELLA DANZA

Project for Professional Excellence in Dance, second edition
La Biennale di Venezia, Venice

Duration: January 18 – May 30, 2010, Venice

ACCADEMIA NAZIONALE DI DANZA

Rome

Visiting lecturer: Ismael Ivo
Artistic director AND: Margarita Parrilla
Präsident AND: Bruno Borghi
Block seminars: April, May, and June 2010

CAPTURING EMOTIONS

La Biennale Danza
7th International Festival of Contemporary Dance, Venice
La Biennale di Venezia, Venice

Director of dance section: Ismael Ivo
Organization management DMT: Massimo Ongaro
Artistic collaboration: Rino Achille de Pace
Organization: Stefania Lora
President of the Biennale: Paolo Baratta
General director: Andrea Del Mercato

Duration: May 6 – June 12, 2010, Venice

SYMPOSIUM *CAPTURING EMOTIONS*

Ca' Giustinian, La Biennale di Venezia, Venice

Duration: May 27/28, June 3/4/9, 2010

XXI

LEONE D'ORO FOR THE LIFETIME ACHIEVEMENT OF WILLIAM FORSYTHE

eulogy by Ismael Ivo
La Biennale di Venezia, Venice

Award ceremony: June 5, 2010

EQUITAZIONI & APOTEOSI DELLO SPORT

contribution to the program BALLO SPORT (2 of 8 scenes)
Teatro Grande di Accademia Nazionale di Danza, Rome

Choreographer: Ismael Ivo
Director: Arturo Cirillo
Dancers: Student of the Accademia Nazionale di Danza
Producer: Accademia Nazionale di Danza
Artistic director: Margherita Parrilla
Music (recordings): Francesco Lanzillotta
Premiere: June 16, 2010, Rome

OXYGEN

Arsenale della Danza
Teatro alle Tese, La Biennale di Venezia, Venice

Concept: Ismael Ivo
Choreographer: Ismael Ivo
Dancers: Marta Lastowska (soloist); visiting dancers at Arsenale della Danza 2009: Ivelice Braun, Valeria Galluccio, Stefano Roveda; dancers at Arsenale della Danza 2010: Jessica Bova, Ivelice Brown, Antonino Casile, Ariella Maria Casu, Francesco Colaleo, Laura De Nicolao, Sandra Français, Valeria Galluccio, Jan Jamrich, Roberto Lazzari, Isabella Legato, Chiara Montalbani, Gioia Maria Morisco, Andrea Orlandi, Amandine Petit, Stella Picariello, Claudio Pisa, Stefano Roveda, Teresa Santos, Hema Sundari Vellaluru, Pavel Zhukov
Singer: Maddalena Calderoni
Stage design & costumes: Marcel Kaskeline
Lighting: Delio Baoduzzi
Makeup concept: Servullo Mendez Rey
Assistant choreographers: Franca Pagliassotto, Karl Schreiner
Assistant producer: Joseph Candeloro
Technical director: Carlo Pallieri
Producer: La Biennale di Venezia – Settore Danza in cooperation with Teatro Comunale Treviso, Italy
Music: Johann Sebastian Bach: *Erbarme dich, mein Gott*, Arvo Pärt: *Fratres*, John Adams: *Shaker Loops*, Maddalena Calderoni & Roberto Olzer: *My Breath*
Conductor: Maffeo Scarpis
Live music: Orchestra di Padova e del Veneto
Violin solo: Paolo Chiavacci

Premiere: May 26, 2010, Venice
Duration: 80 minutes

XXII

A FLOR DA PELE

Teatro Castro Alves, San Salvador da Bahia, Brazil
Balé Teatro Castro Alves

Concept: Ismael Ivo
Director & Choregraphy: Ismael Ivo
Artistic director: Jorge Vermelho
Dancers: Adriana Bamberg, Agnaldo Fonseca, Ajax Vianna, Alice Becker, Ãngela Bandeira, Dina Tourinho, Evandro Macedo, Gilberto Baia, Iracema Cersósimo, José Antônio Sampaio, Konstanze Mello, Lícia Morais, Lila Martins, Lilian Pereira, Luis Molina, Maria Ãngela Tochilovsky, Mônica Nascimento, Paullo Fonseca, Renivaldo Nascimento, Rita Brandi, Rosa Barreto, Solange Lucatelli, Sônia Gonçalves, Ticiana Garrido
Stage design: Marcel Kaskeline
Costumes: Miguel Carvalho
Lighting: Irma Vidal, Ismael Ivo, Jorge Vermelho
Dramaturge: Jorge Vermelho
Music selection: Ismael Ivo
Assistant choreographers: Anna Paula Drehmer, Dina Tourinho
Head of production : Ramonah Gayão
International production: Julia Gomes
Producer: BTCA Balé Teatro Castro Alves
Director BTCA: Jorge Vermelho
Artistic director TCA: Rose Lima
Music: Gustav Mahler, Johann Sebastian Bach, Dmitri Schostakovich, Andreas Bick, Thom Willems
Live music: Orquestra de Cordas do Neojiba
Conductor: Ricardo Castro
Premiere: October 29, 2010
Salvador da Bahia, Brazil
Duration: feature-length piece

XXIII

LE SACRE DU PRINTEMPS

Campania Festival Italia / Paestum Festival
Archeological Zone of Paestum – Cultural World Heritage, Paestum, Italy

Director & choreographer: Ismael Ivo
Dancers: Dance company Les Danseurs Napolitains: Mariella Celia, Francesco Colaleo, Maria Carmela d'Angelo, Gianluca d'Aniello, Valentina Schisa, Roberta de Berardinis, Luca Della Corte, Roberta de Rosa, Valeria Galluccio, Giuseppe Paolicelli, Claudio Pisa, Armando Rossi, Elisabetta Violante, Mirco Visconti
Stage design: Marcel Kaskeline
Costumes: Annamaria Morelli
Lighting: Marco Policastro
Assistant choreographers: Franca Pagliassotto, Karl Schreiner
Head of production: Mario Crasto di Stefano
Producer: Napoli Teatro Festival Italia in cooperation with Paestum Festival, Leuciana Festival and Pompei Festival
Premiere: July 16, 2010
Paestum, Italy
Duration: 65 minutes, no interval

PHÄDRA

based on the play by Jean Racine
Salzburg Festival / Burgtheater Wien

Director: Matthias Hartmann
Stage design & costumes: Johannes Schütz
Lighting: Peter Bandl
Dramaturge: Andreas Erdmann
Choreographer: Ismael Ivo
Actors: Paulus Manker (Theseus), Sunnyi Melles (Phädra), Philipp Hauß (Hippolytos), Sylvie Rohrer (Arikia), Hans-Michael Rehberg (Theramenes), Therese Affolter (Önone), Merle Wasmuth (Ismene), Brigitta Furgler (Panope)
Producer: Salzburg Festival in cooperation with Burgtheater Wien
Premiere: August 18, 2010
Salzburg
September 8, 2010
Vienna
Duration: 120 minutes, no interval

RUSALKA

Lyrical Fairy-tale in Three Acts by Antonín Dvořák
Opernhaus Zürich

Music: Antonín Dvořák
Libretto: Jaroslav Kvapil
Director: Matthias Hartmann
Choreographer: Ismael Ivo
Dancer: Adamo Dias
Singers: Krassimira Stoyanova (Rusalka), Piotr Beczala (prince), Alfred Muff (water goblin), Liliana Nikiteanu (witch Ježibaba), Michelle Breedt (the foreign princess), Miroslav Christoff (gamekeeper), Eva Liebau (kitchen boy), Tomasz Slawinski (hunter), Sandra Trattnigg (first wood sprite), Judith Schmid (second wood sprite), Katharina Peetz (third wood sprite)
Stage design: Karl-Ernst Herrmann, Martin Kinzlmaier
Costumes: Victoria Behr
Lighting: Martin Gebhardt
Producer: Opernhaus Zürich
Musical director: Vladimir Fedoseyev
Chorleiter: Jürg Hämmerli
Orchestra: Orchestra of Oper Zurich
Choir: Choir of Oper Zurich
Premiere: May 30, 2010
Zurich
Duration: 165 minutes, interval after 2nd act

ORDEM DO MERITO CULTURAL DO BRASIL

Brazilian Cross of Merit, presented by the President of the Republic
Theatro Municipal de Rio de Janeiro

President of the Republic: Luiz Inácio da Silva
Minister of Culture: Juca Ferreira
Award ceremony: December 2, 2010
Rio de Janeiro

2011 ARSENALE DELLA DANZA

Project for Professional Excellence in Dance, third edition
founder and artistic director
La Biennale di Venezia, Venice

Duration: January – May 2010
Venice

XX *Apoteosi dello Sport*, Stadio dei Marmi, Rome, 2009
XXI Golden Lion Award for Dance for William Forsythe with Ismael Ivo and Paolo Baratta, Venice, 2010
XXII Oxygen, Teatro alle Tese, Venice, 2010
XXIII *A Flor da Pele*, Teatro Castro Alves, Salvador da Bahia, 2011

MOVING THE CITY

Student project
The city as a performance space
Laboratorium Biennale Danza / Università Iuav di Venezi, Venice

Concept & project: Ismael Ivo
Choreographer: Ismael Ivo
Coordination IUAV: Cristina Barbiani
Performer: participants Arsenale della Danza, students of the University IUAV
Duration: February 13 – March 1, 2011
Venice

ACCADEMIA NAZIONALE DI DANZA

Rome, Italy

Guest lecturer: Ismael Ivo
Artistic director AND: Margarita Parrilla
President AND: Bruno Borghi
Block seminars: March, April, and June 2011

DAS BLINDE GESCHEHEN

(The Blind Happening)
Salzburger Festspiele / Burgtheater Wien

Text: Botho Strauß
Director: Matthias Hartmann
Actors: Regina Fritsch, Maria Happel, Sabine Haupt, Alexandra Henkel, Robert Hunger-Bühler, Michael König, Fabian Krüger, Dörte Lyssewski, Johann Adam Oest, Falk Rockstroh, Hermann Scheidleder, Adina Vetter, Moritz Vierboom, Christiane von Poelnitz, Bibiana Zeller
Stage design: Stéphane Laimé
Costumes: Victoria Behr
Music: Arno Waschk
Choreographer: Ismael Ivo
Lighting: Peter Bandl, Plinio Bachmann
Video: Hamid Reza Tavakoli
Producer: Burgtheater Wien
Artistic director: Matthias Hartmann
Premiere: March 11, 2011
Vienna
Duration: 120 minutes, no interval

SACRIFICIUM
VICTIMS OF MUSICAL SENSUALITY

Napoli Teatro Festival Italia
Real Albergo dei Poveri, Naples

Idea: Ismael Ivo
Director & choreographer: Ismael Ivo
Dance: Dance company Les Danseurs Napolitains: Valentina Schisa, Luca Della Corte, Roberta De Rosa, Giuseppe Paolicelli, Claudio Pisa, Armando Rossi, Elisabetta Violante
Stage & props: Marcel Kaskeline
Lighting: Stefano Stacchini
Assistant choreographers: Franca Pagliassotto / Il Gabbiano, Luca Della Corte
Artistic director of the Festival: Renato Qualia
Music (recordings): extracts from *Sacrificium* by Cecilia Bartoli, Alessandro Moreschi: *The Last Castrato*
Premiere: June 27, 2011
Naples
Duration: 20 minutes
double bill with *Le sacre du printemps*

PREMIO ROMA DANZA
CONCORSO INTERNAZIONALE COREOGRAFIA

(international choreography competition)

Artistic directors: Margherita Parrilla, Ismael Ivo
Sponsor: Academia Nationale di Danza, Rome
Duration: June 2 – 6, 2011
Rome

XXIV

BABILONIA – IL TERZO PARADISO

La Biennale di Venezia – Arsenale della Danza
Teatro Malibran, Venice

Concept: Ismael Ivo
Choreographer: Ismael Ivo
Dancers: Arsenale della Danza: Sara Angius, Emanuela Biazzi, Noelle Cotler, Patrick Cubbedge, Loretta D'Antuono, Flavio Arco-Verde, Laura De Nicolao, Roberta De Rosa, David Lagerqvist, Leonardo Magalhães Muniz, Ariadne Mikou, Giuseppe Paolicelli, Claudio Pisa, Andrea Rampazzo, Cristian Rebouças Da Silva, Lucas Ribeiro Saraiva, Armando Rossi, Claudia Sansone, Valentina Schisa, DuJuan Smart Jr., Pamela Tzeng, Felipe Vieira Vian, Elisabetta Violante, Chiara Vittadello, Anastasia Voronina
Stage design: Marcel Kaskeline
Costumes: Marcel Kaskeline
Lighting concept: Ismael Ivo
Lighting: Delio Baoduzzi
Assistant choreographers: Franca Pagliassotto, Luca Della Corte
Head of production : Andrea Buonadio
Production management: Marcel Kaskeline
Producer: La Biennale di Venezia in cooperation with SESC São Paulo and Fondazione Teatro La Fenice
Music (recording): Andreas Bick (composer), Denis Duarte, Antonio Caldara, Carl Heinrich Graun, Leonardo Leo, Riccardo Broschi, Geminiano Giacomelli
Premiere: May 11, 2011
Venice
Duration: feature-length piece

2012

ARSENALE DELLA DANZA

Project for Professional Excellence in Dance
Artistic director
La Biennale di Venezia, Venice

Duration: January 30 – June 9, 2012

AWAKENINGS

La Biennale Danza
8th International Festival of Contemporary Dance, Venice
La Biennale di Venezia, Venice

Director of dance section: Ismael Ivo
Assistant director: Rino Achille de Pace
President of the Venice Biennale: Paolo Baratta
Board of directors: Massimo Cacciari
General director: Andrea Del Mercato
Production manager dance: Massimo Ongaro
Duration: June 2 – 6, 2012
Venice

LEONE D'ORO FOR THE LIFETIME ACHIEVEMENT OF SYLVIE GUILLEM

eulogy by Ismael Ivo
La Biennale di Venezia, Venice

Award ceremony: June 20, 2012

LOGOS – DIALOGOS

Suite V for violincello by Johann Sebastian Bach
Teatro Alfa, São Paulo
SESC Vila Mariana, São Paulo

Idea: Luiz Felipe d'Avila, Ana Maria Diniz
Concept: Dimos Goudaroulis
Choreographer: Ismael Ivo
Dancer: Ismael Ivo
Live music & performance: Dimos Goudaroulis (baroque cello)
Lighting: Joyce Drummond
Producer: Sergio Ignacio
Music: Johann Sebastian Bach (composer): *Cello Suite No. V c-Moll BWV 1011*
Premiere: May 9, 2012
São Paulo
Duration: 30 minutes

BIBLIOTECA DEL CORPO

La Biennale di Venezia
Teatro alle Tese, Venice

Concept: Ismael Ivo
Choreography: Ismael Ivo
Dancers: Arsenale della Danza: Patrícia Bergantin, Giulia Brenzan, Elisa Capecchi, Marina Cervo, César Dias Cirqueira, Martina Fasano, Giampaolo Gobbi, Arianna Henry, Tunai Denise Jones, Malcolm Matheus, Stefano Marietta, Jane Alison McKinney, Ariadne Mikou, Antonio Nicastro, Guilherme Nunes, Giuseppe Paolicelli, Domenico Russo, Valentina Schisa, Paulo Sousa, Leilane Teles, Felipe Torquatto, Lucas Valente, Richard Villaverde, Elisabetta Violante, Miles Edward Yeung
Stage design: Marcel Kaskeline
Costumes: Gabriele Frauendorf
Lighting: Marco Policastro
Assistant choreographers: Franca Pagliasotto, Claudio Pisa
Pastoral care: Cléo Regina Miranda
Assistant producers: Andreas Bonadio Italy, Cena Cultural produções Brazil / Julia Gomes
Producer: La Biennale di Venezia in cooperation with Arteve, Veneto, Teatro Comunale Treviso, and SECS São Paulo
Music selection: Ismael Ivo
Premiere: June 8, 2012
Venice
Duration: 70 minutes, no interval
Restaging: 2018 São Paulo

XXV

BUTTERFLY EFFECT

Cava Minerali Industriali marble quarries, Verbania, Italy
open air

Concept: Ismael Ivo
Choreography: Ismael Ivo
Dancers: Compagnia Danza Fedora
Award: Laura de Nicolao, Roberta De Rosa, Ariadne Mikou, Valentina Schisa, Elisabetta Violante, Giuseppe Paolicelli, Matteo Cravone, Stefano Roveda, Fabrizio Varriale, Marco delle Foglie
Singer: Maddalena Calderoni (soprano)
Stage design & props: Marcel Kaskeline
Costumes: Gabriele Frauendorf
Lighting: Nevio Cavina
Live electronics and web links to weather stations in the Atlantic: Luigi Pizzaleo
Assistant choreographers: Franca Pagliassotto, Claudio Pisa
Producer: Atelier La Voce dell'Arte in cooperation with Arsenale della Danza / La Biennale di Venezia
Music: Luigi Pizzaleo (composer)
Live music: Lorenzo Gabriele (glass harp and bansuri) Paolo Pasqualin and Davide Merlino (percussion)
Premiere: July 7, 2012
Mergozzo de Verbania VB, Italy
Duration: feature-length piece

DAS LABYRINTH

The Magic Flute's Second Part
A grand heroic-comic opera in two acts
Residenzhof, Salzburger Festspiele 2012

Music: Peter von Winter
Libretto: Emanuel Schikaneder
Director: Alexandra Liedtke
Choreography: Ismael Ivo
Singers: Christof Fischesser (Sarastro), Julia Novikova (Queen of the Night), Malin Hartelius (Pamina), Michael Schade (Tamino), Thomas Tatzl (Papageno), Regula Mühlemann (Papagena), Anton Scharinger old (Papageno), Ute Gfrerer (old Papagena) and others
Stage design: Raimund Orfeo Voigt
Costumes: Susanne Bisovsky, Elisabeth Binder-Neururer
Lighting animation: Philipp Haupt
Lighting: Peter Bandl
Dramaturge: Christian Arseni
Producer: Salzburger Festspiele
Conductor: Ivor Bolton
Live music: Mozarteum Orchestra Salzburg, Salzburger Bachchor
Premiere: August 3, 2012
Salzburg
Duration: 180 minutes, interval after 1st act

FRANCIS BACON REENACTMENT

Odeon Theater, Vienna
SESC Pinheiros, São Paulo

Director: Johann Kresnik
Director & choreography: Ismael Ivo
Dancers: Ismael Ivo, Elisabetta Violante, Valentina Schisa, Giuseppe Paolicelli
Set design & costumes: Penelope Wehrli
Lighting: Stefan Pfeistlinger
Head of production: Marcel Kaskeline
Producer: Karl Regensburger, ImPulsTanz – Vienna International Dance Festival
co-producers: Plataforma Internacional Estado da Dança, Brazil / Associação Paulista dos Amigos da Arte / Secretaria de Estado da Cultura, Governo de São Paulo
Music: Paulo C. Chagas (composer)
Premiere: August 8, 2012
Vienna
Duration: 70 minutes, no interval

2013–2015 MAX-REINHARDT-SEMINAR

visiting professorship at the University of Music and Performing Arts Vienna
training of actors in physical theater

XXIV *Babilonia — Il Terzo Paradiso*, Teatro Malibran, Venice, 2011
XXV *Biblioteca del Corpo*, Teatro alle Tese, Venice, 2012

2013

MISHIMA
THE GARDEN OF FORBIDDEN DREAMS

Napoli Teatro Festival Italia
Museo Nazionale Ferroviario di Pietrarsa, Naples and
Belvedere of Villa Rufolo, Ravello, Italy (Ravello Festival)

Choreography: Ismael Ivo
Dancers: Compagnia Arabesque / Les Danseurs Napolitains: Gabriet Beddoes, Francesco Saverio Cavaliere, Roberta De Rosa, Martina Fasano, Giacomo Lugi, Giuseppe Paolicelli, Stefano Roveda, Marianna Russo, Valentina Schisa, Elisabetta Violante
Visiting soloist: Khãi Ngọc Vũ
Stage design: Marcel Kaskeline
Costumes: Gabriele Frauendorf
Lighting: Marco Policastro
Assistant choreographers: Valentina Schisa, Elisabetta Violante
Special thanks to: Tonino Di Ronza
Production management: Maria Teresa Scarpa
Executive producers: Compagnia Arabesque, director Annamaria Di Maio
Producers: Fondazione Campania Dei Festival, Napoli Teatro Festival Italia, Arb Dance Company, Compagnia Arabesque in cooperation with Accademia Di Belle Arti Di Napoli and Conservatorio Di Musica S. Pietro a Majella
Organization: Mario Crasto de Stefano, Mascia Pavon
Artistic director Naples: Luca de Fusco
Music (recordings): Arvo Pärt, Kodō, Eugène Ysaÿe, Reynaldo Hahn, Richard Wagner (composer)
Live music: Angela Luglio (voice), Federica Severino (violin)
Premiere: June 15, 2013 Naples
Duration: 70 minutes, no interval

BIBLIOTECA DO CORPO®

Project for Professional Excellence in Dance
ImPulsTanz – Vienna International Dance Festival

Artistic director: Ismael Ivo
Interaction & group dynamics: Cléo Regina Miranda
In cooperation with: ImPulsTanz – Vienna International Dance Festival SESC São Paulo, Brazil, and SEC – Secretaria de Estado de Cultura, São Paulo, Brazil
Duration: June 30 – August 13, 2013 Vienna, Austria

WINTERBALLET

contribution to *aufspiel 2013* / with students of the University of Music and Performing Arts, Palais Auersperg, Vienna

Choreography: Ismael Ivo
Performers: students of the Max-Reinhardt-Seminar, Vienna
Premiere: November 21, 2013 Vienna

NO SACRE

Biblioteca do Corpo®
ImPulsTanz – Vienna International Dance Festival;
SESC São Paulo; Secretaria de Estado da Cultura São Paulo
Odeon Theater, Vienna

Idea: Ismael Ivo
Choreography: Ismael Ivo
Dancers: Mary-Dora Bloch-Hansen (Canada), Hillary Bodin (USA), Elisabeth Hillinger (Austria), Agnieszka Jachym (Poland), Ilaria Orlandini (Italy), Romina Simone (Argentinia), Ruimin Li (China), Tavares Anádria Rassyne (Brazil), Bruna Pereira Barbosa (Brazil), Cláudia Stephany Chiamakaeze Nwabasili (Brazil), Hellen Karoline Mesquita Oliveira (Brazil), Malki Sanae Takeshita Hora Pinsag (Brazil), Valentina Schisa (Italy), Elisabetta Violante (Italy), Giovanfrancesco Giannini (Italy), Ka-chun Kenneth Hui (China), Wei Mao (China), André Rodolfo de Oliveira (Brazil), Luan Fonseca Torralbo Gimenez (Brazil), Roges Doglas Leal da Conceição (Brazil), Tiago Salezio Weber (Brazil), Vilson Domingo Junior (Brazil), Giuseppe Paolicello (Italy), Stefano Roveda (Italy)
Stage design: Marcel Kaskeline
Costumes: Annamaria Morelli
Lighting: Marco Policastro
Assistant dramaturge: Catherine Jennings
Assistant choreographers: Elisabetta Violante, Giuseppe Paolicelli, Stefano Roveda, Valentina Schisa
Producer: ImPulsTanz – Vienna International Dance Festival
Coproducers: SESC São Paulo, Brazil; Secretaria de Estado da Cultura / Governo de São Paulo, Brazil; in cooperation with Foundation Paestum festival / Mario Crasto di Stefano; L'Associazione Arabesque / Annamaria di Maio;
Head of production: Marcel Kaskeline (Vienna), Julia Gomes (São Paulo)
Biblioteca do Corpo® is supported by: SESC São Paulo; SP Escola de Teatro / Secretaria de Estado da Cultura, São Paulo; Governo do Estado São Paulo; ImPulsTanz – Vienna International Dance Festival
Music (recordings): Igor Stravinsky: *Le sacre du printemps*; Andreas Bick: *Fire and Frost Pattern*
Premiere: August 9, 2013 Vienna August 17, 2013 São Paulo
Duration: 75 minutes, no interval
Restaging: 2018, São Paulo

XXVI

2014

BIBLIOTECA DO CORPO®

Project for Professional Excellence in Dance
ImPulsTanz – Vienna International Dance Festival
SESC São Paulo

Artistic director: Ismael Ivo
Interaction & group dynamics: Cléo Regina Miranda
In cooperation with: ImPulsTanz – Vienna International Dance Festival, SESC São Paulo, and SEC – Secretaria de Estado de Cultura, São Paulo
Duration: July 6 – August 18, 2014 Vienna August 19 – 24, 2014 São Paulo

XXVII

ERENDIRA

Biblioteca do Corpo®
ImPulsTanz – Vienna International Dance Festival
Volkstheater, Vienna

Director: Ismael Ivo
Choreography: Ismael Ivo
Artistic concept: Ismael Ivo & Marcel Kaskeline
Actor: Cleide Queiroz
Visiting dancers: Valentina Schisa, Stefano Roveda
Dancers: Alexandre Cardoso, Alice Vasconcelos, Carolina Vilela Abrão, Claudia Sibille, Daniel Rolim, Emma Rehnberg, Elayna Waxse, Felipe Guedes, Kate Page, Letícia Mantovani, Levana Prud'homme, Li Tuokun, Lindsay Head, Lo Pan Chi Pansy, Lucas Borges, Mainá Santana, Mayra Maris, Olivia Coombs, Pablo Lozano, Robson Ledezma, Rony Leão, Thaís Diniz, Vagner Cruz, Vinicius Francês, Sarah Xiao, Jodie Judy Lu YingChu, Esl Kim
Stage design & props: Marcel Kaskeline
Costumes: Gabriele Frauendorf
Lighting: Marco Policastro
Interaction & group dynamics: Cléo Regina Miranda
Assistant choreographers: Valentina Schisa, Stefano Roveda
Assistant dramturge: Catherine Jennings
Producers: SESC São Paulo; ImPulsTanz – Vienna International Dance Festival; SEC – Secretaria de Estado da Cultura de São Paulo
Artistic production management: Marcel Kaskeline and Karl Regensburger
Organization BdC: Olivia Schellander
Production management: Cena Cultural produções / Julia Gomes for Brazil
Premiere: August 23, 2014
Duration: 75 minutes, no interval

PROJETO DE QUALIFICÃO EM DANÇA

Project for the promotion of dance in the State of São Paulo

Artistic curator: Ismael Ivo
Consultant: Cassia Navas
Head of artistic analysis: Valquiria Vieira
Coordination: Poiesis, FUNACC
Artistic coaching: Carolina Natal, Deise de Brito, Érika Moura, Fernando Machado, Igor Gasparini, Lara Pinheiro, Morgana Sousa, Ramiro Murillo, Robson Ferraz
Guest artist: Francisco Medeiros, Maria Thaís
Head of programing: Aldo Valentim
Producer: Government of the State of São Paulo
Minister of State for Culture: Marcel Mattos Arauja
Director art & education: Renata Bittencourt
Duration: September 4 – 28, 2014 and December 13 – 23, 2014
State of São Paulo

2015 PROJETO DE QUALIFICÃO EM DANÇA

Project for the promotion of dance in the State of São Paulo

Artistic curator: Ismael Ivo
Consultant: Cassia Navas
Head of artistic analysis: Valquiria Vieira
Coordination: Poiesis, FUNACC
Artistic coaching: Carolina Natal, Deise de Brito, Érika Moura, Fernando Machado, Igor Gasparini, Lara Pinheiro, Morgana Sousa, Ramiro Murillo, Robson Ferraz
Visiting artists: Francisco Medeiros, Maria Thaís
Head of programing: Aldo Valentim
Producer: Government of the State of São Paulo
Minister of State for Culture: Marcel Mattos Araújo
Director art & education: Renata Bittencourt
Duration: January 2 – October 30, 2015
State of São Paulo

THE 120 DAYS OF SODOM

after Marquis de Sade and Pier Paolo Pasolini
Volksbühne am Rosa-Luxemburg-Platz, Berlin

Director: Johann Kresnik
Libretto: Christoph Klimke
Choreography: Ismael Ivo
Actors: Roland Renner, Helmut Zhuber, Enrico Spohn, Hannes Fischer, Ismael Ivo, Inka Löwendorf, Ilse Ritter
Singer: Sarah Behrendt soprano
Dancers: Juan Corres Benito, Andrew Pan, Valentina Schisa, Sylvana Seddig, Sara Simeoni, Osvaldo Ventriglia, Elisabetta Violante, Yoshiko Waki
Supernumeraries: Günter Cornett, Helmut Gerlach, Wagner Peixoto Cordeiro, Arnd Raeder, Christian Schlemmer, Leandro Tamos
Actors (girl): Katia Fellin, Paula Knüpling, Ruby Mai Obermann, Estefania Rodriguez, Nathalie Seiß, Marlon Weber
Breakdance: David Eger, Lukas Steltner
Actors (children): Lucia Itxaso Kühlmorgen Unzalu
Stage design: Gottfried Helnwein
Costumes: Gottfried Helnwein
Lighting: Torsten König
Sound: Jörg Wilkendorf, Gabriel Anschütz
Dramaturge: Sabine Zielke, Christoph Klimke
Producer: Volksbühne am Rosa-Luxemburg-Platz
Artistic director: Frank Castrof
Music (recordings): Ali Helnwein composer
Premiere: May 27, 2015
Berlin
Duration: 100 minutes

BIBLIOTECA DO CORPO®

Project for Professional Excellence in Dance
ImPulsTanz – Vienna International Dance Festival
SESC São Paulo
SEC São Paulo

Artistic director: Ismael Ivo
Interaction & group dynamics: Cléo Regina Miranda
In cooperation with: ImPulsTanz – Vienna International Dance Festival, SESC São Paulo, and SEC – Secretaria de Estado de Cultura, São Paulo
Duration: July 17 – August 17, 2015
Vienna
August 20 – September 19, 2015
São Paulo

XXVIII

DAS TRIPAS ... CORAÇÃO

SESC Vila Mariana, São Paulo

Director: Ismael Ivo
Choreography: Ismael Ivo
Artistic concept: Ismael Ivo & Marcel Kaskeline
Visiting dancers: Valentina Schisa, Elisabetta Violante
Dancers: Chang Hu, Mengmeng He, Wai Shan Vivian Luk, May Jean Teo, Anahi Poty Corteletti Jiménez, Caio Rodrigues Moreira, Caroline Zito Siqueira, Lucas Oliva Ferreira, Mariana Miranda de Oliveira Silva, Mariana Yoshida, Milton César Fernandes Oliveira Junior, Rodrigo Rivera, Vitor dos Santos Rodrigues, Willian Silva
Stage design: Marcel Kaskeline
Costumes: Marcel Kaskeline
Lighting: Andre Boll
Assistant choreographers: Valentina Schisa, Elisabetta Violante
Interaction & group dynamics: Cléo Regina Miranda
Head of production: Cena Cultural Produções / Julia Gomes
Producer: SESC São Paulo
Director SESC: Danilo Miranda
Premiere: September 5, 2015
São Paulo, Brazil
Duration: 85 minutes, no interval
Restaging: 2017, Balé da Cidade de São Paulo / Theatro Municipal São Paulo, Brazil

2016 PROJETO DE QUALIFICÃO EM DANÇA

Project for the promotion of dance in the State of São Paulo

Artistic curator: Ismael Ivo
Consultant: Cassia Navas
Head of artistic analysis: Valquiria Vieira
Coordination: Poiesis, FUNACC
Head of programing: Aldo Valentim
Producer: Government of the State of São Paulo
Duration: February 1 – September 31, 2016
State of São Paulo

XXVI *No Sacre*, Odeon Theater, Wien, 2013, photographer: Karolina Miernik
XXVII *Erendira*, Volkstheater, Wien, photographer: Gabriela Frauendorf
XXVIII *Das Tripas ... Corção*, São Paulo, 2015, photographer: Clarissa Lambert

BIBLIOTECA DO CORPO®

Project for Professional Excellence in Dance
ImPulsTanz – Vienna International Dance Festival
Tanzwerk101, Zurich

Artistic director: Ismael Ivo
In cooperation with: ImPulsTanz – Vienna International Dance Festival (artistic director Karl Regensburger); Tanzwerk101, Zurich (director Frank Rutishauser)
With support from: The Hong Kong Academy for Performing Arts
Duration: July 8–16, 2016 Zurich
July 17–August 15, 2016 Vienna

BLACK OUT

Biblioteca do Corpo®
ImPulsTanz – Vienna International Dance Festival
Arsenal

Concept: Ismael Ivo
Choreography: Ismael Ivo in cooperation with the dancers
Dancers: Group Biblioteca do Corpo® 2016
Visiting dancers: Elisabetta Violante, Valentina Schisa
Stage design: Marcel Kaskeline
Assistant choreographers: Valentina Schisa, Elisabetta Violante
Dramaturge: Catherine Jennings
Producer: ImPulsTanz – Vienna International Dance Festival (artistic director Karl Regensburger)
In cooperation with: Tanzwerk101, Zurich (director Frank Rutishauser)
With support from: The Hong Kong Academy for Performing Arts
Music (recordings): *The songs and sounds of the humpback whale* recorded by Lon Brocklehurst, Apocalyptica with the MDR-Sinfonieorchester: *Wagner Reloaded*, David Bowie: *Blackstar*
Premiere: August 13, 2016 Vienna
Duration: 70 minutes, no interval

XXIX

DISCORDABLE BACH

ImPulsTanz – Vienna International Dance Festival
Volkstheater

Concept: Dimos Goudaroulis
Choreography: Ismael Ivo
Dancer: Ismael Ivo
Live-performance: Dimos Goudaroulis (baroque cello)
Stage design: Marcel Kaskeline
Lighting: Marco Policastro
Music: Johann Sebastian Bach: *Cello Suite No. 2 in D Minor*, *Cello Suite No. 5 D Minor*; improvisations by Dimos Goudaroulis; variations on *La Folia*
Premiere: August 6, 2016 Vienna
Duration: 60 minutes, no interval

OXYGEN

Anacã Companhia de Dança, São Paulo
ImPulsTanz – Vienna International Dance Festival, Vienna
Arsenal
Auditorio Oscar Niemeyer, Iberapuera, São Paulo

Choreography: Ismael Ivo
Concept: Ismael Ivo & Marcel Kaskeline
Solo dancers: Elisabetta Violante, Valentina Schisa, Fernanda Bueno
Dancers: Anacã Companhia de Dança: Alessandro Silva, Carlos Veloso, Daniela Correa, Jonatha Martins, Kamila Oliveira, Karine Miranda, Letícia Alfenas, Lucas Martinelli, Rafael Luz, Rafael Trevisan, Thaynara Gomes
Stage design: Marcel Kaskeline
Video design: Marcel Kaskeline
Costumes: Angélica Chaves
Lighting: Marcel Kaskeline
Assistant choreographers: Elisabetta Violante, Valentina Schisa
Producer: ImPulsTanz – Vienna International Dance Festival (artistic director Karl Regensburger); Tanzwerk101, Zurich (director Frank Rutishauser); Anacã Companhia de Dança (director Ana Maria Diniz)
Premiere: August 12, 2016 Vienna
Revised version: Anacã Companhia de Dança, October 21, 2017 São Paulo

2016–2017 INTERWEAVING PERFORMANCE CULTURES

artist-in-Residence
Fellow at International Research Center for Advanced Studies
Freie Universität Berlin

Director: Erika Fischer-Lichte
Co-director: Gabriele Brandstetter
Senior advisor: Christel Weiler
Research associate: Stefan Donath
Duration: November 1, 2016–February 28, 2017

2017–2020 BALÉ DA CIDADE DE SÃO PAULO

director of dance company
at Theatro Municipal de São Paulo

Artistic director: Ismael Ivo
Governor of São Paulo: João Doria
Minister of State for Culture: André Sturm
Artistic director of the theatre: Cleber Papa

In December 2016, São Paulo's Governor-designate João Doria and Secretary of State for Culture-designate André Sturm offered Ismael Ivo the directorship of the Balé da Cidade dance company at the Theatro Municipal.

Assumption of office: February 1, 2017

2017 BIBLIOTECA DO CORPO®

Program for Professional Excellence in Dance
ImPulsTanz – Vienna International Dance Festival
Tanzwerk101, Zurich

Artistic director: Ismael Ivo
In cooperation with ImPulsTanz – Vienna International Dance Festival (artistic director Karl Regensburger); Tanzwerk101, Zurich (director Frank Rutishauser)
With support from: Anacã Companhia de Dança, São Paulo (director Ana Maria Diniz)
Duration: July 8–14, 2016 Zurich
July 16–August 13, 2016 Vienna

RISCO
Balé da Cidade de São Paulo / Theatro Municipal, São Paulo

Concept: Ismael Ivo
Artistic director: Ismael Ivo
Director: Sergio Ferrara
Dancers: Ana Beatriz Nunes, Ariany Dâmaso, Bruno Gregório, Bruno Rodrigues, Camila Ribeiro, Cleber Fantinatti, Erika Ishimaru, Fabiana Ikehara, Fabio Pinheiro, Fernanda Bueno, Hamilton Felix, Harrison Gavlar, Igor Vieira, Isabela Maylart, Juruam Miguez, Joaquim Tomé, Julie Endo, Leonardo Hoehne Polato, Lucas Axel, Luiz Crepaldi, Luiz Oliveira, Manuel Gomes, Marcel Anselmé, Marcos Novais, Marina Giunti, Marisa Bucoff, Rebeca Ferreira, Renata Bardazzi, Reneé Weinstrof, Thaís França, Victor Hugo Vila Nova, Victoria Oggiam, Vivian Navega Dias, Yasser Diaz
Stage design: Marcel Kaskeline
Film & video: Marcel Kaskeline
Costumes: Archiv Balé da Cidade, curated by Juliana Andrade
Lighting: Sueli Matsuzaki
Video camera & editing: Joachim Tomé
Assistant choreographers: Fernando Machado, Carolina Franco, Roberta Botto
Director Balé da Cidade: Ismael Ivo
Artistic director of drama: Cleber Papa
Music: Gustav Holst: *The Planets op. 32, Mars*, Ottorino Respighi: *Festas Romanas*
Live music: Orquestra Sinfônica Municipal de São Paulo
Conductor: Luis Gustavo Petri
Premiere: March 24, 2017 São Paulo
Duration: 35 minutes (part of a double bill)

WINTERREISE
Balé da Cidade de São Paulo / Theatro Municipal, São Paulo

Idea & concept: Ismael Ivo & Marcel Kaskeline
Director & choreography: Ismael Ivo
Dancers: Fabio Pinheiro, Reneé Weinstrof, Ariany Damaso Vidal, Renata Alves Bardazzi, Victoria Oggiam, Marina Giunti, Leonardo Hoehne Polato, Harrison Gavlar, Cleber Fantinatti, Manuel Gomes
Dancers (understudies): Hamilton Felix, Receca Ferreira, Isabela Maylart, Ana Beatriz Nunes, Erika Ishimaru, Julie Endo, Yasser Diaz, Bruno Gregório, Luiz Crepaldi, Victor Hugo Vila Nova
Stage design: Marcel Kaskeline
Costumes. Juliana Andrade
Lighting: Valeria Lovato
Assistant choreographer: Fernando Machado, Carolina Franco, Roberta Botta
Director Balé da Cidade: Ismael Ivo
Artistic director of drama: Cleber Papa
Live music: Franz Schubert: *Winterreise, op. 89*, Vinícius Atique (baritone), Anderson Brenner (piano)
Premiere: May 15, 2017 São Paulo
Duration: 70 minutes

PROJETO DE QUALIFICÃO EM DANÇA
Project for the promotion of dance in the State of São Paulo

Artistic curator: Ismael Ivo
Consultant: Cassia Navas
Head of artistic analysis: Valquiria Vieira
Coordination: Poiesis, FUNACC
Head of programing: Aldo Valentim
Producer: Government of the State of São Paulo
Duration: April and August–September 2018 State of São Paulo

TRÓFEU RAÇA NEGRA

The award is a Brazilian award that has been given annually since 2004 to individuals and groups who have achieved social and economic improvements for Afro-Brazilians. It is organized by the NGO Afrobras.

Award ceremony: November 23, 2017 São Paulo

2018 NUCLEO ARTISTICO DO THEATRO MUNICIPAL DE SÃO PAULO
joint artistic director of the Theatro Municipal, São Paulo

Artistic directors: André Sturm, Roberto Minczuk, Ismael Ivo, Carlos Gradim, Tatyana Rubim, Renata Araújo

MEDALHA DA CIDADE DE SÃO PAULO
cross of Honor of the City of São Paulo

Award ceremony: January 30, 2018 Theatro Municipal, São Paulo

UM JEITO DE CORPO
Balé da Cidade de São Paulo / Theatro Municipal, São Paulo

Concept: Ismael Ivo
Artistic director: Ismael Ivo
Choreographer: Morena Nascimento
Dancers: Balé da Cidade de São Paulo: Ana Beatriz Nunes, Ariany Dâmaso, Bruno Gregório, Bruno Rodrigues, Camila Ribeiro, Cleber Fantinatti, Erika Ishimaru, Fabiana Ikehara, Fabio Pinheiro, Fernanda Bueno, Hamilton Felix, Harrison Gavlar, Igor Vieira, Isabela Maylart, Jaruam Miguez, Joaquim Tomé, Julie Endo, Leonardo Hoehne Polato, Lucas Axel, Luiz Crepaldi, Luiz Oliveira, Manuel Gomes, Marcel Anselmé, Marcos Novais, Marina Giunti, Marisa Bucoff, Rebeca Ferreira, Renata Bardazzi, Reneé Weinstrof, Thaís França, Victor Hugo Vila Nova, Victoria Oggiam, Vivian Navega Dias, Yasser Diaz
Stage design: Marcel Kaskeline
Costumes: Isadora Gallas
Lighting: Aline Santin
Makeup: Luiz Parisi,
Dramaturge: Vadim Nikitin
Consultant: José Miguel Wisnik
Assistant choreographers: Fernando Machado, Carolina Franco, Roberta Botto
Producer: Theatro Municipal de São Paulo
Director Balé da Cidade: Ismael Ivo
Artistic director of drama: Nucleo Artistico do Theatro: André Sturm, Roberto Minczuk, Ismael Ivo, Carlos Gradim, Tatyana Rubim, Renata Araújo
Music (recordings): Caetano Veloso (composer & voice)
Musical director: Cacá Machado
Premiere: March 16, 2018 São Paulo
Duration: 60 minutes, no interval

PRAÇA DAS ARTES
move to the new, definitive headquarters of the Balé da Cidade
Av. São João, 281—Centro—São Paulo

With the political support of Governor João Doria, Ismael Ivo manages to secure the completion of the planned premises in the Praça das Artes building complex on Vale de Anhangabaú in the center of São Paulo. After 50 years in provisional premises, the Balé da Cidade will be given its definitive headquarters in September 2018.

Moving in: March 31, 2018
Official handover: September 2018

PROJETO DE QUALIFICÃO EM DANÇA
project for the promotion of dance in the State of São Paulo

Artistic curator: Ismael Ivo
Consultant: Cassia Navas
Head of artistic analysis: Valquiria Vieira
Assistant curator: Andrea Thomioka
Coordination: Poiesis, FUNACC
Head of programing: Aldo Valentim
Producer: Government of the State of São Paulo
Duration: April–September 2018 State of São Paulo

ORDEM DO MÉRITO CÍVICO CULTURAL AFRO BRASILEIRO

The Afro-Brazilian Medal for Civic and Cultural Merit is awarded by the private, non-profit educational institution Faculdade Zumbi dos Palmares to personalities who have contributed directly or indirectly to the moral, socio-economic, cultural and educational advancement of Black Brazilians.

Award ceremony: May 14, 2018 Auditório Simón Bolívar im Memorial da América Latina, São Paulo

EPÍLOGO – UM ÍCONE

part of the dance evening *Danças e Quimeras – homenagem a David Bowie*
Balé da Cidade de São Paulo / Theatro Municipal, São Paulo

Concept & artistic director *Danças e Quimeras*: Ismael Ivo
Choreography *Epílogo*: Ismael Ivo
Soloist: Uátila Coutinho
Dancers: Alyne Mach, Fabio Pinheiro, Grécia Catarina, Julie Endo, Leonardo Muniz, Marisa Bucof
Costumes: Juliana Andrade
Lighting: Sueli Matsuzaki
Sound: Leandro Lima
Design throne: Roberto Mainieri
Assistant choreographers: Fernando Machado, Carolina Franco, Roberta Botta
Music (recording): David Bowie
Premiere: July 6, 2018
São Paulo, Brazil
Duration: 10 minutes

HARPIAS

video production
Cataratas do Iguaçu Iguazú waterfalls, Brazil

Concept: Fábio Caramuru
Choreographer: Ismael Ivo
Dancer: Ismael Ivo
Live music: Fábio Caramuru composer & piano
Time of shooting: July 2018
Foz do Iguaçu, Brazil

A SAGRAÇÃO DA PRIMAVERA

(Le sacre du printemps)
Balé da Cidade de São Paulo / Theatro Municipal de São Paulo

Idea & concept: Ismael Ivo & Marcel Kaskeline
Choreographer: Ismael Ivo
Dancers: Balé da Cidade de São Paulo: Alyne Mach, Ana Beatriz Nunes, Antônio Adilson Jr., Ariany Dâmaso, Bruno Rodrigues, Camila Ribeiro, Carolina Martinelli, Cleber Fantinatti, Erika Ishimaru, Fabiana Ikehara, Fabio Pinheiro, Fernanda Bueno, Grécia Catarina, Harrison Gavlar, Igor Vieira, Isabela Maylart, Jessica Fadul, Leonardo Hoehne Polato, Leonardo Muniz, Luiz Crepaldi, Luiz Oliveira, Manuel Gomes, Marcel Anselmé, Márico Filho, Marina Giunti, Renata Bardazzi, Reneé Weinstrof, Uátila Coutinho, Victor Hugo Vila Nova, Victoria Oggiam, Yasser Diaz
Dance residency: Lincoln Sampaio, Micaella Rodrigues
Stage design: Marcel Kaskeline
Costumes: Gabriele Frauendorf
Lighting: Marisa Bentivegna
Assistant choreographer: Elisabette Violante
Artistic coordination: Fernando Machado,
Head of rehearsals: Carolina Franco, Roberta Botta
Production: Theatro Municipal de São Paulo
Director Balé da Cidade: Ismael Ivo
Artistic directors of drama: Nucleo Artistico do Theatro: André Sturm, Roberto Minczuk, Ismael Ivo, Carlos Gradim, Tatyana Rubim, Renata Araújo
Music (recording): Andreas Bick: *Fire and Frost Pattern*,
Live music: Igor Stravinsky: *Le sacre du printemps*, Orquestra Sinfônica Municipal
Conductor: Roberto Minczuk
Premiere: September 15, 2018
São Paulo
Duration: 60 minutes

ASAS PARA VOLAR
ILLUMINATIONS

an interaction in dance and music, in response to the exhibition *Histórias Afro-Atlânticas*
Instituto Tomie Ohtake, São Paulo
12 Choreografies, of these 3 by Ismael Ivo

Asas para Volar is a format created by Ismael Ivo whereby dancers from Balé da Cidade de São Paulo create choreography for other dancers from the company.

Concept & artistic directors: Ismael Ivo & Rodolfo Stroeter
Choreographers: Ismael Ivo and members of the Balé da Cidade: Igor Vieira, Fabio Pinheiro, Luiz Crepaldi, Ariany Dâmaso, Raymundo Costa, Manuel Gomes, Fernanda Bueno, Marisa Bucoff, Mariama Camara
Dancers: Balé da Cidade de São Paulo
Producer: Balé da Cidade de São Paulo in cooperation with Instituto Tomie Ohtake
Singer: Nduduzo Siba
Music: Rodolfo Stroeter, Lelo Nazario, Celine Rudolph, Humberto Maracanã, Folclore Cubano

DELÍRIO DE UMA INFÂNCIA

Fragment in memorian Takao Kusuno and Felicia Ogawa

Choreographer: Ismael Ivo
Dancer: Uátila Coutinho
Music: Lambarena: *Bach to Africa*
Duration: 16 minutes

GATE OF NO RETURN

Choreographer: Ismael Ivo
Dancers: Ariany Dâmaso, Fabio Pinheiro, Fernanda Bueno, Igor Vieira, Luiz Crepaldi, Manuel Gomes, Marisa Bucoff
Music: Espreita
Rodolfo Stroeter, Lelo Nazario
Duration: 10 minutes

LITANIAS DE SATÃ

Choreographer: Ismael Ivo
Dancer: Fernanda Bueno
Text: Federico García Lorca

Performances: October 20–21, 2018
São Paulo
Duration: 100 minutes

PRÊMIO MESTRE DA CRIATIVIDADE

Organized by Catraca Livre Portal e Comunicacao LTDA
São Paulo

Award ceremony: November 7, 2018
(Black Awareness Day)

Since 2019 CONSELHO ESTADUAL DE CULTURA E ECONOMIA CRIATIVA DO ESTADO DE SÃO PAULO

(State Council for Culture and Creative Economy of the State of São Paulo)

President: Eduardo Saron
(director of Itaú Cultural)
Vice presidents: Fernanda Feitosa & Ismael Ivo
Governor of São Paulo: João Doria
Official announcement: April 15, 2019

2019 LAUNCH OF *50 ANOS DA TV CULTURA*

Theatro Municipal, São Paulo

Ceremony: June 11, 2019
São Paulo
Duration: 2 minutes 30 seconds

XXX

A BIBLIOTECA DE BABEL
based on the story of the same name by Jorge Luis Borges
Balé da Cidade de São Paulo / Theatro Municipal, São Paulo

Choreographer: Ismael Ivo
Idea & concept: Ismael Ivo & Marcel Kaskeline
Dancers: Ana Beatriz Nunes, Ariany Dâmaso, Bruno Gregório, Bruno Rodrigues, Camila Ribeiro, Cleber Fantinatti, Erika Ishimaru, Fabiana Ikehara, Fabio Pinheiro, Fernanda Bueno, Hamilton Felix, Harrison Gavlar, Igor Vieira, Isabela Maylart, Juruam Miguez, Joaquim Tomé, Julie Endo, Leonardo Hoehne Polato, Lucas Axel, Luiz Crepaldi, Luiz Oliveira, Manuel Gomes, Marcel Anselmé, Marcos Novais, Marina Giunti, Marisa Bucoff, Rebeca Ferreira, Renata Bardazzi, Reneé Weinstrof, Thaís França, Victor Hugo Vila Nova, Victoria Oggiam, Vivian Navega Dias, Yasser Diaz
Stage design: Marcel Kaskeline
Costumes: Gabriele Frauendorf
Lighting: Marco Policastro
Assistant choreographers: Valentina Schisa, Elisabetta Violante
Artistic coordination: Fernando Machado
Head of rehearsals: Carolina Franco, Roberta Botto
Producer: Theatro Municipal de São Paulo
Director Balé da Cidade: Ismael Ivo
Artistic director of theater: Hugo Possolo

Music (recordings): Ivan Fedele Canone: *Infinito 2.2*, György Ligeti: *Jupiter and Beyond*, Ivan Fedele Canone: *Infinito 1.2*, Kodō and Yosuke Yamashita: *Monochrome*, Steve Reich: *Drumming*, Kodō & Leonardo Eto: *Zoku*
Premiere: June 14, 2019
São Paulo
Duration: 75 minutes

AUSTRIAN CROSS OF HONOR FOR SCIENCE AND ART

Award ceremony: July 23, 2019
Burgtheater, Vienna

IN MEMORIAM JOHANN KRESNIK
solo
artistic contribution to the memorial service for Johann Kresnik
Kulturni dom, Pliberk / Bleiburg, Austria

Memorial service: October 5, 2019
Pliberk / Bleiburg, Austria
Duration: 15 minutes

INSTITUTO ARTXS
establishment of institute
establishment of Organização Social OS
(umbrella body for cultural and social institutions)

Founding Members: Ismael Ivo (executive director), Fabio Mazzoni (Fabio Roberto Elias), Willian Pereira Alexandrino, Fernando de Brito Macchado, Pagú (Kleber de Barros Dias)

The Instituto Artxs was meant to apply as sponsor for the management of the planned SP Escola de Dança.

Date of incorporation: November 18, 2019
São Paulo

2020 SP ESCOLA DE DANÇA
founding initiative and development of project
initiative for the establishment of a training center for choreographic arts

With the political support of Governor João Doria, Ismael Ivo plans to establish a reference center for dance education in Brazil, modeled after the Juilliard School in New York and based on the method and structure of the proven SP Escola de Teatro, along with an affiliated junior dance company, Companhia Jovem de Dança do Estado de São Paulo. The sponsor is to be the State of São Paulo.

Official presentation of the project to Governor of the State of São Paulo, João Doria: February 3, 2020
Palácio dos Bandeirantes, São Paulo

DANÇANDO PALAVRAS
video series
Balé da Cidade de São Paulo / Theatro Municipal, São Paulo

Artistic director: Ismael Ivo
Choreography & dance: Balé da Cidade de São Paulo

Ismael Ivo's contract as director of the Balé da Cidade de Sao Paulo is not renewed.

End of tenure: end of 2020

2021 TV CULTURA
artistic consultant

Announcement: November 2020
Start of contract: beginning of 2021

DIED ON APRIL 8, 2021, 20:10 UHR, IN SÃO PAULO
Hospital Sirio Libense, Bela Vista, São Paulo

ÖSTERREICHISCHER KUNSTPREIS FÜR DARSTELLENDE KUNST
awarded to Karl Regensburger and to Ismael Ivo in memoriam

Announcement: August 5, 2021
Vienna

TRÓFEU RAÇA NEGRA
receipt of award in memoriam

Award ceremony: November 21, 2021
São Paulo

SÃO PAULO ESCOLA DE DANÇA ISMAEL IVO
initiator
establishment of training center for choreographic arts
Júlio Prestes Cultural Complex; São Paulo

The government of the State of São Paulo under Governor João Doria decides to establish the SP Escola de Dança Ismael Ivo. The public tender is won by Associação Pró-Dança, and the new training center is headed by dancer Inês Bogéa. Secretary of Culture and Creative Industries Sérgio Sá Leitão writes: "It will be the most important dance school in Latin America."

Announcement: December 30, 2021

XXX *Biblioteca de Babel*, São Paulo, 2019

Image credits

Clara Crocodilo, Jazzfest Berlin (1982)

53 97 113

Studio photographs, TanzTangente, Berlin (1982)

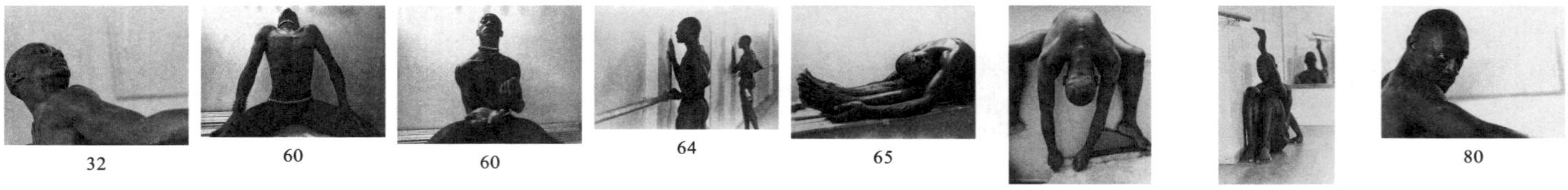

32 60 60 64 65 68 73 80

80

Bowery, New York (1983)

89 89 89

Ritual of a Body in Moon, rehearsal, Berlin (1983)

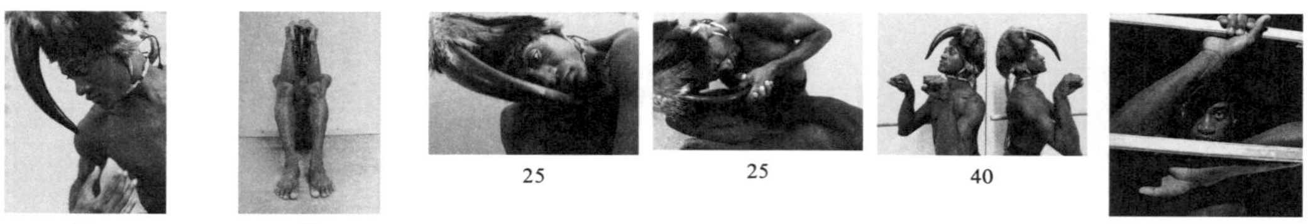

24 25 25 25 40 100

Berlin (1984)

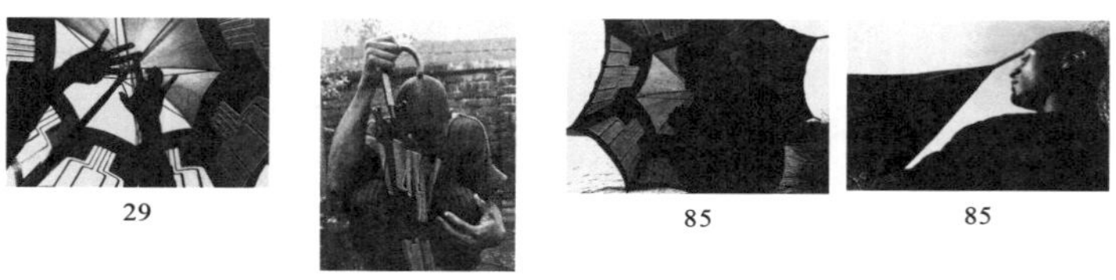

29 84 85 85

Ritual of a Body in Moon, Schaubühne am Lehniner Platz, Berlin (October 1984)

13 13 32 40 41 56 56 56

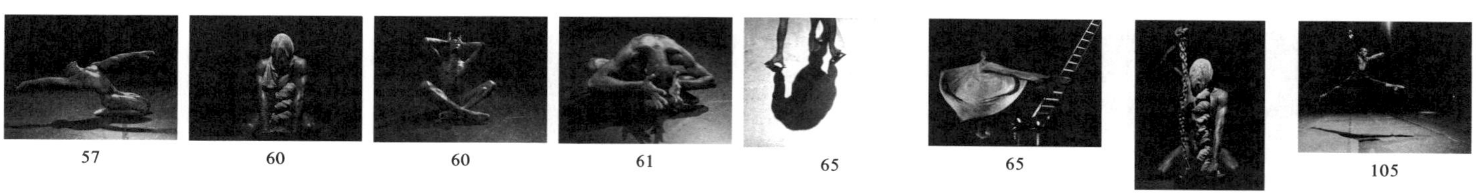

57 60 60 61 65 65 76 105

105 113

Café Orlin, New York (1984)

65

Phoenix, rehearsal at Schaubühne am Lehniner Platz, Berlin (September – November 1985)

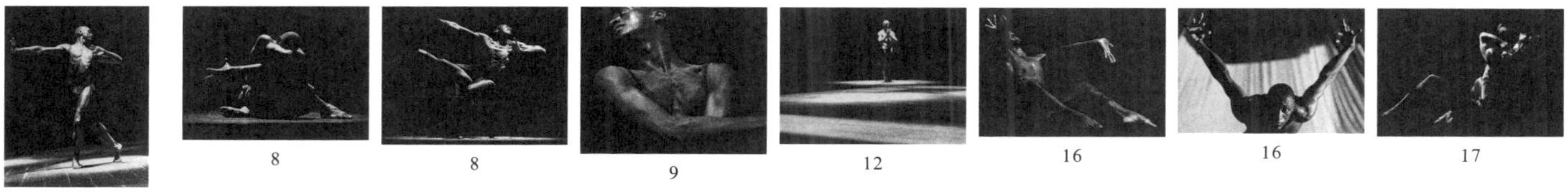

5 8 8 9 12 16 16 17

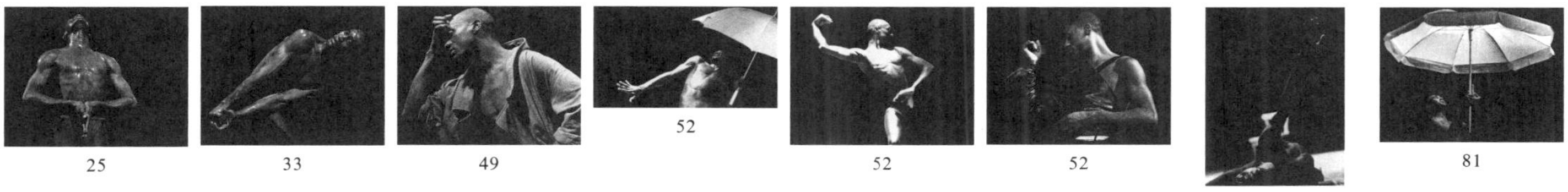

25 33 49 52 52 52 53 81

81 88 93 104 105

Studio photographs, Berlin (November 1985)

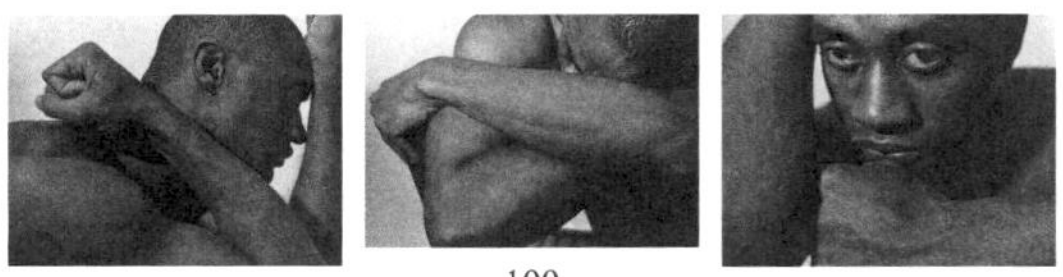

9 100 108

Phoenix, Schaubühne am Lehniner Platz, Berlin (1985)

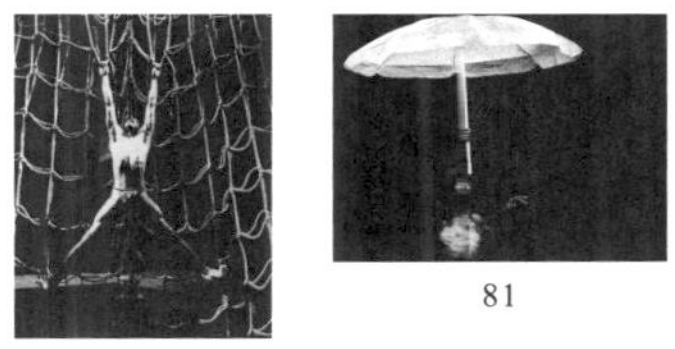

69 81

Delirium of a Childhood, studio photographs, Berlin (December 13, 1988)

33 101 109

Studio photographs, Berlin (1988)

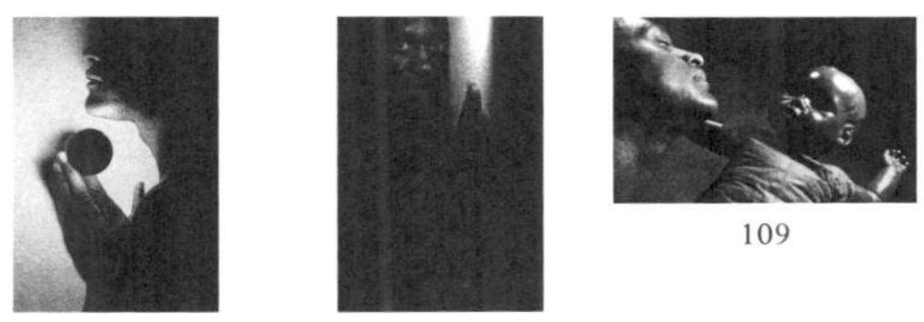

17 45 109

Studio photographs, Berlin (January 28, 1989)

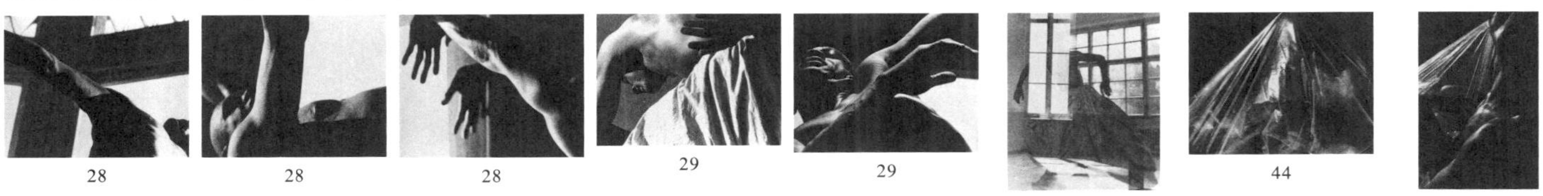

28 28 28 29 29 36 44 45

45 57 96

Berlin (1991)

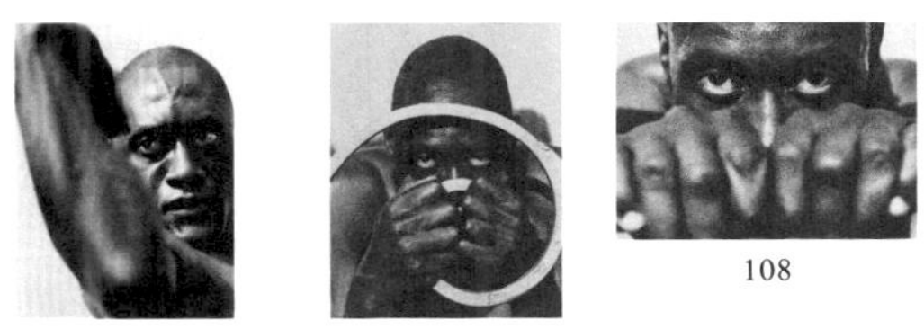

20 92 108

ANNO WILMS photographed Ismael Ivo in his first performance in 1982 at the Jazzfest Berlin in the Philharmonie. This resulted in an ongoing congenial collaboration during rehearsals, on stage, and in photo sessions dedicated to the dialogue between photographer and performer. The photo series for the productions *Ritual of a Body in Moon, Phoenix, Under Skin,* and *Delirium of a Childhood* date from 1982 to 1991.

Francis Bacon, Theaterhaus Stuttgart (1993)

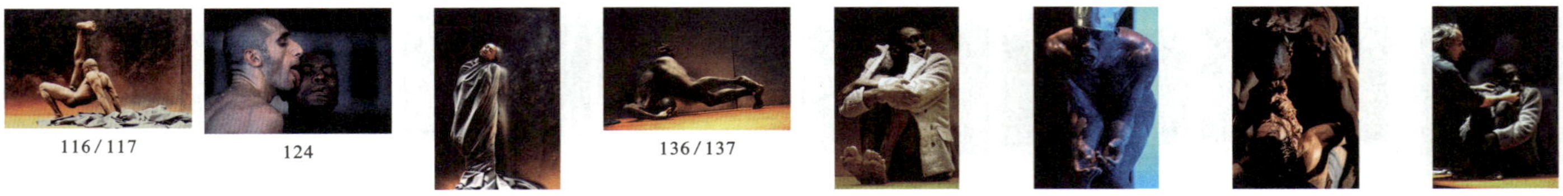

116 / 117 124 129 136 / 137 141 144 149 161

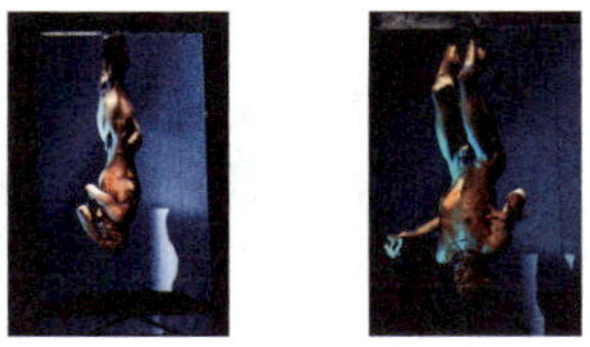

168 169

Othello, Theaterhaus Stuttgart (1995)

133 165 193

Journey with Ismael Ivo to Brazil in preparation for the project *Der Black Atlantic* (2004)

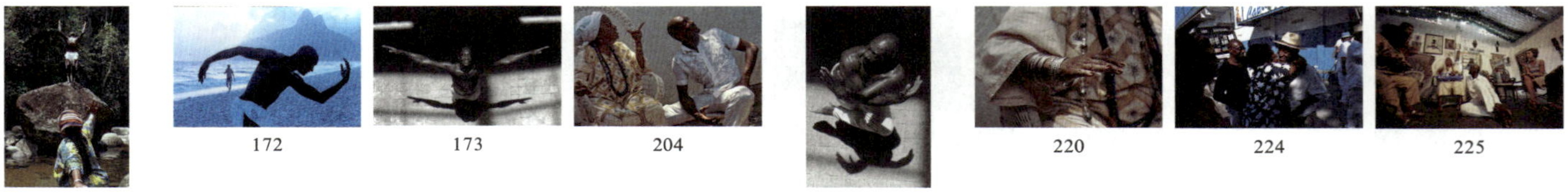

152 172 173 204 209 220 224 225

229 233 236 237 244 / 245 252 / 253 256

Die Zofen, Theaterhaus Stuttgart (2001)

156 / 157

Mapplethorpe, La Biennale di Venezia (2002)

120 177 180 240 / 241 248

Tristan Isolde, Theaterhaus Stuttgart (1999)

185

Collaboration with Hans Kresnik, George Tabori, and Márcia Haydée

188 189 197 200 201 221

At the studio of Elvira Bach, Berlin (2005)

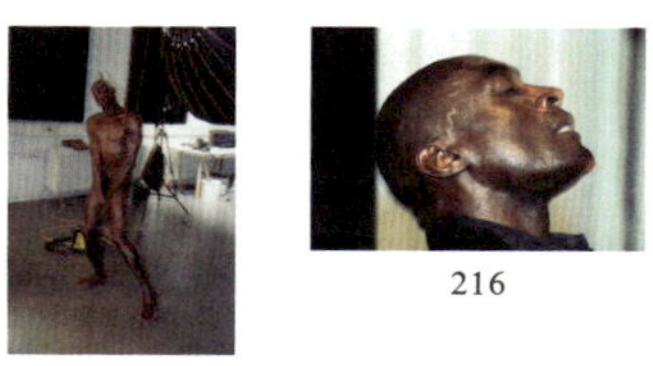

213 216

DIETER BLUM worked with Ismael Ivo for more than 15 years (1993–2012) on all important productions, including in Brazil in 2004. Several times, he invited Ismael Ivo for photo sessions in Esslingen and other places, where he was able to stage the dancer's compelling presence for the photos. Inspired by the rehearsals of *Francis Bacon* in particular, which he attended, he developed further series of images that closely followed the plays. This resulted in a corpus of images that include some of Ismael Ivo's most iconic portraits.

Acknowledgements

The driving forces behind this book were Marcel Kaskeline, Ismael Ivo's set designer and life partner, and Karl Regensburger, the festival director and Ismael Ivo's closest companion.
We would especially like to thank the authors and interviewees who describe and reflect on Ismael Ivo's work from various perspectives.
Without the financial support of the ImPulsTanz Festival as well as the Cultural Office of the City of Vienna and the Austrian Federal Ministry of Culture, the Theaterhaus Stuttgart, the Akademie der Künste, Berlin, the publisher Spector Books, Leipzig and the Goethe-Institut, this publication would not have been possible.
The cooperation with the publisher has resulted in a book that approaches the ephemeral performative work of Ivo Ismael in a congenial way. Our thanks go to the publisher Jan Wenzel, the graphic designer Elias Erkan, the translators, especially Jan Caspers, the editor Martin Hager and the proofreaders of the catalogue raisonné, Jan-Frederik Bandel and Christin Krause.
The photographic works of Anno Wilms and Dieter and Daniela Blum are an essential part of the book. With their generous support, Nina Zenker (Anno Wilms Foundation) and Dieter Blum made the success of the project possible.

Johannes Odenthal

JOHANNES ODENTHAL studied art history and archaeology in Cologne, Bonn, and Paris. Together with Angelika Peters, he founded the magazine *tanz aktuell* in 1986, which was relaunched in 1995 as *tanz aktuell / ballett international* and is now called *tanz*. In November 1986, he conducted the first interview for *tanz aktuell* with Ismael Ivo, which was followed by numerous other interviews until 2015. His interview collection *Ismael Ivo*, was published in Italian in the series "dance for word, Intervista sulla coreografia contemoranea" by L'EPOS. Between 1997 and 2006, Odenthal was artistic director for music, dance, and theater at the Haus der Kulturen der Welt. He developed a close artistic cooperation with Ismael Ivo on topics such as the Black Atlantic. Since 2006 Odenthal has been program officer at the Academy of Arts, Berlin. In this position, he was editor of various publications including *Contemporary Artists from Brazil* in the series "Positions" by Steidl (Göttingen 2013).

KARL REGENSBURGER graduated in business administration from the Vienna University of Economics and Business Administration in 1981. In the early 1980s, he met Ismael Ivo and organized a dance series at the Serapion Theater. The performances became a huge success, paving the way for the *ImPulsTanz* festival they both founded in 1984 in Vienna, which today is the most important dance festival in Europe. *ImPulsTanz—Research* followed in 1990, and in 1996 an independent *danceWEB scholarship program* was established for more than 60 dance artists from 40 countries each year. In 2006, Ismael Ivo and Karl Regensburger were awarded the Golden Order of Merit of the Federal State of Vienna. In 2008, Regensburger was awarded the prestigious title Officier de l'Ordre des Arts et des Lettres by the French Minister of Culture. The promotion of a new generation in dance has been the motivation for the establishment of the *Prix Jardin d'Europe—European Prize for Emerging Choreography* that same year, which has been continued under the name *ImPulsTanz—Young Choreographers' Award* since 2018. In 2021, the Austrian State Prize for the Performing Arts was awarded to Karl Regensburger and in memoriam to Ismael Ivo.

MARA BORBA graduated in Fine Arts in 1974 and appeared on stage for the first time that same year. Until today, at the age of 71, she is dedicated to all forms of physical expression. She has had a remarkable career as a director, choreographer, performer, creator, and composer. Both as a dancer and as a choreographer, she has won several awards, including for her work with actor William Hurt in the film *The Kiss of the Spider Woman*. She has worked with Ismael Ivo in Vienna and Weimar, among other places, and most recently staged *Lady x Macbeth* with Márcio Aurelio at the Teatro Anchieta in São Paulo.

GABRIELE BRANDSTETTER is a senior professor of theater and dance studies at Freie Universität Berlin and has been co-director of the International Käte Hamburger College "Interweaving Theater Cultures" since 2008. Her research focuses on the history and aesthetics of dance, theater, and literature from the 18th century to the present, virtuosity in art and culture, the relationship between body, image, and movement; and issues of border crossings, migration, and decolonizing dance.

FERNANDA BUENO is a dancer, choreographer, journalist, curator, producer, and manager. At the age of 10, she began her dance training at the Escola Municipal de Bailados, now the Escola de Dança de São Paulo of the Theatro Municipal. In 2012, she created her first choreography, *Tempo*, with the Corpo de Baile Jovem. In 2013, she produced her first solo, *Fino Fio Frio*. Together with Kleber Pagu, she is a cultural activist, provocateur, entrepreneur, and patron of public art projects. Since 2021 she has been the director of the Arts Institute in São Paulo.

FRANCESCA HARPER started her professional dance career with the Dance Theater of Harlem. She danced with William Forsythe's Ballett Frankfurt from 1991 to 1999, and became a Principal Dancer in 1994. She has performed in Broadway productions including *Fosse, All Shook Up*, and *The Color Purple*. She has choreographed works for The Alvin Ailey American Dance Theater, Ailey II, Tanz Graz, The Ailey School, and her own company, The Francesca Harper Project. The Francesca Harper Project has performed at La Biennale di Venezia, Holland Dance Festival, Central Park SummerStage, New York City Center, and many other festivals and venues. As an educator, Francesca Harper has served as a professor at The Juilliard School, an adjunct professor at NYU, a former associate professor at Barnard College, and a professor in the Ailey / Fordham BFA program. In 2021, she was appointed Artistic Director of the Ailey II Company.

GOTTFRIED HELNWEIN is one of the best known but at the same time one of the most controversial German-speaking artists after the Second World War. He made his name primarily through his hyper-realistic paintings of wounded and bandaged children. Throughout his oeuvre, he deals with the themes of pain, injury, and violence, touching on topics of recent history that are deemed irritating or taboo. His works thus also deal with the subject of National Socialism in particular; however, the focus of his work is above all on the depiction of the child.

RICCARDA HERRE completed her training as a dancer at the Hamburg State Opera Ballet School in 1987. Afterwards, she danced as a soloist with various companies in Germany and abroad, including the Choreographic Theater of the Volksbühne Berlin and the Tanztheater of the Deutsches Nationaltheater Weimar. In 2004 she graduated as a cultural and media manager at the Hamburg University of Music and Theatre. Since 2002, she has worked in this capacity for the festivals Tanz im August, Tanzplan Deutschland, and, since 2012, for Diehl + Ritter, among others. Since 2017, she has been the project manager of the development fund Tanzpakt Stadt-Land-Bund there.

MARCEL KASKELINE studied architecture at the Technical University of Berlin. In 1995, he met Ismael Ivo in Berlin. The encounter shaped his life decisively, and a private partnership was complemented by an artistic one in 1999. He began to design the stage spaces for Ismael Ivo's choreographies. He deepened his knowledge in a postgraduate course in stage design for architects at TU Berlin. In addition, he took over the production management as well as the private management of Ismael Ivo. Since 2002, he was increasingly involved in the ideas and artistic concepts of the dance productions. Altogether 38 joint pieces were created.

KOFFI KÔKÔ, dancer and choreographer from Benin, West Africa, is one of the most important artistic personalities of the African continent and a key figure for the identity of a contemporary African dance scene. With his more than 40 choreographies, he has developed a unique body of work in Europe that translates the philosophy of voudoun and the potential of ritual for the Western dance stage. Koffi Kôkô had formed a deep friendship with Ismael Ivo, which found its artistic expression in the joint production of *The Maids* after Jean Genet in 2001.

CÁSSIA NAVAS holds a Ph.D. in Dance / Semiotics from Pontifícia Universidade Católica, São Paulo, she has completed postgraduate studies in Cultural Policy and Management at Université Dijon, and graduated with a Bachelor of Law from Universidade de São Paulo. She is a researcher, lecturer, and collaborator in the Postgraduate Program in Performing Arts at the Universidade Estadual de Campinas, São Paulo, as well as a dance and performing arts consultant, essayist, and writer.

RINO ACHILLE DE PACE has been artistic director of the MILANoLTRE International Festival since 2010. From 1985 to 1999 he was in charge of production and distribution in Italy and abroad for the Teatro dell'Elfo, Milan. From 1999 to 2010, he worked in the Dance, Music, and Theatre Department for the Venice Biennale, where he was in charge of production and co-production projects; he was artistic secretary to Carolyn Carlson, Frédéric Flamand, Peter Sellars, Romeo Castellucci, Karole Armitage, and Ismael Ivo.

FRANCA PAGLIASSOTTO, born in Volpiano in 1957, is a dancer and choreographer. She broadened her classical and modern studies at the Alvin Ailey New York, approaching the Horton technique with Milton Meyers and Max Luna III. In Paris, she studied with Peter Gross and in Vienna with Ismael Ivo. In 1984, she founded the dance school Il Gabbiano of which she is still the director. From 2004 she was assistant to Ismael Ivo with whom he collaborated at the Venice Biennale until 2012. Since 2006 she has been teaching yoga Ballet at the ImPulsTanz Vienna.

DANILO SANTOS DE MIRANDA graduated in Philosophy and Social Sciences and completed complementary specialization studies at the Pontifícia Universidade Católica and the Getúlio Vargas Foundation in São Paulo as well as the IMEDE—Management Development Institute, in Lausanne, Switzerland. He was Chairman of the Steering Committee of the World Cultural Forum in Barcelona in 2004 and Chairman of the Brazilian Commission of the Year of France in Brazil in 2009. He has been honored with the title of Commander of the National Order of Merit of France and was awarded the Grand Cross of the Federal Republic of Germany as well as the National Order of the Belgian Crown, among others.

PETRA SCHAEBER is a freelance writer living in Salvador / Bahia. She studied economics and politics at the University of Cologne and the Pontifícia Universidade Católica in Rio de Janeiro and holds a Ph.D. in Education from the Free University of Berlin on Afro-Brazilian culture and race relations in Brazil. She has published several books on travel, culture, and language. She first saw Ismael Ivo in *Phoenix* and remained friends with him for years—in Berlin, Salvador, Rio de Janeiro, and São Paulo.

VALENTINA SCHISA, born in Naples, graduated from the dance school of Patty Schisa. In 2010 she was selected by Ismael Ivo as a dancer for *Sacre du Printemps* and the professional dance program *Arsenale della Danza*. From 2010 she was principal dancer of Ismael Ivo and became his choreographies assistant for the *Biblioteca do Corpo* project. Additionally, she was responsible for the staging of Ismael Ivo's repertoire for the Balè da Cidade de São Paulo, which Ivo was in charge of as the director at the time. She also performed with Ivo in other pieces such as *Francis Bacon* or *Die 120 Tage of Sodom*, co-directed by Ivo and Hans Kresnik.